Volume 2: Since 1500

# Women and Gender in the Western Past

*Katherine L. French*
*State University of New York–New Paltz*

*Allyson M. Poska*
*University of Mary Washington*

Houghton Mifflin Company     Boston     New York

Publisher: Patricia Coryell
Senior Sponsoring Editor: Nancy Blaine
Senior Development Editor: Jennifer Sutherland
Editorial Assistant: Tawny Pruitt
Senior Project Editor: Jane Lee
Editorial Assistant: Kristen Truncellito/Carrie Parker
Senior Art and Design Coordinator: Jill Haber
Senior Photo Editor: Jennifer Meyer Dare
Composition Buyer: Chuck Dutton
Associate Strategic Buyer: Brian Pieragostini
Senior Marketing Manager: Katherine Bates
Marketing Assistant: Lauren Bussard
Cover Design Manager: Anne S. Katzeff

Cover image: Copyright © De Kooning, Elaine (1920–1989). *Self-Portrait, 1946.* Oil on masonite. Credit: National Portrait Gallery, Smithsonian Institution, Washington, DC/ Art Resource, NY.

Printed in the U.S.A.

Library of Congress Control Number: 2006926566
ISBN 13: 978-0-618-24625-0
ISBN 10: 0-618-24625-8

1 2 3 4 5 6 7 8 9-QUF-10   09   08   07   06

Text credits: pp. 242–243: Sarah Fyge Egerton, compiled and edited by the Beck Center at Emory University, *The Female Advocate: or, an Answer to A Late Satyr against The Pride, Lust and Inconstancy, &c. of Woman Written by a Lady in Vindication of Her Sex* (London: Printed by H. C. for John Taylor 1686). Reprinted by permission of the Beck Center at Emory University. p. 231: *The Witch Hunt in Early Modern Europe*, 2d ed., Brian Levack, Pearson Education Limited. Copyright © 1995 by Pearson Education Ltd. Reprinted by permission of Pearson Education Limited. pp. 282–283: Copyright © Marie Madeleine Jodin, 1741–1790, Felicia Godon and P. N. Furbank, 2001, Ashgate Publishing Ltd. Reprinted by permission of Ashgate Publishing Ltd. pp. 300–301: pp. 7–10 from *Mrs Beeton's Book of Household Management* by Isabella Beeton, edited by Humble, N. (2000). Reprinted by permission of Oxford University Press. pp. 350–351: Robert Nemes, "Getting to the Source: Women in the 1848–1849 Hungarian Revolution," *Journal of Women's History* 13:3 (2001): 193–209. Copyright © *Journal of Women's History.* Reprinted with permission of The Johns Hopkins University Press. pp. 390–391: Patricia Clarker (ed.) and Dale Spender (ed.), *Life Lines: Australian Women's Letters and Diaries, 1788–1840,* Allen & Unwin Pty., Limited, Australia (August 1992). Reprinted by permission of Allen & Unwin Pty., Limited. www.allenandunwin.com.au. pp. 430–431: From Agnes Warner, *My Beloved Poilus,* Barnes & Co., Limited, Publishers (St. John, N.B.), 1917. pp. 466–467: From Women's International League for Peace and Freedom, Fifth Congress, Dublin, July 8–15, 1926. Reprinted by permission of the Women's International League for Peace and Freedom. pp. 516–517: From *Fresh Wounds: Early Narratives of Holocaust Survival* by Donald L. Niewyk. Copyright © by 1998 the University of North Carolina Press. Used by permission of the publisher. pp. 552–553: Alfred C. Kinsey, Wardell B. Pomeroy, Clyde E. Martin, Paul H. Gebhard, The Kinsey Institute, *Sexual Behavior in the Human Female* (WB Saunders, 1953). Reprinted by permission of The Kinsey Institute for Research in Sex, Gender, and Reproduction, Inc. pp. 598–599: From *Women, Art, and Power and Other Essays,* by Linda Nochlin. ISBN: 064301834. Copyright © 1988 Linda Nochlin. Reprinted by permission of WESTVIEW PRE, a member of Perseus Books, L.L.C.

# Contents

Maps   ix

Special Features   x

Preface   xi

About the Authors   xvi

## Chapter 7

### Early Modern Europe, 1500–1700   217

The Protestant Reformations   218
  The Lutheran Reformation   218
  Calvinist Discipline   221
  The Radical Reformation   223
  Women and the Formation of the Anglican
    Church   224
The Catholic Reformation   225
  Laywomen and the Catholic
    Reformation   226
  Women and the Inquisitions   227
  The Permeable Cloister: Women Religious
    After Trent   228
Life on the Margins: Witches, Jews, and
Muslims   229
  The Early Modern Witch-Hunts   229
  Expulsions and New Communities   232
  The End of Islam in Western Europe   234
Queens, Patrons, and Petitioners   235
  Unifying Queens   235
  The Monstrous Regiment of
    Women   235
  Other Avenues to Power   236

Gender, Politics, and the English
  Civil War   238
Art, Literature, and Science   239
  Gender Theory and Reality in Early
    Modern Thought   239
  Enlivening the Arts   241

*Sources from the Past: Female Advocate,
A Defense of Women by Sarah Fyge
Egerton*   242

  Behind Closed Doors: Women in Early
    Modern Science   245
European Expansion   246
  Life on the Periphery: European Women
    and the Colonization of Asia and the
    Americas   246

*Women's Lives: Catalina de Erauso, Soldier
and Adventurer*   248

  Women and the Missionary Effort   250
  Native Women in the Conquest of the
    Americas   250
Conclusion   252

## Chapter 8

### Whose Enlightenment? Whose Revolution? 1700–1815   255

Society at the End of the Old
Regime   256
  Royal and Aristocratic Women   256

Women and Rural Life  258
Urban Women  259
**Enlightenment Ideas**  261
Women and the Birth of Modern
Science  261
Enlightenment Ideas About Women  262
The *Salonières* and the Philosophes  263

*Women's Lives: Lady Mary Wortley
Montague*  266

**The Enlightenment in Eastern Europe and
Russia**  267
Gendering Enlightened Absolutism in
Austria and Prussia  267
The Westernization of Russia  270
**Women, Art, and Culture in the Eighteenth
Century**  271
Women as Professional Artists  271
Music  272
Literature by and for Women  273
**Gender in the Colonies**  275
Colonial Economies  275
Slavery and the Abolitionist
Movement  276
The American Revolution  277
Women in Spanish America  278
**Women and the French Revolution**  279
Women and the Start of the
Revolution  280
Women and the Radical Phase of the
Revolution  281

*Sources from the Past: Marie-Madeleine Jodin
on Women's Rights*  282

Women and the Napoleonic Era  286
Women and Resistance to Napoleon  288
**Conclusion**  289

*Chapter 9*

**Women and the New Industrial
Society, 1800–1900**  293

**Women's Work and the Creation of Industrial
Society**  294
Gendering Factory Work  296

Domestic Work  298
Women and the Industrialization of
Agriculture  298

*Sources from the Past:* Mrs. Beeton's Book
of Household Management  300

**Gendered Spaces in the New Urban
Landscape**  302
Moving Around the City  302
New Destinations  304
Shopping  305
Urban Problems  306
**Urban Reform and the Control of
Women**  308
Regulating Women's Work  308
Reforming the Poor  310
Prostitution  311
**Sex and Gender: Theory and
Reality**  312
The Cult of Domesticity  312
Social Darwinism and Eugenics  314
Sexology and Sexual Identity  315
Sexual Realities  317

*Women's Lives: Martha Carey Thomas,
Education Pioneer*  318

**Piety and Charity**  319
Religious Revival  319
Women and Judaism  320
Women and Philanthropy  321
**Educating Women**  324
Educational Reform and Higher Education
for Women  324
Women and Science at the Turn of the
Century  326
**Conclusion**  327

*Chapter 10*

**Resistance, Revolution, and Reform,
1815–1900**  332

**Politicizing Women in the Early Nineteenth
Century, 1815–1848**  333
Abolitionism  333
Women in English Politics  336

Women and Utopian Socialism   338
Founding the Women's Movement   340
**The Crises of 1848**   342
Fomenting Revolution   342
Women and the Revolution of 1848 in
France   345
The Revolution in Central Europe   347
**Forging International Connections Among
Women**   349
Shared Texts and Shared Ideas   349

*Sources from the Past: Demands of
the Radical Hungarian Women,
1848*   350

The Right to Walk the Streets   352
Women and Pacifism   353
Formalizing Connections   354
**Radical Actions and Liberal
Reforms**   356
The Franco-Prussian War and the Paris
Commune, 1870–1871   356
Women and Early Marxism   358
Liberal Reforms   359
**Women and the Creation of National
Identities**   361
German Unification   361
Women and Italian Unification   363
Russia and the Baltic   365

*Women's Lives: Sofia Perovskaia, Russian
Radical*   368

**Conclusion**   369

**Chapter 11**

**Gender and Imperialism,
1830–1930**   372

**Sex and Gender in the Empire**   374
Race, Gender, and Colonialism   376
Concubinage and Prostitution   378
Mixed-Race Children   380
Native Men and European Women   381
**Spreading the Gospel: Female Missionaries
Around the World**   381
Missionary Values   382

Catholic Missionaries   383
Protestant Missionaries   385
**Life in the Colonies**   386
Women and the Maintenance of Empire:
The Wives of Colonial Officials   386
Working Overseas   388

*Sources from the Past: Isabella Gibson on the
Immigrant Experience in Australia*   390

Going Native   392
**Collaboration and Resistance**   394
Imperialist Women   394
Imperial Feminism and Feminist
Anti-Imperialists   395

*Women's Lives: Olive Schreiner, Writer and
Activist*   396

Suffrage and the Imperial World   397
**Traveling the World**   399
Travel and Study   400
Noncolonial Migration   402
**Conclusion**   407

**Chapter 12**

**The New Woman from War to
Revolution, 1880–1919**   411

**Women in the Belle Époque**   412
The New Woman   412
The New Woman and the Art of the Belle
Époque   415
The Dangers of the New Woman   417
**Women and Political Activism**   418
Women and Radical Politics   418
Women and the Russian Revolution of
1905   419
The Push for the Vote   421
Racism and Nationalism Before the
War   424
**Women and the Great War**   425
Women in the Military and at the
Front   426

*Sources from the Past: Letters from a
Canadian Nurse in France*   430

Women at Home: Inventing the Home
  Front   432
Antiwar Activism   435

*Women's Lives: Aletta Jacobs, Physician,*
*Suffragist, Pacifist*   436

The World Turned Upside Down: Gender
  and World War I   437
**New States, New Citizens**   440
  The Great Influenza Epidemic   440
  The End of the War   441
  Postwar Politics   442
  Gender and the Russian Revolution   444
**Conclusion**   446

## Chapter 13

### The Modern Woman Between the Wars, 1919–1939   449

**A Modern Society**   450
  The Modern Woman   450
  Gender and Consumer Culture   453
  Birth Control   454
  Modern Relationships   455
**Women and Work**   457
  The Interwar Workplace   457
  Women and Trade Unionism   459
  New Careers   460
**Women in Postwar Democracies**   462
  Suffrage and Its Impact   462
  After the Vote   463
  New Relations Between Women and
    the State   465

*Sources from the Past: Resolutions of the*
*Women's International League for Peace*
*and Freedom, 1926 and 1932*   466

**Women Under Authoritarian Rule**   468
  Nationalizing Women in Mussolini's
    Italy   468
  Fascism and Its Opponents in Spain   470
  Other Authoritarian Regimes   473
**Women Under the Soviet State**   473

Women and Early Soviet Society: Theory
    Versus Reality   473
  Economic Revolutions   475
  Soviet Regulation of the Family   476
  Politics   477
**Gender and New Forms of Expression**   478
  The Avant-Garde   478
  New Forms of Entertainment   481

*Women's Lives: Jessie Redmon Fauset, Writer*
*of the Harlem Renaissance*   482

**Conclusion**   483

## Chapter 14

### New Possibilities, New Perils: Women in World War II, 1939–1945   487

**Race, Sex, and the National Socialist Agenda**   488
  Nazi Racism   489
  Nazism, Sex, and the Family   491
  Nazi Women's Organizations   492
**Women at War**   493
  Reactions to War   495
  Women in Uniform   497
  The Resistance   500
  Female POWs   501

*Women's Lives: Marie-Madeleine (Meric)*
*Fourcade, Resistance Fighter*   502

**On the Home Front**   504
  Women and Wartime Work   504
  The Kitchen Front   506
  Other Pressures at Home   508
  The Home Front in Germany   510
**The Holocaust**   511
  Life in the Ghetto   511
  Labor and Extermination Camps   512
**The End of the War**   514
  Occupation and Liberation   515

*Sources from the Past: A Woman's Story*
*of the Holocaust*   516

Returning to "Normal"  518
Out of the Service  520
**Conclusion**  521

## *Chapter 15*

## Women and the Postwar Generation, 1945–1970  525

**Gender and the Cold War**  528
The Creation of the United Nations  528
Women and International Conflict in the Cold War  530
Anti-Communist Hysteria in the United States  531
Dividing German Women  531
**Postwar Society**  533
The Postwar Family  533
Women and the European Welfare State  534
Women and the Postwar Economy  535
**Gender Behind the Iron Curtain**  537
Women and Politics in the Soviet Union  537
Communism, the Family, and the State  538
Gender, Production, and the Soviet Economic System  539
Women Against the Regime  541
**Women and Decolonization**  543
Native Women and Nationalist Movements  543
Gender and the Wars of Independence  545
Postcolonial Repercussions  546
**Agitating for Change**  548
The Antinuclear and Environmental Movements  548

*Women's Lives: Dorothy Crowfoot Hodgkin, Scientist and Peace Activist*  550

The Pill and the Sexual Revolution  551

*Sources from the Past: The Kinsey Report*  552

Social Protest Movements  554
A New Woman's Movement  556

**Gender and Postwar Culture**  558
The Transformation of the Modern Home  558
Creating an Image: Women in Film and Television  559
The Rise of Rock 'n' Roll  560
**Conclusion**  561

## *Chapter 16*

## Gender at the Turn of the Millennium  565

**Feminist Action**  567
Women's Liberation and Second Wave Feminism  568
The Push for Reproductive Rights  569
Ending Violence Against Women  570
Lesbian Rights  571
**Political Transformations**  572
Women and the Democratic Transition in Southern Europe  573
Violent Reactions  574
Transformations in the Soviet Union  575
The Limits of Progress in Eastern Europe  576
German Unification: Hope and Disappointment  578
The Fall of the Soviet Union  580
**Recent Trends in Gender and Politics**  581
Electoral Quotas and Women's Representation  581
Women at the Helm  582
Women in Radical Politics  583

*Women's Lives: Gro Harlem Brundtland, Politician and Human Rights Activist*  584

**Gender Politics Beyond Nations**  585
The UN and the Internationalization of the Women's Movement  585
Gender Politics in the European Union  586
Nongovernmental Activism  588
**Changes in the Family and at Work**  590
A New Demographic Regime  590
New Relationships  591

Aging   592
New Opportunities   593
Gender Equity in the Workplace   593
**Women and Culture**   595
Women's Studies and Feminist
Theory   595
Feminist Culture   596

*Sources from the Past:* **Why Have There Been No Great Women Artists?**   598

Women in Mainstream Culture   600
**Conclusion**   601

**Index**   605

# *Maps*

7.1   The Protestant and Catholic Reformations     220
7.2   European Overseas Expansion, 1715     247
8.1   Europe in 1789     269
8.2   Napoleonic Europe in 1810     287
9.1   The Industrial Revolution in England     302
9.2   Industrialization on the Continent     303
10.1  Europe's Age of Revolutions     343
10.2  Peoples of the Habsburg Monarchy, 1815     344
10.3  The Unification of Germany, 1866–1871     362
10.4  The Unification of Italy, 1859–1870     364
11.1  European Imperialism in Africa (1914)     375
11.2  Imperialism in Asia (1914)     377
12.1  Europe During World War I, 1914–1918     427
12.2  Territorial Changes in Europe After World War I     443
14.1  World War II in Europe, 1939–1945     494
14.2  World War II in the Pacific, 1941–1945     496
15.1  Cold War Europe, 1949–1989     529
16.1  Democratic Movements in Eastern Europe, 1989     579
16.2  Contemporary Europe     587

# Special Features

## Women's Lives

Catalina de Erauso, Soldier and
   Adventurer   248
Lady Mary Wortley Montague   266
Martha Carey Thomas, Education
   Pioneer   318
Sofia Perovskaia, Russian Radical   368
Olive Schreiner, Writer and
   Activist   396
Aletta Jacobs, Physician, Suffragist,
   Pacifist   436
Jessie Redmon Fauset, Writer of the Harlem
   Renaissance   482
Marie-Madeleine (Meric) Fourcade,
   Resistance Fighter   502
Dorothy Crowfoot Hodgkin, Scientist and
   Peace Activist   550
Gro Harlem Brundtland, Politician and Human
   Rights Activist   584

## Sources from the Past

*Female Advocate, A Defense of Women* by
   Sarah Fyge Egerton   242
Marie-Madeleine Jodin on Women's
   Rights   282
*Mrs. Beeton's Book of Household
   Management*   300
Demands of the Radical Hungarian Women,
   1848   350
Isabella Gibson on the Immigrant Experience
   in Australia   390
Letters from a Canadian Nurse in
   France   430
Resolutions of the Women's International
   League for Peace and Freedom, 1926
   and 1932   466
A Women's Story of the Holocaust   516
The Kinsey Report   552
*Why Have There Been No Great Women
   Artists?*   598

# Preface

Women's history has transformed our understanding of the past and the historical profession itself. Only three decades ago, the field was in its infancy. Scholars who asked questions about the role of women in the past faced the bafflement of their colleagues and struggled to teach and research women's history with little institutional support. Although these conditions persist on many campuses, the field has flourished. Women's historians have produced scholarly studies of the highest quality, and the dynamism of the field is evident in the many conferences, book series, and journals dedicated to the subject. Women's history courses have become a regular part of many college and university curricula, and high school teachers increasingly integrate the historical experiences of women into their classes.

Despite these successes, teaching women's history continues to be a challenge, because many students see women's history as marginal to their education. In recent years, we have worked to bridge the gap between what our students perceive as "important" and women's history by blurring the line between women's history and more traditional fields of historical inquiry. We have integrated women's history into our Western Civilization courses and brought more of the narrative of traditional history into our women's history classes. We have shown our students that women's history is not a secondary topic to be relegated to elective courses, but an indispensable part of the study of history. However, in the process, we found that the available textbooks on European women's history did not serve our needs. Some were collections of essays that did not provide the larger historical framework; others

were survey textbooks organized in ways that made them difficult to teach.

In response, we decided to write a textbook that would integrate the critical themes of women's history into the historical narrative. *Women and Gender in the Western Past* brings students the most up-to-date scholarship on women, from the earliest days of human experience to the present. We examine the experiences of women of all classes, religions, and ethnicities and provide the most extensive coverage of women in Western political, social, economic, intellectual, religious, and cultural history available.

We recognize that students come to this course with varying levels of historical knowledge and preparation. Written at an introductory level, *Women and Gender in the Western Past* provides enough historical context to make it accessible to students from a wide variety of majors and educational backgrounds.

*Women and Gender in the Western Past* focuses on five major themes:

1. *The relationship between historical events and ideas and women's lives.* Our text shows women as vibrant creators of and participants in the events, ideas, and movements that shaped the past. We reject the notion that women were mostly passive victims without influence on their own lives or the world around them.

2. *The history of the family and sexuality.* For much of history, women were defined by their marital and family status. But ideas of women's place in the family and societal norms about sexuality have evolved over time, influenced by developments in religion, law, and technology. We

emphasize the scholarship that has shown that the family and sexuality are not natural categories that transcend historical forces but shifting realities that have a history of their own.

3. *The social construction of gender.* Like the family and sexuality, gender has a history. Every society constructs its own gender norms based on religious beliefs, cultural stereotypes, and other societal forces. We include extensive discussions of the evolution of gender ideologies as they apply to both women and men, as well as to relations between the sexes. Although our discussions of masculinity are limited by space constraints and the relative newness of masculinity studies, we understand that men and masculinity are integral to gender studies.

4. *The differences between cultural ideals and the lives of women.* Over the centuries, Western society has formulated and reformulated its expectations for how women should behave. We explore changes in gender expectations and how and why some women willingly acquiesced to them while others rejected them.

5. *Women's perceptions of themselves and their roles.* One of the most important contributions of women's history has been the discovery and rediscovery of writings and other works by women. Women's perspectives on their own lives and the issues facing their societies further illuminate how women understood and interacted with social expectations. Women's voices provide an important corrective to the male-dominated historical narrative and challenge assumptions about the development of Western society.

*Women and Gender in the Western Past* consistently addresses these five major themes as it integrates women's history into the familiar narrative of Western Civilization, making women's history easier for faculty to teach and for students to learn.

## FEATURES

We have included a number of features to supplement the narrative and engage students. We encourage students to personalize historical experience by examining the lives of individual women. Each chapter includes a biography feature called "Women's Lives." We have selected women of different classes, nationalities, religions, and occupations, showing how each was shaped by and responded to historical forces and constraints. For instance, in Chapter 4, students meet Perpetua, who was imprisoned for practicing Christianity in the Roman Empire. In Chapter 11, we show how author Olive Schreiner challenged both sexism and racism in colonial South Africa.

Each chapter also includes "Sources from the Past"—short excerpts from primary sources written mostly by women. Students will learn how these writers viewed women and how women used writing to communicate their feelings and concerns. The excerpts reflect the diversity of sources that scholars use to investigate women's history. For example, the selection of Egyptian legal texts found in Chapter 1 reveals the protections and rights of Egyptian women. In Chapter 8, Marie-Madeleine Jodin's proposal on women's rights to the National Assembly may be the first signed, female-authored, feminist work of the French Revolution.

Each chapter also includes a Chronology to highlight key developments in the chapter and integrate women's history into the traditional historical narrative. Students can see at a glance the relationship between women's experiences and the major historical events of the period.

We have tried to make this text visually appealing to both faculty and students. A generous selection of maps provides geographic context for the events discussed in each chapter. The illustrations include images from a wide array of media and, whenever possible, women's representations of themselves and each other. Images of material culture created by women demonstrate women's creativity, resourcefulness, and priorities. For example, in Chapter 14, the Changi Quilt, made by women in a Japanese prisoner of war camp during World War II reveals how under the most horrific circumstances, women found ways to use traditional skills to preserve their identity and communicate with others.

We were determined to credit the work of scholars who have transformed our understanding of women's place in the past and to give students access to the sources on which our book is based. As a result, in addition to a short list of Suggested Readings at the end of each chapter, we provide extensive footnotes to the primary and secondary sources that we used to write this book. We hope that *Women and Gender in the Western Past* will inspire students and make it easier for them to pursue topics in women's history that they find particularly intriguing.

## CHALLENGES

Writing this textbook forced us to deal with some of the most controversial issues in the historical profession. Our decision to refer to *the West* will be problematic for some scholars. We wholeheartedly agree that the term *Western Civilization* is problematic because it implies a particular notion of Western progress and privileges the history of white Europeans. However, we decided to work within that framework in order to make the text useful as a core or supplemental text in Western Civilization courses and to meet our goal of viewing the familiar narrative of Western Civilization through the lens of gender. We believe that women's history fundamentally challenges any teleological notion of Western progress, and we have consciously addressed the issue of ethnocentrism by being racially, ethnically, and religiously inclusive.

Chronology has also been problematic for women's historians. The traditional Western Civilization narrative was focused on powerful and influential men and events that historians believed were central to the creation of the modern Western world. However, the trajectory of women's history does not necessarily follow the traditional divisions of history. Although we generally work within that framework, some events that loom large in Western Civilization texts, such as the Peloponnesian wars, play a minimal role in *Women and Gender in the Western Past* because of the limited influence of or impact on women. In addition, based on the research in those fields, we have reconceptualized the traditional periodizations of the Middle Ages and Renaissance to reflect the transformations that most affected women. Chapter 5, "Women in the Early and High Middle Ages," covers the 400–1200 period, when most women followed the distinct rhythms of rural life, while Chapter 6, "Women and Urban Life: The Late Middle Ages," covers the 1200–1500 period, when women increasingly

participated in life and work in European towns and cities. In Chapter 6, we examine the Renaissance as an intellectual and artistic movement rather than as a time period.

Every historian must confront the problem of sources. For the ancient period, there is little written by women and, in some cases, very little written by men about women. Instead, we turned to literature, art, and archaeology to supplement the written record. Even during the modern period, there are topics that remain largely unstudied, such as the role of women in the Thirty Years War. Women's history is an evolving field, and our text reflects the limits of our current knowledge.

Space constraints also limited our ability to provide significant discussions of historiography; however, the relationship between historiography and the creation of the historical narrative was always in the forefront of our work. We have tried whenever possible to convey a sense of historical debate, as we believe that it is important for students to recognize that history is created and that the process of creation is dynamic.

Women's history is the product of many social and intellectual changes. Although previous generations of historians did not ignore women entirely, until the middle of the twentieth century, both male and female historians demonstrated little interest in the lives of women other than rulers and women directly associated with major political changes. Then, during the 1930s, the *Annalistes* and their successors in the burgeoning field of social history reconceptualized historical time to focus on the *longue durée*. They introduced the use of quantitative analysis, anthropology, sociology, and geography, in order to explore the lives of people who left no written records. These changes would prove critical for the study of women, because many of the basic structures of women's lives change very slowly and in response to factors unrelated to political events.

Women's history as a subfield of the historical discipline emerged in the 1960s and early 1970s, when the widespread application of these innovations in the historical profession came together with the social and political movements of that era. Galvanized by the second wave of feminism, many female scholars began to investigate the role of women in history. They understood the potential of historical study to gain not only a more comprehensive understanding of the past but also to contextualize their own place in society.

Women's history would challenge some of the most fundamental historical concepts. In her groundbreaking essay "Did Women Have a Renaissance?" (1977), Joan Kelly forced scholars to reconsider the meaning of the term *Renaissance*, as she asserted a decline in women's status at the height of that period. Kelly demonstrated how the traditional historical narrative and notions of progress systematically excluded women and that the inclusion of women challenged some of the dearest assumptions about Western progress. A decade later, Joan Scott, in "Gender as a Useful Category for Historical Analysis" (1988), argued that gender is central to power relations and a primary aspect of social organization. Therefore, understanding gender is critical even to the study of subjects that traditionally excluded women, such as politics.

These are just a few of the ideas that have shaped the field of women's history. For a more extensive discussion, we recommend Merry E. Wiesner-Hanks, "Gender" in *Writing Early Modern History,* edited by Garthine Walker (London: Hodder Education, 2005): 95–113. Wiesner-Hanks provides an excellent overview of the field of women's history in general and early modern women's history in particular. We also recommend the remarkable three-volume collection, *Women's History in Global Perspective,* edited by Bonnie G. Smith (Urbana: University of Illinois Press, 2005). Written with the teacher in mind, these essays provide clear, accessible introductions to the historiography in many fields of women's history.

Finally, we have taken an explicitly feminist approach to *Women and Gender in the Western Past.* We believe that patriarchy is systemic in Western culture and has been the central force curtailing the movement and rights of women. However, we do not view patriarchy as stagnant. We explore how technology, politics, religion, economics, and a variety of social forces have interacted with patriarchal norms to influence women's lives.

Gerda Lerner once said, "Women's history is the primary tool for women's emancipation." We hope that this textbook can be one small part of that project.

## WEBSITE

The *Online Study Center* has been developed as a companion website for *Women and Gender in the Western Past.* Created by Marybeth Carlson, University of Dayton; Holly Hurlburt, Southern Illinois University; and Annette F. Timm, University of Calgary, it includes chapter outlines, web exercises, and pre-class quizzes to help students master the material.

## ACKNOWLEDGEMENTS

We are grateful for the care with which the many reviewers read the chapters of this text. Whenever possible, we integrated their suggestions, and their insightful comments and corrections made the manuscript stronger.

Marybeth Carlson, University of Dayton

Laurel Carrington, St. Olaf College

Craige Champion, Syracuse University

Ann Chirhart, Indiana State University

Susan Conner, Florida Southern College

Michelle Den Beste, California State University, Fresno

Susan Freeman, Minnesota State University, Mankato

Jennifer Heuer, Middlebury College

Holly Hurlburt, Southern Illinois University

Erika Kuhlman, Idaho State University

Lynn MacKay, Brandon University

Amy Thompson McCandless, College of Charleston

John McClymer, Assumption College

Elizabeth Green Musselman, Southwestern University

Kenneth Orosz, University of Maine

Brian Pavlac, King's College

Tammy Proctor, Wittenberg University

Judith Sebesta, University of South Dakota

Phyllis Soybel, College of Lake County

Emily Tai, Queensborough Community College

Annette Timm, University of Calgary

Deborah Valenze, Barnard College

Marta Vicente, University of Kansas

Leigh Whaley, Acadia University

This project has been an intellectual and emotional challenge that we could not have completed without the support of many people. At the University of Mary Washington, Allyson Poska would like to thank Jeff McClurken, Claudine Ferrell, Porter Blakemore, Carole Garmon, Leonard Koos, Liane Houghtalin, Lisa Patton, Mary Rigsby, and Steve Hanna, all of whom patiently answered questions, lent books, read sections of the text, and helped in a myriad of other ways. Lorene Nickel's spinning lesson helped her to better understand that critical aspect of women's work. Jack Bales, Beth Perkins, Carla Bailey and the rest of the staff at Mary Washington's library dedicated extra time and energy to fulfilling seemingly endless, and often quite unusual, requests.

At SUNY New Paltz, Katherine French would like to acknowledge the assistance of Lee Bernstein, Stella Dean, Kathleen Dowley, Andrew Evans, Barbara Hollingshead, Susan Lewis, and John Vander Lippe.

The staff at the Sojourner Truth Library was generous with their time, expertise, and support. We would also like to thank Sandy Bardsley, Stephen Bensch, Eric Carlson, Angela Creager, Emma Dench, Ellen Eisenberg, Robin Fleming, Christine Kraus, Amy Leonard, Nancy McLoughlin, Bella Millett, Lydia Murdoch, Hal Parker, Kevin Perry, Wim Phillips, Mary Louise Roberts, John Shinners, Thomas Sizgorich, Wendy Urban-Mead, and Merry Wiesner-Hanks. Each of these scholars willingly gave of their time and knowledge. We hope that we have not forgotten anyone, but if we have, please know that we valued your assistance just as much. Christopher Kilmartin went beyond the call of duty as he proofread and commented on every chapter. However, his contributions were more than technical. His knowledge of men's studies and masculinity was critical to our conceptualization of the project.

The staff at Houghton Mifflin—Jean Woy, Nancy Blaine, Jennifer Sutherland, Tawny Pruitt, and Jane Lee, as well as freelance art editor George McLean, Maria Sas at New Graphic Design, copyeditor Laurie McGee, proofreader Ruth Jagolinzer, and photo researcher Linda Sykes— guided us through what was a very challenging process. We are grateful for their dedication to this project.

Of course, our students offered challenging questions and often heard the first formulations of our ideas. Their interest in women's history was the spark for this project.

Katherine L. French
Allyson M. Poska

# About the Authors

Katherine L. French is Associate Professor of History at the State University of New York–New Paltz, where she teaches medieval and women's history. She received her Ph.D. from the University of Minnesota in 1993. She is the author of several articles on women and medieval popular religion. She is also the author of *The People of the Parish: Community Life in a Late Medieval English Diocese* (2001) and *Good Women of the Parish: Gender and Religion in Late Medieval England* (forthcoming).

Allyson M. Poska is Professor of History at the University of Mary Washington in Fredericksburg, Virginia, where she teaches European and Latin American history. She received her Ph.D. from the University of Minnesota in 1992. In addition to numerous articles, she is the author of *Regulating the People: The Catholic Reformation in Seventeenth-Century Spain* (1998) and *Women and Authority in Early Modern Spain: The Peasants of Galicia* (2005).

## Chapter 7

# Early Modern Europe, 1500–1700

*Sofonisba Anguissola, Self Portrait at an Easel (ca. 1556). Anguissola's talents as a portrait painter won her international acclaim, despite the fact that many people believed that self-portraits compromised a woman's femininity. (Muzeum Zamek w Lancucie, Lancut, Poland/Erich Lessing/Art Resource, NY.)*

■ **The Protestant Reformations** 218

   *The Lutheran Reformation* 218
   *Calvinist Discipline* 221
   *The Radical Reformation* 223
   *Women and the Formation of the*
     *Anglican Church* 224

■ **The Catholic Reformation** 225

   *Laywomen and the Catholic*
     *Reformation* 226
   *Women and the Inquisitions* 227
   *The Permeable Cloister: Women*
     *Religious After Trent* 228

■ **Life on the Margins: Witches,
Jews, and Muslims** 229

   *The Early Modern Witch-Hunts* 229
   *Expulsions and New*
     *Communities* 232
   *The End of Islam in Western*
     *Europe* 234

■ **Queens, Patrons, and
Petitioners** 235

   *Unifying Queens* 235
   *The Monstrous Regiment of*
     *Women* 235
   *Other Avenues to Power* 236
   *Gender, Politics, and the English*
     *Civil War* 238

■ **Art, Literature, and Science** 239

   *Gender Theory and Reality in Early*
     *Modern Thought* 239
   *Enlivening the Arts* 241
   *Behind Closed Doors: Women in*
     *Early Modern Science* 245

■ **European Expansion** 246

   *Life on the Periphery: European*
     *Women and the Colonization of*
     *Asia and the Americas* 246
   *Women and the Missionary*
     *Effort* 250
   *Native Women in the Conquest of*
     *the Americas* 250

Between 1500 and 1700, Europeans' understanding of the world was transformed. Protestant reformers successfully challenged the Catholic Church's monopoly on Christian belief, and the Catholic Church responded with its own program of reform. Women enthusiastically entered these religious conflicts, some joining new Protestant churches and others defending Catholic orthodoxy. However, both Protestant and Catholic leaders reaffirmed traditional beliefs about women's inferiority and attempted to constrain women's religious activities, forcing women to come up with new, innovative forms of religious participation. The religious turmoil led to anxiety about the state of society, and both Catholics and Protestants persecuted witches and non-Christians. Women were frequently the victims of these pressures for cultural homogeneity. Nevertheless, from queens to artisans' wives, women struggled for power against enemies of their countries and opponents of their sex. They eagerly ventured into new creative arenas and new lands, taking advantage of the unsettled nature of early modern life.

## THE PROTESTANT REFORMATIONS

Despite the many unsuccessful attempts to reform the Catholic Church during the Middle Ages, the pressure for reform did not abate. At the beginning of the sixteenth century, Martin Luther's attacks on the Catholic Church found enthusiastic support across Europe, and other Protestant reformers quickly offered their own novel interpretations of the Christian theology (see Map 7.1). Many women were attracted to Protestant ideas and even risked their lives to support their faith; however, Protestant leaders continued to defend traditional gender roles and hierarchies, rejecting women's attempts to become leaders in their religious communities.

### The Lutheran Reformation

Although many others had criticized Catholic doctrines and practices, Martin Luther (1483–1546), an Augustinian monk, formulated the most successful challenge to the power of the Catholic

## Chapter 7 ❖ Chronology

| | |
|---|---|
| **1492** | Defeat of Muslim Kingdom of Granada and Expulsion of Jews from Spain |
| **1519** | Martin Luther posts his ninety-five theses |
| **1525** | Caritas Pirckheimer defends her convent from assault by Lutherans |
| **1534** | King Henry VIII of England breaks with the papacy |
| | Anabaptists establish religious state in Münster |
| **1535** | Angela Merici founds the Order of St. Ursula |
| **1541** | Calvin reforms Geneva |
| **1545–1563** | The Council of Trent meets to define Orthodox Catholicism |
| **1553** | Mary Tudor becomes the first English queen since the formation of the monarchy |
| **1559** | Elizabeth I becomes head of the Church of England |
| **1572** | Thousands of Protestants killed in Saint Bartolomew's Day Massacre |
| **1598** | Henry IV of France issues the Edict of Nantes granting limited toleration to Protestants |
| **1609** | Moriscos expelled from Spain |
| **1685** | Revocation of the Edict of Nantes |

Church. Angered by the church practice of granting *indulgences* for the remission of sins in purgatory, he came to believe that the institution of the Catholic Church stood in the way of Christian salvation. In 1517, hoping to spark a debate, Luther posted ninety-five theses that questioned both church doctrine and papal authority. The theses enraged church authorities and Luther fled into the protection of Frederick, the Duke of Saxony (r. 1486–1525). Luther was later declared a heretic and excommunicated.

Challenging Catholic doctrine, Luther asserted that God granted salvation through faith alone and that no amount of good works could alter one's relationship with God. He also denied the special authority of the clergy, instead declaring that Christians belonged to a "priesthood of all believers." He believed that Scripture contained everything necessary for individual salvation, and that Christians should learn to read and interpret Scripture on their own. Luther denied the value of the sacraments not explicitly mentioned in Scripture and decreed that the intercession of saints, pilgrimages, relics, and miracles were useless. He also rejected monasticism and clerical celibacy.

Luther's views on women were complex. He believed that women were created by God and could be saved by faith alone. Thus, women, like men, no longer had to rely on the intervention of priests for their salvation. However, unlike Catholicism, Luther did not promote female models of spiritual power. Luther's God was not influenced by the Virgin Mary or supported by the work of female saints. Instead of the Virgin Mary, Luther extolled the virtues of Martha, the sister of Lazarus, who stayed in the kitchen, prepared the food, and oversaw the household. In fact, the image of woman as wife and mother dominated Luther's life and work. Soon after leaving the monastery, he married a former nun, Katherine von Bora (1499–1550), who eventually bore him nine children. He believed that men and women fulfilled God's will through

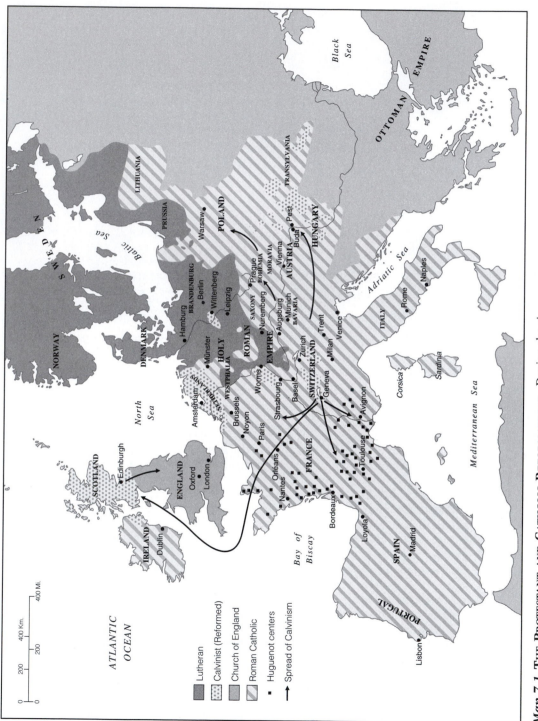

*Map 7.1* THE PROTESTANT AND CATHOLIC REFORMATIONS. During the sixteenth century, Protestantism broke the religious monopoly of the Catholic Church in western Europe. Many women converted to the new faiths, although the majority of men and women remained Catholic.

marriage. The decision not to marry went against the natural sex drive, which he believed was greater in women than in men.

The conversions of monarchs and municipal authorities to Luther's ideas changed the lives of women in their jurisdictions. Every Protestant territory passed a marriage ordinance that stressed wifely obedience, and city officials established new courts to handle marriage and morals cases that had previously fallen under the jurisdiction of church courts. Luther's emphasis on reading Scripture led authorities to establish schools for both girls and boys. However, Luther opposed too much learning for women, saying, "There is no dress that suits a woman as badly as trying to become wise."[1] As a result, Lutheran education for girls focused on religious morality, not intellectual achievement, and often lagged far behind men's. Protestantism also affected female artisans and merchants in unanticipated ways. People bought fewer votive candles, which were often made and sold by women, and as people began to eat meat on Fridays, the demand for fish declined, cutting into the profits of female fishmongers.[2] Poor women also suffered as Luther dissolved Catholic charitable institutions.

When local authorities assumed control over convents and their property, they released nuns from their vows and usually offered them dowries so that they would marry. Women who had entered the convent unwillingly or who were attracted by Luther's message rejoiced at leaving their convents, thrilled to be freed from their vows. However, others who remained Catholic or wanted no other life resisted. Caritas Pirckheimer (1467–1532), the abbess of a Clarissen convent in Nuremberg, refused to comply with that city's demand that she release her nuns from their vows. The city pressured the nuns to leave voluntarily, but they refused. According to Pirckheimer, when family members entered the convent and tried to drag their daughters out, "The children cried out that they did not want to leave the pious, holy convent, that they were absolutely not in hell, but if they broke out of it they would descend into the abyss of hell."[3] In Strasbourg, nuns in three convents refused to leave, and the city's elite, who relied on the convents to educate their daughters until they were married, supported their resistance. In the end, the city allowed the convents to remain open only as schools for girls. Even when the convents defied city laws by encouraging girls to become nuns, city magistrates did not close them.[4]

Beyond these pockets of resistance, many women displayed remarkable enthusiasm for the new faith; however, that enthusiasm threatened many men. City officials prohibited women from preaching and discouraged them from even gathering to discuss religion. Lutheran men silenced even their most prominent female supporters. Argula von Grumbach (1492–1563), a noblewoman from Bavaria, wrote open letters to the Duke of Bavaria and other officials protesting the treatment of Lutherans in Catholic territories, urging them to support the reformers, and arguing for open debate on religious issues in which women could participate. Her letters were printed and widely distributed, selling nearly thirty thousand copies in two years. She even met with both Martin Luther and a representative of the Holy Roman Emperor to press her case. However, Protestant men attacked her, not because they disagreed with her ideas, but because she was a woman. She received threats to wall her up, to break her fingers, and even to kill her. Her husband lost his job because of his failure to keep her under control. She eventually stopped writing but continued to support local Protestants.

Luther's reforms provoked a war between Lutheran and Catholic forces that devastated the continent for nearly forty years. Thousands died, and economic disruption and destruction was widespread. The violence only ended with the Peace of Augsburg (1555) in which the Lutheran princes and Charles V (r. 1519–1556), the Holy Roman Emperor, guaranteed a degree of religious toleration in the Empire. According to the settlement, the ruling prince would decide the religion of all the people in his territory. Subjects who disagreed with the ruler's faith would have to move elsewhere. As a result, some women followed family members or husbands into the new faith and new lands; for others, the adoption of Lutheranism by local authorities compelled them to convert.

## Calvinist Discipline

Following on the heels of Martin Luther, John Calvin (1509–1564), a French humanist and legal scholar, became committed to church reform in his early twenties and converted to Protestant beliefs around 1533. In 1536, when he was only twenty-seven years old, Calvin published his major theological work, *The Institutes of the Christian Religion*. He had much in common with Luther; but, according to Calvin, God decided a person's fate before his or her birth and few would receive God's grace. Nevertheless, Calvin declared that Christians should try to please God at all times and make every effort to lead lives worthy of those few, the elect, who were predestined for salvation.

Calvin took his reformed ideas to Geneva (Switzerland) in 1536, but city officials rejected them as too radical. When new elections brought Calvin's supporters to power in 1541, he returned to establish a perfect Christian community based on strict discipline. The Consistory, a group of carefully chosen male citizens, enforced adherence to Calvin's theology. Laws forbade everything from decorative buttons to gossip, and the Consistory had jurisdiction over a wide variety of infractions, including blasphemy, divorce, marriage disputes, and the practice of Catholicism. It had the authority to excommunicate and even execute offenders, but more often it merely admonished Genevans to behave appropriately.

Like Luther, Calvin believed that both men and women were created in the image of God and had equal opportunity for both sin and salvation. But, unlike many reformers, Calvin insisted that both sexes were responsible for sin and evil, as both Adam and Eve had sinned in the Garden of Eden. However, Calvin clearly asserted the inferiority of women to men. He described women with the same misogynist stereotypes as Catholic theologians, stating, "Men are preferred to females in the human race. We know that God constituted man as the head and gave him a dignity and preeminence above that of the woman. . . . It is true that the image of God is imprinted on all; but still woman is inferior to man."[5] He promoted motherhood as women's true calling and made clear that women's inferiority began with Eve's creation. As a result, he denied women positions of authority in his church.

The Consistory adopted Calvin's views on women and particularly monitored women's lapses in faith. At first, the Consistory did not punish women more often or more harshly than men, although it regularly interrogated women about their attendance at church and their knowledge of prayers. However, after Calvin's death, the Consistory reverted to a pre-Reformation double standard, sentencing female adulterers to be whipped and/or banished while punishing men with only fines and excommunication.[6]

Reformed missionary efforts were remarkably successful. John Knox (1513–1572) spread reformed ideas across Scotland where Calvinist ministers worked alongside *kirks,* parish committees of lay male elders similar to the Consistory. The kirks punished an array of moral offenses, but they focused on extramarital sex. They fined people who had sex outside of marriage and forced them to appear in church on the "stool of penitence" for three successive Sundays. Adulterers had to face the same humiliation for twenty-six consecutive Sundays. Sometimes the kirk punished recently married couples because it was clear that the wife had become pregnant before the wedding.[7]

Calvinism attracted many converts in France, where members became known as Huguenots. Violent conflict between Huguenots and French Catholics culminated in the deaths of more than six thousand Huguenots during and after the Saint Bartholomew's Day Massacre in 1572. Calvinist narratives describe incredible violence directed at Huguenot women, including the murder of pregnant women and the desecration of female bodies. Women were the perpetrators as well as the victims of the violence. In one case, in the city of Aix-en-Provence, a group of Catholic women butchers harassed and eventually hanged a Protestant woman from a nearby tree. In reaction, Protestant women marched through the streets and rioted alongside their husbands.[8]

Huguenots suffered through years of civil war, eventually moving their families to Protestant strongholds created by the Edict of Nantes (1598). The Edict, issued by King Henry IV (r. 1589–1610), granted limited toleration of Calvinism. However, that toleration did not last long. Louis XIV (r. 1643–1715) revoked the Edict in 1685, forcing nearly a quarter of a million Huguenot women and their families to flee France for the safety of Germany, England, and North America.

Calvinism also spread to parts of the Netherlands, Germany, Poland, and Hungary, and Dutch traders took Calvinism to Indonesia where they converted native islanders from the Catholicism that the Portuguese brought. Most converts to Calvinism were members of Europe's growing middle class. By the end of the sixteenth century, it had become the largest Protestant denomination.

## The Radical Reformation

Luther's belief that every Christian should read and interpret the Scriptures paved the way for many varieties of religious thought. The Anabaptists were among the most radical of the Reformation sects. The word *Anabaptist* comes from the Greek word meaning "to baptize again," and Anabaptists believed that only adults could make free choices about religious faith, baptism, and entry into the Christian community. They considered the idea of baptizing infants preposterous and wanted to rebaptize all adult believers. Anabaptists took the Gospels literally and favored a return to the kind of church that they believed had existed among the earliest Christians—a voluntary community of believers who had experienced an inner light.

Anabaptist communities developed in Switzerland, southern Germany, Moravia, the Baltics, and the Netherlands, but they never formed any overarching institutions or hierarchy. Indeed, women may have been attracted to Anabaptism because its lack of a formal hierarchy allowed some female leadership. At least in the early stages of the Anabaptist movement, numerous women chose Anabaptism over the objections of their spouses. Some divorced their unbelieving husbands and married other Anabaptists. Many women sought to convert others, and at least one fervent Anabaptist, Hilla Feicken, attempted to assassinate the Catholic bishop of Münster.[9] A number of women became Anabaptist prophets, and some Anabaptist communities even admitted women to the ministry. However, Anabaptist women did not enjoy leadership or clerical roles in the most infamous Anabaptist community, Münster, Germany.

Anabaptism's hold on Münster began with the migration of large numbers of followers from the Netherlands in the early 1530s. Led by the prophet Jan Matthys (d. 1534) and his loyal follower Jan Bockelszoon (d. 1535), the immigrants intended to make Münster into the New Jerusalem. They took over the city and created a utopian community. Anabaptist leaders outlawed private property and money, confiscated the property of Catholics, and began to stockpile food and clothing.

Once Matthys and Bockelszoon had established Anabaptism as the sole religion, it took a much less woman-friendly turn. They introduced polygyny in 1534, when the already-married Jan Bockelszoon wanted to marry Jan Matthys's widow to bolster his claim to the community's spiritual leadership. The authorities decreed that all women under a certain age must marry or face expulsion, justifying their decision through Biblical references to "be fruitful and multiply" and "to fill the earth with 144, 000." However, the male leadership also encouraged polygyny because women made up nearly 80 percent of the city's population. Although most early modern cities had a surplus of women, the demographic imbalance in Münster was especially severe after thousands of men fled during the Anabaptist takeover. They left their wives to look after family property, believing that the Anabaptists would be less likely to kill non-Anabaptist women. When the Anabaptists forced all the city's inhabitants to be rebaptized, the female majority could not flee and most probably did not convert to Anabaptism willingly. Polygynous marriages to Anabaptist men helped the city's leaders ensure that no women lived outside of male control. In fact, when some inhabitants rose up in opposition to polygny, the authorities fiercely crushed their movement, killing more than two hundred rebels. Women who opposed polygyny, including one of Jan Bockelszoon's many wives, were imprisoned or even executed.[10]

In addition, the city established a legal code that decreed the death penalty for insubordinate wives and forbade religious ecstasy and prophecy, both of which were associated with women. Münster's political-religious leadership even tried to deny Anabaptist women direct access to salvation and sanctity. They asserted that women were to their husbands as their husbands were to Christ and that they could only receive salvation through their husbands and then through Christ.

Anabaptist Münster only lasted for about a year. Catholic troops besieged the city and famine soon followed. Finally, in June 1535, a mercenary opened the city gates and, after bloody fighting, Bockelszoon and his supporters were captured, tortured, and executed.

Anabaptists in other communities often suffered persecution from both Protestants and Catholics. In Amsterdam, a small group of Anabaptists (seven men and five women) ran through the streets without clothes, proclaiming that the truth had to appear naked. They later stormed the city hall. In reaction, city authorities moved to repress the sect, executing seven Anabaptist women by drowning.[11] However, many less radical Anabaptist communities survived, and many members eventually emigrated to the Americas. These small, often isolated communities advocated pacifism, lived communally, and provided women with new forms of spiritual comfort.

## Women and the Formation of the Anglican Church

In England, conflict between King Henry VIII (r. 1509–1547) and the papacy, rather than theological differences, led to religious change. Soon after Henry succeeded to the throne in 1509, he married Catherine of Aragón, the widow of his deceased elder brother, Arthur. However, she bore him only a daughter, Mary, and as a queen had not ruled England since the formation of the monarchy, Henry feared that without a male heir England would be plunged into civil war. Henry wanted his marriage to Catherine annulled so that he could marry Anne Boleyn (1507–1536), a beautiful young courtier just arrived from France. When Pope Clement VII (r. 1523–1534) denied Henry's request, Henry broke with the papacy and forced Parliament to make him the head of the English, or Anglican, Church. Anne and Henry were secretly married in 1533. Anne supported Protestant clergy and writers and discussed religious reform with members of the royal court. She may even have influenced Henry's decision to sever all ties with Rome in 1534.

Despite his break with the Catholic Church, the theology of the English Church was still essentially Catholic and Henry actively persecuted self-identified Protestants. In one of the most famous cases, Anne Askew (1521–1546), a well-educated

member of a gentry family, defied her husband and joined the reformed church. In 1545, authorities charged Anne with heresy for preaching in London. When she refused to recant, she was tortured and executed in 1546 at the age of twenty-five.

However, even women who remained faithful Catholics felt the impact of Henry's policies. In Exeter, when officials arrived to shut Saint Nicholas's Hospital as a part of Henry's dissolution of the monasteries, women appeared with pitchforks to run off the workmen dismantling the building. Many women also were angered when Henry closed England's convents. In doing so, he abolished Englishwomen's primary means to an education and removed any trace of female authority from the English church. Parliamentary legislation even limited women's access to the English Bible. Among the nobility and gentry, both men and women could read the Bible in private, but only men could read aloud to their families. Male merchants, but not their wives or daughters, could read Scripture in private. Lower-class men and women were prohibited from reading the Bible at all.[12]

Henry's marital life continued to affect England's political and religious situation. Disappointed that his relationship with Anne did not produce a male heir, Henry had her arrested, charged with adultery and treason, and beheaded. He then married another courtier, Jane Seymour, who died giving birth to Henry's only son, Edward, in 1537. Henry had three more wives before dying in 1547. His last wife, Catherine Parr, was also an enthusiastic Protestant.

Despite Henry's split with Rome, the monarchy only began to create a truly Protestant church in England during his son, Edward's, short reign (r. 1547–1553). As Edward was still a minor, England was governed by regents, first the Duke of Somerset and then the Duke of Northumberland, both Protestants. They instituted a Protestant liturgy, created the Anglican prayer book, the *Book of Common Prayer,* and forced Catholics into hiding. However, England's flirtation with Protestantism ended at Edward's death at the age of sixteen. When Mary (r. 1553–1558), Edward's half sister, succeeded him in 1553, she returned the country to Catholicism by force. She condemned almost three hundred Protestants, nearly 20 percent of whom were women, to death in heresy trials. Most of the female Protestant martyrs were married, poor, and steadfast in their advocacy of the new faith.[13] The wives of Anglican bishops and clergy also suffered. Mary required clergymen to reject their wives and be celibate.

The English Reformation ultimately succeeded during the reign of Edward's other half sister, Elizabeth I (r. 1558–1603), daughter of Anne Boleyn. In 1559, Parliament reinstated the Act of Supremacy, which made Elizabeth the Supreme Governor of the Church of England and the first female head of a Protestant church. Although she pursued and executed staunch Catholics and forbade Catholic services, she paced her reforms and the reinstitution of Protestantism so that England avoided the religious violence that plagued the continent. The Anglican liturgy was similar to the Catholic services, except that it was in English. Elizabeth even allowed her clergy to redefine the meaning of the Eucharist to suit her style of reform, taking a middle ground between Catholic and Protestant thought.

Some members of the Church of England believed that the church should undergo more intense reform than Elizabeth had allowed. They wanted the church to be purified. Their detractors often referred to them as Puritans, but they called themselves, "the godly." Puritanism was attractive to women because they were free to participate in the two critical aspects of the Puritan experience, the pursuit of a personal experience of God and the practice of godly behavior that reflected their standing as God's elect. They could also be spiritual advisors to both men and women.[14]

During the transition to Protestantism, many women continued to be active Catholics. Although *recusants*, those who refused to attend Protestant services and use the *Book of Common Prayer,* were a small percentage of the population, many were women. Recusant women continued Catholic practices at home, gave religious instruction to their children, and sent their daughters to convents on the Continent. Some recusant women harbored priests, despite the fact that such an act was punishable by death.

Women across Europe enthusiastically accepted Luther's call for Christians to read and interpret Scripture and Calvin's injunction to live a disci-plined, Christian life. However, both men promoted traditional views of women. Anabaptism provided the most flexible gender expectations, but its lack of centralized authority led to both horrific abuses and widespread discrimination against its adherents. In England, religious instability challenged pious women of all beliefs. Although the new Protestant churches offered women alternative paths to salvation, men continued to control their public displays of faith.

## THE CATHOLIC REFORMATION

The Catholic Church was not unaware of the problems that Luther highlighted. Indeed, attempts to reform the Catholic Church from within began long before Martin Luther. Among others, humanist theologian Desiderius Erasmus (1469–1536) criticized the clergy's ignorance, the luxurious lifestyles of the church hierarchy, ostentatious liturgies, and the superstitious beliefs of the masses. However, these critiques had little impact on Catholic institutions and clergy until 1545 when Pope Paul III (r. 1534–1549) called a church council to stop the spread of Protestantism and end abuses within the clergy. The council met on and off in the Italian city of Trent for nearly twenty years (1545–1563), dodging wars, plagues, and international politics. The decrees the Council of Trent issued clearly defined orthodoxy and presented a program of reform that came to be known as the Catholic or Counter Reformation.

Among its many decrees, the Council of Trent condemned Lutheran ideas, reasserted that both church tradition and Scripture formed the basis of church doctrine, and reiterated that both faith and good works were necessary for salvation. The decrees insisted on clerical celibacy and promoted the education and reform of the clergy at all levels by directing bishops to establish seminaries to train priests. The Council also attempted to end clerical corruption, reform the monastic orders, and strengthen the power of bishops. Finally, the Council encouraged the expansion of extended religious education for the laity and emphasized participation in the seven sacraments and the veneration of saints. As the Catholic Church attempted to clearly explain doctrine and behavioral expectations, and to ensure consistency of practice and beliefs, it expressed increased suspicions about women and worked hard to constrain female sexuality.

## Laywomen and the Catholic Reformation

Laywomen were most affected by the church's regulation of the sacraments of baptism and marriage and its enforcement of prohibitions on extramarital sex. For centuries, midwives had baptized newborn babies who were in danger of dying; however, reforming bishops attempted to end that practice, urging parishioners to call the parish priest to the woman's bedside. If a priest was not available, the church preferred that a layman administer the sacrament. According to the reforms, a midwife was only supposed to administer baptism when no knowledgeable man was present. Bishops also increasingly required the examination of midwives to make certain that they understood the ritual and added no unorthodox words or ceremonies.

The church's emphasis on sexual morality led to renewed attempts to end clerical concubinage. At the time of the Reformation, many parish priests had concubines. These women often played critical roles in local religious activities, including acting as godmothers for parish children, helping administer last rites to the dying, and distributing charity to the needy. Bishops forced clergymen to remove their concubines and their children from their homes without making any provisions for their care. Both the priest and his concubine suffered. When a church official confronted a parish priest from Catalonia about his concubine, the priest replied, "that in conscience he could not do anything about it because he had lived with her for so long that to leave her now would destroy her."[15] As a result, some priests merely moved their female companions to nearby homes and continued their relationships in secret.

In a move that affected millions of Catholics, the church standardized marriage ceremonies. Prior to the Council of Trent, people relied on local customs and sexual mores when they decided to marry. Generally, families considered couples who promised marriage and had sexual intercourse married even if there were no witnesses. Although binding, these clandestine marriages often circumvented church prohibitions against marrying blood relations and frustrated family marriage strategies. According to the new decrees, a marriage was not legal until a priest had announced it three times from the pulpit of the parish church (a practice known as posting banns) and a clergyman had administered the nuptial blessing in front of witnesses. Women often benefited from the new procedures as they helped prevent bigamy and protected women from the unscrupulous behavior of men who promised marriage only to seduce them.

Church authorities hoped to end extramarital sex by shaming unmarried sexually-active women and their illegitimate children. The Council's decrees required parish priests to keep records of each child's birth that included the name and marital status of both parents. Priests and midwives were expected to pressure women to reveal the names of the fathers of their illegitimate children at the moment of the most intense labor pain. These decrees had little impact on fathers and did not take into account the circumstances of the sexual encounter, such as rape. Enforcement varied from parish to parish. In central areas and in large cities, efforts to end nonmarital sexual activity were quite successful, and in much of Europe, illegitimacy rates dropped to less than 2 percent. However, in many rural and peripheral areas of Europe, from northern Portugal to parts of Austria, illegitimacy rates remained high. The church even tried to control sex within marriage, by reiterating prohibitions against sexual activity during Advent and Lent and on a variety of holy days throughout the year.

The Catholic Reformation Church also attempted to make parish religious activity more uniform and solemn. Church officials rededicated many of the local shrines that women favored to more universally recognized venerations such as the Virgin Mary and the Holy Sacrament. As bishops made regular visits to parishes to ensure compliance with the decrees, they increasingly deemed local religious practices in which women played critical roles as "superstitious," such as the use of holy water for fertility rites. Bishops and priests carefully supervised local pilgrimages and festivals to prevent the sexual activity, drunkenness, and brawling that had become commonplace. For instance, in the bishopric of Speyer (Germany), ecclesiastical authorities were appalled to find that on Ash Wednesday, women controlled the village, chased after men, and drank heavily during the "women's carnival."[16] Despite their efforts, that festival, like many others across Europe, continued into the eighteenth century.

Church officials urged cities to close brothels and establish asylums, called Magdalene houses, to shelter repentant prostitutes. Some of these institutions were very strict. Female supervisors oversaw an exhausting regimen of work and prayer intended to prevent the women from returning to their immoral lives. In some Magdalene houses, the women learned Christian doctrine, lived by strict enclosure, and eventually professed as nuns. In Spain, in response to King Philip II's (1556–1598) request that she run a women's prison in Madrid, Madre Magdalena de San Jerónimo proposed a program of hard work, silence, and shaven heads. Madre Magdalena boasted that her regime to rehabilitate prostitutes was particularly harsh because it had been "invented by a woman against women."[17] Although these measures may have helped some women leave the streets, they did little to end prostitution.

## Women and the Inquisitions

Ecclesiastical officials in southern Europe turned to the Inquisition to discipline Catholics who did not conform to the church's expectations. During the Middle Ages, the Inquisition was established by papal decree only when the authorities uncovered potential heretics and was disbanded as soon as the heresy was suppressed. However, during the early modern period, monarchs established permanent Inquisitions in the Spanish kingdoms, Portugal, and parts of Italy. The Inquisition in Castile was created in 1483 at the request of Queen Isabel (r. 1474–1504) to ensure that her kingdom's population of newly converted Jews and Muslims, known in Spain as *New Christians*, did not relapse to their old faiths. Over the next century, the Spanish monarchy established twenty-one Inquisitional tribunals across the peninsula and in Spanish territories in Europe and the Americas.

Because women made up only a minority of defendants who faced the Inquisition, for that reason alone, it must have been a particularly frightening experience. All the Inquisition officials, from its judges and jailers to its executioners, were male. In addition, the punishments often had a different impact on women than on men. For instance, for many crimes, Inquisitors sentenced the guilty person to be stripped naked to the waist and whipped as he or she rode a mule through the city streets. For men, such punishment may have been painful, but women also had to endure the humiliation of public nudity.

*Old Christian* women, those free of Muslim or Jewish blood, were most often accused of blasphemy for asserting that the virginity of Mary was impossible, that marriage was better than celibacy, or that it was better to be the concubine of a good man than to be married to a bad man. They were mostly illiterate and misinformed peasant women, who saw themselves as righteous Catholics and loyal believers, not heretics. Inquisitors reacted accordingly. Most of the guilty were forced to publicly recant and pay a fine.

The Spanish Inquisition rarely pursued witchcraft accusations. Prosecutions for crimes involving superstition and witchcraft accounted for only 7.9 percent of the total number of cases between 1540 and 1700.[18] However, some women were accused of both asking for and providing love magic. A woman who desired the attentions of a particular man sought out a healer who then gave her incantations and recipes for concoctions that would make the man love only her. In one incantation, the woman repeated, "I conjure you / blood from the crimson fountain—or my fountain— make [man's name] follow [woman's name] like the lamb after the sheep."[19] Other women looked to healers to help them end abuse, impotence, or adultery by their husbands. The church viewed love magic as dangerous because the incantations often used the names of saints and God blasphemously and because such magic infringed on the man's free will.

As early modern people did not really understand female homosexuality, few women were charged with having sex with other women. In one case, in the mid 1650s, community members denounced two women for their sexual activity to the Aragonese tribunal, and they were convicted, while in another case, the officials of the Inquisition in Madrid told the Saragossa tribunal not to prosecute two women since they had not used an artificial phallus.[20] In contrast, thousands of men were denounced to both the Spanish and Portuguese Inquisitions for having sex with other men. Inquisitors were more likely to convict and burn a foreigner, particularly a native of France, or a slave of sodomy than a Spaniard. Both accusers and Inquisitors associated sodomy with foreignness and religious heresy, especially Lutheranism. Sexual activity between slaves and freemen, especially black slaves, disrupted class and racial hierarchies.

## The Permeable Cloister: Women Religious After Trent

Reiterating medieval papal decrees, the Council of Trent demanded that all female religious live in cloistered religious communities. Reformers pursued a two-pronged approach to enclosure: active enclosure, which completely prohibited nuns from leaving the cloister, as well as passive enclosure, which limited the access of outsiders to the convent. Bishops frequently wanted convent buildings altered to make them as impenetrable as possible. They ordered convent doors locked and garden walls constructed and instructed abbesses to guard the keys to doors and windows. If male visitors, such as confessors and doctors, had to enter the community, a trustworthy, often older nun had to accompany them. The abbess appointed a listener to monitor conversations between nuns and laypeople in the convent's visiting parlors. In Milan, officials attempted to prevent even accidental contact between nuns and the outside world by mandating that nuns could only take in washing if both the wearer and the washer were anonymous.[21]

Some communities willingly accepted enclosure and retreated from the world. However, across Europe, many convents obstinately resisted the reformers' demands. Convents refused to undertake the required alterations to their facilities and chased off clergy charged with enforcing enclosure. Frequently, they claimed that these demands ran counter to the customs and traditions of their communities and argued that their observance of monastic rules was already sufficiently rigorous.

Full enclosure also threatened the ability of convents to maintain their ties to their secular patrons and their economic interactions with local communities. As owners and administrators of nearby towns and lands, convent officers had to interact with municipal authorities on a regular basis, and many continued to do so despite the prohibitions. Because many nuns were supported by income from family property, convents continued to enter into litigation to protect their incomes. Thus, although enclosure changed the functioning of many Catholic Reformation convents, for others it never became a reality.

The Council of Trent also acted to end abuses in convents. Women had to be sixteen years old before taking final vows, and the Council reiterated previous decrees that prohibited families from forcing young women to profess. Finally, the church prohibited women from joining tertiary orders in which they took simple vows but lived outside of convents. As a result, one-third of the women in a Franciscan tertiary convent in Munich left rather than submit to full enclosure.[22]

Both the Inquisition and other church courts grew increasingly suspicious of female mystical activity. Church officials regularly accused female mystics of preaching, engaging in inappropriate relationships with confessors, and even faking their mystical ecstasies. To avoid suspicion, the Spanish abbess and reformer Teresa of Avila (1515–1582) counseled the nuns in her convent not to do anything to provoke religious raptures, such as fasting or not sleeping enough.

Despite the restrictions, many women believed in the goals of the Catholic Reformation. In her reform of the Carmelite Order, Teresa of Avila embraced the goals of the Catholic Reformation Church, emphasizing obedience and contemplation, while still meeting the spiritual needs of her nuns. She encouraged mental prayer, which many church officials feared would lead women into diabolical possession. Teresa argued that she and her nuns used their prayers as a weapon in the church's struggles. Even when her ideas led to conflicts with her opponents and investigations of heresy by the Inquisition, Teresa remained enthusiastically supportive of the reformers' goals.

A number of women attempted to fulfill the gender expectations of Catholic orthodoxy and work in the world at the same time. Angela Merici (ca. 1471–1540), founder of the Order of St. Ursula (the Ursulines) in 1535, established a community of pious laywomen who worked in orphanages and schools for abandoned girls and reformed prostitutes. Initially, the Ursulines effectively avoided enclosure, purposely dressing differently from nuns and living among those they served. However, despite their piety, Catholic Reformation clerics felt threatened by these independent, chaste women. After Merici's death, authorities gradually forced most members into the cloister.

English Catholic Mary Ward (1585–1645) encountered similar obstacles when trying to work outside the convent. Beginning in 1609, Ward established schools known as the "Institutes of the Blessed Virgin Mary" across the continent from the Netherlands to eastern Europe. Ward modeled her organization after the Jesuits, a monastic order founded in 1540 by the Spaniard Ignatius Loyola (1491–1556). He and his followers preached throughout Europe and the Spanish colonies and staffed the new seminaries designed to educate the Catholic clergy. Although Loyola did not allow women to join his order, Ward and her followers sought to emulate the Jesuits' great learning and strict Catholicism. In her schools (some of which were free and open to the poor), female lay teachers taught Latin, Greek, mathematics, religion, and the arts. However, her assertiveness and the success of the Institutes incurred the disapproval of the ecclesiastical authorities. Gossipmongers accused her of being sexually intimate with her Jesuit confessor and even of living disguised as a man in a Jesuit community. More dangerous yet, many clergy and powerful laymen believed that Ward and her followers were improperly usurping men's roles in the reassertion of Catholicism in England. In 1630, Pope Urban VIII suppressed the Institutes and Ward was denounced as a heretic for refusing to submit to enclosure.

Only Vincent de Paul's (1581–1660) Daughters of Charity successfully avoided enclosure. In 1633, he asked his friend Louise de Marillac (1591–1660) to help him train women to minister to the community. The women took private vows that each renewed annually. To prevent enclosure, De Paul never constructed any building to house the Daughters, so that nothing existed that church authorities might call a cloister. Backed by powerful, wealthy patrons, the Daughters ran hospitals, hospices, and insane asylums across northern France, and by the eighteenth century, they were France's premier nursing community.

In response to criticism from both Protestants and Catholics, the Catholic Church aggressively pursued its own reforms. Some women's lives changed substantially as ecclesiastical officials attempted to end nonmarital sexual activity, control marriage, and regulate life within the convent. However, not all women eagerly accepted the new restrictions. They challenged the church's reforms and found creative ways to fulfill their spiritual goals.

## LIFE ON THE MARGINS: WITCHES, JEWS, AND MUSLIMS

The same religious enthusiasm that energized the Protestant and Catholic Reformations also produced fears about the presence of evil in Christian society. As a result of those fears, both faiths persecuted witches and non-Christians—people who were viewed as dangerous. The fight against evil and the pursuit of religious homogeneity had serious implications for women living on the margins of Christian society.

### The Early Modern Witch-Hunts

Medieval and early modern Europeans believed in the constant presence of the supernatural in the world and in the ability of some people to access supernatural power. The clergy could access that power through the administration of the sacraments and through their access to certain objects, such as holy water, holy oils, and the Eucharist. Other people, including mystics, healers, and midwives (all occupations associated with women) could also call upon supernatural power through the use of magic. Good magic, like healing and divination, existed for everyone's benefit. Black magic (*maleficia*) caused harm. Although people might believe that witches existed and that some people practiced magic, no one identified himself or herself as a witch. People used "witch" as a slur against men and women whose magical abilities had become suspect.

Although local people made the initial accusations against witches, educated government and ecclesiastical officials controlled the judicial processes. Many of these men were influenced by a famous treatise on witch-hunting known as the *Malleus Malificarum* (1486), (*The Witches Hammer*), by two Dominican inquisitors, Heinrich Kramer and Jacob Sprenger. The *Malleus* emphasized the relationship between women and witchcraft and put forward the notion that some women who practiced magic had sex and made pacts with the devil. Witches supposedly danced naked with the devil, kissed his ass, and engaged in sexual relations with him.

Witchcraft trials had taken place in the Middle Ages, but witch-hunts (large-scale trials) were purely an early modern phenomenon. In addition to the general anxiety of the period, many scholars have attributed early modern witch-hunting to some key changes in the way that witchcraft was prosecuted. During the Middle Ages, the injured party accused a witch in public. If the accused confessed or if the accuser offered substantive proof, the judge would find the defendant guilty. If

not, the judge would look to God to judge the accused through an ordeal, such as carrying a hot iron or placing a hand in boiling water. By the early modern period, most courts had adopted inquisitorial systems in which local authorities might also bring accusations. The judges and judicial systems then undertook investigations that included interrogations and witness depositions. Trials were no longer contests of right and wrong before God, but rather official procedures in which judges decided results based on the rules of law. The use of torture also changed witch trials. Although the Mediterranean Inquisitions required that any confession made under torture had to be repeated without torture, other judicial systems did not have that safeguard. Torture often elicited the names of supposed accomplices in addition to confessions, thus creating a witch-hunt from a single accusation. In England, the system was different, as torture was prohibited in witchcraft cases and juries of laymen decided the guilt or innocence of the accused.

**WITCH GIVING RITUAL KISS TO THE DEVIL (1626).** During the early modern period, elite ideas about witchcraft increasingly associated women with the devil. This image from Francesco Maria Guazzo's *Compendium Maleficarum,* an early modern witchcraft manual, vividly portrays contemporary connections between gender, sex, and the devil. *(The Granger Collection, New York.)*

Table 7.1

## SEX OF ACCUSED WITCHES

| Region | Years | Male | Female | % Female |
|---|---|---|---|---|
| Southwestern Germany | 1562–1684 | 238 | 1,050 | 82 |
| Bishopric of Basel | 1571–1670 | 9 | 181 | 95 |
| Franche-Comté | 1559–1667 | 49 | 153 | 76 |
| Geneva | 1537–1662 | 74 | 240 | 76 |
| Pays de Vaud | 1581–1620 | 325 | 624 | 66 |
| County of Namur (Belgium) | 1509–1646 | 29 | 337 | 92 |
| Luxembourg | 1519–1623 | 130 | 417 | 76 |
| City of Toul | 1584–1623 | 14 | 53 | 79 |
| Dept. of the Nord, France | 1542–1679 | 54 | 232 | 81 |
| Castile | 1540–1685 | 132 | 324 | 71 |
| Aragon | 1600–1650 | 69 | 90 | 57 |
| Venice | 1550–1650 | 224 | 490 | 69 |
| Finland | 1520–1699 | 316 | 325 | 51 |
| Estonia | 1520–1729 | 116 | 77 | 40 |
| Russia | 1622–1700 | 93 | 43 | 32 |
| Hungary | 1520–1777 | 160 | 1,482 | 90 |
| County of Essex, England | 1560–1675 | 23 | 290 | 93 |
| New England | 1620–1725 | 75 | 267 | 78 |

Source: Brian P. Levack, *The Witch-Hunt in Early Modern Europe*, 2nd ed. (London: Longman, 1995), 134.

Between roughly 1450 and 1750, approximately one hundred thousand Europeans were tried for witchcraft. The enthusiasm for witch-hunting varied greatly across Europe. About half of the trials took place in the German lands of the Holy Roman Empire, and authorities in the adjacent lands of Poland, Switzerland, and France also conducted large numbers of trials. In contrast, the number of witch trials in Spain and Italy was much lower, probably no more than ten thousand. Across Europe, approximately forty thousand to sixty thousand people were executed as witches, although the rates of execution varied from 90 percent of those tried in the Pays de Vaud (France) to only about 12 percent in Iberia and Italy.[23]

The relationship between witchcraft and women was complex. Scholars consider it a sex-related but not a sex-specific crime, as women were the frequent, but not the only subjects of witchcraft accusations (see Table 7.1). In Denmark, Switzerland, and Hungary, women made up 90 percent or more of those accused. In contrast, in the Baltic nations of Finland, Estonia, and Russia more men were accused than women, and the same was true in the Spanish Kingdom of Aragón and in Iceland. Overall, women were more than 75 percent of those accused of witchcraft. The fact that officials hunted witches in both Catholic and Protestant regions of Europe indicates that adherents of both faiths shared similar ideas about witchcraft and witches and similar fears about women.[24]

It is difficult to create a profile of the typical witch, but certain women were more susceptible to charges of witchcraft than others. Neighbors sometimes denounced women healers and midwives as witches because of their knowledge of women's bodies and their presence at the death of mothers in childbirth and infants. Older women also regularly fell victim to witchcraft charges. Women older than age fifty, although not rare, were less common than they are today. These independent, sexually experienced women could be threatening to other community members. Moreover, women accused of witchcraft may have tended to be older because they had been healers or midwives for many decades, and tensions about their supposed powers had built up over the years.

Finally, the early modern women accused of witchcraft were often poor. Generally, they were not the poorest people in the community, but they lived on the margins of subsistence and had no families to help them. As a result, they often relied on charity for their survival. During economic crises, when these women begged for food from already impoverished neighbors, they provoked guilt and resentment. Women frequently accused other women, reminding us that both men and women believed that women were more likely to engage in witchcraft.

Another component of early modern witch-hunting was the prosecution of cases of demonic possession. Traditionally, people believed that those possessed by the devil could be "cured" by exorcism. In early modern society, women were most often considered possessed, and many believed that women were responsible for causing the devil to enter their bodies and that therefore they had to be punished. Cases of demonic possession often led to multiple accusations of witchcraft. In one of the most famous cases, seventeen Ursuline nuns in a convent at Loudon in southern France allegedly were possessed by demons. The witch trials in Salem, Massachusetts (1692), in which hundreds of people were accused of witchcraft, began with the accusation that two girls were possessed.

The role of sex was clearly evident in trial procedures. Judges frequently searched women's bodies for the devil's mark. Many judges believed that the devil branded his followers with a scar or that witches had an extra nipple. Accused women were stripped and shaved before being thoroughly searched. Although midwives or other women might be trusted to search for the mark, most of the humiliating and erotically charged inspections were done by male judges in front of all-male audiences. Additionally, as mentioned in the previ-

ous section, men often watched, touched, or hurt partially naked women during tortures and punishments.

Early modern witch-hunting met a rapid end. By the seventeenth century, as authorities relied more on empirical investigation, the numbers of witchcraft accusations quickly dwindled. As early as 1610–1614, after mass accusations led to a witch panic in Logroño in the Spanish Basque country, Inquisition officials in Madrid put a halt to the trials and investigations. The new Inquisitor used empirical study to prove that the ointments witches allegedly used were harmless and concluded that witchcraft had not taken place. Moreover, some European intellectuals had long expressed skepticism about the existence of witchcraft, asserting that it contradicted the belief in an all-powerful God. By 1700, witchcraft trials had almost entirely disappeared from western Europe, although they continued in Hungary and other parts of eastern Europe for another half century.

## Expulsions and New Communities

Early modern Europeans not only feared the existence of witches in their communities, but also the presence of non-Christians. Early modern anti-Semitism was driven by a desire for religious homogeneity that had its roots in the Middle Ages. As a result, by the end of the late Middle Ages, monarchs had expelled Jews from much of northern Europe. Queen Isabel of Castile and her husband, Ferdinand of Aragón, ordered the expulsion of the remaining unconverted Jewish population of the Spanish kingdoms on March 31, 1492. Within six months, Spanish Jews had to accept baptism or leave the country.

Recent scholarship suggests that despite the edict only some of the Spanish kingdoms' eighty thousand Jews left Spain. Approximately ten thousand Jews left the Mediterranean coast in 1492 and 1493, and another thirty-five thousand spent some time in exile in neighboring Portugal and Navarre, where Judaism was still tolerated. To remain in Spain, Jews had to convert to Christianity. Many Jews sincerely converted and quickly assimilated into Christian culture. For those women, this meant altering the family's eating habits (for instance, by including pork), having their children baptized, and attending Mass on a regular basis. However, many women secretly adhered to Jewish tradition and became known as crypto-Jews. These women maintained Jewish culture by continuing to clean meat according to Jewish law. They also followed Sabbath traditions like wearing freshly laundered clothes and avoiding work.

Although the Inquisition had no jurisdiction over Jews who had not yet converted, it took a special interest in crypto-Jews. In fact, during the first fifty years of its existence, the majority of Inquisition cases dealt with recently converted Jews accused of relapsing to their Jewish faith. Female converts from Judaism, *conversas,* were regularly accused of cooking "Jewish" foods, trimming or washing meats according to Jewish law, and/or preparing clean clothing and linens for the Sabbath. Their Christian servants often denounced them. While many conversas confessed to their "crimes" in the hope of avoiding execution, at least one accused Judaizer, María López, argued that she had been falsely accused and that her suspicious laundry and food habits had been those of a conscientious, clean housewife, not those of a clandestine Jew.[25] She was convicted and handed over to the secular authorities for execution. Between 1480 and 1530, thousands of converted Jews were executed as heretics.

After their expulsion from Spain, many Jews fled to Portugal, where they eventually made up nearly a fifth of the Portuguese population. The Portuguese monarchy expected these immigrants to convert, but promised not to introduce the Inquisition for twenty years. When the Portuguese king finally established the Inquisition in 1536, thousands of New Christians fled the country.

As a result of these expulsions, during the sixteenth century the Netherlands became a major center of early modern Sephardic (from the Hebrew word for Spain, *Sepharad*) Jewish culture. Wealthy Sephardic families contributed to its rich, cosmopolitan culture. They built fabulous synagogues that attracted non-Jewish visitors, and patronized artists and musicians. The Duarte family, affluent Antwerp jewelers and diamond merchants, made their home into a center of music and the visual arts. Their daughter, Leonora Duarte (ca. 1610–1678), composed music, and the family was renowned for its musical abilities. Sephardic women benefited from their commu-

nity's economic and social success; they were twice as likely to be literate as their counterparts in the Christian community.[26]

After the expulsions, many Sephardic Jews, like Doña Gracia Mendes Nasi (1510–1569), were caught precariously between Christian and Jewish cultures. Born in Portugal to a recently converted family of Spanish emigrants, she was baptized Beatriz de Luna. She later married the son of a wealthy Spanish Jewish family, Francisco Mendes, who had also recently fled to Portugal. During their short marriage, the crypto-Jewish couple maintained connections with their Jewish heritage and other converso families. When Francisco died, he left Doña Gracia with a daughter and half of his extensive properties. She and her daughter then fled the Portuguese Inquisition for Antwerp, where her husband's family had a successful business in luxury goods. In Antwerp, Doña Gracia grew wealthy through the family business, using her money to aid conversos fleeing the Iberian Peninsula and to support the publication of works by Jewish scholars and rabbis. Her powerful social and business alliances included both Christians and Jews.

Despite her baptism, Doña Gracia continued to practice Judaism and was, therefore, a Christian heretic. To punish her, Holy Roman Emperor Charles V ordered the confiscation of the Mendes family records and assets, but Doña Gracia prevented the destruction of her financial empire by bribing the emperor with a substantial loan. She then dismantled the family business in Antwerp and moved her family and her wealth to the relative safety of Venice. In 1552, she and her daughter moved to Constantinople where they could practice Judaism openly. There, Doña Gracia became a leader in the Jewish community and a great philanthropist and businesswoman who was influential at the sultan's court. She even pressured Jewish shippers and traders to boycott the Italian port of Ancona after the Inquisition burned twenty-six of the city's Jews. Jewish and Ottoman leaders enforced the embargo, which only collapsed after the economic pressure on Ancona's Jewish community became too great. When Doña Gracia died in 1569, twenty thousand people attended her funeral.

While the Netherlands became the center of Sephardic Jewry, large numbers of central European

Jews emigrated to Poland, which became home to the largest Jewish community in the world at the time. The Jewish population grew from approximately one hundred thousand at the end of the sixteenth century to more than five hundred thousand by the middle of the eighteenth century. The Polish monarchy allowed Jews to freely practice their religion and engage in most occupations.

## The End of Islam in Western Europe

Unlike the Jewish population, Europe's remaining Muslims were expelled entirely from western Europe. At the end of the fifteenth century, the only significant populations of Muslims lived in the Kingdom of Aragón, where they made up nearly one-third of the population, and in the Kingdom of Granada, the last Muslim stronghold in western Europe. In Aragón, most Muslims worked as farmers or peasants on large estates owned by Christians. When they lived in Christian cities, Muslims were forced to live in ghettos.

With the final destruction of the Muslim kingdom in 1492, Isabel and Ferdinand promised this large minority population a degree of religious toleration. However, under pressure to convert, Muslims in Granada revolted in 1499. After the revolt, the Spanish monarchs declared the treaty null and void, offering Muslims living in the Crown of Castile the choice of conversion or expulsion. Thousands left for North Africa, but many more converted, at least nominally. Many others just kept to themselves, remained loyal to their Islamic faith in private, and hoped to avoid confrontation with Christian officials.

In 1527, in an attempt to end an uprising of Muslim peasants, Charles V reached an agreement with Muslim authorities that the Inquisition would not be too rigorous in seeking out relapsers and that they could retain their own customs for the next forty years. During this transitional period, women were central to the Muslim community's resistance to Christianization. Without mosques, Arabic books, or official religious leaders, the home became the secret center of Islamic life. The fact that Muslims were forced to live in ghettos reinforced the ability of women to maintain Islamic culture in secret. Under the careful supervision of women, families could even continue to celebrate the Muslim holy month of Ramadan in the privacy of their homes, and newborns could be presented in traditional Muslim ceremonies before being taken to the church for baptism. *Moriscas*, Muslim women who had converted to Christianity, hid Arabic books and taught their children Islamic prayers. As a result, Moriscas were frequently denounced to the Inquisition for maintaining Islamic rituals, dietary laws, and fast days, and Christian clerics accused Moriscas of preventing their children from attending compulsory Christian schools.[27]

Not all Morisca resistance took place within the home. When the Morisco population in the mountains outside of Granada revolted in 1568, women armed with stones and roasting spits joined in the rebellion. However, the results were disastrous. Once the revolt was suppressed, the Spanish government dispersed the remaining population across the kingdom. Many were enslaved, and young children were removed from their families to ensure that they were raised as Christians. Finally, in April 1609, King Philip III (r. 1598–1621) decided in favor of the expulsion of the Moriscos. Forced to pay their own passage, authorities herded more than 275,000 Moriscos aboard waiting vessels that left under naval escort for North Africa. Without further research, we can only speculate on the impact of the expulsion on women. Mothers must have suffered as they were forced to leave their young children behind to be converted to Christianity. The expulsion also must have increased their economic stress, as few Moriscos were wealthy and many had to leave most of their belongings behind. Finally, Moriscas were no doubt critical in the establishment of new households in foreign lands.

As both Catholics and Protestants attempted to consolidate authority in their respective territories, they worked to purify their communities of people whom they saw as threatening. Thousands of poor and old women were victims of witch-hunts, and Jews and Muslims faced expulsion in the name of religious homogeneity. Gender played a central role in these events. Regardless of their beliefs or social status, suspicions about women's knowledge and their authority in the home made them particularly vulnerable to marginalization and persecution.

# QUEENS, PATRONS, AND PETITIONERS

During the early modern period, many European kingdoms developed into strong, centralized monarchies, a process that has traditionally been viewed as the product of masculine accomplishments on the battlefield and at the negotiating table; however, in their formative periods, powerful female monarchs led many of these nations. Despite obstacles to their rule, these women ruled adeptly, molding gender ideologies to reinforce their authority. Behind the scenes, noblewomen used their resources and influence to support their families and beliefs. By the end of the seventeenth century, even savvy nonaristocratic women dared to enter the political arena and express their political opinions in public.

## Unifying Queens

During the late Middle Ages and early modern period, women regularly ruled in Europe, as both queens and regents. They exercised power with authority, never shirking from diplomatic or military confrontation. Indeed, the fifteenth century began and ended with powerful queens successfully unifying large kingdoms and establishing new models for female rule. Margaret of Denmark (1353–1412) rose to power as regent for her son Olaf in 1375. As regent, she consolidated power by forcing the return of royal castles that had been taken by the Hanseatic League, an association of northern German merchants, and laid the groundwork for Olaf's expansion of Danish territory. However, Olaf died suddenly in 1387 and in a curious turn of events, the Danish nobility chose Margaret to succeed her childless son as "guardian" of the kingdom. Quickly, Margaret had the nobility declare her queen of Denmark and the following year she convinced the Norwegian nobles to elect her as their queen following the death of her husband, King Haakon VI (r. 1340–1380). She even won the support of the Swedish nobility who proclaimed her queen of Sweden in 1388. Margaret signed the Union of Kahlmar in 1397, uniting the three kingdoms under one rule. She chose her great-nephew, Erik of Pomerania (1382–1439), as the ruler of the three kingdoms, but she never gave up her guardianship of the thrones. She successfully fought off German incursions until her sudden death in 1412. The Scandinavian union that she created lasted until 1523.

Similarly, Isabel of Castile fought for the consolidation of her kingdom and set the stage for the eventual unification of the Spanish kingdoms under one monarch. Before becoming queen, Isabel and her supporters had to defeat Castile's stubborn nobility, many of whom supported her niece Juana as the legitimate heir to the throne. Isabel secretly arranged to marry Ferdinand, the prince and soon to be king of the neighboring Kingdom of Aragón. While each continued to rule separately in their respective kingdoms, the alliance helped solidify her own succession and Castile's defeat of the Muslim Kingdom of Granada. Isabel further expanded her power when she petitioned for the establishment of a permanent Inquisition. She made certain that it fell under royal, not papal jurisdiction. Isabel brought religious unity to the peninsula by defeating the Kingdom of Granada and expelling the Jewish population. She also strengthened royal authority by placing royal officials in each city and by creating a rural police force.

## The Monstrous Regiment of Women

Despite these powerful late medieval precedents, most early modern political thinkers declared that women were unsuited to politics. In one of the most virulent attacks on female rule, in 1558 the Scottish Calvinist John Knox (1505–1572), faced with the rule of Mary Tudor in England, Mary Stuart (1542–1587) in Scotland, and Catherine de Médicis (1519–1589) in France, termed their rule "the monstrous regiment of women." Many thinkers fervently believed that men had to rule over women to maintain the order God created. Clerics, aristocrats, and intellectuals challenged women's right and ability to govern based on their sex. As a result, early modern queens either creatively employed different strategies to overcome opposition to their rule or suffered severe consequences.

Despite the fact that Henry VIII legitimized his daughters' successions in the 1544 Act of Succession, Elizabeth I had to transcend the expectations of her gender and act like a man without appearing manly, and therefore unnatural, in order to govern effectively. Hoping to prevent her enemies from marking her as weak because of her sex, Elizabeth I remained unmarried and childless despite the succession problems that dogged her reign. By remaining the "Virgin Queen," she de-emphasized her sexuality to such a degree that men could respect her as a monarch. Her strategy was largely successful. According to her advisor Robert Cecil, she became "more than a man and in truth somewhat less than a woman."[28]

In contrast, Mary, Queen of Scots fell victim to early modern gender expectations, as her enemies manipulated her through her lovers and husbands. Mary became queen of Scotland before she was a week old, but was reared in France and married the young king Francis II (r. 1559–1560). He died shortly after, but she did not return to Scotland to take the throne until she reached the age of majority in 1561. Although Catholic, she agreed to rule alongside her half brother's Protestant-led government that was in place when she arrived. She faced constant and strong opposition. Her detractors accused her of sexual promiscuity (a typical argument against women's ability to rule), charges that seemed to be confirmed by her many marriages and lovers. Her second husband, Lord Darnley, sided with the nobility against her and had her secretary (and rumored lover) murdered. Accusations of adultery, lust, and "unbridled licentiousness" plagued her. Eventually, Darnley was strangled and blown up in a Protestant plot in which Mary was implicated. She then eloped with the man who had murdered Darnley. Her decision to marry again, this time to a Protestant, caused a revolt by the Catholic nobility. They quickly defeated her armies and forced her to abdicate in favor of her son, who was crowned as James VI (r. 1567–1625) while still an infant. Mary then sought refuge at the court of Elizabeth I. Protestants unfavorably compared the thrice-married Mary to the virginal Elizabeth. When she arrived in England, Elizabeth had her seized and kept under house arrest. The English eventually charged her with conspiracy to assassinate Elizabeth. Elizabeth had Mary tried and executed for treason in 1587. Unlike Elizabeth I, Mary never found a way to move beyond the negative expectations of her sex.

Catherine de Médicis used a different strategy to maintain her authority, basing her rule on traditional expectations of motherhood. In the fourteenth century, the French monarchy invoked medieval Salic laws of inheritance to prevent women from succeeding to the throne; however, women like Catherine regularly ruled as regents for their minor sons. Catherine had little power during the reign of her husband and that of her first son, Francis II, but upon Francis's death in 1560, the government fell entirely into her hands. She ruled as regent for her second son, Charles IX, until he reached the age of majority in 1563, and she dominated him for the duration of his reign. Catherine exerted power in ways that Elizabeth could not. She presented herself as the pious widow, devoted to her late husband and the mother of future kings of France. She put motherhood at the heart of her queenship, making it the source of her power. When she brought peace or formed alliances, it was not as a ruler but as the mother of France. This strategy seems to have worked during her lifetime. In the earliest stages of the Catholic-Protestant conflict, she played the role of the peacemaker, encouraging Huguenot noblewomen to live at court and allowing them to worship as they pleased.[29] She continued to pursue peace, both at home and internationally, but religious partisans on both sides hindered her efforts. Although this emphasis on her femininity brought her power, it also left her vulnerable to attacks. After the plot to assassinate the Protestant leader Gaspar de Coligny (1519–1572) and the deaths of an estimated six thousand other Huguenots in the Saint Bartholomew's Day Massacre, both sides were eager to believe that she condoned if not initiated the violence. Her enemies turned her maternal identity upside down, describing her as a corrupt, unnatural mother who either dominated her children to further her own ambitions or a dangerous mother who put the good of her children over the needs of the state. Catherine's power declined after Charles died and her third son, Henry III (r. 1574–1589), succeeded to the throne.[30]

## Other Avenues to Power

Royal women often exercised considerable power even when they did not rule directly. Their ability to affect the course of events through their influence and wealth is most evident as leaders and supporters of both sides in the French Wars of Religion. Well-educated and powerful noble-women often supported Protestant forces using what historian Sharon Kettering has called "domestic patronage"—their access to economic resources and authority over family members—to support men with certain religious beliefs. Early on, church reformers found support at the French court from Marguerite of Navarre (1492–1549), the influential sister of the French king Francis I (r. 1515–1547). A humanist and author of *The Heptameron* (published in 1559), Marguerite carefully protected religious reformers at court, although she never converted to Protestantism. Madaleine Mailly (d. 1567) was one of the earliest French noblewomen to convert to Calvinism. In an attempt to influence royal policy, she arranged an early meeting between Calvinist pastors and Catherine de Médicis, and although she was imprisoned during the wars, she was influential in arranging the Edict of Amboise (1563) that ended the first of the Wars of Religion. Jeanne d'Albret (1528–1572), the daughter of Marguerite of Navarre, became an enthusiastic supporter of French Calvinism and converted her husband, the king of Navarre, to the faith. She pawned her jewels in 1569 to pay the expenses of a Huguenot army that reconquered the city of Béarn from the Catholics.[31]

Queen regents were frequently able to fulfill their duties without explicitly addressing the issue of gender. Although no Habsburg woman ruled on her own until the eighteenth century, Habsburg women regularly ruled on behalf of their male relatives in the Holy Roman Empire, parts of the Low Countries, and Spain. On four different occasions when the Holy Roman Emperor Charles V left Spain for the wars in Germany, he appointed his wife, Isabel of Portugal (1503–1559), as his regent. Later in his reign, he chose his sister María and his daughter Juana to watch over his Iberian possessions. His aunt, Margaret of Austria (1480–1530), acted as Charles's regent in the Low Countries from 1507 to 1530. At her death, Charles's sister, Mary of Hungary (1505–1558), replaced her and ruled until 1555. As representatives of the most power-ful man in Europe, their authority faced few challenges.

Other Habsburg women influenced court politics from behind the scenes. Margaret of Austria (1584–1611) was not only the wife of the Spanish king Philip III and his second cousin, but also the sister of Ferdinand II, the Holy Roman Emperor (r. 1620–1637). She regularly wrote her relatives in central Europe to pressure them with specific demands that were favorable to her husband and to Spain. She also used her influence with Philip to negotiate aid for her brothers, Austrian archdukes who needed funding for their military exploits. Philip's aunt, the Empress María (1528–1603), was a daughter of Charles V and widow of the Holy Roman Emperor Maximilian II. Although she made her home in a Madrid convent, she actively engaged both Philip and his advisors in policy conversations. She acted as a conduit for information between the Spanish and the Austrian courts and promoted the interests of friends and relatives. Philip regularly came to her for political advice. Empress María's voluntary enclosure in the Carmelite convent in Madrid protected her from court gossip and intrigue, and unlike other courtiers, she could regularly speak with the king in complete privacy. Her reputation for piety actually allowed her to undertake political critique that was impossible for other women (and for many other men).[32]

One of the most unconventional examples of female power was Queen Christina of Sweden (1626–1689). Lutheran Sweden, a longtime bystander in Continental politics, came to international prominence during the Thirty Years' War (1618–1648) under the leadership of Christina's father, King Gustav II Adolf (1594–1632). The Thirty Years' War was a complex multinational conflict that highlighted Europe's long-standing political antagonisms and unresolved religious tensions. When Christina came to the throne in 1644 after a twelve-year regency, she was critical in ending the war with the Peace of Westphalia in 1648. However, after the war, she converted to Catholicism. As Swedish law forbade a Catholic from ruling, she abdicated the throne in 1654. Despite her status as a former monarch, Christina refused to submit to traditional gender expectations by either marrying or entering a convent.

Her rejection of the roles of queen, wife, and nun were controversial as was her decision to wear men's clothing while traveling and her well-documented romantic relationship with an Italian cardinal. Instead, Christina went to Rome where she became active in papal and international politics, urging war against the Turks and making unsuccessful attempts to seize the thrones of Naples and Poland. She was also a prominent patron of the arts and sciences. Even without a crown, Christina remained a powerful force in European politics.

## Gender, Politics, and the English Civil War

Women also found opportunities for political action when political and religious strife struck England during the last half of the seventeenth century. Unlike other similar bodies in Europe, the English Parliament had acquired significant authority, and its willingness to use that power to limit royal power led to ongoing tensions with King Charles I (r. 1625–1649). Charles further antagonized Parliament with his Catholic sympathies. Despite the fact that he was the head of the Church of England, he married a Catholic and granted Catholics some freedom to practice their religion. Charles also persecuted Puritans, many of whom fled to North America. As the Parliament was overwhelmingly Protestant, these actions eventually provoked the English Civil War (1642– 1649).

Even before the outbreak of war, women attempted to employ the English political system to express their opinions. Although voting had been limited to upper-class men, in the 1640 election to Parliament, some upper-class women attempted to vote for Puritan candidates. Officials rejected their votes, not because it was illegal for them to vote, but they argued that women's support would dishonor the candidates.[33] Nevertheless, Englishwomen believed in their right to take political action, and women boldly asserted their right to petition the government for political change. In 1642, a number of Protestant women led by a brewer's wife named Ann Stagg petitioned Parliament to send troops to put down a Catholic rebellion in Ireland. The petition also called upon the House of Commons to expel the bishops and Catholic nobles from the House of Lords. The next day four hundred more women and children appeared at the House of Commons demanding a response to the petition. Members of the House of Commons gave it serious consideration.

Once the English Civil War began, women used violence to support their side or to protect their homes and families. In 1643, a mob of women who shouted for peace in the Palace Yard responded to calls to disband by throwing stones.[34] Rumors that women were fighting among the soldiery were pervasive enough that Charles I felt compelled to issue a proclamation intended to prevent women from joining the army by punishing them for wearing men's clothing.[35]

During the Civil War, the majority of Englishwomen remained Anglican or secretly Catholic; however, Protestant radicals split into a number of small sects. Women were particularly attracted to the new congregations. In overall numbers, members of these sects made up less than 5 percent of the population, but women outnumbered men in nearly all of them. These new congregations frequently met in women's homes, and during the early stages, female members frequently preached and prophesied. Mrs. Attaway, a lace maker in London, was a member of a Baptist congregation and held regular religious meetings. By 1645, women preached there regularly on Tuesday afternoons.[36] Many prominent female preachers were members of the Society of Friends, also known as the Quakers. Unlike many sects, Quakers did not preach but spoke when inspired, and they believed that godly inspiration was open to both men and women. Margaret Fell (1614–1702), a Quaker leader, wrote eloquently about women's right to preach. Historian Phyllis Mack has identified more than two hundred female Quaker visionaries, many of whose messages included political as well as religious ideas.[37]

As members of the Levellers, women explicitly connected Christian equality and political equality. The Levellers argued that all men were equal and that the government should be a secular state created by a contract between equal citizens with rights to vote, freedom of speech, and religious toleration. Leveller women took this emphasis on equality even further:

> *That since we are assured of our creation in the image of God, and of an interest in*

*Christ, equal unto men, as also of a proportionable share in the Freedoms of this Commonwealth, we cannot but wonder and grieve that we should appear so despicable in your eyes, as to be thought unworthy to petition or represent our grievances to this honorable house. Have we not an equal interest with the men of this Nation in those liberties and securities, contained in the Petition of Right and other good Laws of the Land?*

Asserting those rights, in 1649, they petitioned Parliament to release Leveller leaders from prison. However, they were brusquely rebuffed. Parliament refused to accept the petition, telling the women:

*That matter you petition about, is of an higher concernment then you understand, that the House gave an answer to your Husbands, and therefore that you are desired to go home, and look after your owne businesse, and meddle with your housewifery.*[38]

In the ongoing war between supporters of the king and those of Parliament, Parliamentary forces eventually prevailed. Led by Oliver Cromwell (1599–1658), Parliament tried and executed Charles I in 1649 and a Puritan Commonwealth replaced the monarchy. As head of this Puritan state, Cromwell also faced female critics. Anna Trapnel (fl. 1642–1660), a member of the millenarian Fifth Monarchist sect, was imprisoned for her political prophecies against Cromwell's regime. She was in a trance for ten months from October 1657 to August 1658, during which time she continued to criticize the government.

Cromwell created a state based on Puritan principles that prohibited ostentatious dress and public entertainments. Intolerant of dissent, the government subjected members of other Protestant sects, especially Quaker women, to harassment and imprisonment. Dissatisfaction with Cromwell's regime led to the restoration of the monarchy in 1660. However, religious differences continued to divide the Protestant Parliament from the Catholic kings Charles II (r. 1660–1685) and James II (r. 1685–1688). By

1688, to ensure Protestant rule, Parliament arranged for the succession of James II's eldest daughter, Mary (1662–1694), and her husband, William of Orange (1650–1702). When the couple died without an heir, Parliament chose another woman to rule, Anne, James II's other Protestant daughter (r. 1701–1714). By the end of the seventeenth century, female rule was no longer monstrous, but politically and religiously expedient.

At the end of the Middle Ages, queens were central to the creation of early modern nation states. Although many women came to power during the next two centuries, early modern intellectuals expressed deep suspicions about the abilities of women rulers. Indeed, early modern queens had to develop strategies to negotiate gender expectations. However, queenship was not the only means for women to exercise power. Noblewomen used patronage and familial connections to participate in politics, and by the end of the seventeenth century, Englishwomen asserted their rights through prophecy and petitions.

## ART, LITERATURE, AND SCIENCE

Women's increased engagement in public discussions of religion and politics was complemented by their growing visibility in intellectual and scientific debates and the artistic world. A combination of increased literacy and the invention of the movable type printing press significantly increased their participation in discussions about sex and gender. Female artists became famous in their own right and created large bodies of work. However, women continued to be frustrated by their inability to be seen as equals by male writers, artists, and scientists.

### Gender Theory and Reality in Early Modern Thought

The debate over the role of women in society, the *querelle des femmes,* that received so much attention from European intellectuals in the late Middle Ages, intensified during the early modern period. Writers from many backgrounds, some known, others anonymous, composed hundreds of texts on the subject of women. Much like their medieval predecessors, most male writers were unquestionably antifeminist, regularly referring to Eve's role in the temptation of Adam and asserting that women were inferior and by nature subordinate to men. Some of the most misogynist, presumably satirical, works questioned whether women were human beings at all.

Whether Catholic or Protestant, most of these male thinkers asserted that women needed to be carefully supervised, and they produced instructional manuals for women that clearly expressed gender expectations and described how women might fulfill those expectations. One such manual, Juan Luis Vives's *The Education of a Christian Woman* (1523), extolled the virtues of chastity, marriage, and subservience to one's husband. According to Vives, "Not only the tradition and institutions of our ancestors but all laws, human and divine, and nature itself, proclaim that a woman must be subject to a man and obey him."[39] Many male writers emphasized the importance of female honor based on virginity or chastity. Male honor was dependent on men's ability to ensure the chastity of their female relatives. Women who were not chaste not only threatened their own reputations but also dishonored their families. Although this emphasis on honor was generally associated with Catholic thinkers, conduct manuals by Protestant authors, such as the Swiss reformer Henry Bullinger (1504–1575), also emphasized the preservation of chastity. In fact, as far away as Russia, men voiced their concerns about female honor. During the sixteenth century, the *Domostroi*, a manual of household management, praised female obedience, submission, and the need to preserve female chastity. Elite Russian women were secluded in the women's quarters, the *terem*, to protect their virginity.[40]

However, even in the societies that produced works advocating the most rigid controls of women, such as Spain and Russia, the emphasis on female honor was not as inflexible as the prescriptive works would have us believe. For instance, in both societies, uxoricide (wife killing) was rare and women of all social classes could use the judicial system to help defend and even restore their honor. Moreover, class played a key role in determining the degree to which a woman was expected to conform to honor codes. Elite women no doubt faced great pressures to be chaste and submit to male control, while nonelite women may have had greater latitude in both their public and private activity.

Women had some male defenders. These intellectuals generally asserted that biological difference did not make women naturally inferior and that only the lack of opportunity (especially in terms of education) kept women from being the equals of men. One of the most important defenses of women was *Of the Nobilitie and excellencye of woman kynde* (1509) by Heinrich Agrippa von Nettesheim (1486–1538), a German humanist. In this work, which was reprinted many times and translated into numerous languages, he argued that Adam was responsible for the Fall, not Eve. According to Agrippa, women were not only equal to men in reason, but superior to men in many ways. He argued that women had the capacity to rule and that society controlled women through marriage laws and convents. Agrippa believed that men should not deny women full economic and political equality.

Women were also active defenders of their sex. Moderata da Fonte's (also known as Modesta dal Pozzo, 1555–1592) *The Worth of Women* (1600) is a conversation among seven women, each of whom proclaim their independence from men. One character, Cornelia, asserts the independence of women, saying, "Wouldn't it be possible for us just to banish these men from our lives, and escape their carping and jeering once and for all? Couldn't we live without them? Couldn't we earn our living and manage our affairs without help from them? Come on, let's wake up and claim back our freedom, and the honor and dignity that they have usurped from us for so long."[41] Fonte contrasts the natural superiority of women with the inferiority of men who are dangerous, unreliable, and liars. She praises singleness and condemns marriage for the way it subordinates women. Ironically, Fonte died giving birth to her fourth child, one day after finishing *The Worth of Women*.

Fonte was far from alone. Among some of the notable treatises in defense of women is that of the young Englishwoman Rachel Speght (1597–ca. 1630). At the age of twenty, she wrote a response to Joseph Swetnam's misogynist tract, *The*

*Arraignment of Lewd, Idle, Froward and Unconstant Women* (1615). Speght used biblical passages to argue that God had made women and men equal. In fact, in seventeenth-century England, defenses of women outnumbered anti-woman texts three to one.[42] Even fourteen-year-old Sarah Fyge Egerton felt driven to compose a compelling defense of her sex (see **Sources from the Past:** *Female Advocate, A Defense of Women* by Sarah Fyge Egerton).

The *querelle des femmes* intensified during the early modern period, presumably in response to women's increased public activity. Although many writers reaffirmed traditional gender expectations, not all intellectuals readily accepted assertions of female inferiority. Both men and women published passionate responses that promoted the intellectual, moral, and physical equality, and even superiority, of women.

## Enlivening the Arts

As intellectuals debated the role of women in society, many successful and innovative female painters thrived. Giorgio Vasari's *Lives of the Painters* (1550) includes a number of women artists whose work was highly regarded. Of those female artists, Sofonisba Anguissola (1532–1625) was the most famous during her lifetime. The eldest of six daughters of an aristocratic family from Cremona, she studied informally with Michelangelo. Anguissola quickly became famous for the naturalness of her portraits and was invited to the court of the Spanish king Philip II to serve as a court painter. Like many female painters who followed in her footsteps, Anguissola excelled at portraying intimate moments. Vasari noted that her paintings were "truly alive and are wanting nothing save speech" (Vasari, *Lives of the Painters*, vol. 3).

While Anguissola worked in Spain, Lavinia Fontana's (1552–1614) artistic talents were being heralded in Bologna. Trained by her father, also a well-known artist and teacher, she supported her family with her paintings. In her father's studio, she met another painter, Gian Paolo Zappi, whom she married in 1577. Zappi appears to have given up his artistic career to assist his wife in her studio, handle the accounts of her numerous commissions, and help care for their eleven children. Fontana is remarkable for the variety of works that she produced. She became famed as a portraitist as well as for her biblical and mythological works. She was also commissioned to paint large public altarpieces, a rare distinction for a woman artist. After moving to Rome around 1603, she created the best known of her public commissions, the altarpiece for the pilgrimage church of San Paolo Fuori le Mura in Rome, *The Stoning of Saint Stephen Martyr.* Although scholars have documented over one hundred works by Fontana, only thirty-two signed and dated or datable works exist, and a smaller number of paintings are attributed to her on stylistic grounds. Nevertheless, hers is the largest surviving body of work by any woman artist active before 1700.

Women's personal experiences often informed their painting. For many scholars, Artemesia Gentileschi (1593–1653) epitomizes the close relationship between art and life. When she was refused admission to art academies because she was a woman, her father, Orazio Gentileschi (1563–1644), a well-known artist, arranged for her to study with a friend, Agostino Tassi (1578–1644). Her early works, like *Susanna and The Elders* (1610), communicate a decidedly feminine point of view. However, Gentileschi is best known for her scenes of graphic violence, especially her *Judith Decapitating Holofernes* (1620). Some feminist art historians assert that this and similar works reflect the violence to which Artemisia had been subjected. At age nineteen, Artemisia was allegedly raped by her instructor, Tassi. The seven-month trial that resulted was quite sensational and did more harm to Artemisia than to her assailant, who served only a brief prison sentence. One month after the trial, Gentileschi married and moved to Florence where she produced some of her finest paintings.

As still lifes and flower paintings grew popular during the seventeenth century, Dutch women like Clara Peeters (1594–ca. 1657), Maria van Oosterwyck (1630–1693), and Rachel Ruysch (1666–1750) found audiences for their talents. Peeters was one of the first painters to work in the genre, and all three women were important innovators in the field.

Despite these successes, female artists faced innumerable obstacles. They had to overcome the traditional male expectation that women could not create art, a perception that made it difficult

## Female Advocate, A Defense of Women by Sarah Fyge Egerton

*At the age of only fourteen, Sarah Fyge Egerton (1670—1723) wrote this response to the misogynist literature of late-seventeenth-century England. The poem was published without her consent, and her parents banished her to live with relatives in the countryside. She then revised the poem and had it reprinted a year later. Her second volume of poems,* Poems on Several Occasions, *was published in 1703.*

### Female Advocate or, an Answer to a Late Satyr Against the Pride, Lust and Inconstancy, &c. of Woman. Written by a Lady in Vindication of Her Sex (1686)

Blasphemous Wretch, thou who canst think or say
Some Curst or Banisht Fiend usurp't the way
When Eve was form'd; for then's deny'd by you
Gods Omniscience and Omnipresence too:
Without which Attributes he could not be,
The greatest and supremest Deity:
Nor can Heaven sleep, tho' it may mourn to fee
Degenerate Man utter Blasphemy.
When from dark Chaos Heav'n the World did make,
Made all things glorious it did undertake;
Then it in Eden's Garden freely plac'd
All things pleasant to the Sight or taste,
Fill'd it with Beasts & Birds, Trees hung with Fruit,
That might with man's Celestial Nature suit:
The world being made thus spacious and compleat,
Then Man was form'd, who seemed nobly great.

When Heaven survey'd the Works that it had done,
Saw Male and female, but found Man alone,
A barren Sex and insignificant;
So Heaven made Woman to supply the want,
And to make perfect what before was scant:
Then surely she a Noble Creature is,
Whom Heaven thus made to consummate all Bliss.
Though Man had been first, yet methinks She
In Nature should have the supremacy;
For Man was form'd out of dull senceless Earth;
But Woman she had a far nobler Birth:
For when the dust was purify'd by Heaven,
Made into Man, and Life unto it given,
Then the Almighty and All-wise God said,
That Woman of that Species should be made:
Which was no sooner said, but it was done,
'Cause 'twas not fit for Man to be alone.
Thus have I prov'd Woman's Creation good,
And not inferior, when right understood:
To that of Man's; for both one Maker had,
Which made all good; then how could Eve be bad?
But then you'll say, though she at first was pure,
Yet in that State she did not long endure.
'Tis true; but if her Fall's examin'd right,
We find most Men have banish'd Truth for spight:
Nor is she quite so guilty as some make;
For Adam did most of the Guilt partake:
For he from God's own Mouth had the Command;
But Woman she had it at second hand:
The Devil's Strength weak Women might deceive,
But Adam tempted only was by eve.
Eve had the strongest Tempter, and least Charge;
Man's knowing most, doth his Sin make most large.
But though Woman Man to Sin did lead?

Yet since her Seed hath bruis'd the serpent's
   Head:
Why should she be made a publick scorn,
Of whom the great Almighty God was born?
Surely to speak one slighting Word, must be
A kind of murmuring Impiety:
But still their greatest haters do prove such
Who formerly have loved them too much:
And from the proverb they are not exempt;
Too much Familiarity has bred contempt;
For they associate themselves with none,
But such whose Virtues like their own, are
   gone;
And with all those, and only those who be
Most boldly vers'd in their debauchery:
And as in Adam all Mankind did die,
They make all base for ones Immodesty;
Nay, make the name a kind of Magick Spell,
As if 'twould censure married Men to
   Hell. . . .

But if all Men should of your humor be
And should rob Hymen of his Deity,
They soon would find the Inconveniency.
Then hostile Spirits would be forc'd to
   Peace,
Because the World so slowly would increase.
They would be glad to keep their Men at
   home,
And each want more to attend his Throne;
Nay, should an English Prince resolve that he
would keep the number of of 's Nobility:
And this dull custom some few years
   maintin'd,
There would be none less than a Peer oth'
   land.
And I do fancy 'twould be pretty sport
To see a Kingdom cramb'd into a Court.
Sure a strange world, when one should
   nothing see,
unless a Baudy House or Nunnery.

Or should this Act ere pass, woman would
   fly
With unthought swiftness, to each Monastry
And in dark Caves secure her Chastity.
She only in a Marriage-Bed delights;
The very Name of Whore her Soul affrights.
And when that sacred Ceremony's gone,
Woman I am sure will chuse to live alone.

There's none can number all those vertuous
   Dames
Which chose cold death before their lovers
   flames.
The chast Lucretia whom proud Tarquin
   lov'd,
Her he slew, her chastity she prov'd.
But I've gone further than I need have done,
Since we have got examples nearer home.
Witness those Saxon Ladies who did fear
The loss of Honour when the Danes were
   here:
And cut their Lips and Noses that they
   might
Not pleasing seem, or give the Danes delight.
Thus having done what they could justly
   do,
At last they fell their sacrifices too.
Thus when curst Osbright courted Beon's
   wife,
She him refus'd with hazard of her life.
And some which I do know but will not
   name,
Have thus refus'd and hazarded the same.
I could say more, but History will tell
Many more things that do these excel.

Source: The Emory Women Writers Research Project:
http://chaucer.library.emory.edu/cgi-bin/sgml2html/
wwrp.pl?act=contents&f=%2Fdata%2Fwomen_writers%2F
data%2Fegerton.sgm

for women to find teachers and patrons. They also had to reject cultural norms about female modesty in order to use male models, to paint nudes, and even to paint self-portraits.

Women writers took advantage of increased literacy to express their opinions on particularly female concerns. Veronica Franco (1546–1591) was a Venetian courtesan, a highly paid prostitute, famed for both her beauty and her poetry. As a courtesan, she was free from the social constraints placed on respectable women. Well-educated and cultured, her relationships with powerful men provided her with the influence and finances necessary to edit anthologies and publish her poetry. She deeply believed in women's abilities and recognized their subordination by men. In response to a famous attack by another poet, Franco asserted that women's inequality was not natural but was due to a lack of education. "When we women too, have weapons and training, we will be able to prove to all men that we have hands and feet and hearts like yours." Using the weapons of language and poetry, Franco vowed to show her opponent, "how far the female sex excels your own."[43]

Maria de Zayas y Sotomayor (1590–ca. 1660) used her literary skills to attack the sexual double standard and violence against women in *The Disenchantments of Love* (1647). The disenchantments are ten stories told by guests to entertain a bride-to-be. The tales all include gruesome depictions of women tortured and/or murdered by men whom they loved or trusted. In addition to the violence against women that marks most of the stories, Zayas reveals her disdain for Spanish gender norms when, in the end, all the women who survive in the stories as well as the bride-to-be enter convents where they find safety and comfort away from men.

By the seventeenth century, women began to make their livings from writing. The English author Aphra Behn (ca. 1640–1689) began her career as a successful dramatist. Between 1670 and 1689, Behn had nineteen plays produced on the London stage. However, the use of her talents for profit did not stop her from expressing her views on politics and gender. Her play *The Rover, or the Banished Cavaliers* (1677) voiced her disappointment with the limited options available to women. Her female characters refused to consent to either life in a convent or arranged marriages. These were not merely literary images for Behn; she also served as a spy for the English king.

Women also became more prominent in early modern music as the result of both the Reformation and changes in musical aesthetics. As had been true for centuries, women expressed their religious piety through music. Protestant women including Katherine Zell (1497–1562), a prominent reformer, and the Norwegian noblewoman Inger of Austrät (fl. 1530) composed early Lutheran hymns.

The Catholic Church's desire to control convent life affected the composition and performance of convent music. Some church officials argued that nuns should refrain from polyphonic chant, fearing that such music "distracted [the nuns] from their ceremonial duties and spiritual exercises to which they are dedicated because of the dissolute rhythms they produce in sinuous voices."[44] More broadly, the decree on enclosure hindered nuns' ability to hear new compositions and receive instruction. Nevertheless, Isabella Leonarda (1620–1704), enclosed in an Ursuline convent in Novara, Italy, was amazingly prolific. She composed and published more than two hundred works and was the first woman to publish sonatas.

Dramatic changes also took place in secular music. Prior to the early modern period, vocal performances had been group performances, but during the sixteenth century, composer Giulio Caccini promoted what is often referred to as "the new music," based on solo performances. His daughter, Francesca Caccini (1587–ca. 1645), one of three musical sisters, was not only renowned for her performances of the new music, but she also composed and published dozens of secular and sacred pieces. Her most famous work, *La liberazione di Ruggiero dall'isola d'Alcina* (1625), was the first extant opera by a woman.

Female artists, writers, and musicians flourished during the early modern period. They defied the skeptics who denied their abilities and bravely displayed their passions on canvas, print, and in song. For the first time, people were reading, seeing, hearing, and even purchasing works by women. For a few special artists, it was truly a new age.

## Behind Closed Doors: Women in Early Modern Science

During the seventeenth century, European intellectuals increasingly relied on empirical investigation in their attempts to understand the world. This scientific revolution transformed philosophy, biology, physics, and astronomy, yet women remained on the margins of these disciplines. Women were prohibited from earning university degrees or joining the growing number of scientific academies, yet they gained access to scientific study through other avenues. Some women used their noble status to learn from the great thinkers of their time. For example, Princess Elizabeth of Bohemia (1618–1680) corresponded extensively with French philosopher Rene Descartes (1595–1650), and Descartes' work, *The Passion of the Soul* (1649), resulted from her questions about the interactions between the soul and the body. Other women married scientists as a means to pursue scientific study, as did Elizabeth Koopman (1647–1693). Eager for a career in astronomy, she married the prominent German astronomer Johannes Hevelius (1611–1687) and served as his chief assistant.

No matter how they acquired their knowledge or how sophisticated their participation in the sciences, women found little respect among male scientists. When Maria Cunitz (1610–1664), who learned the skills that she used as an astronomer from her father, published her collection of astronomical tables, *Urania propitia*, in 1650, her husband had to deny that the work was actually his in the preface to later editions. Critics also accused her of neglecting her domestic duties by sleeping during the day so she could observe the stars at night.[45]

During the early modern period, the relationship between female and male medical practitioners began to change. Some historians assert that although female healers and midwives had provided most medieval medicine to women, professionally trained physicians gradually removed women from obstetrical care. However, recent scholarship presents a much more complicated picture of early modern medicine. Although male midwives increasingly attended births, especially in emergencies, in most parts of Europe, women continued to prefer female midwives to help during labor. Moreover, professional medical knowl-

POLISH ASTRONOMER JOHANNES HEVELIUS AND WIFE ELIZABETH KOOPMAN WORKING TOGETHER USING THEIR LARGE BRASS SEXTANT (DANZIG, 1673). The exclusion of women from university study made it difficult for them to engage in scientific experimentation. However, some women, like Elizabeth Koopman, found scientist husbands whom they worked alongside. *(The Granger Collection, New York.)*

edge and medical theory were not solely available to men, as is evident in the obstetrical treatises written by Louise Bourgeois (1563–1636), midwife to the French queen Marie de Médicis (1573–1642). Midwives' role in childbirth would not be supplanted for another century.[46]

During the early modern period, women vigorously defended their intellectual abilities as a part of the ongoing querelle des femmes. They also found new prominence as artists and writers. However, women continued to be limited in their ability to enter scientific professions. Few in the European intellectual community could comprehend that women might have the rational skills to undertake empirical investigation and analysis.

## EUROPEAN EXPANSION

During the religious strife and political consolidation that swept the Continent, early modern Europeans expanded their wealth and power through overseas exploration and conquest. During the fifteenth century, the Portuguese headed east, slowly traversing the coast of Africa in the hope of finding a sea route to the rich kingdoms of the East. They set up colonies in Africa, India, China, and Southeast Asia. By 1492, Christopher Columbus had chosen a westward path to Asia and established permanent contact between Europeans and Native Americans. The consequences of the conquest of the Americas were disastrous. European disease rapidly killed off more than 90 percent of the native population, as Native Americans' immune systems proved unable to resist European diseases such as smallpox and typhus. In the Western Hemisphere, as native peoples from the Mississippi Valley to Peru died, the Spanish, French, Dutch, and Portuguese toppled powerful native empires, converted the survivors, and set up colonies (see Map 7.2). In Africa and Asia, the Portuguese became the great colonial power. Gender roles were critical in the creation of the European empires. From the beginning, European women traveled to these colonial outposts in search of wealth, spiritual fulfillment, or husbands. With them, they brought their religion, their cultures, and their capacity to produce European children. In contrast, native women bore the brunt of the conquest as victims of rape, enslavement, and cultural conquest.

## Life on the Periphery: European Women and the Colonization of Asia and the Americas

Although the military conquest was largely a masculine effort, early modern Europeans believed that women were integral to successful colonization. Imperial authorities thought that women would tame the largely unsupervised soldiers and help to establish permanent European settlements. They feared that soldiers and settlers without wives would be unruly and their behavior could compromise the evangelization and "civilizing" processes.

European women arrived in the Americas on Columbus's third voyage to the Caribbean in 1498. Initially, the numbers of female settlers were small, but women traveled to conquer Mexico with Hernán Cortés (1485–1547). Five women were among the founders of the city of Puebla in 1531. Some were single female servants, but many were the wives and daughters of the conquistadores. Between 1598 and 1621, 42 percent of the immigrants to Peru and 32 percent of immigrants to Mexico were female.[47]

Across the Americas and Asia, the scarcity of European women, racial concerns, and individual ambition increased the value of European women in the colonies. They not only produced white children to populate the new colonies, but their dowries were essential to the establishment of colonial businesses. Moreover, the fact that single and widowed Iberian women could inherit, administer, and dispose of property without the intervention of men made the wealthiest women highly sought after. As a result, the colonial powers enacted policies to ensure a regular supply of European women overseas. The Portuguese crown set up a scheme to bring orphan girls and reformed prostitutes to its overseas possessions, and the French undertook a similar project in Quebec. Certain Portuguese orphan girls, living in government-sponsored shelters known as *Recolhimentos*, were chosen to move to the colonies. They had to be between the ages of twelve and thirty, and free of Jewish, Muslim, or African blood. In addition, authorities preferred girls whose fathers had died in service overseas. These "orphans of the king" were sent to both Brazil and to India in small batches and "rewarded" with dowries of minor posts in the imperial bureaucracy. Potential husbands petitioned for the posts and, upon marriage, accepted the jobs as the women's dowries. Once orphanages were set up in Goa (India), local Portuguese orphans were also included in the project. In Portuguese Sri Lanka and a few parts of Portuguese India, some women

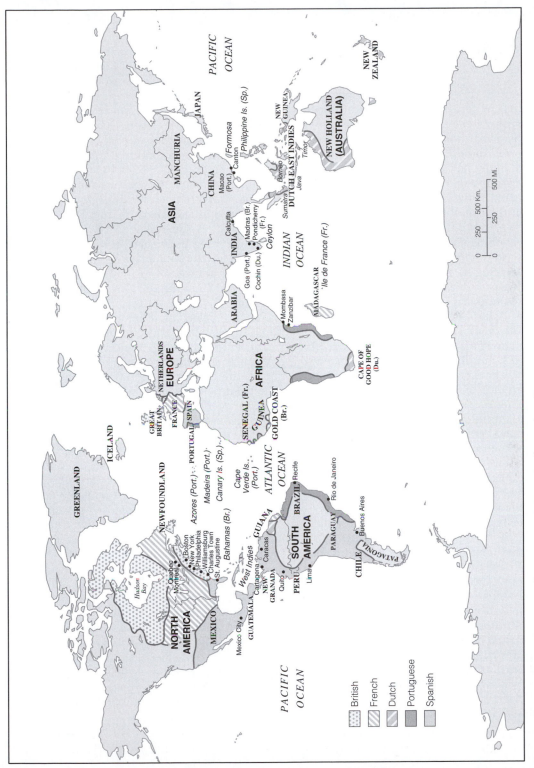

*Map 7.2* **European Overseas Expansion, 1715.** Early modern European expansion has often been characterized as a male enterprise, but European women were central to the creation of colonies around the world.

# Women's Lives

## Catalina de Erauso, Soldier and Adventurer

As early modern explorers and conquerors opened up new continents to European settlement, they also created new possibilities for personal transformations. Catalina de Erauso was born to a well-to-do Basque family in 1592. At the age of four, her parents took her to the Dominican convent to be educated along with her two sisters. However, she hated the religious life, and at the age of fifteen, Catalina escaped from the convent. Erauso made her nun's habit into boy's clothing and cut her hair. She changed her name and began to live as a man.

After working as a boy page in a number of different households, Catalina traveled to the Americas where she could more easily escape detection. After crossing the Atlantic on a Spanish galleon as a cabin boy, she jumped ship at what is now Panama. Passing as a man, she worked for a merchant. Erauso then moved to Peru where she took the name Alfonso Ramírez de Guzmán.

During her stay, she attracted the attention of one of her employer's sisters-in-law. Erauso seems to have reciprocated her affections as, at one point, the two were caught in an intimate moment. However, she never engaged in a long-term relationship with a woman either for fear of being exposed or out of discomfort with her feelings for other women.

After killing a man in a brawl, Erauso joined a group of Spanish soldiers fighting the Araucanian Indians in Chile. Her bravery in battle won her the title of lieutenant. Remarkably, despite living among men in military camps, her secret was never revealed. Supposedly, as a youth, she had used a poultice to dry up her breasts and those who met her rarely noticed that she had no beard. How she dealt with menstruation remains a mystery. She was not discovered until after she killed her brother in a duel and was twice seriously injured in deadly brawls. Fearing death, she confessed her true sex to the bishop and allowed local women to examine her. They confirmed her femininity and her virginity. Upon hearing her story, church officials forced her to live in a convent for two and a half years until word came from Spain that she had not taken vows as a nun and therefore was free to leave.

When Erauso arrived back in Spain, she returned to men's clothing. She was arrested twice more, once in Madrid and again in Piedmont as a Spanish spy. In 1626, she returned to Madrid and requested a pension in reward for her service in the Americas from King Philip IV. In the petition, she explained how she had served as a soldier for his majesty in Peru as a man and her valiant efforts on his behalf. The Council of the Indies approved her request, granting her a pension of eight hundred escudos. Erauso then traveled to Rome, where Pope Urban VIII (r. 1623–1644) granted her a license to continue dressing as a man, despite biblical injunctions against cross-dressing. Sometime between 1626 and 1630, she either wrote or dictated a memoir of her life. She returned to the Americas, where she lived in Mexico as a muleskinner and merchant named Antonio de Erauso. She disappears from the historical record after 1645.

Although born female, Catalina de Erauso found success and independence living as a man. On the one hand, she transgressed gender norms, denying her biological sex for most of her adult life. On the other hand, as a man she accepted masculine notions of violence and power. Known in literature and folklore as the lieutenant nun, Catalina de Erauso was both a product of and a rebel against early modern society.

---

Sources: Mary Elizabeth Perry, "From Convent to Battlefield: Cross-dressing and Gendering the Self in the New World of Imperial Spain," in *Queer Iberia: Sexualities, Cultures, and Crossings from the Middle Ages to the Renaissance*, ed. Josiah Blackmore and Gregory S. Hutcheson (Durham: Duke University Press, 1999), pp. 394–419; and Catalina de Erauso, *Lieutenant Nun: Memoir of a Basque Transvestite in the New World*, trans. Michele Stepto and Gabriel Stepto (Boston: Beacon Press, 1996).

received their dowries in the form of land or taxes from villages to encourage settlement. In addition, Portuguese officials severely limited the establishment of convents in its Asian possessions. In a setting where white women's reproductive abilities were so valuable, government officials did not want any women taking vows of celibacy. The population of the convent of Santa Clara in Portuguese Macau (now China) was limited to thirty-three nuns, so that few women left the marriage market. Between 1550 and 1755, probably no more than one thousand orphans and reformed prostitutes left Lisbon to colonize the empire; however, the project offers a fascinating look into the use of women to pursue certain racial policies. The goal was always to have more whites in the territories and to perpetuate European culture. However, by the end of the seventeenth century, Portuguese authorities had decided that families were the best means of colonizing its territories. Portuguese women and their husbands traveled to places as diverse as Angola, São Tomé, Mozambique, Monomotapa (modern-day Zimbabwe), and the Maranhão in the interior of Brazil.[48]

The English also wanted more white women in their North American colonies. To make the colony more attractive to women, the first session of the Virginia legislative assembly in July 1619 granted husbands shares of land for their wives so that women could claim land in their own right. They also wrote to England requesting more women. In response, ninety single women arrived later that year. In 1620, authorities requested another hundred women to fill the need for wives among the colonists. Each woman cost 120 pounds of tobacco, six times the cost of a young male servant. Unfortunately, by 1625, three-quarters of these women had died of starvation or disease, and men outnumbered women in Virginia four to one.[49]

Life for white women in colonial possessions must have been difficult. They were far from their families. The customs and gender expectations of their home countries often pressured them to wear heavy clothes that were popular in Europe, but uncomfortable and unhygienic in the tropics. Husbands and fathers often restricted their movements to prevent them from interacting with indigenous men. For all but the most wealthy, the work was hard and the living conditions difficult.

Their husbands and fathers were frequently away on business or defending the settlements, leaving them in charge of large farmsteads and family businesses. In the Catholic colony of Maryland, Margaret Brent (1601–1671) owned thousands of acres of land, which she vigorously protected from mutinous soldiers and government criticism. In peripheral areas like Chile, Angola, and Canada, white women often had few social opportunities. No doubt, their sense of loneliness and isolation was heightened as their husbands entered into sexual relationships with local women and the growing numbers of African slaves in both North and South America.

In the anonymity of Europe's colonies, people could undergo striking transformations. Although thousands of men, women, and children were taken captive by native tribes during the colonial period, most were "redeemed" or, like Hannah Dustin (1657–1737), murdered their abductors and escaped. However, many women who were taken captive in colonial North America chose to remain among their captors. They adopted native dress, bore children to native men, and spoke native languages. They took native names and adopted the religion of the tribe. Their choices shocked their contemporaries, who saw their decisions not only as betrayals of Christian civilization, but also as transgressions of race and gender hierarchies.

A few people took the opportunity to redefine their sexual identities (see **Women's Lives: Catalina de Erauso, Soldier and Adventurer**). Virginia colonist Thomas Hall certainly took advantage of the colonial setting to remake him/herself in ways that confounded colonial officials. In 1629, Hall became the subject of rumors of sexual misconduct that prompted a local investigation. The investigators found that he had been christened Thomasine and raised as a girl, but at the age of twenty-four he had cut his hair, wore men's clothing, and became a soldier. After fighting in France, he resettled in England as a woman. In 1627, Hall returned to life as a man but occasionally wore women's clothing and performed traditional women's work. Hall crossed the Atlantic as a man, but once in Virginia he sometimes wore women's clothing. When asked whether he was a man or a woman, he replied that he was both. A group of women who examined his body concluded that he was a man, but the plantation commander overturned that decision and ordered Hall to wear women's clothing. Authorities never reached a clear conclusion on Hall's gender. The General Court in Virginia eventually sentenced him to wear men's clothing but also to wear an apron to mark him as a woman. In the colonies, gender and even sex could be difficult to unravel.[50]

## Women and the Missionary Effort

The European colonies offered new religious opportunities and constraints for women. For example, female monastics in or close to major European settlements were carefully cloistered. Their mission was to pray for the success of the evangelization effort, to provide homes for white women with religious vocations or those who were unmarriageable, and to educate the daughters of colonists. The first convent in New Spain (Mexico) was founded in 1540. Although there were few Spanish women, colonists across the Americas wanted a convent in which to place mestizo (mixed-race) daughters produced by European men's relationships with native women. Nuns taught these girls European ways and protected their virginity until the time came for them to marry. Although in the early years of the conquest, convents eagerly sought out mixed-race students and boarders, as time passed convents often replicated colonial race and class hierarchies. In Spanish America, where women of color were forbidden to take final vows, a two-tiered system developed within many convents. European nuns wore black veils and held monastic offices, while women of color wore the white veil of the novice or lay sister and were not allowed to take final vows or hold offices. In wealthier convents, dozens of black, mixed-race, and native slaves served European white nuns. Many of these slaves were orphaned girls who had been raised in the convent but were not permitted to leave.

In contrast, the first convents were founded in Portuguese Brazil only in the last half of the seventeenth century, nearly two hundred years after the territory's settlement by Europeans. Until that time, European women were in short supply and those few who actively sought the religious life were sent to convents in Portugal. Only when European women were plentiful did the Crown allow for the foundation of the Destêrro Convent in Bahia in 1677. The Destêrro served an elite clientele of Brazil's wealthiest families, protecting and educating their daughters until marriage.

Nuns in peripheral areas brought Christianity and European culture to Native Americans. The French Ursuline convent in Quebec under the supervision of Mother Superior Marie de l'Incarnation (1599–1672) took in Algonquin, Huron, and Iroquois girls. In addition to teaching Christian doctrine and prayer, the sisters dressed their students in French clothing and taught them how to speak French, embroider, and paint. The sisters hoped that the girls would bring Catholicism and French customs to their families when they returned to their villages.[51]

Like Catholic women, the Puritan women who fled persecution in England for the shores of North America could neither evangelize to natives nor engage in any activity that might be construed as preaching to other members of their own communities. Nevertheless, carried away by religious enthusiasm, Anne Hutchinson (1591–1643) began informal prayer groups for Puritan women. When her preaching began to attract large audiences, Boston's clergy and magistrates rebuked her. They eventually excommunicated Hutchinson and banished her from Massachusetts. Quaker women met similar fates. Twenty-six female Quaker preachers journeyed from England between 1656 and 1663, among them Mary Dyer (ca. 1611–1660) who had returned to England and joined the Quakers after hearing Anne Hutchinson preach. In 1657, she returned to New England but was banished from Massachusetts. More than once, she defied the ban and returned to preach. Massachusetts magistrates sentenced her to death for her actions and then commuted her sentence to banishment, but she returned again to Boston. The governor of Massachusetts ordered her to be executed the next day.

## Native Women in the Conquest of the Americas

While European women were critical to colonization and settlement, those processes took a heavy toll on native women, especially in the Americas. Thousands of women died, victims of murder and disease. Survivors faced the disruption and destruction of their families, homes, and cultures. Enslavement, rape, and abduction marked native women's experience of conquest.

As slaves or newly conquered peoples, native women frequently served as guides and interpreters for Europeans. Doña Marina (d. ca. 1530) has come to epitomize this interaction between native women and European men. Sold into slavery by her Maya kin, she was either given or sold to the Spanish conqueror Hernán Cortés soon after his arrival on the Mexican mainland in 1519. Upon taking possession of her, Cortés had her baptized and gave her the Christian name Marina. She proved to be a skilled linguist and interpreter whose proficiency included a special form of Nahuatl (the language of the Aztecs) only used in the presence of the emperor. As Cortés's translator during the conquest of the Aztec Empire, she was central to negotiations between Cortés and members of the Aztec Empire and eventually in the meetings between Cortés and the emperor

**Doña Marina Translating for Hernan Cortés During His Meeting with the Aztec Ruler Moctezuma (ca. 1560).** As Europeans explored and then conquered new lands, Native women often acted as cultural mediators. Whether willingly or by force, they provided European explorers with food, acted as guides, and even translated critical diplomatic moments. *(The Granger Collection, New York.)*

Moctezuma. She later gave birth to Cortes's son, Martín, and many consider her the mother of the mestizo race in Mexico, a title with both positive and negative connotations; she was also called La Malinche, a nativized version of Marina, which has come to mean "traitor."

Abduction was another way that European men controlled native women. Pocahontas (1595–1617), a famous native captive, first entered the historical record in 1607 in Captain John Smith's description of his capture by the Powhatan Indians in Virginia. Although much of Smith's narrative has come under scrutiny (curiously he is rescued on three different occasions by prepubescent native girls), it seems clear that his relationship with Pocahontas began her lifelong contact with the English. Beginning in 1608, Pocahontas (a nickname; her real name was Matoaka) made frequent trips to Jamestown, delivering messages from the Powhatan and arranging for the exchange of food and supplies.

In 1613, English settlers abducted her so that they could exchange her for English prisoners and weapons held by the Powhatan. While in captivity, she converted to Christianity, supposedly becoming the first native in Virginia to do so. In 1614, she married John Rolfe, a prominent settler, changed her name to Rebecca Rolfe, and bore a son. In 1616, Rebecca, her husband, their son, and several other Indian men and women traveled to England. The Indian woman captivated English royalty, and the publicity surrounding her visit sparked interest in the colonies. Sadly, onboard ship, Rebecca Rolfe became gravely ill and died far from her native land. She was buried in England.

Like many native women, Doña Marina and Pocahontas became chattel, taken from their families and exchanged among Europeans, for whom they became critical in the process of cultural exchange. They translated for European men and taught them native languages. They instructed the European men who controlled them about native plants, foods, and customs. Their captors and husbands renamed them, converted them to

Christianity, and introduced them to European ways. In the process, the women often lost much if not all of their cultural identity. In time, they no longer used natives words, ate native foods, wore native clothes, or practiced native religions.

Over the centuries, these women have faced considerable criticism from their own peoples. They have been accused of betraying their race and culture. From the European perspective, they were model women who acted as good Christian women, helping them conquer uncivilized peoples. Whatever the case, they are testaments to survival. They employed their strengths and skills to overcome the traumas of conquest, abduction, slavery, and rape.

Women continued to shape the European colonial experience. In eighteenth-century Latin America, women made up the majority of the population of most colonial Latin American cities. While military might and technological superiority were critical in the early stages of early modern European colonization, the ultimate success of those efforts relied on women's emotional, productive, and reproductive abilities. Through their persistence and determination, European and native women created new colonial cultures.

## CONCLUSION

The religious turmoil of the early modern period turned women's lives upside down. Although Protestantism offered women new possibilities for salvation, it often did little to change their place in society. The Catholic Church reacted to the challenge of Protestantism with increased controls on women's sexuality. Across Europe, religious tensions erupted in anti-Semitic violence and witch-hunts. Nevertheless, as women faced increasing criticism for their participation in public life, they found new sources of power, new creative outlets, and new worlds in which they could express their priorities, their personalities, and their promise.

## NOTES

1. Merry Wiesner, "Luther and Women: The Death of Two Marys," in *Disciplines of Faith: Religion, Patriarchy, and Politics*, ed. Raphael Samuel, James Obelkevich, and Lyndal Roper (London: Routledge, 1987), 300.

2. Merry Wiesner, "Women and the Reformation," in *The German People and the Reformation*, ed. R. Po-Chia-Hsia (Ithaca: Cornell University Press, 1988), 156.

3. Margaret L. King, *Women of the Renaissance* (Chicago: University of Chicago Press, 1991), 100–101.

4. Amy Leonard, *Nails in the Wall: Catholic Nuns in Reformation Germany* (Chicago: University of Chicago Press, 2005), chapter 4.

5. Cited in Mary Potter, "Gender Equality and Gender Hierarchy in Calvin's Theology," *Signs* 11:4 (Summer 1986): 727.

6. E. William Monter, "Women in Calvinist Geneva," *Signs* 6:2 (1980): 192.

7. Julian Goodare, "Scotland," in *The Reformation in National Context*, ed. Bob Scribner, Roy Porter, and Mikulás Tech (Cambridge: Cambridge University Press, 1994), 102–103.

8. Natalie Zemon Davis, *Society and Culture in Early Modern France* (Stanford: Stanford University Press, 1975), 183.

9. R. Po-Chia Hsia, "Münster and the Anabaptists," in *The German People and the Reformation*, 58.

10. Po-Chia Hsia, "Münster and the Anabaptists," 59.

11. Marybeth Carlson, "Women In and Out of the Public Church in the Dutch Republic," in *Women and Religion in Old and New Worlds*, ed. Susan E. Dinan and Debra Meyers (New York: Routledge, 2001), 118.

12. Diane Willen, "Women and Religion in Early Modern England," in *Women in Reformation and Counter-Reformation Europe: Private and Public Worlds*, ed. Sherrin Marshall (Bloomington: Indiana University Press, 1989), 144.

13. Willen, "Women and Religion in Early Modern England," 146.

14. Diane Willen, "Godly Women in Early Modern England: Puritanism and Gender," *Journal of Ecclesiastical History* 43:4 (1992): 563, 578.

15. Henry Kamen, *The Phoenix and the Flame: Catalonia and the Counter Reformation* (New Haven: Yale University Press, 1993), 326.

16. Marc Forster, *The Counter-Reformation in the Villages: Religion and Reform in the Bishopric of Speyer, 1560–1720* (Ithaca: Cornell University Press, 1992), 237.

17. Mary Elizabeth Perry, *Gender and Disorder in Early Modern Seville* (Princeton: Princeton University Press, 1992), 142.

18. Jaime Contreras and Gustav Henningsen, "Forty-four Thousand Cases of the Spanish Inquisition (1540–1700): Analysis of a Historical Data Bank," in *The Inquisition in Early Modern Europe*, ed. Gustav Henningsen and John Tedeschi (Dekalb, IL: Northern Illinois University Press, 1986), 114.

19. María Helena Sánchez Ortega, "Sorcery and Eroticism in Love Magic," in *Cultural Encounters: The Impact of the Inquisition in Spain and the New World*, ed. Mary Elizabeth Perry and Anne J. Cruz (Berkeley: University of California Press, 1991), 82.

20. William E. Monter, *Frontiers of Heresy: The Spanish Inquisition from the Basque Lands to Sicily* (Cambridge: Cambridge University Press, 1990), 281–282, 316–317.

21. P. Renée Baernstein, *A Convent Tale: A Century of Sisterhood in Milan* (New York: Routledge, 2002), 88.

22. Ulrike Strasser, "Cloistering Women's Past: Conflicting Accounts of Enclosure in a Seventeenth-Century Munich Nunnery," in *Gender in Early Modern German History*, ed. Ulinka Rublack (Cambridge: Cambridge University Press, 2002), 225.

23. Brian P. Levack, *The Witch-hunt in Early Modern Europe* (New York: Longman, 1995), 23.

24. Levack, 133.

25. Reneé Levine Melammed, "María López. A Convicted Judaizer from Castile," in *Women in the Inquisition: Spain and the New World*, ed. Mary E. Giles (Baltimore: The Johns Hopkins University Press, 1999), 58–59.

26. Daniel Swetschinski, *Reluctant Cosmopolitans: The Portuguese Jews of Seventeenth-Century Amsterdam* (London: The Littman Library of Jewish Civilization, 2000), 88.

27. Mary Elizabeth Perry, "Patience and Pluck: Job's Wife, Conflict and Resistance in Morsico Manuscripts Hidden in the Sixteenth Century," in *Women, Texts, and Authority in the Early Modern Spanish World*, ed. Marta V. Vicente and Luis R. Corteguera (Burlington, VT: Ashgate Press, 2003), 94.

28. Anne MacLaren, "Gender, Religion, and Early Modern Nationalism: Elizabeth I, Mary Queen of Scots, and the Genesis of English Anti-Catholicism," *American Historical Review* 107:3 (June 2002): 759.

29. Nancy Roelker, "The Appeal of Calvinism to French Noblewomen in the Sixteenth Century," *Journal of Interdisciplinary History* 2 (1972): 400.

30. Elaine Kruse, "The Blood-Stained Hands of Catherine de Médicis," in *Political Rhetoric, Power, and Renaissance Women*, ed. Carole Levin and Patricia A. Sullivan (Albany: SUNY Press, 1995), 146.

31. Sharon Kettering, "The Patronage Power of Early Modern French Noblewomen," *Historical Journal* 32:4 (December 1989): 825.

32. Magdalena S. Sánchez, *The Empress, The Queen, and the Nun: Women and Power at the Court of Philip III of Spain* (Baltimore: The Johns Hopkins University Press, 1998).

33. Sara Mendelson and Patricia Crawford, *Women in Early Modern England, 1550–1720* (Oxford: Clarendon Press, 1998), 396–397.

34. Alison Plowden, *Women All on Fire: The Women of the English Civil War* (Phoenix Mill, England: Sutton Publishing, 1998), 62.

35. Plowden, 67.

36. Patricia Crawford, *Women and Religion in England, 1500–1720* (London: Routledge, 1993), 135.

37. Phyllis Mack, "Women as Prophets During the English Civil War," *Feminist Studies* 8 (1982): 24.

38. Ann Hughes, "Gender and Politics in Leveller Literature," in *Political Culture and Cultural Politics in Early Modern England*, ed. Susan D. Amussen and Mark A Kishlansky (Manchester: Manchester University Press, 1995), 163.

39. Juan Luis Vives, *The Education of a Christian Woman: A Sixteenth-Century Manual*, ed. and trans. Charles Fantazzi (Chicago: University of Chicago Press, 2000), 193.

40. Natalia Pushkareva, *Women in Russian History: From the Twelfth to the Twentieth Century*, trans. Eve Levin. (Armonk, NY: M. E. Sharpe, 1997), 88–93.

41. Moderata da Fonte, *The Worth of Women: Wherein Is Clearly Revealed Their Nobility and Their Superiority to Men*, trans. Virginia Cox (Chicago: University of Chicago Press, 1997), 237.

42. Frances Teague and Rebecca De Haas, "Defenses of Women," in *A Companion to Early Modern Women's Writing*, ed. Anita Pacheco (London: Blackwell, 2002), 250.

43. Veronica Franco, "A Challenge to a Poet Who Has Defamed Her," *Poems and Selected Letters* ed. and trans. Ann Rosalind Jones and Margaret R. Rosenthal (Chicago: University of Chicago Press, 1998), 163,165.

44. Kimberlyn Montford, "L'Anno Santo and Female Monastic Churches: The Politics, Business and Music of the Holy Year in Rome (1675)," *Journal of Seventeenth-Century Music* 6:1 (2000): par. 3.3 http://www.sscm-jscm.org/jscm/v6/no1/Montford.html

45. Londa Schiebinger, *The Mind Has No Sex: Women in the Origins of Modern Science* (Cambridge, MA: Harvard University Press, 1989), 80–81.

46. Lianne McTavish, *Childbirth and the Display of Authority in Early Modern France* (Aldershot, England: Ashgate Press, 2005), esp. 2, 43, 103.

47. Auke P. Jacobs, *Los movimientos migratorios entre Castilla e HispanoAmerica durante el reinado de Felipe II, 1598–1621* (Amsterdam: Editions Rodopi, 1995), 281.

48. Timothy J. Coates, *Convicts and Orphans: Forced and State-Sponsored Colonizers in the Portuguese Empire, 1550–1755* (Stanford: Stanford University Press, 2001), esp. 143, 155, 173.

49. Kathleen Brown, *Good Wives, Nasty Wenches, and Anxious Patriarchs: Gender, Race, and Power in Colonial Virginia* (Chapel Hill: University of North Carolina Press for the Institute of Early American History and Culture, 1996), 80–83.

50. Brown, 75–80.

51. Natalie Zemon Davis, *Women on the Margins: Three Seventeenth-Century Lives* (Cambridge: Harvard University Press, 1995), 96–97.

## SUGGESTED READINGS

Brown, Kathleen. *Good Wives, Nasty Wenches, and Anxious Patriarchs: Gender, Race, and Power in Colonial Virginia*. Chapel Hill: University of North Carolina Press for the Institute of Early American History and Culture, 1996. Brown examines not only the role of women in Colonial British America, but also the interactions between white settlers and native and African Americans.

Davis, Natalie Zemon. *Women on the Margins: Three Seventeenth-Century Lives*. Cambridge, MA: Harvard University Press, 1995. These portraits of a Catholic nun, a Jewish woman, and a Dutch artist bring the complex world of early modern women to life.

Giles, Mary E. *Women in the Inquisition. Spain and the New World*. Baltimore: The Johns Hopkins University Press, 1999.

Levack, Brian P. *The Witch-hunt in Early Modern Europe*. 2nd ed. London: Longman, 1995. This works provides the most detailed and the broadest examination of the phenomenon of witch-hunting.

Schiebinger, Londa. *The Mind Has No Sex: Women in the Origins of Modern Science*. Cambridge, MA: Harvard University Press, 1989. This pioneering study looks at the changing roles of women during the scientific revolution.

# Chapter 8

# Whose Enlightenment, Whose Revolution? 1700–1815

*Women's March on Versailles, (October 1789).* In the French Revolution, women's public protests and violence changed from demands for food for their families to demands for equality and citizenship. (Musée Carnavalet, Paris, France/ RMN/Art Resource, NY.)

- **Society at the End of the Old Regime**  256
    - *Royal and Aristocratic Women*  256
    - *Women and Rural Life*  258
    - *Urban Women*  259

- **Enlightenment Ideas**  261
    - *Women and the Birth of Modern Science*  261
    - *Enlightenment Ideas About Women*  262
    - *The* Salonières *and the* Philosophes  263

- **The Enlightenment in Eastern Europe and Russia**  267
    - *Gendering Enlightened Absolutism in Austria and Prussia*  267
    - *The Westernization of Russia*  270

- **Women, Art, and Culture in the Eighteenth Century**  271
    - *Women as Professional Artists*  271
    - *Music*  272
    - *Literature by and for Women*  273

- **Gender in the Colonies**  275
    - *Colonial Economies*  275
    - *Slavery and the Abolitionist Movement*  276
    - *The American Revolution*  277
    - *Women in Spanish America*  278

- **Women and the French Revolution**  279
    - *Women and the Start of the Revolution*  280
    - *Women and the Radical Phase of the Revolution*  281
    - *Women and the Napoleonic Era*  286
    - *Women and Resistance to Napoleon*  288

The eighteenth century was a period of intense social, political, and intellectual change. Class differences increased as the nobility lived in luxury while peasants continued to starve. Inspired by the scientific revolution, Enlightenment intellectuals debated the inevitability of social and gender inequality and laid the groundwork for the revolutions in the Americas and France. They also struggled with the question of whether women could be citizens or whether motherhood demanded their confinement to home and domesticity. Women were both patrons of and participants in these debates. The impact of the Enlightenment was not the same everywhere. In Austria, Prussia, and Russia, Enlightened rulers manipulated gender expectations in different ways to maintain their authority. The Enlightenment also inspired new artistic forms, and women critiqued their experiences through their artistic participation. Ultimately, the revolutions in North America and France brought short-term gains to women and raised new issues about the nature of political participation.

## SOCIETY AT THE END OF THE OLD REGIME

Increasing class tensions marked the end of the Old Regime. The aristocracy lived in luxury and had almost exclusive access to political power. Although the wealthiest members of the middle class could live like the aristocracy, they lacked the status and privileges that came with nobility. At the bottom of the social hierarchy, poor women struggled to make ends meet, resenting the ostentatious luxury and leisure of the upper classes. Although these tensions were nothing new, changing economies accentuated class divisions.

### Royal and Aristocratic Women

Wealth and leisure defined the lives of aristocratic women. Their families' personal holdings were often enormous. In Hungary, 40 percent of the land belonged to 150 or so families.[1] In Naples, eighty-four noble families controlled at least ten thousand peasants each, over two million people

## Chapter 8 ❖ Chronology

| | |
|---|---|
| **1720** | Rosalba Carrira paints in Paris |
| **1740** | Emilie du Châtelet published translation and commentary on Newton's *Principia mathematica* |
| | Maria Theresa first woman ruler of the Habsburg monarchy |
| | Prussia invades Silesia, initiating the War of Austrian Succession |
| **1757** | Louis XVI bans the *Encyclopédie* |
| **1758** | Jean-Jacques Rousseau writes *Emile* |
| **1759** | Marie Thiroux d'Arconville publishes *Ostéologie* |
| **1764** | Catherine the Great founds first secular school for girls in Russia |
| **1776** | Declaration of Independence, start of American Revolution |
| **1786** | Carona Schröter publishes first of two collections of songs |
| **1789** | Start of French Revolution |
| **1791** | Olympe de Gouge writes *Declaration of the Rights of Women and Female Citizen* |
| **1792** | Mary Wollstonecraft publishes *Vindication of the Rights of Woman* |
| **1793** | Executions of Marie Antoinette and Louis XVI |
| **1804** | Napoleonic Code |
| **1807** | New Jersey terminates women's right to vote |
| **1815** | Napoleon defeated at Waterloo |

total.[2] This wealth allowed aristocratic women to live in remarkable opulence. Palaces, like that of Queluz built by the Portuguese king consort Dom Pedro III (1717–1786) between 1747 and 1780, held splendid furnishings imported from around the world. A lavish life required an elaborate wardrobe. When Empress Elizabeth of Russia (1709–1762) died, she left fifteen thousand dresses in her wardrobe, and the trousseau of Archduchess Maria Josepha of Austria (1699–1757) included ninety-nine dresses made of rich silks decorated with gold and silver lace.[3] The aristocracy filled their considerable leisure time with racing, card playing, balls, and other social events.

Aristocratic women's sole duty was to produce male heirs who would perpetuate the lineage and increase the family's political and economic power. Families looked for suitable matches based on political connections and family wealth. Elite women married around age sixteen, nearly a decade younger than most peasant women, and their husbands were often considerably older. By marrying young and sending their children out to wet nurses, noblewomen tended to have large families. In France at the beginning of the century, noble families had an average of 6.5 children.[4] Considering that nearly half of all children did not live to adulthood, noblewomen often had more than ten pregnancies in a lifetime.

Some historians argue that aristocratic attitudes toward motherhood changed considerably over the eighteenth century. At the beginning of the century, elite mothers often took little interest in their children. Their wealth allowed them to employ large numbers of servants to cook, clean, sew, attend to the needs and wants of their masters and mistresses, and take care of the children. One French noblewoman remembered her childhood as a time of neglect and frequent accidents. "My mother . . . neglected me a little, and left me too much in the care of the women [servants], who neglected me also."[5] However, as the century progressed, elite society began to emphasize the importance of maternal love. In his 1758 novel *Emile,* the Swiss social theorist Jean-Jacques Rousseau (1712–1778) encouraged mothers to breastfeed to strengthen the maternal bond. Letters between husbands and wives and between female friends indicate a greater interest in child-rearing. Even the French queen, Marie Antoinette (1755–1793), had a model dairy farm built for her and her ladies in waiting so that they could "return to nature" and practice nurturing. Increasingly, mothers looked after their children's education and supervised nannies, governesses, and tutors. Both breastfeeding, which suppressed fertility, and an increased use of birth control led to a decline in the number of children born to noblewomen.

Despite the importance of marriage, family strategies prevented many noblewomen from marrying. Nearly one-third of elite Englishwomen never married because their families could not afford dowries or find appropriate spouses.[6] Because women assumed the status of their husbands, noblemen could find spouses among the daughters of the urban elite, but sisters who married down in the social hierarchy brought shame to their families. As a result, many women remained single, living at home and receiving only modest inheritances. These women were doubly disappointed; they were unable to fulfill the goals of marriage and motherhood for which they were raised and unable to afford the lifestyle of their class.

Aristocratic women's wealth gave them access to court life and royal politics. Indeed, many contemporaries complained that women had taken over politics. Some women used their sexuality to achieve their personal and political goals. Claudine-Alexandrine Guérin de Tencin (1681–1749) first seduced the French regent Philippe Duc d'Orléans (1674–1723) and then became the mistress of the abbé Dubois (1656–1723), who went on to become an archbishop and cardinal. Through her liaisons, she hoped to promote the career of her less ambitious brother, Cardinal Pierre Guérin de Tencin. Even more influential was Jeanne Poisson, mistress to the French king, Louis XV (r. 1715–1774), and better known as the Marquise de Pompadour (1721–1764). Her affair with the king brought her more than riches; she controlled all access to the king and placed her allies in important political positions.

Increasingly, the new elites who had earned great fortunes from business rather than family wealth clamored to become members of the aristocracy. They wanted access to the power and privileges that came with hereditary titles. Eager for alliances and money for the treasury, the French monarchy sold noble titles to those ambitious families. As a result, over the course of the century, the French aristocracy nearly doubled in size.

## Women and Rural Life

As had always been true, peasant women produced much of the wealth enjoyed by elite women. Although rural women's work remained much as it had for centuries, overseas trade, increased consumption and manufacturing, and new farming techniques changed the organization of peasant women's work. Across Europe, peasant households were less often self-supporting. Women now produced goods and food for markets in a process known as *protoindustrialization.*

Landowners drove much of the change in rural life. They introduced a variety of new farming techniques and new crops like the potato and the turnip, which allowed for more efficient use of land and healthier, more productive livestock. Just as important, landowners enclosed fields, forcing thousands of peasant families off lands that they had worked for generations. After enclosure, peasants no longer farmed primarily for themselves, but to harvest crops that would be sold in the marketplace and whose profits went to the landowner.

While peasant men continued to work in the fields, businessmen purchased raw materials such as linen, cotton, or wool and employed peasant women to turn it into cloth. Some women produced the entire product from thread to finished cloth, while others completed only one part of the production process, such as spinning or weaving. The businessman returned to collect the finished product, paying the women by the piece. He then sold the cloth at regional, national, and international markets. This process is known as "cottage industry," since it took place in peasant cottages, or as the "putting-out system." Although this system of production was not new, it became much more common in the eighteenth century. Women's paid labor integrated easily into their traditional household duties. The cash they earned paid for the goods that their families no longer produced. Often, women earned the only cash families ever saw.

Their ties to national and international economies left women and their families increasingly vulnerable to economic crises. The changing price of manufactured goods affected families' survival, and crop failures in France in 1725, 1739–40, 1752, and 1768, caused an increase in bread prices and hunger. One French police officer testified that a pregnant woman, desperate to feed her children, had come up to him before a riot crying, "Help me, help me. My husband and me and my three children will starve to death if you don't get us corn [grain]. I'll stab myself before your very eyes."[7] A group of women then attacked the local grain store. Unable to grow their own food and without the cash to buy basic foodstuffs, women resorted to violence to feed their families.

In eastern Europe, the living and working conditions of peasants declined as most were forced into serfdom. Faced with lower profits and higher labor costs, aristocratic Austro-Hungarian, Polish, Prussian, and Russian landowners held on to their shrinking rural workforce by tying them to the land. Peasants owed their lords as many as three hundred days of labor a year in exchange for a plot of land and a house. Typically, they supplied their own tools and draft animals, which added to their burden. Life was hard and living conditions squalid. Attempts to flee brought severe penalties. In many areas, serfs were no better off than slaves. In Poland, landlords had the power of life and death over their serfs until 1768. The impact on women was especially severe. To alleviate their labor shortage, eastern European lords encour-

aged or coerced their serfs into marrying early and raising more children. Russian peasant women could expect to marry in their early teens and bear numerous children. Widows made up the poorest segment of the serf population; often lacking male help to perform the onerous labor services, they had to sell off livestock and household goods to feed and support themselves.

These harsh conditions did not prevent thousands of serf families from either fleeing to cities or revolting against their lords. In Russia, seventy-three peasant uprisings took place between 1762 and 1769. After nearly one-quarter million Bohemian peasants died between 1770 and 1772 from famine, the survivors launched a massive revolt in 1774.

Although life expectancy increased during the eighteenth century, rural life was still very difficult, especially for those trapped in serfdom. With poor medical care and long workdays, malnutrition and poor hygiene remained constant threats. For women, this meant continued high rates of death from childbirth and high infant mortality rates.

## Urban Women

While peasant women toiled in their homes and fields, cities became the centers of a new consumer-oriented society that fostered new values and behavior. New manufacturing techniques and cheaper raw materials now made it possible for nonelite women to afford items that had been previously beyond their reach. Many of those goods imitated the styles of the wealthy. They bought fashionable clothing and home furnishings rather than utilitarian goods. At all levels of urban society, women's wardrobes became larger and more expensive. Manufacturers and shopkeepers encouraged this consumption by advertising the latest fashions from Italy and France in newspapers. The first color fashion advertisements appeared in the British publication *The Lady's Magazine* in 1771. Ads targeted women, as they made most of the basic household expenditures, and manufacturers eagerly accommodated women's changing tastes. When British women sought to make their skin pale by washing in arsenic, they then wanted black tea sets to set off their skin. Josiah Wedgwood (1730–1795), who had pioneered the mass production of fine china, quickly capitalized on this trend by producing an inexpensive set of black china.[8]

Formerly exotic goods like coffee and tea became commonplace and changed urban society. Coffeehouses replaced taverns as public gathering spots where men met to discuss business and politics. To distinguish themselves from lower-class taverns, coffeehouses prohibited swearing, gambling, and fighting on their premises. Teahouses and tea drinking became associated with women and feminine behavior. Some moralists even worried that women's control of tea serving would lead to a rise in effeminate men and a weakened military.[9]

Nevertheless, tea imports increased steadily throughout the eighteenth century, especially in England. Tea gardens and teahouses such as the Golden Lion, opened by the Twinings Company in 1706, catered to women. Men and women also drank tea at home, and by the 1740s, English women routinely presided over afternoon tea. At tea, parents taught their children upper-class manners, emphasizing that moderation, self-control, and domestic order conferred respectability rather than birth and wealth.

The city offered women a wider array of life choices than the countryside. Although most women married, between 15 and 25 percent of urban middle-class women remained single.[10] As sons and daughters inherited equally, middle-class single women often used their inheritances to set up their own households in the city. Others shared lodgings with another woman or a relative. Over the course of the eighteenth century, illegitimate births in much of the rest of Europe more than doubled, evidence that many of these single women did not wait for marriage to engage in sexual relationships. Other women chose to spend their time with women, both as friends and as lovers. To support themselves, single women worked in occupations that their socially mobile families found acceptable, such as milliners, shopkeepers, and glovers. Single women with some education became governesses and boarding school teachers.

European cities were also home to a range of working-class women whose work options reflected the growing urban economy. Although some were born in the city, most had moved from

the countryside seeking a better life. Domestic service drew the largest numbers of young women to urban areas. During the eighteenth century, one-quarter of London's women worked in domestic service. Changes in the cloth industry also offered women new work opportunities, as the growth of overseas trade brought in more raw materials and new manufacturing techniques weakened the guild system. In Florence, thousands of women wove silk cloth for a living; in German cities, they dominated the spinning industry; and in France they made lace. With such a variety of occupations available, many women found they did not have to marry to support themselves. In London between 1695 and 1725, 78 percent of single women and 71 percent of widows claimed that they were wholly self-supporting.[11]

However, the changing economy endangered widows' abilities to earn livings. As guild masters saw their livelihoods threatened, they tried to protect themselves by excluding women from the few remaining guilds. Legislation prevented widows from taking over their deceased husbands' trades and, as a result, widowhood in urban areas became increasingly associated with poverty. Across Europe, urban widows tended to be poorer than women living in households headed by men. Many rented dank and cramped rooms and had little opportunity to enjoy urban life.

Most urban married women also worked. One historian found that between 1695 and 1725, 60 percent of London wives who testified in court claimed that they were at least partially employed. No doubt, many more women worked informally for or with their husbands.[12] The wealthier a woman was, the less likely she was to work outside the home for pay. However, her domestic work, including the supervision of servants, left her with little leisure time.

Differences between social classes intensified during the eighteenth century. Elite women lived in magnificent palaces, surrounded by the finest clothing and furnishings that money could buy. They built their success on the labor of peasant women, whose livelihoods became increasingly fragile as family economies became integrated into regional and national markets. At the same time, successful middle-class women enjoyed the benefits of an ever more consumer-oriented society.

The differences among women reflected broader social divisions that would erupt in violence in many parts of Europe by the end of the century.

## ENLIGHTENMENT IDEAS

Conscious of the increasing disparities in wealth and driven by the intellectual achievements of the scientific revolution, intellectuals began to explore the possibilities for changing society. In this intellectual revolution, known as the Enlightenment, thinkers used rational observation to understand the laws that governed the universe, nature, and social and political organization. They questioned the legitimacy of monarchies and the social order, as well as the role of women in politics and society. Although male intellectuals used a wide array of scientific and philosophical arguments to marginalize women from scholarly and political pursuits, across Europe, women found innovative ways to participate in intellectual debate and artistic achievement.

### Women and the Birth of Modern Science

At the end of the seventeenth century, scientific inquiry captured the imagination of many. Interested men and women observed and experimented in an effort to explain the natural world. Mathematics became particularly popular, and women of all classes attended public lectures on mathematics and astronomy. Several popular publications, such as the *Ladies' Diary* published in England from 1704 to 1841, promoted women's education in the "mathematical sciences."[13] Many aristocratic women used their connections to explore the world of science. Emilie du Châtelet (1706–1749) took advantage of this new enthusiasm. Emilie married the Marquis du Châtelet when she was nineteen years old. While raising three children, she surrounded herself with mentors who instructed her in science and mathematics. Her most famous association was with Voltaire (1694–1778), the French writer and satirist with whom she formed a close physical and intellectual relationship. He introduced her to Newtonian physics, and she actively participated

in the debates about the role of metaphysics in natural science that raged between the Newtonian and Cartesian (followers of Descartes) thinkers in France. In 1740, she published her French translation and commentary on Newton's *Principia mathematica*.

Female artisans also became interested in scientific inquiry. Maria Sibylla Merian (1647–1717) learned illustration, engraving, and painting from her father. After successfully printing textiles for many years, she began to study nature in search of better colors and new images for her textiles. Merian illustrated the works of other naturalists, and then in 1699, she set sail for the Dutch colony of Surinam to continue her research into plants and insects. She returned to Amsterdam in 1701 to begin her major scientific work the *Metamorphosis Insectorum Surinamensium*, an illustrated study of New World insects.

However, men continued to limit women's access to higher education and the most elite intellectual circles. Officially unable to attend universities, few women could obtain the university degree required to do scientific research in academies or universities. Laura Bassi (1711–1778) held a chair in physics, and Maria Gaetana Agnesi (1718–1799) succeeded her father as professor of mathematics at the University of Bologna. Agnesi felt closely connected to other ambitious women. She dedicated her most famous mathematical treatise to Maria Theresa of Austria (see below). In the dedication she noted, "Nothing has encouraged me as much as your madam being a woman, which luckily applies to me."[14] Maria Theresa sent Agnesi a basket of jewels in appreciation. However, these women were exceptional. Most of the newly formed scientific societies, such as the Royal Society of London (1662), the Parisian Royal Academy of Science (1666), or the Royal Society of Sciences in Berlin (1700) also excluded women from membership, thus denying women the economic and intellectual networks that Europe's male intelligentsia gained from their membership.

Science was men's work, and most women who wanted to pursue scientific investigation could only do so as assistants to their fathers, husbands, and brothers. Caroline Herschel (1750–1848), born in Hanover, Germany, served as her brother's assistant while he was astronomer to King George

MARIA SIBYLLA MERIAN
Nat: XII. Apr: M D C X L V II. Obiit XIII. Jan: M D C C X V II.

**MARIA SIBYLLA MERIAN (1647–1717).** Merian's work as an artist for silk cloth led to her interest in the natural world. She traveled to Surinam to catalogue, collect, and illustrate the insects' life there. *(Offentliche Kunstsammlung Kunstmuseum, Basel.)*

III of England (r. 1760–1820). She could only have access to his high-quality telescopes when her brother traveled, yet between 1789 and 1797, she discovered eight comets and three nebulae and published her *Catalogue of Stars* with the Royal Society. Nonetheless, she described herself as "a well-trained puppy-dog," not an independent thinker.[15]

## Enlightenment Ideas About Women

As Enlightenment thinkers explored the basic structures of nature and society, debates about gender revolved around the nature of sex differences and their role in social organization. Although French philosopher René Descartes

(1596–1650) did not directly address the issue of gender, his ideas became central to Enlightenment defenses of women's intellectual abilities. According to Descartes, the mind functioned independently of the body. Men's bodies differed from women's bodies only in the sex organs; therefore, all minds were potentially equal. This idea led many followers of Descartes to reconsider their views on women. Philosopher and former Jesuit Francois Poullain de la Barre (1647–1725) said, "When I was a scholastic, I considered [women] scholastically, that is to say, as monsters, as beings inferior to men, because Aristotle and some theologians whom I had read, considered them so." Changed by his encounter with Cartesian ideas, Poullain de la Barre later enthusiastically proclaimed, "The mind has no sex."[16]

Similarly, political theorist John Locke (1632–1704) almost unintentionally provided a philosophical foundation for women's political roles. In his *Two Treatises on Government* (1680–1690), he refuted traditional justifications for absolutism and in doing so, he provided a critique of patriarchy. Supporters of absolutist monarchies argued that the king was analogous to a father and children were to honor their father. However, Locke pointed out that the biblical commandment was to honor fathers *and mothers*. Moreover, Locke asserted that marriage was a voluntary relationship, and while husbands might rule their wives, that hierarchy was not inevitable.[17]

However, not everyone agreed with these radical views of human equality. Eighteenth-century anatomists began to reconsider the theories of bodily humors that had dominated classical and medieval understandings of the body and sex differences. In the process, they formulated views of male and female bodies that emphasized sex differences beyond those found in the reproductive organs. Marie Thiroux d'Arconville (1720–1805) played a critical role in both defining and illustrating these differences. Although she argued that women should not get involved in medicine, in 1759, she produced the most important illustrations of the female skeleton of her time. Published under a male pseudonym, her *Ostéologie* became the standard view of female skeletons, with a small head, enlarged pelvis, and narrow ribs.[18] Such a body was perfect for childbearing, but

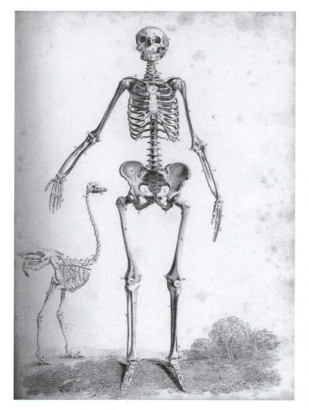

**D'ARCONVILLE'S FEMALE SKELETON (1759).** Marie Thiroux d'Arconville produced the standard view of female skeletons, with a small head, enlarged pelvis, and narrow ribs. *(Courtesy Special Collections, Dalhousie University Archives and Special Collections.)*

woefully inadequate for intellectual or physical exertion.

The new belief that women's bodies differed fundamentally from men's and were not just inferior versions of them was known as *complementarity*; men's and women's bodies had differing but complementary roles in society and biology. Complementarity had profound social implications. On the one hand, because anatomists believed that women's bodies were designed only for motherhood, they came to view the womb as an amazing organ, instead of the source of hysteria and confusion advanced by Aristotle. On the other hand, complementarity provided the basis for the idea that women were built for domesticity

and child-rearing, and men were built for rule, rationality, and public duties. This understanding of sex differences justified the different educations and political rights that men and women received.

Rousseau was a vocal advocate of complementarity. Men and women were physically, intellectually, and morally different and those innate and unalterable differences determined women's inferior place in society.[19] Tapping into the new emphasis on domesticity that was sweeping Europe, Rousseau believed that women had the capacity to develop, learn, and grow, but that their talents lay only in the domestic realm. Thus, women's education must be different from men's in order for them to reach their full potential as mothers and helpers to their husbands.

Although popular, Rousseau's ideas faced criticism. The Marquis of Condorcet (1745–1793) argued that granting women rights did not imply a social revolution, only that it would give them basic rights due to all humans. Because society had advanced to a peaceful, sedentary, and civilized level, it should foster greater equality between men and women. Condorcet also believed that the physical differences between men and women should not stand in the way of social equality and citizenship. There were many physical differences between people, not the least of which were differences between men and women. To those who believed that pregnancy made women incapable, Condorcet responded that other people became incapacitated by rheumatism or ill with gout. To those who argued that women had not made important scientific discoveries or written literary masterpieces, he replied that was also true of most men.[20] At the heart of Condorcet's disagreement with Rousseau and other proponents of complementarity was whether the social differences between men and women were natural or, to use a modern phrase, "socially constructed."

## The *Salonières* and the Philosophes

Enlightenment thinkers debated these and other issues in intellectual gatherings known as *salons*, most of which were organized and supported by noble and bourgeoisie women. Salons took place in private homes and women, the *salonières*, presided over them. At a salon, intellectuals, usually men, debated ideas, read new literature, and performed music. The men who embraced this new emphasis on intellectual inquiry, particularly in order to critique religion and politics, called themselves *philosophes.*

Although many salon participants were connected to the king, the salon as an institution was the antithesis of the monarchy in its appreciation of criticism, debate, and republican sentiments. In fact, the salon had much in common with the workshop, because members saw it as a place of work, not play, and like a workshop, it depended on the labor of both men and women. Although members valued wit, good manners, and a pleasant personality, in a salon one also had to produce, debate, and defend ideas; frivolous activities such as gambling and parlor games were largely absent. One of the leading salonières, Marie-Thérèse Rodet Geoffrin (1699–1777), specifically rearranged the schedule of her salon to encourage its work. Instead of hosting the traditionally sociable late-night supper, she moved her salon to one o'clock in the afternoon so as to leave the afternoon free for conversation. To focus discussions, she held her Monday salon for artists and her Wednesday salon for writers. This regular schedule made the salon a social center for those who saw themselves as public intellectuals or as they referred to themselves, "citizens in the Republic of Letters."[21]

Mentoring between women also made the salon much like an artisan's workshop. For instance, salonières served informal apprenticeships before opening their own salons. Geoffrin began her salon career as a very young, devout wife of a man five times her age. To educate herself, she attended the salon of her neighbor, Claudine-Alexandrine Guérin de Tencin. When Tencin died in 1749, Geoffrin formalized her own salon. In turn, Geoffrin "trained" Suzanne Necker (1739–1794) and Julie de Lespinasse (1732–1776) who eventually ran their own salons in concert with Geoffrin. Julie de Lespinasse, the illegitimate daughter of a countess, had no dowry and few prospects in eighteenth-century society. Her letters acknowledge the value of the friendships that she had formed in salons. For the salonières, salons offered ideas, friendship, leadership, and work in contrast to the rest of elite society where women were only expected to be beautiful when they were not producing heirs. In fact, historian Dena Goodman has argued that the salon's primary relationship was not between a woman and a group of men, but between female mentors and their students.[22]

Women set the agenda for much of the debate and scholarship that emerged from the salons. Members of Julie de Lespinasse's salon planned the *Encyclopédie,* the most ambitious Enlightenment project; indeed her salon came to be known as the "laboratory of the *Encyclopédie.*"[23] Initially intended to be a translation and expansion of a popular English encyclopedia, it soon became an undertaking in its own right, embodying, so its editors believed, the spirit and goals of the Enlightenment. Two Frenchmen, Denis Diderot (1713–1784) and Jean Le Rond d'Alembert (1717–1783), the illegitimate son of the salonière Tencin, directed this work. They attempted to use the expertise of a variety of thinkers to catalogue and explain all human knowledge.

The editors funded production of the *Encyclopédie* through subscriptions, a new system recently imported from England. They increased circulations by bringing out cheap editions and abridged versions, and with the appearance of pirated copies, the *Encyclopédie* enjoyed a wide audience. Because of its broad readership and its open examination and criticism of many aspects of society, such as organized religion and monarchies, the king of France banned the *Encyclopédie* in 1757, forcing it underground after only seven volumes had been published. Soon thereafter, Madame de Pompadour came to the project's defense at a dinner party attended by the king. The host raised the question of how gunpowder was made and Madame de Pompadour countered by wondering about the ingredients of face powder. She then added that had the king not banned the *Encyclopédie,* they might know the answers to these and other interesting questions. The king then sent for his own copies, which had not been confiscated, and soon thereafter allowed Diderot and d'Alembert to continue their work.[24] When completed in 1766, the project consisted of seventeen volumes of articles and eleven volumes of illustrations. Despite the important role that Lespinasse played in fostering this project, only two women actually contributed to it. Both articles were on garments or fashion, and one of these women remains anonymous.[25]

The most famous salons were in France, but the idea spread to other parts of Europe, where salons often took on other agendas. In Prussia, Berlin's salons attracted Jews and Christians from all walks of life, and Jewish women ran some of the most influential gatherings. They introduced French style and culture to attendees and emphasized common interests over their cultural differences. One of the products of the Prussian salons was Moses Mendelssohn (1729–1786), the father of the Jewish Enlightenment known as the *Haskalah,* which encouraged Jews to study secular subjects and to assimilate into European society. Mendelssohn attempted to integrate reason into Jewish understandings of God, and his daughter, Dorothea von Schlegel (1763–1839), carried on this intellectual inquiry with her own popular salon. Although the salons offered Jewish women new educational opportunities, they also attracted them away from their traditional culture. Many Jewish salon women took Christian names, divorced their Jewish husbands, converted, and married Christian men.[26]

In Spain, female participants in the Enlightenment did not criticize Catholicism or the monarchy as they did in France, but directed their attention to social reforms. In Madrid, a group of about thirty women formed a women's council attached to the Economic Society of Madrid, whose work focused on women's education and the reform of foundling hospitals. As the first female member of a Spanish Economic Society, Josefa Amar y Borbón (1749–1833) turned her considerable intellectual powers to translating and composing treatises on new agricultural techniques for the Royal Aragonese Economic Society. She argued passionately for female membership in the Economic Society. She also created her own catalogue of worthy women for other women to emulate and produced an important work on women's education.[27]

In England, women gathered in reading groups to discuss ideas and promote social change (see **Women's Lives:** Lady Mary Wortley Montagu). These reading societies drew some of their inspirations from the writings of David Hume (1711–1776) and other Scottish Enlightenment thinkers. He argued for women's education and their important role in civilizing society. Members of these reading groups often pooled their resources to open their own libraries or publish their own books and pamphlets. One of the most famous of these groups was the *bluestockings,* who focused on women and women's social concerns. Led by Elizabeth Montague (1720–1800), they challenged the limitations placed on women, in particular the frequency with which women had to marry for money or social standing and the vapid pleasure-seeking lives that often followed such marriages. Among the most active English bluestockings, Hannah More (1745–1833) wrote and spoke publicly on behalf of women's education, and Elizabeth Carter (1717–1806) translated Greek classics and was fluent in many other languages. Samuel Johnson (1696–1772), the great lexicographer, declared of Carter that she "could make a pudding as well as translate Epictetus [first century C.E.] and work a handkerchief as well as compose a poem."[28]

Run by women and organized around the principles of mutuality and friendship, the salon was the opposite of the academy, which excluded women and likened academic debate to combat. However, in the end, the association of the salon with femininity was the salon's undoing. The most pointed attack came from Rousseau. He argued that society grew out of man's need to be judged by others and that putting the role of judge in the hands of women, as was done in the salons, was corrupt. Salons feminized knowledge and made thinkers effeminate or womanish. These and other criticisms had their effect. By the end of the century, the new professional and scientific academies and the resurgence of universities had eclipsed the great influence of the salons. Yet the role of women in salons meant that for most of the century, gender, either implicitly or explicitly, was a regular topic of conversation.

The Enlightenment arose out of the passion for intellectual inquiry brought about by the scientific revolution. Although male scientists often excluded women from traditional but important educational and research institutions, many women found alternative avenues to scientific exploration. The desire for a greater understanding of the world around them led to passionate debates over sex differences, the nature of government, and social hierarchies. If men's and women's minds were equal, then society needed to be reformed to reflect that

## Lady Mary Wortley Montague

Lady Montague's life exemplifies the opportunities and limitations of the Enlightenment. She traveled extensively, engaged in literary debates about the rights and privileges of women, and applied her observations to improving society. Resistance to her and her ideas reveals the limits of the Enlightenment when it came to gender.

Born Mary Pierrepont, the eldest daughter of a Yorkshire gentry family, Lady Montague received a limited education but taught herself Latin in order to read Ovid. Her father then arranged to have her taught Italian and French. Instead of marrying a suitably rich aristocrat, Mary eloped with Edward Wortley Montague, the brother of a girlhood friend. Edward believed that women should be educated and was impressed with his wife's erudition.

In 1714, Edward became Lord of the Treasury and moved his family to London where Lady Montague joined London's literary scene. She became a close friend of poet and social critic Alexander Pope (1688–1744) and began writing. Although relatively few works appeared in her name, she was instrumental in developing a genre of writing, town eclogues, which celebrated urban life, particularly London, in the way that pastoral literature idealized the countryside.

In 1716, the couple traveled to Istanbul where her husband had been appointed ambassador. Lady Montague toured the country, learned Turkish, visited with harem women, and often dressed in local clothing. She kept a journal of her observations, which served as a source for her letters back home and her famous *Embassy Letters*, fifty-two letters written or assembled shortly after she returned to London in 1718 and published after her death.

In Turkey, she observed inoculations for smallpox, a practice unknown in Europe. Lady Montague had been scarred by the disease before leaving for Turkey and when an epidemic threatened London in 1721, she had her children inoculated. However, when some patients died after being inoculated, doctors and scientists condemned her and the practice of inoculation, accusing her of feminine gullibility.

Lady Montague's notoriety reached into the literary and political world. In 1722, when she rejected Pope's declaration of love, he began a sustained and public attack on her. He accused her of infidelity, manliness, and lesbianism. Lady Montague composed public replies published under a pseudonym. Her replies only made Pope angrier and his attacks threatened her husband's political career. In response, Lady Montague turned to writing political commentary in defense of her husband's political party. These tracts were also published anonymously. They were a huge success, but did not restore her reputation and that of her husband.

In 1734, Lady Montague left England for a self-imposed exile in France and Italy. Some claimed that she was following a lover, but she never lived with one. She traveled extensively and even managed a farm in Italy. She lived on the Continent for twenty-seven years, corresponding with her husband and daughter regularly. Her husband gave her a generous allowance, but they never met again.

Meanwhile, her daughter, also Mary, had married one of King George III's (r. 1760–1820) most trusted advisors. The younger Mary, fearing the impact of her mother's unorthodox ways on her own husband's reputation, destroyed her mother's journals after she died and tried unsuccessfully to prevent the publication of *The Embassy Letters*.

Lady Mary Wortley Montague was an adventurer, deeply influenced by the scientific and romantic ethos of the period. She immersed herself in Turkish culture and society and tried to pursue the new ideas current in intellectual circles. Her success threatened many. In her confrontations with Pope and British physicians, she faced the limitations of her society and her sex, even as she broadened their horizons with her writings.

Sources: Robert Halsband, ed., *The Complete Letters of Lady Mary Wortley Montague*, 3 vols. (Oxford: Oxford University Press, 1965–67); and Isobel Grundy, *Lady Mary Wortley Montague* (Oxford: Oxford University Press, 2001).

equality. The emphasis on intellectual equality was most evident in the salons that appeared across Europe. Organized and supported by women, these intellectual gatherings produced some of the great achievements of the Enlightenment.

# THE ENLIGHTENMENT IN EASTERN EUROPE AND RUSSIA

Many Europeans reacted to the Enlightenment with horror, afraid of its potential to disrupt the social hierarchy and monarchical authority. However, even the most absolute monarchs of the period expressed some interest in pursing limited reforms based on Enlightenment ideas. As *enlightened despots*, they implemented changes that benefited their kingdoms and increased monarchical power. Enlightened monarchs in Austria and Prussia used gender in very traditional ways to both maintain power and impose reform, while in Russia, absolutist pressures tempered enthusiasm for Western ideas.

## Gendering Enlightened Absolutism in Austria and Prussia

The Habsburg monarchy ruled over Austria, Hungary, and Bohemia, the southern Netherlands, and parts of Italy and the Balkans, was one of the most powerful absolute monarchies in the West. However, the Habsburg rulers constantly struggled to maintain control over this multicultural, multilingual, and multireligious empire. By the eighteenth century, a succession crisis threatened to end centuries of Habsburg rule. Historically, the Habsburg monarchy had excluded women from the throne based on medieval Salic law that had prohibited women from inheriting property. In an effort to keep Habsburg possessions intact, Emperor Charles VI (r. 1711–1740) spent much of his reign persuading the many territories under Habsburg rule and the rest of Europe to accept the Pragmatic Sanction, a decree that provided for his daughter's succession and the indivisibility of Habsburg lands. When Maria Theresa (r. 1740–1780) succeeded him, she became the first female ruler in the dynasty's 650–year history.

When Maria Theresa became empress at the age of twenty-three, she was four months pregnant and woefully unprepared to govern. Despite her father's work on behalf of the Pragmatic Sanction, he had done little to educate her to rule and had even excluded her from official meetings. Charles just assumed that Maria Theresa's husband would be the true power behind the throne.[29]

From the outset, she faced regular challenges to her authority. Almost immediately Bavaria, France, Prussia, and Saxony reneged on their support of the Pragmatic Sanction. Prussia invaded Silesia, initiating the War of the Austrian Succession. Soon, France, Spain, and Prussia formed a coalition against her. Things at home were no better. Her own subjects knew little about her and hated her French-speaking husband.

However, Maria Theresa proved to be an adept ruler, who was always willing to use her femininity to her advantage. In 1741, she went to the Hungarian diet to request military support. She stood before the Hungarian nobles with her four-month-old son in her arms and tears in her eyes. Her feminine wiles and some skillful negotiation persuaded the Hungarians to raise an army of fifty-five thousand men on her behalf.[30] With their aid, Maria Theresa quickly recovered her occupied lands. In 1742, she sent a letter and picture of herself and her infant son to the commander of her army hoping to rally him and his troops with a rousing reference to her femininity:

> *Here you see before you a queen and her masculine inheritance who have been abandoned by the whole world. What do you think will become of this child? Look at this poor woman who must place in your loyal hands, herself, her whole power, her authority, and everything that our empire stands for and is capable of achieving. Act, O hero and true vassal, as if you will have to justify yourself before God and the world.*[31]

Her military successes attracted Austria's traditional allies especially England. The war dragged on, but when peace was negotiated in 1748, Maria Theresa emerged with her claim to the monarchy secure (see Map 8.1).

Domestically, Maria Theresa liked to be called "Mother of the Country," *Landesmutter*, and she skillfully introduced a wide array of reforms that affected nearly all aspects of life in her domains. She revised the Austrian law code and abolished judicial torture. Within a decade, her administrative reforms had doubled state revenue and professionalized the civil and military bureaucracies. Despite her personal piety, she decreased the power of the church, particularly the Jesuit Order that controlled most educational institutions. When the pope suppressed the order in 1771, Maria Theresa appropriated its holdings to help finance expansion of the public school system. She believed that her subjects should be educated, as education was an avenue to greater productivity, better armies, stronger morality, and orthodox Catholicism. She also decreased the work required of serfs and abolished some feudal dues. However, her commitment to her people came from her personal piety and humanitarian concerns rather than an Enlightenment sense of social justice. She supported the social hierarchy that allowed her and her nobles to control most of the population and believed that calls for liberty and freedom would lead to chaos and disorder.

When not actively engaged in governing her empire, Maria Theresa was dedicated to her family. She was remarkably fertile. She gave birth to sixteen children, five sons and eleven daughters, and used their marriages in to the ruling houses across Europe to secure important alliances. Her most famous match was the marriage of her youngest daughter, Marie Antoinette, to the future French king, Louis XVI (r. 1774–1793). After her husband's death in 1765, Maria Theresa assumed the title *kaiserinwitwe,* empress-widow, cultivating the image of the sad widow and dressing in mourning for the rest of her life.[32]

From 1765, Maria Theresa ruled the hereditary Habsburg lands jointly with her son Joseph II (r. 1765–1790) until her death in 1780. More influenced by Enlightenment thought than his mother, Joseph II abolished serfdom in 1781 and reversed many of Maria Theresa's policies that had been motivated by religious intolerance. In 1745, she had expelled the Jews from Prague, accusing them of siding with Prussia against her. Joseph II condemned this decision and lifted the prohibition. He allowed Protestant clergy to proselytize, as long as they did not insult Catholicism. He continued his mother's policy of closing contemplative monasteries and limiting new monastic vocations, a process that constrained the opportunities for many aristocratic women He also ended censorship of the press and curtailed the activities of the secret police. Unfortunately, his progressive ideas met with considerable criticism, and the nobility and the clergy compelled him to rescind many of his reforms on his deathbed.

While Maria Theresa promoted an image of a powerful mother in Austria, her greatest rival, Frederick II (r. 1740–1786), fashioned a masculine, military society in neighboring Prussia. Frederick, who came to the throne only five months before Maria Theresa, viewed himself as the consummate enlightened monarch. He was an intellectual, a poet, a musician, and a lover of French culture. However, in reality, he was one of the most conservative monarchs in Europe.

By the end of the eighteenth century, Prussia had become the dominant military power on the European continent. Frederick's father, Frederick William I (r. 1713–1740), had created this powerful military by raising taxes, re-enserfing the peasantry, employing new technologies and strategies to modernize the troops, and setting up military academies. By 1740, the army had become the preeminent institution in the country, and Frederick was eager to use it to expand his territories. Upon coming to power, he rejected the Pragmatic Sanction and invaded Silesia in 1740, challenging Maria Theresa's succession to the throne.

To sustain his aggressive foreign policy, Frederick created a masculine culture focused on the military. The officers all came from the nobility, and the troops were conscripted peasants. His taxation system and bureaucracy were designed to support the army and he maintained a close alliance with the *Junkers*, the landed aristocracy who served as the officers in his army. To improve the health of the soldiers and the women who bore them, Frederick moved villages to more fertile lands and introduced potato cultivation. Frederick believed that social segregation ensured strict military discipline, and he used legislation to enforce class distinctions. Noble officers could not socialize with commoners, and he prohibited marriages between people of different social standings. Each social group paid different taxes and a noble could

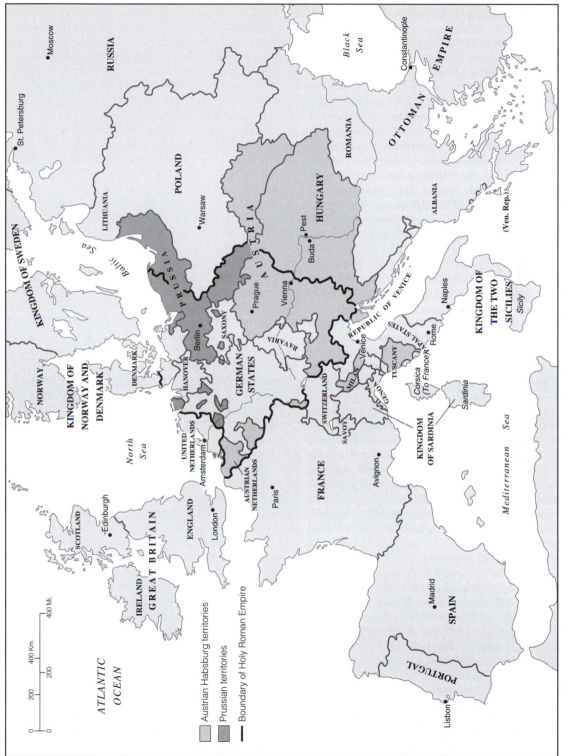

*Map 8.1* **Europe in 1789.** When Maria Theresa became the first woman to rule Habsburg lands, she adopted a policy of "enlightened despotism," tempering centralized rule with Christian charity.

not sell land to a commoner or a member of the middle class.

Frederick's conservative ideas are evident in the Prussian law code of 1747. The code reveals the contradictory views of gender that Enlightenment thought provoked in Prussia. On the one hand, it proclaimed both sexes as equal unless otherwise indicated by law. On the other hand, the code contained numerous exceptions to that equality. For instance, it declared that "the man is the head of the marriage, and his decision prevails in common affairs" and went on to urge men to support their wives appropriately, unless they could not, at which point wives had to be content with lower social standing. Women were "obligated to preside over the household." Thus, in legal terms, the code designated public life as men's sphere and the home as women's sphere.[33]

Although Frederick II may have wanted to be remembered for his enlightened ideas, his conservative reforms and laws reinforced class distinctions and traditional gender norms. Moreover, the centrality of the Prussian military created a masculine culture based on hierarchy and obedience.

## The Westernization of Russia

Until the eighteenth century, Russia had only limited contact with western Europe. Only the determination of Peter I, also known as Peter the Great (r. 1682–1725), finally ended Russia's isolation. During his reign, he brought western European culture to Russia and made Russia a recognized European power. Although peasant women lives remained the same, elite women's lives changed dramatically as Peter transformed Russian society.

Peter believed that Russia had to adopt European culture in order to compete successfully with Western powers. He built a new capital in St. Petersburg with western European–style architecture. At court, the Russian nobility spoke French, dressed in European fashions, and attended western European–style social gatherings, where men and women talked, ate, and danced together. Peter did not achieve this social transformation easily. Most memorably, he insisted that nobles cut their beards. Noble women had to wear Western-style clothing that showed off the waist and the bust and left their heads uncovered, instead of tradi-tional Russian tunics, cloaks, and kerchiefs that had hid women's bodies and covered their heads. He moved elite women out of seclusion in the *terem* and encouraged them to mix with men in public celebrations and court festivities. These women were not necessarily well prepared for public interactions. One British visitor commented on Russian women's awkwardness, stating they "appear indeed perfectly well dressed after the foreign Fashion; but in conversation with strangers, they cannot yet conquer their in-born bashfulness and awkwardness."[34] Other visitors to Peter's court noted that the women danced poorly and that Peter had to post guards at the doors of court balls to stop guests from leaving early. In 1700, Peter expanded his reforms to the lower classes, decreeing that women in towns also adopt Western dress.[35]

Peter used his family to model behavior and appearance. His half sister Praskovia Saltykova (1664–1723) was one of the first women at court to adopt European dress, participate in public assemblies, and host European-style parties. Her daughters received European educations, which focused more on language and natural philosophy than the traditional terem education of needlework and religious piety. When they were old enough, Peter married his nieces to European, not Russian, nobles in order to expand his political connections with western Europe. When Praskovia died, Peter arranged a grand European-style funeral.

Peter's second wife, Catherine I (1684–1727), was a Lithuanian peasant whose intelligence and interests matched Peter's. She came to Peter's attention after one of his field marshals captured her and made her his mistress. Peter married Catherine in 1712 and crowned her his consort in 1724. Peter included Catherine in his government, and when he died in 1725, she ruled successfully for two years, continuing Peter's pro-Western policies. For example, she sponsored expeditions to Siberia in search of furs for export; one expedition discovered the Bering Strait between Russia and Alaska. She also founded the Russian Academy of Sciences.

Catherine came to power because Peter declared his right to designate his successor. In fact, for much of the eighteenth century, women ruled Russia. After Catherine's death, Peter's great-niece Anna (r. 1730–1740) ruled, followed by his daughter Elizabeth (r. 1741–1760), and finally Catherine II (r. 1762–1796). Her son, Paul I (r. 1796–1801), then established hereditary rule, excluding women from the throne.

Russia's enthusiasm for Western ideas and practices continued but without much direction or commitment until the reign of Catherine II "the Great." Born Sophia Frederika Augusta, the daughter of a minor German prince, she married Tsar Peter III in 1733 at the age of fourteen. She took the name Catherine when she converted to Russian Orthodoxy. Unlike her husband whose only interest was drilling his troops, Catherine enthusiastically read Enlightenment writers. When she discovered that her husband wished to concede vast tracks of land won by Russians in hard-fought battles to Prussia, she led a coup and had Peter killed. She then ruled on her own, styling herself as an Enlightened ruler, but actually ruling as an absolute monarch.

Catherine's rule was filled with contradictions. On the one hand, she was a great supporter of education and the arts. She opened the first secular school for elite girls in 1764 and followed with plans for public schools in 1786. She also founded the Free Economic Society that produced up-to-date information on agriculture and industry. She corresponded with Voltaire and promoted many noble women to positions of public responsibility. Among them, Princess Ekaterina Vorontsova-Dashkova (1743–1810) became one of the great intellectuals of the Russian Enlightenment. She was the first women president of the Academy of Sciences and the Academy of the Study of the Russian Language. Vorontsova-Dashkova traveled around Europe, met Diderot and Voltaire among others, and oversaw the publication of the first Russian dictionary. She was also a naturalist, particularly interested in mineralogy.[36]

On the other hand, the condition of most of Russia's population worsened during Catherine's reign. Continual warfare and an ostentatious nobility cost the Russian peasantry dearly. Although initially Catherine expressed some interest in reforming serfdom, a series of rebellions prompted a change in her attitude. She issued decrees in 1765 and 1767 that reduced the serfs nearly to slave status. It became illegal for a serf to file a complaint against his or her master. Lords could sell serfs away from their families or exile them to Siberia for minor infractions. Class tensions came to a head in 1773 when a local uprising led by Emilian Pugachev (ca. 1740–1775), an illiterate Cossack (an ethnic group known for their military prowess) who claimed to be Catherine's murdered husband, erupted into an enormous peasant rebellion. It took two years and extreme measures to put it down. After the rebellion, Catherine dropped all pretense of enlightenment or liberalism, ruling harshly for the rest of her life.

The spread of Enlightenment ideas across Europe prompted some absolutist monarchs to pursue limited reforms. The absolutist rulers of the Habsburg monarchy and Prussia were both heavily influenced by gender expectations in their paths to reform. Maria Theresa of Austria relied on traditional representations of femininity to maintain power during her reign, and Frederick II of Prussia consciously created a very masculine, military culture during his. In Russia, although elite women benefited from the monarchy's Westernization policies, most Russian women experienced no improvement in their lives. For many, Enlightenment ideas about social reform and reconsiderations of gender expectations were too dangerous to even consider.

# WOMEN, ART, AND CULTURE IN THE EIGHTEENTH CENTURY

During the late seventeenth and eighteenth centuries, changes in the art world transformed artisans into artists and provided women with a wide array of new opportunities. However, much like scientific inquiry, men worked to exclude women from the highest levels of artistic recognition. They attacked not only women's talents, but also the genres of painting, music, and literature typically associated with women. Nevertheless, women not only excelled at art, but created new forms of expression in painting, music, and literature that addressed the limitations of their gender.

## Women as Professional Artists

The creation of artistic academies, such as the French Royal Academy of Painting and Sculpture founded in 1648, clearly established the position of the artist as a trained theoretician, not a tradesman or an amateur; however, painting's transition from a guild-controlled occupation to a profession did nothing to aid the artistic careers of women. The Royal Academy offered a rigorous course of instruction and hosted juried art shows that attracted thousands of visitors. It also established a hierarchy of painting genres. History paintings with their representations of Enlightenment themes of advancing civilization and republican sentiments were the most prestigious form, followed by portraiture, still life, and landscape. However, the Academy prevented women from obtaining the skills necessary to participate in the most prestigious genres. Women could not attend human drawing classes because it would expose them to naked bodies. This restriction made it difficult for women to get the training necessary to execute history scenes. Instead, women were relegated to portraiture, still lifes, and landscapes, the lesser forms of painting.

Fortunately, urban middle-class tastes helped to cultivate women's talents. They often hired women to immortalize their social and economic success in portraits and encouraged their daughters to learn painting and drawing because of the new availability of prepared colors, colored chalk, and inexpensive paper.

Indeed, paintings were often important illustrations of the emphasis on family and domesticity that men like Rousseau promoted. Images of mothers and women performing women's traditional "minor arts" of embroidery or sewing became particularly popular, such as depicted by Catherine Read's (1723–1778) *Lady Anne Lee Embroidering* (1764).

Despite these attempts to feminize certain artistic media and subjects, women transformed even popular genres. The Venetian painter Rosalba Carriera (1675–1757) revolutionized the use of pastels. By employing white chalk over a darker under drawing, she was able to create luminescent highlights. In 1720, she joined a group of artists in Paris working in the sensuous rococo style, popular among the wealthy urban elite. Carriera was so influential that the royal family commissioned her to paint the ten-year-old monarch, Louis XV. She was accepted as a member of the Roman Academy in 1705, and in 1720, she was elected to the Royal

Academy in France, which had not admitted a woman in thirty-eight years. After Carriera, the Academy returned to its original policy of excluding women.[37]

In contrast to the restrictive policies of the Royal Academy, the *Académie de Saint-Luc*, founded in 1751, not only allowed women artists to exhibit, but its membership included a wide array of women artists and artisans. The two most famous French female painters, Adélaïde Labille-Guiard (1749–1803) and Elisabeth-Louise Vigée-Lebrun (1755–1842), began their careers there. The popular press created a rivalry between them, encouraging critics to compare the women to each other, rather than to their male contemporaries. However, this supposed rivalry generated accusations of sexual immorality and obscured both the quality of these women's works and the similarities in their styles. Labille-Guiard and Vigée-Lebrun were famed for introducing a "natural" and unencumbered image of women and motherhood into aristocratic portraiture, and their works reflect elite women's increasing emphasis on maternity and domesticity.[38] In particular, Vigée-Lebrun's famous painting of Marie Antoinette tried to redefine the foreign-born queen as a tender mother and domesticated queen.[39]

Breaking the boundaries of genre, Angelica Kauffmann (1741–1807) became renowned as one of the great history painters of her day. Having studied in Italy, she returned to her native England in 1766 and two years later was one of the founding members of the Royal Academy of Arts in London. She clearly fostered her unique position as a female history painter by consciously choosing subjects that had not been portrayed before and giving them innovative interpretations. Her royal patrons included Emperor Joseph II of Austria, Catherine II of Russia, and Queen Carolina of Naples (1752–1814). Engravers often copied her paintings and used them as china patterns and other decorative pieces, allowing her ideas to reach beyond those who could attend urban art exhibitions.[40]

## Music

During the eighteenth century, although religious music was still popular, public secular music began to draw large audiences and created new opportunities for talented women. In fact, the most eminent names in eighteenth-century music, Antonio Vivaldi (ca. 1680–1743), Franz Josef Haydn (1732–1809), and Wolfgang Amadeus Mozart (1756–1791), employed female musicians, taught female students, and competed with female composers. Among the most celebrated female composers was Maria Theresia von Paradis (1759–1824). She studied with Mozart's rivals Leopold Kozeluch (1747–1818) and Antonio Salieri (1750–1825), and both Mozart and Haydn composed pieces for her. Mostly blind, she wrote more than thirty works, including at least five operas, as well as cantatas and numerous piano pieces.

In Venice, four *Ospedali*, or conservatories, trained talented orphan boys and girls. Donations and noble patronage provided the children with quality educations and dowries for the girls. The girls received ten years of rigorous training and those who completed the course could stay on at the conservatory as *maestrae*. Their concerts drew audiences from all over Europe. Antonio Vivaldi composed many of his celebrated works for the choirs and orchestras of girls in the *Ospedale della Pietà*. At least twenty-eight concertos were for violinist Anna Maria della Pietà (ca. 1689– after 1750). Although she never performed outside the conservatory, she was hailed as the greatest violinist in Europe. For other students of the Ospedale, a career in performance and teaching provided an alternative to marriage. Although generally women could not marry and maintain the status of maestrae, Maddalena Lombardini (later Sirmen) (1745–1785) was the exception. The daughter of poor aristocrats, she was raised in an ospedale and became both a virtuoso violinist and composer. Her talent was so great that she received permission to train with notable musicians outside of the conservatory and to occasionally tour with them as a singer, solo violinist, and a member of an opera orchestra. Sixty years after her death, her music was still in print and regularly performed.

Female opera singers gained increasing renown during this period, although they often had to compete with *castrati*, castrated men whose voices remained high, for roles. However, private training with male teachers, the gender-bending of operatic roles, and the androgynous or effeminate castrati left women vulnerable to questions about their morality and sexuality. One exception was Faustina Bordoni (later Hasse) (1700–1781), whose noble background afforded her the best private teachers and lifted her above the suspicions associated with opera. She made her debut at age sixteen and became a star on the great stages of Europe. In the 1720s, she sang with Frederic Handel (1685–1759) in London. She then married operatic composer Johan Adolph Hasse (1699–1783), and both went to work at the court of Dresden, where she earned twice his salary.[41]

Choral music, which blended Protestant musical styles of Germany and the operatic traditions of Italy and France, also enjoyed great popularity. German concertmaster Johann Adam Hiller (1728–1804) of Leipzig argued for the inclusion of women's voices in choral music, and in 1771, he opened a school for male and female singers. He taught Corona Schröter (1751–1802), who went on to perform in royal German courts as a singer and actress and moved in the highest intellectual circles. In 1786 and 1794, she published two collections of her own songs, called *lieder,* experimenting with a range of styles, some drawn from the folk tradition.

## Literature by and for Women

With the expansion of literacy, women produced and purchased books, pamphlets, and newspapers as never before, and the formation of lending libraries gave a broad segment of society access to the world of literature. One enthusiastic Spanish intellectual declared that the *Biblioteca Real,* which opened in Madrid in 1722, was "full of the best Spanish books which anyone is allowed to read."[42] As more people demanded printed material, literary styles multiplied and the printing industry expanded to accommodate the tastes of the reading public.

To meet the demands of this reading-hungry public, women founded popular magazines directed at female audiences. In England, Sarah Trimmer (1741–1810), who along with Hannah More had instigated the Sunday school movement, founded *The Family Magazine* in 1788. Their goal was to introduce middle-class manners, morals, and interests to the lower classes. To this end, Trimmer also wrote a religious history for young people in 1805. Women often risked their lives by expressing radical political opinions in the press. In Naples, Italy, Eleanor Pimentel (1752–1799) founded the republican newspaper the *Il Monitore*. She supported education for the lower classes, arguing that illiteracy hindered true political reform. When the monarchy cracked down on its opponents in 1799, she was arrested and executed.[43]

The eighteenth century saw the rise of the female novelist. Extremely popular among European women, the novel was a flexible form that allowed the author to include social commentary and explore personal development while entertaining the public. By the end of the century, female novelists nearly outnumbered male ones. As a popular genre, female authors had to find ways to express themselves while meeting the demands of critics and the reading public. Critics urged female novelists to avoid bawdy, sexually explicit prose in favor of sentimental tales of virtuous heroines, while the middle class, who purchased most novels and had the time to read them, wanted authors to write about family issues, interpersonal relationships, and feelings.

Novels in the form of letters became very popular. One of the first of these epistolary novels was *The Persian Letters* (1721), by Charles-Louis de Secondat, Baron de Montesquieu (1689–1755). Through the fictional letters of two Persians, Rica and Usbek, who are visiting Paris at the end of Louis XIV's reign, Montesquieu mocked French society and questioned its restrictions on women. Montesquieu likened Usbek's dominance of the wives in his harem to that of a despotic monarch who deprived his subjects of their happiness. After the success of *The Persian Letters*, Françoise de Graffigny (1695–1758) used the same medium of fictional letters to discuss women's roles in society. Whereas Montesquieu presented a male-voiced debate over the relative merit of a wife's fidelity or freedom, in *Letters from a Peruvian Woman* (1747), Graffigny chronicled the travels of Zilia, an Incan princess. Captured and sent to France, most of the letters are to her Peruvian lover, who in the end, betrayed her. Zilia admires French culture, even as it treats her with disdain. In her Spanish translation of *Letters from a Peruvian Woman*, María Romero Masegosa y Cancelada manipulated Graffigny's social commentary to suit Spanish concerns. She refashioned Graffigny's negative portrayal of Spanish conquest into something more positive. Rather than maintain the common Enlightenment stance that Catholicism was a source of ignorance and superstition, Romero argued in her translation that hypocrisy and ignorance were far more dangerous.[44]

Gothic novels also became popular among women writers. Ann Radcliffe (1764–1823) wrote five such novels between 1789 and 1797. This style owed much to both the Enlightenment and colonial expansion. Gothic novels favored exotic locations, heavy atmospheres, and a standard plot of danger, lost inheritances, hidden crimes, and interactions with the supernatural. Authors contrasted scientific discoveries, travel, and empirical observation by the hero and heroine with the villain's superstitious behavior. Characters traveled to Catholic countries, where such "enlightened inquiry" was forbidden and whose "backward" customs set up obstacles for the hero to overcome. This genre became even more popular as industrialization and colonization expanded during the next century.

Readers' changing tastes did not prevent women writers from criticizing society. German author Sophie von La Roche (1731–1807), author of *The Story of Miss Von Sternheim* (1771), created a heroine, Sophie, who grew in wisdom and accomplishments as she fled a bad marriage and a seductive prince. While focusing on Sophie's personal moral development, von La Roche used her as a medium to express concerns about women's role in society at large. Similarly, Jane Austen (1775–1817) wrote with great irony and wit about women's lack of money, their need to make a good marriage, and the shallowness and greed of English society. Through observations of her characters, such as Elizabeth Barrett in *Pride and Prejudice* (1813), Jane Austen criticized society's constraints on women.

Until recently, women's artistic endeavors from the eighteenth century have been largely ignored. Their paintings fell into obscurity, their musical compositions were lost, and many of their novels only had one printing. Yet contemporaries noted the growth in women's artistic production, and the enthusiasm with which women engaged in artistic pursuits brought their ideas to larger audiences than ever before. Even as men sought to limit women's artistic activity, female artists persistently challenged those constraints.

## GENDER IN THE COLONIES

During the eighteenth century, Europe's changing relationship with its colonial possessions altered the lives of women of all races and classes. European nations' increasing dependence on their colonies to supply the raw materials for the early stages of their industrial development came at the expense of women from Mexico to Calcutta and the expansion of the slave trade. At the same time, Enlightenment critiques of tyranny and debates about individual rights laid the foundation for the American Revolution. On both sides of the Atlantic, women fought for republican liberty and struggled with the social and moral implications of slavery.

## Colonial Economies

During the seventeenth century, to ensure control over their expanding colonial possessions, many European nations adopted French minister of finance Jean-Baptiste Colbert's (1619–1683) economic policies aimed at increasing the power of the state. In terms of colonial economics, these *mercantilist* policies tightly regulated trade between the mother country and the colony. The colony extracted raw materials, which were then shipped to the mother country to be manufactured into finished goods. Laws required that colonists then buy the finished goods only from the mother country. They could not buy cheaper goods elsewhere, nor were they encouraged to manufacture their own finished products.

Mercantilism led to the expansion of enormous plantations across the Americas, most of which relied on slave labor. Because of the transient nature of colonial life, women often managed these large estates. For example, when Eliza Lucas Pinckney (1722–1793) was sixteen, her father left her in charge of the family plantation on the island of Antigua. After the family moved to South Carolina, he became lieutenant governor and again left his family and estate in her hands. An able and innovative manager, Eliza introduced indigo (a plant that produces a bright blue dye) on her plantation worked by hundreds of slaves. This crop quickly became the foundation of South Carolina's agricultural economy. Eliza married and bore four children, but she continued her pur-

suit of agricultural innovations, experimenting with hemp and flax, and revived the silk industry in the region. After her husband's death, she managed many of his properties.

With its victory over France in the Seven Years War (1756–1763), England added Canada, all of France's North American territories east of the Mississippi River, and most of France's possessions in India to its already extensive empire. In India, rather than directly administer its Indian possessions, the British government relied on the British East India Company to represent it and facilitate trade. These kinds of state-sponsored trading companies were very popular across Europe. Individuals invested in the companies, receiving a portion of the profits in return. Women eagerly participated in these financial opportunities. Women made up more than one-third of the investors in the East India Company in 1756. Interestingly enough, the majority of these female investors were not Englishwomen, but Dutch widows and single women attracted by the stability of the British company.[45]

The English government gave the East India Company extensive control over its dominions. Between 1763 and 1857, the East India Company directly managed many formerly independent Indian states and reduced others to vassal or dependent status with a native army led by a few European officers. It established major settlements in Bombay, Madras, and Calcutta, where white merchants and soldiers lived separate from the Indian population. At least during the eighteenth century, few English women traveled to India. Some wives of company employees settled with their husbands, but soldiers were prohibited from taking their wives. English society, both at home and in India, assumed that single women who emigrated to India were only seeking rich husbands. A ceremony called "sitting up" displayed newly arrived single women to marriageable men, and the women were referred to as "the fishing fleet."[46]

The Company ruled harshly and without regard for local custom, while making huge profits by exporting spices, cotton cloth, and tea to Europe. Indian women worked in the tea fields, harvested cotton and spices, and spun, wove, and dyed cotton into colorful cloth. Because female labor was cheap, the East India Company was able to export these goods inexpensively to England.

European demand for cotton and the British East India Company's successes led to important technological innovations. Manufacturers developed a series of new technologies to speed spinning and weaving, including the flying shuttle and the spinning jenny. In terms of colonial trade, these inventions had a powerful impact. With the ability to easily harvest and finish cotton at home, English merchants no longer needed to buy finished cloth from India, and by 1830, India's cotton trade was dead, putting thousands of women out of work.

## Slavery and the Abolitionist Movement

Enlightenment ideas clashed with European economic growth over the issue of slavery. As economies boomed, the production of raw materials for use in Europe and the United States soared, and the United States increasingly relied on slave labor to keep up with demand. Over the course of the century, the British exported more than three million slaves from West Africa to its colonies and former colonies in North America and the Caribbean.

Male slaves outnumbered women by about two to one. Although some slave women worked in plantation houses caring for children, cooking, and cleaning, most worked in the fields planting and harvesting cotton. Slave owners routinely separated mothers and children and had little respect for the emotional ties between men and women. Women were brutalized and raped by slave traders and masters, and while infant mortality was much higher among slave than free women, those infants who survived assumed their mother's slave status.

Europe also had a small population of slaves. European elites prized African children as house slaves, where they served as accessories to the elite's lavish lifestyles. In addition, runaway and freed slaves established communities in places like London and Bristol. One scholar has estimated that there were as many as fourteen thousand blacks in eighteenth-century England.[47] These communities cultivated some of the earliest resistance to slavery, sheltering runaways and writing accounts of the slave trade.

Some of the most radical Enlightenment thinkers opposed slavery and were horrified to realize that their refined lifestyles and creature comforts depended on the wealth produced by slaves. The philosophe abbé Guillaume Thomas François Raynal (1713–1796) pointedly reminded his readers, "They [African slaves] are tyrannized, mutilated, burnt, and put to death, and yet we listen to these accounts coolly and without emotion. The torments of a people to whom we owe our luxuries, can never reach our hearts."[48] To address the issue, in 1788, Jacques-Pierre Brissot de Warville founded the Society of the Friends of Blacks, a French antislavery group. Unfortunately, both the ideals and most members of the Society would fall victim to the violence of the French Revolution.

England had a much larger and longer-lived abolition movement. Led by Hannah More, a bluestocking who grew up in the slave-trading town of Bristol, England, and Anna Laetitia Barbauld (1743–1825), Englishwomen pressed for abolition on both sides of the Atlantic. Quaker women, who were allowed to travel and preach, became important in these transatlantic discussions. For example, Mary Peisley (1717–1757) of County Kildare in Ireland and Catherine Phillips (1727–1794) of Worcestershire, England, traveled extensively in the United States organizing and speaking to groups of Quakers about abolition. Women also collected money for antislavery groups and gathered signatures for antislavery petitions that they submitted to Parliament. Many women boycotted sugar grown with slave labor. Antislavery literature enjoyed great popularity in England. One of the most famous antislavery pieces, *A Poem on the Inhumanity of the Slave-Trade* (1788), was written by Ann Yearsley, a working-class woman who sold milk for a living. Irish abolitionist poet Mary Birkett (1774–1817) admonished women to consider the role of slaves when buying goods: "yes, sisters, to us the task belongs / 'Tis we increase or mitigate their wrongs. / If we the produce of their toils refuse, / If we no more the blood-stain'd lux'ry choose."[49] England and the United States criminalized the slave trade in 1806. However, the impact of those decisions was limited as slavery remained legal in the Americas.

## The American Revolution

Inspired by Enlightenment criticisms of absolutism and debates over individual rights and social equality, colonists in British America began to agitate for representation in the English Parliament. Much of this rhetoric was highly gendered, likening England to a corrupt and evil mother and the colonies as strongholds of manly virtue. Politician John Adams (1735–1826) worried about the threat of European "elegance, luxury, and effeminacy" on "colonial vigor, industry, and frugality."[50] Female writer Mercy Otis Warren (1728–1814) of Massachusetts understood the gendering of the colonial relationship quite differently. In her anonymously published

**EUROPE SUPPORTED BY AFRICA AND AMERICA, WILLIAM BLAKE (1796).** Beliefs in women's need for domination and support were employed by intellectuals to conceptualize the relationship between Europe and the colonies. *(The Bridgeman Art Library.)*

satire, *The Adulateur* (1772), villainous governor Rapatio figuratively set out to rape the colony.

Colonists were particularly outraged at progressive increases in their taxes, much of which was used to pay for England's wars. The Stamp Act of 1765 taxed all paper, including newspapers, legal documents, and stationery. Angry mobs of men and women rioted and Parliament withdrew the tax the next year. However, Parliament also reaffirmed its right to tax the colonies in the Declaratory Act, and in 1767, the Townsend Act imposed new duties on all imports into the thirteen colonies, prompting colonists to boycott British products.

The boycotts that arose in response to the Townsend Act drew women into politics in unprecedented ways. The most famous of these political acts was the tea boycott, which followed the Tea Act of 1773. In 1773, Parliament withdrew the Townsend Act but replaced it with a tax on tea. Colonists retaliated by boycotting tea. The success of the boycott required male organizers winning over women to the cause, because purchasing tea, like all foodstuffs, was a part of women's domestic work. Newspaper editorials called upon women to participate in the boycott, and, in response, both individuals and groups of women publicly asserted their opposition to British taxes. In 1774, one landlady refused to serve tea to John Adams, even though he specifically requested smuggled, untaxed tea. In Boston in 1773, three hundred women publicly agreed to refrain from serving any tea, and in October 1775, fifty-one women from North Carolina publicly declared their support of the tea boycott. Conversely, prominent Loyalist women drank tea in public as an assertion of their political stance.[51] Other boycotts included women organizing or hosting spinning bees to make their own cloth, in order not to buy cloth manufactured in England. Such political behavior on the part of women shocked many, and British newspapers lampooned colonial women's efforts.

Women's efforts did not end with the outbreak of war in 1776. Although General George Washington (1732–1799) did not like the large numbers of women in his camps, his continually undersupplied army needed women to make uniforms, cook food, tend the sick and wounded, and do anything necessary to keep the colonial army fighting. Women even raised money to help the revolutionary forces. In Philadelphia, New Jersey, and Maryland, women went door-to-door soliciting money to help the troops, an act which would have been shocking in other circumstances.[52]

Many women took up arms to defend their houses and farms. After Margaret Corbin's (1751–ca.1800) husband died during an assault on Fort Washington, she loaded his cannon and fired until she was wounded by enemy fire. The Continental Congress granted her a pension as a disabled soldier. However, a few women fought in the army disguised as men. Perhaps the most famous is Deborah Samson (1760–1827), who was only discovered when she fell sick with a fever, after fighting for two years. When she died, her husband received a pension as a widower of a revolutionary soldier.

The American Revolution, like all wars, was dangerous for noncombatants. Both British and American troops plundered towns and farms and killed civilians. The British practice of billeting troops in civilian homes left women particularly vulnerable to sexual assault. Hunger, disease, and economic devastation left many families ruined, not to mention the many women widowed by the rebellion.

With the defeat of the British in 1781, the elite men who had led the Revolution debated the qualifications for citizenship in the new nation. From the outset, some had argued that women who met property requirements should be granted certain rights as citizens. Indeed, Abigail Adams (1744–1818) admonished her husband, John, to grant women rights, noting that, "all men would be tyrants if they could. If particular care and attention is not paid to the ladies, we are determined to foment a rebellion, and will not hold ourselves bound by any laws in which we have no voice or representation" (*Letter from Abigail Adams to John Adams, March 31, 1776*). However, the Declaration of Independence, issued only three months later, stated only that "all men are created equal." The presumption of women's inequality persisted throughout the creation of the legislative and judicial institutions of the new nation. Women were neither involved in their formation nor allowed to serve in their halls.

However, at least at first, individual states had considerable freedom in defining citizenship within their borders, and some propertied women had limited voting rights in New York, New Hampshire, New Jersey, and Massachusetts. Moreover, New Jersey's Constitution of 1776 gave all inhabitants worth fifty pounds and over the age of twenty-one the right to vote regardless of race or gender, and its election law of 1790 refers to voters as both "he" and "she." As married women had few independent legal rights, only single and widowed adult, property-owning women met New Jersey's criteria as voters. Yet, by 1784, the tide had turned and all states except New Jersey had rescinded women's voting rights. Following their lead and encouraged by charges of voter fraud, New Jersey legislators terminated women's right to vote in 1807.

Instead of supporting women as active voting citizens, American leaders created a new political role for women that historian Linda Kerber has called *Republican motherhood*. That is, rather than direct engagement in politics as a citizen, a woman's role as mother determined her participation in politics. She was to train her children in civic virtue, educate her sons for civic participation, and correct her husband when he failed to uphold civic values.[53] Women could not be citizens in the United States; they could only contribute to the political culture of the new nation through their influence over men.

## Women in Spanish America

In Spanish America, Enlightenment intellectuals had to negotiate the strong presence of the Catholic Church and a strong monarchy back in Spain. There were few calls for republican government and almost none for social equality, yet eighteenth-century intellectual and economic trends still shaped Spanish colonial life. In particular, the Spanish monarchy attempted to reformulate the mother country's relationship with its colonies to increase its colonial income to pay for its Continental wars and the defense of its extensive colonial borders.

Women in Spanish America played an ever-larger role in the changing economy. In addition to administering large estates, wealthy white women often invested in companies that manufactured or sold goods. Doña María Paulía y Aguirre (d. 1789), the daughter of one of Mexico City's most important textile factory owners and widow of a wealthy merchant, owned a store and two factories. Some women, like María Magdalena de Mérida of Caracas, could be quite successful. The widow of a military man, she increased her husband's estate by two thousand silver pesos in the first five years after his death.[54]

Farther down the social scale, women owned shops or worked in factories. According to a 1795 survey of Mexico City, 7 percent of the shop owners were women.[55] In cloth production and some areas of food preparation, women were so numerous that by the end of the eighteenth century, guilds began to admit them. Women also worked in cigarette factories. Indian and mestiza women (part Indian and part European) dominated the manufacturing and retail of some alcoholic beverages, and women of all races worked in domestic service, although white women generally did not do the most menial jobs, leaving those tasks to women of color—Indians, black women (both free and enslaved), and mestizas and mulattas (part black and part European). In the countryside, poor free and slave women worked in the fields and the mines.

White women in Spanish American cities tried to emulate the lavish lifestyles of their European relations. They imported expensive clothes and jewelry and were attended by entourages of black or mixed-race servants. Since wealthy European women were in short supply, they often married young and had many children. Francisca Moreno de Mendoza, the wife and daughter of military men, married at fifteen and had sixteen children, one child every thirteen months for the next twenty-one years.[56]

As far away as Bógota, elite Spanish women tried to form their own versions of European salons. Doña Manuela Sanz de Santamaría held a weekly salon called *El Buen Gusto*, where attendees discussed science, literature, and radical politics. However, unlike Spain or France, we have no female writers commenting on women's status in the colonies. Woman may not have participated in these debates due to the conservative nature of the Enlightenment in Spanish America and the rarity of advanced female education.

The most dramatic change in the lives of Spanish American women came with the Spanish monarchy's regulation of marriage. In Catholic countries, the church had sole authority over marriage, emphasizing an individual's free will and the right to marry even without parental consent. However, many Spanish thinkers believed that the growth of the nonwhite population in Spanish America threatened the social and racial hierarchy because women married men who were not their social, economic, or racial equals. As a part of its program to remove authority from the church, the Spanish monarchy issued the Royal Pragmatic in Spain in 1776 and in Spanish America in 1778. The Pragmatic protected families from "unequal" marriages and preserved the social and economic hierarchy by requiring a parent's or guardian's consent to all marriages under threat of disinheritance. Although the crown intended to prevent interracial marriage, parents used it to stop marriages of unequal status or wealth. The Pragmatic resulted in a flood of lawsuits, like that of Don Manuel Valdivieso y Carrión from Quito Ecuador, who sued Juan Teodoro Jaramillo, his daughter's fiancé. Don Manuel argued that Jaramillo was of too low a social standing for his daughter and he wanted the royal authorities to intervene and prevent the marriage.[57] For women in Spanish America, the Enlightenment was less about freedom and more about increased government regulation and control.

Women did not always benefit as colonial society became a testing ground for Enlightenment ideas. Although North American women challenged British rule, their participation went unrewarded as men relegated them to the margins of American politics. In Spanish America, many European women lost the critical right to choose their own marriage partners as the monarchy used marriage laws to reinforce social, economic, and racial hierarchies. Nevertheless, many women adopted Enlightenment ideas of social equality, working tirelessly to end the injustice of slavery.

## WOMEN AND THE FRENCH REVOLUTION

The most radical manifestation of the Enlightenment was the French Revolution (1789–1798). Revolutionaries developed doctrines of human rights and citizenship and fostered institutions that opened politics to all levels of society. Unlike the American Revolution, where women's involvement drew largely on their domestic experiences, French women's participation in the Revolution was much more extensive, as they questioned the quality of their citizenship and their place in the new revolutionary society.

## Women and the Start of the Revolution

One of the major issues that led to the French Revolution was the absolutism of King Louis XVI. Known for his harsh and inconsistent laws and his wild spending habits, he exacerbated an ongoing fiscal crisis, which he and his ministers tried to resolve by raising the already high taxes. Peasants and urban laborers bore the brunt of these taxes, from which the nobility and rich middle classes were exempt. Much of the population also resented the church, which they saw filled with unproductive, frivolous, and immoral aristocrats whose prying eyes and greed further burdened the population. Food shortages in the late 1780s brought these tensions to a head.

In 1788, the king again raised taxes, but the nobility resisted, and in desperation, the king and his ministers summoned the Estates General, an assembly representing the three estates of society (the clergy, the nobility, and the common people) to approve new taxes. The Estates General had not met since 1614, as French monarchs had ruled with limited input from their subjects. Much had changed in the intervening century and a half. By 1788, the Third Estate included not only the peasantry, but also the urban middle classes, some of whom were richer than the nobility. Calling the Estates General necessitated elections for deputies to represent the three estates. Traditionally, few people had participated in this process, but in the Enlightenment spirit of public debate, intellectuals and officials widely publicized the election and men and women of all classes enthusiastically debated political issues. Local deputies assembled lists of people's concerns. Assembling the lists of grievances involved both men and women of all classes in the political process. Female artisans wanted protection for their crafts and rural women wanted better prices for their grain, and women across France complained about unhappy marriages.[58] These complaint books demonstrate French women's determination to be a part of political reform.

Once the Estates General assembled in Paris in the late spring of 1789, the members quickly realized that the king had no interest in their reform agenda. In anger, the Third Estate split off and formed a new body called the National Assembly. Members of the National Assembly drew on Enlightenment ideas that state power resided with the people, not an absolutist monarch. They argued that they had a mandate to govern from the people and vowed not to disband until they created a new constitution for France.

The National Assembly worked throughout 1789. They kept the people apprised of their efforts despite resistance from the king, who refused to acknowledge the Assembly's legitimacy. On July 14, an angry mob of men and women stormed the Bastille prison. Although largely a symbolic act, it demonstrated the people's strong opposition to royal power. In August, the National Assembly abolished all feudal privileges and sent to the king a *Declaration of the Rights of Man and Citizen*, which stated that based on natural law, the people were the source of his sovereignty, and that he could not rule without their consent. Throughout the summer, people demonstrated in Paris and other cities almost daily. Women played a key role in these disturbances. Police reports even include accounts by women who felt coerced into joining for fear of reprisals by other women. Although women had long been part of mob violence and demonstrations, the events of the summer of 1789 gave new meaning to their actions and drew a larger cross section of women.

When the king refused to ratify the *Declaration of the Rights of Man and Citizen*, a mob of women, angered by high bread prices and food shortages, marched on the king's palace of Versailles, outside of Paris. Demanding that the king and his family move back to Paris, they broke into the palace and killed two bodyguards. A small delegation met with the king and his queen, Marie Antoinette, and fearing more violence, the king and queen returned with the women to Paris where they were kept under guard.

With the royal family under lock and key, the National Assembly began a radical restructuring of French government and society (see **Sources from the Past: Marie-Madeleine Jodin on Women's Rights**). They created a new national administration, eliminated church power, and ended privileges based on birth. They instituted new holidays, such as Bastille Day, adopted the Tricolor flag, and tried to impose a new state religion dedicated to the Supreme Being. The Assembly also abolished slavery in the colonies. In 1792, the National Assembly adopted a new set of laws designed to end the patriarchal family, which reformers argued replicated the relationship between the king and his subjects. The laws ended distinctions between legitimate and illegitimate children and primogeniture, allowing younger sons and daughters to inherit. New laws made it easier for women to file for divorce. However, women did not gain full equality. Basing citizenship on the concept of "public utility," the constitution classified women with foreigners, domestic servants, and men who could not pay the value of three days of labor as passive citizens, unable to vote. Men who paid this rate were active citizens and could vote. Although radical for the time, the National Assembly could not disassociate women from the domestic realm.

By 1791, the church and the nobility who had fled into exile began financing a counterrevolutionary movement. The king and his family escaped Paris with the intent of joining supporters at the Belgian border. On the way, revolutionaries recognized, captured, and brought them back to Paris where they faced a hostile crowd. The royal family's arrest ushered in a new phase of the Revolution. Whereas the revolutionaries had been fighting for liberty and an end to what they saw as feudal traditions that privileged the aristocracy, the next phase focused on citizenship and equality and brought increased revolutionary activity by urban women.

## Women and the Radical Phase of the French Revolution

The new government faced many problems. When Louis fled, the National Assembly suspended his executive powers. To prove its legitimacy, the Assembly assumed France's massive debts and suffered a devastating combination of rising prices and no new sources of revenue. Tensions developed between urban radical revolutionaries and the National Assembly, and Austria amassed armies along France's borders.

A variety of political clubs, such as the radical *Cercle Social* and the Cordeliers Club, contributed to Parisians' radicalism. The Cercle Social was the first club to admit women. Members challenged the legitimacy of both the king and the National Assembly. The Cercle Social argued that women should be granted citizenship and without that provision, France's democracy was incomplete. One male member declared: "Women be a citizen! Until now you have only been a mother."[59] Members of the club did not accept the idea that motherhood disqualified women from equal rights.

On July 17, antagonisms between the people of Paris and the National Assembly came to a head. The National Assembly's troops fired on a peaceful demonstration at the Champ de Mars, killing dozens of people. The massacre outraged the citizens of Paris, who believed that the National Assembly had betrayed them and that their constitution of 1791 was invalid.

The next year, revolutionary leaders encouraged women to challenge the constitutional monarchy by demanding the right to carry a pike: an affordable and easy-to-use weapon of self-defense. It became a symbol of equality, independence, and the recovery of liberty. In newspapers, at clubs, and on broadsheets, men and women debated women's ability to carry pikes. Pauline Léon (1768–after 1793), who had been at the massacre at Champ de Mars, presented a petition of more than three hundred signatures to officials and declared, "You cannot refuse us and society cannot remove from us this right which nature gives us, unless it is alleged that the Declaration of Rights is not applicable to women and that they must allow their throats to be slit, like sheep, without having the right to defend themselves."[60] While the National Assembly debated, the mayor of Paris granted them this right, thus creating a model of women's citizenship that combined their right to defend themselves with their civic obligation to defend the nation. By the spring of 1793, Léon and other women used this new authority to form an all-women's political group, the Society of Revolutionary Republican Women, which

# Marie-Madeleine Jodin on Women's Rights

*Marie-Madeleine Jodin (1741–1790) was an actress, a protegée of the great philosophe Diderot, and a strong advocate for women's rights. Published at the height of the French Revolution, her argument that women should be granted full citizenship based on their moral perfectibility is a sharp critique of Rousseau's ideas about women. Jodin's treatise may be the first signed, female-authored, feminist work of the Revolution.*

### LEGISLATIVE VIEWS FOR WOMEN ADDRESSED TO THE NATIONAL ASSEMBLY BY MADEMOISELLE JODIN

Now that the French have declared their zeal for the regeneration of the State and for basing its happiness and glory on the eternal foundations of Virtue and Law, the thought has struck me that my sex, which constitutes an attractive half of that fair Empire, could also claim the honour, and even the right, of contributing to the public welfare; and that in breaking the silence to which politics seems to have condemned us, we could usefully say: 'And we too are Citizens.'

As such, have we not our rights as well as our duties, and must we remain purely passive at a moment when all fruitful thinking about the public good must also touch on this delicate point, the happy bond which attaches us to good? No, there is a plan necessary to the health of our Legislation; and this plan, founded upon ancient and pure foundations, shaken by the vicissitudes of time and the alteration of manners, can only, it seems to me, be revived by ourselves.

I mean to do no more than announce this plan. The programme is a simple one; it invites my fellow Citizenesses to take part in an undertaking altogether worthy of them and of the motives which led me to conceive it. Happy woman that I am! Able to pay to my country the debt, not of talents, but of the heart; and to my sex, that of my esteem.

### LEGISLATIVE VIEWS FOR WOMEN

At a time when true Philosophy is beginning to enlighten all minds, when the defeat of Despotism leaves the prejudices which owed their existence to it helpless and without defence, shall the weaker sex, excluded by force from public deliberations, demand its inalienable rights in vain? Shall that essential half of Society not have any share in the legislative Code proclaimed in the name of Society as a whole? I can picture the reason and equity which animate the august Assembly of Representatives of the Nation, amazed that these questions have not been raised before, hastening to welcome them. So let us obey the general impulse which directs all ideas towards the goal of liberty regained, a liberty usurped by oppression from all of us equally. . . .

Do you wish to raise us to great things? All that is necessary is to excite our emulation. Now, this can only be brought about by a new mode of political organization—one which grants full rights to opinion and frees us from the species of tutelage which, in a sense, separates us from public concerns, leaving us linked with them only by our heart's vows and irresistible attraction to that imperious sex which enslaves our wills as it does our affections. But whilst the subordination thus inseparable from our condition bends us under its Laws, it has not succeeded in stifling our sense of our rights. We claim them today, Sirs, when a new scheme of Legislation is to consider the bonds connecting us with civic harmony. If our private advice has benefited you, when esteem and love have admitted us into your confidence, what even greater advantages will you not derive from our gratitude (for we shall have to owe it to your goodwill) when you restore to us the rights which are ours by Nature and by the social compact. . . .

Love of country, of liberty and of glory animate our sex as much as they do yours, Sirs; we are not, on this earth, a different species from yours. The mind has no sex, any more than does Virtue; but the vices of intelligence and the heart belong almost exclusively to your sex. It is painful for me to declare this harsh truth, but one is sometimes allowed to take one's revenge. . . .

We deserve no fewer eulogies, and no less censure, than yourselves, Sirs. Some women are the shame of their sex, some are its glory; nothing will curb the former in vice, nothing will arrest the latter in the painful path of Virtue. Your sex is not more free than ours from this contrast; for what motives, then, could you pronounce a *nolle prosequi* on this demand of ours to the right to contribute with you to the public welfare, in the legal sphere which concerns us alone? One sex has not been appointed the oppressor of the other, and these ridiculous debates about superiority offend against Nature. You are born our friends, not our rivals, and we emulate you. To reduce us to slavery is to abuse a force which was given you to defend us; it is to deprive Society of what gives it charm and life. . . .

The empire which we wield through beauty is only given us for the good of the human species. The character of the male, destined to strong actions, has a roughness which it is our task to correct; a gentleness in our manners, even more than in our features, is designed to soften that natural pride of yours which otherwise degenerates into ferocity. From every point of view, man would be less perfect, less happy, if he did not converse with women. He who is insensible to commerce with women, who refuses it, has an inflexibility that renders his very Virtues dangerous. . . . In our absence, Sirs, your imagination is inactive, your productions are without grace, your philosophy is sombre and harsh; in your absence, ours become too frivolous. It is by commerce with you that our talents and qualities develop and acquire solid-ity. From this exchange of mutual aid there flows a happy concord which brings both of us nearer to perfection, the faults of one sex correcting those of the other, and in this way women, whatever you do, will always be central to life in Society. Your having charge of public affairs only reinforces our value. The human species conducting itself more by the heart than by the mind, the direction of public affairs, whoever is responsible for it, is always influenced by what is loved. Accordingly, Sirs, you will always do what we want. Where women command, men reign, and when women reign, they prove that they possess the science of government in the highest degree.

The English were never so powerful as under the reign of Elizabeth. Women in France, though excluded from the throne, have none the less played their part in government during various royal minorities. Queen Blanche proved that she deserved more than a mere regency; her maxims are the Code of good kings. Catherine II, reigning in the north at this moment, will be the model for conquerors. Though the snarls of jealous pride endeavour to tarnish the splendour of her great qualities, she will none the less occupy an honourable place in history! The men of Rome, too jealous of their own authority, allowed women no part in government; but in France, where custom and Nature grant them an influence, one could not fail to benefit by entrusting to them Legislation on manners and morals, . . .

If order, the foundation of Society, depends especially on the Virtue and decency of women, if regard for this constitutes their honour, as your 'point of honour' is courage, and if your Laws—refer matters of masculine honour to a unique and supreme tribunal, why should we not have ours too? . . .

Source: Felicia Gordon and P. N. Furbank, *Marie Madeleine Jodin, 1741–1790: Actress, Philosophe and Feminist* (Burlington, VT: Ashgate Press, 2001), 176–191.

worked to curb prices on food and limit the influence and power of the aristocracy.

Gender did more than inform the debates over citizenship. Revolutionaries also used sexually charged rhetoric to press their claims and humiliate the royal family. Some pamphlets even argued that the right to sex with anyone, in any position, was a natural and inalienable right. The queen, Marie Antoinette, was a particularly popular subject. Her foreign origins, frivolous nature, and her difficult relationship with the king, who was impotent for the first seven years of their marriage, inspired anonymous attacks, satires, and criticisms in both newspapers and broadsides. One frequent accusation, featured in such pamphlets as *The Royal Dildo* or *The National Bordello Under the Auspices of the Queen*, was that she was a lesbian. Anonymous writers asserted that because the king could not satisfy her, she found comfort in the arms of other women and in the bed of her brother-in-law. By questioning the queen's sexuality, pamphleteers criticized the royal family and the aristocracy for adhering to a different moral code than the rest of the nation, further undermining the legitimacy of the monarchy.[61]

As the violence escalated, it became clear that the Parisian revolutionaries were far more radical than their rural counterparts. Most peasants had fairly conservative political ideas. They were happy to have their taxes lowered and were not opposed to the republic, but they disagreed with the extreme goals of the Revolution. Rural women particularly resisted the campaign to de-Christianize the nation, which they saw as an attack on their families and traditions. They believed the abolition of church bells, which regulated the day, and the ecclesiastical calendar, which ordered the year, as too radical. Instead of the Trinity and the Virgin Mary, the Revolution promoted alternative deities such as the Supreme Being, Reason, and Liberty. This part of the revolutionary program failed dramatically and villagers engaged in both active and passive resistance to it. For example, in 1794, a governmental official arrived in a Loire village to preach on the Supreme Being at the local Temple of Reason. When he began, the women stood up, turned around, and lifted their skirts revealing naked backsides.[62] Women could also secretly

**MARIE ANTOINETTE AND HER CHILDREN (1788).** Elisabeth-Louise Vigée-Lebrun's (1755–1842) picture of the unpopular queen in a domestic setting did not change her image with the public. They were unable to see her as maternal, but only as frivolous and decadent. *(Art Resource, NY.)*

baptize an infant, pray over a dying person, or provide a Christian burial service at night—all in opposition to revolutionary dictates.

Women who supported the Revolution became more radical and more vocal, articulating distinct political programs from men. Two pieces of writing stand out as statements on women's rights in the new nation: Olympe de Gouge's *Declaration of the Rights of Woman and Female Citizen* (1791) and Mary Wollstonecraft's *Vindication of the Rights of Woman* (1792). Both women had been on the fringes of the salons, and Enlightenment thinking influenced their ideas. Olympe de Gouge (ca. 1748–1793) came from an uneducated, provincial family, but she later claimed to be the illegitimate child of a nobleman. At sixteen, she married a man she did not love and had at least one son.

She left her husband for Paris in 1770, where she developed her political ideas living on the fringes of the salons, supported by a male companion. During the Revolution, she frequented many of the radical political clubs and wrote political pamphlets and political dramas. Her most famous work, her *Declaration,* was largely unknown during her lifetime. Modeled on the *Declaration of the Rights of Man and Citizen,* published by the National Assembly, it was a call for action by women. She based women's right to citizenship on the fact that women gave birth to citizens, an act that contributed to the state. Therefore, women should be granted equal citizenship with men. For de Gouge, gender and sex differences were important, but they did not justify political exclusion. She also demanded equal opportunities in employment and women's right to economic support by the fathers of their children.[63]

Mary Wollstonecraft (1758–1797), an English journalist and teacher, became involved in the French Revolution when she moved to France. Her *Vindication of the Rights of Woman* celebrated women's involvement in the Revolution and challenged Rousseau's belief that women should have only limited education. According to Wollstonecraft, because women were rational creatures, they had a right to the same education as men in order to develop the dignity of their work as partners to their husbands in the household. Without such education, women could not adequately perform the natural duties of motherhood. She also decried conceptions of women's femininity, believing that they developed out of women's dependence on men and kept them in an inferior position. The equal treatment of the sexes should result from their separate but equal human duties to community and nation.

Increased radicalism led to more violence. In August of 1792, the constitutional monarchy collapsed. In January of 1793, after a brief trial, the king was executed for treason and a new legislative body, the National Convention, took over the government. The National Convention tried the queen separately on charges that included incest and executed her as well.

With the ongoing war with Austria needing urgent attention, the National Convention turned over concern for counterrevolutionaries to the Committee of Public Safety, a group of twelve men

lead by Maximilien Robespierre (1758–1794). Relying on Rousseau's rhetoric, Robespierre argued that sovereignty resided with the people and that he would root out all opposition to their will. However, he ruled as a virtual dictator and executed twenty-five thousand people for their real and imagined counterrevolutionary beliefs or activities. In July of 1793, Charlotte Corday (1768–1793) assassinated Jean-Paul Marat (1743–1793), the radical pamphleteer, while he bathed. Corday, outraged that Marat had supported Robespierre and what became known as the Reign of Terror, wanted to avenge his betrayal of the Revolution. For this act, she was guillotined in 1793. Ironically, because Olympe de Gouge had dedicated her *Declaration of the Rights of Women* to the queen, she was executed as a royalist in 1793.

The Committee of Public Safety found women's agitation so threatening that they outlawed women's political groups such as the Society of Revolutionary Republican Women. Later the Committee banned women from attending public meetings or assembling in groups. At the same time, the government also imposed price controls on foodstuffs, which won the support of many women. A combination of the Terror's violence and legislation that prevented women's participation as citizens pushed women back into their homes.

Robespierre's popularity declined as his fanaticism grew. The National Convention began refusing to pass his decrees, and in September 1794, the Committee of Public Safety executed Robespierre as an enemy of the state, ending the Terror. A new, governing body, called the Directory, was elected and took over the government. Made up of many members of the previous National Convention, the Directory withdrew from the radical ideas of the Revolution and tried to negotiate between royalists and radical republicans. Because of its general Napoleon Bonaparte (1769–1821), the Directory achieved considerable military success, expanding France's territory to include Belgium, the Netherlands, Switzerland, and much of Italy. However, it was unable to reconcile opposing political factions. In 1798, Napoleon overthrew the Directory and declared himself the leader of the new French government. In 1802, the French people gave him the title "consul for life."

## Women and the Napoleonic Era

Following his conquest of France, Napoleon turned his attention to the rest of Europe. In 1801, Napoleon defeated Austria. In 1802, he signed a treaty with Great Britain that assured his continued rule of the Low Countries and the rest of Italy. In 1804, Napoleon crowned himself emperor. By 1806, the Holy Roman Empire had collapsed and Napoleon controlled its territories. He conquered Spain and Portugal and had weakened Russia, Austria, and Prussia through diplomatic maneuvers and outright military defeat. By the 1807 Treaty of Tilsit, he dominated Europe (see Map 8.2). His conquests made him adored in France and reviled throughout the rest of Europe.

Napoleon created a highly efficient and centralized government to regulate the lives of his subjects. At the heart of his government was the 1804 legal reform called the Napoleonic Code, which he imposed on all social classes and all conquered territories. The Code was a radical departure from traditional ideas of law and privilege. There were no exceptions for the rich and aristocratic and no feudal privileges. At the same time, it was very conservative, enshrining Napoleon's belief in separate spheres for men and women. Napoleon believed that women needed protection, not liberty. He did not believe that they could be citizens, or that they should have public legal rights. He had vivid memories of women marching with weapons in the French Revolution and wanted to ensure that women never took up arms against him. By reestablishing the patriarchal family and subordinating women to male authority, the Napoleonic Code undid most of the social and legal gains French women made in the Revolution.

Central to redefining women's status were changes to the laws surrounding married women and marriage. The Code also made it difficult for married women to inherit property. While married a woman could not undertake legal transactions without her husband's permission and she could not appear in court. Her husband controlled any property she brought to the marriage, and it became difficult for women to inherit property. The Code made it harder for a wife to initiate divorce than a husband. A wife's adultery was grounds for divorce without her consent, but a woman could only sue for divorce without her husband's permission if he kept his mistress in the same house with his wife. In keeping with the idea that women needed protection, these divorce laws tried to protect middle-aged women from abandonment. Even if both parties agreed to the divorce, the Code forbade it if it was within the first two years of marriage, if the wife was over forty-five years old, or if the couple had been married for more than twenty years.[64] The Code served as a model for the legal codes of Italy, Portugal, Spain, and parts of Switzerland.

To enforce his Code, Napoleon created an extensive bureaucracy that kept track of population size, how many children women had, how much land families owned, how much money they earned, and what they thought about him and his government. With this information, he created a taxation and military system that helped further his conquests and silenced political opposition. His bureaucracy changed the relationship between women, families, and the state.

Napoleon's imperial ambitions required an immense army. Napoleon argued that families should willingly work and fight for his empire, and that women should bear and raise the sons who would sacrifice themselves for him and the greater glory of France. Motherhood was not just a biological function, it was also a patriotic duty. His bureaucracy identified male babies and kept track of them as they grew to military age. Since not enough men would volunteer, Napoleon conscripted most of his army. Scholars estimate that between 1799 and 1812, Napoleon had 1.3 million men in arms.[65] An army of six hundred thousand, over half of whom came from outside of France, invaded Russia.

Conscription created hardship and disrupted families. Although the rich could pay someone to serve in the military for them or pay the fines imposed for resisting the draft, the working and peasant classes could not. Familiar with the soldiers' stories of poor treatment, loneliness, and homesickness, large numbers of men resisted conscription. Throughout 1802 and 1803, entire villages in Italy violently resisted conscription by burning birth registers, draft notices, and other evidence of military eligibility. Government officials responded by imposing travel restrictions, which hindered peasants' ability to flee. These regulations also limited women's ability to go to mar-

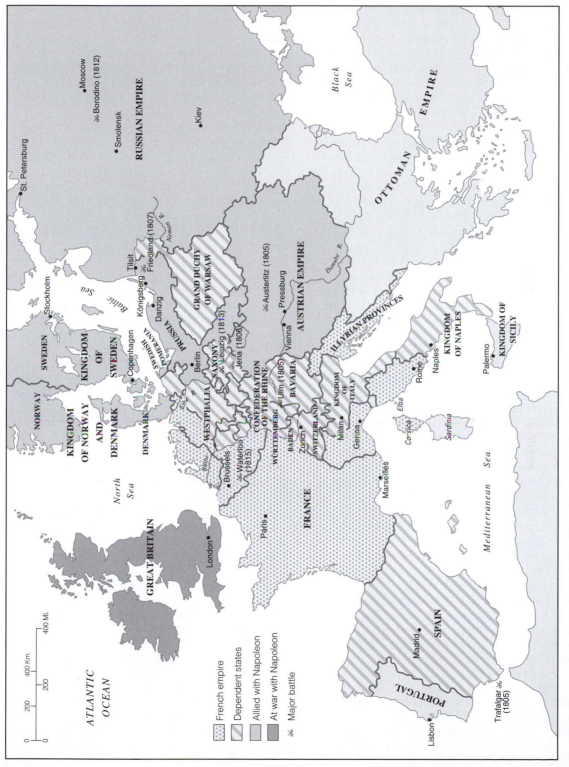

*Map 8.2* **Napoleonic Europe in 1810.** Napoleon's conquest put most European women under his restrictive legal code.

ket and men's ability to search for work or follow their herds to better grazing. Women frequently helped individual men resist the draft by hiding them in barns, cellars, or in nearby woods, and by supplying them with food and clothing until the recruiters left. In 1805, police in the department of Seine-et-Oise arrested and punished a woman for providing shelter for numerous deserters.[66] Widows, even elderly widows, offered themselves as brides to young men to make them ineligible for the draft. In 1809, Gerolamo Uglio of Breme (Italy) married a seventy-two-year-old widow in an effort to avoid the draft.[67] Napoleon's desire for a glorious empire imposed great hardship on the European peasantry.

## Women and Resistance to Napoleon

Napoleon's charismatic personality and military success made him immensely popular in France. However, he did not rule unopposed. Liberals were unhappy with military rule and limitations on their ability to participate in government. Monarchists wanted a strong king and a restoration of aristocratic privilege. The working classes resented the imposition of harsh rules, conscription, taxes, and limited suffrage. Outside of France, his conquered subjects hated him.

One of Napoleon's most celebrated opponents was the novelist and essayist Germaine de Staël (1766–1817). De Staël was born to a wealthy Swiss family but lived nearly all of her life in France, where she received an excellent education and traveled in the best social circles. The heroines of her romantic novels lived in worlds quite different from the society that Napoleon envisioned. In *Delphine* (1802), the story of an impetuous but generous heroine, her characters argued for the need for divorce, criticized stifling social conventions, and discussed the benefits and problems of the Revolution. In *Corinne* (1807), de Staël's descriptions of Italy drove home the point that great civilizations had existed before Napoleon and that their citizens had enjoyed greater freedoms than they did under the emperor. De Staël's work *On Germany* celebrated German culture and ideas as the antithesis of Napoleonic France. Although Napoleon originally permitted its publication, upon learning of its contents, he changed his

mind. De Staël escaped France just ahead of the police with a copy of the manuscript and published it in Britain in 1813. De Staël's opposition to Napoleon cost her dearly. Not only was she was forced into exile several times, but she saw many of her friends and lovers persecuted, and Napoleon's secret police and spies continually followed and harassed her.

Outside of France, Napoleon and his troops faced strong opposition. The most serious revolt erupted in Spain in 1808. Monarchists, Catholics, and Spanish patriots rebelled when Napoleon replaced the Spanish king with his brother Joseph Bonaparte (r. 1808–1813). Spanish women risked their lives for their country's independence and Spanish accounts hailed their valor. Agustina of Aragon took over the firing of cannons in defense of the city of Zaragoza after the men had been killed. Her quick actions reportedly saved the city and later she received a medal, an officer's commission, and a military pension for her bravery.[68] Spanish women taunted also French soldiers and impugned their masculinity. When the French soldiers went on parade in Madrid in May of 1808, a group of "beautiful young women" straddled the French cannons and yelled at the French soldiers, "Your dinky pistols do not frighten those of our regiment."[69]

Napoleon's conquests brought war to much of Europe. As in every other era, women accompanied men into battle. Although "camp followers" had unsavory reputations, most were not prostitutes but soldiers' wives with nowhere else to go. By holding lotteries, the British military maintained strict quotas on the number of women allowed to follow regiments. Women who won their lottery received official rations, although less than their husbands. To augment their meager rations, women bartered, took in mending, or simply stole. The British general leading the army in Spain repeatedly issued orders prohibiting women from pillaging local gardens. Following the army meant marching with them, sleeping outside in tents or huts (often close to battle), and facing the danger of snipers and attack. When James Anton of the Forty-Second Highlanders sailed to Spain to fight Napoleon, his wife, Mary, accompanied him. He turned his daily rum ration over to the ship's cook so that he and Mary could sleep undisturbed in one of the lifeboats. Mary commented that they were the "most comfortable of the uncomfortable."[70]

The scarcity of women turned them into a commodity. When camp life or marital life became too difficult, soldiers made a practice of "selling their wives" to other men. A German soldier serving in Spain wrote, "In Palermo I had also the opportunity of witnessing the singular English custom of the sale of wives. A soldier of the 10th regiment of infantry sold his wife to a drummer for two pounds sterling; he, however, did not keep her long, but parted with her to the armourer of the regiment for two Spanish dollars."[71] Women were not always the innocent victims. One Anne Duke, tired of her husband, took up with the higher-ranked soldier who "purchased" her from her husband. Her new "husband" left her behind when he was transferred to another post and Anne found another "husband' of even higher rank.[72]

In 1812, Napoleon turned on his former ally, Russia, but the harsh combination of winter weather, lack of food, and the Russian army handed Napoleon a major defeat. Most of his army never returned. He then attacked Prussia and Austria, who quickly formed a coalition with Great Britain to defeat him in 1814. The coalition exiled Napoleon to the island of Elba off the coast of Italy. They then installed a Bourbon king, Louis XVIII (r. 1814–1824), the brother of the executed Louis the XVI, as France's ruler. (Louis XVI and Marie Antoinette had a son who died in prison. He never ruled but is considered Louis XVII.) In February 1815, Napoleon escaped from Elba to reclaim his empire; however, within months, the British, led by the Duke of Wellington (1769–1852), defeated Napoleon at the Battle of Waterloo. The coalition exiled Napoleon again, this time to the rocky and desolate island of Saint Helena off the coast of Africa, where he died in 1821.

After Napoleon's defeat, the victors, Britain, Prussia, Russia, and Austria, gathered at the Congress of Vienna to divide Napoleon's conquests and redraw the map of Europe. The settlement was very harsh, pushing the borders of France back to its 1792 territory and imposing reparations. The Congress compensated the victors for their participation in the wars and balanced Europe's military power in the hope of preventing further conflict.

## CONCLUSION

In the eighteenth century, debates about women's political participation reached new heights. Encouraged by Enlightenment ideas and pushed by economic change, women marched in the streets, debated in salons, and fought on the battlefield. However, many continued to believe that women were only fit for motherhood, did not need citizenship, and did not belong in politics. In the end, the few citizen rights that women won in the American and French Revolutions would be short-lived. Conservative thinkers and monarchs pushed women to embrace motherhood and domesticity over voting and economic independence. Nevertheless, women found outlets for their ideas and emotions in art, and debate about women's proper roles would provide the basis for political and social action in the nineteenth century.

## NOTES

1. Jerome Blum, *The End of the Old Order in Europe* (Princeton: Princeton University Press, 1978), 25

2. Isser Woloch, *Eighteenth-Century Europe: Tradition and Progress, 1715–1789* (New York: Norton, 1982), 80–81.

3. Aileen Ribeiro, *Dress in Eighteenth-Century Europe*, 2nd ed. (New Haven, CT: Yale University Press, 2002), 77.

4. Cissie Fairchilds, "Women and Family," in *French Women in the Age of Enlightenment*, ed. Samia I. Spencer (Bloomington: Indiana University Press, 1984), 101.

5. Quoted in Fairchilds, 100.

6. Lawrence Stone, *The Family, Sex and Marriage in England, 1500–1800* (New York: Harper and Row, 1977), 44, 47.

7. Quoted in Olwen Hufton, *The Prospect Before Her: a History of Women in Western Europe* (New York: Alfred Knopf, 1996), 473.

8. Neil McKendrick, Colin Brewer, and J. A. Plumb, *The Commercialization of Eighteenth-Century England* (Bloomington: Indiana University Press, 1982), 76.

9. Ross W. Jamieson, "The Essence of Commodifications: Caffeine Dependencies in the Early Modern World," *Journal of Social History* 35:2 (Winter 2001): 284.

10. E. A. Wrigley and R. S. Schofield, *The Population History of England, 1541–1871* (Cambridge: Cambridge University Press, 1989), 262–265.

11. Margaret R. Hunt, "The Sapphic Strain: English Lesbians in the Long Eighteenth Century," in *Singlewomen in the European Past, 1250–1800,* ed. Judith M. Bennett and Amy M. Froide (Philadelphia: University of Pennsylvania Press, 1999), 280.

12. Margaret R. Hunt, *The Middling Sort: Commerce, Gender, and the Family in England, 1680–1780* (Berkeley: University of California Press, 1996), 128.

13. Londa Schiebinger, *The Mind Has No Sex? Women in the Origins of Modern Science* (Cambridge, MA: Harvard University Press, 1989), 41.

14. Quoted in Maria Cieslak-Golonka and Bruno Morten "Two Women Scientists of Bologna," *American Scientist* 88 (January 2000): 68.

15. Schiebinger, 262.

16. Quoted in Schiebinger, 174, 176.

17. Linda K. Kerber, "The Republican Mother: Women and the Enlightenment—An American Perspective," in *Toward an Intellectual History of Women*, ed. Linda Kerber (Chapel Hill: University of North Carolina Press, 1997), 43–44.

18. Schiebinger, 197.

19. Schiebinger, 221–222.

20. Schiebinger, 232.

21. Dena Goodman, *The Republic of Letters: A Cultural History of the French Enlightenment* (Ithaca, NY: Cornell University Press, 1994), esp. 74, 90–91.

22. Goodman, *The Republic of Letters*, 76.

23. Sara Ellen Procious Malueg, "Woman and the *Encyclopédie*," in *French Women in the Age of Enlightenment*, 260.

24. Malueg, 259.

25. Mme Delusse wrote the commentary for two plates in volume 22, and an anonymous woman wrote the entries for "Falbala," and "Fontange," both decorative elements in women's clothing. Malueg, "Woman and the *Encyclopédie*," 260–261.

26. Deborah Hertz, "Emancipation Through Intermarriage? Wealthy Jewish Salon Women in Old Berlin," in *Jewish Women in Historical Perspective*, 2nd ed., ed. Judith Baskin (Detroit, MI: Wayne State University Press, 1998), 193–204.

27. Constance A. Sullivan, "Constructing Her Own Tradition: Ideological Selectivity in Josefa Amar y Borbón's Representation of Female Models," in *Recovering Spain's Feminist Tradition*, ed. Lisa Vollendorf (New York: Modern Language Association of America, 2001), 142.

28. *Johnsonian Miscellanies*, vol. 2, ed. George Birkbeck Hill (London: Constable and Co., 1966), 11.

29. Charles Ingrao, *The Habsburg Monarchy, 1618–1815* (Cambridge: Cambridge University Press, 1994), 150.

30. Ingrao, 155.

31. Quoted in Karl A. Roider Jr., *Maria Theresa* (Englewood Cliffs, NJ: Prentice Hall, 1973), 23.

32. Michael E. Yonan, "Conceptualizing the *Kaiserinwitwe*: Empress Maria Theresa and Her Portraits," in *Widowhood and Visual Culture in Early Modern Europe*, ed. Allison Levy (Burlington, VT: Ashgate Press, 2003), 113.

33. Marion W. Gray, *Productive Men, Reproductive Women: The Agrarian Household and the Emergence of Separate Spheres During the German Enlightenment* (New York: Berghahn Books, 2000), 162.

34. Quoted in M.S. Anderson, *Peter the Great* (London: Thames and Hudson, 1978), 123.

35. Lindsey Hughes, *Russia in the Age of Peter the Great* (New Haven, CT: Yale University Press, 1998), 187–188.

36. Natalia Pushkareva, *Women in Russian History from the Tenth to the Twentieth Century*, trans. Eve Levin (New York: M. E. Sharpe, 1997), 149–150.

37. Whitney Chadwick, *Women, Art, and Society* (London: Thames and Hudson, 1990), 143.

38. Chadwick, 161, 166, 168.

39. Melissa Hyde, "Under the Sign of Minerva: Adélaïde Labille-Guiard's *Portrait of Madame Adélaïde*," in *Women, Art, and the Politics of Identity in Eighteenth Century Europe*, ed. Melissa Hyde and Jennifer Milam (Burlington, VT: Ashgate Press, 2003), 144.

40. Wendy Wassyng Roworth, "Ancient Matrons and Modern Patrons: Angelica Kauffman as a Classical History Painter," in *Women, Art, and the Politics of Identity in Eighteenth Century Europe*, esp. 197.

41. Barbara Garvey Jackson, "Musical Women of the Seventeenth and Eighteenth Centuries," in *Women and Music*, ed. Karin Pendle (Bloomington: Indiana University Press, 1991), 116.

42. Quoted in Nigel Glendinning, *A Literary History of Spain: the Eighteenth Century* (London: Ernest Benn Limited, 1972), 18.

43. Bonnie Smith, *Changing Lives: Women in European History Since 1700* (New York: D. C. Heath, 1988), 112.

44. Theresa Ann Smith, "Writing Out of the Margins: Women, Translation, and the Spanish Enlightenment," *Journal of Women's History* 15:1 (Spring 2003): esp. 116.

45. H. V. Bowen, "Investment and Empire in the Later Eighteenth Century: East India Stockholding,

1756–1791," *Economic History Review* 42:2 (1989): 202.

46. P. J. Marshall, "The White Town of Calcutta Under the Rule of the East India Company," *Modern Asian Studies* 34:2 (2000): 312.

47. Gretchen Holbrook Gerzina, *Black London: Life Before Emancipation* (New Brunswick: Rutgers University Press, 1995), 5.

48. Quoted in Dena Goodman, "Women and the Enlightenment," in *Becoming Visible: Women in European History*, 3rd ed., ed. Renate Bridenthal, Susan Mosher Stuard, and Merry E. Wiesner (Boston: Houghton Mifflin, 1998), 241.

49. Clare Midgley, *Women Against Slavery: The British Campaigns, 1780–1870* (London: Routledge, 1992), 15, 36.

50. Quoted in Sara Evans, *Born for Liberty* (New York: Free Press, 1989), 47.

51. Evans, 49–50.

52. Evans, 50.

53. Kerber, 58.

54. Susan Migden Socolow, *The Women of Colonial Latin America* (Cambridge: Cambridge University Press, 2000), 113.

55. Socolow, 113.

56. Socolow, 86.

57. Christian Büschges trans. "Don Manuel Valdivieso y Carrión Protests the Marriage of his Daughter to Don Teodoro Jaramillo, a Person of Lower Social Standing, Quito, 1784–85," in *Colonial Lives: Documents on Latin American History, 1550–1850*, ed. Richard Boyer and Geoffrey Spurling (Oxford: Oxford University Press, 2000), 224–235.

58. Darline Gay Levy and Harriet B. Applewhite, "A Political Revolution for Women? The Case of Paris," in *Becoming Visible*, 270.

59. Quoted in Gary Gates, "The Powers of Husband and Wife Must Be Equal and Separate: The *Cercle Social* and the Rights of Women, 1790–91," in *Women and Politics in the Age of Democratic Revolution*, ed. Harriet B. Applewhite and Darline G. Levy (Ann Arbor: University of Michigan Press, 1990), 172.

60. Quoted in Levy and Applewhite, "A Political Revolution for Women?" 280.

61. Elizabeth Colwill, "Pass as a Woman, Act Like a Man: Marie-Antoinette as Tribade in the Pornography of the French Revolution," in *Marie-Antoinette: Writings on the Body of a Queen*, ed. Dena Goodman (London: Routledge, 2003), 139–169.

62. Olwen Hufton, "Counter-Revolutionary Women," in *The French Revolution in Social and Political Perspective*, ed. Peter Jones (London: Arnold, 1996), 299.

63. Joan W. Scott, *Only Paradoxes to Offer: French Feminists and the Rights of Man* (Cambridge: Harvard University Press, 1996), 33ff.

64. Theresa McBride, "Public Authority and Private Lives: Divorce after the French Revolution," *French Historical Studies* 17:3 (Spring 1992): 750.

65. Alexander Grab, "Army, State, and Society: Conscription and Desertion in Napoleonic Italy (1802–1814)," *The Journal of Modern History* 67:1 (March 1995): 26; Eric A. Arnold Jr., "Some Observations on the French Opposition to Napoleonic Conscription," *French Historical Studies* 4:4 (Autumn 1966): 453.

66. Arnold, 455.

67. Grab, 41.

68. John Lawrence Tone, "Spanish Women in the Resistance to Napoleon, 1808–1814," in *Constructions of Spanish Womanhood: Female Identity in Modern Spain*, ed. Victoria Lorée Enders and Pamela Beth Radcliff (Albany, NY: SUNY Press, 1999), 263.

69. Quoted in Tone, 259.

70. Quoted in F. C. G. Page, *Following the Drum: Women in Wellington's War* (London: Andre Deutsch, 1986), 39.

71. Quoted in Page, 50.

72. Page, 51–54.

## SUGGESTED READINGS

Brophy, Elizabeth Bergen. *Women's Lives and the Eighteenth-Century English Novel*. Tampa: University of South Florida Press, 1991. A study of the relationship between the presentation of everyday life in eighteenth-century novels and the social history of ordinary women.

Goodman, Dena. *The Republic of Letters: A Cultural History of the French Enlightenment*. Ithaca, NY: Cornell University Press, 1994. Feminist history of the salons that argues for the centrality of women's roles in the Enlightenment debates that preceded the Revolution.

Kerber, Linda. *Towards an Intellectual History of Women*. Chapel Hill: University of North Carolina Press, 1997. Collection of essays that looks at the issues of women's political identity and involvement in the American Revolution and early republic.

Schiebinger, Londa. *The Mind Has No Sex? Women in the Origins of Modern Science.* Cambridge, MA: Harvard University Press, 1989. Looks at how the changing understanding of sex differences gave rise to the idea that science was a masculine enterprise.

Scott, Joan Wallach. *Only Paradoxes to Offer: French Feminists and the Rights of Man.* Cambridge, MA: Harvard University, 1996. An analysis of the paradox of French feminists' demands that both accept and reject the significance of differences between men and women with respect to citizenship.

Valenze, Deborah. *The First Industrial Woman.* Oxford: Oxford University Press, 1995. A study of the underlying gender assumptions behind women's work at the beginning of the Industrial Revolution.

# Chapter 9

# Women and the New Industrial Society, 1800–1900

**Swedish Woman on a Bicycle.** *The invention of the bicycle gave women more freedom of movement. It also compelled a change of fashion, revealing more leg. (Courtesy of the author.)*

■ **Women's Work and the Creation of Industrial Society**   294

  *Gendering Factory Work*   296
  *Domestic Work*   298
  *Women and the Industrialization of Agriculture*   298

■ **Gendered Spaces in the New Urban Landscape**   302

  *Moving Around the City*   302
  *New Destinations*   304
  *Shopping*   305
  *Urban Problems*   306

■ **Urban Reform and the Control of Women**   308

  *Regulating Women's Work*   308
  *Reforming the Poor*   310
  *Prostitution*   311

■ **Sex and Gender: Theory and Reality**   312

  *The Cult of Domesticity*   312
  *Social Darwinism and Eugenics*   314
  *Sexology and Sexual Identity*   315
  *Sexual Realities*   317

■ **Piety and Charity**   319

  *Religious Revival*   319
  *Women and Judaism*   320
  *Women and Philanthropy*   321

■ **Educating Women**   324

  *Educational Reform and Higher Education for Women*   324
  *Women and Science at the Turn of the Century*   326

D uring the nineteenth century, industrialization transformed economies and women's lives. The technological and organizational changes that accompanied industrialization altered women's work both inside and outside of factories. The industrial revolution while difficult and socially dislocating, raised living standards for many people, by giving them access to cheaper goods. The industrial revolution also revolutionized women's leisure time. Innovations in transportation and expanding cities opened new urban spaces for women of all classes. Women's increased visibility and independence caused considerable anxiety among those who believed that a woman's place was in the home. In response, intellectuals searched for biological and psychological explanations for traditional gender roles. However, the tide had turned. Determined women would not be denied the opportunity to work for social, religious, and scientific change.

## WOMEN'S WORK AND THE CREATION OF INDUSTRIAL SOCIETY

New ways of organizing production and new technologies dramatically altered women's work over the course of the nineteenth century. As we saw in Chapter 8, businesses increasingly contracted parts of the production process to women working in their homes. This challenged male monopolies over many trades. As the century progressed, industrialization and mechanization moved economic activity away from agriculture and cottage industries and into centralized manufacturing. Most production no longer took place in the home, but in factories owned by entrepreneurs and worked by hired labor. Rather than create goods by hand, workers increasingly used machines to produce more and cheaper goods. Although employers often preferred to hire women to work in factories, domestic service and agriculture continued to be the largest employers of women. Yet, even these traditional forms of women's labor felt the impact of industrialization.

# *Chapter 9* ❖ Chronology

| | |
|---|---|
| **1814** | French government creates bureau to oversee abandoned and orphaned children |
| **1818** | First Reform Synagogue founded in Hamburg |
| **1832** | Amalie Sieveking founds the Female Association in Germany |
| **1834** | Britain's New Poor Law Passed |
| **1836** | Alexandre-Jean-Baptiste Parent-Duchâtelet's posthumous study of Parisian prostitutes published |
| **1837** | Beginning of reign of Queen Victoria in Britain |
| **1838** | Aristide Boucicaut founds the store that would become Bon Marché Department Store |
| **1842** | Mines and Collieries Act |
| **1843** | Jeanne Jugan founds Sisters of the Poor |
| **1845** | Mill workers in Lowell, Massachusetts found Female Labor Reform Association |
| **1848** | Elizabeth Blackwell admitted to Geneva Medical College |
| **1851** | London's Great Exhibition |
| **1853–1856** | Crimean War |
| **1859** | Charles Darwin publishes *Origin of the Species* |
| **1861** | Russia's Great Reforms and the abolition of serfdom |
| **1861–1865** | American Civil War |
| **1864** | Britain's first Contagious Disease Act |
| **1867** | Nadeshda Suslova first woman to receive a PhD |
| **1868** | Elizabeth Blackwell founds Women's Medical College of the New York Infirmary |
| **1874** | Paris establishes municipal daycares |
| **1875** | Mary Baker Eddy publishes *Science and Health with Key to Scriptures* |
| **1882** | Aletta Jacobs opens Europe's first birth control clinic |
| **1886** | Kamilla Odynets founds Saint Petersburg's first Industrial Home |
| | Marie Béquet de Vienne establishes the *Asile Maternel* |
| | Jane Addams founds Hull House |
| **1890** | Austria and the Netherlands legislate against married women working outside the home |
| **1894** | Havelock Ellis publishes *Man and Woman* |

## Gendering Factory Work

As we saw in the previous chapter, during the early stages of industrialization, companies contracted out much of the finish work to women, such as assembling artificial flowers or sewing buttons onto clothes. Women did piecework in their homes while they tended children, cooked meals, and did other chores. In search of the cheapest labor, companies began employing women in traditionally male-dominated trades such as tailoring. However, women's entry into such trades threatened male artisans' livelihoods and masculinity. In an effort to preserve their honor, artisans linked specific skills with masculinity. For example, tailors only allowed women to do undesirable tasks, such as sewing military uniforms. Male tailors considered this work demeaning because it employed coarse material, required little skill, and earned low pay. They also made it clear that quality work was completed in a workshop. In 1806, 1810, and 1811 the skilled tailors of London went on strike after some journeymen took work home to complete. Other groups of artisans followed suit; hatters, calico printers, and framework knitters all struck to prevent women from working in their trades.[1] However, their tactics were unsuccessful. Employers broke the strikes by hiring women who would work for lower wages at home.

Employers often preferred to hire women in the new mechanized factories. They believed that women were docile, industrious, and submissive workers and, therefore, ideally suited for repetitive, low-paid, and low-skilled labor. Indeed, employers relied on those same traditional stereotypes to divide factory work according to gender. In particular, many assumed that women could not or should not work with machines. Thus, although cotton mill owners held that women could tend the fine threads on looms better than men, men repaired and adjusted the machines. In addition, they only allowed men to work heavy broadlooms and work more than one loom at a time. As mining became mechanized, mine owners also limited women's contact with heavy machinery, restricting them to basic tasks such as carting and sorting ore and coal. Because women were not allowed to work with most machines, they could not hold managerial positions and were more likely to lose their jobs during economic downturns.

Factory work attracted both married and single women. Some found factory work more exciting and better paying than farm work or domestic service. They appreciated the independence that accompanied work outside the home and viewed it as a temporary means to make money until they married. Although factory work paid well at the beginning of the century, by midcentury many more women took up factory work as a result of poverty or family crisis. For example, Verena Conzett was forced to take a job in a wool factory at the age of twelve when her father went blind.[2] The death of a parent also pushed many women into the factory as teenagers.

While factory work provided single women with the income necessary to live independently, many middle-class men and women grew uncomfortable with the social liberties that accompanied that independence. Factory workers had unsupervised contact with men before and after work and during breaks. They also met men as they traveled to and from work. Single women were quite conscious of the suspicions surrounding factory girls. After Anneliese Rüegg's father died when she was fourteen, she went to work in a Swiss cloth factory. She had not wanted to become a factory girl, "because I knew that factory workers weren't worth much and were suspect in many people's minds."[3] In fact, most single women aspired to quit their factory work as soon as they married.

Although most factory workers were single, across Europe, working-class families relied on married women's wages to make ends meet. Married women faced considerable criticism for working in factories. They were often accused of ignoring their children and household duties. Moreover, illness and economic downturns forced couples to adopt unconventional gendered divisions of labor in order to survive. In 1886, after their husbands were laid off, married women workers in a French braid factory petitioned for changes in laws to limit their ability to work. The next year, their petition noted:

> *The effects of this crisis have been to reduce a large number of households to destitution bordering on misery; to attenuate the sad consequences, many wives of workers have*

*not hesitated to solicit night work, an option that is better paid and that their age permits. We have thus often seen the singular spectacle of the woman working outside in order to bring in some small resources for the household, while the husband, confined to the house by lack of work, is occupied in the preparation of food and child care.*[4]

Such upheavals in the division of labor no doubt occurred regularly in the preindustrial world; however, they were usually temporary and happened privately—one family at a time. During the nineteenth century, when a factory closed, entire communities of working-class families might be turned upside down as unemployed men undertook domestic tasks while their wives went off to work.

Factories were notorious for their loud, dirty, dangerous, and unhealthy working conditions. Hours were long and discipline was harsh. Women complained of sexual harassment and unfair treatment by male supervisors and coworkers. A member of the British Parliament expressed his horror at the conditions he witnessed in 1838:

*Amongst other things I saw a cotton mill—a sight that froze my blood. The place was full of women, young, all of them, some large with child, and obliged to stand twelve hours each day. Their hours are from five in the morning to seven in the evening, two hours of that being for rest, so that they stand twelve clear hours. The heat was excessive in some of the rooms, the stink pestiferous, and in all an atmosphere of cotton flue. I nearly fainted. The women were all pale, sallow, thin, yet generally fairly grown, all with bare feet—a strange sight to English eyes.*[5]

While mill work had been a positive experience for young women working in Lowell, Massachusetts, by the 1840s conditions and wages had declined because of increase competition from other mills and an influx of cheap labor from immigrant women. In 1847, a woman mill worker, writing about her work experience in a labor newspaper explained that she had worked in the mill since she was seven years old, standing for fourteen hours a day. She also complained that "some of the clocks are so fixed as to lose ten minutes during the day and gain ten minutes during the night," in order to lengthen their day. When she worked as an overseer, she frequently saw girls faint because the air was so poor.[6]

Pushed to the brink of despair, workers organized to demand better conditions. In 1830, three thousand female workers in a tobacco factory in Madrid rioted for five days against a wage cut and poor working conditions.[7] That same year, twenty Frenchwomen fur cutters went on strike when the workshop owner cut their wages. Authorities arrested five women, four of whom received prison sentences for illegal organizing. The next year, women shawl cutters struck for a week, but this time authorities did not arrest them because they believed that the leaders were men disguised as women.[8]

These spontaneous work actions led to the formation of labor unions. Unions demanded shorter hours, better pay, improved conditions, and health insurance. Generally, women were slow to join unions. Many were too poor to pay the dues, did not identify themselves as permanent factory workers, or did not have the time to go to meetings. Moreover, male-dominated unions often discouraged women from joining and participating in the movement. During the 1870s, the French association Workers of Northern France required that women who wanted to speak at meetings have written approval from their fathers or husbands.[9] Male labor organizers argued that women were victims of bourgeois exploitation that took them away from their families. Others feared the uncontrolled sexuality of working women, especially those without families to support, arguing that women without adequate male supervision were more likely to become prostitutes or corrupt other women.[10]

In response, women organized their own labor unions. Women working in the cotton mills of Lowell formed the Female Labor Reform Association in 1845. Led by Sarah Bagley (1806–1848), it pressured employers to improve working conditions and even bought a labor journal, *The Voice of Industry*, to publicize its efforts. The union was strong enough to help defeat a local politician who opposed their campaign for a ten-hour workday.

The Knights of Labor, founded in 1869 by garment cutter Uriah Stephens (1821–1882), was the first union in the United States to organize women on a national scale, hiring activist Leonora Barry (1849–1930) to be its national organizer. It pushed for equal pay for equal work and was the first major labor organization to accept black members into the movement. By the 1880s, it claimed more than seven hundred thousand members, but fell into decline by the end of the century.

Female labor organizers had different demands than men. They pressed for equal pay for equal work, daycare for their children, and safe working conditions. Authorities tended to see workers as a genderless class, but labor organizers and workers increasingly understood that female workers faced issues particular to their gender.

## Domestic Work

Although large numbers of women went to work in factories, many more worked as domestic servants. As the urban middle class grew and became wealthier, they sought young women to help with work in the home. Employing a servant was an important sign of financial success and upward mobility. Having worked their way up in the expanding commercial and industrial sectors of the economy, middle-class families saw servants as a reward for their years of hard work. By 1828, domestic servants were 14 percent of Munich's population. During the 1860s, approximately one-third of all urban working women in London, Berlin, and Paris worked as domestic servants. The numbers of female servants did not peak until the turn of the twentieth century.[11]

Although they had less freedom, many women preferred domestic service to factory work. Positions were plentiful, the wages were good, and one was guaranteed room and board. As we have seen in previous chapters, some servants suffered physical and verbal abuse, but domestic work generally seemed safer than managing alone in a big city and much less dangerous than many factories. Moreover, domestic work required no special training, so even young girls could find work.

Most servants were rural single women in their midteens to midtwenties. Parents placed them in domestic service often because they could not afford to apprentice them. As they migrated to the cities, networks of clergy, family, and friends helped women deal with the city's employment bureaus. One young woman, Doris Viersbeck, stayed with her aunt in Hamburg until she found employment. Her aunt helped her choose among three job offers and negotiate her wages.[12]

Domestic service was hard work. Doris Viersbeck recalled that she got up at five thirty in the morning and did not finish until ten or eleven at night.[13] Most families only had one servant, who worked at all tasks. Maids like Viersbeck cleaned rooms, cooked, washed dishes, did laundry and ironing, carried coal and wood, and took care of the personal needs of the mistress, master, and their children. One maid recalled that in addition to shopping, housework, and heavy laundry, she looked after "two spoiled and insolent children—though their mother would not hear a word against them."[14] Servants' responsibilities were great, but their authority was limited.

The majority of these women worked for middle-class employers, who accentuated the class differences between themselves and their servants. They treated their servants more like employees and less like family members. They also imparted their values to servants, stressing self-discipline and hard work. Building on their experience in the workplace, employers emphasized the importance of rationality and efficiency as a part of housekeeping (see **Sources from the Past:** *Mrs. Beeton's Book of Household Management*).[15]

Although most young women left domestic service after marriage, some women could not afford to stop working. They cooked or took in washing and ironing while living on their own. Others worked as charwomen, cleaning offices. Wages were low, and the hard work ruined many women's health.

## Women and the Industrialization of Agriculture

Although industrialization and population growth swelled urban populations, most women still lived in the countryside and worked in agriculture or cottage industries. However, the continued consolidation of land that began in the eighteenth century led to the decline of small farms in favor of large commercial farming. As large landowners introduced new crops and put more acres into cultivation, they created many new agricultural jobs for women. Like their counterparts in industry, agricultural employers preferred women workers because they could pay women lower wages than men. However, female workers were not as popular with local residents. The boisterous female fieldworkers, who moved about the countryside and worked for wages, challenged many traditional assumptions about femininity and rural life. People complained about the loud gangs of migrant women farm workers who had no domestic skills. One English clergyman explained that fieldwork degraded women, "their skin is wrinkled, their faces burnt, their features masculine."[16] In the 1870s, Italian women who weeded the rice fields were assumed to be promiscuous. One contemporary Italian study described them as damaged "in their most delicate feelings as a consequence of the promiscuity of the lodgings, and by the loose morals that are its results."[17]

By the end of the century, technological innovations changed agricultural work habits even more. Seed drills sped up beet planting and displaced the women who had previously done this work by hand. The scythe, heavier and bigger than the sickle that women used, became associated with men. Women lost jobs as reapers and worked instead at gathering, binding, and stacking sheaves of grain. These poorly paid jobs encouraged rural women to move into domestic service.

Dairying also became more industrialized. Dairymaids, who were usually single, had been romanticized as the ideal of rural femininity. Traditionally, rural women worked in dairies and in family kitchen gardens, spaces associated with women's work. The public associated the cleanliness necessary to produce fresh healthy milk with housekeeping. Early industrialization benefited dairywomen. In 1836, new training enabled Danish women to take charge of butter making in large commercial dairy farms, earning them high wages as skilled workers. Hanne Nielsen, a Danish dairy specialist, traveled across Europe studying and lecturing on cheese making. She trained over one thousand women during her career, and in 1874, she invented Havarti cheese. However, at the end of the century, the dairy industry mechanized; and the association of men with machines, already evident in factory work and agriculture, made dairying less feminine. Men became technical experts, supervisors, and managers. Their scientific knowledge of milk production gradually replaced that of the traditional dairymaid.

While industrialization changed rural women's work in western Europe, the gradual abolition of serfdom in eastern Europe slowly transformed rural society there. Prussia and Poland began the process in 1807, followed by Russia's Baltic provinces from 1816 to 1819. Austria finally abolished serfdom in 1848. In the Baltic provinces, serfs were less secure after abolition because landowners retained title to all their lands, forcing former serfs to pay rents on their holdings. In contrast, in the lands of the Habsburg monarchy, freed serfs became landowners immediately. In the long run, most former serfs benefited from their new freedom. They could grow products for market, work as wage laborers, and even become small business owners. They were also free to move, marry, and bequeath property without interference from landowners.

In 1861, Russia became the last nation to abolish serfdom. Scholars estimate that prior to emancipation, 4 percent of Russian landowners controlled 54 percent of the serfs.[18] However, by the 1840s, Russian elites increasingly saw serfdom as a relic of the past and a sign of Russia's backwardness. They also realized the dangers of a large and miserable population. In addition to these concerns, Russia's defeat by France and Britain in the Crimean War (1853–1856) made it clear that the country needed extensive reform in order to compete with Western nations. In response, in 1856 the new tsar, Alexander II (r. 1855–1881), began the Great Reforms, the most important of which was the abolition of serfdom.

Legislation in 1861 proposed emancipation in a multistage process. The laws gradually redefined the relationship between serf and owner until they required that serfs redeem or purchase the land they worked from their former owners. The government spread these redemption payments over a forty-nine-year period. In the end, emancipation freed forty million Russian serfs.

The process of emancipation created confusion in many communities and did little immediately to improve the quality of life for most serfs. The proclamations read to the peasants by their local priests explained that most of men's labor obligations would continue for the immediate term, while dues on items collected or produced by

## Mrs. Beeton's Book of Household Management

*Advice manuals proliferated during the nineteenth century, reinforcing the ideology of separate spheres. They described social expectations and gender norms to the growing numbers of literate middle-class women and popularized new ideas of domestic science and household management. This excerpt comes from* Mrs. Beeton's Book of Household Management, *one of the most popular of the genre.*

THE MISTRESS:

> Strength and honour are her clothing; and she shall rejoice in time to come. She openeth her mouth with wisdom; and in her tongue is the law of kindness. She looketh well to the ways of her household, and eateth not the bread of idleness. Her children arise up, and call her blessed; her husband also, and he praiseth her. Proverbs xxxi. 25–28.

1. AS WITH THE COMMANDER OF AN ARMY, or the leader of any enterprise, so is it with the Mistress of a house. Her spirit will be seen in the whole establishment; and just in proportion as she performs her duties intelligently and thoroughly, so will her domestics follow her path. Of all those acquirements, which more particularly belong to the feminine character, there are none which take a higher rank, in our estimation, than such as enter into a knowledge of household duties; for on these are perpetually dependent the happiness, comfort, and well-being of the family. In this opinion we are borne out by the author of the "Vicar of Wakefield,"[1] who says: "The modest virgin, the prudent wife, the careful matron, are much more serviceable in life than petticoated philosophers, blustering heroines, or virago queens. She who makes her husband and her children happy, who reclaims the one from vice and trains up the other to virtue, is a much greater character than ladies described in romances, whose whole occupation is to murder mankind with shafts for their quiver or their eyes."

2. PURSUING THIS PICTURE, we may add, that to be a good housewife does not necessarily imply an abandonment of proper pleasures or amusing recreation; and we think it the more necessary to express this as the performance of the duties of a mistress may, to some minds, perhaps seem to be incompatible with the enjoyment of life. Let us, however, now proceed to describe some of those home qualities and virtues which are necessary to the proper management of a Household, and then point out the plan which may be the most profitably pursued for the daily regulation of its affairs.

3. EARLY RISING IS ONE OF THE MOST ESSENTIAL QUALITIES which enter into good Household Management, as it is not only the parent of health, but of innumerable other advantages. Indeed, when a mistress is an early riser, it is almost certain that her house will be orderly and well-managed. On the contrary, if she remained in bed till a late hour, then the domestics who, as we have before observed, invariably partake somewhat of their mistress's character, will surely become sluggards. To self-indulgence all are more or less disposed, and it is not to be expected that servants are freer from this fault than the heads of the houses. The great Lord Chatham thus gave his advice in reference to his subjects: "I would have inscribed on the curtains of your bed and the walls of your chamber, 'If you do not rise early, you can make progress in nothing.'"[2]

4. CLEANLINESS IS ALSO INDISPENSABLE TO HEALTH, and must be studied both in regard to the person of the house, and all that it contains. Cold or tepid baths should be employed every morning, unless, on account of illness or other circumstances, they should be deemed objectionable. The bathing of *children* will be treated under the head of "MANAGEMENT OF CHILDREN."

5. FRUGALITY AND ECONOMY ARE HOME VIRTUES, without which no household can prosper. Dr. Johnson says: "Frugality may be termed the daughter of Prudence, the sister of Temperance, and the parent of Liberty. He that is extravagant will quickly become poor, and poverty will

enforce dependence and invite corruption."[3] The necessity of practicing economy should be evident to every one, whether in the possession of an income no more than sufficient for a family's requirements, or of a large fortune, which puts financial adversity out of the question. We must always remember that just as a great merit in housekeeping is to manage a little well. "He is a good waggoner," says Bishop Hall, "that can turn in a little room. To live well in abundance is the praise of the estate, not the person. I will study more how to give a good account of my little, than how to make it more."[4] In this there is true wisdom, and it may be added, that those who can manage a little well, are most likely to succeed in their management of larger matters. Economy and frugality must never, however, be allowed to degenerate into parsimony and meanness.

6. THE CHOICE OF ACQUAINTANCES is very important to the happiness of a mistress and her family. A gossiping acquaintance, who indulges in the scandal and ridicule of her neighbours, should be avoided as a pestilence. It is likewise, all-necessary to beware, as Thomson sings,

> the whisper'd tale,
> That, like the fabling Nile, no fountain knows;
> Fair-faced Deceit, whose wily, conscious eye
> Ne'er looks direct; the tongue that licks the dust
> But, when it safely dares, as prompt to sting.[5]

If the duties of the family do not sufficiently occupy the time of the mistress, society should be formed of such a kind as will tend to the natural interchange of general and interesting information.

7. FRIENDSHIPS SHOULD NOT BE HASTILY FORMED, nor the heart given, at once, to every newcomer. There are ladies who uniformly smile at, and approve everything and everybody, and who possess neither the courage to reprehend vice, nor the generous warmth to defend virtue. The friendship of such persons is without attachment, and their love without affection or even preference. They imagine that every one who has any penetration is ill-natured, and look coldly on a discriminating judgment. It should be remembered, however, that this discernment does not always proceed from an uncharitable temper, but that those who possess a long experience and thorough knowledge of the world, scrutinize the conduct and dispositions of people before they trust themselves to the first fair appearances. Addison, who was not deficient in a knowledge of mankind, observes that "a friendship, which makes the least noise, is very often the most useful; for which reason I should prefer a prudent friend to a zealous one."[6] And Joanna Baillie tells us that

> Friendship is not plant of hasty growth,
> Thought planted in esteem's deep-fixed soil,
> The gradual culture of kind intercourse
> Must bring it to perfection.[7]

8. HOSPITALITY IS A MOST EXCELLENT VIRTUE; but care must be taken that the love of company, for its own sake, does not become a prevailing passion; for then the habit is no longer hospitality, but dissipation. Reality and truthfulness in this, as in all other duties of life, are the points to be studied; for as Washington Irving well says, "There is an emanation from the heart in genuine hospitality, which cannot be described, but is immediately felt, and puts the stranger at once at his ease."[8]

---

[1] A novel written in 1766 by British novelist Oliver Goldsmith (1728–1774).

[2] William Pitt, Earl of Chatham (1708–1778), Prime Minister of Britain (1757–1761).

[3] Samuel Johnson (1709–1784), British lexicographer, critic, author, and conversationalist.

[4] Bishop Joseph Hall (1574–1656), poet and bishop of Exeter.

[5] James Thomson (1700–1748), Scottish poet dramatist.

[6] Joseph Addison (1672–1719), British poet and essayist.

[7] Scottish poet (1762–1851).

[8] American novelist and short story writer (1783–1859).

Source: *Mrs. Beeton's Book of Household Management* (London: S. O. Beeton, 1861), 1–3.

women, such as eggs, mushrooms, cloth, and yarn, were terminated first. Many villages mistakenly believed that women earned their freedom first and demanded that the tsar abolish labor dues and thus free the men as well.[19] The process of abolition was further complicated by the fact that peasants received only small plots to work and many were unhappy with the clause that made the entire village responsible for the rents on individual's land.

By the end of the century, women's work across Europe had changed dramatically both in form and in organization. Whether in the country or city, women increasingly worked away from their families and homes. Despite the long hours, dangerous conditions, low pay, and lack of respectability, they did whatever was necessary to support themselves and their families.

## GENDERED SPACES IN THE NEW URBAN LANDSCAPE

During the nineteenth century, cities expanded to meet the needs of the new industrial society. In 1800, London was the largest city in Europe or America with a million people. By 1900, London had grown to 3.3 million, and the five boroughs of New York City had a population of nearly 3.5 million, most of whom were immigrants.[20]

Many of these immigrants were women. By 1860, there were 125 single women of marrying age for every 100 men of the same age in New York City.[21] At the end of the century, Paris had 111 women for every 100 men.[22] The same was true in cities across Europe; however, whatever the statistical reality, by midcentury people believed that most cities suffered from a surplus of women.

Population growth and technological change transformed the lives of urban dwellers. Public transportation allowed women to move around the city easily. There were also more places for them to go, as cities created more public spaces that were considered acceptable recreational destinations for women. Even shopping became a more leisurely activity. However, urban life was not always pleasant. Urban growth and mobility also led to an increase in crime that compromised

women's reputations and endangered their lives. (See Maps 9.1 and 9.2.)

## Moving Around the City

At the beginning of the century, people still relied on private horse-drawn carriages and hired coaches or hackney cabs to move about the city. As cities grew, improvements in transportation allowed more people to move into and across them for business and pleasure. In 1826, horse-drawn "omnibuses" started carrying large numbers of people through French cities, and the innovation quickly spread to

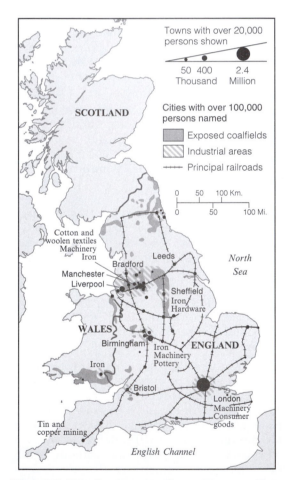

*Map 9.1* THE INDUSTRIAL REVOLUTION IN ENGLAND. The Industrial Revolution dramatically changed the organization of women's work.

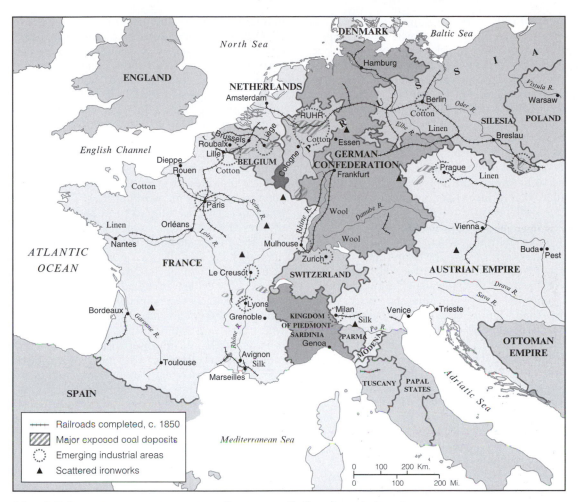

***Map 9.2*** **INDUSTRIALIZATION ON THE CONTINENT.** Railroads made it easier to transport both goods and people over long distances and gave women more geographic mobility.

other countries. By the 1830s, railroads powered by steam connected northern and southern London, and in 1863, the Metropolitan Line opened the first underground railway. At the end of the century, electric trolleys and subways connected neighborhoods while trains created links between cities and between the city and the surrounding countryside. By the end of the century, gaslights allowed people to move through the city at night.

Women took advantage of new forms of travel, creating controversy and anxiety by moving from place to place so freely. For many observers,

women's mobility added to the decadence of urban life. One London critic described women traveling into the city as "barbarians dressed in silk and sealskin." Some of this anxiety came from the mixing of social classes in stations and on trains, while others worried that women would be easy victims of crime. In 1860, a murder in an English railway compartment brought these two concerns together and led to half-hearted attempts to create women-only compartments to protect them. Women tended to reject this solution, advocating instead that railroad officials control working-class men more.[23]

By the 1880s, women riding bicycles caused a sensation. Bicycles gave women new independence, as they could travel cheaply and unchaperoned. Advertisers worked to feminize the bicycle to make this mobility acceptable, but journals such as the *Georgia Journal of Medicine and Surgery* still warned in 1899 of its potential dangers. The bicycle brought on a dangerous female medical condition when "the body is thrown forward, causing the clothing to press against the clitoris thereby eliciting and arousing feelings hitherto unknown and unrealized by the young maiden."[24] The idea that a woman might experience sexual pleasure (even inadvertently) made bicycle travel all the more dangerous.

Women's clothing changed to accommodate their increased mobility. The hoop skirts and tight corsets that were fashionable at midcentury represented idealized womanhood to many, but they were impractical for riding bicycles and traveling on buses and trains. Moreover, they were expensive and dangerous to wear in factories. As a result, they became associated with middle-class and elite women who did not have to worry about such issues. Working-class women adopted slim skirts, and some members of the women's movement wore bloomers. As these new styles emphasized women's figures and bloomers showed women's legs, they tapped into anxieties about the relationship between women's appearance, social freedom, and femininity.

Women also began demanding accommodations to make their urban experience more comfortable. As they moved through the city, women found that there were few if any public lavatories for women. Ursula Bloom recalled in her diary that "in London, fashionable ladies went for a day's shopping with no hope of relief for those faithful tides of nature until they returned home again."[25] Beginning in the 1870s, women activists campaigned for public restrooms for women. However, many locals resisted the establishment of such facilities, arguing that they brought in foreigners and unchaperoned women and contributed to social disorder.[26]

## New Destinations

Not only could women travel with greater ease in nineteenth-century cities, but cities boasted more public attractions such as libraries, parks, and museums, sites that civilized the chaos of urban life and extended domestic space. Libraries, previously male bastions, opened children's rooms and reading areas that looked like living rooms and parlors. In the 1850s, Baron von Haussman (1809–1891) transformed Paris with his large avenues and the Bois de Boulogne where Parisians could spend leisurely afternoons, and Frederick Law Olmsted (1822–1903) built New York's Central Park to provide a place for families to gather and relax.

Pubs and cafés attracted a variety of urban residents, particularly the working class. These establishments not only offered food and drink, but they provided a better atmosphere for socializing than the dank tenements that housed the urban poor. Although middle-class moralists might have assumed that women in cafés were prostitutes, there is little evidence that café proprietors or the working-class customers made this assumption.[27] Indeed, women of all classes spent leisurely hours with friends and family in cafés. Describing a café in Paris, an American observer noted, "In a distant corner a dark-skinned beauty of not more than eighteen is engaged in an exciting game of dominoes with an elderly women evidently her mother . . . other women are sewing and chatting busily."[28] Cafés were available for a wide range of activities that the middle class performed at home.

Theaters also become respectable destinations for women. Theater had long been popular among the urban working class; however, during the nineteenth century, the stage began to lose its seamy reputation. Governments were important in legitimating the theater. Napoleon nationalized four Parisian theaters to promote French patriotism and culture, and by the middle of the century, the British government censored scripts to prevent inappropriate subject matter from being performed. As transportation improved, more middle-class men and women attended performances. Theaters also accommodated this new diverse audience. New buildings, such as London's Majesty Theatre, which opened in 1897, divided seating into sections, each with its own entrances and exits to keep the classes apart. This arrangement helped insulate middle- and upper-class women from contact with their lower-class counterparts.

From time to time, elaborate international exhibitions drew enormous crowds into Europe's major cities. London's Great Exhibition of 1851, "A Great Exhibition of the Works of Industry of All Nations," focused attention on Great Britain as a world leader in industry and art. The centerpiece of the Exhibition was the prefabricated cast-iron and glass exhibition hall called the Crystal Palace. In it, tens of thousands of displays introduced new inventions such as the Colt revolver and exotic finds such as the first-ever life-size reproductions of dinosaurs and the priceless Koh-i-Noor diamond. Exhibits also showed women new home products and styles such as bentwood rocking chairs, whose ease of manufacturing, affordable price, and graceful style made them very popular. The Exhibition promoted the benefits of industrialization but highlighted the new products and improved living standards now available. The London Exhibition was a huge success. Train travel helped bring six million people to London in five and a half months, and the social classes mingled in ways unprecedented in English society.[29]

Other cities produced similar exhibitions. These later fairs introduced women to domestic improvements such as the sewing machine in 1855 and indoor electric lighting in 1878. At its World's Fair in 1889, the French government encouraged women to purchase French items that they saw at the exhibitions. The exhibitions made consumerism respectable. Women could properly represent their husbands, class, and nation by acquiring the right kinds of household goods.[30]

## Shopping

As the urban population traveled about town, shopping changed for upper and middle class women from essential household provisioning to a leisure and social activity. Increasingly, consumers purchased mass-produced rather than custom-made clothing and furniture. The department store played an important role in changing consumer habits and gendering different kinds of shopping. The first such enterprise was Aristide Boucicaut's (1810–1877) Parisian Bon Marché, which opened as a dry goods store in 1838. Boucicaut sold a wide variety of goods, attractively displayed under one roof. Fixed low prices made shopping less stressful,

**CRYSTAL PALACE.** The London Exhibition in 1861 attracted millions of women to exhibits that promoted technology and the British Empire. The exhibits inspired new consumerism among women. *(Historical Picture Archive/Corbis)*

as female shoppers no longer had to haggle for bargains, and customers received help from large staffs of clerks dressed in uniforms. Department stores emphasized the convenience of being able to buy whatever one wanted at a moment's notice. Store credit, concerts, and in-store dining added to the leisurely nature of shopping. Bus lines facilitated travel from middle-class neighborhoods to shopping districts so that women could travel without chaperones.

However, not everyone was thrilled with the new emphasis on female consumption. When William Whiteley (1831–1907) transformed his London dry goods store into a department store, critics reacted angrily, accusing him of luring women into the city in search of pleasure and thereby encouraging immoral behavior. Moreover, by attracting a diverse clientele, he upset class, gender, and moral boundaries. In 1872, when Whiteley wanted to serve alcohol at his newly opened refreshment room, the local press denounced him, stating that serving alcohol would attract the wrong sort of women to the neighborhood and Whiteley already drew in too many women.[31] Critics in France reacted in similar ways, even equating unregulated female consumption with seduction and adultery. Women could betray their husbands and families with their desire for objects.[32]

Nineteenth-century shops and department stores were stocked with a dizzying array of new products. Europe's colonies (see Chapter 11) provided many exotic goods that became very popular in the mother country. Expensive shawls imported from India were all the rage among wealthy Englishwomen and shawl shops opened across the country. Store shelves were also stocked with curry pastes and chutney.[33] The exotic did not always come from far away, however. Lower- and middle-class women also flocked to stores to purchase cheap imitations of upper-class clothing and furniture.

This new world of consumerism was driven by an increase in advertising, much of which was aimed at women. Retailers encouraged women to purchase more products, in order to beautify themselves and reflect their families' social positions.[34] Some advertisements revealed a new obsession with purity in food, medicine, and soap that played on women's anxieties as mothers and caretakers.

Others, like a turn-of-the-century advertisement for the Bon Marché Department Store, looked to attract a different female customer, featuring independent women bicycling and strolling in front of the store.[35] Finally, in an attempt to catch the eye of new customers, many advertisements included boldly sexual pictures of scantily clad, seductive women that appealed to both male and female consumers.[36]

As shopping became more feminine, collecting became a male activity. Men hunted for desirable objects at auctions, flea markets, or galleries—places respectable women avoided. Collectors had to negotiate prices, trying to convince the seller through knowledge and intrigue to sell at a lower price. This process was active and aggressive. Collecting also involved traveling to out-of-the-way places or even the colonies, where the collector had to mix with the lower classes, possibly even criminals, and compete with other buyers.[37]

## Urban Problems

Alongside their grand promenades, lush parks, and stately museums, industrial cities were also home to poverty, crime, and violence. Most rural immigrants came to the city with little in their pockets. They lived in cheap, poorly ventilated, disease-ridden tenements, which were vulnerable to fire. Sewers dumped waste into rivers, polluting the drinking water and causing illness. Politicians hoped that railroads would ease the overcrowding, but they only added to urban pollution. Although it became easier for residents and visitors to move around the city, urban life, which had never been healthy, became increasingly dangerous.

As unemployment rates rose, men and women turned to theft, prostitution, and other crimes to survive. Petty crimes, including pickpocketing, made the city an increasingly dangerous place. Gangs of children, as immortalized by Charles Dickens (1812–1870) in his serial novel *Oliver Twist* (1837–1839), often became pickpockets in order to survive. Children could easily snatch purses, lift wallets, and steal produce displayed on sidewalks. Cities also had numerous back alleys to stash stolen goods. Moreover, most cities did not have police departments until the end of the century. London was unique in turning over responsibility for crime to a metropolitan police department in 1829 rather than leaving it in the hands of the army as it was in Paris and other cities.

Prostitution particularly troubled government authorities and they went to great measures to study and regulate it. Governments saw prostitutes as lascivious and threatening to the reputations of respectable women. Women activists countered that prostitution grew not out of women's moral failings, but from poverty and lack of jobs. These divergent attitudes toward the growing population of prostitutes reflected competing ideas about the role of the state, femininity, and the presence of women in public places. Some urbanites confused well-dressed prostitutes and middle-class matrons out in public, a situation that provoked a great deal of humor. The cartoon pictured at the right from 1865 shows an evangelical clergyman trying to give a reforming pamphlet to a well-dressed woman. She replied, "You're mistaken. I am not a social evil, I am only waiting for a bus."[38]

Most prostitutes came from families of unskilled and semiskilled workers and had come to the city to work as domestics or in some other female-dominated occupation. They were young, between sixteen and twenty-five years of age, with little education. Nearly half of the prostitutes who registered with the Italian police were illiterate.[39] Contemporaries who studied prostitutes remarked on how frequently these young women grew up in "broken homes" or orphanages. Some women turned to prostitution when their families could not afford to feed them. One British prostitute explained to a charity worker that she did not go home because, "Father couldn't afford to keep me at home; and I was ashamed for mother to know I was so bad off."[40] Women seldom saw prostitution as a permanent career; most only worked for a few years before moving on to another job or setting up house with a spouse or lover.

Prostitutes either worked on their own or in brothels. Women who worked the streets usually worked in pairs for protection, as they were often the victims of harassment and violence from clients, the authorities, and nearby residents. Some prostitutes were quite successful. One London prostitute, Sarah Tanner, began as a servant and then worked as a prostitute for well-to-do middle-class men for three years. She then retired with her savings to open a respectable coffeehouse.[41] At the other end of the spectrum,

**SCENE IN REGENT STREET.** This cartoon highlights the tension between changes in women's behavior and changes in social expectations. While women could travel more readily, many thought that unchaperoned women were sexually available. (*Linda Nead,* Victorian Babylon: People, Streets and Images in Nineteenth-Century London, *New Haven, CT: Yale University Press, 2000, 63.*)

many prostitutes were sick and malnourished and suffered from alcoholism.

Brothels offered some protection, but it came at a price. The police or municipal authorities regulated and licensed brothels in Germany, Italy, and France. Brothel keepers had to keep the windows closed and shuttered at all times, residents could only leave every few weeks for a day off, and sanitary conditions inside were usually poor. One French observer described the seedy conditions in a brothel as "an attic furnished with two or three iron beds, where the girls sleep two by two. Large tin basins full of dirty water show how these women prepare themselves. Along the length of the walls, with hanging strips of loose wallpaper, one perceives long trails of the soot that forms part of the prostitute's makeup."[42] Even in luxury bordellos, only paying customers used the nicely furnished rooms. The women slept in the attic, usually two to a bed, prompting accusations that brothels were hotbeds of lesbianism. Brothel life was also tedious. Isolated and required to keep a schedule unlike the rest of society, prostitutes spent their leisure hours playing endless card games, drinking, smoking, reading light romances if they could read, and talking.[43] Madams often hindered prostitutes' ability to leave the brothel by charging them exorbitant rates for clothes, food, makeup, and other accessories and putting them heavily in debt.

In addition to petty crime and prostitution, cities could be violent, and nineteenth-century journalists contributed to cities' reputations as dangerous and disreputable places by publishing voyeuristic stories about sensational crimes. Accounts of Jack the Ripper, who murdered and dismembered five London prostitutes in the autumn of 1888, terrified Britons. The police never identified or caught the killer, contributing to a media frenzy that fed on stereotypical images of class and gender.[44] As journalists speculated about the killer's identity, their theories drew on the fears of London's ethnically and socially diverse population. The sexual mutilation of many of the victims convinced some that the murderer was a physician. Others believed the killer was an aristocrat. Still others blamed the new Jewish immigrants who were fleeing eastern European pogroms. The police's heavy-handed investigation and lack of success further alienated the working class, who lived in the Whitechapel neighborhood where the murders took place, from the government and middle-class establishment. As a result of the newspaper coverage, men formed vigilante groups to patrol the streets. To many, the murders were clear evidence that women belonged indoors, protected by men.

Nineteenth-century cities were bustling centers in which people of all classes mingled much more freely. Streetcars took women to different parts of town to shop, stroll through parks, and see public exhibitions. However, the sharp increase in population and the freedom with which city dwellers moved also made cities dangerous. The fact that women were both victims and perpetrators of crimes encouraged male vigilance over their movements and morality.

## URBAN REFORM AND THE CONTROL OF WOMEN

Distressed by increasing urban poverty and crime, reformers took action to alleviate the ills of industrial society. They were outraged at the appalling conditions in which many women worked, concerned about the growing numbers of poor, single mothers, and upset by the rise in prostitution. However, rather than deal with the social and economic issues that caused those problems, most reform efforts focused on women's activities and morality.

### Regulating Women's Work

As we have already seen, women workers organized to improve working conditions; however, they were not alone in their desire to make factories and other workplaces safer for women. Politicians argued that factory work and mining jeopardized women's femininity and threatened their children's health and welfare. In response, during the 1830s and 1840s, the British Parliament passed a series of laws to protect women at work. The Factory Acts reduced the hours that women and children could work in textile factories and limited the machines that women could use. In 1842, the British Parliament passed the Mines and Collieries Act, which prevented women and children from working in mines. Health was not the only issue. Female miners wearing pants, going shirtless, and working in dark close quarters with men provoked moral outrage. One writer feared that the women might "lose every quality that is graceful in women, and become a set of coarse licentious, wretches, scorning all kinds of restraint and yielding themselves up, with shameless audacity to the most detestable sensuality."[45] Other reformers believed that unsanitary mines hindered female miners' ability to maintain a clean household. French and Belgian legislation imposed similar restrictions on women

**TWO BELGIAN PIT GIRLS.** Women mine workers adopted clothing and behavior that the middle class believed to be unfeminine. Belgian pit girls, however, took great pride in their work. *(Munby Documents, Trinity College, Cambridge, UK.)*

miners in the early 1870s, and Germany and Austria followed soon after. In 1877, Switzerland curtailed women's night work in factories and forced women to take unpaid maternity leave.

Motivated more by paternalistic concerns about the propriety of women working for wages than by a desire to improve working conditions or to improve pay, politicians and reformers often focused on removing married women from the workforce. In 1890, both Austria and the Netherlands passed laws limiting married women's ability to work outside the home. The same year, the Swiss and German governments held a joint convocation in Berlin on worker protection. The conference produced legislation that curtailed the hours and types of women's work and their ability to work during pregnancy. However, owners frequently ignored these laws or paid off enforcers in order to maintain a cheaper female

workforce, and women who needed work often encouraged factory and mine owners to flout these regulations.

Women activists were divided on the issue of protective legislation. Many opposed such reforms, asserting that women had a right to work when and where they wanted. French activist Paule Mink (1839–1901) spoke out vigorously for women's right to work:

> *By denying women the right to work, you degrade her, you put her under man's yoke and deliver her over to man's good pleasure. By ceasing to make her a worker, you deprive her of her liberty, and, thereby, of her responsibility (and this is why I insist so much on this issue), so that she longer will be a free and intelligent creature, but will merely be a reflection, a small part of her husband.[46]*

Others advocated for government-sponsored paid maternity leave so that female workers would not have to depend on male breadwinners. Probably the most radical idea to emerge from this debate was French women's activist Léonie Rouzade's (1839–1916) argument that motherhood was so important to the nation's well-being that it should be a paid social function.[47]

## Reforming the Poor

Efforts to address the problem of urban poverty reflect the tensions between new scientific approaches to the problem and the middle-class morality that drove many reformers. At the beginning of the century, French civil servant Dr. Alexandre-Jean-Baptiste Parent-Duchâtelet (1790–1835) revolutionized urban reform efforts by collecting extensive public health data for the government. In fact, his study of prostitutes, published just after his death, became a model for other countries.[48] Based on his work, reformers across Europe tabulated the numbers of abandoned children, deaths by different diseases, the social and geographic origins of urban immigrants, and the numbers and origins of prostitutes in order to better understand the extent of the problem; however, they then categorized the poor in terms of deserving and undeserving. Only those who expressed a desire to change received help. Reformers labeled the rest of the poor population as lazy or immoral and in need of punishment.

Increasingly, liberal politicians and reformers pushed for government intervention. However, laissez-faire economics held that such regulation was bad for business, even if businesses contributed to the population's ill health and poverty. Thus, the Poor Laws passed by the British Parliament in 1834 regulated the poor, rather than encouraging businesses to pay fair wages. The bill specifically tied government aid to a willingness to work in state-sponsored workhouses. Women's activist and liberal economist Harriet Martineau (1802–1876) supported such efforts, arguing that traditional charity encouraged dependence and sexual promiscuity. She believed that workhouses would act as a deterrent to such behavior and teach self-sufficiency. By claiming to teach the poor independence and a work ethic, the Poor Laws treated poverty as a moral failing rather than an economic condition.

Women particularly suffered from the Poor Laws' harsh measures. Most reformers saw single mothers as the primary cause of increasing poverty and believed that charity allowed them to reproduce without considering their ability to support their children. The bastardy clause of the Poor Laws made women financially responsible for their children; if they could not support them, they had to enter a workhouse. Single women could not name the fathers of their children, thereby holding them responsible for child support, because reformers and civil authorities believed that women intentionally named innocent men. One London overseer of the poor told the story of a young woman who had accused a gentleman of fathering her child. When asked why, she replied, "Because I choose that he shall be the father of my child." A subsequent medical exam proved his erectile dysfunction.[49] The moral of the story was that poor women could not be trusted.

Married women also suffered from the contradictory logic of the Poor Laws, which required all able-bodied workers to work, despite the fact that most people believed that married women should not work. Women whose fathers or husbands could not or would not support them were sent to workhouses. Conditions in workhouses were deplorable, and wages were worse than those of the lowest-paid laborers.

Britain's Poor Laws inspired Russian reformers. With the abolition of serfdom in Russia, peasants flocked to cities in search of new jobs; however, relative to the rest of Europe, Russia was slow to industrialize and suffered periodic economic depressions. Coupled with peasants' lack of training and education, unemployment became a serious problem. As in western Europe, Russian reformers such as Kamilla Odynets also classified the poor as either deserving or undeserving. Odynets believed that the alms degraded the deserving poor who needed instead "a safe port . . . a school of work and morality."[50] She founded the first Industrial Home in Saint Petersburg in 1886 to provide such a place, and soon others opened up across Russia. They housed and fed the deserving poor and trained them in useful skills. Many Industrial Homes had to set up nurseries for small children so that their mothers could work. However, Industrial Homes faced huge obstacles as many of the poor had health problems and physical disabilities or were either too young or too elderly to work.

Charity became a public duty rather than a religious calling. As early as 1814, the French government created bureaus to oversee the care of abandoned children and provide some hospital care for destitute women. By the 1860s, the government took responsibility for all abandoned children, opening orphanages for infants. By the age of six, children went to foster homes, usually in the countryside to provide needed labor. The state considered twelve-year-olds old enough for occupational training. One scheme even proposed filling the military with teenage orphans. In 1874, Paris established municipal daycare centers so that working women could leave their children in safety. By the end of the century, sixty-seven daycare facilities in the department of the Seine provided care for more than six thousand babies.[51] Government health inspectors traveled the countryside teaching mothering skills to the working classes.[52]

Reformers had a particularly difficult time grappling with the rapid rise in illegitimacy. The numbers of children born out of wedlock rose dramatically over the course of the century. During the 1880s, 29 percent of babies born in Paris were illegitimate, as were half of all children in Vienna and Prague. Between one-third and one-half of the children born in Rome, Budapest, and Moscow were born out of wedlock.[53] Their mothers tended to be single immigrants, who were sexually vulnerable. Some worked as domestic servants and had no protection from men in the household or whom they met on the streets, while others had little leverage with which to pressure sexual partners into marriage. Urban circumstances were part of the problem. These women were far from family or village culture which would have otherwise provided pressure on the father to marry the women. Pregnant women often lost their jobs, and without family to care for them, they fell into poverty. Many gave birth in the growing number of free state-run hospitals like La Maternité in Paris. Frenchwomen could also apply for public assistance programs, but they had to appear at the office with their babies, had to have given birth in

a public hospital, and had to have threatened to abandon the baby.[54] Those women were judged to be so desperate that only government intervention could prevent family catastrophe.

## Prostitution

Nineteenth-century reformers and politicians expended considerable energy in the battle to control prostitution. Although politicians argued endlessly about prostitution and moral decay, to many urban reformers, the real danger in prostitution was disease. Syphilis reached epidemic proportions in the nineteenth century. Among the British military hospitals in 1862, one in eleven patients suffered from venereal disease, and by 1864, that number rose to one in three. In the first six months of 1846, syphilis caused 57 percent of London's infant deaths.[55] Public health officials worried that men unknowingly infected their wives and that pregnant women passed the disease to their children.

Medical opinion held that prostitutes, not their clients, spread venereal disease. In response, medical authorities advocated routine medical examinations of prostitutes to curb the spread of syphilis, although they required no such checks of men. In France, Napoleon (r. 1798–1814) developed a complex regulatory system in which morals police attempted to register all prostitutes, consign them to brothels, and routinely check them for syphilis. Prostitutes who resisted went to prison without trials. In England, prostitution came under government scrutiny with the Contagious Disease Acts (CDA) of 1864, 1866, and 1869. These acts specifically sought to control venereal disease among enlisted men in port and garrison towns. In eighteen districts, plainclothes policemen could identify any woman as a prostitute and subject her to biweekly medical exams. They locked up sick women in special hospitals. Italy and Germany followed in the 1870s with similar legislation.

Nineteenth-century medicine further humiliated infested women. Doctors relied solely on observation, making it easy to misdiagnose visible genital lesions as syphilis. Moreover, for a long time, doctors believed that syphilis and gonorrhea were the same disease. Even when they could differentiate among venereal diseases, most did not believe gonorrhea posed a threat to women because it showed few symptoms. Doctors could not accurately diagnose syphilis until the invention of the Wassermann test in 1907, and even with a diagnosis, the disease remained incurable until the development of sulfa drugs and antibiotics in the twentieth century. The most common treatment was mercury inhaled as a vapor, taken as pills, or administered directly to the vaginal walls, a process made easier with the invention of the speculum. Mercury treatment caused a variety of dangerous side effects, including loss of teeth and hair, mental illness, and ultimately death.

Doctors examined prostitutes' cervixes and vaginal openings for venereal disease with the newly invented speculum, but their contemptuous attitudes toward accused prostitutes turned examinations into punishments and contributed to the spread of disease. Women complained that these examinations were degrading and humiliating, and they referred to the process as "instrumental rape." In one Italian health office, a critic observed, "the doctor, having withdrawn the speculum from one [patient], had hardly rubbed it on a sponge full of oil before he applied it to another. After about fifty examinations, the sponge was loaded with mucus and blood, but the doctor continued unperturbed."[56]

Government regulation of prostitutes outraged many people. Nighttime dragnets often arrested innocent working women because police did not consider the possibility that poor, but respectable women might have to go out in public at night. In the roundup of suspected prostitutes, the economic realities of working-class women clashed with societies' expectations of proper female behavior. As we will see in the next chapter, campaigns to repeal these laws galvanized women across Europe into political action.

The social and economic changes that accompanied industrialization created new problems in the workplace, exacerbated urban poverty, and increased prostitution. Conscious of the scope of these problems, politicians and concerned citizens pushed for a wide array of reforms, most of which focused on women's behavior. Although the conditions in many factories and the large numbers of women and children toiling in them horrified reformers, for the most part, they did not regulate the businesses and employers. Instead, they constrained the ability of women, particularly married women, to work. When the numbers of urban poor exceeded the ability of parishes and other local religious organizations to meet their needs, governments offered some social services, but only to women whom they categorized as deserving. Unwilling to address the issue of male extramarital sex, the reform of prostitution focused on controlling women rather than morality. Few reforms even began to address the root causes of unhealthy workspaces, poverty, or prostitution.

## SEX AND GENDER: THEORY AND REALITY

As we have seen, women's increased public activity did not always conform to middle-class ideas of respectability and femininity. The ideology of separate spheres associated women with the home and childbearing and men with work and public life. Ensconced at home, women were expected to dedicate themselves to the care of their children, their households, and their husbands. Separate spheres not only dominated expectations for normal family life, it also influenced scientific research, as scientists theorized the roots of male dominance and the fragility of female sexuality. However, women were far from the weak, one-dimensional beings that separate spheres idealized. They led complicated lives enriched by a wide array of sexual and emotional relationships with both men and women.

### The Cult of Domesticity

As we saw in Chapter 8, many Enlightenment thinkers argued that home and motherhood were women's natural domains; however, the connection between women and the home took on new meaning in the mid-nineteenth century. Journalists, etiquette books, and clergymen equated the home with women, creating what scholars have referred to as the cult of domesticity. Respectable women did not engage in wage labor but instead remained at home and cared for the house and children. The phrase "angel in the house," a term drawn from Coventry Patmore's

(1823–1896) 1854 poem of the same name, vividly described society's perfect woman. Women were expected to create a private haven for their husbands to return to from their work in the public sphere. In return, the husband supported his wife financially and morally, protecting her from the dangerous public world that might jeopardize her reputation and her femininity. Many middle- and upper-class women embraced this ideal. One such woman, Margaretta Greg, wrote in her diary "a lady, to be such, must be a mere lady, and nothing else. She must not work for profit, or engage in any occupation that money can command, lest she invade the rights of the working classes."[57] A woman was to submit completely to her husband. Sarah Stickney Ellis (1812–1872), who authored behavioral guides for women, reminded her readers that "As women, the first thing of importance is to be content to be inferior to men—inferior in mental power, in the same proportion that you are inferior in bodily strength."[58]

This cult of domesticity sentimentalized the family and mother-child relationships. Increasingly, nineteenth-century families celebrated children's birthdays with parties and presents. With photography, a new technology, families memorialized children's growth, family occasions, and departed members. Children's literature became increasingly popular, and mothers bonded with their children over bedtime stories. Christmas became an occasion of family gatherings, gift giving, and secular traditions. The British queen Victoria (r. 1837–1901) and her German-born husband celebrated highly publicized German-style Christmases with their large family, even introducing Christmas trees and Father Christmas to Britain. Through holiday food and decorations, women created a domestic culture that identified the home as a refuge from the outside world.

Industrialization created the cult of domesticity, altering middle-class women's domestic activities. By midcentury, the home was a unit of consumption rather than production. Women bought rather than made goods and remained at home caring for their possessions. Isabella Mary Beeton (1836–1865), an English author of advice books, encouraged women to run their homes like their husbands ran their businesses, employing concepts of thrift, rationality, and order (see **Sources from the Past:** *Mrs. Beeton's Book of Household Management*.) The domestic maxim "A place for everything and everything in its place" emphasized the new value of regimentation. Rational and businesslike housekeeping required inventories of the linen and china cupboards and a schedule for maintaining them. The German-language magazine *Schweizer Frauenheim* (*Swiss Womanhood*) reminded its readers that a tidy and organized linen closet was every woman's pride.[59]

Moralists reinforced these ideas by promoting a new standard of cleanliness. John Wesley (1703–1791), the founder of Methodism, even claimed that "cleanliness was next to Godliness," thus linking housework to moral worth. Like the housewife's virtue, the house had to be spotless. The increased affordability of household furnishings and knickknacks meant that a home included a large number of items that needed constant attention. Women were expected to keep their sheets white; their floors swept, mopped, and polished; and their household decorations dusted without the aid of chemical cleaners or household appliances. Cleanliness also signaled affluence and assimilation. Wealthy, educated, middle-class German Jews used these higher standards of cleanliness to distinguish themselves from working-class Russian and eastern European Jews. For instance, middle-class German Jewish housewives cleaned fastidiously to disassociate their houses and their families from the garlic smell that pervaded the homes of their lower-class immigrant neighbors.[60]

Because the working class could not afford to do without women's wages, they could not observe separate spheres for men and women nor could working-class women achieve the middle-class ideal of the angel in the house. Unwilling to acknowledge their economic plight, many in the middle class judged women who worked outside the home as unfeminine, sexually suspect, and bad mothers. They even attempted to teach working-class women the value of domesticity through lessons in housewifery, cooking, and hygiene. However, some working-class women rejected these values, asserting their own worth to their families through their wage labor and mothering. Mrs. Williamson, a widow with eight young children, told charity workers who wanted to put her children in an orphanage that no matter how poor the family, a mother's love was indispensable.[61]

By the end of the century, a combination of economic changes, government regulation, and the cult of domesticity meant that only about 10 percent of English working-class wives engaged in paid labor by 1900.[62] Upwardly mobile women aspired to become housewives.

## Social Darwinism and Eugenics

Scientific theory also influenced people's ideas on sex and gender. One of the most transformative works of the period was Charles Darwin's (1809–1882) *The Origin of the Species* (1859). This book, published in six editions by 1872, revolutionized scientific thought. Darwin argued that changes in species were random and that those changes that helped an organism survive in its environment could be inherited by the next generation, a process known as natural selection. Natural selection explained how species adapted to their environment. *The Origin of the Species* generated considerable controversy, as Darwin denied both creation as described in the Bible and the existence of a divine plan.

Addressing the issue of sexual difference in his 1871 work *Descent of Man*, Darwin explained the process of sexual selection. He argued that the male domination resulted from the competition among men for survival and attractive mates. During that process desirable traits were "transmitted more fully to the male than to the female offspring. . . . Thus man has ultimately become superior to woman." Moreover, men were inherently more intelligent than women. "Man is more courageous, pugnacious and energetic than woman, and has a more inventive genius" (*Descent of Man*, Chapter 19). By the end of his life, Darwin's ideas were widely accepted in both the scientific community and the reading public.

However, many women were unhappy with Darwin's characterization of them, arguing that their inferior status was the result of social forces, not biology. One of his earliest female critics was Antoinette Brown Blackwell (1825–1921), the first woman ordained as a Christian minister in the United States. She had studied natural philosophy and metaphysics at Oberlin College in Ohio, and in her collection of essays, *Studies in General Science* (1869), she accepted the basic premise behind evolution. More important, she was

excited by the promise of Darwin's ideas; she believed that unfettered by traditional prejudice, evolutionary theory and scientific investigation would allow a reconsideration of women's rights and abilities.[63] However, she believed in a moral universe guided by a divine plan and that humans played a special role in God's plan.[64]

Some of Darwin's supporters, such as sociologist Herbert Spencer (1820–1903), applied Darwin's biological theories to social organization. These theorists, called Social Darwinists, used Darwin's ideas about the survival of the fittest (a phrase coined by Spencer) to explain social, sexual, economic, and racial differences. They argued for the superiority of the white race and the inferiority of Africans and Jews. Economic wealth and class privilege reflected moral worth and biological superiority. Based on that formula, women were less developed than men.

Rejecting the misogynist aspects of Darwinian thought, Charlotte Perkins Gilman (1860–1935) employed the essential components of Darwin's and Spencer's works in support of a women's activist agenda, albeit one limited to whites only. According to Gilman, evolution provided a scientific basis for the expansion of women's rights. In her treatise *Women and Economics: A Study in the Economic Relation Between Men and Women as a Factor in Social Evolution* (1898), Gilman bemoaned the fact that "Women have been checked, starved, aborted in human growth" and that men had limited women to merely a sexual role in society. However, industrial society had brought significant changes to male-female relations. Using the language of evolution, she went on to assert that "Now that it is no longer of advantage to society, the 'woman's movement' has set in; and the relation is changing under our eyes from year to year" (Chapters 4 and 7). Gilman also argued passionately against separate spheres: "As a natural consequence of our division of labor on sex-lines, giving to the woman the home and to the man the world in which to work, we have come to a dense prejudice in favor of the essential womanliness of the home duties, as opposed to the essential manliness of every other kind of work" (Chapter 11). Rather than bind them to the home, she believed that women's cooperative nature prepared them perfectly for the new economy.

Social Darwinism also attracted upper-class nationalist politicians who felt threatened by the growing political power of the working class and the fast pace of technological and economic change. Many Social Darwinists declared that welfare programs were fruitless because they could not change the evolutionary trajectory of the lower class and nonwhites. Some thinkers, such as Sir Francis Galton (1822–1911), who coined the term *eugenics* in 1885, believed that governments should encourage marriages and large families among the wealthy and gifted. His followers argued that the only solution to the high birthrate among the poor and less intelligent was birth control and family planning. Proponents of eugenics also employed the ideology of separate spheres, asserting that women had to be properly educated to be the mothers of superior races and that motherhood was a national duty. To prevent national or race suicide, white middle-class women had to be inculcated with the desire to have large families. As eugenicist Caleb Saleeby explained in his book *Parenthood and Race Culture* (1909), "the history of nations is determined not on the battlefield but in the nursery, and the battalions which give lasting victory are the battalions of babies."[65]

By asserting that social organization and gender roles resulted from biology, not culture, Darwin and his followers gave scientific validity to the ideology of separate spheres. Darwin's observations about the development of new species would not only remain central to modern science, but the application of his theories to society would also perpetuate and justify social and gender inequality into the next century.

## Sexology and Sexual Identity

Darwin's discussion of sexual selection and sex differences gave rise to the new science of sexology. Some doctors believed that women were passionless beings. In 1861, a British physician wrote, "the majority of women (happily for society) are not very much troubled with sexual feelings of any kind."[66] Indeed, many doctors believed that women's sexual arousal was dangerous, causing a variety of diseases from insanity to epilepsy, and that women who desired sex were more likely to become prostitutes and engage in socially deviant

behavior. By the end of the century, some physicians identified sexuality as a chief cause of men's and women's psychological problems.

Early psychologists and psychoanalysts pathologized women's sexuality. By defining some women's behavior as disease, doctors sought cures for their "afflictions." Cures and control often took the form of gynecological exams, drugs, and even clitoridectomies, the surgical removal of the clitoris. One historian estimated that in England between 1860 and 1866 when the practice was outlawed, six hundred women received clitoridectomies, often without their consent. London gynecologist Isaac Baker Brown reported curing a "Mrs. O" of her distaste for her husband by removing her clitoris. According to the doctor, "After two months treatment, she returned to her husband, resumed cohabitation, and stated that all her distaste had disappeared; soon she became pregnant, and resumed her place at the head of the table, and became a happy and healthy wife and mother."[67] From his perspective, only women devoid of sexual feelings could succeed in Victorian society.

Several male scholars looked beyond physical explanations for sexual problems and pioneered the new science of psychology. Richard von Krafft-Ebing (1840–1902), Henry Havelock Ellis (1859–1939), and Sigmund Freud (1856–1939) all explored the role of sexuality in human development and the causes of different sexual practices and problems.

Krafft-Ebing's interest in sexuality grew out of an interest in so-called sex-crimes. As a professor of psychiatry at Strasbourg, Krafft-Ebing identified and discussed sexual behaviors such as homosexuality, fetishism, sadism, and masochism—behaviors and acts he defined as deviant because they were nonreproductive. Sadism, he believed, was a pathological intensification of the masculine character while masochism was the pathological degeneration of the female character. He based his research on the premise that the sex drive was "the most important factor in social existence." Civilization came only when humans contained their lust with altruism and restraint. According to Krafft-Ebing, "Only characters endowed with strong wills are able to completely emancipate themselves from sensuality and share in the pure love from which springs the noblest joys of human life."[68] Although willing to explore the diversity of human behaviors, Krafft-Ebing was a man of his time, confident in his belief that the only natural sex was procreative sex.

Havelock Ellis, a British sexologist, accepted many of Krafft-Ebing's observations about the varieties of human sexual behavior but was less judgmental. Ellis was interested in the degree to which sex differences were socially or biologically constructed. In *Man and Woman* (1894), he concluded that men were naturally active while women were naturally passive. However, because more women deviated from this norm than men, civilization drew its inspiration from men.

Ellis's interest in human relationships led him to study homosexuality, which he believed could be both inborn and learned. He believed that society should accept inborn homosexuality, but that learned homosexuality might be curable. In describing homosexuality, he coined the term *sexual inversion*, which he defined as "sexual instinct tuned by inborn constitutional abnormality towards a person of the same sex." His use of the term abnormal was less a condemnation than an observation that homosexuality was statistically less common in the population than heterosexuality. According to Ellis, many prominent women in history had been "homosexual, bisexual, or at least, of pronounced male temperament" and that social norms that encouraged women to associate almost exclusively with other women fostered lesbianism.[69] He also argued that women's sex drives were weaker and more passive than men's, but that women enjoyed sexual feelings throughout their bodies, not just in their clitorises. Thus, women's sexual enjoyment was more diffuse than men's, which focused only on penile erection, making courtship a necessary part of women's sexuality.

Sigmund Freud (1856–1939) expanded on these ideas in his theories of personality and sexual development. He began his career as a specialist in nervous diseases, but at the time, most physicians believed that these problems were untreatable because they were caused by hereditary degeneration or lesions on the nerves. However, Freud had trained in France, where physicians appeared to be having some success with hypnosis. Returning to Vienna, he collaborated with his friend and fellow psychiatrist Josef Breuer (1841–1925), who believed that neurotic symptoms were the physical manifestations of repressed emotions or experiences and that these symptoms could be cured through hypnosis.

As a result of his early work with female patients, Freud came to believe that childhood sexual trauma caused many neuroses. By 1905, he argued that personality and sexual development began in infancy and progressed in stages that were defined by reactions to erogenous zones (mouth, then anus, and finally genitals). He revolutionized the understanding of human sexuality by asserting that infants were sexual beings and that masturbation was a natural part of infant and childhood sexuality. In his view, as a girl began to focus on her genitals as a source of sexual pleasure, she came to identify as a castrated male and began to suffer from what Freud called *penis envy* (a term that was first coined by Freud's colleague Karl Abraham). For Freud, successful female development resulted from transforming this envy into a desire for children. As a boy began to desire his mother sexually, Freud argued that he began to view his father as a rival for his mother's affection and feared that his father would punish him by removing his penis (Freud called this fear *castration anxiety*, although the term castration actually refers to the removal of the testicles and not the penis). Freud concluded that the healthy resolution of this *Oedipus conflict* required the boy to identify with his father and displace his desires for his mother onto a safer object, such as the girl next door. The resolution of the girl's Oedipal conflict was the same; she should identify with her mother and displace the desire for her father onto a safer object. Freud believed that castration anxiety was a great motivator for boys to identify with their fathers. However, because girls perceived themselves as already castrated and blamed their mothers for their loss, they would not identify as strongly with their mothers as boys would with their fathers. Since identification with the parent is critical for developing a sense of morality, Freud believed that women could not be as moral as men.

The bourgeois experience of heterosexuality and motherhood shaped many of Freud's ideas. In addition to believing that women were not as morally strong as men, he reduced many women's childhood traumas to fantasies, thereby denying women's experiences as causes of their suffering.

By claiming that a female patient's sexual assault by a family friend was really a fantasy, Freud blamed the patient for her illness and perpetuated the idea that women were hysterical, emotional, and unreliable. Yet, at the same time, Freud was willing to take women's sexuality seriously and he did not pathologize their sexual arousal.

## Sexual Realities

For all the theorizing about women's biological and social roles, the reality was quite different for most women. Working-class women could not afford the bourgeois luxury of remaining at home and demonstrated little interest in middle-class sexual morality. However, even upper-and middle-class women experienced much more complex sexual and emotional relationships than male sexologists understood.

Although Victorian culture idealized dominating husbands and asexual women living in separate spheres, many progressive authors, including Friedrich Schlegel (1772–1829) and Jane Austen (1775–1817), praised companionate marriages based on mutual respect and even sexual intimacy. German writer Louise Aston (1814–1871) described her unhappy arranged marriage in her 1847 novel *Aus dem Leben einer Frau* (*About the Life of a Wife*). Even as medical discourse argued that good women should have no interest in sex, many writers asserted that sexual intimacy was an important component of a happy marriage. In his best-selling instructional book *Monsieur, Madame, et Bébé* (*Mr., Mrs., and Baby*) (1886), French author Gustave Droz (1832–1895) celebrated sexual love between married men and women. The Danish play *A Doll's House* (first performed in 1880), written by Henrik Ibsen (1828–1906), in which the heroine, Nora, leaves her stifling husband and children in order to pursue personal fulfillment, was also important to discussions of women's sexuality. The play created controversy, and women across Europe debated about their social and sexual choices as a result.

Moreover, men were not always the focus of women's emotional attachments. Intimate relationships between women were an important part of nineteenth-century women's lives. Female friends came for visits that lasted many months. At finishing schools, and later colleges, women often shared

the same beds and wrote each other passionate letters. Women also fell in love. In 1778, despite their families' disapproval, two Irish women named Eleanor Butler (1739–1829) and Sarah Ponsonby (1755–1831) eloped to Wales, where they set up a household until Butler's death.[70] College professors at these women's schools shared homes and engaged in long-term relationships that Americans called "Boston marriages." Martha Carey Thomas, the president of Bryn Mawr College, preferred such living arrangements. In a letter to her mother, she posited, "If it were only possible for women to select women as well as men for a '[life's] love' . . . all reason for an intellectual woman's marriage [would] be gone"[71] (see **Women's Lives**: Martha Carey Thomas, Education Pioneer). Whatever the nature of these relationships, early nineteenth-century society did not sexualize them. Society understood female intimacy as a natural extension of female emotionalism and domestic life. With the exception of Austria, no country even had a legal category for female homosexuality, although male homosexuality was illegal across Europe.

The application of scientific study to sexuality changed how society and women viewed same-sex relationships. Although some continued to see women's same-sex desires as abnormal or even perverted, Havelock Ellis's discussions of homosexuality as a natural part of human sexuality allowed women to assume the new sexual identity of "lesbian" and claim sexual fulfillment from sex with women. By the 1890s, many cities, including Paris and Rome, had identifiable lesbian subcultures, and novelists such as Colette (1873–1954) celebrated love between women.

For historians, the sexual relationships and attitudes of working-class women are more difficult to recover because they left few sources. Novelists and moralists tended to assume that working-class sex was more animalistic. They often justified their claims based on the fact that working-class women had higher levels of illegitimate children and fewer working-class women married. However, these differences often reflected the legal barriers to marriage rather than inherent sexual or moral differences. Although many working women remained single or lived with other women, these relationships may have been economically motivated, but they might also have had strong sexual and emotional components.

## Martha Carey Thomas, Education Pioneer

Martha Carey Thomas (1857–1935) was a pioneer in women's education. The eldest child in a large and politically active Quaker family, she first attended a local Quaker school and then a Quaker boarding school in New York, where she studied Latin, Greek, mathematics, and literature. She then attended Cornell University in Ithaca, New York, which had just begun accepting women.

After graduation, Carey rejected marriage, believing that it entailed repeated pregnancies and stifled ambition. Eager to pursue a doctorate, Carey sought admission to the Johns Hopkins University, but the university refused to allow her to attend classes with men. Undeterred, she enrolled at the University of Leipzig in Germany. She took with her as a traveling companion Mary "Mamie" Qwinn (1861–ca. 1945).

Unable to earn a degree at Leipzig, Carey transferred to the University of Zurich in 1882. She graduated summa cum laude, the first women to do so, and returned to the United States in 1884 the first American woman to earn a doctorate. It is now clear that Mamie wrote much of Carey's thesis, and when Carey began teaching, Mamie composed many of Carey's lectures. Mamie never received credit for her work.

Carey wanted to be president of Bryn Mawr, the Quaker women's college founded by her father and uncle, but the trustees instead hired her to be dean and professor of English. From this position, Carey built Bryn Mawr into a secular intellectual center, rather than a provincial Quaker school. She envisioned a Leipzig in America,[1] where women would meet the same academic standards as men's universities.

In 1895, Carey became president of Bryn Mawr, a position she held until her retirement in 1922. Although the trustees did not approve of Carey's secular vision or her lavish personal spending, Thomas proved to be a successful fundraiser, established a rigorous curriculum, and allowed students to create the first student government in the United States. She built Bryn Mawr into one of the foremost centers for white women's higher education.

Carey's personal life was remarkably unconventional. Mamie lived with Carey and taught English literature, eventually receiving her PhD from Bryn Mawr. Carey likened her relationship with Mamie to marriage. However, Carey was not content to love only Mamie and pursued Mary Garrett (1854–1915), the daughter of a railroad magnate. This new relationship made Mamie unhappy, and Mary resented Carey's time away from her. Carey's letters make her passion for both women clear. In 1895, Mamie left Carey for a male English professor, and Mary Garrett moved in with Carey, placing her considerable fortune at Carey's disposal.

Through Mary's influence, Carey began to support women's suffrage and expand her interest in women's education beyond Bryn Mawr. She and several others founded the Bryn Mawr School for Girls in Baltimore, which trained students for admission to Bryn Mawr. In 1889, Carey and some of these same women raised $100,000 to endow a medical school at the Johns Hopkins University, stipulating that it must admit women. Although unenthusiastic about coeducation, Johns Hopkins' trustees could not refuse such a generous gift. Thomas's devotion to women's education had its limits, however. She refused to accept blacks and Jews to either Bryn Mawr College or the Bryn Mawr School, believing they were morally and socially unfit.

After her retirement, Thomas spent her last years traveling and spending most of Garrett's fortune. All her life, Carey ignored nineteenth-century society's gender and sexual expectations. She was determined to obtain the best education possible and provide a high standard of learning for younger generations of women. Both publicly and privately, Carey Thomas lived according to her own rules.

---

[1] Helen Lefkowitz Horowitz, *The Power and Passion of M. Carey Thomas* (New York: Alfred A. Knopf, 1994), 158–159.

Source: Helen Lefkowitz Horowitz, *The Power and Passion of M. Carey Thomas* (New York: Alfred A. Knopf, 1994).

It is difficult to know how women felt about these issues. In the 1890s, American physician Clelia Mosher (1863–1940) began a thirty-year survey of a group of forty-five middle-class married American women. The majority of these women, forty-four of whom were college educated, expressed desires for sexual intimacy and most reported having had at least one orgasm. Most had sex on average once a week, and while some claimed they would have liked it less often, most declared it important to their marriages. One woman wrote, "Men love their wives more if they continue this relation and the highest devotion is based upon it, a very beautiful thing and I am glad nature gave it to us."[72] This limited evidence suggests that many women did not believe that women should repress their sexuality.

Changes in how women expressed their sexuality both initiated and reflected demographic changes in Western society. Women gave birth less often, changing how they interacted with their children and with their partners. At the beginning of the century, women had as many as twelve pregnancies, with as many as five or six children surviving. Emblematic of the amount of time women spent either pregnant or in confinement was the British queen Victoria who had nine pregnancies in seventeen years. By the end of the century, Jewish and Protestant women had successfully begun to limit their fertility to only three or four children.

A variety of birth control methods made fertility control easier. Condoms were introduced in 1844 after manufacturers learned to vulcanize rubber, but they remained too expensive for the working class, and the public associated them with prostitutes. Dutch physician Aletta Jacobs (1851–1929) opened Europe's first birth control clinic in 1882 in the Netherlands, where she dispensed the newly invented "Dutch cap," a cervical cap. Nonetheless, coitus interruptus (early withdrawal by the male) and abstinence were probably the most common. One German Jewish man wrote in his memoirs that his wife insisted on "protected years" when the couple practiced abstinence so as to space the births of their children.[73]

Women were divided over access to birth control. German socialists Clara Zetkin (1857–1933) and Luise Zietz (1865–1922) believed that birth control was a decadent bourgeois practice. However, French activist Madeleine Pelletier (1874–1939) believed that women should have access to birth control and even abortions in the first trimester. In Britain, the first woman pharmacist, Alice Vickery (1844–1929), drawing from both a women's activist and eugenics perspective, advocated "preventatives" for working-class women because too many children contributed to poverty. Most governments opposed such open discussions of "obscene" topics. Women would have to wait until the next century before birth control became readily available.

The turmoil of industrialization led to the formation of new ideologies of gender and sex that identified women with home and men with the public sphere. New scientific theories both justified this gendered division of life and provoked debate about the relationship between biology and society's expectations of women. However, for all the theorizing, women's behavior belied most men's ideas about female sexuality, which was as diverse and complex as the women themselves.

## PIETY AND CHARITY

Alongside the mechanization and capitalist fervor of the Industrial Revolution, the nineteenth century witnessed a significant resurgence of religious activity by middle-class women. Women found spiritual comfort and outlets for their reforming energies in both Catholicism and many Protestant denominations. At the same time, Judaism underwent significant changes, offering women new styles of worship and new ideas about the relationship between religious and secular life. Across denominations, religious devotion played an important role in the expansion of women's charitable activities.

### Religious Revival

In the wake of Napoleon's defeat, the Catholic Church reasserted its place in European society, leading many women to take religious vows. Between 1800 and 1880, some 200,000 Frenchwomen became nuns, while in Germany the number of nuns increased from 7,794 in 1866 to almost 50,000 in 1908.[74] For the most part, these women joined new monastic orders dedicated to public charity and missionary work. In contrast to the seclusion of most early modern religious women, nineteenth-century Europeans believed that women were particularly well suited for mission work because they were naturally driven to serve others and deny their own needs. In fact, many new orders worked specifically with the growing urban population and supported themselves rather than living in cloisters. Nuns ran schools, collected donations, and manufactured and sold the religious items that decorated pious laywomen's homes. One of the most popular of these new orders was the Little Sisters of the Poor, founded in 1843 by Frenchwoman Jeanne Jugan (1792–1879). In particular, the Sisters aided elderly poor women displaced by industrialization and urban expansion. As Irish immigrants flooded American and British cities, and overwhelmed urban parishes and their priests, the Irish Sisters of Charity (1815) and the Sisters of Mercy (1831) established hospitals, orphanages, and schools for needy children.

Women also played an important role in spreading new forms of Protestant devotion. German women formed religious congregations independent of both the Catholic and Protestant Churches. The German Free Churches vigorously promoted women's equality. One group, the German-Catholics, a splinter group of the Roman Catholic Church, only acknowledged marriages based on mutual affection and respect. Marriages arranged for political and economic purposes would be invalid. German women's activist Louise Dittmar (1807–1884), who founded a Free congregation, stated, "Our church is the world, our religion is reason, our Christianity is humanity, our creed is freedom, our worship, the truth."[75] Under the guise of religious discussion, members of the German-Catholic or Free Evangelical Church met with agnostics, freethinkers, and Jews to debate political reform, family life, and economics. Women joined these Free congregations in numbers greater than any other movement of the time. Another German women's activist, Malwida von Meysenbug (1816–1903), declared that joining a Free congregation "separated me forever from my past; by it I publicly renounced the Protestant church and joined a truly democratic society."[76] Activist journalist Louise Otto (1819–1895) believed that, "It is

above all the religious movement to which we are indebted for the rapid advance of female participation in the issues of the times."[77]

In the United States, Mary Baker Eddy (1821–1910) became the first woman to found her own denomination, the Church of Christ, Scientist (or Christian Science). Eddy suffered for many years with incurable illnesses. In desperation, she turned to the Bible for healing, and gradually she eschewed physicians for faith in God's healing powers. In 1875, she published her theology and healing system in her book *Science and Health with Key to Scriptures*, and four years later she founded a church in Boston, Massachusetts. After ten years as the pastor, she reorganized the church and allowed both women and men to lead church services. Eddy promoted her ideas by founding the Massachusetts Metaphysical College in 1881 and a monthly magazine called *The Christian Science Journal* in 1883. In 1908, she founded the internationally respected newspaper the *Christian Science Monitor*.

## Women and Judaism

Divisions among European Jews also created new possibilities for women. Hoping to counteract rising anti-Semitism through assimilation, many Jews were attracted to the Reform movement, which rejected many traditional Jewish rituals including the need for circumcision, kosher butchering, and the mikvah, the ritual bath after menstruation and childbirth. The first Reform services took place in Seesen, Germany, in 1810, followed by the founding of the first Reform synagogue in 1818 in Hamburg. Reform services made religious practice more appealing to assimilated Jews by adopting vernacular prayers, organ music, and family seating. Jewish reformers also advocated giving women greater roles in synagogue worship. Abraham Geiger (1810–1874), a founder of Reform Judaism, argued that there should be "no shaping of public worship, in form or content that closed the doors of the Temple to women."[78] Although by 1900, 85 percent of Jews in Germany followed Reform practices, these reforms were slow to take hold.[79] Women's religious practice remained largely a private affair.

In response to the Reform movement, Samson Raphael Hirsch (1808–1888) led a movement called Orthodox Judaism or Neo-Orthodoxy that reasserted the importance of traditional Jewish practices in the modern world. Hirsch's work countered both the popular urban-based Reform movement as well as government demands that Jewish children attend state schools, where they received a secular or Christian-based education. The religious schools in Germany that Hirsch established to offset state-mandated curricula were the first Jewish schools for girls.

Many Jews in eastern Europe still lived in rural villages where Hasidism, an eighteenth-century movement, had taken hold. *Hasid* means pious and developed out of the teachings of Israel ben Eliezer (ca. 1700–1760), known as Ba'al Shem Tov, a Polish Jew who spread a new form of prayer in which the believer suppressed his or her own individuality so that God could speak through him or her. Across Poland and Lithuania, his followers adopted behavior and dress that distinguished them from other Jewish communities. They wore rustic peasant clothing and broad fur hats as signs of simplicity and prayed loudly and joyfully. Life revolved around Jewish rituals and followers relied on guidance from the community's spiritual leader, or *rebbe*.

Hasidic Jews believed in a strict separation of men and women in work and education and the preservation of girls' modesty. By the age of three, girls wore long stockings, long sleeves on their dresses or blouses, and high-necked collars. Generally, Hasidim did not believe that women and girls had the same intellectual capabilities as boys and men, so girls received only enough education to familiarize them with the Bible, dietary laws, and religious holidays. Boys and girls remain segregated until marriage.

Despite these constraints, Hannah Rochel Verbermacher, known as the Maiden of Ludmir (modern-day Vladimir Volinski, Ukraine), became a Hasidic holy woman. She is the only woman in the three-hundred-year history of Hasidism to function as a rebbe in her own right. Born around 1809, much of her life remains clouded in folklore. Her followers venerated her as a master of the Kabbalah (Jewish mystical texts), teacher, and visionary, but her detractors believed that she was possessed, crazy, or irrelevant. Verbermacher broke traditional gender roles by building her own prayer house and holding gatherings, healing the ill, wearing the *tallit* (prayer shawl), and refusing to marry. Eventually, she immigrated to Ottoman-controlled Palestine, where she reestablished herself as a holy woman.[80]

## Women and Philanthropy

The revitalization of religious life and the growing numbers of urban poor encouraged middle-class women of all faiths to devote their time and energy to charitable work. Many saw charity as an extension of mothering. They established homes for unwed mothers and worked in hospitals and orphanages. Women advocated on behalf of a variety of causes from antianimal cruelty campaigns, which worked to end dog and cock fighting, to groups that encouraged vegetarianism. Most women believed that charity was both their Christian responsibility and a natural extension of their mothering and domestic duties into the public sphere. However, such work also increased women's public visibility, as they raised money and petitioned for social change, went door-to-door seeking funds, and spoke at public meetings to mixed audiences. Critics condemned such behavior as inappropriate and unfeminine.

Guided by their Christian faith, many women established their own charitable organizations. Amalie Sieveking (1794–1862), the daughter of a prominent Hamburg family, founded the Female Association in 1832. Modeled on the Catholic Daughters of Charity, this group of upper-middle-class Protestant women visited poor women to teach them self-discipline, frugality, and personal piety. Sieveking's organization was very innovative for Germany, where women could not engage in politics and the government tolerated no criticism. Her model for women's charity quickly spread to other cities. By 1848, more than forty-five organizations were affiliated with Sieveking's Female Association.[81]

The religious focus of Sieveking's work compelled her to refuse membership to Charlotte Paulson (1799–1862) in 1844 because she suspected Paulson of atheism. In response, in 1849, Paulson formed her own organization, the Women's Association for the Support of Poor Relief. Paulson committed herself and her organization to religious ecumenism. Her association attracted radical Protestants and local Jewish groups such as the Society for Social and Political Interests of the Jews, rather than Sieveking's wealthy women. Paulson's group made home visits, and ran a daycare center and a school for working women's children.[82]

Across Europe, as many as one hundred thousand infants were abandoned annually, and epidemics of cholera, illegitimacy, and widespread poverty added to the numbers of orphans.[83] Traditionally, nuns cared for these children, but even the rapidly expanding religious orders could not meet the growing need. Marie Béquet de Vienne (1854–1913) dedicated her life to preventing women from aborting or abandoning their babies. Believing that a strong maternal bond would curtail this behavior, she founded the Society of Maternal Breastfeeding in 1876. Members of this society worked with midwives and visited poor new mothers regardless of their marital or religious status.[84] They provided clothes and milk bottles if the mother could not breastfeed. In 1886, Béquet de Vienne founded a shelter for abandoned pregnant women and new mothers. Her *Asile Maternel* accepted both married and single women. It began with only twenty beds, but by 1910, it had doubled in size. Patients learned hygiene, childcare, and morality. The home provided them with paid work and helped them find jobs when they were ready to leave. It also provided daycare facilities for former residents when they found jobs. Between 1886 and 1906, 12,314 women and 11,893 infants lived at the Asile Maternel.[85] Indeed, many governments relied on women's charitable activities. In 1875, the Spanish minister of the interior created a Women's Committee to assist the government in welfare matters, encourage the foundation of more charitable organizations, and supervise the running of the Foundling Hospital.[86]

Women who conducted home visits and ran orphanages or homes for unwed mothers regularly confronted the problems of disease, the lack of good medical care, and inefficiency or corruption in hospitals. Medical care improved considerably during the nineteenth century, but it remained outside the reach of the poor and indigent. Their contact with medicine was confined to the chronically underfunded poorhouses or charity hospitals where nurses had no training. Florence Nightingale (1820–1910) believed that with proper training, nursing could improve health care and provide meaningful and respectable work for legions of unemployed women.

Born to a wealthy and very religious Unitarian family, Nightingale felt called by God to help the needy. Despite her family's considerable resistance, she volunteered in a London hospital during the 1854 cholera epidemic. The high quality of her work earned her respect, and she and a group of nurses traveled to the Crimea to address the shocking lack of medical care for British troops serving in the Crimean War. She returned home a national hero and parlayed her renown into campaigns to reform military hospitals and to make nursing a respectable career for women. Women's problems, she argued, resulted from their own laziness, and she decried women who retreated into helplessness, subservience, and unhappy marriages. By the end of the century, Nightingale Nurses set the standard for care and nursing had become an acceptable, even desirable occupation for middle-class women.

Women of color faced additional obstacles when trying to perform charitable work. One example is Mary Seacole (1805–1881), the daughter of a Jamaican mother and a Scottish father. Seacole, who learned nursing from her mother, traveled widely and augmented her traditional medical knowledge with Western medicine. In 1854, she went to England to offer her services as an army nurse, but the War Office refused to meet with her because of her race. Undeterred, she financed her own travel to the Crimea, where she established a hotel for convalescing soldiers and used the money she earned to treat soldiers wounded on the battlefield.

Alcoholism's link to poverty and domestic violence drove many women in both Europe and the United States to support the temperance movement, which had its roots in Evangelical Christianity. Whisky, gin, and beer were inexpensive, and tavern life was deeply entrenched in the working-class and rural cultures. The movement began with a message of moderation, but by the 1830s, the two major U.S. temperance groups, the American Temperance Society and the American Temperance Union, advocated total prohibition.

Although women participated in the movement from the beginning, the male leadership denied women leadership and influence. After the U.S. Civil War (1861–1865), midwestern women took the cause into their own hands in a social protest movement called the Women's Crusade. Ultimately, fifty-six thousand women participated in protests against liquor stores and saloons. The enthusiasm generated by the Crusade led to the founding of the Women's Christian Temperance Union (WCTU) in 1874. Members saw their mission as an extention of women's need to protect their home and their children.

In 1883, Frances Willard (1839–1898) won the presidency of the WCTU, and under her guidance, the organization internationalized. Willard's political interests were wide-ranging, and she added women's suffrage and drug abuse to the causes the WCTU's international campaign supported. Willard worked closely with her longtime companion and the WCTU's secretary, Anna Gordon. Under WCTU's patronage, Mary Clement Leavitt (1830–1912) traveled the world for eight years spreading the message of temperance. By 1897, the WCTU had five hundred thousand members worldwide (see Chapter 11).

Some of the prohibitionists' strategies turned violent. After a brief and disastrous marriage to an alcoholic, American Carrie Nation (1846–1911) embraced the temperance movement and joined the WCTU. Beginning in 1900, Nation and other members closed down saloons in her home of Medicine Lodge, Kansas, by holding prayer meetings. Then she and other women went to neighboring Kiowa and attacked three bars with stones, bricks, and bottles. Because the saloons she destroyed were illegal, authorities did not prosecute Nation. As she continued her campaigns, she used her famous hatchet to attack bars and liquor stores.

By the end of the century, many women dedicated themselves to work in the settlement houses that were springing up in cities. First established by Anglican priest Samuel Barnett (1844–1913) and his wife, Henrietta (1851–1936), in 1884, settlement houses quickly spread to other European countries and the United States. The concept of a settlement house grew out of Barnett's familiarity with women's charity work, which emphasized

neighborliness and community. Barnett believed that by living and working among the poor and working class, the middle class could both teach and learn from their working-class neighbors. Unlike urban missions, such as the Salvation Army, which promoted religious conversions, settlement houses fostered mutual understanding and cooperation without a religious agenda. The movement quickly attracted women, and many women's settlement houses soon opened. By 1900, there were approximately one hundred settlement houses in the United States.[87]

Jane Addams (1860–1935) founded Hull House in Chicago in 1886. Her work attracted graduates of the new women's colleges. Hull House, and many other settlement houses, ran daycare centers, soup kitchens, participated in cooperatives, taught first aid classes, and ran discussion groups. Addams also encouraged residents to work on their own projects and follow their own interests. Addams resisted the label of social worker, believing that both the residents and their neighbors were learning from each other and that Hull House was not a charity. In 1892, Jane Addams integrated Hull House by admitting African American Harriet Rice, a graduate of Wellesley College and a physician. Other houses were not as comfortable with racial integration, but the settlement movement was not an exclusively white project. Middle-class African Americans participated in the movement almost from the beginning. In 1890, Janie Porter Barrett (1865–1948), an African American and graduate of the Hampton Institute, opened the Locust Street Social Settlement in Hampton, Virginia.

The nineteenth century witnessed a religious revival in which women played prominent roles. Motivated by religious enthusiasm and the shocking poverty and crime of the industrial city, middle-class women dedicated much of their time and energy to charitable works, founding philanthropic organizations and inventing innovative ways to address social problems. As we will see in the next chapter, this emphasis on charitable work had important implications, drawing women into politics and influencing the trajectory of the women's movement.

## EDUCATING WOMEN

Western society's association of women and domesticity often prevented women from obtaining more than the most basic education. Yet, by the middle of the nineteenth century, reformers encouraged the expansion of women's education at all levels, arguing that education made women better mothers, wives, and citizens. However, women's increased access to education had some unintended social consequences, as graduates often rejected traditional female roles and strove to use their education to change society or pursue careers, including the fields of science and medicine.

## Educational Reform and Higher Education for Women

Because of the emphasis on middle-class domesticity, many parents lost interest in formal academic training for their daughters. Most countries did not require even an elementary education for girls. Although Prussia made elementary education compulsory for girls in 1812 and Denmark in 1814, the rest of the West did not address this issue until late in the century. At the beginning of the century, some schools provided vocational training, such as that provided by Madame Lemire's School of Fine Arts for Women, which trained girls to become porcelain artists. The education of middle-class girls depended on their parents' interests and concerns. They might be educated at home with their brothers as many nineteenth-century women's movement reformers were, but they might also be sent to finishing schools where music, embroidery, French, and etiquette dominated the curriculum. Families expected finishing schools to replicate the family, with the headmistress acting as the surrogate mother. These schools did not offer academic training because such programs bore no relationship to family life.[88] In Spain and Italy, girls could also attend convent schools, but these institutions emphasized devotional practices rather than scholarship. Many wanted women to obtain the cultural benefits of higher learning, but no one expected middle- or working-class women to have careers.

The situation was quite different in the United States, where secondary and college education had become more common for American women. Reformers argued that women's education was critical to a democracy. In a petition to the New York State legislature to fund her school, the Troy Seminary, Emma Willard (1787–1870) pointed out that the Greek and Roman republics failed to educate their women and, as a result, both failed as governments.

Reformers differed over whether women's education should be single sex or coeducational. The Vassar brothers, who founded Vassar College in 1865, believed that women needed sexually segregated schools. After the U.S. Civil War, members of the African American community began founding women's colleges, and in 1881, Spelman College opened in Atlanta, Georgia. However, Evangelical Christians established a number of coeducational schools, such as Oberlin in Ohio (1833) and Carleton in Minnesota (1866), designed to prepare students for missionary work, often in China; and state universities, whose charters also enshrined republican sentiments, began admitting women.

Progress was slower in Europe. In 1849, sympathetic professors at the University of Zurich in Switzerland began admitting women to lectures. Although few Swiss women took advantage of this privilege, many foreign women did. Between 1864 and 1872, 203 women from six different countries enrolled at the university, 148 of whom were Russian.[89] Russian women reformers saw science and technology as key to transforming their nation. In 1867, Nadeshda Suslova (1843–1918), the daughter of freed serfs, became the first woman to graduate with a doctorate in medicine. She had begun her education in Saint Petersburg, where reforms had opened university lectures to women. However, when student protests following the abolition of serfdom caused the government to shut down the university, radicals, including Suslova, who had not been exiled to Siberia fled to western Europe. Zurich's openness attracted other female students. American reformer Martha Carey Thomas received her doctorate from the University of Zurich in 1882 (see **Women's Lives**: Martha Carey Thomas, Education Pioneer). Upon returning to the United States, Carey Thomas took a position at the new women's college, Bryn Mawr, in Pennsylvania and became its president in 1895. During her tenure, she fought to give her students the same curriculum as men's colleges.

In England, the Taunton Commission's 1867 report attacked the weaknesses of girls' education, providing women's activists with ammunition for reform. Like Carey Thomas, Emily Davies (1830–1921) believed that the only way to improve women's education was to provide them with the same educational opportunities as men. Unlike Thomas, she had received only a minimal education and often felt hampered by her lack of intellectual preparation. She established Girton College in 1869 outside of Cambridge and convinced university authorities to allow her students to sit for the same examinations as the male students, although they would not receive degrees. Davies's insistence that women receive the same education as men led to rivalry with Professor

**NADESHDA SUSLOVA.** In 1867, Nadeshda Suslova, the daughter of serfs, became the first women to receive a Ph.D. She wanted to use her medical training to help the Russian peasants. *(University of Zurich.)*

Henry Sidgwick (1838–1900). He believed that the Cambridge curriculum, which emphasized classics, was outdated and that students needed to study natural and social sciences. He wanted to use the introduction of women's colleges as an opportunity to reform the entire university curriculum. Sidgwick founded Cambridge's second women's college in 1871, which became Newnham College. Reforms at Oxford led to the founding of two women's colleges there in the late 1870s.

Europeans often commented on how emancipated American women were and how daring their coeducational colleges, but only Thomas Holloway (1800–1883) attempted to emulate American education. Impressed with Vassar's philanthropic backing and the size of its campus, he hoped to bring these advantages to British women. In 1879, he opened a women's college, Royal Holloway, later admitted as part of the University of London.[90]

Women's colleges on both sides of the Atlantic imitated male college life. College administrators encouraged sports to foster competition and to demonstrate that college life did not make women sick. They discouraged wild fashions and uncontrolled emotions. Clubs tested women's leadership and engaged them in social activism. Many of the first generation of female college students became teachers, worked in settlement houses, or trained as doctors and social workers. Influenced by pioneers like Carey Thomas, many women eschewed marriage in favor of careers, financial independence, and the companionship of other women. Between 1885 and 1910, 62 percent of Bryn Mawr graduates pursued graduate school, 90 percent worked for a salary at least briefly, and only 45 percent married.[91] Their life choices differed significantly from other women in American society.

However, by the end of the century, attitudes again changed, as critics claimed that college made women mannish and unmarriageable. In 1873, Harvard professor and physician Dr. Edward Clark published his *Sex in Education: Or a Fair Chance for the Girls*, in which he argued that education would permanently damage women's reproductive organs. Many graduates of the new coeducational colleges found life after college difficult because they had been taught not to conform to traditional notions of femininity. By the 1890s, women's journals began promoting a new image of the college woman as feminine, lively, and healthy, but not too studious or serious. Magazines published lively stories of the pranks and parties that made up the college women's lives. Descriptions of cozy dormitory rooms and fashionable clothes softened the dour image of the old-maid college student.[92]

Despite the fact that women's journals often negatively portrayed education as promoting singleness, more women than ever flocked to colleges and universities. However, influenced by these negative stereotypes, the second generation of college women had a very different experience. In addition to the traditional curriculum that included Latin, Greek, and mathematics, women at many schools could take home economics and sanitation science courses, which prepared them for middle-class domestic life. By the second decade of the twentieth century, 67 percent of Bryn Mawr's graduates married and fewer went to graduate school or worked outside the home.[93]

## Women and Science at the Turn of the Century

Over the course of the nineteenth century, scientists made many important discoveries, from new comets and stars to bacteria and germs. Scientists made most of these discoveries in research universities, not in private laboratories. Although science continued to be a masculine endeavor, as women began attending college in larger numbers, they increasingly demanded that schools include science in their curricula. Educational reformers believed that science would make women better mothers and citizens and would offer them important career opportunities.

Despite gains in undergraduate science education, graduate education remained out of the reach of many women. German universities, which had some of the best scientists and facilities, refused to admit women. In fact, an 1804 Bavarian law actually prevented women from studying science. Thus, although administrators of the new women's colleges wanted to hire the best-trained female teachers, few women had the required academic credentials. Many of the earliest female science professors, such as noted astronomer Maria Mitchell (1818–1889) who taught at Vassar College, lacked

formal science training. Mitchell studied with her father and, in 1847, charted and calculated the position of a new comet and then observed it. This feat won her fame and a gold medal from the king of Denmark, but until the founding of Vassar College in 1865, she worked as a part-time librarian. To help alleviate the problems of female scientists, Cambridge University's two women's colleges, Girton and Newnham, pooled their resources and prevailed upon sympathetic male professors at the university to help them build the Balfour Biological Laboratory in 1881. It provided women students with the most up-to-date equipment and an important meeting place, since the university continued to exclude women from its scientific societies.

Although women excelled in the world's most rigorous scientific graduate programs, most could not find employment as scientists. Teaching jobs at women's colleges were the best jobs for women scientists, despite heavy teaching loads and limited or nonexistent research budgets. Minimal laboratory or observatory facilities made it difficult for professors to continue their research, and male-dominated research universities refused to hire women, no matter how qualified. To make a living at science, many women accepted low-paying jobs in data and specimen collecting or mathematical analysis. In the United States, women often worked as "computers" in observatories where they made tedious astronomical calculations. Many British women opted for teaching careers at secondary schools rather than take that type of work. Despite these obstacles, Elizabeth Knight Britton (1858–1934) became an expert on mosses. When she married a Columbia University professor, she was put in charge of the botany department's moss collection. Her work led her to be the only female charter member of the Botanical Society of America.

For Russian women, scientific education went hand in hand with radical activism. They wanted to instigate revolution by providing former serfs with better medical treatment, nutrition, sanitation, and farming techniques. From the 1860s to the 1880s, Russia had more licensed women physicians than any other European country. Maria Bokova-Sechenova (1839–1929), who had trained with Nadeshda Suslova in Zurich, worked as a researcher in the Russian Academies of Science and

Medicine. When she inherited a small estate from her grandmother, she turned to agronomy to improve crop yields. Russia needed women researchers' scientific and medical expertise, especially after its humiliating loss in the Crimean War, but feared their radical politics. In 1873, the government made it difficult for women to obtain an education at home or abroad, and graduates found it difficult to get jobs. Award-winning mathematician Sofia Kovalevskaia (1850–1891) taught in Sweden because her political activism made it impossible for her to teach in Russia.

Although women had to fight for science education, medicine seemed less problematic, as women were traditionally associated with healing and caregiving. In 1848, Elizabeth Blackwell (1821–1910) gained admission to Geneva Medical College in New York. She believed that women's modesty prevented them from seeking medical care, dooming them to a lifetime of sickness and poor health. She also argued that women's natural sympathy would make them better physicians. However, once Blackwell completed her studies, hospitals prevented her from obtaining the necessary clinical experience. She had to move to Paris in order to work in the public maternity hospital. While some colleagues resisted her presence, her hard work also won her supporters. Blackwell returned to the United States and established her own practice. In 1857, she founded the New York Infirmary for Indigent Women and Children, and in 1868, she established the Women's Medical College of the New York Infirmary with her sister Emily, who had also become a physician. Gradually other medical schools for women opened across the United States, and by 1900, women made up 4 to 5 percent of American physicians, a figure that remained constant until the 1960s.[94]

Blackwell's medical ideas reveal the persistence of very traditional notions of medical care. Blackwell was drawn less to the science of medicine than to the nurturing of patients. She believed that the behavior of the person contributed to the progress of disease. Doctors had to treat the whole person, a notion that included addressing their patients' morality. However, Blackwell's ideas clashed with the discoveries in bacteriology that identified germs as the cause of disease, causing tension with another prominent female physi-

cian, Dr. Mary Putnam Jacobi (1842–1906). Trained at the Women's Medical College in Philadelphia, Jacobi continued her studies in Paris, where Louis Pasteur (1822–1895) had discovered germs and was making rapid advances in vaccinations. In 1871, Jacobi returned to the United States and went to work at Blackwell's medical school. She wanted to bring the new science to her practice but the two physicians disagreed over the future of medicine. Several prominent Boston women asked Jacobi to compete for the Boylston Medical Prize for 1876. The topic that year was Edward Clark's book *Sex in Education* and the effects of menstruation on women. Jacobi used the latest methods of statistical analysis to prove Clark wrong. Because the essays were submitted anonymously, the judges did not know she was a woman and awarded her the prize.

During the last half of the nineteenth century, women's access to education expanded dramatically. Women in the United States were the first to benefit from the creation of secondary schools and colleges for women, and gradually, European women gained entry to prominent educational institutions. As a part of their studies, female students demanded more science instruction. However, male-dominated research institutions demonstrated little interest in mining the intellectual and creative capabilities of women scientists. In fact, European governments were often threatened by women's social and intellectual aspirations. In the long run, women would make important achievements in science, but as those disciplines accepted more women, they earned less prestige and lower wages than men.

## CONCLUSION

From dairywomen to college girls, women's lives underwent tremendous changes during the nineteenth century. Working-class women found their lives altered as their work took them out of their homes and away from their families. Work also brought women to cities where they enjoyed new opportunities for leisure. The new theory of evolution and the new science of psychology tried to justify traditional expectations for women's behavior, but few women in the new urban industrial society remained at home and out of the public eye. In fact, women used their new visibility to work for social reform and to demand better educations. In the next chapter, we will explore women's involvement in the changing world of nineteenth-century politics.

## NOTES

1. Anna Clark, *Struggle for the Breeches: Gender and the Making of the British Working Class* (Berkeley: University of California Press, 1995), 120, 122.

2. Mary Jo Maynes, *Taking the Hard Road: Life Course in French and German Worker's Autobiographies in the Era of Industrialization* (Chapel Hill: University of North Carolina Press, 1995), 122.

3. Quoted in Maynes, 121–122.

4. Quoted in Elinor Accampo, *Industrialization, Family Life, and Class Relations: Saint Chamond, 1815–1914* (Berkeley: University of California Press, 1989), 96.

5. Quoted in Louise A. Tilly and Joan W. Scott, *Women, Work, and Family* (New York: Holt, Rinehart and Winston, 1978), 64.

6. "The Condition of the Operatives," *Voice of Industry* (March 26, 1847) in *The Factory Girls*, ed. Philip S. Foner (Urbana: University of Illinois Press, 1977), 87–88.

7. Adrian Shubert, *A Social History of Modern Spain* (London: Unwin Hyman, 1990), 40.

8. Judith DeGroat, "The Public Nature of Women's Work: Definitions and Debates During the Revolution of 1848," *French Historical Studies* 20:1 (1997): 35.

9. Joan W. Scott, "The Woman Worker," in *A History of Women: Emerging Feminism from Revolution to World War*, ed. Geneviève Fraisse and Michelle Perrot (Cambridge, MA: Harvard University Press, 1993), 418.

10. DeGroat, 34.

11. Deborah Simonton, *A History of European Women's Work: 1700 to the Present* (London: Routledge, 1998), 97–98.

12. Katharina Schlegel, "Mistress and Servant in Nineteenth-Century Hamburg: Employer/Employee Relationships in Domestic Service, 1880–1914," *History Workshop* 15 (1983): 60–61.

13. Schlegel, 61.

14. Simonton, 104.

15. Theresa M. McBride, *The Domestic Revolution: The Modernisation of Household Service in England and France, 1820–1920* (London: Croom Helm, 1976), chap. 1.

16. Quoted in Katrina Honeyman, *Women, Gender, and Industrialization in England* (New York: St. Martin's Press, 2000), 80.

17. Quoted in Elda Gentili Zappi, *If Eight Hours Seem Too Few: Mobilization of Women Workers in the Italian Rice Fields* (Albany, NY: SUNY Press, 1991), 29.

18. Steven L. Hoch, *Serfdom and Social Control in Russia: Petrovskoe, a Village in Tambov* (Chicago: University of Chicago Press, 1986), 3.

19. David Moon, *Abolition of Serfdom in Russia: 1762–1907* (Harlow, England: Longman, 2001), 93.

20. Roy Porter, *London: A Social History* (Cambridge, MA: Harvard University Press, 1994), 186; Ira Rosenwaike, *Population History of New York City* (Syracuse, NY: Syracuse University Press, 1972), 58, 90.

21. Christine Stansell, *City of Women: Sex and Class in New York, 1789–1860* (New York: Alfred A. Knopf, 1986), 83.

22. Rachel G. Fuchs and Leslie Page Moch, "Pregnant, Single, and Far from Home: Migrant Women in Nineteenth-Century Paris," *American Historical Review* 95:4 (October 1990): 1010.

23. Quoted in Erica Rappaport, *Shopping for Pleasure: Women and the Making of London's West End* (Princeton, NJ: Princeton University Press, 2000), 123.

24. Quoted in Robert Atwan, Donald McQuade, and John W. Wright, *Edsels, Luckies, Fridgidaires: Advertising the American Way* (New York: Dell, 1979), 151–151.

25. Quoted in Rappaport, 82.

26. Rappaport, 85.

27. W. Scott Haine, *The World of the Paris Café* (Baltimore: The Johns Hopkins University Press, 1996), 199–200.

28. Haine, 201.

29. Porter, 291; John R. Harris, *The Great Exhibition* (Stroud, England: Sutton, 1999) 171.

30. Leora Auslander, "The Gendering of Consumer Practices in Nineteenth-Century France," in *The Sex of Things: Gender and Consumption in Historical Perspective*, ed. Victoria de Grazia and Ellen Furlough (Berkeley: University of California Press, 1996), 95.

31. Rappaport, 29–30.

32. Lisa Tiersten, *Marianne in the Market: Envisioning Consumer Society in Fin-de-Siècle France* (Berkeley: University of California Press, 2001), 17, 24, 43.

33. Nupur Chauduri, "Shawls, Jewelry, Curry, and Rice in Victorian Britain," in *Western Women and Imperialism: Complicity and Resistance*, ed. Nupur Chauduri and Margaret Strobel (Bloomington: Indiana University Press, 1992), 233, 240.

34. Leora Auslander, *Taste and Power: Furnishing Modern France* (Berkeley: University of California Press, 1996), 221, 292.

35. Tiersten, 26.

36. Lori Ann Loeb, *Consuming Angels: Advertising and Victorian Women* (New York: Oxford University Press, 1994), 57, 62.

37. Auslander, "The Gendering of Consumer Practices," 85.

38. Quoted in Judith Walkowitz, *City of Dreadful Delight* (Chicago: University of Chicago, 1992), 50.

39. Mary Gibson, *Prostitution and the State in Italy, 1860–1915* (New Brunswick, NJ: Rutgers University Press, 1986), 113.

40. Quoted in Judith Walkowitz, *Prostitution and Victorian Society: Women, Class, and the State* (Cambridge: Cambridge University Press, 1980), 16.

41. Walkowitz, *Prostitution*, 23.

42. Quoted in Jill Harsin, *Policing Prostitution in Nineteenth-Century Paris* (Princeton: Princeton University Press, 1985), 299.

43. Harsin, 116.

44. Walkowitz, *City of Dreadful Delights*, 191.

45. Quoted in Honeyman, 71.

46. Speech by Paule Mink in *Victorian Women: A Documentary Account of Women's Lives in Nineteenth-Century England, France, and the United States*, ed. Erna Olafson Hellerstein, Leslie Parker Hume, and Karen Offen (Stanford, CA: Stanford University Press, 1981), 399

47. Karen Offen, *European Feminisms, 1700–1950: A Political History* (Stanford, CA: Stanford University Press, 2000), 163–164.

48. Harsin, 96.

49. Quoted in Lisa Forman Cody, "The Politics of Illegitimacy in the Age of Reform: Women, Reproduction and Political Economy in England's New Poor Law of 1834," *Journal of Women's History* 11 (2000): 143–144.

50. Quoted in Adele Lindenmeyer, "Charity and the Problems of Unemployment: Industrial Homes in Late Imperial Russia," *The Russian Review* 45 (1986): 4.

51. Rachel Fuchs, *Poor and Pregnant in Paris: Strategies for Survival in the Nineteenth Century* (New Brunswick, NJ: Rutgers University Press, 1992), 144.

52. Rachel Fuchs, *Abandoned Children: Foundlings and Child Welfare in Nineteenth-Century France* (Albany, NY: SUNY Press, 1984), 26.

53. Fuchs and Moch, "Pregnant, Single, and Far from Home," 1010.

54. Fuchs, *Poor and Pregnant in Paris*, 156.

55. Walkowitz, *Prostitution*, 49.

56. Quoted in Gibson, 186.

57. Quoted in F. K. Prochaska, *Women and Philanthropy in Nineteenth-Century England* (Oxford: Oxford University Press, 1980) 5.

58. Excerpt from Sarah Stickney Ellis, "The Daughters of England (1850)," in *Free and Ennobled: Source Readings in the Development of Victorian Feminism*, ed. Carol Bauer and Lawrence Ritt (Oxford: Pergamon Press, 1979), 13.

59. Simonton, 92.

60. Marion A. Kaplan, *The Making of the Jewish Middle Class: Women, Family, and Identity in Imperial Germany* (Oxford: Oxford University Press, 1991), 35–36.

61. Ellen Ross, *Love and Toil: Motherhood in Outcast London, 1870–1918* (Oxford: Oxford University Press, 1993), 129.

62. Joanna Bourke, "Housewifery in Working-Class England," in *Women's Work: The English Experience, 1650–1914*, ed. Pamela Sharpe (London: Arnold, 1998), 333, 337.

63. Penelope Deutscher, "The Descent of Man and the Evolution of Woman," *Hypatia* 19:2 (Spring 2004): 37.

64. Elizabeth Cazden, *Antoinette Brown Blackwell: A Biography* (Old Westbury, NY: Feminist Press, 1983), 147.

65. Quoted in Anna Davin, "Imperialism and Motherhood," in *Tensions of Empire: Colonial Cultures in a Bourgeois World*, ed. Frederick Cooper and Ann Laura Stoler (Berkeley: University of California Press, 1997), 108.

66. Quoted in Susan K. Kent, *Sex and Suffrage in Britain* (Princeton, NJ: Princeton University Press, 1987), 38.

67. Kent, *Sex and Suffrage*, 47.

68. Quoted in Bullough, *Science in the Bedroom* (New York: Basic Books, 1994), 41.

69. Havelock Ellis, *Studies in the Psychology of Sex*, vol. 2, *Sexual Inversion*, Chapter 4 (New York: Random House, 1937), 1, 197.

70. Martha Vicinus, *Intimate Friends: Women Who Loved Women, 1778–1928* (Chicago: University of Chicago Press, 2004), 5–6.

71. Lillian Faderman, "Acting 'Woman' and Thinking 'Man': The Ploys of Famous Female Inverts," *GLQ: A Journal of Lesbian and Gay Studies* 5:3 (1999): 320.

72. Clecia Duel Mosher, *The Mosher Survey: Sexual Attitudes of 45 Victorian Women*, ed. James MaHood and Kristine Wenburg (New York: Arno Press, 1980), 416.

73. Kaplan, 44.

74. Susan O'Brian, "French Nuns in Nineteenth-Century England," *Past and Present* 154 (1997): 142; Margaret Lavinia Anderson, "The Limits of Secularization: On the Problem of the Catholic Revival in Nineteenth-Century Germany," *The Historical Journal* 38 (1995): 653.

75. Quoted in Bonnie S. Anderson, *Joyous Greetings: The First International Women's Movement, 1830–1860* (Oxford: Oxford University Press, 2000), 12.

76. Anderson, 149.

77. Quoted in Catherine Prelinger, *Charity, Challenge, and Change: Religious Dimensions of the Mid-Nineteenth-Century Women's Movement in Germany* (New York: Greenwood Press, 1987), 1.

78. Quoted in Kaplan, 67.

79. Kaplan, 13.

80. Nathaniel Deutsch, *The Maiden of Ludmir: A Jewish Holy Woman and Her World* (Berkeley: University of California Press, 2003).

81. Prelinger, 43.

82. Prelinger, 57, 61.

83. Lynn Abrams, *The Making of Modern Women* (London: Longman, 2002), 120.

84. Fuchs, *Poor and Pregnant*, 133–134.

85. Fuchs, *Poor and Pregnant*, 109.

86. Shubert, 55.

87. Louise W. Knight, "Jane Addams and the Settlement House Movement," in *Against the Tide: Women Reformers in American Society*, ed. Paul A. Cimbala and Randy M. Miller (Westport, CT: Praeger, 1997), 88.

88. Rebecca Rogers, "Boarding Schools, Women Teachers, and Domesticity: Reforming Girls' Secondary Education in the First Half of the Nineteenth Century," *French Historical Studies* 19 (Spring 1995): 174–175.

89. Ann Hibner Koblitz, "Science, Women, and the Russian Intelligentsia: The Generation of the Sixties," *Isis* 79 (1988): 214.

90. James C. Albisetti, "American Women's Colleges Through European Eyes, 1865–1914," *History of Education Quarterly* 32:4 (1992): 439–458.

91. Roberta Wein, "Women's Colleges and Domesticity, 1875–1918," *History of Education Quarterly* 14 (Spring 1974): 37.

92. Lynn D. Gordon, "The Gibson Girl Goes to College: Popular Culture and Women's Higher Education in the Progressive Era, 1890–1920," *American Quarterly* 14 (1974): 211–230.

93. Wein, "Women's Colleges and Domesticity," 44.

94. Regina Markell Morantz-Sanchez, *Sympathy and Science: Women Physicians in American Medicine* (New York: Oxford University Press, 1985), 234.

## SUGGESTED READINGS

Bullough, Vern. *Science in the Bedroom: A History of Sex Research.* New York: Basic Books, 1994.

Clark, Anna. *The Struggle for the Breeches: Gender and the Making of the British Working Class.* Berkeley: University of California Press, 1995.

Fuchs, Rachel. *Abandoned Children: Foundlings and Child Welfare in Nineteenth-Century France.* Albany: State University of New York Press, 1984.

Kaplan, Marion A. *The Making of the Jewish Middle Class: Women, Family, and Identity in Imperial Germany.* Oxford: Oxford University Press, 1991.

Prelinger, Catherine. *Charity, Challenge, and Change: Religious Dimensions of the Mid-Nineteenth-Century Women's Movement in Germany.* New York: Greenwood Press, 1987. Studies the connection between women's religious activities and their developing sense of the need for political reform.

Stansell, Christine. *City of Women: Sex and Class in New York, 1789–1860.* New York: Alfred A. Knopf, 1986.

Walkowitz, Judith. *City of Dreadful Delights: Narratives of Sexual Danger in Late-Victorian London.* Chicago: University of Chicago Press, 1992. An innovative work that studies the impact of sensational journalism on perceptions of urban life in Victorian London.

## Chapter 10

# Resistance, Revolution, and Reform, 1815–1900

*French Political Cartoon: "Camille, Je Vais Au Club" ("Camille, I'm Going to the Club").* *In this cartoon, the wife goes out to her club, leaving instructions with her husband to care for the baby and dinner. Cartoonists and journalists poked fun at the women's movement, arguing that women's demands would feminize men and destroy family life. (Bibliothèque Nationale, Paris.)*

- **Politicizing Women in the Early Nineteenth Century, 1815–1848** 333

  *Abolitionism* 333

  *Women in English Politics* 336

  *Women and Utopian Socialism* 338

  *Founding the Women's Movement* 340

- **The Crises of 1848** 342

  *Fomenting Revolution* 342

  *Women and the Revolution of 1848 in France* 345

  *The Revolution in Central Europe* 347

- **Forging International Connections Among Women** 349

  *Shared Texts and Shared Ideas* 349

  *The Right to Walk the Streets* 352

  *Women and Pacifism* 353

  *Formalizing Connections* 354

- **Radical Actions and Liberal Reforms** 356

  *The Franco-Prussian War and the Paris Commune, 1870–1871* 356

  *Women and Early Marxism* 358

  *Liberal Reforms* 359

- **Women and the Creation of National Identities** 361

  *German Unification* 361

  *Women and Italian Unification* 363

  *Russia and the Baltic* 365

During the nineteenth century, the numbers of politically active women grew. Women's political awareness began with their religious and charitable work and their involvement in with abolitionist, democratic, and utopian groups. As they struggled for the social, economic, and political equality of others, they became keenly aware of the discrimination that they faced because of their sex. In response, women activists organized the women's movement so that they could dedicate their energies to improving the status of women in society. From the outset, the women's movement was diverse. Some women preferred to press for change through governmental and legal reform, while others believed that women's emancipation would come only through revolution. Their goals also differed. Some wanted greater legal protections, others full equality with men. Despite their differences, female activists of different classes and ethnicities shared a belief in the need for women's emancipation and created a strong, international women's movement.

## POLITICIZING WOMEN IN THE EARLY NINETEENTH CENTURY, 1815–1848

As we saw in the previous chapter, across Europe and North America, women's philanthropic work propelled them into social activism. Politicization came first to Anglo-American women. Through their work in abolitionist and workers' movements, British and American women learned to challenge government and social discrimination. However, for many women, the pace of change was too slow. Some looked to utopian communities for more rapid social transformation. Frustrated by the unwillingness of male-dominated groups to address the issues facing women, women dedicated themselves to the creation of a political movement focused on the struggle for women's emancipation.

### Abolitionism

Although Great Britain and the United States criminalized the slave trade in 1807, they did not

333

# Chapter 10 ❖ Chronology

| | |
|---|---|
| **1807** | Great Britain and United States criminalize the slave trade |
| **1815** | Congress of Vienna |
| **1825** | Founding of the Birmingham Ladies Society for the Relief of Negro Slaves |
| **1843** | Flora Tristan publishes *The Workers Union* |
| **1845** | Sweden gives women equal inheritance rights |
| **1848** | Revolutions across Europe |
| | Seneca Falls Convention |
| | Marx and Engels publish the *Communist Manifesto* |
| **1849** | Louise Otto founds her newspaper, *Frauenzeitung* |
| **1855** | Fredrika Bremer publishes her novel *Hertha* in England |
| **1869** | John Stuart Mill publishes *The Subjection of Women* |
| **1870** | Start of the Franco-Prussian War |
| | Unification of Germany |
| | Unification of Italy |
| **1871** | Paris Commune |
| | Foundation of Danish Women's Association |
| **1878** | Women's Rights Congress held in Paris |
| **1881** | Sofia Perovskaia and the People's Will assassinate Tsar Alexander II |
| **1886** | Repeal of Contagious Disease Acts in Great Britain |
| **1905** | Finnish women gain the right to vote |

abolish slavery. In fact, even abolitionists were divided over how emancipation should ultimately take place. Many insisted that abolition come gradually in order to acclimate slaves to freedom and avoid the racial violence that had devastated the island of Haiti during its slave revolt and subsequent independence. However, many others decried the immorality of allowing people to remain enslaved. In 1824, Elizabeth Heyrick (1769–1831) responded to that faction of the abolition movement with her pamphlet entitled *Immediate Not Gradual Abolition*, in which she addressed fears about black insurrections and

challenged supporters of gradual abolition to take action: "The cause of emancipation calls for something more decisive, more efficient than words. . . . Give the slave his liberty,—in the sacred name of justice, give it him at once. Whilst you hold him in bondage, he will profit little from your plans of amelioration."[1] Her pamphlet enjoyed widespread popularity in both Britain and the United States and gave impetus to the cause of immediate abolition.

Frustrated by the insistence on gradual abolition by the major abolitionist organization, the male-run Anti-Slavery Society, in 1825, Heyrick and a group of other white Englishwomen formed the Birmingham Ladies Society for the Relief of Negro Slaves. Later renamed the Female Society for Birmingham, it was not a women's auxiliary but an independent association with its own budget, policies, and strategies. It inspired the formation of seventy-three other independent women's antislavery groups between 1825 and 1833.[2] These groups raised money, sent petitions to Parliament, sponsored speakers, and wrote pamphlets. Women went door-to-door talking to other women about abolition and urging them to boycott sugar grown on slave plantations.

The older generation of abolitionists was often uncomfortable with the overtly political nature of these women's activities. They urged women to return to the more feminine role of behind-the-scenes supporters. In particular, many were disturbed by women's petitions to Parliament. Most men believed that women could petition the monarch because they were subjects of the Crown, but that they could not petition Parliament because it was a political body and women did not belong in politics. Nevertheless, in 1833, through her work with the Chelmsford Ladies' Anti-Slavery Society, Quaker activist Anne Knight (1781–1862) initiated a national petition drive that collected nearly two hundred thousand signatures, more than half of which were women's. Knight presented the petition to abolish slavery to Parliament in 1833, the same day that the government introduced its Emancipation Act, which phased out slavery in England and its colonies.

The importance of these women's organizations to the success of abolition in Britain cannot be overstated. Even contemporaries acknowledged their contribution. In a letter to Anne Knight, one male abolitionist wrote, "Where they [female societies] existed, they did everything. . . . In a word they formed the cement of the whole anti-slavery building—without their aid we should never have been united."[3]

American women were also frustrated by the slow pace and conciliatory attitude of abolitionist leaders. In the late 1820s and early 1830s, two women, Elizabeth Chandler (1808–1834), a white Quaker from Delaware, and Maria W. Stewart (1803–1879), a black widow from Boston, pushed for a more aggressive campaign against slavery. Before her early death at age twenty-six, Chandler

wrote a woman's newspaper column for the abolitionist newspaper *Genius of Universal Emancipation* and organized female abolitionists in Philadelphia and Michigan. She worked to foster empathy between white and black women, arguing that all women could be leaders in the antislavery movement. For her part, Stewart called upon African American men to be more assertive in demanding their rights and black women to set both public and private examples of moral righteousness. Her criticism angered the male leadership of Boston's free black community and they forced her to leave the city in 1831. However, her example led African American women in Salem, Massachusetts, to form the first women's antislavery society in the United States in 1832.[4]

Soon thereafter, radical Quaker William Lloyd Garrison (1805–1879), who published the abolitionist newspaper *The Liberator*, called for women's support. In response, many women, most notably Maria Weston Chapman (1806–1885), and the Grimké sisters, Sarah (1792–1873) and Angelina (1805–1879), joined local antislavery groups. Chapman led the Boston Female Anti-Slavery Society and edited abolitionist periodicals. The Grimké sisters left their slaveholding family in South Carolina, became Quakers, and challenged the expectation that respectable women did not speak in public. In their addresses to state legislatures, they connected the treatment of slaves and women. Angelina's frank discussion of slave women's sexual abuse by their masters shocked many.

At the same time, Quaker preacher Lucretia Mott (1793–1880) became one of the founders of the American Anti-Slavery Society (AASS). Mott was a vocal proponent of immediate abolition, having traveled in Britain and worked with British abolitionists. Despite her high profile at the convention, male leaders did not ask her to sign the organization's founding document, but encouraged Mott and other women to found their own antislavery societies. Five days later, Mott and others formally established the Philadelphia Anti-Slavery Society, which included both white and black women. Most of the African American women members belonged to prominent, wealthy Philadelphia families who worked tirelessly to end slavery and to improve the situation of free blacks.[5]

The experiences of black men and women on both sides of the Atlantic motivated and informed the abolition movement. One of most famous of these women was Mary Prince (ca. 1788–ca. 1834), a slave from Antigua. When slave owners brought their slaves to Britain, the slaves were free as long as they remained in Britain, but if they returned to the British West Indies without formal manumission, they were reenslaved. Mary Prince's owners, the Woods, brought her to Britain but would not formally free her so that she could return to Antigua where her free husband lived. Prince's situation came to public attention when she dictated her autobiography, *The History of Mary Prince* (1831), to a literate white woman, Susannah Strickland. Mary's personal history of slavery became a critical text in the abolition campaign.

With the emancipation of slaves in Great Britain and its colonies, many turned their attention to the United States. In 1840, the British and Foreign Anti-Slavery Society (BFASS) held its first World Anti-Slavery Convention in London. American abolitionist groups sent female delegates to the conventions, among them Lucretia Mott. Elizabeth Cady Stanton (1815–1902) went with her husband who was also a delegate. However, the BFASS would not allow them to sit with the rest of the convention because they were women. When male supporters challenged this ruling, delegates spent the first day debating women's rights instead of abolition.

The BFASS's refusal to let female delegates participate as full members of the convention was one in a series of discriminatory acts that catalyzed the women's movement. Fifty years later, Stanton remembered that this slight, "stung many women into new thought and action [and gave] rise to the movement for women's political equality both in England and the United States."[6] Mott and Stanton spent their time away from the convention meeting with other women, making connections that would be fundamental in the creation of the women's movement.

The abolition movement not only gave women extensive experience in political activism, it led them to compare their own limited legal and economic options to those of slavery. American Lydia Maria Child (1802–1880), the editor of the AASS's newspaper, the *National Anti-Slavery Standard*, and a member of the group's executive council, drew trenchant comparisons between how women and blacks were characterized. She

wrote: "the comparison between [white] women and the colored race is striking. . . both are characterized by affection more than intellect; both have strong development of the religious sentiment; both are excessively adhesive in their attachments' both . . . have a tendency to submission; and hence have been kept in subjection by physical force, and considered rather in the light of property, than as individuals."[7] As white activist women came to identify with black men and women rather than men of their own race and class, they began to articulate the need for a women's movement to redress long-standing social, political, and economic inequalities.

## Women in English Politics

Abolition was not the only political cause that attracted British women. Many women entered politics during the Queen Caroline affair. Caroline (1768–1821) was the unfortunate wife of George, the Prince of Wales and regent of England for his ailing father, George III (r. 1760–1820). The Prince of Wales lived a lavish and dissolute life with his mistress and was very unpopular with the British public. In 1795, when he appealed to Parliament to pay his gambling debts, Parliament insisted that he marry Princess Caroline of Brunswick, a German principality. The couple did not get along, and George regularly humiliated her, even sending his mistress to be her lady in waiting. In 1814, Caroline left him to live on the Continent where she remained until he ascended the throne in 1820 as George IV (r. 1820–1830). When Caroline returned to Britain to become queen, George put her on trial for adultery, hoping she would be convicted and he could divorce her. Caroline was acquitted, but died four months later.

The publicity surrounding Caroline's trial was unprecedented. Radical journalists manipulated the public's sympathy for her, hoping to undermine the monarchy. The public identified with Caroline, seeing her as the wronged wife and a symbol of purity among a corrupt aristocracy. George's attack on her was an attack on the middle-class family. To the working class, less concerned with Caroline's guilt or innocence, she was a symbol of aristocratic oppression and family upheaval. Caroline's trial reminded women of their powerlessness in the face of unjust accusations and the sexual double standard. One broadside published the following verse to gain women's support:

> *Attend ye virtuous British wives,*
> *Support your injur'd queen,*
> *Assert her rights; they are you own,*
> *As plainly could be seen.*
> *Could you sustain the injuries,*
> *Your Queen has undergone?*
> *You answer no, her cause is yours,*
> *Then make her cares your own.*[8]

Through the popular media, the Queen Caroline affair drew Englishwomen into a royal scandal that had implications for their own lives.

Although Englishwomen may have become more interested in politics, politicians demonstrated little interest in women's rights. British politics were dominated by two parties. The conservatives, or Tories, favored maintaining the status quo, believing that the upper class, which had governed for centuries, knew what was best for society. In contrast, British Liberals promoted suffrage for men with property and education; a representational form of government that employed people based on talent rather than birth; freedoms of speech, assembly, and the press; and policies that favored economic development and free trade. Liberalism's emphasis on property ownership and minimal government intervention appealed to the expanding middle class. Smaller numbers of radicals, drawn predominantly from the working class, advocated a range of ideas from abolishing the monarchy and private property to universal suffrage.

Beginning in 1830, Liberals controlled the British government, and in 1832, Parliament passed the first Reform Bill, which redistributed parliamentary representation so that the new northern manufacturing districts received greater representation. It also expanded the vote to male heads of house worth £10, but it did not enfranchise the working class or women. Socialist Anna Wheeler (1785–1848) wrote angrily that the Reform Bill "had not a word about justice to women."[9] When Mary Smith from Yorkshire petitioned Parliament for the right to vote because she paid taxes and was subject to the law, Parliament denied her request.

The failure of the Reform Bill to expand suffrage to working-class men attracted many to Chartism. Chartism advocated parliamentary democracy as a means of ending social and economic inequality. The People's Charter had six demands for parliamentary reform, including the extension of the vote to all men. Although the Chartists' class politics were radical, they espoused traditional ideas about gender. Chartists argued that men should be paid a living wage so that they could support their wives. Working-class women were expected to aspire to a middle-class lifestyle in which they did not work outside of the home.

Women's participation in the Chartist movement reveals its traditional gender expectations. They organized teas, concerts, and boat, theater, and rail trips that raised money, educated followers, and increased support for the Chartist cause. They also participated in "exclusive schemes," which meant shopping only at places that supported the Charter. Mothers taught their children about Chartism at Chartist Sunday schools and grammar schools.

The Chartists' conservatism was also reflected in their response to the demands of women workers. Although single women made up a significant portion of the workforce, the Chartists continued to see women workers as oppressed mothers who needed liberation from wage labor. For example, in 1838, the Chartists called a public meeting in Newcastle, where female glassworkers had gone on strike. Although they invited the women to the meeting, Chartist organizers praised "manly conduct" and looked forward to "the day when the working man should not be looked upon as a mere tool of the capitalists."[10] They did nothing to address the decrease in pay that caused the women to strike in the first place.

Nevertheless, many Chartists were deeply interested in women's rights. Women from Newcastle upon Tyne published a petition in 1839 in *The Northern Star* that stridently declared women's right to a voice in politics:

> *We have been told that the province of woman is her home, and that the field of politics should be left to men; this we deny. . . . Is it not true that the interest of our fathers, husbands, and brothers, ought to be ours? If they are oppressed and impoverished, do we*

*not share those evils with them? If so, ought
we not to resent the infliction of those wrongs
upon them? We have read the records of the
past, and our hearts have responded to the
historians' praise of those women, who
struggled against tyranny and urged their
countrymen to be free or die.*[11]

However, when faced with the decision to include
women's suffrage in the People's Charter, the
drafters acknowledged both the legitimacy of the
women's demands and their fear that its inclusion
would be detrimental to the Chartist cause.[12]

## Women and Utopian Socialism

Not all women were willing to wait for legal
reforms to create a more egalitarian society. In
their desire for immediate equality, many radical
women were attracted to the messages of utopian
socialists. Several groups created egalitarian communes in the 1820s and 1830s in which women
experimented with new social and sexual relationships; however, in the long run, many became dis-
enchanted with utopianism's inability to embrace
complete sexual equality.

The Saint-Simonians and Fourierists undertook
some of the earliest utopian socialist experiments.
Count Henri de Saint-Simon (1760–1835), a
French aristocrat who renounced his title during
the French Revolution, was one of the first social
critics to understand the negative implications of
industrialization. He argued that a scientifically
organized society was the only way to move
beyond the problems of industrialization. Charles
Fourier (1772–1837) envisioned a socialist utopia
based on detailed mathematical calculations. He
wanted his carefully planned communities to
function based on cooperation and a distribution
of labor based on one's skills and preferences.
The former had its greatest impact in France; the
latter began in France and spread to the United
States, where there were twenty-four Fourierists
communities from Massachusetts to Iowa and
Wisconsin.

The Saint-Simonians fused planned scientific
progress with a radical interpretation of Christianity that followers believed would herald a new
age of economic and social harmony. Their interpretation of the New Testament demanded they foment

social revolution by creating Jesus's mission of
heaven on earth. Advocating sexual equality, Saint-
Simonian lectures drew thousands of women. The
Saint-Simonians argued that progress would require
the work of both men and women, and that most of
society's problems grew out of the oppression of
women.

In Saint-Simonian communities, leaders
believed that motherhood was the source of
women's equality. In 1831, a new leader, Prosper
Enfantin (1796–1864), assumed the title of
"Supreme Father" and specifically advocated for
women's emancipation:

*The man and the woman, that is the social
individual, this is our deepest belief about the
relationship of the two sexes; this is the basis
for the morality of the future. The
exploitation of woman by man still exists,
and this is why our apostolate is so necessary.
This exploitation, this subordination—
contrary to nature as far as the future is
concerned—has for its effects* lying *and fraud
on the one hand, and violence and brutal
passions on the other. These are the vices that
must be ended.*[13]

However, in practice, Enfantin excluded women
from the collective's hierarchy. He claimed that
women could not achieve equality without
redemption by men, which required the "rehabili-
tation of the flesh." Saint-Simonians could achieve
this redemption through sexual freedom, which he
believed would benefit women because they were
by nature fickle and inconstant.[14]

Many Saint-Simonian women felt betrayed by
Enfantin, left the communities, and formed splinter groups. In 1832, a group of working-class
Saint-Simonian women established their first
newspaper, *La Femme Libre* (*Free Woman*),
which published only articles written by women.
Between 1832 and 1834, they produced thirty-one
issues, which they sold in the movement's book-
stores across Europe and the United States.
Through this newspaper, Jeanne Deroin (1805–
1894) and Pauline Roland (1805–1852) quickly
realized that their goals as women went far
beyond those of the Saint-Simonians. Deroin
knew firsthand the problems of working-class
women. She had worked as a seamstress and

joined the commune hoping to improve her life. For Deroin and other working-class women in the movement, sexual liberation was less of a concern than access to education and good jobs. Roland denounced the ideology of sexual freedom because it left women vulnerable and provided no guarantees for male responsibility. She had two children by two different Saint-Simonian men who in the end would not support them. Instead, Roland and Deroin advocated marriages of equal and loving partners.

Flora Tristan (1803–1844) was one of the most influential women drawn into the orbit of the utopian socialists. An advocate of socialism, she focused much of her writings on the need for women's rights and economic self-sufficiency. Born to a rich Peruvian father and French mother, Tristan grew up in poverty after her father's death in 1807. After fleeing an abusive marriage to her employer, the owner of a print shop, she supported herself as a ladies companion and writer. She traveled unaccompanied to Peru to reestablish connections with her father's family and wrote about her experiences in *Peregrinations of a Pariah* (1838). She tried to divorce her husband and gain custody of her children, both illegal in France at this time. Her husband also demanded part of her earnings. In 1838, he shot her. She recovered and only then was able to gain a legal separation.

The publicity of the court case popularized Tristan's writings, allowing her to support herself. In 1839, she wrote about working-class poverty in London in her *London Journal* and followed it with her most famous work, *The Workers Union* (1843), in which she advocated organizing the working class so that they could realize their collective strength and resist oppression. In this work, she also argued for women's emancipation, including access to divorce and the right to work. According to Tristan, women's emancipation was in men's best interests. Women could gain better educations, support themselves, marry for love, and be better wives and mothers. Like the Saint-Simonians and Fourierists, she envisioned the possibility of social transformation. However, rather than change one community at a time, she sought complete social and economic transformation.[15]

In Britain, industrialist Robert Owen (1771–1858) formulated his own utopian communities.

According to Owen, competition, not moral weakness, caused crime and poverty. He hoped to eradicate these ills by providing his workers in New Lanark, Scotland, with schools, decent working conditions, food, and housing. Convinced that cooperative working communities would provide the greatest happiness for the greatest number, Owen promoted legislation to regulate and reform factories. In the 1820s, he traveled across England and the United States, speaking and establishing Owenite communities in places such as New Harmony, Indiana, and Skaneateles, New York. Ultimately, there were ten such communities in the United States.

Owenites based their communities on equality and cooperation between men and women. They ran labor exchanges and cooperative stores. Most women who joined Owen's communities were from the upper ranks of the working class, the wives and daughters of skilled factory workers, who typically had worked as dressmakers, weavers, and domestic servants.[16] The Owenites were broadly condemned for their labor activism, their denunciation of organized religion, and their rejection of marriage.

Although Owen was paternalistic and most women in his communities were relegated to traditionally female tasks, women also wrote for Owenite newspapers and spoke publicly for the Owenite cause. One of Owen's female associates, Scottish heiress Fanny Wright (1795–1852), who had a son by him, came to Owenism after a bad marriage. She founded an Owenite community in the Tennessee wilderness at Nashoba. Fanny Wright's community tried not only to redress the inequities of marriage but also those of race and slavery. She even advocated racially mixed marriages, although they were illegal in most of the United States. However, the Owenites at Nashoba did not free blacks; rather, white community leaders forced black members to work as indentured servants to pay off their purchase prices. Although both black and white men had free sexual access to the women, white leaders raised the children of these unions away from their mothers in order to prepare the children for freedom. Like many abolitionists, Wright did not believe that blacks were ready for equality. Nashoba, along with other Owenite communities, depended on subsidies from Owen himself. When Nashoba failed because of financial troubles and government harassment, Wright sent the blacks to Haiti where they would be assured of their freedom, and she continued to advocate the mixing of the races as a means to bring about equality. The Owenite experiment declined in the 1840s because of financial mismanagement, but members took many of his radical ideas with them when they left their communities.

## Founding the Women's Movement

By drawing women into political and social action, each of these political causes contributed to the formation of the women's movement. Abolitionism and labor activism provided women with the vocabulary to describe sexual inequality and strategies to combat discrimination. Utopian socialism provided new frameworks for women to understand sexual, economic, and social relationships. Most important, women's political action led them to believe that a change in women's status was both necessary and possible.

The early women's movement was led by liberal middle-class women from the United States and Great Britain. They had the time and money and more experience with representative government than their Continental peers. Indeed, transAtlantic connections were critical to women's activism. American Quaker women had longstanding connections through the abolition movement, and Lucretia Mott's 1840 travels to England for the World Anti-Slavery Society Convention forged many new ties. Englishwomen were often transformed by their travels across the Atlantic. After British journalist and political economist Harriet Martineau visited the United States, she quickly penned three important books. In her *Society in America* (1837), Martineau argued that it was profoundly undemocratic for a government to tax, punish, and even enslave women while denying them the right to vote.

In 1848, momentum for women's rights was strong enough that Elizabeth Cady Stanton, and Lucretia Mott convened the Women's Rights Convention in Seneca Falls, New York, near Stanton's home. The convention ran for two days in July and attracted about three hundred people, more than half of whom were women. Stanton told the audience that women must work for their own liberation; they could not expect men to give it to them. Freed slave Frederick Douglass (1818–1895) also spoke on behalf of women's rights. Energized by their shared dedication to improving the lives of women, the Seneca Falls convention attendees produced the Declaration of Sentiments, a rewriting of the Declaration of Independence. According to the preamble, "the history of mankind is a history of repeated injuries and usurpations on the part of man toward women, having in direct object the establishment of an absolute tyranny over her. To prove this let facts be submitted to a candid world." The document went on to assert that men had "never permitted [women] to exercise her inalienable right to the elective franchise," and "had compelled her to submit to laws, in the formation of which she had no voice." The text articulated fifteen demands, including the right to vote—a controversial idea that nearly did not receive the convention's approval. Not all women believed that voting would bring equality, and many feared domestic conflict when a husband and wife voted differently. Two weeks after Seneca Falls, the convention reconvened in a larger venue in Rochester, New York, for further discussion. The Rochester Convention highlighted economic injustices and cofounded a Working Woman's Protective Union, which advocated for factory and labor reforms. In 1850 and 1851, the women's rights convention met in Worcester, Massachusetts, and subsequent meetings convened in Syracuse (1852), Cleveland (1853), and New York (1853). Susan B. Anthony (1820–1906), the other great women's suffragist, was not at Seneca Falls. She did not begin her suffrage activism until she met Stanton in the spring of 1851.

The burgeoning activist press in both the United States and Europe provided coverage of the meetings and printed the speeches, helping to internationalize the movement. After the second Worcester convention, Harriet Taylor Mill (1807–1858) praised American women's activism in the progressive English journal *The Westminster Review*. Jeanne Deroin and Pauline Roland, who were imprisoned in Paris (see below), were elated by the coverage of the Declaration of Sentiments. Their appeal for support, which was read at the Worcester convention, began, "Dear Sisters: — Your courageous declaration of Women's Rights

**SUSAN B. ANTHONY AND ELIZABETH CADY STANTON.** Anthony and Stanton were leaders of the women's suffrage movement in the United States. Their emphasis on the right to vote influenced women on both sides of the Atlantic. *(Bettmann/Corbis.)*

has resounded even to our prison, and has filled our souls with inexpressible joy."[17] After her release, Deroin covered the later conventions in her London-based *Almanack des femmes* (*The Women's Almanac*).

The early women's movement had diverse goals. Most participants believed that married women's ability to control their own property and earnings was crucial for women's independence. Many also advocated easier divorce for women and the ability of mothers to retain custody of their children in order to protect women and children from domestic violence. Women across Europe and the United States pursued greater access to education, which would help women support themselves and be better mothers and wives. As we saw in the previous chapter, many activists dedicated themselves to women's right to

work. Women's suffrage was the most controversial goal of the women's movement, as we will discuss later. Although a central component of some Anglo-American women's activism, most European women had little interest in obtaining rights that the state denied their fathers and husbands. Moreover, many women believed that suffrage was unnecessary and distracted from the more important need for legal reforms.

Although most women focused on basic legal and political rights, some women equated women's emancipation with sexual freedom. Indeed, many early women activists were associated with the "free love" ideas of the utopian socialists. In particular, the popular novels of French author Aurore Dupin (1804–1876), who wrote under the pseudonym George Sand, attracted large audiences and inspired many women to activism. Her celebrated novels such as *Indiana* (1832) criticized women's lack of education and legal rights, but her works also caused controversy by advocating "freedom of the heart," by which she meant freedom to pursue sexual relationships unencumbered by social convention. Sand also led a very unconventional life. She fled an unhappy marriage for Paris and lived scandalously, dressing as a man, smoking cigars, and engaging in a number of passionate and public love affairs. However, many women distanced themselves from such radical sexual ideas. German journalist Louise Otto (1819–1895) felt compelled to distinguish between the sexual liberation embodied by Sand, which Otto did not support, and the emancipation of women, sought by "all who prize progress."[18] Similarly, the founders of the Parisian Society for the Emancipation of Women defined emancipation as a moral and intellectual condition, not a physical one.[19]

During the first half of the nineteenth century, women, particularly in Britain and the United States, became engaged in politics. They worked for an end to slavery, greater political participation for workers, and joined utopian communities designed to create a better, more egalitarian society. Through these experiences, women learned to analyze the social, economic, and political constraints placed upon them and gained the skills necessary for successful political action. With the founding of the women's movement, women activists dedicated those experiences and skills to improving the lives of women, but it did not mean an end to competing goals and solutions to the problem of women's status.

## THE CRISES OF 1848

Although they had abhorred Napoleon's rule, most Continental politicians proved equally hostile to women's political demands. The memory of women's military and political activities in the French Revolution remained fresh in many leaders' minds, and they equated women's political demands with the radicalism of the Reign of Terror (see Chapter 8). The conservative politicians who took over after Napoleon's defeat embraced a romantic vision of the past in which both peasants and warriors sacrificed for the betterment of their society. In the kingdoms of Prussia, Russia, and the Austrian Empire, which included northern Italy, Hungary, and Bohemia, monarchs reasserted absolute rule. Royal whim, state churches, and old feudal obligations again regulated people's lives. The newly reestablished monarchies in Spain and France also relied on traditional beliefs to reestablish their authority and control attempts at liberal reforms.

These conservative politics provoked considerable unrest. As we saw in the last chapter, separate spheres did not describe the experiences of most women, and increasingly women of all classes resented the political and social limitations that society imposed on them. The working class and subject minority groups in Austria and the German lands became more restive, and members of the middle class demanded inclusion in the political system. Finally, in 1848, violence erupted across Europe (see Map 10.1). Known collectively as the Revolutions of 1848, these uprisings expressed a variety of political sentiments from radicalism to nationalism. Although women of all classes participated in the revolutions, revolutionaries never made women's rights central to their demands. Some women fought to have their concerns included in revolutionary programs, but many others joined the uprisings on behalf of their families, their ethnic group, or their class and devoted little attention to the issues affecting them as women.

## Fomenting Revolution

The decades following Napoleon's defeat were turbulent for France. The elderly king Louis XVIII who had succeeded Napoleon died in 1824, and his brother Charles X (r. 1824–1830) assumed the throne. A staunch enemy of Republicanism, Charles had watched the French Revolution from exile and despised the radicalism of the Terror and the execution of his fellow aristocrats. Working with a group called the ultraroyalists or the "Ultras," he restored absolute monarchy to France. The Ultras limited freedom of the press, curtailed the political participation of nonaristocrats, and encouraged a return to traditional farming and manufacturing methods. They argued that production for the market eroded traditional village lifestyles and family structure. They believed that women did not belong in the workplace, but should be at home raising children. Many peasants initially supported the Ultras' program, but worsening economic conditions changed many minds. Poor weather between 1827 and 1832 caused repeated crop failures. Prices rose, families went hungry, and wine producers and farmers went bankrupt. Investors pulled out of France, spreading hardship to the working class, especially men and women working in the silk and cloth industries. Riots in Paris early in the summer of 1830 compelled Charles to abdicate, and the Duke of Orleans, Louis-Philippe I (r. 1830–1848), agreed to rule as a constitutional monarch. The July monarchy would prove no more responsive for calls for reform from liberals and the working class than its predecessor.

Social tensions were also increasing in central Europe. After Napoleon's defeat, the Congress of Vienna (1815) created the German Confederation, which included all German-speaking lands. However, with no common currency, legal system, or shared political ideology, it was a weak association dominated by Austria and Prussia, both of whom were distrusted by the smaller principalities.

Prussia was a conservative, rural kingdom, dominated by a conservative military and civil service. It had only a tiny middle class and an oppressed peasantry that had only recently been released from serfdom. In 1840, when Frederick William IV (r. 1840–1861) became king of Prussia, many Germans hoped for change. His

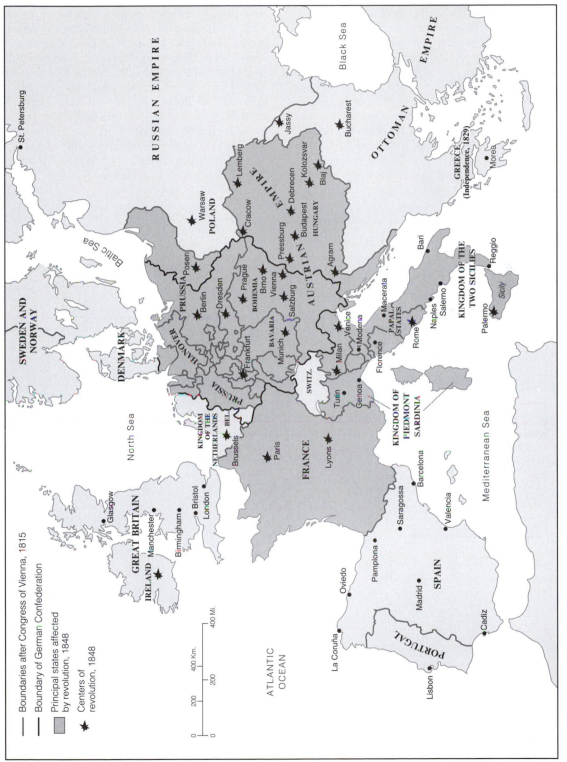

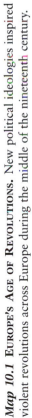

***Map 10.1*** **Europe's Age of Revolutions.** New political ideologies inspired violent revolutions across Europe during the middle of the nineteenth century.

early criticism of the civil service and willingness to release most political prisoners gave him a reputation as a reformer and earned him the support of many Germans. However, far from being a reformer, Frederick William saw himself as the father of Prussia. He tolerated no criticism and demanded complete loyalty from his subjects. His intractability soon found him at odds with both the small middle class, who wanted economic reform to further trade and industrialization, and much of the nobility, who hoped to check his power with a constitutional monarchy.

The Austrian Empire was also very conservative. The minister of foreign affairs, Prince Metternich (1773–1859), created a system of police surveil-lance, strict censorship, and political exile to deal with all those suspected of opposing the government. Metternich's iron rule kept in check the restive subject populations that made up the empire (see Map 10.2). Although German language and culture dominated and Germans ran the government and made up the political elite, they only comprised a quarter of the population.[20] The majority of the population were Slavs, Hungarians, Romanians, and Italians. Religious differences between Roman Catholics, Orthodox Christians, Protestants, and Jews added to the empire's diversity. Non-Germans resented the primacy of German culture and language at the expense of their own traditions.

*Map 10.2* **PEOPLES OF THE HABSBURG MONARCHY, 1815.** The Habsburgs ruled over a multiethnic and multireligious empire that proved increasingly unmanageable, as nationalists and liberals demanded greater political participation.

Tensions over the lack of political and economic reform accelerated in 1846 and 1847 after disease devastated the potato crop and pushed millions of European peasants to the brink of starvation. German governments, fearful of urban unrest, requisitioned food to feed the cities, which worsened the situation in the countryside. Between 1845 and 1847, the price of bread in Paris rose 50 percent while the price of potatoes doubled.[21] As the economic crisis deepened, urban workers could no longer afford to feed their families or purchase goods. With consumption down, many lost their jobs. In April of 1847, crowds of women in Berlin attacked merchants over high prices. At bakeries, women weighed the bread and if they found it priced well according to its weight, they hung a sign on the door declaring the baker's honesty. If the price was too high, they stole the bread without paying.[22]

In this time of crisis, people turned to revolutionary solutions. When violence broke out in 1848, class and nationalist demands were at the forefront of revolutionary thought.

## Women and the Revolution of 1848 in France

The revolutions began in France. Agitation increased as King Louis-Philippe's constitutional monarchy ignored calls for reform from both the working and the middle class. The working class wanted better working conditions and higher wages. The middle class demanded a voice in politics. Even among men, political participation was limited, as only one of every thirty-six adult males were eligible to vote.[23] Louis-Philippe also kept to the treaties of 1815, which had deprived France

**GERMAN BREAD RIOT, 1847.** Some women joined the Revolutions of 1848 in hopes of bringing about profound social and political change. Others responded to immediate concerns, such as the high cost of food and their inability to feed their families. *(© Corbis.)*

of Savoy, Nice, and the lands along the Rhine. His refusal to go to war angered the strongly nationalistic working class and peasantry. By 1848, much of France resented Louis-Philippe for his inaction.

As social tensions mounted, revolutionaries began stockpiling weapons, and even before the violence began in earnest, the uprising forced King Louis-Phillipe to abdicate in late February 1848, and the revolutionaries declared the Second French Republic. The provisional government chosen by the Chamber of Deputies abolished slavery in the French Empire and compensated the former owners, thereby keeping resistance to a minimum. This act attracted female abolitionists around the world to the revolutionary cause and was one of the government's lasting achievements.

To undertake economic reforms, the provisional government assembled the Luxembourg Commission to study the working conditions of laborers. Women from many trades testified about their working conditions and their need for economic assistance. In response, the government established national workshops. In March 1848, the mayor of Paris opened a workshop for women to sew shirts for the National Guard, although revolutionary Désirée Gay (1810–1891) criticized him for assuming that all women knew how to sew. The Parisian women workers proved to be far from docile. They petitioned the mayor for the right to work at home so that they could also care for their children and do their housework. They also demanded pay equal to that earned by the men in workshops.

In early March, the provisional government expanded suffrage to all males over twenty-one years of age and set elections for mid-April. When the expansion of suffrage did not include women, a group of women calling themselves the Committee on the Rights of Women went to the government demanding to know why they had been excluded. They argued, "You say 'there are no more proletarians,' but if women are not included in your decrees, France can still count more than seventeen million of them."[24] In defiance, Pauline Roland attempted to vote in her local municipal elections. Although the mayor accompanied her, authorities refused to allow her to cast her ballot, an act that received extensive coverage in the French press.

Most radicals did not support women's voting rights. They believed that the enfranchisement of all men had already put them in a difficult position. Most French were peasants and politically conservative, and most radical Parisians did not want France's fate determined by the peasants, whom Parisians believed were dominated by both landowners and the Catholic Church. Indeed, when the government held parliamentary elections in April, the countryside voted overwhelmingly for local men of property, most of whom had served in previous regimes and nearly half of whom were monarchists.

By late spring, the workshop program had failed. Half the workforce had lost their jobs due to the continuing recession, and peasants resented paying for urban programs when they were struggling in the countryside. In response, Parisian workers and the urban poor marched on Parlement on May 15, demanding its dissolution. Activist women kept up ideological pressure by continuing to write newspaper articles and editorials to keep their concerns at the forefront.

Following the march on the Parlement of Paris, two women's groups, the Society for the Emancipation of Women and the Committee for the Rights of Women demanded full female equality. One of their petitions bluntly stated that, "There cannot be two liberties, two equalities, two fraternities. . . . Men's liberty and quality are clearly those of women as well."[25] In fact, French women activists argued that the first French Revolution had failed because it had not included women and thus lacked the female virtues of peace, reconciliation, and social harmony. They contended that without women, this revolution would also fail, and despotism, militarism, and the restoration of the monarchy would result. Moreover, women should be central to the new regime. According to Jeanne Deroin:

> *The reign of brute force has ended; that of morality and intelligence has just begun. The motives that led our fathers to exclude women from all participation in the governance of the State are no longer valid. When every question was decided by the sword, it was natural to believe that women—who could not take part in combat— should not be seated in the assembly of warriors. In those days it was a question of destroying and conquering by the sword;*

*today it is a question of building and of organizing. Women should be called on to take part in the great task of social regeneration that is under way. Why should our country be deprived of the services of its daughters?*[26]

Frustrated by government inaction, at the end of June, revolutionaries began erecting barricades. Many women participated in the ensuing violence by nursing the wounded, carrying ammunition, and throwing stones. The government tried to limit the bloodshed, but to no avail. To retake the city, the government relied on National Guard troops from the rural provinces, who used extreme violence against Parisians whom they believed were anarchists and a threat to French society. When the fighting from the "June Days" ended, five hundred insurgents and one thousand soldiers lay dead. With superior numbers and supplies, the government ultimately emerged victorious. The soldiers then retaliated against the surviving revolutionaries by killing another three thousand and arresting twelve thousand. Many died in labor camps in the French colony of Algeria.[27] To reassert public order, the government again banned women from political activity; shut down their clubs, newspapers, and journals; and forbade them from public speaking and organizing. Socialist Pierre Joseph Proudhon (1809–1865) argued that just as men could not be wet nurses, women could not be legislators. Jeanne Deroin tartly replied in her newspaper *l'Opinion de femmes* (*The Opinion of Women*), "Now we know what organ is needed to be a legislator."[28]

Newspapers spread the news of France's revolution across Europe. The internationalism of nineteenth-century activism that had connected abolitionists and socialists before 1848 bound revolutionaries together and mobilized them to fight against oppression. They shared their ideas and strategies, supported one another's activities, and encouraged the spread of the revolution.

## The Revolution in Central Europe

The revolutionary fervor that overtook Paris quickly spread into Germany, Austria, Hungary, and Italy. The causes of these outbreaks were often similar to those in France, including worker and peasant poverty and middle-class alienation, yet each revolution also addressed local issues. For instance, although nationalism played a major role in Hungary's uprisings, in southern Germany, revolutionaries called for liberal reforms. When the revolutions spread to northern Italy and Vienna, subject peoples in the Habsburg Empire, including Bohemians, Hungarians, Piedmontese, and Venetians, pressed for more autonomy. Germans in the Rhineland, who had come under Prussian domination as a result of the Congress of Vienna, also saw the revolution as a chance for liberation. These nationalist attacks on both the Habsburg Empire and Prussian domination inspired countermovements in support of Habsburg and Prussian claims in these areas.

German women lived under much greater political constraints than their British, French, or American counterparts. They were not as well organized and had not fully articulated an activist program. However, as the crisis intensified, some women, including journalist and activist Louise Otto, tried to expand the revolution's goals to include rights for women. Louise Otto came from a middle-class German family. She reportedly astonished a suitor by her ability to read philosophy and knit at the same time. In 1842, she published her first articles about women's issues under a male pseudonym and only later published under her own name. She also attended labor meetings and published articles about the need for economic reform. In 1849, Otto founded her own weekly newspaper, *Frauenzeitung* (*The Women's Newspaper*), the longest-lasting German revolutionary newspaper.

Otto's ideas combined nationalism with her concern for women. She believed that women needed to focus on building a new German state. Through her newspaper, Otto campaigned for education reforms and better working conditions for both male and female workers. She argued that social norms and marriage laws kept women passive and "characterless," and that in this degraded condition women were incapable of acting on their own interests or those of their families. To overcome this situation, women needed moral and economic independence, which was only possible with economic reform and greater educational opportunities. In April of 1849, she proclaimed in her newspaper, "We shall demand to have as our share the right to accomplish with all our strength and in unrestricted development that in us which is purely human, and the right to come of age and enjoy independence with the State."[29] However, the demand for such basic rights would find little support in German society.

Otto was only one of many German women active in revolutionary journalism. Musician Johanna Kinkel (1810–1858) came to journalism after founding a literary group, the Ladybug Society, in 1840, which satirized complacent middle-class society. As revolution approached, she took over the editorship of the *New Bonn Newspaper* and advocated for the democrats, who supported the formation of a democratic republic. When her husband was imprisoned for his revolutionary activities, she helped him escape and then, together with their children, they fled to London. There she continued to write and raise money for the cause.

Women's participation in central Europe's revolutions drew not only on the ideas and strategies of suffragists and socialists, but also on traditional ideas of women's behavior. As in earlier political movements, women's roles as mothers and housewives gave them opportunities for political action. In Germany, women boycotted foreign goods, and in Vienna, they wore clothes in the German colors to protest the anti-German sentiments of the Hungarians and Czechs. In Prague and Budapest, Czech and Hungarian women also wore their national colors and costumes and taught their children their own languages instead of German. In Hungary, the most nationalistic of the 1848 revolutions, the anonymous group "Radical Hungarian Women" published a list of demands in the patriotic newspaper *Pesti Dvatlap* (*Pest Fashion Magazine*) (see **Sources from the Past: Demands of the Radical Hungarian Women**). They asserted women's right to public and political participation even as they recognized their traditional roles as mothers and consumers.[30]

One of the most vocal supporters of the Hungarian revolution was the countess Blanka Teleki (d. 1862). In the 1840s, she founded a school for girls in which the language of instruction was Hungarian. She did not believe that Hungarian women were yet ready for emancipation, and she advocated that women start their

political involvement by staying home and raising patriotic children. In her article entitled "First Reform Then Women's Emancipation," Teleki warned against superficial involvement: "You are not allowed to flirt with freedom, to dress yourself in it because it is a fashion, because it looks good—sacrilege! It is the responsibility of everyone to be able to grasp the complete meaning of this holy word in all its grandeur."[31] Threatened by her nationalistic curriculum, the government closed her school in December of 1848. Teleki was undeterred; when the city of Pest fell to the Austrian army, she spent most of her time nursing wounded revolutionaries and caring for their families. With the end of the revolution late in the following year, the Habsburg government closed all political clubs, censored the press, and arrested political leaders, including Teleki and two female associates. She served six years of a ten-year prison sentence.[32]

The revolutions in Hungary, Germany, and Italy were brutally suppressed by the superior military power of the Prussian and Austrian armies. With the end of the revolutions came an end to immediate hopes for a unified Germany under a liberal constitution and an end to Austrian dominance in Hungary and Italy. In the aftermath of the revolutions, the Austrian and Prussian governments became even more repressive and distrustful of women's activism. Although Metternich fled Austria and died in exile as a consequence of the revolution, his successors continued to believe that women's political activities led to violence and social disorder. In Prussia, laws forbade women to engage in politics.

For many women, the Revolutions of 1848 were testing grounds for their ideas about women's equality. As revolutionaries advocated political change, female activists worked to incorporate their concerns into the new political order. The brutality with which governments suppressed the revolutions and women's involvement in planning and fighting made many middle-class men and women wary of addressing the issue of women's rights. They associated women in politics with violence and political excess. However, despite the backlash, the revolutions attracted many new women into the movement. They understood more clearly than ever the connection between the plight of workers and peasants and that of women of all classes and ethnicities.

# Forging International Connections Among Women

In the wake of the Revolutions of 1848, the women's movement gained more momentum. Transcending national boundaries, women united in their opposition to the sexual double standard and the unfair treatment of prostitutes. Pacifism also brought many women together in common purpose. In new organizations and conferences, female activists met like-minded women from other nations, reinforcing the increasingly international character of the movement.

## Shared Texts and Shared Ideas

Sex alone could not unite Europe's diverse female population. Women from different classes and cultures needed to have a sense of common obstacles and inspirations in order to feel a part of the women's movement and forge international bonds. Often seen as a particularly female genre, novels became a critical medium for women to express their frustrations and introduce women's concerns to new audiences. As they read the ordeals faced by their fictional characters, women came to understand that their frustrations were not unique. Women's novels not only educated women across Europe and the United States about their common problems, but also provided many with their first glimpse of the possibilities for change.

English novelist Charlotte Brontë (1816–1854) inspired women and provoked controversy with her novel *Jane Eyre* (1847). This story of a poor orphan girl who overcomes adversity and marries her wealthy employer while remaining true to her values detailed the appalling conditions of the poor and disenfranchised and the limited opportunities for single women. Critics denounced it because the heroine did not remain within her class, but women activists including the Swede Fredrika Bremer (see below), the American Susan B. Anthony, and the eastern European activist Helen Ghika (1829–1888), who wrote under the pseudonym Dora d'Istria, all admired the powerful English work. In fact, one of Brontë's American obituaries extolled the book's ability to transcend national boundaries: "Women of the broad earth—whether English or American, French or German, it was for you that Charlotte Brontë wrote. . . . Jane Eyre was a fearfully honest book. That was why it startled the echo of all the corners of the earth and gathered them into one hoarse cry of opprobrium."[33]

The next year, Charlotte's sister Anne's novel *The Tenant of Wildfell Hall* appeared under the pseudonym Acton Bell. Widely read and critically acclaimed, it told the story of Helen Huntington, who was married to a selfish and brutal man. Unwilling to submit to him, Helen left with her young son and was forced to support herself. The novel was very radical because Helen's behavior defied both convention and British law. Moreover, Anne rewarded Helen's behavior with a happy ending rather than condemnation and more tragedy.

*Hertha, or the Story of a Soul*, written by Swedish novelist Fredrika Bremer (1801–1865), first appeared in England in 1855 and was published in Sweden a year later. Hertha is an unconventional homely young woman who lives under the control of her despotic father. Bremer's sharp critique of Sweden's laws that kept unmarried women under their fathers' guardianship regardless of their age provoked public outcry and helped contribute to the extension of rights to Swedish women over the next two decades.

In southern Europe, women writers struggled to have their voices heard in cultures marked by very conservative gender norms and low rates of female literacy. Spanish author Concepción Arenal (1820–1893) was amazingly prolific, publishing more than four hundred books and essays. She was a vocal opponent of separate spheres in a cultural milieu that promoted the separation of the sexes. Although radical for a Spaniard, her ideas about women's place in society were usually based on very traditional notions of feminine virtue. As a result, Arenal doubted women's ability to engage in politics, believing that they lacked the education and inner fortitude for such endeavors.[34] Novelist and critic Emilia Pardo Bazán (1852–1921) expressed the same complicated view of women. An ardent supporter of the women's movement, she argued that it was a

# Demands of the Radical Hungarian Women, 1848

*In Hungary, six weeks after the beginning of the revolution, this remarkable document appeared in the newspaper* Pesti Divatlap (Pest Fashion Magazine). *This document expresses concerns common to European women in 1848, as well as the particular issues facing Hungarian women at the time.*

1. We demand: that in addition to expertise in ordinary housekeeping, household management, and female labors, the true Hungarian woman comprehensively fulfill the requirements of intellectual development and know, at least in outline, and have clear ideas about the situation, constitution, laws, political relations, and history of Hungary and the world. Indeed, she should be able to speak modestly as befits a female, but also sensibly on every public affair. She should, however, avoid endless, pedantic politicizing, and instead occupy herself more frequently with matters agreeable to a woman's temper, such as the vital branches of knowledge, the arts, literature, social life, and more of this kind.

2. We demand: that the Hungarian woman actively take part in public affairs as much as possible. She should do everything possible in her circle to facilitate the triumph of rightful and good causes; gather loyal friends and strong supporters for everything that is beneficial and praiseworthy for the homeland. If by chance a man, who is bound to her heart by love, kinship, or feelings of friendship, should want to swerve off the proper course of patriotism . . . or be a detriment to the community . . . let her work . . . to return him to the right path.

3. We demand: that Hungarian women, according to their talents, support every undertaking, institution, association, and cause that aims at the advancement of the interests of humanity, homeland, or nation.

4. We demand: that in our resurrected nation every good mother raise ardent, loyal Hungarian sons and daughters for the homeland, a praiseworthy goal which can best be achieved through early maternal instruction.

5. We demand: that the minister of education shut down as soon as possible every foreign-spirited girls' school that stunts the growth of Hungarian pupils with respect to nationality or morals, and establish a model girls' school at national expense in the capital and in each district as well. . . .

6. We demand: that the wealthier Hungarian women effectively promote the instruction of not only their own offspring but the children of poor people as well—especially by means of beneficial kindergartens.

7. We demand: that all true Hungarian women know the most sacred patriotic requirements: to strengthen and assist the general diffusion of our nationality, which still stands on weak footing in more cultured circles, into every branch of public and private life, and make it a thing of respect and honor not only at home but abroad as well. . . .

8. We demand: that in general Hungarian be the reigning language of domestic and social circles, that in addition it be held in respect by foreigners appearing among us, and that it be the foreign language of conversation for all those who, as the result of adverse circumstances, have not yet had the opportunity to make the national language their own.

9. We demand: that everyone who knows Hungarian not address us in other languages; otherwise we will not converse with her or him.

10. We demand: that the true Hungarian mother neither teach nor have her children taught any foreign languages as long as the children do not speak the national one clearly, beautifully, and fluently.

11. We demand: that Hungarian women patronize and support above all the national literature and arts. That is why we also declare that those Hungarian women who avoid the national literature and arts and deem only foreign ones wor-

thy of attention—women who, for example, only subscribe to German or French papers and read only foreign books—are forever despised, and we will expel these traitorous, degenerate girls from our circles.

12. We demand: that every Hungarian woman who possesses a real vocation take pen in hand and work for the benefit and honor of freedom, the homeland, and women. But do not forget, however, about the woman's realm and responsibilities.

13. We demand: that Hungarian women train themselves in the fine arts, especially in those suited to the weaker sex—painting, singing, and music, with national progress always in view.

14. We demand: that Hungarian women not waste their money on foreign goods. . . .

15. We demand: that Hungarian women keep Hungarian servants in their homes.

16. We demand: that the most beautiful characteristics of an uncorrupted Hungarian, such as: pride in honor, honesty, trustworthiness, sobriety, generosity, and noble simplicity, united with a genuine and national-spirited culture, take hold particularly in domestic and social circles.

17. We demand: that every Hungarian patriot protect herself as much as possible from the corruption of foreign habits and fashions injurious to our nationality and morals.

18. We demand: that Hungarian women's fashion, free from apish imitation and developing through original initiative, have as its cornerstone: love of country, nationality, womanliness, domesticity, and simplicity.

19. We demand: that Hungarian women . . . be as thrifty as possible now and also later in this new world of scarce money, and not try to darken their domestic happiness with useless luxuries and vanities.

20. We demand: that the Hungarian woman's dress be national, attractive, but as simple as possible. It would be a true national sin for us to ignore or neglect the Hungarian dress, as there is none more beautiful in the whole world. We should wear our strikingly beautiful Hungarian costume not only on holidays, but constantly in domestic circles; we should display it, however, with all possible simplicity and at the lowest cost. . . .

21. We demand: that especially our larger social gatherings, parties, and particularly balls, be purely Hungarian-spirited and Hungarian-colored. In addition to our own folk dances we will only perform the dances of those nations for whom we feel real sympathy, and at whom we have no reason to be angry because of past deeds,—that is, the Poles and the French.

22. We demand: that indecent flirting, affectation, stiff correctness, ostentation, shrewishness, and other weaknesses that are so opposed to the genuine character of a Hungarian woman be forever banished from our circles.

23. We demand: that with the general diffusion . . . of these demands, Hungarian women's associations be formed across the country.

24. We demand: and finally . . . we ask Archduke Stephen, the royal viceroy, that because His Highness's good example will be widely followed, that he . . . establish and conduct a court that is outwardly and inwardly wholly Hungarian, which, on the ruins of the German courtiers' stockinged world, will reflect a true picture of our good old kings' national courtly and domestic life, and whose leading star—we are convinced—will be an enthusiastic Hungarian-speaking and Hungarian-spirited woman.

Published on the authority of the Radical Hungarian Women Imre Vahot.

This petition has already been signed by several hundred Hungarian women, and later thousands more will sign it.

Source: Robert Nemes, "Getting to the Source: Women in the 1848–1849 Hungarian Revolution," *Journal of Women's History* 13:3 (2001): 193–209.

serious error not to consider women as individuals, and she advocated for women's education and entry into the professions. Her 1896 novel, *Memories of a Bachelor*, applauded middle-class women's independence and productivity; however, many of her works reveal Pardo Bazán's conservative upper-class bias. Although she praised working-class women for their hard work and intelligence in her novel *The Tribune of the People* (1882), she also criticized the main character, Amparo, for getting pregnant outside of marriage and foolishly believing that her lover would marry her. Having published many articles on the condition of women, in 1900, Pardo Bazán was the only Spanish woman to attend the international Conference on the Condition and Rights of Women. As she became more involved in the women's movement, she was increasingly disappointed by the disinterest in it in Spain.

## The Right to Walk the Streets

The problem of prostitution also drew women to political activism. In particular, the campaign to repeal Britain's Contagious Diseases Acts (CDA) attracted worldwide attention and propelled women from around the world into politics. By 1885, 250,000 men and women gathered in London to demonstrate against the laws.[35] The ultimate success of this campaign owed much to the political knowledge that activist women had acquired in the preceding decades.

As we saw in the previous chapter, Britain passed a series of laws in the 1860s that gave the police the right to arrest any woman on suspicion of prostitution. Women could be forcibly tested for venereal disease, based on the rationale that prostitutes, not their clients, spread disease. Sick women could be imprisoned without trial. Similar laws existed in much of the rest of Europe. In response, many female reformers turned their attentions to ending the double standards of sexual behavior codified in the regulations. Purposefully associating their cause with antislavery activism, they called themselves Abolitionists, as they worked to abolish regulations against prostitutes and end the so-called white-slave trade. Angered by the laws' classist and sexist assumptions that trapped working-class women and made any woman on the street suspect and

liable for arrest, Josephine Butler (1828–1906) led the campaign against the CDA. Raised in a socially progressive family, she was active in the abolition movement. As a young woman, she had tried to attend a session of Parliament but was refused because she was a woman. She returned dressed as a boy. After the accidental death of her young daughter in 1864, Butler turned to rescuing prostitutes. She wrote that she needed to "find some pain keener than my own, to meet with people more unhappy than myself."[36] She eventually took over the leadership of the Ladies National Association for the Repeal of the Contagious Diseases Acts (LNA). Butler argued that the CDA violated British law because it allowed the police to arrest, convict, and imprison women without trial. In 1869, the London *Daily News* newspaper published a protest article written by Harriet Martineau and signed by 127 other women, including Florence Nightingale (1820–1910). They argued that "it was unjust to punish the sex who are the victims of a vice, and leave unpunished the sex who are the main cause, both of the vice and its dreaded consequences."[37] Their activism was controversial not only because women were engaging in public political activity, but also because they were talking about sex, prostitution, and rape—inappropriate topics for respectable women. As a result, many women faced criticism from their friends and families. Nevertheless, committees working for repeal of the CDA formed throughout Britain and actively engaged large numbers of middle-class women in their first political cause.

Working across the country, the LNA intervened in police raids, provided prostitutes with legal council and advice, and petitioned Parliament. The campaign was long and hard fought, and its success in 1886 came in no small part from Josephine Butler herself, whose physical beauty, charismatic speaking style, and respectable behavior made her a formidable advocate for prostitutes' rights. Her strategy also relied on building alliances between middle-class women and working-class men. In her public appearances, Josephine catered to men by urging them to take up their masculine roles of protective father and noble hero.[38]

Butler also took her campaign outside of England where she inspired other women to lead similar campaigns in France, Germany, Italy, and

India. In these areas, the campaign was tied to ongoing debates about the role of government in society. Butler helped found the British and Continental Federation against State Regulation of Vice, headquartered in Switzerland. It sponsored several international conferences and published a monthly newsletter. Through their efforts to end the regulation and imprisonment of prostitutes, activists argued against legal double standards for men and women, and they worked for labor reform so that women could find jobs that would pay enough to support them and their families. Although many women remained uncomfortable with their frank discussions of sex, the work of this organization introduced a new generation of women to the struggle for equality and emancipation.

In Berlin, Butler's campaign clashed with the work of the *Verein Frauenwohl* (Women's Welfare Association), founded in 1888. The Frauenwohl advocated abolition of government-controlled brothels but continued to see imprisonment of prostitutes and moral education to reform them as worthy goals. Led by Hanne Bieber-Böhm (1851–1910), this movement had strong ties to the conservative evangelical movement that believed that prostitutes were evil and in need of tough regulation. However, by 1898, Butler's ideas had inspired a new generation of women activists who agreed with Butler's abolitionist platform. They competed with Bieber-Böhm for control of the Frauenwohl and used the issue of prostitution to take over the organization. In Hamburg, the disagreements among women's groups were especially bitter. Led by radical Lida Gustava Heyman (1868–1943), Abolitionists made little headway against the police or the local government. In the end, the power of the newly unified government proved too strong and prostitutes continued to be harshly regulated, ostensibly for the good of German society.[39]

When Butler took her campaign to Italy in 1874 and 1875, it also was a newly united nation, still unsure of what role the state would play in society. Many liberal men supported the abolition of prostitution, arguing that regulation of prostitutes denied women equal rights and that the regulations promoted corruption among the police. Reformer Anna Maria Mozzoni (1837–1920) had extensive contact with Butler and led the Milanese branch of the International Abolitionist Federation. However, reform proved difficult under the new Italian constitution that left the parliament weak and gave the prime minister most of the power.

Finally, in 1888, the Crispi regulations (named after the prime minister) eased the pressure on prostitutes. Italian police continued to regulate brothels, and brothel keepers had to supply lists of their employees to the police. However, the police could not arrest women unless they were breaking the law, and simply being out in public was not a breach of the penal code. The government was also expected to provide treatment to both men and women infected with venereal disease. Finally, the police had to protect prostitutes from violence and help those who wanted to leave the profession. Unfortunately, poor enforcement and a dearth of government funds to run clinics led to a resurgence in syphilis and new demands for regulating prostitutes. In 1891, the Nicotera Laws reinstated some of the old regulations, including the surveillance of single women in public.

## Women and Pacifism

Women activists also joined forces in international campaigns against war. In the second half of the century, state-against-state aggression increased. Nations anticipated warfare with larger investments in military equipment and greater numbers of men in uniform. As conflicts erupted, women were particularly angered by the scale of the violence, as technological advances made weapons more deadly and more destructive. The Crimean War provoked considerable outrage from novelist Fredrika Bremer. In 1853, Britain and France invaded the Crimea to halt Russian encroachment in the Black Sea region. The campaign was marked by military incompetence, horrific conditions, and poor leadership. In an article for the *Times of London* in 1854, Bremer called on Christian women's associations across Europe to join forces to end the suffering. She hoped that "through women a peaceful alliance might be concluded, embracing the whole earth—an alliance opposing the direful effects of war." For Bremer, women's natural predilection for peace and their Christian duty obligated them to work to end the violence.

Prussian military expansion into the rest of Germany and France in the 1860s also motivated calls for peace. Marie Goegg (1826–1899), a Swiss pacifist, worked with her husband Amand for the Swiss-based International League of Peace and Liberty, founded in 1867. Although the League was primarily focused on the creation of a European federation, Marie pushed for the inclusion of women's issues in the League's agenda. In her speech to the 1868 congress, Marie specifically referred to the French Revolution's failure to include women rights: "Men have paid dearly for their mistake and their descendants still suffer. By denying women as their equal, arrogant men lowered their own stature. If women had been called from 1789 to develop their own abilities . . . society . . . would have progressed."[40] The League added women's emancipation to its demands in 1868, but Goegg also founded the International Association of Women. Entirely run by women, this organization advocated an end to war and the militaristic values that led to war. In speeches and articles, Goegg called on mothers to reeducate their sons so that they would disavow military glory and conquest. The International Association of Women attracted female intellectuals from across Europe, including Clemence Royer (d. 1902), the French translator of Darwin.

In 1868, the overthrow of Spanish queen Isabella II (1830–1904) led France into a war against Prussia over who would fill the empty Spanish throne. This war was very unpopular with activists. Journalist Léodile Bera Champseix (1832–1900), who wrote under the pseudonym André Leo (a name taken from her twin sons), and teacher Louise Michel (1830–1905) organized demonstrations and petition drives to protest the war. When the war began, they demanded the right to fight.[41]

After the Franco-Prussian War, women took up new efforts at establishing a permanent peace. In 1888, American women formed the National Council of Women, a branch of the International Council of Women that had been founded by May Wright Sewell (1822–1920), an educator. With permanent committees on peace and arbitration, both the National and International Councils focused on the need for peace education in families and public schools. In its pursuit of peace, Sewell's group also tried to reform children's literature, opposing violent games and harmful topics.[42]

Most of these groups worked with middle-class women, but French activist Sylvie Flammarion (1842–1919) and Séverine (a pen name for journalist Carolyn Rémy) worked with working-class women through the Association of Peace and Disarmament by Women. Flammarion hoped to attract the working class to her disarmament campaign by arguing that cuts in governmental investment in the arms race would ease their impoverishment. The initiative also drew women from the newly formed women's societies in Norway and Sweden.

By the 1890s, women were becoming a major force in international peace organizations. Prominent peace activists included Belva Lockwood (1830–1917), the first woman lawyer to argue before the U.S. Supreme Court, and Bertha von Suttner (1843–1914), a Czech-born peace activist. Both women sat on the executive board of the International Peace Bureau.[43] Suttner's 1889 work about the horrors of war, *Dei Waffen Nieder* (*Lay Down Your Arms*), became the most important antiwar novel of the period. She was awarded the Nobel Peace Prize in 1905.

The connections between the women's movement and the peace movement are vividly expressed in the life of Lucretia Mott. In addition to her work in the abolition and women's movements, Mott's Quaker faith pushed her into international peace activism. Frustrated by the failure of the American Peace Society to end the American Civil War, Mott and others founded the Universal Peace Union in 1866. Women made up half of the Union's membership, which included Belva Lockwood. The Union opposed imperialism, supported the rights of Native Americans, and tried to prevent U.S. entry into the Spanish-Cuban conflict in 1898 and U.S. interference in the Dominican Republic. Mott for her part also organized a peace petition to Britain, when tensions erupted between the United States and Britain over control of the Oregon Territory. For women like Mott, peace, freedom, and women's emancipation were all components of a lifelong quest for justice.

## Formalizing Connections

Toasting an audience of women activists convened in honor of the one-hundredth anniversary of the French Revolution, León Richer (1824–1911) said, "A principle has no country; truth knows no frontiers. The question of women's rights is the same everywhere; everywhere it can be summarized in two words: Equality, Justice."[44] Richer's focus on women's shared concerns reflected the internationalist vision of the women's movement during the 1870s. Buoyed by the associations formed over issues like prostitution, activists worked to build on the common obstacles facing women and their common goals through the creation of international organizations and regular international congresses. Although founded as a women's pacifist society affiliated with the International League of Peace and Liberty, by the 1870s, Marie Goegg's International Association of Women quickly adopted a much broader women's agenda. As explained on its membership card, the organization intended to "work for the moral and intellectual advancement of women, for the gradual amelioration of her position in society by calling for her human, civil, economic, social, and political rights." In practice, this meant advocating for equal pay with men, access to education, and equality before the law, issues that resonated among women activists across Europe. Although her organization was short-lived, Goegg's internationalism was carried on by its successor, Solidarity: Association for the Defense of Women's Rights.[45]

In 1878, women activists held a women's rights congress to coincide with the International Exposition in Paris. Participants came from as far away as Brazil and Russia. They debated legal and moral double standards, government-regulated prostitution, equal pay for equal work, government subsidies for motherhood, unionization, the effects of war on women, and perpetuation of the patriarchy. However, the decision to table the issue of suffrage provoked great debate and signaled a division within the women's movement. As had been true earlier in the century, many women believed that advocating suffrage would incite opposition and detract from the movement's other goals. Moreover, it was a moot point for women living under monarchical rule. Nevertheless, French suffragist Hubertine Auclert (1848–1914) argued that the right to vote was fundamental to changing women's position in society, "The weapon of the vote will be for us, just as it is for man, the only means of obtaining

the reforms we desire. As long as we remain excluded from civic life, men will attend to their own interests rather than to ours."[46]

After the congress, Elizabeth Cady Stanton's son Theodore (1851–1925), who had attended with his wife, French suffragist Marguerite Berry (b. 1861), toured Europe studying the status of women. His goal, was "to secure, in each country of Europe, the collaboration of one or more women, who, in connection with a literary training, had participated, either actively or in spirit, in some phase of the women's movement,—that remarkable social revolution now going on in old Europe as well as in young America."[47] His goal was a factual study that would be useful to future endeavors, rather than a political treatise. The essays were composed by women activists from various nations. The work exposed the expectations and assumptions of women in different countries, as well as the varying level of political involvement of women. Anna Schepeler-Lette (1827–1897) and Jenny Hirsch (1829–1902), who wrote the essay on Germany, noted that, "Many excellent reforms have encountered a long and obstinate resistance on this side of the Rhine because they were said to be a product of the upheaval of 1789, and in addition to its unfortunate origins, was brought into disrepute as the 'Emancipation of Women.'"[48] Concepción Arenal had a similarly dismal view of women's status in Spain and critiqued Spain's lack of industrialization and work opportunities for women. Likewise, Elise van Calcar (1822–1904) decried the pace of change in the Netherlands, "I am sorry to confess that, as regards the general emancipation of women, we have accomplished but very little."[49] Stanton's authors vividly described the successes, failures, hopes, and desires of a generation of women activists.

During the second half of the nineteenth century, the women's movement in Europe and North America built on the momentum gained during the Revolutions of 1848. The international connections among activists flourished as they found shared concerns in the growing numbers of women's novels. They also focused on international initiatives that brought activist women from many cultures together for specific goals, such as the abolition of prostitution and an end to warfare.

They learned that despite cultural and linguistic differences, they could find common purpose in the struggle for women's emancipation.

## RADICAL ACTIONS AND LIBERAL REFORMS

Despite an enhanced sense of unity among many women activists and a shared sense of women's oppression, activists remained divided by class and political ideologies, differences that produced competing visions of reform in the last half of the century. Some wanted full equality with men, others wanted better protection to help them raise their families. Inspired by socialism and the social theorists Karl Marx (1818–1883) and Freidrich Engels (1820–1895), radical activists demanded social revolution that would empower the working class and bring an end to private property. In contrast, liberals believed that the best strategy to resolve social problems was to legislate social change that would create conditions whereby the individual could thrive and fulfill his, and sometimes her, potential. Rather than overhaul the system, liberals relied on legal reforms that accepted governmental processes and protected individual liberty. The conflicts between liberals and radicals reveal the difficulties involved in integrating class and gender into a coherent plan for social transformation.

### The Franco-Prussian War and the Paris Commune, 1870–1871

The growing strength of the radical left first showed itself in France. With the extension of universal male suffrage in France in 1848, voters elected the nephew of Napoleon Bonaparte, Louis Napoleon (1808–1873), as president. However, Louis Napoleon quickly lost interest in maintaining the republic. In 1851, unable to run for a second term, he overthrew the government in a coup d'état. Then, to legitimize his government he called a plebiscite, a national referendum, which overwhelmingly affirmed his rule as Emperor Napoleon III. Then in a poorly conceived move to exert his imperial authority, Napoleon III engaged his longtime nemesis, Prussia, in the brief but disastrous Franco-Prussian War. On September 3, 1870, just two months after hostilities broke out, the Prussians captured the emperor and one hundred thousand troops. Upon hearing the news, the citizens of Paris proclaimed a new revolution and a new republic with a provisional government. However, this nonviolent revolution did not prevent Prussia's advance, and on September 18, Prussian troops besieged Paris.

When the French Army was delayed in coming to Paris, Parisians bolstered the National Guard's defense of the city. One plan suggested the creation of all-women's battalions, called "Amazons of the Seine." Supporters argued that women would make ideal soldiers because, among other things, they "drink little and above all do not smoke."[50] Plans called for wealthy women to fund these battalions with their jewelry, which would be confiscated if the Prussians invaded. Although fifteen hundred women signed up to be Amazons of the Seine, the National Guard was not interested and abandoned the plan.

With Paris under siege, the rest of France established a new government. The French electorate chose an elderly and conservative statesman, Adolphe Thiers (1797–1877), to lead the nation. However, to the surprise of many, Thiers immediately surrendered to Prussia and accepted all of Prussia's demands. Although Thiers successfully ended the siege of Paris, the subsequent settlement forced France to cede most of Alsace, part of Lorraine, and the city of Metz to Prussia and to pay an indemnity of five billion francs. Moreover, Thiers allowed the Prussians to hold a triumphal military march through the city of Paris. These terms outraged the Parisians, who had sacrificed much during the siege. Thiers further angered the poor and working-class citizens of Paris when he ended the wartime moratoria on debts and the sale of pawned goods. Finally, adding insult to injury, Thiers decided that the National Assembly would reside in Versailles, not Paris, and that army would take the cannons left in the city from the National Guard.

On March 18, 1871, in the working-class neighborhood of Montmartre, military discipline broke down and angry Parisian workers took control of the cannons, initiating another siege of Paris. However, this time, the enemy spoke the same language, as the National Guard defended Paris from the French Army. During the siege, Parisians formed a radical new leftist government, the Commune. The Commune enforced the separation of church and the state, secularized education, and made plans to abolish the class structure. Fearful for their property and livelihoods, many members of the bourgeoisie hunkered down in their homes to wait out the crisis or fled.

The Commune's leaders were mostly radical members of the bourgeoisie, while their supporters were working-class men and women. Although women had no official role in either the Commune's government or the National Guard, many, such as Russian émigré and radical activist Elizabeth Dmietrieff (1851–1910), formed political clubs including the Union des Femmes (Union of Women) to act as intermediaries between the Commune and working women. The Union demanded that the Commune end all discrimination against women, provide meeting halls for women, and subsidize the printing of materials. Members of the Union also marched in the streets and wrote editorials for Commune newspapers.

During the violence, working-class women worked as *cantinières* and *ambulancières*, providing the National Guard troops with food, drink, and medical care. One ambulancière, Alix Milliet Payen, wrote to her mother that she was stationed in the southwestern part of Paris, where the army was bombarding the city. She was camped in a cemetery in the rain. The men had no tents and blankets. Despite their hard work, these women were not always appreciated, and many suffered sexual and physical abuse at the hands of the National Guard.[51]

Female Communards struggled to convince Commune leaders to include their concerns in the revolutionary program. André Leó repeatedly denounced women's exclusion from direct political action and their poor treatment by the National Guard. Prior to the Commune, Leó had written on a number of women's issues, including the uneasy relationship between women and revolutionaries. In one of her Commune publications, Leó noted that, "From a certain perspective, one could write our [women activists'] history since [17]89 under the title: 'History of the Revolutionary Party's Inconsistencies.' The woman question would make up the largest chapter, and it would show how this

party successfully pushed half of its troops over to the enemy's side, troops who only wanted to march and fight for the revolution."[52] During the Commune, Leó focused her outrage on those advocates of democracy who continued to deny women the vote. Leó worked alongside Louise Michel, without a doubt the most famous female Communard.

During the Commune, Michel undertook a variety of tasks. She headed the women's vigilance committee of Montmartre that cared for workers' children, set up a soup kitchen, organized and staffed ambulance stations, and tended to the wounded. Despite these many responsibilities, she could not stay away from the heat of battle. Dressed in a National Guard uniform, she fought alongside her male comrades. According to her own account, Michel used her sex to challenge the enemy, "You are men, I am only a woman, yet I look you in the eye. . . . Kill me if you are brave enough."[53]

The Commune lasted only ten weeks. Thiers refused to negotiate with them and in May 1870, the army broke into the city and slaughtered twenty-five to thirty thousand men, women, and children. As the Communards retreated behind barricades, many set fire to the city. The image of women incendiaries, or *pétroleuses*, is one of the most enduring of the Paris Commune. Although few women actually set fires, fear of these women spread among the bourgeoisie. Artists and caricaturists portrayed pétroleuses as madwomen irrationally bent on the destruction of property and home, the very place where women belonged.

The army then marched thirty-eight thousand Communards to Versailles to face trial. The prisoners suffered humiliation and brutality at the hands of their jailers. In one prison, an enclosed field with no shelter, the only water to drink was a pond into which executed prisoners were thrown. More than one thousand women were accused of participating in the uprising. According to the official account of the trial, "All or almost all live indecently . . . even the married women. . . . The immense majority . . . could be easily won over by the appealing prospect of disorder. . . . Idleness, envy, and thirst for unknown and ardently desired pleasures all contributed to blinding them. Hence they threw themselves into the revolutionary movement which was to engulf them."[54] The government sentenced forty-five hundred people to prison terms, and an additional forty-five hundred, including Louise Michel, were deported to the prison camp at New Caledonia (see Chapter 11). Many others, including André Leó, went into exile. The government used the trials to discredit the Commune and to define female rebels as unwomanly and unfeminine. Politics, the government asserted, was for men; women should stay home. Although the violence that the French government used on its citizens shocked Europe, women's visible participation perpetuated the belief that women in politics equaled anarchy and violence.

## Women and Early Marxism

The Communards relied heavily on the ideas of Karl Marx and Freidrich. In the *Communist Manifesto* (1848), Marx and Engels argued for the need to reinterpret history from a material rather than a moral perspective, privileging workers' exploitation in historical narrative rather than intellectuals and ideas. They argued that a socialist order run by the working class after the overthrow of the capitalist system was inevitable.

According to Marx, capitalism destroyed the family and harmed men, women, and children by forcing them into factory work. Prostitution provided even more dire evidence of the control of capital over people's bodies and minds. However, Marx did not see the oppression of working women as different from the oppression experienced by working men. In fact, he emphasized the similarities between men and women of the same class and reminded working women that bourgeois women activists were working for goals that

**COMMUNARDS IN A VERSAILLES PRISON CAMP AFTER THE FALL OF THE COMMUNE.** The government believed that female Communards were unwomanly and unfeminine, and they treated them with particular brutality after their arrest. *(Hulton-Deutsch Collection/Corbis.)*

would not ultimately remedy their class-based oppression.

During the government repression that followed the Commune, some Marxists began to grapple with the relationship between their ideas and gender. In 1878, August Bebel (1840–1914) wrote his critical work, *Women in the Past, Present, and Future,* later republished as *Women and Socialism.* Bebel predicted that women's emancipation would come only as a result of the socialist revolution:

> The complete emancipation of woman, and her equality with man, is the final goal of our cultural development, the achievement of which no power on earth can prevent. But it is possible only on the basis of a transformation that abolishes all domination of man by man, and hence also that of the worker by the capitalist. Only now will human development reach its peak. The "Golden Age" men have been dreaming of for millennia and for which they have yearned, will come at last. An end will be put to class domination once and for all, and with it too man's domination of woman.[55]

By arguing that women's oppression was a component of capitalism and that the socialist future held promise for women as women, not just as workers, Bebel helped to relate Marxism to the expanding women's movement.

Following from Bebel's work, Friedrich Engels reflected on women's oppression in *The Origins of the Family, Private Property, and the State* (1884). Engels argued that women's oppression was rooted in the ancient past and in the connection between property and monogamous marriage. Ancient societies established slaves and breeding herds as property and then transferred inheritance systems from females to males. According to Engels, "The overthrow of the mother-right was the world historical defeat of the female sex."[56] Engels argued that only women's economic independence and the end of the monogamous family as an economic unit would restore women's power. In response, opponents accused Marxists of being antifamily.

The most vocal proponent of integrating the women's movement and Marxism was Clara Zetkin (1857–1933). From a working-class background, she joined the Socialist Party (SPD) while still in high school, although German chancellor Otto von Bismarck (1815–1898) outlawed the party in 1878. In 1881, she followed her lover, Russian socialist Ossip Zetkin (1848–1889), into political exile in Paris. Although she used his name and had two children by him, Zetkin did not marry Ossip and his sudden death only a few years later left her with two small children and no support. Familiar with the issues facing working women, she pressured socialist leaders to form the International Socialist Women's Secretariat and urged the annual celebration of an International Proletarian Women's Day. Zetkin argued that until women achieved economic independence, they would be enslaved to men, just as workers were enslaved to capital. In 1890, she returned to Germany when the SPD again became legal. Two years later, she assumed the editorship of the socialist women's magazine *Die Gleicheit* (*Equality*). By 1894, Zetkin had formed the German Social Democratic Women's movement and had severed her connections with other Marxists groups.

## Liberal Reforms

Leftist violence in 1848 and 1871 and the Marxist insistence on an end to private property concerned liberals and pressured them to take substantive action to ameliorate women's inferior status. Many politicians focused on the reform of marriage as it was legally constituted. Marriage not only made women subject to the rule of their husbands but also made them legal nonentities, as married women in many countries lost their legal personhood. They argued that marriage constituted a form of prostitution in which women purchased their economic security with their bodies. Moreover, laws gave them no protection from domestic violence or men's financial mismanagement. In England, women activists opposed the law of coverture, which denied married women control of their property.

At least two famous couples made strong public stands against marriage laws. Before John Stuart Mill (1806–1873) married writer and activist Harriet Taylor in 1851, he made a formal written protest against England's marriage laws. His brief statement included a public assurance that "she [Taylor] retains in all respects whatever the same absolute freedom of action and freedom of disposal of herself and of all that does or may at any time belong to her, as if no such marriage had taken place; and I absolutely disclaim and repudiate all pretension to have acquired any rights whatever by virtue of such marriage."[57] Taylor also expressed concerns about the impact of matrimony on a relationship in her essay, "The Enfranchisement of Women" (1851). She argued that marriage laws made men "either the conscious or unconscious despot of his household."

Similarly, in the United States, when abolitionists Lucy Stone (1818–1893) and Henry Blackwell (1825–1909) married in 1855, they published their "Marriage Protest," which began:

> *While acknowledging our mutual affection by publicly assuming the relationship of husband and wife, yet in justice to ourselves and a great principle, we deem it a duty to declare that this act on our part implies no sanction of, nor promise of voluntary obedience to such of the present laws of marriage, as refuse to recognize the wife as an independent, rational being, while they confer upon the husband an injurious and unnatural superiority, investing him with legal powers which no honorable man would exercise, and which no man should possess.*[58]

The protest went on to list laws related to marriage that the couple found unjust. Stone also refused to take her husband's surname.

In 1869, eleven years after Harriet Taylor's death, Mill published *The Subjection of Women*. He argued that legal and cultural constraints, particularly marriage, prevented women from fully developing their intellectual and social potential. Laws concerning inheritance, divorce, and even women's participation in politics and the professions denied women basic rights merely because of their sex without any acknowledgment of individual abilities. He compared married women's legal status to that of slavery. Thus, the law required extensive reform: "The equality of married persons before the law, is not only the sole mode in which that particular relation can be made consistent with justice to both sides, and conducive to the happiness of both, but it is the only means of rendering the daily life of mankind, in any high sense, a school of moral cultivation" (Chapter 2). Indeed, women's subjection was so complete that the responsibility for change lay with men, "Women cannot be expected to devote themselves to the emancipation of women, until men in considerable number are prepared to join with them in the undertaking" (Chapter 3). Widely translated and read, this work became a major influence on the women's movement in Europe, inspiring liberal men and women to pursue political and marriage reform across the continent.

Although many considered these couples' positions extreme, liberal reformers worked to temper the negative implications of marriage for women. After much lobbying, pressure on male relatives who were politicians, and publicity, reformers could celebrate some successes. In 1857, the British Parliament passed the Divorce Act, which made it easier for women to terminate a marriage, although it was still difficult and costly. After 1869, British women who met property qualifications could vote in municipal elections. This limited franchise also allowed women to run for local public offices, particularly school boards and poor-law boards, positions that fell within women's traditional spheres. By 1879, there were seventy women on British school boards and by 1885, fifty women served on poor-law boards.[59] Finally, in 1882, Parliament passed the Married Women's Property Act, which gave married women control over their property and access to the same legal remedies available to unmarried women. The British parliament also slowly expanded the voting rights of women, allowing them to vote in county council elections after 1888.

In Sweden, Denmark, and Norway, legislators passed a series of laws that improved women's status despite the fact that Scandinavian conservatism hindered the formation of a strong women's movement. Initially, liberals improved women's civil and legal standing as part of a broad attempt to reform the government and break the power of the hereditary nobility and powerful monarchs. In Sweden, liberal politicians passed legislation giving women equal inheritance rights in 1845. During the next two decades, they lifted guild restrictions on women, allowed single women to become legal adults at age twenty-five, and granted women the right to marry without a male relative's consent. The debates over these reforms, which expanded middle-class income and gave unmarried women respectable occupations, largely ignored the issue of women's rights, focusing instead on broader economic concerns. In 1873, the first women's association, the Association for Married Women's Property Rights, demanded that married women be allowed to control their own property. However, the campaign hit a glitch when the Association proposed the complete abolition of marital property. Women's progress was further slowed when, although property-owning women had been voting in local elections since 1862, the legislature firmly rejected female suffrage in 1884. Even when the Swedish women's movement began in earnest in 1885 with the founding of the Fredrika Bremer Society, its programs were quite moderate and focused on improving women's legal status. The Society stressed education and self-help programs that included employment bureaus for women, educational funds, and pension funds. Only later did the organization broaden its work to include more controversial issues like sex education and suffrage.

Danish women followed a similar path to legal reform. They passed the Majority Act in 1857, which gave single adult women full civil and legal standing. Women's activism only emerged in the 1870s. In 1871, Mathilde Bajer (1840–1934) and her husband, Fredrik (1837–1922), founded the Danish Women's Association, inspired in part by the translation and publication of Mill's *Subjection of Women* in 1869. Because the legislation of the 1850s had largely benefited single women, the Danish Women's Association focused on bringing economic equality to married women. Fredrik Bajer left the Association when he was elected to Parliament; however, from his new position he ensured the passage of the law giving married women economic independence in 1880. Despite these successes, the Association remained small and generally conservative in its goals and strategies. As more radical groups emerged in the 1880s, the organization lent its general support for suffrage, but it refused to promote the cause itself for fear of appearing partisan and losing influence with the legislature.

Differences between radicals and liberals divided the campaign for women's rights during the last half of the nineteenth century. Although Marxists and members of the women's movement did not always agree on priorities and strategies, many Marxist women worked to end working-class exploitation without neglecting the cause of women's emancipation. Liberals pursued a more moderate path, pushing for legislative reform of marriage and women's property rights. In both cases, broader political agendas often slowed the campaign for women's rights.

## WOMEN AND THE CREATION OF NATIONAL IDENTITIES

During the nineteenth century, many of Europe's smaller political entities united to form larger nation-states. In terms of women's rights and women's social roles, the nationalism that drove these movements objected to women's emancipation. Nationalists wanted women to be good patriotic mothers, educating their children in the native language and culture. They believed that men and women should put the state's interests ahead of individual concerns. Across Europe, women struggled to forge a space for themselves that did not conflict with their newfound national identities.

### German Unification

With Germany's defeat of France in the Franco-Prussian War, the many independent German principalities united under Prussia's military leadership (see Map 10.3). Although much of the day-to-day business of government remained in the hands of local governments, Chancellor Otto von Bismarck headed a militaristic, autocratic central government. Bismarck ruled with an iron hand and limited the amount of political agitation by citizens. However, autocratic rule did not erase religious, class, regional, or gender differences.

One of the first challenges facing the German government was the worldwide economic crisis of 1873. During the crisis, cheap grain from Russia, the United States, and Canada flooded Germany's markets, hurting local producers. To protect

***Map 10.3* The Unification of Germany, 1866–1871.** Germany was unified under conservative Prussian leadership, which prevented women from engaging in any political activities.

German agriculture and industry and maintain the support of Catholic and Protestant landholders, Bismarck imposed high tariffs on imports. Although his economic policies favored factory and landowners, they did not particularly address the concerns of workers. To win their support, Bismarck pushed through a series of social reforms, including insurance for sick and injured workers and social security for retirees. At the same time, he banned the Socialist Party and imprisoned many of its leaders.

Bismarck demonstrated little interest in the problems facing women. He supported the traditional middle-class ideal that placed women at home subject to the rule of their husbands. In fact, laws prohibited women from political activities, keeping them out of the public eye and further hampering women's demands for equality and suffrage. Many described women's emancipation as unpatriotic, asserting that it would prevent Germany from fully developing its potential as a nation. The only way that women could work on behalf of the nation was through charitable activities that served Germany's military aims. Through their churches and independent associations, middle-class women dispensed charity to the poor, the sick, and orphans. German society saw these efforts as an extension of the female virtues of warmth, care, tenderness, and nurturance.[60] After unification, women's charitable societies were organized under the League of German Patriotic Women's Societies, affiliated with the International Red Cross. By 1877, there were four hundred branches of Patriotic Women's Societies, and by 1891, nearly eight hundred.[61] During wartime, women trained as nurses and raised money to build hospitals and clinics. During peacetime, they assisted in relief work in natural disasters such as floods. Because these groups aided the military, an unquestioningly masculine institution, the state approved of them as appropriately feminine. Dominated by middle-class women, these patriotic societies did not demand social or legal equality.

## Women and Italian Unification

After the overthrow of Napoleon, the Italian peninsula also included many independent states, each with its own political culture. The pope ruled the Papal States. The Kingdom of Sardinia developed a liberal constitutional monarchy after 1848. Much of the north remained in the hands of the autocratic Habsburg Empire. In the poor, rural, and undeveloped south, a large oppressed peasant population lived under the rule of the Kingdom of the Two Sicilies.

Italian unification, *Il Risorgimento*, came in stages (see Map 10.4). First, the great Sardinian statesman Count Cavour (1810–1861) wrestled Lombardy from the Austrian Empire for his monarch, King Victor Emmanuel (r. Sardinia from 1849; r. Italy 1861–1878). At the same time, the revolutionary and republican-minded Giuseppe Garibaldi (1807–1882) led the fight to unite southern Italy. Concerned about Garibaldi's military success, Cavour sent an army to invade the Papal States and regain control of the unification process from his much more colorful rival. Cavour's plan worked and, in 1860, much of central Italy voted to join the new Kingdom of Sardinia. Unification was completed in 1870 when Rome and Venice agreed to join the Kingdom of Italy ruled by Victor Emmanuel II.

Garibaldi was a romantic figure. He fought all over the world for republican causes and attracted many women to his side. His first wife, Brazilian Ana Maria de Jesus Ribeiro da Silva, better known as Anita Garibaldi, dressed as a man and fought alongside him. She died in 1849, helping him besiege Rome at the end of the Revolution of 1848. After her death, Garibaldi had many mistresses, some of whom were wealthy and influential and funded his campaigns for Italian unification.

The process of unifying the Italian peninsula sparked debates about the status of women and women's citizenship. During these debates, Anna Maria Mozzoni demanded full equality, including suffrage, for Italian women. Mozzoni argued:

> *To deny woman complete educational reform, to deny her access to higher levels of instruction, to deny her work, to deny her a living in the city, to deny her a life in the nation, to deny her a public voice, is no longer possible. Those interests hostile to the resurgence of women can delay it with an unworthy battle, but they will never be able to prevent it.*[62]

Mozzoni fought vigorously for women's rights. In 1881, she founded the first Italian woman's rights organization, the League to Promote the Interests of Women. As we have seen, she was also active on the international stage. In addition to her work on the abolition of prostitution laws, she was well connected with leaders in the women's movements in other nations, attending international conferences and giving the opening address at the 1878 Women's Rights Congress.[63] She also translated Mill's treatise *The Subjection of Women* into Italian.

Many of the women active in Italy's fight for unification were either educated in other parts of Europe or foreigners married to Italian men, such as Jesse White Mario (1832–1906). She had raised

**Map 10.4** THE UNIFICATION OF ITALY, 1859–1870. The unification of Italy resulted in the melding of different legal systems, economies, and political ideologies, but women still remained without an official political role.

money for the cause of Italian republicanism and unification, and after moving to Italy, she fought with Garibaldi on the battlefield. Inspired by Marx, she worked in the early stages of unification to build bridges between different classes of women and obtain equal rights for women.

In 1865, the new government in the north accepted a modified form of the Napoleonic Code that limited suffrage to men who met certain property requirements, a small sector of the male middle class and aristocracy, and sanctioned the legal inferiority of women. However, the Code included a provision that the property that women brought to their marriages would remain in their name and under their control.

Despite their disappointment, women continued to fight for equality. Gualberta Alaide Beccari (1842–1890) founded the journal *La Donna* (*Woman*) in 1869. Beccari had a long history of republican activism, having been born while her parents were in exile for their political activities. Mozzoni, for her part, continued her work for women's suffrage. Firm in the belief that men were not "the natural representatives of women's interests," she submitted a petition requesting the vote for women to each new parliament beginning in 1874. By 1907, her petition had ten thousand signatures.[64]

Italian women faced a formidable opponent in the papacy, which vigorously opposed women's rights. Forced to flee Rome during the Revolution in 1848, Pope Pius IX (r. 1846–1878) rejected any nationalist agenda or attempt at modernization that diminished the role of the church or removed women from their family responsibilities. Pope Leo XIII (r. 1878–1903), Pius's successor, reaffirmed men's role in supporting the family, "Women, again, are not suited for certain occupations; a woman is by nature fitted for home-work, and it is that which is best adapted at once to preserve her modesty and to promote the good bringing up of children and the well-being of the family" (*Rerum Novarum*, 1891).

Women activists responded that the state must create a legal and economic environment that allowed women to be the best mothers possible. In 1890, Milanese women organized the League for the Defense of Women's Interests. They wanted the government to establish a maternity insurance fund. The money was to come from wealthy women, the state, and workingmen's associations. Women in other Italian cities formed similar groups.

At the beginning of the twentieth century, Catholic women's organizations hoped to integrate religion and rights for women. These groups, which drew more women than secular women's organizations, advocated greater educational and employment opportunities for women. They founded trade unions for women and benevolent societies aimed at helping poor women. The pope affirmed many of their goals by granting an audience to the Italian Union of Catholic Women in 1909.

## Russia and the Baltic

Nationalism was not limited to the emerging states of Italy and Germany. Ethnic groups that had failed to achieve independence and states with long histories of territorial conquest, such as Russia, experienced the demands of nationalists as well. These demands cast women in the role of patriotic mothers, who as consumers and housewives could promote the nationalist agenda by teaching children their heritage. The Russian Empire was a large multiethnic and autocratic state. Russian nationalists wanted to reform the tsarist government, and ethnic minorities such as the Finns wanted independence. Ukrainians, who lived under both Russian and Austro-Hungarian domination, also had a nationalist movement. Both Finnish and Ukrainian nationalist movements involved women and women's issues, but to very different ends.

Until the beginning of the nineteenth century, Sweden ruled Finland. In 1809, Finland achieved partial autonomy when the Russian tsar also became the Grand Duke of Finland. However, Russian overlordship did not preclude Finland from developing its own representative government. Socialists dominated this government and made independence from Russia one of their goals. Mother-educators played a large role in the rhetoric of Finnish independence. Mothers taught their children Finnish rather than Swedish or Russian. Activists founded Finnish language newspapers and schools to perpetuate Finnish identity. By 1880, many of these schools were coeducational. The interactions of boys and girls

**EXECUTION OF SOFIA PEROVSKAIA.** Sophia Perovskaia was born to an elite family. Her education introduced her to Russia's social inequities and radical political ideas. Despairing of any hope for reform, she joined a terrorist group who assassinated the tsar. She was executed for her participation. *(© Corbis.)*

overcame preconceived ideas about women's inferior intellectual capabilities. At about the same time, John Stuart Mill's *Subjection of Women* appeared in Finnish and inspired women to organize for greater rights. Women's rights advocate Baroness Aleksandra Gripenberg (1857–1913) explained, "The leading men appealed to the mothers, through whom the ideas were to go to the coming generation by the education of the children in their native tongue. The women did not remain indifferent, and for them this movement became the plow which prepared the field for another idea—that of their own rights."[65]

Russia viewed the Finnish cultural campaign with great concern and in 1899 countered with a Russification program, provoking a political crisis. Finnish men and women fought to extend self-determination and maintain their culture. In October 1905, Finns called a national strike and the tsar, preoccupied with a revolution in Russia (see Chapter 12) capitulated to their demands. He granted the Finnish diet (legislature) virtual independence and universal suffrage. Finnish women had been voting in municipal elections for more than a decade and universal suffrage extended this right to national elections. Never complacent, Gripenberg, who was ultimately elected to the Finnish parliament, noted Finnish women's debt to other suffragists: "Our victory is in all cases great, and more so as the proposal has been adopted without opposition. The gratitude which we women feel is mingled with the knowledge that we are much less worthy of this great success than the women of England and America, who have struggled so long and so faithfully, with much more energy and perseverance than we."[66] Indeed, with the success of the Finns, the fight for suffrage would intensify over the coming decade in the rest of Europe and the United States.

In the Ukraine, nationalists were unsuccessful in their bid for independence from either Russia or the Habsburgs. As ethnic minorities, Ukrainian men and women had few rights in either empire. However, the women's movement within the Ukrainian independence movement had to contend as much with sexual discrimination from the nationalists as with resistance from the Russian and Austro-Hungarian governments. The leader of the Ukrainian women's movement was the German-educated Natalia Ozarkevych Kobryns'ka (1855–1920). She was widely read in political theory, including Mill, Marx, and Engels, and believed that the emancipation of women would only come with greater education and economic opportunities. She founded women's groups in her hometown of Stanyslaviv to help women educate themselves about their oppressed conditions. In the 1890s, she published a woman's almanac, *Nasha dolia (Our Fate)*. Although sympathetic to socialism, she did not believe that it would automatically bring emancipation to women. To immediately improve women's lives, she opened kitchens and daycare centers to help peasant women while they worked in the fields. The kitchens and daycares not only cared for and fed children, but also taught them Ukrainian to counter Polish Catholic efforts to teach Polish. Kobryns'ka also formed alliances with Czech women, and together they petitioned the Viennese Reichstag (legislature) for greater educational opportunities. Her petition of 1890 had 226 signatures from Ukrainian women. Kobryns'ka's father, a member of the Reichstag, presented her petition, but the body never discussed it. Kobryns'ka's efforts did not find support among men in the independence movement either. Like many nationalists, they believed that the woman question diverted attention away from the more important issue of independence and that women should support the men's work. Kobryns'ka bitterly denounced this position as "the blind faith of our

women in male authority and the tragic economic dependence of women upon men."[67]

Russia presented an altogether different situation for women. With only minimal industrialization and a highly autocratic government, most women in Russia had been serfs with few rights and no education. Much of the impetus for reform in Russia came with Russia's defeat in the Crimean War (1853–1856). In analyzing the war, it became clear that Russia's lack of industry and railroads played a major role in its defeat, and serfdom prevented Russia's economic development. Tsar Alexander II (r. 1855–1881) believed that the government should initiate all reforms. As we saw in the last chapter, his scheme to emancipate the serfs forced them to purchase their land. As a result, they became further impoverished and alienated rather than productive farmers. Government reforms increased industrialization and the number of railroads, but the pace of reform was slow and focused largely on the military. Few attempts were made to expand political participation or liberalize the laws.

Among the nobility and the small middle class, Russian women had property rights but remained under their fathers' legal authority. In the 1860s, many middle-class women, in an effort to free themselves from their fathers' despotism, entered into "white marriages" to like-minded men to gain independence from their families. Husbands in white marriages did not exercise their legal and sexual prerogatives, and couples often did not live together. Espousing a doctrine of *nihilism*, which negated all old ways of living, these young women participated in a counterculture that accepted them as equals of men. They attended universities and joined underground political groups. Women nihilists dressed in ways that displayed their political ideologies. They wore short hair, dark glasses, and mannish clothing. They behaved in unfeminine ways that showed their disrespect for old institutions such as the Russian Orthodox Church and the government.

For some nihilists, it was not enough to dress and act in new ways. Underground groups of revolutionaries wanted faster reform. They spread propaganda that advocated overthrowing the government. When the peasantry did not rise up, they began a campaign of terrorism and assassination. In 1878, prompted by the beating of a friend who

## Sofia Perovskaia, Russian Radical

Women's activism in nineteenth-century Russia had a moral fervor absent from western Europe and the United States. Sofia Perovskaia was the daughter of a dictatorial military officer and a shy provincial woman. Her politicization began in 1869 when she and some two hundred other women began attending lectures in Saint Petersburg. Energized by the lectures, Perovskaia and others formed women's groups to discuss politics, social reform, and the woman question. Through these discussions, Perovskaia came to oppose the economic exploitation of the masses and understand the need for women's rights. She believed that women had the right to share public privileges and responsibilities with men because women were morally superior to men.

Perovskaia fled her father's wrath and joined the Chaikovskii Circle. Until its demise in 1874, this group ran an underground printing press and worked to educate peasants about their economic exploitation. Perovskaia found work among peasants difficult. Her short hair, utilitarian clothing, and confident behavior led many peasants to believe that she was a witch.

Perovskaia returned to Saint Petersburg to open a school for factory workers and organize a correspondence program with prison inmates. Although the members of the Chaikovskii Circle did not engage in violence, their radical politics attracted the government's attention, and they were arrested in 1874. Many of her companions were convicted, but the court found Perovskaia innocent. Seeing no other way to reform, she reluctantly joined the terrorist group the People's Will in 1879. This group was intent on assassinating the tsar. Perovskaia's motives were less ideological than personal. She told her brother "I'm simply taking my revenge for my good friends who have died on the scaffold and in the fortresses [prisons]."[1] Perovskaia served on the group's executive council, which was nearly one-third female.

The People's Will made several attempts on the tsar's life before finally succeeding. Each attempt required a great deal of planning and was exceedingly dangerous. After a third attempt failed, Perovskaia became discouraged and she contemplated suicide. However, while planning the final attempt on the tsar, Sofia and the leader of the People's Will, Andrei Zheliabov, became lovers.

Only Zheliabov and Perovskaia knew the entire plot to kill the tsar. Police arrested Zheliabov the day before the attempt, leaving Perovskaia in charge. The conspirators planned to mine a street used by the tsar. If this failed, the revolutionaries would throw a bomb into the tsar's carriage. When the tsar took a different route, Perovskaia anticipated the change, and the assassination finally succeeded. Nine days later, on March 10, 1881, the police arrested her, and four others. At the trial, she did not deny her own role in the plot but tried to protect the other defendants. The six-day trial ended with the conviction of all the defendants, who were hanged. Writing to her mother the day before her death, Perovskaia tried to reassure her, "my fate isn't all that dismal. I have lived according to my convictions; I could not have acted otherwise, and so I await the future with a clear conscience."[2]

Sofia Perovskaia and the other women in Russia's revolutionary movement took traditionally female expectations of service and self-sacrifice and employed them on behalf of their radical politics. They engaged in violence and risked their lives to fight the injustice and oppression that plagued nineteenth-century Russia. Fervent and determined, Sofia Perovskaia would become a model for Soviet revolutionaries in the tumultuous revolutions of the twentieth century.

[1] Barbara Alpern Engel, *Mothers and Daughters: Women of the Intelligentsia in Nineteenth-Century Russia* (Cambridge: Cambridge University Press, 1983), 178.
[2] Engel, 199.

Source: Barbara Alpern Engel, *Mothers and Daughters: Women of the Intelligentsia in Nineteenth-Century Russia* (Cambridge: Cambridge University Press, 1983).

was being held as a political prisoner, Vera Zasulich (1851–1919) assassinated the governor of Saint Petersburg. An independent judiciary, one of Alexander II's new reforms, found her innocent because it believed that her actions were justified. Although Zasulich had worked alone, her trial set off a wave of assassinations by underground groups such as the People's Will and the Land and Liberty parties. During the 1880s, eighty-two women were tried in political cases. Their crimes ranged from harboring fugitives and recruiting new members to their underground cells to assassinations.[68] In 1881, after several failed attempts, revolutionaries finally assassinated Alexander II. His son and successor, Alexander III (r. 1881–1894), presided over a reactionary backlash. The government arrested and executed four men and two women, Gesia Gel'fman, who was pregnant, and Sofia Perovskaia (1853–1881), the daughter of a respected general. Perovskaia became the first woman executed in Russia for a political crime (see **Women's Lives:** Sofia Perovskaia, Russian Radical). In response to the assassination, Alexander III stopped all political modernization and increased police surveillance and prosecution of political crimes. In 1889, four women were convicted of political crimes and sentenced to corporal punishment while in prison in Siberia. They defiantly committed suicide. Nevertheless, increased government repression did not dampen Russian revolutionaries' commitment to change. Women continued to participate in underground movements and to suffer exile, imprisonment, and execution.

At midcentury, many women hoped that the creation of new nation-states would create new possibilities for women. However, the reality was often disappointing. Although liberal politicians often risked their lives for unification and democracy, they were unwilling to do so for women's rights. New governments ignored women's demands for legal and educational rights and suffrage, arguing that such radical notions might compromise national stability. By the end of the century, only Finnish women had reaped the benefits of their hard-fought struggle for political equality.

## CONCLUSION

Women's political activism changed considerably over the course of the nineteenth century. Inspired by liberalism, Marxism, and nationalism, women joined political causes in unprecedented numbers. By midcentury, a separate women's movement emerged as few other reform movements proved willing to include women's emancipation among their goals. Although often focused on basic legal and economic rights, over the course of the century, the goals and strategies of the women's movement expanded. By the end of the century, women activists themselves disagreed over the direction they should take. Some wanted a broad agenda of reform, while others focused only on the issue of the vote.

## NOTES

1. Elizabeth Heyrick, *Immediate, Not Gradual Abolition; or an Inquiry into the Shortest, Safest, and Most Effectual Means of Getting Rid of West-Indian Slavery* (Philadelphia: Merrihew and Gunn, 1836), 6, 8.

2. Clare Midgley, *Women Against Slavery: The British Campaigns, 1780–1870* (London: Routledge, 1992), 47.

3. Quoted in Midgley, 44.

4. Stanley Harrold, *American Abolitionists* (Harlow, England: Longman, 2001), 42.

5. Carolyn Williams, "The Female AntiSlavery Movement: Fighting Against Racial Prejudice and Promoting Women's Rights in Antebellum America," in *The Abolitionist Sisterhood: Women's Political Culture in Antebellum America,* ed. Jean Fagan Yellin and John C.

Van Horne (Ithaca, NY: Cornell University Press, 1994), 164–165.

6. Elizabeth Cady Stanton, *Eighty Years and More: Reminiscences 1815–1897* (Boston: Northeastern University Press, 1993), 82.

7. Quoted in Ronald G. Walters, *American Reformers, 1815–1860* (New York: Hill and Wang, 1978), 105.

8. Quoted in Anna Clark, "Queen Caroline and the Sexual Politics of Popular Culture in London, 1820," *Representations* 31 (1990): 60.

9. Barbara Taylor, *Eve and the New Jerusalem: Socialism and Feminism in the Nineteenth Century* (New York: Pantheon Books, 1983), 61.

10. Anna Clark, "Rhetoric of Chartist Domesticity," *Journal of British Studies* 31 (1992): 82.

11. "Address of the Female Political Union of Newcastle upon Tyne to their Fellow Countrywomen," in *The Early Chartists*, ed. Dorothy Thompson (Columbia: University of South Carolina Press, 1971), 128.

12. Jutta Schwarzkopf, *Women in the Chartist Movement* (New York: St. Martin's Press, 1991), 59.

13. Prosper Enfantin, "Extrait de la parole du Père dans la reunion générale de la famille, le 19 Novembre 1831," in *Women, the Family and Freedom: The Debate in Documents, vol. 1, 1750–1880*, ed. Susan Groag Bell and Karen M. Offen (Stanford, CA: Stanford University Press, 1983), 144.

14. Claire Goldberg Moses, *French Feminism in the Nineteenth Century* (Albany, NY: SUNY Press, 1984), 47.

15. Moses, 109.

16. Taylor, 57.

17. Jeanne Deroin and Pauline Roland, "Letter to the Convention of the Women of America," June 15, 1851, in *Women, the Family and Freedom*, vol. 1, 287.

18. Quoted in Bonnie S. Anderson, *Joyous Greetings: The First International Women's Movement, 1830–1860* (Oxford: Oxford University Press, 2000), 108.

19. Anderson, 109.

20. Jean Sigmann, *1848: The Romantic and Democratic Revolutions in Europe*, trans. Lovett F. Edwards (New York: Harper and Row, 1973), 138.

21. Peter N. Stearns, *1848: The Revolutionary Tide in Europe* (New York: Norton, 1974), 33.

22. Pracilla Smith Robertson, *The Revolutions of 1848: A Social History* (Princeton, NJ: Princeton University Press, 1952), 112.

23. Anderson, 154.

24. Quoted in Karen Offen, *European Feminisms: 1700–1950, A Political History* (Stanford, CA: Stanford University Press, 2000), 111.

25. Quoted in Anderson, 157–158.

26. Jeanne Deroin, "Aux Citoyens Français!" in *Women, the Family and Freedom*, vol. 1, 247.

27. Stearns, 92.

28. Quoted in Anderson, 8.

29. Louise Otto, "Program," in *Women, the Family and Freedom*, vol. 1, 263.

30. Robert Nemes, "Getting to the Source: Women in the 1848–1849 Hungarian Revolution," *Journal of Women's History* 13:3 (2001): 197.

31. Quoted in Nemes, 196.

32. Nemes, 197.

33. Quoted in Anderson, 105.

34. Lou Charnon-Deutsch, "Concepción Arenal and Nineteenth-Century Spanish Debates About Women's Sphere and Education," in *Recovering Spain's Feminist Tradition*, ed. Lisa Vollendorf (New York: Modern Language Association, 2001), 205.

35. Gisela Bock, *Women in European History* (Oxford: Blackwell Publishers, 2002), 122.

36. Quoted in Judith Walkowitz, *Prostitution and Victorian Society: Women, Class and the State* (Cambridge: Cambridge University Press, 1980), 116.

37. Gayle Graham Yates, ed., *Harriet Martineau on Women* (New Brunswick, NJ: Rutgers University Press, 1985), 266.

38. Judith Walkowitz, *City of Dreadful Delight: Narratives of Sexual Danger in Late-Victorian London* (Chicago: University of Chicago Press, 1992), 93.

39. Richard Evans, *The Feminist Movement in Germany, 1894–1933* (London: Sage, 1976), 63.

40. Quoted in Sandi E. Cooper, *Patriotic Pacifism: Waging War on War in Europe: 1815–1914* (Oxford: Oxford University Press, 1991), 41.

41. Gay L. Gullickson, *Unruly Women of Paris: Images of the Commune* (Ithaca, NY: Cornell University Press, 1996), 148.

42. Cooper, 79.

43. Cooper, 63.

44. Offen, 159.

45. Offen, 150–151.

46. From Hubertine Auclert, "Le Droit politique des femmes, question qui n'est pas traitée au Congrès international des femmes," in *Women, the Family and Freedom*, vol. 1, 515.

47. Theodore Stanton, *The Woman Question in Europe* (New York: G. P. Putnam and Sons, 1884), v.

48. Anna Schepeler-Lette and Jenny Hirsch, "Germany: A General Review of the Women's Movement in Germany," in *The Woman Question in Europe*, ed. Theodore Stanton (New York: Source Book Press, 1884), 140.

49. Elise van Calcar, "Holland," in *The Woman Question in Europe*, 174.

50. Quoted in Gullickson, 100.

51. Gullickson, 92.

52. Quoted in Carolyn J. Eichner, "'Vive la Commune!' Feminism, Socialism, and Revolutionary Revival in the Aftermath of the 1871 Paris Commune," *Journal of Women's History* 15 (2003): 70.

53. Marie Marmo Mullaney, "Sexual Politics in the Career and Legend of Louise Michel," *Signs* 15:2 (1990): 302–303.

54. Quoted in Eugene Schulkind, "Socialist Women During the 1871 Paris Commune," *Past and Present* 106 (February 1985): 126.

55. August Bebel, *Woman Under Socialism* (New York: Schocken Books, 1971), 349.

56. Friedrich Engels, *The Origins of the Family, Private Property, and the State*, chapter 2, "The Family" (New York: International Publishers, 1942).

57. John Stuart Mill, *Essays on Equality, Law, and Education*, ed. John M. Robson (Toronto: University of Toronto Press, 1984), 99.

58. "Lucy Stone's Marriage Protest," in *Early American Women: A Documentary History, 1600–1900*, ed. Nancy Woloch (New York: McGraw-Hill, 2002), 246.

59. Walkowitz, *City of Dreadful Delights*, 65–66.

60. Roger Chickering, "'Casting Their Gaze More Broadly': Women's Patriotic Activism in Imperial Germany," *Past and Present* 118 (1988): 160.

61. Chickering, 162.

62. Quoted in Sharon Wood, *Italian Women's Writing 1860–1994* (London: Athlone Press, 1995), 14.

63. Offen, 151.

64. Quoted in Bock, 139.

65. Quoted in Offen, 215.

66. Alexandra Gripenberg, "The Great Victory in Finland," in *Women, the Family and Freedom*, vol. 2, 230.

67. Quoted in Offen, 218.

68. Natalia Pushkareva, *Women in Russian History: From the Tenth to the Twentieth Century*, trans. Eve Levin (London: M. E. Sharpe, 1997), 206.

## SUGGESTED READINGS

Anderson, Bonnie S. *Joyous Greetings: The First International Women's Movement, 1830–1860*. Oxford: Oxford University Press, 2000. This text looks at the international relationships that women activists shared in creating the first women's movement.

Engel, Barbara Alpern. *Mothers and Daughters: Women of the Intelligentsia in Nineteenth-Century Russia*. Cambridge: Cambridge University Press, 1983. Study of how elite women's upbringing attracted them to anarchist movements, and why so many were willing to die for their beliefs.

Gullickson, Gay L. *Unruly Women of Paris: Images of the Commune*. Ithaca, NY: Cornell University Press, 1996. A study of the press and government use of women's images to promote or undermine the Paris Commune.

Harrold, Stanley. *American Abolitionists*. Harlow, England: Longman, 2001.

Midgely, Clare. *Women Against Slavery: The British Campaigns, 1780–1870*. London: Routledge, 1992.

Schwarzkopf, Jutta. *Women in the Chartist Movement*. New York: St. Martin's Press, 1991.

# Chapter 11

# Gender and Imperialism, 1830–1930

*Mixed-Race Dutch East Indies Family (1922).* As few European women traveled to Southeast Asia, many European men formed long-term relationships with local women. However, they rarely married those women and often left them and their children behind when they returned to Europe. (©Corbis.)

■ **Sex and Gender in the Empire**  374

  *Race, Gender, and Colonialism*  377
  *Concubinage and Prostitution*  378
  *Mixed-Race Children*  380
  *Native Men and European Women*  381

■ **Spreading the Gospel: Female Missionaries Around the World**  381

  *Missionary Values*  382
  *Catholic Missionaries*  383
  *Protestant Missionaries*  385

■ **Life in the Colonies**  386

  *Women and the Maintenance of Empire: The Wives of Colonial Officials*  386
  *Working Overseas*  388
  *Going Native*  392

■ **Collaboration and Resistance**  394

  *Imperialist Women*  394
  *Imperial Feminism and Feminist Anti-Imperialists*  395
  *Suffrage and the Imperial World*  397

■ **Traveling the World**  399

  *Travel and Study*  400
  *Noncolonial Migration*  402

Most of the early modern European colonial system collapsed during the political, economic, and intellectual changes of the eighteenth and early nineteenth centuries. Britain lost its American colonies, Haitians revolted against French rule, and in the wake of Napoleon's conquest of Iberia, nearly all of Spain's extensive overseas empire became independent. However, these losses did not hinder Europe's expansionist ambitions. By the nineteenth century, Europe looked to Asia, Africa, and the Pacific to satisfy its imperial desires.

The British led the imperial push. In addition to abolishing the British East India Company and administering India directly, Britain wrestled control of much of the Middle East from local authorities. The British took the Cape Colony in South Africa from the Dutch during the Napoleonic wars, and during the 1890s, English settlers set up protectorates over large parts of Africa.

In fact, during the last quarter of the nineteenth century, Africa became the site of intense political maneuvering by European nations. In addition to the Portuguese, who maintained their early modern colonies in Angola and Mozambique, the French conquered and annexed Algeria (1834) and Tunisia (1881) and then pushed inland through west and central Africa. In the 1870s, Leopold II of Belgium (r. 1865–1909) sent explorer Henry Stanley (1841–1904) to central Africa to lay claim to the Congo basin. Despite European attempts to regulate European control over Africa at the 1884 and 1885 Berlin Conferences, Germany asserted its claim to Tanganyika (now Tanzania), parts of southern and central Africa, as well as some Pacific Islands (see Map 11.1).

In Asia, the Dutch had controlled substantial possessions in the East Indies since the early modern period, but during the nineteenth century, France acquired dominion over all of Indochina (what is now Laos, Cambodia, and Vietnam), and Russia conquered parts of northern China. In the Pacific, Japan never fell under European rule, although European influence brought substantial changes to Japanese society. British control of Australia and New Zealand was countered by the French acquisition of large parts of Melanesia and Polynesia. The United States also became active in the imperial scramble, annexing Hawaii after business interests overthrew the islands' monarchy and

# *Chapter 11* ❖ Chronology

| | |
|---|---|
| **1817** | Anne-Marie Javouhey founds the Sisters of Saint Joseph |
| **1857** | Rebellion in India |
| **1884** | Ilbert Bill |
| **1885** | Berlin Conference divides Africa among the European Powers |
| **1888** | Flora Annie Steel writes *The Complete Indian Housekeeper and Cook* |
| **1893** | U.S. business interests overthrow the Hawaiian monarchy |
| | Women in New Zealand obtain the right to vote |
| **1896** | First Chinese women graduate from the University of Michigan medical school |
| **1897** | Flora Shaw coins the term Nigeria |
| | Founding of Canadian Methodist Missionary Society |
| **1898** | Spanish-American War |
| **1901** | Founding of the pro-imperialist Victoria League |
| **1902** | New York City Kosher Meat Boycott |
| **1905** | German authorities ban interracial marriages in Southwest Africa |
| **1911** | Triangle Shirtwaist Factory fire kills immigrant women in New York |
| **1912** | Lawrence textile mill strike |
| | Carrie Chapman Catt and Aletta Jacobs travel around the world on behalf of the International Woman Suffrage Alliance |
| **1919** | Constance Markievicz becomes first Labour minister in Ireland |
| | Women allowed to take jobs in the British colonial civil service |

taking control of Cuba, Puerto Rico, and the Philippines after the Spanish-American War (1898) (see Map 11.2). By 1914, European nations controlled most of Asia, Africa, and the Middle East. Europe held approximately 85 percent of the earth's land mass as colonies and in other formal and informal governing arrangements.[1]

A variety of forces drove imperialism, among them intra-European politics and the desire for new markets for Europe's industrial economy. Once they asserted control, European powers used gender inequality to help maintain their imperial authority. They reinforced race and gen-

der hierarchies that privileged the masculinity of white men at the expense of white women and native men and women. As European women migrated to the far ends of these empires as missionaries, as wives, and as workers, some challenged their place in the colonial race and gender hierarchy, while others became important agents of imperial ideology.

## SEX AND GENDER IN THE EMPIRE

Although Europeans initially took control over much of the world through military conquest and

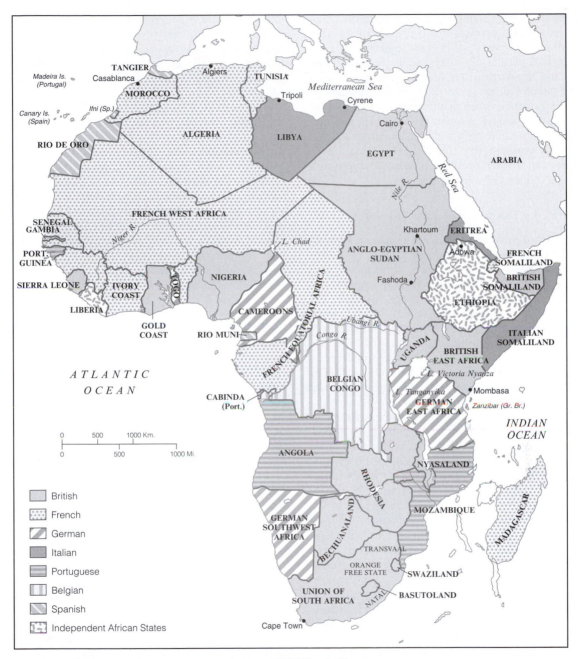

***Map 11.1*** **EUROPEAN IMPERIALISM IN AFRICA (1914).** As European powers divided Africa into colonies, women from many walks of life took the opportunity to explore, study, and migrate to the continent.

diplomatic maneuvering, they maintained their colonies based on clear distinctions between colonizer and colonized, rulers and subjects, based on race and gender. As they established authority around the world, they defined conquered lands and peoples as feminine and in need of control by white European men. They used sexual relationships with native women to assert their dominance over native men and women. However, that control was fragile, and the mere presence of European women heightened concerns about race and sex in the colonial setting.

## Race, Gender, and Colonialism

Europeans viewed themselves as naturally superior to all other "races." Their ideas of race went beyond biology to include a combination of skin color, culture, and religion. For followers of Social Darwinism (see Chapter 9), science provided clear evidence of European superiority. Indeed, some Europeans even believed that non-European peoples belonged to another species.

In addition to presumed biological differences, Europeans viewed most non-European societies as depraved. Their social practices, customs, and beliefs, including polygamy, child marriage, and the poor treatment of women, clearly marked them as inferior. In fact, Europeans believed that their "civilized" treatment of women was proof of their racial and cultural superiority. Ironically, European men saw no relationship between women's subordination in non-European societies and the gender inequalities that pervaded European society.

Ideas of masculinity also influenced colonial interactions. European masculinity extolled sexual virility, physical strength, and rationality. They described unexplored lands with feminine terms like "virgin territory" and sexualized the geography, referring to mountains as breasts and mountaintops as nipples.[2] French colonial writers depicted the conquest of North Africa in terms of sexual penetration and used the metaphor of insemination to describe the renewal that would come with French imperial authority.[3] In the process, Europeans also sexualized the inhabitants of those lands, portraying non-European women as sexually available and lustful. Some viewed native women as inherently sexually promiscuous, while others believed that natives' interactions

with Europeans had led them into vice. Sexuality defined not only native women, but European women as well. European men described European women as racially and morally superior, but also as passive, vulnerable, and unable to fulfill male sexual desire.

In contrast, throughout the colonial world, Europeans stereotyped men of other races and ethnicities as effeminate. Effeminate men were not the same as women; they were failed men. European men unfavorably compared native men's bodies with their own. According to many British observers, Bengali men had effeminate physiques. In French Indochina, Europeans described Vietnamese men as fine jointed, slim, elegant, slender, and supple—adjectives typically used to describe women in European society. French journalist and novelist Pierre Mille (1864–1941) observed that the Vietnamese have "such frailty that the men have the air of women, and the women have the air of children."[4] Asian men's lack of facial hair accentuated their effeminacy to Europeans, as they viewed beardlessness as a sign of immaturity and impotence. The fact that many European and American women were taller than Chinese men reinforced the sense of European physical superiority, even among women. Europeans often found that they had difficulty distinguishing Asian men from Asian women, confounding their preconceptions about sex and gender.

Europeans also demasculinized non-European men by comparing them with children. One female American missionary in China noted, "I have no more fear of these Chinese men than of a child, and there is no reason to have."[5] Female missionaries in China often referred to their male servants as "boys" and sometimes gave Chinese men American women's names. One missionary called her male cook "Betty" while another called her Chinese teacher "Pansy."[6]

European men's portrayal of non-European men as effeminate also became a critical part of imperial rhetoric, as was evident in the debate over the Ilbert Bill (1884) in India. This legislation granted Indian officials limited criminal jurisdiction over Euro-British subjects under their rule and gave Anglo-Indians the right to demand a trial by jury made up of at least half Euro-British subjects. Although this legislation did not explicitly address

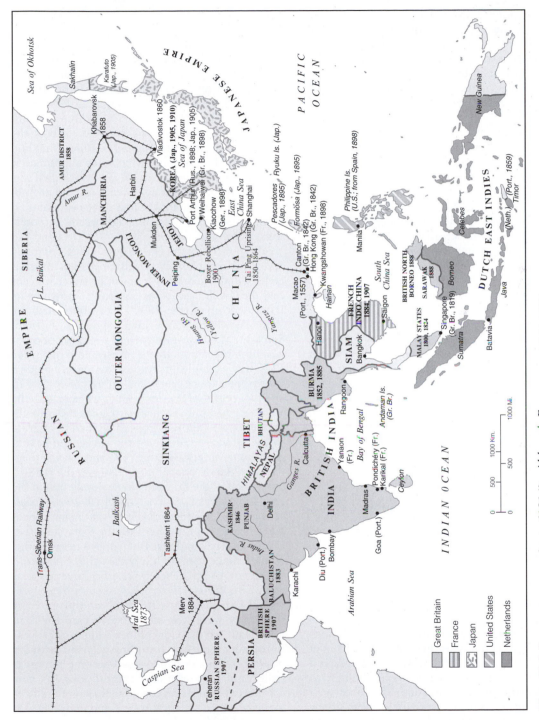

**Map 11.2** **IMPERIALISM IN ASIA (1914).** Although European women were rare in Asia during the nineteenth century, increasing numbers emigrated to Europe's colonial possessions at the beginning of the twentieth century.

gender, opponents asserted that Indians were effeminate and therefore unfit to try men and women of the more "civilized" race.[7] During heated debates about legislation to prohibit child marriage in British India, the English constantly challenged Bengali men's masculinity. Bengali men who opposed the legislation were accused of effeminacy.[8]

Concerns about European and American masculinity also drove nineteenth-century men toward military conquest. Traditionally, European men had proven their masculinity through warfare. Indeed, much of the rhetoric of early American masculinity had been based on the conquest of the North American frontier. However, by the end of the nineteenth century, there was no Wild West left to tame. Urbanization and industrialization had created comfortable middle-class jobs that many men feared made them "soft." Moreover, some men believed that the agitation for women's suffrage and women's increased political activity was undermining American democracy and blurring gender norms. A generation of American men feared that they would not be able to live up to the masculine model of their fathers and grandfathers who had fought bravely in the American Revolution and the Civil War. Supporters of intervention in the Spanish-Cuban conflict cultivated the fear that America was becoming effeminate. They portrayed themselves as virile young men and anti-imperialists as old women.[9]

## Concubinage and Prostitution

As European soldiers and businessmen settled across the continents, sexual intercourse became not only the subject of bedrooms and backrooms but also of imperial policy. There were few European women in the colonies, and European men satisfied their sexual and emotional needs with native women; in fact, for most of the imperial period, authorities encouraged such relationships. Native concubines helped European men get accustomed to their new surroundings, and sexual access to native women was thought to keep men virile and heterosexual. Moreover, such relationships forcefully asserted European domination over native men by denying them access to women from their own culture. By controlling native women and men, concubinage reinforced colonial rule.

During the late nineteenth century, European militaries, financial organizations, and governments almost exclusively recruited single men for employment overseas and discouraged or forbade their employees from marrying. Until the early 1900s, the French Bank of Indochina did not allow its employees to be married. Across the empires, European men signed contracts that laid out the conditions under which they might marry, if at all. In India as late as 1929, British civil servants were recruited at age twenty-six and prohibited from marrying for the first three years of their service. As a result, concubinage became a central feature of colonial life.

The policies of the Dutch East Indies Company reveal the complex relationship between imperial control and concubinage. Since the sixteenth century the Dutch East Indies Company (known by its Dutch acronym, the VOC) had controlled the Indonesia archipelago, including Java, Borneo, Sumatra, Malacca, Taiwan, and a number of other islands in the region. By the nineteenth century, the VOC had expanded its trade in spices to include a variety of export crops, including coffee, sugar, and tobacco. As its business interests increased, the VOC selected only bachelors to go to the colonies and refused to allow European women to migrate to the territories. To meet the social and sexual needs of its employees, the VOC encouraged them to take Asian concubines. During the 1880s, nearly half of the European male population in the East Indies was unmarried and living with Asian women.[10] VOC officials believed that Asian concubines made fewer demands on the Company than European wives and that Dutch men's ties to native women made it more likely that the men would settle permanently. There were other advantages as well. The VOC asserted that Asian women prevented European men from falling into poverty since they were less expensive to care for than European wives. Concubines supposedly kept European men away from brothels and sexually transmitted diseases and helped prevent homosexuality and masturbation. Hand-books for new recruits extolled Asian concubines as useful guides to the language and local society and indicated that their medical knowledge might be useful in keeping new immigrants alive.

For native women, concubinage had some advantages but was a risky proposition nonetheless. European men expected women with whom they had long-term relationships to do domestic work without compensation or legal rights and the women had no rights over their children by European men.[11] When European men returned home, they typically abandoned their native concubines. Dutch law actually forbade men from returning home with native wives and children.[12] The persistence of slavery in many societies further complicated the situation for concubines. Although opposed to slavery in theory, many colonial powers turned a blind eye to indigenous slavery in order to maintain good relationships with local elites and have access to local women. It was not unheard of for European men to acquire slaves as concubines, as was true in nineteenth-century Khartoum.[13] When the men returned to Europe or left for another posting, they often exchanged or passed on concubines to other men.[14] In these inherently unequal relationships, European men were always in control, determining the conditions of the couple's daily life, the concubine's future, and the future of any children that the couple produced.

Interracial relationships were so common in Libreville, the capital of Gabon in French Africa, that it became known as the "black Babylon." One priest estimated that 280 out of 300 European men had African concubines in 1896. Some local Mpongwe women entered willingly into these relationships for the social or economic benefits that they brought, while other women were pawns in transactions among men as Mpongwe men often offered wives, daughters, and relatives to foreigners to solidify business relationships.[15]

In addition to provoking tensions with local men, these relationships also pitted European men against one another, as they competed for authority in the colonies. In Libreville, local Catholic priests referred to concubinage in their critiques of anticlerical colonial administrators. At the same time, members of the local community accused the church of supporting concubinage. European men tended to prefer concubines who were the graduates of Catholic mission schools because they spoke European languages and could maintain homes in European fashion. When criticized for their extramarital relationships, European traders and imperial employees responded that Catholic missionaries had "trained" African girls for such relationships.[16]

Prostitution also posed a complicated problem for imperial authorities. On the one hand, they believed in the need for a sexual outlet for soldiers. In fact, during the 1857 rebellion in India, British officials selected and sent for northern Indian courtesans to provide sexual services for soldiers and sent for more prostitutes when their numbers dwindled. On the other hand, venereal disease posed an increasing problem. Diseases caused more English casualties during the Indian rebellion than combat, and one-quarter of European soldiers were infected by venereal disease.[17] These findings prompted the English to pass the Contagious Diseases Acts (1864–1886), which applied both at home and in the colonies. The Acts made colonial officials into regulators of prostitutes and unofficial sponsors of prostitution (see Chapters 9 and 10).

U.S. policy was equally as ambivalent. In the Philippines, the American military established a special district for prostitution in 1901 and issued medical certificates to prostitutes, supposedly as a means to control venereal disease. When the Pershing Expedition took parts of Mexico in 1916 as part of an American intervention in the Mexican Revolution, they surrounded the prostitutes with a barbed-wire fence and forcibly examined each of them. Healthy women were then allowed to engage in sex with soldiers.[18]

Opponents of concubinage and prostitution saw marriage as the most reliable way to end both problems, but rules about marriage between European men and native women varied from colony to colony. Generally, authorities prohibited marriage between Christians and non-Christians; however, in most colonies, authorities recognized some form of customary marriage for interracial/interreligious couples. In French Africa, these relationships, were known as *mariage à la mode du pays* (marriage in the style of the region) and in German Samoa, they were called Samoan-style (*fa'a Samoa*) marriages. Although these "marriages" had no legal or religious foundation, they were respected by many members of the colonial community. Moreover, couples often eluded regulations against such relationships in one colony by eloping to another colony where interracial marriages were legal.[19]

There are some cases of legitimate Christian marriage between European men and native women, but more often such marriages were with mixed-race women. In German territories, female colonial subjects who married German men gained some legal rights. Across Africa and the Pacific, many male missionaries took native women as their wives. Their native wives helped them make contacts with local tribes, learn local customs, and even helped translate the Gospel into local languages.

However, in the British Empire, the situation was considerably different. Although concubinage had been common during the eighteenth century, by the mid-nineteenth century, the tensions between Indians and officials that culminated in the Indian Rebellion of 1857 and the arrival of large numbers of missionaries forced officials to come out against the practice. British men were discouraged from having any contact with native women after the 1860s. Although prohibitions against liaisons between British men and native women were less problematic in India, which was home to significant numbers of European women, European women were quite rare in parts of Africa and concubinage continued well into the twentieth century. Prohibitions against concubinage further disadvantaged native women, as they lost any positive benefits that they garnered from those relationships while they were legal.

Not surprisingly, European women strongly opposed interracial relationships. Those relationships not only compromised white women's place in the race and gender hierarchy, they made white women irrelevant to the imperial project. European men could rely on local women for labor and for sexual satisfaction with few, if any, constraints on their behavior.

## Mixed-Race Children

Interracial relationships often produced offspring and Europeans vigorously debated the status of mixed-race children. They viewed mixed-race children as a threat to European power and prestige and disdained them as evidence of European immorality. Colonial authorities identified them as potentially disloyal, torn by divided identities and unclear allegiances. The poverty of many mixed-race children increased tensions between them and both native and European populations. Moreover, their status was fluid. Mixed-race children might be considered native at home, but French, Portuguese, or Dutch when they moved to other parts of the empires.[20]

These children were often difficult to classify, as authorities could not rely on skin color to determine European status and/or citizenship. As a result, a mixed-race child's status often depended on the situation in which he or she was raised. To be "European," the child had to have a European father and demonstrate his or her Europeanness. Mixed-race children in French and Dutch Asia who had been raised by their white fathers in European households were often afforded the full privileges of Europeans as long as they were Christian, had European names, and spoke the European language of the colony. Such children also had to dress in European clothing, be educated in European ways, and be comfortable with European social norms.[21]

In contrast, mixed-race children who did not demonstrate their Europeanness were legally adrift and sometimes socially ostracized. Authorities designated these children as "abandoned" if they were left in the care of a native mother. The same was true of mixed-race children who were raised among natives even in the presence of their fathers. Such situations blurred the cultural and hierarchical distinctions between ruler and ruled in ways that provoked anxiety among colonial authorities.[22]

Tensions about the status of mixed-race children came to a head in the German empire after colonial authorities banned mixed marriages in three colonies—Southwest Africa (1905), East Africa (1906), and Samoa (1912). The ban on mixed marriages prevented German men from passing German citizenship on to their native wives and mixed-race children. German men involved with native women protested the bans, noting that their inability to marry compromised the legitimacy of their heirs, exposed their children to insults, and prevented those children from traveling with their fathers in European-only train cars. Many of these men had worked hard to raise their children as Europeans only to have them denied equal access to European privilege. The Berlin Colonial Office's decision to uphold existing "respectable" mixed marriages provoked a storm of controversy. Proponents of racial separatism in the German empire pushed to prevent mixed-race children from obtaining citizenship in order to protect German women's status and the privilege of German citizenship.[23]

## Native Men and European Women

Although many Europeans believed that European women could not satisfy the sexual urges of European men as well as native women could, they also asserted that white women's mere presence provoked the uncontrollable lust of native men. As noted in Chapter 7, according to many Europeans, masculinity and honor were based on a man's ability to protect the chastity of the women in his care. Moreover, Europeans believed that the impregnation of European women by native men compromised the health and well-being of the white race. As a result, European men used the rhetoric of European women's vulnerability and native men's unpredictability to prevent any interactions between them.

In the British Empire, the threat of native male sexuality was known as "The Black Peril." Despite the fact that the rape of European women by native men was rare, the English spoke fearfully about the dangers of sexual assault that European women in the colonies faced. Because sexual interactions between African men and European women threatened white dominance, even attempted rapes met with extreme punishments. In Southern Rhodesia, after an African man's death sentence for raping a white woman was commuted to life in prison, outraged European men protested the decision noting that "the honour of the white woman is to be held sacred, and any attempt at rape must be punished with death."[24]

Frequently, there was no evidence that native men had even made sexual advances toward European women. Often Europeans charged native men with rape solely for entering white women's social space. For instance, a native man found near the bed of a sleeping white woman might be accused of rape despite the fact that no sexual intercourse took place.[25] In 1859, Dr. Gillis, a Eurasian physician in India, was accused of breaking the rules on interracial intimacy for having uncovered an Englishwoman while assisting her in childbirth.[26] Rape accusations often unified the European community against the native population during times of economic and political stress. For example, in South Africa between 1890 and 1914, an increase in rape accusations against native men coincided with a series of mining strikes.[27]

European men did not hold native men solely responsible for native lust for European women. For centuries, European men had defined women as temptresses and as susceptible to seduction. Authorities in British Africa were concerned enough that they passed a number of Immorality Acts that prescribed prison sentences for white women who "by words, writing, signs, or suggestion enticed a native to have illicit sex." Yet, few European women's memoirs mention the fear of native men; only European men expressed those anxieties.

Despite European men's self-professed desire to protect women, in the imperial world, rape was race specific. The sexual assault of native women by either European or native men was not classified as rape, and few European men were prosecuted for sexual crimes at all. In fact, the supposed influence of the untamed colonial setting often became an excuse for European sexual predators. When Carl Peters (1856–1918), a German explorer of East Africa, raped and murdered a number of African women, he excused his behavior by claiming that such acts were normal in Africa.[28] In places like Australia, where men far outnumbered women, it was the uncontrolled behavior of European men, not native men, that left women vulnerable to rape and assault.[29]

## SPREADING THE GOSPEL: FEMALE MISSIONARIES AROUND THE WORLD

In most colonies, missionaries were the first European women to have contact with native peoples. Women enthusiastically accepted the opportunity to evangelize, and new Catholic missionary orders dedicated to overseas missions flourished during the nineteenth and early twentieth centuries. Numerous Protestant denominations also sent women overseas, both alone and with their husbands, to convert and educate native peoples around the world.

Often unwittingly, Christian missionaries supported the imperial effort. Their multiple goals, including conversion, the expansion of basic literacy, the implantation of middle-class values, and their desire to save non-Christian women from perceived injustices were critical to the integration of native peoples into colonial structures. For the missionary women themselves, the experience was exhilarating, frustrating, and unlike anything available to them at home.

## Missionary Values

Despite their theological differences, Catholic and Protestant female missionaries shared similar goals and expounded similar values. Certainly, the conversion of native peoples to Christianity was foremost in their minds. Of course, their success varied from place to place. In many colonies, missionaries converted only a handful of native men and women over the course of a lifetime, whereas other peoples converted easily after missionaries persuaded a local leader to adopt Christianity.

Many missionaries also taught their charges that upon conversion, native traditions were no longer relevant and could imperil their souls. Child marriages, footbinding, infanticide, and polygamy all conflicted with European Christian values. Moreover, many missionaries cited native religions as the primary cause of the supposed degradation of native women. Nineteenth-century tracts about India provide lurid, sensationalist descriptions of the horrors imposed upon Hindu women. In particular, they railed against the practice of *sati*, in which widows were burned on their husbands' funeral pyres, and the African practice of clitoridectomy, the removal of women's external genitalia.

Education was central to female missionaries' goals. Mary Louisa Whately (d. 1889), one of the first British missionaries in Egypt, founded a network of schools dedicated to bringing the educational methods created by reformers for the English lower classes to the children of Egypt. Women undertook similar projects around the world. The missionaries' enthusiasm for female education revealed their willingness to believe that, across cultures, women were the primary source of morality. Once exposed to the morals of European civilization, girls would, by nature, help create a moral society. The British Education Dispatch of 1854 noted, "The importance of female education cannot be overestimated. . . . By this means, a far greater proportional impulse is imparted to the educational and moral tone of the people than by the education of men."[30] However, although female education became central to the transformation of native society, missionaries faced innumerable obstacles.

Cultural priorities often clashed with missionary education, and families sometimes married off their daughters during school vacations. The girls also faced considerable social pressure from peers to participate in traditional coming-of-age rituals. To prevent such conflicts, missionaries tried to limit contact between girls and their families. The experience of Norwegian missionaries, who set up a boarding school for girls in Madagascar in the 1870s to educate Malagasy girls, exemplifies the frustration that many missionaries faced. Although the founders of the school set up a rigid schedule of work and learning, their attempts to impose Western gender expectations clashed with Malagasy norms that tolerated nonmarital sexual activity. Despite the school's strict policies, their students regularly became pregnant, sometimes while at school.[31]

While some missionaries worked to change what they perceived as the moral laxity of their charges, other missionaries, both male and female, were surprised to find that in some cultures native norms about sexual interactions were stricter than European norms. In India, many elite Hindu women were confined to the *zenana*, the women's quarters, and males strictly supervised their contact with nonfamily members. Even when missionary women gained access to the zenana, husbands and fathers resisted their attempts to evangelize to the women. Similarly, when Dutch missionaries first opened schools among the Karo in Sumatra, native customs that prohibited many types of male/female interactions, including that of brothers and sisters, initially made coeducation nearly impossible, as boys and girls could not sit on the same benches.[32]

Missionary women emphasized the value of middle-class domesticity for native girls and women and focused their education on training new converts to be good wives for Christian men. Although both boys and girls in mission schools in Mozambique learned to read and write in both Portuguese and the local language, boys also learned math, and agricultural techniques, while girls learned to cook, wash clothes, and iron. Sewing became a critical skill as missionaries encouraged native women to make and wear European clothing. Missionary schools also taught girls the basics of European housework.[33]

In some cultures, the emphasis on domesticity clashed with centuries-old traditions and gendered divisions of labor. Missionaries frequently attempted to force nomadic peoples into becoming sedentary farmers, a lifestyle that they believed was more compatible with Christian society. Even some agricultural societies had to be reformed, as the Victorian ideology of separate spheres (see Chapter 9) clashed with the norms of tribes in which women traditionally farmed. To right what they saw as a topsy-turvy gender order, many missionaries unsuccessfully attempted to force men to work in fields and women to work in the home. Missionaries also showed little regard for native class structures. Wives and daughters of chiefs who attended the Gayaza Girls' School in Uganda complained about the fact that, despite their status, they were expected to engage in household work.[34]

Literacy became a critical marker of Christianization and Europeanization. Of course, missionaries often disregarded literacy in native languages. Emily Hartwell, a Protestant missionary at Foochow College in China, even wrote in 1909 that an alphabetic language "corresponds with the Creator's design" while Chinese characters were "difficult because [they were] artificial and not in accord with the arrangement of nature."[35] From her perspective, Chinese characters were the product of heathens; Christians wrote in Western script.

Missionaries and parents often disagreed on the purpose of education. In most missionary schools, teachers only taught girls to read and to write in order to allow them to read the Bible and other devotional texts so that they could teach Christianity to their children and run orderly homes. Missionaries did not expect girls to use their literacy to improve their economic status by working outside of the home. However, many native parents believed in the benefits of literacy for their children's economic advancement. In fact, native parents were often less than enthusiastic about the missionaries' insistence on evangelization and often withdrew their children from mission schools when students demonstrated too much interest in Christianity.

Finally, missionary education created not only Christians but also good colonial subjects. Imperial authorities believed that the introduction of Christian priorities and European languages and customs to natives would ease their interactions with imperial institutions. The more comfortable natives became with European ways, the less difficult it would be to govern them.

## Catholic Missionaries

The intensification of missionary efforts during the nineteenth and twentieth centuries led to the foundation of new Catholic orders and affiliations created specifically for overseas evangelization. Founded in 1817 by Anne-Marie Javouhey (d. 1851), the Sisters of Saint Joseph de Cluny became pioneers in Catholic missionary work. Javouhey sent nuns to the island of Réunion and then to Senegal in 1819 to run hospitals there. At her settlement in Dagana in Senegal, she taught Africans the principles of modern agriculture, and she was eager to help develop an indigenous clergy. She even established a missionary congregation of African and French priests that brought African children to France for a seminary education. Three of those students eventually became priests. The Sisters of Saint Joseph were also the first female religious in Africa south of the Sahara. Over the course of the nineteenth century, the Sisters expanded their missions around the world, recruiting native women from Africa to the Pacific Islands as lay sisters.

Following in her footsteps, in 1869, Cardinal Martial Allemand Lavigerie (1825–1892) founded the Congregation of Missionary Sisters of Our Lady of Africa, more commonly known as the White Sisters. They worked in Algiers aiding the work of the White Fathers, the primary missionizers in West Africa. Mary Josephine Rogers (1882–1955) founded the Maryknoll Sisters of

**THE MOTHER SUPERIOR AND SISTERS OF ST. JOSEPH AND THEIR CONVERTS AT OLD CALABAR, NIGERIA (CA. 1907).** Many European women participated in the colonial project as nuns and missionaries. Often the only European women in the colonies, they were important transmitters of European culture and imperial power. *(Richard Harding Davis,* The Congo and Coasts of Africa, *Charles Scribner's Sons, New York, 1907.)*

Saint Dominic, known as the Teresians, who first went to China in 1921.

Female missionaries' close contact with native women often brought them into conflict with church directives. Mother Kevin (1875–1957), a Franciscan nun, came to Uganda in 1903 to establish schools and convents and during the expansion of her mission, she actively sought African novices. However, she was frustrated by the poor health conditions in which African women lived. Upon seeing the excellent medical work being accomplished by Anglican women, she pushed for increased medical training for the nuns. However, until 1939, the Vatican opposed her requests to provide medical missionaries trained in obstetrics.

Until the twentieth century, few native women sought admission to Catholic orders. Those who did were models of determination; around the world, long-held ideas about racial inferiority meant that many orders were reluctant to permit native women to take vows. The Sisters of Saint Joseph working in New Zealand did not accept Maori novices until after World War II. Nevertheless, just prior to World War I, native women began to form their own missionary organizations, including the Trinity Sisters, a group of African widows who preferred not to remarry, and the Third Order Regular of Mary, whose missions in Oceania were predominately staffed by native women. However, in many parts of Africa and other colonies, the traditional emphasis on marriage and motherhood meant that few women took the vows of chastity required of Catholic nuns.

## Protestant Missionaries

Across Europe and North America, men and women answered the call to spread the Gospel as Protestant missionaries. Some pious individuals set up missions on their own initiatives, but others traveled under the auspices of the many Protestant missionary societies that formed during the nineteenth century, such as the London Missionary Society, the China Inland Mission, and the American Board of Commissioners for Foreign Missions (ABCFM). Many of these groups included mission societies exclusively for women, such as the Canadian Methodist Women's Missionary Society, founded in 1897. These organizations raised money for missionary activity and organized the missions. Not surprisingly, many leaders of the larger, male-dominated organizations resisted these female mission societies. However, their female leadership persuasively argued that some aspects of missionary work could only be accomplished by women—in particular, evangelizing to non-Christian women.

Women outnumbered men in most mission groups. For example, between 1891 and 1900, there were 450 single female missionaries, 229 married female missionaries, and 380 male missionaries in the Middle East.[36] Female missionaries tended to be single, conservative, middle-aged women, many of whom had training as teachers or nurses. By 1910, about two-thirds of the American mission force was composed of women, many of whom were single recent graduates of Protestant Bible schools.[37]

Female missionaries faced numerous challenges within their own organizations. Despite the centrality of their role, these adventurous women had little standing in the missionary community. They could not vote in missionary organizations, and although many missionary organizations organized separate women's boards to oversee their female missionaries, those boards were limited by the traditional gender expectations of their denomination and were not strong advocates on behalf of the women.

For single women, the minimum uninterrupted term of service was five years, during which time missionary societies expected them to remain unmarried. In the Canadian Methodist Women's Missionary Service, the average age for a female missionary was twenty-nine—much older than the average age at marriage. As a result, single female missionaries became stereotyped as ugly, difficult old maids. In China, single female missionaries initially lived with married couples; however, the mission societies eventually purchased homes in which the women could live collectively. Life was hard for women who lived alone. Martha Cartmell, the first female Canadian missionary in Tokyo, made remarkable progress in a short time, founding a girls' boarding school in 1883, but her letters reveal the frustration, isolation, and helplessness that accompanied her work.[38]

Many missionary societies insisted on sending only married couples, as they feared the sexual temptations that might beset unsupervised single men and women. As a result, many young women simultaneously got married and began their lives as missionaries. Often a young man was accepted for missionary work but was required to find a wife before his ship set sail. The ABCFM actually kept a list of women who might agree to marry men in this situation. The women were also expected to be educated, fit, and reasonably good-looking.[39]

A missionary wife bore significant responsibilities. Her first concern was her husband. She was supposed to meet his sexual needs; be his friend, counselor, and nurse; and maintain a European-styled household that would allow him to accomplish his mission. The presence of wives also allowed native people to witness firsthand a good Christian family life and proper female behavior. In addition to their wifely duties, some missionary wives hoped to share in the preaching and teaching of natives. However, most missionary societies did not recognize these undertakings and provided little support for their extradomestic activities. Other women found that maintaining their Euro-American-style households and raising Euro-American children in remote areas took up too much of their time and energy. As with single women, missionary wives often felt slighted by missionary organizations. In response, missionary wives in the Hawaiian Islands formed their own organization, the Sandwich Islands' Maternal Association (1834), to address the issues that they faced as women in foreign lands.[40]

After the American Civil War, many black educational institutions in the American South emphasized the "special mission" of African Americans to help "redeem" Africa from its non-Christian past. Nancy Jones (b. 1860) of Fisk University became a missionary in Africa, serving first with Henrietta Bailey (b. 1852), the child of runaway slave parents, who was the first unmarried African American woman sent out by ABCFM. Jones later went on to become the first African American missionary in Southern Rhodesia. These women faced multiple challenges. Many were uncomfortable with the cultural differences that existed between themselves and their African charges. In addition, the major European powers often tried to prevent African Americans from engaging in mission work in their territories, believing (without evidence) that they encouraged political instability among native Africans.[41]

Conversion efforts waxed and waned. In some areas, missionaries spent decades evangelizing to only a few native converts. In other parts of the empire, both Catholics and Protestants found many native women who enthusiastically adopted Christian ways. Among them, Caterina Zenab (d. 1921), a Dinka woman from the Sudan, was one of the great early native missionaries. She helped the Catholic Verona Fathers translate biblical texts into Dinka and evangelized to Dinka slave communities. Similarly, the Krio women of West Africa (liberated slaves and their descendants) became important links between Africans and Christian missionaries. The major traders in the region, they spread their faith to communities where Europeans had not yet arrived.[42]

Missionary women of both faiths undertook significant risks in their zeal to spread the Gospel. Travel was slow and dangerous, and their work was hard and often unrewarding. Nevertheless, they had considerable influence on women's lives as they spread middle-class domesticity to women around the world. In addition to the Gospel, they taught non-European women how to meet European social and sexual expectations. In the process, missionary women supported the imperial effort by helping to create submissive, Christian colonial subjects. The missionary experience also offered European women exciting opportunities. They could express their piety, live independently, and face new challenges with little supervision by men.

## LIFE IN THE COLONIES

Although there had always been a few intrepid women in Europe's colonies, their numbers increased significantly during the second half of the nineteenth century and the first decades of the twentieth century. Historians used to believe that the arrival of European women disrupted the positive relationship between Europeans and natives based primarily on concubinage. However, recent research indicates that although European women may have supported racist and separatist policies, they were not the cause of those policies. Nevertheless, European women complicated the colonial hierarchy. The wives of colonial officials and the thousands of adventurous women who traveled to the colonies to work were expected to re-create European culture in the faraway corners of the earth. Much to the dismay of colonists, many new immigrants were unwilling to live according to traditional gender expectations. Indeed, the most unconventional of female travelers found new identities as they shed the restrictions of European dress, religion, and men.

## Women and the Maintenance of Empire: The Wives of Colonial Officials

In most colonial settings, Europeans lived apart from native communities, and colonial authorities attempted to confine women to spaces clearly designated as female and European. Scholar Kumari Jayawardena has described the situation of European women in colonial settings as one of "doubly refined bondage."[43] The colonial wife lived isolated in her home because of her womanhood and was alienated from the rest of the colony as a foreigner. At the beginning of the twentieth century, one colonial official in Nigeria explained that such segregation was necessary not only to protect Europeans from disease and bush fires, but also so that they would not be disturbed by native drumming.[44] They lived in enclosed compounds that included churches, shops with European goods, and dining clubs. Husbands partitioned households to protect European women's modesty and chastity and prevent unanticipated interactions between European women and native men.

European wives had no status of their own; their position derived solely from their husbands' careers. They followed their husbands to new postings, often on short notice. Without family connections and support networks, they were often more dependent on their husbands than was typical of their counterparts in the home country, the *metropole*.

With the arrival of European women in large numbers, European officials changed their views of concubines and their mixed-race children. Rather than being viewed as useful to the colonial project, they came to be seen as contaminating European bloodlines, culture, and language. Instead, officials charged European women with taming European men's sexual desires with cleanliness and order. According to their new vision of colonial society, a happy, well-fed man would no longer need a concubine.[45]

At home, colonial officials' wives were expected to reinforce imperial hierarchies, keep order, and re-create middle-class society; however, it was difficult to set up a European-style household so far from home. When families set out for new postings, they moved their households completely, from china and bedding to clothing and furniture. Women then tried to set up European households in rickety homes in desolate places, often without running water or, later, electricity. Salaries were not sufficient and multiple servants could not compensate for a colonial wife's inability to live and entertain according to metropolitan standards. Nevertheless, while entertaining, administrators' wives were expected to maintain European rules of etiquette and protocol. Occupation and seniority in the community dictated community rank. Administrators ranked above missionaries and businessmen; those who had lived longest in the area ranked above newcomers. The wives of high-ranking officials set the standards of dress, socialization, and behavior for all other European women in the community.

Sometimes Europeans' attempts to live as they did at home seem almost comical. As late as the 1930s, Sylvia Leith-Ross (1883–1980), the wife of a colonial administrator in Nigeria who would later become a noted anthropologist and ethnologist, reported that while traveling upriver in a steel canoe with a young man, each evening they docked the canoe in order to dine. Even in the interior of Africa,

they dutifully followed the traditional British practice of "dressing for dinner." Because completely changing one's clothing in the canoe was impossible, each night, Leith-Ross and her companion would change one part of his or her outfit to ensure that they had, in Leith-Ross's words "obeyed our code and had upheld our own and our country's dignity."[46] Europeans felt compelled to constantly reassert their sense of difference and "civilization."

European women's memoirs demonstrate a preoccupation with clothing. For reasons of modesty and cultural identity, they generally insisted on wearing European clothing even when it was incompatible with the climate. Constance Larymore, the first wife of an administrator to live in northern Nigeria, counseled women to bring six corsets, twelve pairs of stockings, and two evening gowns among other more practical pieces of clothing.[47]

European society also expected colonial wives to produce white Europeanized children, despite fears that the tropical climate would leave European women sterile and anxiety about the conditions in which they would give birth. Colonial authors like Pierre Mille (1864–1941) called the production of children women's "essential contribution to the imperial mission of France."[48] They were expected to create and educate moral, Christian families. Advice manuals counseled European women not to allow their children to eat food given to them by servants, socialize with servants, or even wash the clothes of natives and Europeans together, to prevent any possible social or cultural contagion. Parents watched to ensure that their children did not acquire local words and customs as they played with native children and sent older children off to boarding schools to be certain that they did not absorb the undesirable aspects of local cultures.[49]

Across the empire, British colonial officials' wives, frequently referred to by their title in India, *memsahibs*, had reputations as being petty, frivolous, and racist. Many of them had achieved some upward social mobility through the marriage and overseas posting, and in India they had a higher standard of living than they had back home in Britain, with numerous servants to do the cooking and cleaning. Thus, from the perspective of many Europeans, memsahibs had no productive place in colonial society.

However, many colonial wives took advantage of the colonial experience. They traveled extensively, getting to know native people, customs, and languages. They fashioned new identities by creating projects for themselves, such as setting up maternity clinics and schools. Some were indefatigable. Flora Annie Steel (1847–1929), who arrived in India in 1868 as the wife of a British civil servant, wrote a number of novels and coauthored *The Complete Indian Housekeeper and Cook* (1888), a guide to maintaining a European household. Although she enjoyed the comforts and authority of a memsahib, Steel also designed the town hall and served as the first female school inspector for the British government.[50]

Memsahibs' influence extended beyond their overseas homes. They affected Victorian fashion and interior design with the Indian cloth and artworks that they sent home, and they changed British eating habits as they published recipes for Indian dishes in popular periodicals. Curry and rice recipes began to appear in English cookbooks and the popularization of these tastes led to widespread importation of Indian spices to England.[51]

No matter what their temperament, colonial wives faced considerable emotional hardship. They endured extended separations from family and friends back home in the metropole, and mail was slow and often inconsistent. In addition, they were often separated from their husbands for months at a time. Their husbands often traveled first to new postings, leaving them to move their homes and children by themselves. Many European women returned to Europe prior to childbirth, where they remained with their natal families for a few months or even a year. They often left their children to be raised in Europe to protect them from the dangers of travel and tropical disease. In fact, government prohibitions prevented children of civil servants from coming to Nigeria until after World War II. Sadly, when their husbands died in the colonies, wives often found themselves alone in inhospitable places and left to pack up and return home alone.

## Working Overseas

Although colonial wives did not necessarily travel overseas on their own volition, many other women made a conscious choice to join colonial society.

Some sought refuge from family tensions; others were tempted by promises of wealth or at least better pay (see **Sources from the Past:** Isabella Gibson on the Immigrant Experience in Australia). Many hoped to leave the rigid social and class norms of European society, and still others were drawn by the sense of adventure or desire for the exotic. Women often felt driven by what contemporaries referred to as "the white women's burden": the care of others—first white men, then natives. These European women nearly all worked in educational or caregiving fields. However, European women who worked in the colonies were still constrained by European gender norms, and those who refused to behave accordingly often found themselves isolated from colonial society or returned to the metropole on the next ship home.

During the last half of the nineteenth century, the British Women's Emigration Association (BWEA) and other similar organizations recruited more than twenty thousand women to settle overseas. The French Society for the Emigration of Women to the Colonies was established in 1897, but it was significantly less successful; fewer than five hundred women answered its appeals in French newspapers and magazines.[52] In their recruitment efforts, these organizations stressed the opportunities for advancement and marriage and the need for women to spread European civilization to the far corners of the earth. There were also intra-European rivalries at work in these immigration schemes. For instance, the British hoped to overwhelm South African Boers (South Africans of Dutch descent) with large numbers of English settlers.

European immigration societies were concerned with the increasing "surplus" of single women in the metropoles as men migrated to the colonies. In 1851, there were 1,042 women for every 1,000 men in Great Britain. By 1911, that number had increased to 1,068 women for every 1,000 men.[53] These large numbers of single women did not fit into a society that emphasized marriage and motherhood. Rising female unemployment in the metropoles also factored into the immigration process. Migration to the colonies was one way to solve these problems while supporting the imperialist cause.

Despite women's enthusiasm, job opportunities remained limited. Many businesses refused to hire women, and they could not hold jobs in the British colonial bureaucracy until 1919. Nevertheless, there was much work to be done, particularly in traditionally female occupations. The Female Middle Class Emigration Society recruited women to be domestics in colonial homes. While domestics may have been near the bottom of the socioeconomic hierarchy at home, abroad they held positions of authority over native servants and could take advantage of the privileges available to European colonists. Proponents of emigration asserted that domestic service in the colonies would be more dignified and more egalitarian than the same work in Britain.[54] However, once settled in their new surroundings, many women married rather than continue to work as domestics.

The wives of colonial officials formed the British Colonial Nursing Association (CNA) in 1896 in order to bring medical care to colonial outposts. It was the only branch of the colonial service composed exclusively of women. Although some were better trained than others, these women were attracted by a sense of adventure and the possibility of freedom from the class and gender restrictions of British society. The work was hard and the living conditions often harsh. Despite the tropical heat, they still had to wear a long-sleeved white uniform whose skirt touched the floor in order to protect their modesty and hide their bodies. Some nurses rebelled against clothing and other regulations, frustrating colonial authorities. As single women with little supervision, they gained a reputation for sexual promiscuity. In the first five years of CNA appointments in West Africa, one-third of the nurses were recalled or retired, often under pressure from the European communities that they were supposed to serve.[55]

Some women went to colonial outposts to work as governesses. Because a governess lived in the home of her employer, the family could properly supervise her behavior and thus governess positions were one of the careers considered appropriate for young educated single women. Organizations proliferated to help them find work abroad. The English Society for Promoting the Employment of Women (1859) recruited women to serve as governesses in South Africa and Australia. Other women sought employment overseas on their own. Ina Sofie Amalie von Binzer (1856–ca. 1916) taught for a number of years in German schools before she traveled to Brazil in 1881. She worked for wealthy coffee planter families in São Paolo and Rio de Janeiro and briefly at a private girl's school in Rio de Janeiro. She then documented her experience in her letters, published as *Joys and Sorrows of a School Teacher in Brazil* (1887).

Female medical practitioners were always in short supply in the colonies, despite the fact that many native cultures forbade women from interacting with male doctors. Mary Scharlieb (1845–1930), the wife of a British lawyer in India, struggled to gain access to medical training in Madras in India. It is not surprising that doctors initially opposed her request, as women could still not enroll in British medical schools. Nevertheless, Scharlieb persevered and, in 1875, she and three other women were admitted to the Madras Medical College. She later founded a woman's hospital and became the first female medical lecturer in India. Dr. Edith Pechey (1845–1908), an activist for women's medical education in Britain, went to India to head a government-funded hospital for women and children in Bombay. The hospital was run entirely by female doctors and nurses. In addition to her extensive private practice and clinic work, she started a training school for nurses.[56]

Like their social reforming counterparts in Europe, many women fought to extend education to women across the empires. From the American West to Australia to West Africa, women set up boarding schools to educate native children. While the results may have benefited many native women, their goals were not entirely altruistic. A European education was a critical means of "improving" the status of native women while reinforcing imperial priorities. Generally, these European educators made little or no effort to understand native cultures or the role that native women had in their own societies. Europeans judged native women by the ideals of Victorian femininity with which they had been raised—domesticity and motherhood—and used education to acculturate native women into European gender expectations. Some of the most basic educational efforts aimed to change native women's ideas about health and motherhood. For example, Madame van den Perre founded the League for the Protection of Black

## Isabella Gibson on the Immigrant Experience in Australia

*This letter is from Isabella Gibson, who migrated from England to New South Wales (Australia) in the 1830s. She arrived on the ship* Layton, *which brought 284 single women as a part of a government scheme to encourage women to emigrate. We have maintained the original spelling.*

She may have answered this advertisement published in England:

> Single women and widows of good health and character, from 15 to 30 years of age, desirous of bettering their condition by emigrating to that healthy and prosperous colony, where the number of females compared to the entire population is about one in three, and where, consequently, from the great demand for servants and other female employments, the wages are comparatively high, may obtain a passage by this ship on payment of £5 only, as they will have the advantage of a free grant of £12 each from the Government, which grant, during the present year, will be confined to those females sent out by this Committee, and will cease after this ship is dispatched.

She wrote to her sister Helen in 1834:

> I wrote home on the 17th of Febry last which letter I hope will reach London about this time informing you that we arrvd at Sidney on the 16 Decr and that I had engaged here with a Mr Hunt to do his apholsterary needle work, salary to be at 8 £. For several months after landing I was afflicted with scurvy and other complaints from which I am now got quite better of and at present in good health. I am much surprised and disappointed at receiving no letter from you considering how strictly I charged you to write soon and how faithfully you promised to do so. It is now ten months since I left home yet no letter from any of you. I regularly enquire at the post office every Packet that comes from England and as often return home disappointed. I can get no intelligence of the Mail Brigg the ship which Richard was to come by. It is conjectured here that the owners of it must have failed and in consiquence of that the ship will not come here at all at this time but if so it is strange he has not come out by any other ship whither he has changed his mind and is not coming at all or what has become of him I cannot ascertain. I form numberless conjectures but all in vain every day adds to my anxiety—I still remain at Mr Hunts and at the end of the first quarter had my wages raised from 21 per quarter to 3 10£ which is 14£ a year this is the most they will give they are well satisfied with me or they would not have advanced it so much but in addition to my needlework I have now to make 8 beds and sweep out 6 rooms every morning. If I were assured that Richard would never come I would endeavour to return home as soon as possible if I could find it at all practicable but I doubt whither it will ever be in my power. Today I requested the editor of a newspaper to advertise me to engage with any family that was going to England and wanted a female servant he said that he might do so but that I would find it a difficult matter to succeed there were such numerous applications of the same kind by people that were disappointed in their expectation of endeavouring to return home. He said that by advertising he thought I might procure a larger sallery if I could undertake to be a governess but in no other capacity accordingly I am going to advertise for a nursery governess (that is to begin young children and take the charge of them) free emigrants are sometimes allowed the priviledge of inserting an advertisement gratis in this newspaper so mine is at this

time to be put in free of expense, but I do not well know what is best to do there are so very few places that is any way tolerable here that I am afraid to risk leaving Hunts they are such quiet people and have never once found fault with me since I came to their house. But I trust that providence will direct me for the best for I have none either to care for or assist me. Shop work of any kind is rarely to be had here what is sold in the shops is most all brought from London ready made Millinery and dressmaking are I understand better paid for than what the dressmakers made me to believe when I was trying amongst them for employment they charge from three shillings to 12 for making gowns and from 4 to 7 or 8 shillings for covering a silk or Velvet bonnet willow for bonnet shapes 1/6 per sheet and 2/6 or 3 sh [shillings] when made into a shape it is mostly gause ribbon that they are trimmed with here and that is about 2 sh per yd. I lay out as little as possible on clothing but the family I am in require that their servants well dressed so I am obliged to do so. I had my straw hornet cleaned & pressed lately for which I paid 2/6d. I regret that I have no person to live with me that I could trust or I would take a room and make bonnets and frocks and sell a few toys, penny dolls sell here for 6d each or take in apolstering needlework. Miss Vetch the Scotch woman is the only person I could put my confidence in and I understand she is expecting to he married soon to a farmer 150 miles up the county—A farmer and his family that came out with us in the ship went to live at that place and a few of his neighbour farmers employed him to return to Sidney and bespeak wives for them among the free women that he could recommend he fixed on Miss V. for one and she has had two letters from the man saying that he intends to come to Sidney soon when if they approve of each other at sight they will be directly married. If I was to give the least hint of such a thing being agreeable to me I might have the same opportunity but I could not bring my mind however destitute I may be to think of marrying any person I had no regard for on this account I declined accepting one offer I have had already from a man who has lived a while in this family as cook and butler an Englishman about 45 years of age he has been most of his life time a soldier & has now a pension of 15 £ a year and a house and 20 acres of land from government about 70 miles from Sidney he has now left his service here and gone to live at his little property. A number of women that came out with me have married prisoners—Dear H I hope you will not on any account delay writing to me immediately on receiving this. On my own account I would like to see you here but for my fathers sake and your own I could not advise you to come because I am conscious by doing so you would run the risk of suffering more hardships than I would like to see any of you subjected to. I hope Christina is continuing better that my father is keeping his health and that all of you are well let me know if the cholera has been in London this summer. Being so close confined here I have almost no opportunity of hearing any news or seeing any of my ship acquaintances . . . I dread the coming of the warm weather again if I could get home I would not wish to remain here longer than the month of Feby next. if so I might have time to have an answer to this letter from you before I left here at all events if you are alive and well do not be so long in writing to me again.

*Isabella Gibson's letter was addressed to her sister, care of Mr. Gibson, cowkeeper, I Ashlins Place, Drury Lane, London. There is no record of Isabella marrying in New South Wales; perhaps she returned to England.*

Source: Patricia Clarke and Dale Spender, *Life Lines: Australian Women's Letters and Diaries, 1788–1840* (North Sydney: Allen and Unwin, 1992), 144–147.

Children in Brussels in 1912. She hoped to reduce infant mortality in the Belgian Congo by teaching African women the "arts" of child-rearing, cleanliness, and hygiene.[57] From the perspective of European teachers, once native women received some education, they moved closer in the colonial hierarchy to European women and native men.

Despite the purely domestic goals of European schooling and the protests of British colonial officials, a few women worked to bring an academic curriculum to native girls. At the Hukarere Native School for Girls in New Zealand, European women taught Maori girls English, Latin, algebra, physiology, and history in addition to sewing, cooking, and singing. However, the school's ideas came into conflict with scientific views of gender differences. Lecturers at the University of Otago in New Zealand argued against allowing women to "indulge" in the study of higher mathematics and science because the stress of academic studies might interfere with girls' physical and mental development. One New Zealand scholar even asserted that excessive academic work caused mental illness in girls.[58]

The educational efforts of these women produced the first generation of European-trained native female professionals. Dr. Anandibai Joshi (1865–1887) from India studied medicine at the Women's Medical College of Pennsylvania in Philadelphia. She returned home in 1886 and headed the women's ward at Albert Edward Hospital in Kolhapur before her death a year later. In 1896, two Chinese graduates of Methodist mission schools received medical degrees from the University of Michigan. They later returned to China to work with missionaries. One of them, Dr. Mary Stone (Shi Meiyu) founded two hospitals and was a critical force in the expansion of Western medicine in China.

Male authorities expressed continued ambivalence about single women's immigration. Although in Algeria women ran farms, rooming houses, and shops, French officials in Indochina opposed single female settlers, citing the dangerous possibility that if their businesses did not succeed or they did not marry, they would be forced into prostitution, have sex with native men, and thereby subvert the racial hierarchy.[59]

The lure of land ownership and potential wealth drew many European couples to the colonies. The Danish novelist Karen Blixen (1885–1962), who wrote under the pseudonym Isak Dinesen, moved to Kenya with her husband in 1914 to become plantation owners. They cultivated coffee on six thousand acres of land using local Kikuyu labor. When the couple divorced, Blixen managed the plantation alone until 1931. She later chronicled her experience in her memoir, *Out of Africa* (1937).

A few women did not go to the colonies willingly. According to French law between 1854 and 1900, female prisoners could opt to be sent to prison colonies overseas. Between 1870 and 1885, four hundred women chose exile in the penal colony of New Caledonia. Many of them were participants in the Paris Commune, including the most famous, Louise Michel (1830–1905), an anarchist, poet, and political dramatist (see Chapter 10). Michel was arrested for her participation in the Paris Commune of 1871 and sentenced to lifelong deportation from France. She arrived in New Caledonia in 1873. During her exile, she taught the native people and supported the local Kanak people in their revolt against French rule. Eventually, she was granted amnesty and returned to France. Cayenne in French Guiana also housed female prisoners.

## Going Native

Although most European women struggled to maintain their Europeanness in the colonies, a few "went native," rejecting some or all European gender expectations. Often the products of liberal educations, these women became convinced that they could not find social, sexual, spiritual, or intellectual freedom at home and began lifelong searches for religious and cultural norms that they found less oppressive.

Going native manifested itself in different ways. Some European women shocked their compatriots by choosing to wear native clothing. This visual identification with supposedly inferior cultures made a strong statement, as dress was a critical marker of identity in nineteenth-century Europe. Veils, saris, and other native garments could be signs of either sexual freedom or sexual repression. Jane Digby (1807–1881), the disgraced ex-wife of the Earl of Ellenborough, left her native England for life in the Syrian desert with the tribe of her fourth husband, Sheikh Mejuel el-Mezrab. Her native clothing visually separated her from her privileged life in England. Native dress also closed some of the cultural gaps between European women and native women. Thus, even Charlotte "Lottie" Moon (1840–1912), a Baptist missionary in China, adopted Chinese dress in order to proselytize more effectively.

A few European women found spiritual fulfillment in non-Christian religions. Alexandra David-Néel (1868–1969) studied Sanskrit and Buddhism at the Sorbonne before she set off for India at the age of twenty-one. She spent much of her life studying Buddhism and later met the exiled Dalai Lama in Sikkim. She adopted a Tibetan teenager with whom she illegally entered Tibet. There, she spent three years in a cave studying Tibetan and perfecting her knowledge of Buddhist texts. She even journeyed to Lhasa, "the forbidden city," disguised as a beggar.

Englishwoman Annie Besant (1847–1933) and many other European women found connections to Asian philosophy and religion through *theosophy*, an occult religion with close ties to Eastern religions. Founded by Russian émigré Helena Blavatsky (1831–1891) in New York in 1875, theosophy provided a critique of Western scientific and religious traditions. It attracted many female reformers because it rejected the superiority and traditional patriarchal hierarchy of Christianity and allowed for female leadership. Besant was president of the International Theosophical Society from 1907 until her death in 1933.

When European women married native men, they both gained entry into native society and lost some of the power and privilege that they had as white Europeans. They typically faced severe criticism from other Europeans, who often denounced them as sexually deviant. A turn-of-the-century Englishman once said disgustedly that a woman who married an Indian "has violated her own nature in marrying a man of coloured race."[60] Although race formed the ultimate barrier to these relationships, they became even more inconceivable to Europeans when they transgressed class boundaries. The 1893 marriage between the Maharaja of Patiala and Miss Florry Bryan, a working-class Englishwoman, caused considerable scandal in the British colonial community.[61]

Among Muslims, marriage to native men also meant conversion to Islam. Mary Torok (1877–1968), a Hungarian, married the Khedieve Abbas II, who ruled Egypt between 1892 and 1914. She shared her experiences of converting to Islam and living in the royal harem in Egypt and Turkey in her book *Harem Life* (1930), which she wrote under her Islamic name, Djavidan Hanum. Similarly, Eugenie Le Brun (d. 1908) a Frenchwoman, married Husayn Rushdy, who eventually became prime minister of Egypt (1914–1917). When these women married native men, they lost the social privilege among natives that their European background afforded them. They had little in common with native women, even those of their own social status, and chafed at the restrictions placed on Muslim women. Torok sometimes disguised herself as her husband's bodyguard to escape the restrictions of the harem. Moreover, their writings reveal the degree to which they had internalized European stereotypes. They viewed their relationships as completely different from those between native women and native men. They believed that those relationships were only about erotic pleasure (thus playing into the stereotype of the oversexualized native woman), whereas their own relationships were about a deeper, more intellectualized love. However, they also described their native husbands as being unlike European men; instead, they were childlike, tame, and safe.[62]

Isabelle Eberhardt (1877–1904) ranks as one of the few European women who rejected nearly all European norms. Isabelle grew up in Geneva where she had a very untraditional upbringing and wore boy's clothing as a child. In 1897, at the age of twenty, she arrived in Algeria with her mother. When her mother died shortly after their arrival, she began an extensive refashioning of her own identity. She dressed in men's clothing, took a man's name, Mahmoud Saadi, converted to Islam, and delved into Sufi mysticism. Fluent in Arabic, she wandered the streets and frequented the cafés of the port city of Boné, alone or with male companions. Both her cross-dressing and her decision to dress like an Arab disturbed other Europeans. Although fervent in her prayers and fasting, Isabelle also flouted Islamic norms by praying at the mosques dressed as a man and studying with Muslim scholars. She drank alcohol, smoked hashish, and took many male lovers. In 1901, she married a Muslim military officer in the Sahara.

Eberhardt constantly moved between the two cultures. Periodically, local officials sent her back to Europe into temporary exile for her sexual, political, and cultural transgressions. Once, after being attacked by an Arab man, she traveled to Marseilles as a man. As a male journalist, she went to the desert to cover French attempts to capture Morocco and even undertook some reconnaissance missions. Isabelle survived a bout with malaria but died in a desert flash flood in 1904. Unwilling to inscribe her male Arabic name on her tombstone, the military general who buried her created a female Arabic name for her, Lalla Mahmoud. In death, Isabelle found yet another identity.[63]

Although the military and colonial administrations were exclusively male institutions, European women gradually spread across the empires. Most European women who came to work in the colonies undertook traditional women's work—teaching, nursing, and domestic service. Although they anticipated greater freedoms than they experienced in the metropole, they were often disappointed. The small, insular white communities in which they lived often had little tolerance for even small indiscretions or assertions of independence. Nevertheless, many endured the hardships of colonial life, bringing European-style health care and education to people around the world. For others, the colonies offered newfound freedoms to dress, love, and pray unconstrained by European expectations.

## COLLABORATION AND RESISTANCE

Women's views of European imperialism were as diverse as the women themselves. Each woman's class, education, and experience abroad influenced her understanding of the imperial effort. Women's perspectives on imperialism were deeply connected to their views on the state of women at home. Most women supported the imperial cause, and they whole-heartedly believed that the dominance of non-Europeans was for the betterment of all. Others were openly skeptical of either colonial policies or the entire colonial project. The intersection of feminism and imperialism was most clearly evident in the debates over women's suf-frage. A woman's stance on whether and how colonial women (both European and native) should receive the vote revealed much about her understanding of women's roles in society.

## Imperialist Women

Most European women actively supported imperialism, believing that it was Europe's duty to civilize the world for everyone's betterment. Imperialism also provided women with a sense of importance, power, and privilege. Flora Shaw (1852–1929) was probably the most influential female proponent of European colonization. Although she had no formal schooling, she was bright and well connected to leaders of the imperialist cause. Traveling in Egypt in 1888–89, she became a correspondent for two British newspapers and continued to write on politics after returning to England. She eventually became the first colonial editor for *The Times* of London. During her career, she wrote more than five hundred articles on economic and political issues in the colonies supporting British expansion. As she lived and reported from Egypt, South Africa, Australia, New Zealand, and Canada, her conservative views of colonial life influenced policymakers at home. She even coined the name "Nigeria" in an 1897 article. Despite the fact that her career as a journalist was atypical for a Victorian woman, she identified with imperial ideology and was opposed to suffrage. Shaw eventually married a top colonial administrator, gave up her career, and traveled with him to Nigeria and Hong Kong. She later used her influence to support the British Empire in the debate over Irish Home Rule (see below).[64]

Shaw was not alone. In 1901, Englishwomen formed their own imperial society, the Victoria League. Enthusiastic imperialist women formed the League to "support and assist colonial projects" in ways that conformed to Victorian expectations of female domesticity. Galvanized into action by the Boer War in South Africa, in which the British attempted to displace Dutch settlers, they organized war charities, provided imperial education to children, and supplied art and literature to the far ends of the empire. Of course, not just any books would do. The League hoped to promote the imperial agenda with "books or magazine articles likely to produce appreciation of and attachment towards British institutions." As early as 1905, the president of the League, Violet Markham (1872–1959), worried that Canada was "being Americanised against her will and against what she feels to be the best interests of her people." The League also provided hospitality for colonists visiting England and arranged for the reception of British emigrants in the colonies.[65]

Racism combined with radical nationalism to form the imperialist ideology of Frieda von Bülow (1857–1909). First, she helped establish the German National Women's League to send nurses to the colonies. Then, she became one of the first two nurses to travel to Africa with the League. Eventually, she owned her own plantation in German East Africa. She chronicled her experiences and her beliefs in fictional accounts, which are marked by racist stereotypes and, despite her own unconventional life, profound antifeminism. Although Bülow opposed the exploitation of women and worked to expand women's occupational opportunities, she did so from a radical German nationalist perspective that emphasized the role of women in the reconfiguration of a powerful German state. She viewed the domination of non-Europeans (as well as Jews, Poles, and other marginalized peoples) as a way for German men to prove their masculinity and thereby make themselves suitable for German women.[66]

From the comfort of their homes, most European women saw only the benefits of imperialism. Their access to consumer goods increased and their countries' economies boomed. They enthusiastically accepted the nationalist idea that empire made their countries strong relative to other European nations and to the rest of the world. European newspapers and magazines reinforced women's patriotic fervor by reporting sensational and sordid tales of women's repression outside of Europe. European women's patriotic duty and sense of moral and cultural superiority made them strong defenders of empire.

## Imperial Feminism and Feminist Anti-Imperialists

From the outset, many European reformers were driven by the imperial idea that the protection of native women was Europe's "special burden." These reformers worked to identify their causes with the national interest, asserting that both feminism and empire promoted the political and economic interests of the nation. Advocates of what scholars refer to as *imperial feminism*, they often spoke on behalf of indigenous women rather than empowering native women to act on their own. The sense of responsibility that activist women felt was almost exhilarating, as is evident in the words of Sara Amos, an English feminist, "We are struggling not just for English women alone, but for all the women, degraded, miserable, unheard of, for whose life and happiness England has daily to answer to God."[67] As a result, very few women actively opposed European imperialism.

However, imperialism had a few very vocal opponents (see **Women's Lives**: Olive Schreiner, Writer and Activist). Activist Annie Besant advocated women's suffrage and promoted anti-imperialist ideas. At the age of twenty-five, Besant permanently separated from her husband and began speaking and writing on behalf of liberal causes, including socialism, trade unionism, and the emancipation of Englishwomen. She advocated against the Contagious Diseases Acts and for the dissemination of birth control. She spoke vehemently against British rule in India and Africa and condemned the British invasion of Afghanistan in 1877. After she moved to India in 1895, she praised Hinduism, rejecting the rhetoric of both English imperialists and many Indian reformers who blamed Hinduism for the oppression of women. Her opposition to imperialism led to her involvement in Indian movements for self-government. She helped found the Home Rule for India League in 1916. Her anti-imperial activities caught the eye of colonial officials, and in 1917, she was imprisoned by the British for writing seditious articles. However, Besant was unstoppable. That same year, when the secretary of state for India visited Madras, she was part of a delegation that requested that any plan for Indian self-rule include the vote for women, and she became the first woman president of the Indian National Congress.[68]

While Besant was busy in India, anti-imperialist activity was coming to a fevered pitch closer to home. Ireland had been an English colony since the twelfth century, but by the late nineteenth century, relations between Ireland and England had

## Olive Schreiner, Writer and Activist

Olive Schreiner (1855–1920), a novelist, political writer, and activist, used her notoriety and her skills to bring the sexism and racism of imperial society to the attention of her readers. Schreiner was born in South Africa and grew up on a remote mission. Her German father had joined the London Missionary Society, and he and his wife left for South Africa less than three weeks after their marriage. At age twenty-seven, she briefly joined her brothers in the diamond rush in what was to become Rhodesia. There she began her first novel, *Undine* (published posthumously in 1929), in which the main character, Undine, is frustrated by her exclusion from the profitable world of mining. She also began work on her novel *From Man to Man* (published posthumously in 1927), which posed the dilemma of two sisters, one a prostitute and the other married to a philandering husband. By juxtaposing the two women's lives, Schreiner offered a harsh critique of the sexual double standard and the repression of women's intellect by marriage.

From age fifteen to twenty-two, she worked as a governess, a more appropriate occupation for a young woman. Schreiner then went to England to pursue a career in nursing; however, she had to abandon that goal due to her poor health. Instead, she joined a variety of intellectual clubs and socialist organizations through which she became close friends with London intellectuals including Eleanor Marx (1855–1898), the daughter of Karl Marx, and Havelock Ellis (1859–1939), the British psychologist and sexuality researcher.

While in England she published her first book, *The Story of an African Farm* (1883), under the pseudonym Ralph Iron. A bleak look at the repression of women through the imposition of domesticity and marriage, the book became an overnight success in Britain. Schreiner became the first colonial writer to win acclaim in the metropole.

She returned to South Africa in 1889 and over the next few years became active in South African politics. She also met and married Samuel Cronwright, who changed his name to Schreiner-Cronwright. During this period, Schreiner harshly criticized the British treatment of Boers (descendants of the Dutch settlers) and supported the Boers in the Boer War (1899–1902). Her 1897 book *Trooper Halkett of Mashonaland* criticized the British colonization of Rhodesia.

In her monumental feminist work *Women and Labour*, Schreiner attempted to chronicle the historical plight of women. Unfortunately, the original version of the book was burned by British soldiers who broke into her home during the Boer War. The version of *Women and Labour* that appeared in 1911 was her abbreviated reconstruction of the destroyed book. She was jailed for her anti-British activities, and her political activism brought her into contact with Mahatma Gandhi (1869–1948). Although she was intrigued by his use of nonviolence in defiance of racist imperial policies, she was appalled by his general acceptance of the British Empire.

Later in life, she turned her energies toward the right to vote and became a strong proponent of the suffrage movement in South Africa. However, Schreiner believed that all Africans deserved the right to vote and resigned from the Women's Enfranchisement League when it changed its definition of voting qualification to exclude blacks.

Her ill health forced her to go back to England in 1913, but she returned to South Africa just before she died in 1920. Through her writing, Olive Schreiner exposed the complications of colonial life, campaigning tirelessly against the racism and sexism of the British Empire.

Sources: Ruth First and Ann Scott, *Olive Schreiner* (London: Deutsch, 1980) and Anne McClintock, *Imperial Leather: Race, Gender, and Sexuality in the Colonial Contest* (New York: Routledge, 1995).

seriously deteriorated. The movement for legislative independence for Ireland was gaining support in the English Parliament but passage of a Home Rule Bill failed in 1893. Many Irish suffragists became active in the nationalist movement, including Constance Markievicz (1868–1926). An ardent nationalist, she urged her colleagues in the suffrage movement to channel their energies into Irish independence. In 1909, Markievicz helped found *Na Fianna Eireann*, an organization that prepared young men to fight for Irish independence, and later created the *Cumann na mBan*, a woman's auxiliary to the Irish Volunteer Forces. To prevent civil war in Ireland, Parliament passed a Home Rule Bill in 1914; however, the outbreak of World War I (1914–1918) led to its suspension and the resumption of violence. Markievicz led troops during the Easter rebellion of 1916 and was charged with treason. She served only a few months in jail. Although she was elected to British Parliament in 1918, as a member of *Sinn Fein,* she did not attend. Instead, she went to Dublin where, in 1919, she became the minister for labor in the new Irish government.

Some American women also opposed imperialist policies both at home and abroad. The United States gained its first colonial possessions with its victory in what became known as the Spanish-American War in 1898, and many women and men protested the U.S. acquisition of the Philippines with the formation of the Anti-Imperialist League. Within a year of the founding of the first chapter in Boston, the League had more than thirty thousand members, and half of the attendees at the League's first meeting were women.[69] A petition addressed to "The Women of the United States" from the Women's Auxiliary of the Anti-Imperialist League appealed to women's sense of patriotism: "Believing that, in this national crisis, it is the duty of every American citizen, woman no less than man, to uphold the principles of the Declaration of Independence, and believing that the noble work of the anti-imperialist league should be heartily supported by all true patriots we invite all women of the United States to join us." The petition went on to call for the removal of U.S. troops and Philippine independence.[70] However, despite their activism, women were not allowed to hold offices in the League, forcing them to organize their own Women's Anti-Imperialist League in Massachusetts and Illinois. Later, prominent American social reformers, including Jane Addams (1860–1935), served as officers. American Helen C. Wilson spent five years in the Philippines advocating against U.S. control and working to connect the American and Filipino anti-imperialist movements.

Nineteenth-century European feminism was rooted in notions of women's moral superiority and moral responsibility. European women saw native women as dependents on whom they had to confer aid and comfort. Nevertheless, many women ardently opposed imperialist policies and promoted the cause of self-determination for colonized peoples from Ireland to India.

## Suffrage and the Imperial World

From the outset, the relationship between women's suffrage and imperialism was complex. On the one hand, many conservative women believed that women's votes challenged imperial constructions of gender that asserted European men's right and obligation to govern women and non-Europeans. Moreover, many women feared that giving women the vote would weaken Europe at its most triumphant moment. In fact, antisuffrage forces looked to two prominent supporters of British imperialism to lead their cause; in 1908, Nobel Peace Prize winner Lord Cremer (1828–1908) and Lord Curzon (1859–1925), the former secretary of state for India, helped found the Anti-Suffrage League.

On the other hand, suffrigists more often used their imperial activities to demonstrate women's abilities as citizens and to promote their own imperial ideas. Helena Swanwick, the editor of the prosuffrage journal *Common Cause*, argued for a more feminized "new imperialism" founded "on respect and self-restraint" rather than militarism. In this new imperialism, women's perceived lack of physical strength and military prowess would not hinder their ability to participate in colonial rule.[71]

Like many women, Hubertine Auclert (1848–1914), the founder of the first French suffragist newspaper, *La Citoyenne*, combined her support of suffrage with imperialist attitudes. Auclert lived in Algeria for four years with her husband, a colonial magistrate. From there, she sent articles to Parisian newspapers connecting her campaign for suffrage at home to the plight of women in Algeria. Her writings emphasized the parallel between sexism against women and racism toward colonial subjects. However, she also accepted the basic premise that it was France's mission to civilize non-Europeans, and noting women's moral superiority, she wanted Frenchwomen to have a voice in colonial policy. According to Auclert, undervaluing the abilities of women and North Africans undermined the civilizing effort in both France and its colonies. Her concerns for women in France motivated her desire to improve the lives of women in Africa. She feared that allowing French authorities to denigrate Algerian women would encourage them to treat Frenchwomen the same way.[72]

European suffragists were often slow to include native women in their movements, fully expecting to take the lead in obtaining the vote for women worldwide. Initially, the International Woman Suffrage Alliance sought native women as "auxiliaries" rather than full members, and Carrie Chapman Catt (1859–1947), the organization's president from 1906 to 1923, and Aletta Jacobs traveled around the world in 1912 to recruit auxiliaries, making stops in Egypt, India, Palestine, Japan, and the Philippines. Although suffragists proclaimed their pursuit of internationalism and equality, their efforts were unabashedly hierarchical and imperialist—European women would bequeath suffrage to native women. Nevertheless, their work encouraged the political activism of many native women, including Huda Sharaawi (1879–1924), an Egyptian activist who led the campaign for Egyptian women's rights and even organized an occupation of the Egyptian parliament.

European suffrage movements differed in their enthusiasm and in their success in gaining the right to vote for native and European women in the colonies. One of the more active groups was the World's Women's Christian Temperance Union (WWCTU). Founded by American Frances Willard (1839–1898) and the British Women's Temperance Association president, Lady Isabel Somerset (1851–1920), this organization combined efforts at temperance with agitation for women's rights around the world. The WWCTU's antialcohol message struck a strong chord in colonies like Australia and New Zealand, where

men's drinking led to violence and family problems. Once the organization got the attention of settler women with its antialcohol message, their campaign for suffrage found an enthusiastic audience. In New Zealand, in less than a decade, the WWCTU had successfully lobbied for women's suffrage that included Maori women. However, Maori women did not stand on the sidelines. Meri Mangakahia (1868–1920) proposed that women be allowed not only to vote but also to stand for office. In her 1893 address to members of Parliament, she based her petition for women's enfranchisement on the fact of women's property ownership. At the end of her speech, she referred to ideas of universal womanhood to connect her Maori sisters to Queen Victoria: "Perhaps the Queen may listen to the petitions if they are presented by her Maori sisters, since she is a woman as well."[73] When the bill passed both houses of the New Zealand legislature in September 1893, it was the first modern enfranchisement of native women. Legislators were willing to allow Maori women the vote because of the configuration of New Zealand's parliament. Maori men had been granted the franchise in 1867, but they could only vote for four designated indigenous members of Parliament. Thus, allowing Maori women to vote would not alter the election of Europeans in the colony. The unique circumstances that led to women's suffrage in New Zealand did not have a domino effect in Europe. It would be another thirteen years before European women on the Continent (Finland) received the right to vote.

A similar campaign in the six Australian colonies led to the vote for European women in 1902, but not for Aboriginal peoples. One member of Parliament connected race and gender in his speech during the debate over women's suffrage in western Australia:

> *It is admitted on all sides that, while men are only the progenitors of our race, the women are its saviors; and that on the future of the Anglo-Saxon race to which we are all proud to belong, and on the future of the civilized races of the world, women are exercising a higher influence and playing a more important part and will continue to do so, than men can aspire to do. On these lines I claim the right of woman to have a vote.*

However, legislators found it "repugnant" to provide Aboriginal men and women with the same rights.[74] With the formulation of the new Australian constitution of 1901, Aboriginal men who had been afforded limited voting rights at the state level were denied those rights by federal law. Aborigines would not regain voting rights until 1962.

At the same time, but with very different results, the WWCTU lobbied for women's suffrage in the Hawaiian Islands. In 1893, American business interests overthrew the Hawaiian monarchy. The WWCTU supported the coup over the protests of the women's branch of the Hawaiian Patriotic League. However, in response, the League, with a membership of over eleven thousand Hawaiian women, led an anti-imperial revolt against the U.S.-sponsored Republic of Hawaii in 1895. Undaunted, the WWCTU formed a Hawaiian chapter to agitate for suffrage for Euro-American women; however, both before and after the annexation of the Hawaiian Islands by the United States, its appeals for suffrage went unheeded. American businessmen feared that the Hawaiian population would not support its interests, and demographics fueled their fears—native women outnumbered white women by more than seven to one.[75] Hawaiian women, both native and Euro-American, finally received the vote in 1920 with the passage of the Nineteenth Amendment to the U.S. Constitution.

European women's support of or opposition to imperialism depended not on their understanding of non-European women's status, but on their perceptions of their own place in European society. Women who were comfortable with the status quo were roused by the patriotism and civilizing efforts of imperialism. In contrast, women who struggled for social reform at home often linked their efforts to the end or at least the tempering of imperial institutions. Even as European women worked to bring the vote to women around the world, traditional ideas about race and class permeated their campaigns.

## TRAVELING THE WORLD

Since the eighteenth century elite women had relied on travel to "finish" their educations. During their

**WOMEN'S HAWAIIAN PATRIOTIC LEAGUE PETITION AGAINST ANNEXATION (1897).** The United States' intention to annex Hawaii mobilized native Hawaiian women to take political action. In 1897 and 1898, they collected more than ten thousand signatures in opposition to making the island nation a part of the US. *(University of Hawaii, Manoa.)*

journeys, they could practice their foreign language skills and view great works of art and architecture. Wealthy Europeans also believed that travel could help restore a young woman's physical and mental health. Most European women of sufficient financial means spent a few months or even a year traveling around the Continent or visiting the United States, and American girls traveled to Europe. By the nineteenth century, imperial conquests and improvements in transportation (including the steamship and railroads) allowed women to venture beyond the typical itineraries to the far reaches of the globe.

Although travel may have been easier in the nineteenth century, it could be both dangerous and frustrating. By the end of the century, the steamship voyage from London to Australia still took forty days. After the construction of the Suez Canal, the trip from London to Calcutta was shortened from at least two months to about four weeks. However, one's arrival by ship may have been the easiest part of the journey. To live according to European standards during their travels, women brought along enormous amounts of luggage. Once they arrived in ports like Calcutta or Cairo, they had to engage porters and other native staff to facilitate their travels. For unfamiliar travelers, journey by horseback, carts, or litters carried by bearers could be frightening and uncomfortable. For the most adventurous, unfamiliarity with local dialects, poor roads, and intertribal warfare made land travel difficult, if not impossible, at times. Tropical diseases and lack of European-style medical care in remote areas compounded the dangers.

The transportation revolution of the nineteenth century also opened the world to large-scale migrations from Europe. Women of all social classes, but particularly working-class women, took the opportunity to search for better lives not only in colonial settings, but in new centers of European immigration in North and South America.

## Travel and Study

During the nineteenth century, it became quite fashionable for women not only to travel to exotic locations but also to chronicle their journeys. One of the most remarkable aspects of women's travel writing is that despite the worries European men expressed, most European women reported feeling safe, even in isolated parts of the world that had little if any contact with Europeans. Women generally describe being charmed by the friendliness and curiosity of the native peoples whom they encountered.

Not only did women experience the non-European world differently than men expected, but as they traveled they often wrote about their experiences differently than men did. Scholars of nineteenth-century travel literature have noted that men tended to use the language of domination in their accounts; new lands and peoples they encountered were to be mastered and placed under their control. Male travel writers also tended to focus on overall perceptions of the entire journey. In contrast, female travel writers tended to focus on episodes, and they often denied their ability to dominate new peoples and places. Women's perspectives were also complex as they attempted to reconcile their adventurous and authoritative decision to travel to exotic lands with nineteenth-century expectations that they were timid and subordinate. Most important, female travel writers provide insight into the experience of non-European women because, unlike their male counterparts, they regularly interacted with native women and were interested in their lives. Their diaries, letters, and travel accounts include intimate details about childbearing practices, dietary customs, and mother-child relationships.[76]

Many women traveled purely for pleasure. Fredrika Bremer (1801–1865) was an internationally famous Swedish novelist and activist who toured the United States for two years between 1849 and 1851. She then spent four months in Cuba, ostensibly to restore her health; however, while in Cuba, Bremer spent most of her time on sugar plantations investigating slavery and writing about the lives of slaves. Describing her reaction to the slave society, Bremer wrote, "I have now been here for more than a week in the very lap of slavery, and during the first few days of my visit I was so depressed that I was not able to do much. Close before my window . . . I could not avoid seeing the whole day a group of negro women working under the whip."[77] The social agendas of women such as Bremer were deeply influenced by their experiences abroad.

Ida Pfeiffer (1797–1858) traveled in search of adventure. Forced into an arranged marriage with an older Ukrainian attorney, Ida left her native Vienna for the Ukraine. She did not begin to travel until she was forty-two years old, after she had separated from her husband and her children had grown. Her first voyage was a ten-month pilgrimage to the Middle East. There, she met people easily because, as an older woman, she was not subject to more restrictive gender expectations imposed on young women. Her account of her Middle Eastern voyage became a bestseller in 1844, as did the chronicle of her travels across Scandinavia and Iceland. She later made two trips around the world. During the second voyage, she acquired a number of valuable pieces for the Museum of Natural History in Vienna. At the age of fifty-six, Ida visited California during the gold rush, and she ended her traveling career in 1857 with a trip to Madagascar, where she was briefly imprisoned and had to escape through the jungle. She carefully and vividly chronicled all of her adventures to the delight of European audiences.

Increasingly, women traveled abroad to pursue research and study. Among those, the English-woman Mary Kingsley (1862–1900) attained great fame as both an investigator and a writer. Kingsley, an avid naturalist, traveled to West Africa in 1893 to collect species of fish for scientific study. She returned to Africa again one year later and based on these experiences, she wrote *Travels in West Africa* (1897) and *West African Studies* (1899). She amassed abundant ethnographic information about African society and religion, and when she returned to England, she wrote many articles and gave numerous lectures. Politically, she was very controversial. Kingsley wrote about the failures of missionary efforts, spoke against suffrage, and fought against direct colonial rule in West Africa, not because she was opposed to imperialism, but because she supported rule by British traders. According to Kingsley,

> *I confess I am not an enthusiast on civilizing the African. My idea is that the French method of dealing with Africa is the best at present. Get as much of the continent as possible down on the map as yours, make your flag wherever you go a sacred thing to the native—a thing he dare not attack. Then, when you have done this, you may abandon the French plan, and gradually develop trade in the English manner. (Kingsley,* Travels in West Africa *[Macmillan, 1897], 639).*

She died from disease while working as a nurse during the Boer War.

Although the laboratory remained largely off-limits to women, world travel offered them oppor-tunities for scientific inquiry and discovery. Marianne North (1830–1890), an intrepid traveler and an accomplished naturalist and botanical artist, spent eight months in the jungles of Brazil where she produced more than one hundred paint-ings. Later voyages took her to Japan, Sri Lanka, Java, India, Australia, across Africa, and finally to Chile in 1884. Wherever she went, North painted native plants and, in the process, discovered at least one new species. Five species of plants are named for her. In 1879, she presented her works to the Royal Botanic Gardens and had a friend, an architect, design a new gallery to house them. Today, the gallery houses 823 of her oil paintings.

Such physical and intellectual freedom also appealed to famed archaeologist Jane Dieulafoy (1851–1916). In 1884, she and her husband, Marcel, reopened the excavations of the palaces of Ataxerxes and Darius at Susa in Persia, and she was awarded the prestigious Cross of the Order of the Legion of Honor for her work on the expedi-tion. Her travels allowed her considerable free-doms that she refused to relinquish when she returned to France. For most of her adult life, she refused to wear anything but men's clothing.

Not all female travelers were thoughtful or aca-demically inclined. Many stayed only a short time in each place, and most could not communicate directly with the people they observed. Travelers like Katherine Schuyler Baxter, a pleasure tourist who traveled to Japan in the 1890s, were com-pletely caught up in romanticized ideas of foreign lands. During her travels, she confined her visit to tourist sites and learned little about Japanese peo-ple or culture. In fact, the descriptions of Japanese women in her work *In Bamboo Lands* (1895) tends to treat the women as objects, not unlike the temples and art that Baxter preferred.[78]

The illustrations that women included in their travel writings often offered new and sometimes even the first European views of non-Europeans. Elizabeth Sarah Mazuchelli (1832–1914), the first European woman to visit the eastern Himalayas, recorded the journey in sketches and watercolors. Much more so than male artists, female travelers sketched and painted views of daily life. By the beginning of the twentieth century, photography began to replace sketches. Although some scholars used to believe that few women used photography because of the chemicals and technical knowledge

**JANET WULSIN AND THE MOTHER OF THE PRINCE OF ALASHAN (MONGOLIA, 1923).** In 1923, Janet Wulsin and her husband traveled to Tibet, China, and Mongolia, and took dramatic photographs of the Far East. Female explorers often made contact with local women and noted details of family life. *(Peabody Museum, Harvard University, Photo 56-55-60/15618.)*

necessary, many women quickly adopted the new technology. Janet Wulsin (ca. 1893–1963) and her husband, Frederick, made two expeditions in to China, Mongolia, and Tibet for the National Geographic Society between 1921 and 1925. They documented their travels, which included a seven-hundred-mile trip down the Yangsi River, with photographs. Like the sketches of her predecessors, Wulsin's photographs detailed not only their life in a caravan, but also the daily lives of the people they encountered and preserved them for posterity.

As these women traveled and documented new landscapes and peoples, they redefined their place in the world. Travel gave them access to knowledge and authority outside the supervision of European men. Moreover, their words and pic-

tures forever transformed European understandings of non-European life.

## Noncolonial Migration

The opening of the world that allowed for such remarkable travels also set the stage for the large-scale migration of Europeans to other parts of the world, in particular, the United States, Argentina, Brazil, and Chile. Two great waves of immigrants left Europe, the first between 1830 and 1860 and the second from 1880 to 1920. This migration differed substantially from the immigration to Europe's colonies that we have already described, as most of the immigrants were from the working and lower classes.

Europeans migrated for a variety of reasons. As we have already seen, the nineteenth century was a time of political reorganization in Europe (see Chapter 10), a process that often led to a redistribution or reorganization of peasant lands. Unlike their predecessors whose poverty would have forced them to remain on unproductive land, many European peasants took the opportunity to leave. Famine drove millions of Irish from their homes, and in Germany, rising food prices led to hunger riots and high rates of immigration. Industrialization also transformed the lives of the working classes, as they crossed the ocean in search of better wages. In Russia, the profoundly anti-Semitic regime pressured its Jewish population to leave with violent pogroms, and in response, between 1881 and 1924, 1.5 million Russian Jews emigrated to the United States. Beyond the factors that pushed migrants out of their European homes, both North and South America offered new opportunities that pulled them across the Atlantic. Land was cheap and often available through homesteading and other settlement schemes. Manufacturing was on the rise and factories needed labor. Emigration offered the potential of social mobility, and political freedoms encouraged many to leave their homelands. The largest numbers of immigrants came from Britain, Ireland, Scandinavia, the German Empire, Russia, and Italy. Eight million immigrants arrived in the United States between 1901 and 1910 alone.

The immigration process usually began with a man leaving first. His wife followed later, generally after he had found work and made basic arrangements for his family. That process sometimes took months or even years, during which the wife took on all responsibility for maintaining the family, livestock, and property. Those families not only lacked a man's income, but many men failed to send remittances home, or sometimes the money they sent never arrived. Golda Meir (1898–1978), the former prime minister of Israel whose family immigrated from Russia to Milwaukee, Wisconsin, in 1905, remembered getting word from her father that she, her mother, and her two sisters could join him in America. "It was not a simple matter then for a woman and three girls, two of them very small, to travel all the way from Pinsk to Milwaukee by themselves. . . . Perhaps if we had known that throughout Europe thousands of families like ours were on the move . . . we would have been less frightened." After sneaking across the border to Galicia (now Poland) with fake documents and identities, they boarded a train and then a ship to America. During the two-week journey, Meir recalled being crammed into a stuffy cabin with four other people, sleeping on sheetless beds, and being fed like cattle.[79]

The ocean crossing was only the beginning of the trauma for some women. Emigration ended many marriages. Women arrived in port cities around the world to find that their husbands had deserted them. However, there was no turning back. Those women had to begin new lives in new countries on their own.

Throughout the nineteenth century and early twentieth century, approximately 40 percent of immigrants were women, although eastern European Jewish women and Irish women came at much higher rates. On a few occasions, women actually led families overseas. During the 1870s, female cigar makers in Bohemia migrated to the United States. Their husbands and children followed once they had earned enough money for the passage. Only those women whose skills were highly sought after could migrate under these circumstances.[80]

Approximately 43 percent of female immigrants to the United States were unmarried.[81] Single working-class women often migrated because in parts of Europe it was increasingly difficult for them to find marriage partners. In some countries, there were not enough men and in others, like Germany, laws prohibited domestic servants from marrying. For these women, migration presented the possibility of an expanded marriage market.

Whether married or single, female immigrants tended to be less literate and less skilled than their male counterparts. Not surprisingly, women rarely reported occupations to immigration authorities. By far, the majority of women (87 percent in 1896) said that they were domestic servants. Other women told authorities that they were teachers, seamstresses, and cloth workers.[82]

Life for many newly arrived female migrants to the United States was difficult, and their letters reveal painful homesickness. They rarely knew English and had to learn the language on their own. Even doing the daily shopping was complicated because they did not know the words for different products and were unfamiliar with most of the goods on the shelves. Many became victims of exploitation by unscrupulous merchants. However, in one famous case, Jewish women protested against corrupt business practices. At the turn of the twentieth century, large monopolies controlled the production and distribution of basic foodstuffs in the United States. They increased prices at will and passed them on to the consumer. In 1902, immigrant Jewish women put together a boycott of kosher butchers to protest a sudden rise in kosher meat prices. On May 15, 1902, twenty thousand Jewish immigrant women in New York's Lower East Side broke into butcher shops, looted the meat, soaked it in gasoline, and set it on fire. Armed groups of women prevented other women from purchasing kosher meat. The boycott successfully spread to other northeastern cities through Jewish organizations and synagogues. The *New York Times* called for speedy police action against this "dangerous class . . . especially the women [who] are very ignorant [and] . . . mostly speak a foreign language." Within a month, the prices had returned to normal.[83]

Immigrant women entered the workforce as quickly as possible to help support their families. By 1900, foreign-born women and their daughters were more than half of all female wage earners in the United States. Women generally migrated to cities where women's work was more readily available, while men were drawn to farming and mining. Although many women came to the United States hoping to enter domestic service, the market for servants was not expanding during this period as quickly as manufacturing jobs. In the first quarter of the twentieth century, 34 percent of foreign-born women worked in manufacturing and 25 percent in domestic service. Nationality also factored into the decision to work in domestic service. Although the majority of Norwegian (86 percent), Irish (81 percent), and Slovak (86 percent) women workers were servants, fewer than 10 percent of Jewish and Italian women entered that line of work.[84]

Industrial labor was highly gendered. Men generally took the skilled manufacturing jobs, while women were relegated to the less-skilled jobs of tending machines. Women also tended to work in specific industries, such as the burgeoning textile mills and canning operations. Certain nationalities tended to dominate different industries. New

England's textile mills were largely staffed by French-Canadian and Polish workers, while Jewish and Italian women flocked to New York's garment industry.

Workdays were long, pay was poor, and working conditions often deplorable. However, few people were interested in improving working conditions until the highly publicized Triangle Shirtwaist Fire of 1911. The Triangle Shirtwaist Company in lower Manhattan employed mostly single Jewish and Italian young women between the ages of sixteen and twenty-three. When fire broke out on the eighth floor, the workers were trapped by fire doors that had been locked to prevent the women from stealing or taking unscheduled breaks. Victims who were not burned at their sewing machines died when they fell from deteriorated fire escapes or plunged from windows. In all, 146 women and 3 men died in the tragedy. The flames were so intense that most of the women died within fifteen minutes.

Workplace disasters like the Triangle Fire prompted many female immigrants to become active in the expanding labor movements of the period. Women's exposure to Marxist and other social reform ideas in Europe helped them organize. In an alliance with social reformers including Jane Addams and Lillian Wald (1867–1940), immigrant workers formed their own unions, such as the Women's Trade Union League, and labor organizing among immigrant workers was fundamental in creating powerful union organizations like the International Ladies' Garment Workers Union. These women's unions organized a wave of strikes between 1909 and 1920 that often crippled the clothing industry and led to massive workplace reforms.

Immigrant textile workers undertook one of the most successful strikes in 1912. Like many New England towns, the textile mills of Lawrence, Massachusetts, drew thousands of immigrant workers, mostly single women. The workforce was incredibly diverse. Women from forty different countries who spoke nearly two dozen different languages made up half of the city's workforce. Their squalid living and working conditions led to one of the highest death rates in the country. On January 1, 1912, Massachusetts law reduced the maximum workweek from fifty-six to fifty-four hours. At the same time, mill owners decided to reduce wages to less than six dollars weekly. Finally, on January 11, 1912, a group of Polish women who had been cheated on their paychecks walked out. The next day, Italian workers struck and encouraged workers at other mills to leave their machines. Workers broke machines to ensure that replacement workers could not be used. By the end of the strike, twenty-three thousand female and male workers had walked off the job. When the American Federation of Labor refused to support the strikers, the more radical International Workers of the World (also known as the Wobblies) stepped in to provide organizational support. With the help of this organization, led by Elizabeth Gurley Flynn (1890–1964), the strikers were successful, gaining substantial pay increases and reforms of overtime and bonus pay.

As immigrant women struggled to provide for themselves and their families, they tried to maintain as many traditions from their home country as possible. They adapted traditional recipes using American products. They lived in neighborhoods with other immigrant families from their homelands and joined ethnically based churches that provided religious schooling and services in their native languages. Most important, they formed new associations that reinforced ethnic and religious connections. For instance, Jewish women joined Hadassah, and the National Council of Jewish Women and Polish women in Chicago formed the Polish Women's Alliance of America in 1898.

Immigrant women often faced severe discrimination. Racist rhetoric categorized Jews, Italians, Irish, and others as biologically different from "native" Yankees. Immigrant women's high fertility rates further fueled anti-immigrant sentiment. Although they bore fewer children than their counterparts in Europe, their fertility rate was twice that of the "native" white population of the United States. Anti-immigrant groups asserted that "race suicide" was imminent if quotas were not imposed.

The United States was not the only destination for European immigrants. Another 10 percent settled in Canada, still a British colony, and more than 20 percent of European immigrants went to South America. During the nineteenth and early twentieth centuries, burgeoning economies drew 11.5 million Europeans, mostly Spaniards, Russians, and Italians to Argentina, Brazil, and Uruguay. Although by far the majority of these migrants were single males, during the peak of Spanish migration to Buenos Aires, 36 percent of emigrants were female.[85] For Spanish immigrants, language was not an issue, but they still faced a number of challenges such as poverty and lack of medical care. Elite women in Spain and Latin America were enthusiastic members of beneficent societies in which wealthy women aided women of the lower classes. This charitable ethic led to the formation of organizations like the Patronato Español in 1912 to help young immigrant girls and orphans.

The focus of much eastern European and Russian Jewish immigration was Palestine. Jewish immigration to Palestine was slow until the late nineteenth century, but the revival of Zionist (a movement to establish Israel as a Jewish state) fervor led to a rapid expansion of Jerusalem's Jewish community beginning in the 1840s. Two more waves of immigration followed between 1870 and 1914. Between 1904 and 1914, thirty-five thousand Jews immigrated to Palestine, mainly from Russia and the Austro-Hungarian Empire. Prior to 1904, there was no coordinated effort at immigration. Women like Syla Bergman who came to Israel in 1835 with her husband and children did so on their own accord.[86] However, major Jewish organizations, including the Jewish Colonization Association, created a Central Information Office in Berlin and four hundred Russian cities to help Jews emigrate to Palestine, Canada, and Argentina. As with other groups of immigrants, the decision to leave was often bittersweet, saddened by the separation from friends and family. The journey was perilous. Crooks and dangerous seas often left new arrivals with nothing but the shirts on their backs. For middle- and upper-class Jews, the migration experience often meant a serious decline in economic status. Many new immigrants were forced to accept charity.

Once women arrived in Palestine, they faced surprising impediments, especially if they wanted to farm. Most of the Jewish community lived in farming collectives; however, Zionism promoted very traditional gender expectations. Women were expected to work in the home, in schools, or in offices and were relegated to kitchen and domestic duties. Men did all the manual labor and farmwork. This gendered division of labor fit well with the expectations of early Zionist immigrants;

**IMMIGRANT WOMEN IN BUENOS AIRES (1912).** At the end of the nineteenth and early twentieth centuries, millions of European women immigrated to South America. At the Hotel de Inmigrantes in Buenos Aires, newly arrived immigrants learned how to do domestic chores as a part of their acculturation to Argentine society. *(Archivo General de la Nación, Argentina.)*

however, by the beginning of the twentieth century, more young (sixteen- to seventeen-year-old) single women were emigrating from eastern Europe. These young women were eager to work in the fields alongside men. Finally in 1911, a group of women led by Hanna Meisel (1883–1972) formed a female worker's farm, which functioned until 1917. At the farm, women learned agricultural techniques and self-sufficiency.[87] Such projects were critical in reevaluating the place of women in pre-state Israel.

One of the most problematic results of the arrival of large numbers of new immigrants to Palestine was an increase in prostitution. Brothels flourished in the port town of Jaffa and opened in Jerusalem's most Orthodox neighborhoods. Similar problems with Jewish prostitution arose in other destinations such as South Africa, Argentina, and New York. Jewish procurers and prostitutes even found clientele in the Brazilian Amazon. In fact, a white slave trade developed in which unscrupulous men traveled to Jewish villages in Russia and eastern Europe, courted girls, and proposed marriage and settlement in Palestine. They then sold the girls to pimps. Other pimps would attempt to entrap female immigrants on their way to Palestine by hanging around transit cities like Odessa.[88] Many Jewish women were reduced to prostitution to support themselves. Finally, Bertha Pappenheim (1859–1936), a German-Jewish women's advocate and social worker, founded the Society for the Protection of Women to try to end the white slave trade. Of course, fears of white slavery fed European anxiety about female migration. These prostitutes were vivid reminders that women traveling alone could be easily duped and bring shame to their families.[89]

Imperialism opened the world to women. Wealthier women took the opportunity to travel for study, rest, or curiosity. Lower-class women participated in the enormous waves of migration from Europe. Their adventurousness and perseverance changed Europeans' understandings of themselves and of others. Female travelers returned to Europe with exotic images and tales of far away places, while immigrant women struggled to recreate Europe in distant places through their reconstruction of family life, their food preparation, and their perpetuation of traditional European ways.

## CONCLUSION

From the outset, the formation of European empires during the nineteenth and early twentieth centuries was a highly gendered proposition. Imperial institutions were based on a race and gender hierarchy that placed European males in control of native men and women as well as European women. Some women accommodated that control; other women fought it. Whatever the case, as European women moved to the far corners of the world, they transformed those places as much as they were transformed by them. By 1917, the West was much more connected to the rest of the world than it had ever been, and women were central to those connections.

## NOTES

1. Edward W. Said, *Culture and Imperialism* (New York: Vintage Books, 1994), 8.

2. Anne McClintock, *Imperial Leather: Race, Gender and Sexuality in the Colonial Contest* (New York: Routledge, 1995), 1–4.

3. Jeanne Bowlan, "Civilizing Gender Relations in Algeria: The Paradoxical Case of Marie Bugéja, 1919–1939," in *Domesticating the Empire: Race, Gender, and Family Life in French and Dutch Colonialism*, ed. Julia Clancy-Smith and Frances Gouda (Charlottesville: University Press of Virginia, 1998), 196.

4. Frank Proschan, "Eunuch Mandarins, Soldats Mamzelles, Effeminate Boys, and Graceless Women: French Colonial Constructions of Vietnamese Genders," *GLQ: A Journal of Lesbian and Gay Studies* 8:4 (2002): 439.

5. Cited in Jane Hunter, *The Gospel of Gentility: American Women Missionaries in Turn-of-the-Century China* (New Haven, CT: Yale University Press, 1984), 210.

6. Hunter, 205–206.

7. Mrinalini Sinha, "Chathams, Pitts, and Gladstones in Petticoats: The Politics of Gender and Race in the Ilbert Bill Controversy, 1883–1884," in *Western Women and Imperialism: Complicity and Resistance*, ed. Nupur Chauduri and Margaret Strobel (Bloomington: Indiana University Press, 1992), 99–100.

8. Mrinalini Sinha, *Colonial Masculinity: The 'Manly Englishman' and the 'Effeminate Bengali' in the Late Nineteenth Century* (Manchester: Manchester University Press, 1995), 156–158.

9. Kristin Hoganson, *Fighting for American Manhood: How Gender Politics Provoked the Spanish-American and Philippine-American Wars* (New Haven, CT: Yale University Press, 1998), 202.

10. Ann Laura Stoler, *Carnal Knowledge and Imperial Power: Race and the Intimate in Colonial Rule* (Berkeley: University of California Press, 2002), 48.

11. Stoler, 49.

12. Stoler, 47–48.

13. Ahmad A Sikainga, "Shari'a Courts and the Manumission of Female Slaves in the Sudan, 1898–1939," *The International Journal of African Historical Studies* 28:1 (1995): 5.

14. Stoler, 49.

15. Jeremy Rich, "'Une Babylone Noire': Interracial Unions in Colonial Libreville, c. 1860–1914," *French Colonial History* 4 (2003): 155, 150

16. Rich, 146.

17. Veena Talwar Oldenburg, "Lifestyles as Resistance: The Case of the Courtesans of Lucknow, India," *Feminist Studies* 16:2 (Summer 1990): 260.

18. Cited in Laura Briggs, "Familiar Territory: Prostitution, Empires, and the Question of U.S. Imperialism in Puerto Rico, 1849–1916," in *Families of a New World: Gender, Politics, and State Development in a Global Context*, ed. Lynne Haney and Lisa Pollard (New York: Routledge, 2003), 51.

19. Lora Wildenthal, "Race, Gender, and Citizenship in the German Colonial Empire," in *Tensions of Empire: Colonial Cultures in a Bourgeois World*, ed. Frederick Cooper and Ann Laura Stoler (Berkeley: University of California Press, 1997), 270–271.

20. Stoler, 39.

21. Stoler, 99.

22. Stoler, 89.

23. Wildenthal, "Race, Gender, and Citizenship," 271–272.

24. Quoted in Lynette A. Jackson, "'When in the White Man's Town': Zimbabwean Women Remember Chibeura," in *Women in African Colonial Histories*, ed. Jean Allman, Susan Geiger, and Nakanyike Musisi (Bloomington: Indiana University Press, 2002), 195.

25. Norman Etherington, "Natal's Black Rape Scare," *Journal of Southern African Studies* 15:1 (October 1988): 38.

26. Margaret Strobel, *European Women and the Second British Empire* (Bloomington: Indiana University Press, 1991), 5.

27. Stoler, 59.

28. Lora Wildenthal, *German Women for Empire, 1884–1945* (Durham, NC: Duke University Press, 2001), 73.

29. Marilyn Lake, "Frontier Feminism and the Marauding White Man: Australia, 1890s to 1940s," in *Nation, Empire, Colony: Historicizing Gender and Race,* ed. Ruth Roach Pierson and Nupur Chaudhuri (Bloomington: Indiana University Press, 1998), 95.

30. Quoted in David Savage, "Missionaries and the Development of a Colonial Ideology of Female Education in India," *Gender and History* 9:2 (August 1997): 212.

31. Line Nyhagen Predelli, "Sexual Control and the Remaking of Gender: The Attempt of Nineteenth-Century Protestant Women to Export Western Domesticity to Madagascar," *Journal of Women's History* 12:2 (Summer 2000): 89–90.

32. Rita Smith Kipp, "Emancipating Each Other: Dutch Colonial Missionaries' Encounter with Karo Women in Sumatra, 1900–1943," in *Domesticating the Empire,* 219–220.

33. Kathleen Sheldon, "I Studied with the Nuns, Learning to Make Blouses: Gender Ideology and Colonial Education in Mozambique," *International Journal of African Historical Studies* 31:3 (1998): 603.

34. Nakanyike B. Musisi, "Colonial and Missionary Education: Women and Domesticity in Uganda, 1900–1945," in *African Encounters with Domesticity,* ed. Karen Tranberg Hansen (New Brunswick, NJ: Rutgers University Press, 1992), 175.

35. Carol C. Chin, "Beneficent Imperialist: American Women Missionaries in China at the Turn of the Century," *Diplomatic History* 27:3 (June 2003): 337.

36. Billie Melman, *Women's Orients: English Women and the Middle East, 1718–1918* (Ann Arbor: University of Michigan Press, 1992), 46.

37. Leslie A. Flemming, "A New Humanity: American Missionaries' Ideals for Women in North India, 1870–1930," in *Western Women and Imperialism,* 191–192.

38. Rosemary R. Gagan, *A Sensitive Independence: Canadian Methodist Women Missionaries in Canada and the Orient, 1881–1925* (Montreal: McGill-Queen's University Press, 1992), 71.

39. Patricia Grimshaw, *Paths of Duty: American Missionary Wives in Nineteenth-Century Hawaii* (Honolulu: University of Hawaii Press, 1989), 9.

40. Grimshaw, 115.

41. Sylvia M. Jacobs, "Give a Thought to Africa: Black Women Missionaries in Southern Africa," in *Western Women and Imperialism,* esp. 210, 222.

42. Bengt Sudkler and Christopher Sneed, *History of the Church in Africa* (Cambridge: Cambridge University Press, 2000), 193.

43. Kumari Jayawardena, *The White Woman's Other Burden: Western Women and South Asia During British Colonial Rule* (New York: Routledge, 1995), 4.

44. Helen Callaway, *Gender, Culture, and Empire: European Women in Colonial Nigeria* (Urbana: University of Illinois Press, 1987), 65.

45. Stoler, 71–72.

46. Quoted in Callaway, 72.

47. Callaway, 168–169.

48. Stoler, 73.

49. Elsbeth Locher-Scholten, "So Close and Yet So Far: The Ambivalence of Dutch Colonial Rhetoric on Javanese Servants in Indonesia, 1900–1942," in *Domesticating the Empire,* 138–140; and Stoler, 35, 74–75.

50. Nancy L. Paxton, "Complicity and Resistance in the Writings of Flora Annie Steel and Annie Besant," in *Western Women and Imperialism,* 162.

51. Nupur Chauduri, "Shawls, Jewelry, Curry, and Rice in Victorian Britain," in *Western Women and Imperialism,* 238–240.

52. Michelle Perrot, "Stepping Out," in *A History of Women: Emerging Feminism from Revolution to World War,* ed. Georges Duby and Michelle Perrot (Cambridge: Harvard University Press, 1993), 467.

53. Strobel, 25.

54. Jean Jacques Van-Helten and Keith Williams, " 'The Crying Need of South Africa': The Emigration of Single British Women to the Transvaal, 1901–1910," *Journal of Southern African Studies* 10:1 (October 1983): esp. 21, 32.

55. Dea Birkett, "The 'White Woman's Burden' in the 'White Man's Grave': The Introduction of British Nurses in Colonial West Africa," in *Western Women and Imperialism,* 177–188.

56. Jayawardena, 82–85.

57. Nancy Rose Hunt, "Le Bebe in Brousse: European Women, African Birth Spacing, and Colonial Intervention in Breast Feeding in the Belgian Congo," *International Journal of African Historical Studies* 21:3 (1988): 402–403.

58. Kuni Jenkins and Kay Morris Matthews, "Knowing Their Place: The Political Socialisation of Maori Women in New Zealand Through Schooling Policy and Practice, 1867–1969," *Women's History Review* 7:1 (1998): 90, 97.

59. Penny Edwards, "Womanizing Indochina: Fiction, Nation, and Cohabitation in Colonial Cambodia, 1890–1930," in *Domesticating the Empire*, 113–114.

60. Jayawardena, 4.

61. Strobel, 4.

62. Mervat Hatem, "Through Each Other's Eyes: The Impact on the Colonial Encounter of the Images of Egyptian, Levantine-Egyptian, and European Women," in *Western Women and Imperialism*, 48–55.

63. Julia Clancy-Smith, "The 'Passionate Nomad' Reconsidered: A European Woman in L'Algerie Francaise (Isabelle Eberhardt, 1877–1904)," in *Western Women and Imperialism*, 61–78.

64. Helen Callaway and Dorothy O. Helly, "Crusader for Empire: Flora Shaw/Lady Lugard," in *Western Women and Imperialism*, 79–97.

65. Eliza Riedi, "Women, Gender, and the Promotion of Empire: The Victoria League, 1901–1914," *The Historical Journal* 45:3 (2002): esp. 572, 578, 588, 584.

66. Lora Wildenthal, "'When Men Are Weak': The Imperial Feminism of Frieda von Bülow," *Gender and History* 10:1 (April 1998): 63.

67. Quoted in Antoinette Burton, *Burdens of History: British Feminists, Indian Women, and Imperial Culture, 1865–1915* (Chapel Hill: University of North Carolina Press, 1994), 3.

68. Jayawardena, 128–132.

69. Kristin Hoganson, "'As Badly Off as the Filipinos': U.S. Women's Suffragists and the Imperial Issue at the Turn of the Century," *Journal of Women's History* 13:2 (Summer 2001): 12.

70. Women's Auxiliary of the Anti-Imperialist League, "Women Make an Appeal/In Behalf of the Foundation Principles of the Republic," *Springfield Republican* (May 30, 1899). http://www.boondocksnet.com/ai/ailtexts/wail0599.html. In Jim Zwick, ed., *Anti-Imperialism in the United States, 1898–1935*. http://www.boondocksnet.com/ai/ (Aug. 14, 2005).

71. Burton, esp. 176, 186.

72. Julia Clancy-Smith, "Islam, Gender, and Identities in the Making of French Algeria, 1830–1962," in *Domesticating the Empire*, 169–172; and Joan W. Scott, *Only Paradoxes to Offer: French Feminists and the Rights of Man* (Cambridge: Harvard University Press, 1996), 116.

73. Meri Mangakahia, "So That Women May Receive the Vote," address to Parliament, 1893; http://www.nzhistory.net.nz/Gallery/Suffragists/meri-mang.html.

74. Patricia Grimshaw, "Settler Anxieties, Indigenous Peoples, and Women's Suffrage in the Colonies of Australia, New Zealand, and Hawai'i, 1888–1902," *Pacific Historical Review* 69:4 (November 2000): 560, 565.

75. Grimshaw, "Settler Anxieties," 570.

76. Mary Louise Pratt, *Imperial Eyes: Travel Writing and Transculturation* (London: Routledge, 1992), esp. chap. 9.

77. Cited in June E. Hahner, ed., *Women Through Women's Eyes: Latin American Women in Nineteenth-Century Travel Accounts* (Wilmington, DE: Scholarly Resources, 1998), 71.

78. Seija Jalagin, "Gendered Images: Western Women on Japanese Women," in *Looking at the Other: Historical Study of Images in Theory and Practice*, ed. Kari Alenius and Seija Jalagin (Oulu, Finland: University of Oulu, 2002), 19.

79. Excerpt from Golda Meir, *My Life*, in *Immigrant Women*, ed. Maxine Schwartz Seller (Albany, NY: SUNY Press, 1994), 40–41.

80. Doris Weatherford, *Foreign and Female: Immigrant Women in America, 1840–1930* (New York: Facts on File, 1995), 211.

81. Donna Gabaccia, *From the Other Side: Women, Gender, and Immigrant Life in the U.S., 1820–1990* (Bloomington: Indiana University Press, 1994), 30.

82. Gabaccia, 30.

83. Paula E. Hyman, "Immigrant Women and Consumer Protest: The New York City Kosher Meat Boycott of 1902," *American Jewish History* 70:1 (September 1980): 91–92.

84. Gabaccia, 46–47.

85. José C. Moya, *Cousins and Strangers: Spanish Immigrants in Buenos Aires, 1850–1930* (Berkeley: University of California Press, 1998), 502, n. 94.

86. Margalit Shilo, "Self-Sacrifice, National-Historical Identity and Self-Denial: The Experience of Jewish Immigrant Women in Jerusalem, 1840–1914," *Women's History Review* 11:2 (2002): 201.

87. Margalit Shilo, "The Women's Farm at Kinneret, 1911–1917: A Solution to the Problem of the Working Woman in the Second Aliyah," in *Pioneers and Homemakers: Jewish Women in Pre-State Israel*, ed. Deborah S. Bernstein (Albany, NY: SUNY Press, 1992), esp. 127–130.

88. Gur Alroey, "Journey to Early-Twentieth-Century Palestine as a Jewish Immigrant Experience," *Jewish Social Studies* 9:2 (Winter 2003): 57.

89. Donna Guy, *Sex and Danger in Buenos Aires: Prostitution, Family and Nation in Argentina* (Lincoln, NE: University of Nebraska Press, 1991), 7.

## SUGGESTED READINGS

Allman, Jean, Susan Geiger, and Nakanyike Musisi, eds. *Women in African Colonial Histories*. Bloomington: Indiana University Press, 2002. This collection of articles examines how colonial rule affected the daily lives of African women.

Bernstein, Deborah, ed. *Pioneers and Homemakers: Jewish Women in Pre-State Israel*. Albany, NY: SUNY Press, 1992.

Burton, Antoinette. *Burdens of History: British Feminists, Indian Women, and Imperial Culture, 1865–1915*. Chapel Hill: University of North Carolina Press, 1994. This important work reconsiders the relationship between European women activists and the British Empire.

Chaudhuri, Nupur and Margaret Strobel, eds. *Western Women and Imperialism: Complicity and Resistance*. Bloomington: Indiana University Press, 1992.

Clancy-Smith, Julia and Frances Gouda, eds. *Domesticating the Empire: Race, Gender, and Family Life in French and Dutch Colonialism*. Charlottesville: University Press of Virginia, 1999. These fascinating essays reveal the complex interactions of race and gender in French and Dutch colonial society.

Hoganson, Kristin. *Fighting for American Manhood: How Gender Politics Provoked the Spanish-American and Philippine-American Wars*. New Haven, CT: Yale University Press, 1998.

McClintock, Anne. *Imperial Leather: Race, Gender and Sexuality in the Colonial Contest*. New York: Routledge, 1995. A difficult, but important work on colonialism and how European ideas about race and gender shaped the colonial project.

Stoler, Ann Laura. *Carnal Knowledge and Imperial Power: Race and the Intimate in Colonial Rule*. Berkeley: University of California Press, 2002. An accessible study of the ideas about race that emerged during the nineteenth and early twentieth centuries.

Strobel, Margaret. *European Women and the Second British Empire*. Bloomington: Indiana University Press, 1991. A good general overview of the issues.

Wildenthal, Lora. *German Women for Empire, 1884–1945*. Durham, NC: Duke University Press, 2001. A detailed study of German women's role in their government's colonial enterprise.

## Chapter 12

# The New Woman from War to Revolution, 1880–1919

I-ый Петроградскій женскій батальонъ.
2-я рота.

54

*Petrograd Women's Battalion (1917). After the tsar abdicated in 1917, Maria Bochareva formed an all-women's battalion to fight in World War I. Some reports claimed she had two thousand women under her command, who were to serve as examples to male soldiers. (Special Collections, Brotherton Library, University of Leeds.)*

■ **Women in the Belle Époque**   412
  *The New Woman*   412
  *The New Woman and the Art of the Belle Époque*   415
  *The Dangers of the New Woman*   417

■ **Women and Political Activism**   418
  *Women and Radical Politics*   418
  *Women and the Russian Revolution of 1905*   419
  *The Push for the Vote*   421
  *Racism and Nationalism Before the War*   424

■ **Women and the Great War**   425
  *Women in the Military and at the Front*   426
  *Women at Home: Inventing the Home Front*   432
  *Antiwar Activism*   435
  *The World Turned Upside Down: Gender and World War I*   437

■ **New States, New Citizens**   440
  *The Great Influenza Epidemic*   440
  *The End of the War*   441
  *Postwar Politics*   442
  *Gender and the Russian Revolution*   444

The icon of the new woman grew out of the enormous social and economic changes of the late nineteenth century. She questioned traditional ideals of womanhood and explored new lifestyles. She undertook a greater variety of occupations and sometimes agitated for better working conditions or pressed for women's suffrage. Whatever the new woman did, she challenged and threatened the traditional social order, and defenders of domesticity and motherhood railed against the new woman, blaming her for a wide array of social ills. However, during the chaos of World War I, nations called upon their female populations to work on behalf of their countries and their families. Women took on new roles and faced new hardships as a result. In Russia, revolutionary women also fought for a new society defined by gender and class equality. In the long run, the devastation of those conflicts would take their toll on Europeans, causing a backlash against the new woman once peace returned to the Continent.

## WOMEN IN THE BELLE ÉPOQUE

Europeans would look back at the period between 1880 and 1914 with mixed emotions. Some saw it as the *belle époque*, or the good old days, remembering it as a happier, more carefree time before war ravaged the Continent. Others saw it as the fin-de-siècle, the end of the century, a period of decadence whose economic, political, and social changes heralded further decay. The new woman epitomized both these views, embodying the freedoms and concerns of the turn of the century. She was single, sexually active, and financially independent. She worked hard and spent her income on entertainment that catered to her lifestyle. However, critics derided the new woman as selfish and a threat to femininity, family, and domesticity.

### The New Woman

Everyone recognized the new woman. Usually urban and middle class, she was educated, had a career, and was socially and financially independent. Above all, the new woman refused to define herself solely as a wife and mother. Financial independence

# Chapter 12 ❖ Chronology

| | |
|---|---|
| **1878** | Mary Cassatt exhibits with the impressionists in Paris |
| **1879** | Henrik Ibsen's play *The Doll House* opens in London |
| **1894** | Journalist Sarah Grand defines the new woman |
| | Sydney Gundy's play *The New Woman* opens in London |
| **1897** | Marguerite Durand founds *La Fronde* |
| **1902** | Foundation of the German Union for Women's Suffrage |
| **1903** | Formation of the Women's Social and Political Union in Britain |
| **1905** | Russian Revolution |
| **1907** | International Socialist Congress votes to support women's suffrage |
| | Women's Mud March in London |
| **1908** | German rescinds law prohibiting women's political activism |
| **1914–1918** | World War I |
| **1915** | Execution of British nurse Edith Cavell as a spy |
| | Aletta Jacobs convenes pacifist congress at The Hague |
| | Iceland and Denmark enfranchise women |
| **1916** | Emma Goldman sent to prison for distributing birth control literature |
| | Execution of Gabrielle Petit, member of *La Dame Blanche* |
| | Formation of the WAACs |
| **1917** | Night of Terror for Suffragists in United States |
| | Russian Revolution |
| | Mata Hari executed as a spy |
| | USSR enfranchises women |
| **1918** | Spanish Flu epidemic |
| | Canada enfranchises women |
| | Britain enfranchises some women |
| **1919** | Rosa Luxemburg killed in police custody |
| | United States deports Emma Goldman to USSR |
| | Germany enfranchises women |

was key to the new woman's freedom. Although few women could fully adopt the new woman's lifestyle, many women were empowered by better educations and eagerly entered fields like clerical work, nursing, and teaching. Clerical work became associated with women because many saw the type-writer as analogous to the piano, and thus natural for women to use.[1] Specialists in shorthand had a higher status among women office workers because their skills required extra training and education. Although they worked alone and on demand, they had more freedom and distinguished themselves from other female office workers by wearing a suit and carrying a briefcase.[2] In France by 1906, 40 percent of clerical workers were female.[3] Women also benefited from the expansion of postal, telephone, and telegraphic services. The French postal service began to hire large numbers of women to sell stamps, sort mail, and work as telephone operators. The same was true in England.

Teaching became a respectable occupation and an important avenue for working-class women to improve their social status. In France, primary and secondary schoolteachers made up the single largest group of professionally trained women. These women were the beneficiaries of nineteenth-century education policies. French statesman Jules Ferry (1832–1893) established a national system of women's normal schools in 1879, and by 1900 female graduates outnumbered male graduates. By the 1910s, teacher's professional associations were strong enough to campaign for first a general pay increase and, in 1919, equal pay with men.[4]

More and more often, single women lived alone or shared living spaces with other single women. In 1900, 28 percent of Boston's adult working women lived as boarders or lodgers (excluding servants).[5] An 1894 *Punch* cartoon lampooned the new woman by showing her reading "advanced" books and holding her latchkey aloft. The latchkey was a symbol of her independence, the fact that she did not live with her family, but in an apartment.[6]

Many critics expressed concern about the new woman's clothing. In Paris, female bicyclists tended to wear bloomers, while in New York, they opted for shorter skirts.[7] These outfits, although practical, were often considered "mannish." In response, clothing retailers tried to disassociate their bicycling outfits from association with the new woman. One advertisement for an outfit called "the Luey" assured its readers that "Nothing about 'The Luey' costume suggests masculine attire. . . . No lady cyclist can look other than bewitching in a 'Luey' costume."[8] Critics also accused the new woman of abandoning femininity by wearing "rational" clothing. Rational clothing required less material, was looser and more comfortable, and did not emphasize a woman's figure in the same way that tightly corseted dresses did.

Both the theater and the newly emerging film industry benefited from the image of the new woman. After American inventor Thomas Edison (1847–1931) projected the first silent film in 1896, the new technology quickly caught on and small theaters sprang up across the United States and Europe. Traditional images of women as helpless victims or sexual predators vied with the real lives of the screen actresses who played these roles. One of the first film stars in the United States was Mary Pickford (1883–1979). She played innocent young girls in movies such as *An Arcadian Maid*, *In the Sultan's Garden*, *Little Red Riding Hood*, and *The Little Princess*, all produced around 1910. However, in life, Pickford quickly became a powerful star. In 1909, Biograph Studios paid her $40 per week. By 1911, she earned $275, a huge sum for the time.[9] Pickford went on to help found United Artists Studio. Men found her vivaciousness and virginal onscreen characters appealing and nonthreatening, while the masses of working women identified with her working-class background and her success.

Audiences also loved the vamp, especially as performed on screen by Theda Bara (1885–1955). Between 1915 and 1918, she made forty films for the new Fox Studios.[10] Although she campaigned for roles that matched her intellectual interests, Bara typically played depraved and lustful women, an image she developed for her breakthrough film, *A Fool There Was* (1915), in which she played a vampire. The studio enhanced her popularity by fabricating an exotic background for her and always photographing her with exotic makeup and waist-length hair. Both Pickford and Bara's careers highlight some of the contradictions behind the image of the new woman. Although they were successful career women, their popularity relied on portrayals of stereotypical women.

**THEDA BARA.** When Theda Bara created the image of the vamp, she became a huge star. However, she found it impossible to move away from these roles, to more intellectually satisfying ones. *(The Kobal Collection.)*

For some, the new woman was indistinguishable from the feminist. However, the new woman's desire to rebel against family and domesticity helped distinguish her from the feminists who justified their demands for women's suffrage and marital and economic reforms with their roles as mothers and wives. Moreover, some feminists did not work for wages.

The women who worked for the French newspaper *La Fronde* underscored the complicated relationship between feminism and the new woman. Founded in 1897 by Marguerite Durand (1864–1936), a former actress and divorced single mother, *La Fronde* broke new ground by refusing to be either a feminist newspaper or a traditional women's periodical focusing only on fashion and domestic arts. *La Fronde* covered news, politics, sports, and business. Women typeset the paper,

and only women reporters supplied articles. The only man employed by *La Fronde* was the janitor. The staff included Jeanne Chauvin (1862–1926), one of the first women admitted to the Paris Bar, Clémence Royer (1830–1902), the first woman to teach at the Sorbonne, and Blanche Galien, France's first female pharmacist. The *frondeuses*, as the journalists called themselves, were often the only women present at breaking news. By covering trials and business, the frondeuses interposed women into politics, law, and business, areas usually off-limits to them, and offered a new image of women as knowledgeable and involved in masculine concerns.[11]

Although Durand considered herself a feminist and published feminist editorials in her newspaper, she refused to subscribe to a single image of women, preferring to show them as diverse. She also aspired to create a feminist aesthetic that appealed to men, something feminists rejected. Durand was beautiful and relished her abilities to attract and seduce men. She once famously claimed that "Feminism owes a great deal to my blond hair; I know it thinks the contrary, but it is wrong."[12] Her comment underscores her conflicted relationship with feminism. By 1900, *La Fronde* had lost its edge and became more predictably feminist in its editorials and news stories. Financial problems turned it into a monthly periodical in 1903, and Durand stopped publishing it in 1905.

## The New Woman and the Art of the Belle Époque

Artists and artistic movements celebrated the new freedoms of the belle époque and discussed the new woman's sexual and social independence. The impressionist painters celebrated Paris's new wide boulevards, sidewalk cafés, parks, and restaurants in which men and women of different social classes interacted. Their pointillist style emphasized changing light and the transitory nature of modern life. Many female painters, including Mary Cassatt (1844–1926) and Berthe Morisot (1841–1895), turned to impressionism because the movement celebrated scenes from middle-class daily life instead of the traditional historical subjects that glorified government and the state. Both Cassatt and Morisot came from upper-middle-class families who supported their artistic ambitions. Cassatt, born in Philadelphia, moved to Paris in the 1860s and by 1878 began exhibiting her works with the impressionists. However, unlike their male counterparts, these well-to-do women were uncomfortable socializing in the working-class cafés and dance halls that were the subject of so many impressionist works. Instead, they painted domestic scenes and explored the continuing constraints on women's movement in this more open society.

The Arts and Crafts Movement also challenged assumptions about the role of women in the industrialized world. Adherents of the movement, which was popular in both Britain and the United States, advocated a return to handcrafts and individual skill. Decrying the depersonalization of industrialization, Arts and Crafts leaders such as William Morris (1834–1896) romanticized medieval workshops where workers were not alienated from production as they were in modern factories. Morris and his followers wanted to unite designers, artisans, and artists around ideals of good design and the dignity of labor. His movement elevated to art many crafts traditionally practiced by women, such as embroidery, tile and china painting, and wallpaper design. In the United States, the Arts and Crafts Movement also provided a socially acceptable outlet for many creative and progressive women, whose class did not allow them to embrace all facets of the new woman's lifestyle. Inspired by British Arts and Crafts embroidery, New York socialite Candace Wheeler (1827–1923) believed she could transform women's needlework into something profitable and artistic.[13] Between 1877 and 1883, in association with Lewis Comfort Tiffany (1848–1933), Wheeler organized the Society of Decorative Arts of New York City. By 1883, she managed a successful textile company composed entirely of women workers and designers.

The Arts and Crafts Movement also elevated pottery into an art form. Potters such as Mary Louis McLaughlin (1847–1939) and Maria Longworth Nicholas (later Storer) (1849–1932) experimented with new shapes, glazes, and production methods. McLaughlin, who worked out of Cincinnati Dallas Pottery, created underglazes that became the prototype for American art pottery. Storer, with the help of her wealthy father, founded Rookwood Pottery, also in Cincinnati, in 1880. A year later, intending to provide training for needy women, she opened the Rookwood School of Pottery Decoration. Despite the ideals of the Arts and Crafts Movement, many still accused women artists of amateurism. When Nicholas turned the operations of her workshop and school over to a family friend, he closed the school and replaced the "amateur" women potters with "professional" male potters.

Modernist and abstract artists also challenged traditional definitions of art. One of the greatest influences on the abstract artist Wassily Kandinsky (1866–1944) was Margaretha von Brauchitsch. Her work in embroidery and the Reform Dress Movement linked industrialization, political reform, and feminism by challenging and changing the shape of women's clothing. Under von Brauchitsch's influence, Kandinsky experimented with fashion design, making fashion a place where modern artists could free themselves from the traditions of representation. Kandinsky's partner, painter Gabriele Münter (1877–1962), explored abstract painting, emphasizing color and simplified shapes. Münter's interest in form and color led her to collect examples of folk art and folk motifs, which she then incorporated into her work.

The relationship between modernist artists and their subjects often provoked controversy. In 1910, Russian authorities seized Natalia Goncharova's (1881–1962) modernist paintings of nudes and put her on trial for pornography. Although these large paintings represented only a fraction of her work, they attracted considerable attention, because the idea of a woman painting nude women raised concerns about lesbianism.[14] When female artists used their art to celebrate their love for other women, they met with disapproval from European society.

Novelists also took on issues of female sexuality and morality. Striving for realism and naturalism, novelists like Sigrid Undset (1882–1949) rejected the romanticism and idealism of Victorian literature. A Norwegian novelist, she described the dilemmas facing women who were either unfaithful to their inner selves or who defied traditional gender expectations. Her third novel, *Jenny* (1911), tells the story of Jenny Winge, an aspiring painter who betrays her own ideals and whose affair with a married man ends in tragedy. Despite charges of immorality, Undset won the Nobel Prize for Literature in 1928.

Dance underwent changes that reflected the new woman's physicality and sensuality. At the end of the nineteenth century, ballet was the dominant form of dance, with its highly formalized moves, ethereal quality, and elaborate costumes. Ballet took years of training and dancers lived under the strict discipline of male-run ballet theaters. However, inspired by ancient Greek dance, American Isadora Duncan (1878–1927) explored movement and sexuality through new dance styles and techniques. She brought free movement, unbound hair, and flowing robes to dance. She danced barefooted, ran, jumped, and even skipped in her performances. As her fame grew, her performances commanded large audiences. In 1903, she called for the abolition of ballet because it deformed women's bodies. The following year, she opened a school for poor children in Grunewald, Germany, that incorporated her vision of intellectual and physical education.

## The Dangers of the New Woman

The new woman earned a great deal of negative publicity. Her rebellion against middle-class values, her independence, and her engagement in consumer culture threatened defenders of hearth and home. To counter her popularity, negative stereotypes of the new woman emerged as quickly as glamorous ones. In 1894, Sydney Grundy's comic play *The New Woman* satirized the independent woman. In this play, the main character, Mrs. Sylvester, is not single, but neglected her husband and housekeeping to collaborate with a married man on a book about radical sexual philosophy. Grundy presents the new woman as both a source of ridicule and a danger to masculinity.

Even Russian peasants in remote villages learned of the threat that independent women posed. Films like the 1915 silent film *Deti veka* (*Children of the Age*) portrayed the dangers of social mobility and women's self-determination. This movie revolved around Maria, a young married mother, who was inspired by a friend to visit nightclubs. Her adventures led to her rape by a wealthy businessman, who then promised to support her in luxury. Maria leaves her husband, takes her child, and the film ends with the husband's suicide.[15] The message was clear; abandoning the roles of wife and mother hurt those left behind.

Worried about the new woman's impact on society, authorities often regulated working women's leisure time and forced them to resign once they married. The city council of Saint Petersburg, Russia, imposed strict curfews on female teachers so that they would not become "worldly" and corrupt their students; however, male teachers were free to come and go as they pleased. Female job applicants also had to prove their virginity. However, male teachers could marry and earned higher salaries because they were supporting families.[16] Not all women were willing to submit to such restrictions. In 1902, one teacher, Nadezhda P. Rumiantseva, challenged the marriage ban on the grounds that it violated fundamental notions of equality and women's civil liberties.[17] Married women in England were prohibited from holding positions in the civil service. In the United States, employers used the marriage ban to ensure that men retained the best positions and received most of the promotions. Ironically, given the concerns about single women, marriage bans in several countries hindered many women's professional aspirations and caused others to put off marriage.

Although few women experienced the independence of the new woman, many blamed her for other social tensions and conflicts between husbands and wives. A Russian song of the period, "The Crinoline" (a full stiff underskirt or slip), captures the gender tensions that a piece of lingerie symbolized:

> *Crinoline, crinoline*
> *I'd like to tear you apart!*
> *For, without you, I'd find*
> *My Nadezhda so kind*
> *But with you, so bossy is she*
> *So cross and so full of whimsy.*
> *Such a touch-me-not*
> *Of a wife I've got!*
> *Such a misery never was seen!*
> *And your hoop of steel it's been*
> *That has made her so stony of heart!*
> *Crinoline, crinoline,*
> *I'd like to tear you apart!* [18]

This song expressed the particular frustrations of middle-class Russian men, but men across Europe faced similar challenges to their masculinity. As the song explains, a wife influenced by the new consumer culture became sexually unavailable to her husband. Married men who did not earn enough money to allow their wives to participate in fin-de-siécle culture faced accusations that they were not real men, while the new woman's ability to purchase her own things further challenged the expectation that women were dependent on men.

On top of these anxieties, birthrates across Europe declined. As we saw in Chapter 9, women had greater access to birth control. The decline in birthrates made many government officials anxious. Critics blamed the new woman for the changes; she was selfish and unpatriotic, unwilling to fulfill her motherly role and contributing to the decay and instability of fin-de-siécle society. Suffragists often argued for the right to vote because of women's childbearing capabilities. These criticisms underscore the predicament of many women.

At the turn of the century, the image of the new woman challenged traditional gender expectations and assumptions about women's roles in society. Women entered the workforce in growing numbers and found new ways to act on their newfound economic and physical independence. Art provided both a celebration of women's growing independence and a reflection on its meaning. Yet for many women, the new woman was an unattainable ideal. They did not earn enough money and remained bound by family responsibilities. These struggles also provided female artists, writers, and actresses with material for contemplating the future of gender norms in this changing world.

## WOMEN AND POLITICAL ACTIVISM

Women's political activism continued into the new century. Suffragists believed that the vote was the only way for women to pursue and protect their rights as citizens. Socialists focused on organizing industrial workers, whom they believed would be the backbone of a new, more egalitarian society. Radicals and anarchists sought revolution and abolition of all hierarchies. Like the new woman,

these groups provoked violent reactions from opponents who feared that their demands would lead to the breakdown of traditional society.

## Women and Radical Politics

From the outset, the relationship between women's issues and socialism was tense. Taking their lead from Karl Marx (1818–1883), most socialists saw feminism and women's issues as distracting from the central problem of class exploitation. Instead, they believed that gender equality would automatically follow from class equality. Moreover, the mostly male leadership of socialist organizations focused on educating male industrial workers about unions, socialism, and revolution and spent little time with women workers. As a result, working women often felt divorced from socialism. One German woman explained, "My husband is organized, why should I?" Women workers who combined domestic work with paid labor seldom heard socialists or other union organizers addressing their experiences as mothers, wives, and working women. Despite their neglect by male organizers, the numbers of women joining labor unions grew in the first decades of the twentieth century. In 1896, only 1.4 percent of German working women belonged to unions, but by 1907, that number had grown to 8 percent of the female workforce.[19]

The rise in women's union members was due in large part to socialist activists Rosa Luxemburg (1871–1919) and Clara Zetkin (1857–1933). Luxemburg disdained feminism as a bourgeoisie distraction but believed passionately in the ability of a socialist revolution to change the lives of working-class men and women. In contrast, Zetkin worked intensely to integrate feminism and socialism. In 1907, Zetkin criticized Austrian feminists when they backed off their demands for women's suffrage because it competed with demands for universal male suffrage. Her outspokenness made her unpopular with many socialist leaders. In 1908, when Germany rescinded its law banning women from political participation, the Socialist Democratic Party (SPD) questioned Zetkin's attempt to build a separate women's organization within the SPD. As the SPD incorporated women into the larger party organization, they relegated them to charity and welfare committees and excluded them from leadership positions. When Zetkin opposed Germany's militarization, the party closed her journal and replaced it with a fashion and family magazine edited by a man. Ever the party loyalist, Zetkin accepted these changes, fervent in her belief that socialism would bring about gender equality.

In Italy, women also challenged socialism's commitment to their needs. Anna Kuliscioff (ca. 1854–1925) was forced into exile from her native Russia in 1877. She eventually became a physician and worked in the industrial slums of Milan. In 1884, she met and fell in love with Filippo Turati (1857–1932), a young socialist, and together they founded the Italian Socialist Party and edited the journal *Critica Sociale* (*Social Criticism*). Faithful to the socialist cause, Kuliscioff did not believe that feminism and socialism could be combined. However, her belief in gender equality led to disagreements with the party over its lack of dedication to women's suffrage. After the International Socialist Congress voted to support suffrage in 1907, she focused on organizing women; however, Italian women would not obtain the vote for another thirty years.

Madeleine Pelletier (1874–1939) encountered similar difficulties with French socialists, who remained fragmented and politically weak. Infighting prevented them from gaining much support, and they only organized under the heading of the French Section of the Workers International (SFIO) in 1905. Despite a legacy of French-women's political radicalism, the French associated women with conservatism and support of the church. Thus, the SFIO did not establish a women's organization until 1913. Pelletier, who had fought both poverty and social pressure to train as a physician, attempted to bridge the gap between feminism and socialism. She adapted her arguments to suit her audience. In anarchist publications, she argued for abortion and birth control on demand. In less radical journals, she focused on demands for suffrage and women's economic equality. However, ultimately she failed to convince socialists to focus on women's issues.

Emma Goldman (1869–1940), born to a lower-middle-class Jewish family in Lithuania, found uniting feminism and radical politics less difficult. Her work in a corset factory in Saint Petersburg politicized her. At seventeen she immigrated to the United States, where she continued factory work. She joined with the anarchists after the Haymarket Riots in 1886 led to the botched execution of four rioters on minimal evidence. Goldman was involved in many anarchist and union causes and served numerous prison terms. In 1893, she went to prison for telling workers to steal food if they could not buy it. She was also implicated in the attempted murder of industrialist Henry Clay Frick (1849–1919). To help her lover anarchist Alexander Berkman (1870–1936) raise money for the crime, Goldman tried prostitution. Her first client would not sleep with her but gave her $10 and advice on how to be a successful prostitute. Goldman used the money to purchase a gun for Berkman. He would serve fourteen years in prison for his attempt on Frick. Goldman was also a firm believer in birth control and went to prison in 1916 for distributing birth-control literature. She believed that too many children kept women poor, and women needed to control their fertility to improve their economic conditions. A vocal advocate of women's suffrage, her activism did not end until her death.

## Women and the Russian Revolution of 1905

Like their western European counterparts, Socialist Party organizers in Russia usually ignored issues facing women workers such as unequal pay, sexual harassment, and lack of childcare. However, socialist activist Vera Kareline (b. 1870) found a way to reach women workers through the Assembly of Russian Factory Workers. Unlike other socialist organizations and unions, this group received government approval because it was led by a priest who advocated moral and religious education for workers. Through the Assembly, Kareline ran classes for factory women that addressed issues critical to them, including sexual molestation by guards and brutality at the hands of floor supervisors or male workers. Kareline enjoyed great success. By the end of 1904, she had more than a thousand female members.[20] Kareline's work politicized Saint Petersburg's factory women to a much greater degree than working women in other parts of Russia.

The work of Kareline and others brought new political awareness to Russia's working class. On

January 9, 1905, the Assembly organized a peaceful demonstration of workers and their families outside the Winter Palace in Saint Petersburg. They brought with them a petition for Tsar Nicholas II (r. 1894–1917) that outlined their grievances and asked for redress. The petition's tone was mild and submissive, but the demands were revolutionary. The workers wanted a constitutional government, legal trade unions, and basic civil rights. The soldiers guarding the palace responded to the demonstration by firing upon the assembly, killing hundreds of men, women, and children. The slaughter became known as "Bloody Sunday" and heralded the start of the 1905 Revolution.

The government tried to ameliorate worker outrage over Bloody Sunday by setting up a commission to investigate worker complaints. When the commission failed to address the workers' issues, they struck again. By October, Russia was in the grip of a general strike, accompanied by massive demonstrations and sporadic violence. Even educated professionals, such as doctors, pharmacists, bankers, and artists, joined the protests. Although female factory workers had previously resisted striking, during the Revolution of 1905, women frequently led massive walkouts and demonstrations. On November 6, women workers and the wives of workers staged a huge demonstration on Vasilev Island, an industrialized district of Saint Petersburg. The women demanded political reforms, maternity leave, daycare, and time off for pregnancy and nursing. Their demands make it clear that they hoped to improve their lives as mothers and wives, not as workers.[21]

In the wake of the autumn strikes, workers and revolutionaries formed numerous clubs, unions, and mutual aid societies. The most prominent was the Saint Petersburg Soviet of Worker's Deputies and similar *soviets*, or councils, emerged in other Russian cities. The Saint Petersburg Soviet coordinated strikes, served as a mediator between strikers and the government, and tried to work with the various political parties invested in the revolution. Membership of the executive committee changed frequently, but by mid-November, there were 7 women out of 562 deputies.[22] Only one of these women, Anna Boldyreva (1870–after 1934), was a worker, while the other six were intellectuals allied with the workers' cause. On December 3,

1905, police arrested the executive committee and many members of the soviet, including twenty-one women. The demise of the Saint Petersburg Soviet heralded the end of the revolution.

To restore calm, the government capitulated to middle-class liberals by establishing a representative legislative body, called the Duma. However, only men who met certain property requirements received the vote. Members quickly became bogged down in factional disputes, and women's issues and the working conditions of female factory workers remained far from their minds. Although the centrist liberal Kedet Party ultimately accepted woman's suffrage as part of its platform, the Duma accomplished little in the way of political reform.

Terrorism and anarchism continued to attract women activists. In the early twentieth century, Russian women took leading roles in the Social Revolutionary Party (PSR). Its members advocated terrorism as a means to revolution and refused all political compromises. Like the revolutionaries of the previous century, the men and women in this party were young, idealistic, and generally from the upper and middle classes. Mariia Benevskaia (b. 1883), the daughter of a high-ranking military officer, combined her fervent Christianity with terrorism. Benevskaia saw her terrorist activities as a holy mission and a means to martyrdom. After a bomb exploded prematurely, blowing off one of her hands and maiming the other, the government sent her to exile in Siberia. Jewish women, such as Dora Brilliant (1880–1907), also joined the group and did so in larger numbers than Jewish men.[23] While studying to be a midwife, she met one of the founders of the PSR and began working with the party. In 1904, she was admitted into the elite group within the PSR, the Terrorist Brigade. She prepared bombs and hoped to participate in an assassination. In a roundup of revolutionaries during the 1905 Revolution, Brilliant was arrested and died in prison two years later. Most women who joined the PSR did so out of a desire for personal independence and productive and meaningful political lives and denounced feminism as too complacent. However, the PSR's emotional and physical isolation from the rest of society and its use of terrorism put the PSR on the fringes of Russian political life.

The Revolution of 1905 motivated some middle-class and educated Russian women to demand suffrage. Two days after Bloody Sunday, 150 women from Saint Petersburg petitioned the city council for suffrage "without distinction of class, nationality or religion." Women in Saratov founded the Society for the Mutual Aid to Working Women, and on March 12, 1905, they held a meeting that attracted a thousand people. The meeting passed a resolution calling for equal suffrage, asserting that, "Both as members of families and as citizens, women must take an active part in deciding questions of war and peace."[24] The most visible of the new women's groups was the All-Russian Union of Equal Rights for Women (SRZh), founded in Moscow.[25] Most of the founding members were educated, middle-class women with liberal sympathies. For example, Zinaida Mirovich (1865–1913) studied the French Revolution, translated Ibsen's plays into Russian, and wrote about women's education. Anna Evreinova (1844–1919) was the first Russian woman to earn a doctorate in law. She criticized recent legal reforms, which she explained would take away women's property rights and reduce them to virtual slavery within their families. From the very beginning, the SRZh confronted questions about its mission. Was it to be a broad-based group open to all would-be reformers or would it focus only on feminist issues and women's suffrage? The Union decided upon a "broad path," even though doing so threatened to dilute its feminist agenda.[26] By the end of April 1905, the SRZh had established contacts with eighteen other women's groups around the country. At their first congress, thirty-one delegates from eighteen towns attended, including representatives from Poland, Byelorussia, and Jewish settlements in the Pale. Their representatives agreed to cooperate with the SRZh if it also embraced national and cultural self-determination. However, the government shut down the SRZh in 1908, forcing its members to regroup and undertake a less confrontational stance. A new organization, the League of Women's Equality, took up many of the defunct SRZh's goals and survived until the Revolution of 1917.

By 1907, the government had regained its confidence and refused to listen to any new demands for reform. Instead, it increased political repression and police surveillance. Distrustful of the Duma and its motives, radicals and socialists withdrew from official politics and returned to underground organizations, illegal activities, and terrorism.

## The Push for the Vote

Socialism was only one aspect of women's political activities at the turn of the century. In the United States, temperance activists continued their campaign with some success. Alcohol became illegal in nine states by 1912, and by 1916 fourteen more states had prohibition. Their final triumph would not come until after the war, in 1919, when the Eighteenth Amendment made prohibition the law of the land. Canada and the Scandinavian countries passed similar measures.

Although Iceland and Denmark enfranchised women in 1915, in Britain, suffrage remained a divisive issue. Starting in 1897, British suffrage groups began affiliating themselves with the National Union of Women's Suffrage Societies (NUWSS). By 1909, the NUWSS included some seventy separate societies, a number that swelled to four hundred by 1913.[27] Despite this great interest in women's suffrage, Parliament repeatedly voted down or refused to address bills that would have expanded the voting franchise. In 1903, a new suffrage group, the Women's Social and Political Union (WSPU), formed under the leadership of Emmeline Pankhurst (1858–1928) and her daughters, Christabel (1880–1958) and Sylvia (1882–1960). Believing that polite advocacy and working with politicians would never gain women the vote, the WSPU pursued a policy of confrontational public protest. Its motto was "deeds not words." The WSPU's first demonstration was in 1907, when three thousand women participated in the "Mud March" through London. They shouted slogans, carried banners, and used a brass band to attract crowds, tactics that horrified many in the NUWSS, who preferred subtle pressure and less confrontation. As suffragists' frustration increased, they heckled politicians, obstructed the political process, and damaged property. The police became increasingly intent on stopping their demonstrations, and the Pankhursts resorted to disguises and subterfuge to get into Parliament and disrupt meetings. For the Pankhursts, the suffrage movement was "a revolt against the evil system under which women are regarded as sub-human and as the sex slaves of men."[28]

**EMILY DAVISON'S FUNERAL (1913).** Although thousands attended Emily Davison's funeral, her protest did little to change Parliament's position on women's suffrage. *(Hulton-Deutsch Collection/Corbis.)*

Confrontations between suffragists and the government increased. Once arrested, the Pankhursts and their followers demanded to be classified as political prisoners, which would have gained them better treatment. When the government refused, the women went on hunger strikes and the police responded with forced feedings. Suffragists were tied down and tubes forced down their noses and into their stomachs. Victims likened the treatment to rape, and their descriptions created public outrage. When Parliament seemed likely to pass a new suffrage bill in 1910, the suffragists called a truce. However, when the Conciliation Bill failed, members of the WSPU again became militant. Protesters repeatedly suffered sexual harassment and assault on the streets and in jail. Authorities justified this treatment by claiming that loud and visible women must be prostitutes and that, therefore, they deserved such treatment. By 1912, suffrage demonstrations paralyzed London as police focused on protecting property. In 1913, Parliament passed the "Cat and Mouse Act," which allowed the government to release a suffragist once she became too ill from a hunger strike and to rearrest her when she recovered. Emmeline Pankhurst was repeatedly imprisoned and released under this act. Subsequent confrontations became even more violent. On May 31, 1913, Emily Wilding Davison (1872–1913) threw herself in front of the king's racehorse at the Derby. She was trampled to death, an event that was caught on film. The police refused to allow Emmeline Pankhurst to march in the funeral.

In the United States, five western territories had already granted women the vote before they became states. Their reasons varied. Oregon wanted to attract women settlers. Wyoming hoped that white women's votes would nullify African American votes. In Utah, Mormons wanted women to vote to preserve polygamy, a common practice among this new religious group. However, most states and the federal government demonstrated no interest in giving women the vote.

Like their British counterparts, U.S. suffragists split over tactics. The National Women's Suffrage Association (NWSA) was the largest and most influential suffrage organization. Its president, Carrie Chapman Catt (1859–1947) had revitalized the group at the beginning of the century and worked tirelessly to lobby Congress and the president on the cause of women's suffrage. The NWSA was largely a white and middle class organization. Its tactics of letter writing and personal persuasion frustrated radical members, who left the group in 1913. They formed a new militant group, the National Women's Party (NWP). Alice Paul, a Quaker (1885–1977) from Philadelphia, and Lucy Burns (1879–1966), an Irish Catholic from New Jersey, led the NWP. They took much of their inspiration from the Pankhursts, as Paul and Burns had marched in several of the Pankhursts' protests and met in a London police station. Members of the NWP peacefully demonstrated day after day at the White House; however, their presence attracted hateful crowds who jeered at them and the police, who beat, jailed, and force-fed them. On November 10, 1917, Washington, D.C., police beat the more than 150 women picketing the White House. They arrested Paul and confined her to a mental hospital and even threw a sixty-year-old protester down the stairs. Other detainees refused to give their names, eat, or cooperate in any way with authorities during what became known as the "Night of Terror." Police justified their brutality because the country was at war and these women posed a security threat.

Militant suffragists attracted a great deal of media attention, both as legitimate news stories and as comic characters satirized by moviemakers and cartoonists. Activists on both sides of the debate sought popular support by satirizing their opponents. In 1912, the WSPU produced *80 Million Women Want—?*; not to be outdone, the NWSA produced *Votes for Women* the following year. Several antisuffrage films, including two produced by Thomas Edison. Charlie Chaplin's (1889–1977) 1914 film *A Busy Day* (also known as *Militant Suffragette*), featured Chaplin as a suffragist who abandoned her children and husband, disrupted society, and dominated men.

Opposition to women's suffrage was strongest in Massachusetts. Beginning in the 1890s, opponents published an annual journal called *Remonstrance* that emphasized the dangers of extending the franchise; the vote for women would destroy families and women's protected status. Antisuffrage campaigners, or Antis as they were called, preferred to express their ideas in writing, asserting that it was more feminine than public speaking. Ironically, as the suffragists escalated their activities, the Antis had to adapt their strategies to maintain their visibility.[29] In 1911, the Antis formed the National Association Opposed to Woman Suffrage (NAOWS), headquartered in New York City. Josephine Dodge (1855–1928), a daycare provider and child-welfare reformer, led the group, and most of its membership came from the East Coast. Under Dodge's leadership, the Antis took their campaign to labor unions, state legislatures, and even suffrage meetings. Boasting the support of two former first ladies, Frances Folsom Cleveland (1864–1947) and Helen Herron Taft (1861–1943), the Antis successfully fought the suffragists' state-by-state campaign. However, the Antis lost their advantage when suffragists took their battle to the Congress.

Although some two thousand German women owned enough property to qualify them to vote in some local elections through a male proxy, few women did.[30] German feminists were disadvantaged when trying to expand women's suffrage because until 1908 it was illegal for women to engage in politics in Prussia and much of the rest of Germany. Despite these constraints, in 1902, radicals finally convinced the *Bund Deutscher Frauenvereine* (BDF) (German Women's Associations) to support the issue. Veterans of Germany's failed Abolitionist campaign (see Chapter 10), led by Anita Augspurg (1857–1943), founded the German Union for Women's Suffrage. They advocated a liberal vision of suffrage, which included universal suffrage except in Prussia, where the organization worked for property-based suffrage. This later position lost them the support of working-class women.

The Women's Suffrage Union organized in Hamburg, where women's political activities were not illegal. Their campaign involved letter writing, newspaper articles, publication of leaflets, and support of other causes, such as temperance, the end of regulation of prostitutes, and a general reduction of state interference in the lives of individuals. In 1907, left-wing liberals who had supported women's suffrage formed a voting bloc in the legislature with the conservatives who had not, and the issue died.

Disillusioned by what they saw as a liberal betrayal, Augspurg and others demanded more militant tactics. Yet, militancy never caught on in Germany. Most German feminists shunned street marches, which they associated with the SPD. Although membership in the Women's Suffrage Union grew from 1908 to 1914 to nearly ten thousand members, it never achieved the visibility of the U.S. and British movements.[31] Outside the movement, the middle class was growing more conservative in the face of socialist activism, and the uncompromising stance of the Suffrage Union cost it the support of many members.

## Racism and Nationalism Before the War

In the United States, racial discrimination also pushed women into political activism. Segregationists justified keeping the races apart by combining antiquated notions of women's honor with new ideas of racial purity. Although the Fifteenth Amendment to the Constitution had enfranchised black men, "Jim Crow" laws continued to exclude blacks from the political process and segregated blacks and whites socially. African Americans who rejected segregation ran the risk of being beaten or lynched. Nearly one hundred lynchings took place each year between 1900 and 1910.[32] Despite a widespread antilynching campaign led by journalist Ida B. Wells-Barnett (1862–1931), authorities turned a blind eye to these attacks. Wells-Barnett worked tirelessly to publicize the violent incidents, build networks among blacks, and forge alliances with reformist whites. One of her associates was Jane Addams (see Chapter 10).

Together with other civil rights leaders, they helped found the National Association for the Advancement of Colored People (NAACP) in 1908 and made antilynching legislation a priority.

Racism found new support in film director D. W. Griffith's (1875–1948) 1915 melodrama *Birth of a Nation*. This silent film tells the story of a white southern family, the Stonemans, who were terrorized by former slaves and northern whites after the Civil War. The movie perpetuated the belief that black men were a threat to white women's honor and that without the heroic intervention of the Ku Klux Klan (KKK), blacks would dominate whites. The heroine, the pure Elsie Stoneman, played by Lillian Gish (1883–1993), is nearly raped by a black man, but members of the KKK rescue her in the nick of time. However, her younger sister flings herself off a cliff to escape another predatory black man. Elsie's counterpart is the sexually voracious Lydia, a woman of mixed race, who seduces Elsie's father and becomes mistress of the house. Inspired by *Birth of a Nation*, white men and women in the South and Midwest refounded the KKK, which had disbanded in the 1870s. The organization would grow in popularity over the next decade, terrorizing African Americans and promoting an ideology of racial purity.

American racists often used nationalist ideology to defend their segregationist beliefs. They claimed that they were defending the United States from blacks and foreigners bent on destroying the country and its way of life. Nationalism also attracted followers across Europe, not only in the newly united countries of Germany and Italy, but also in old states such as France and Russia, and among subjected ethnic groups such as the Hungarians who lived under the rule of the Austrian Empire. Nationalist ideologies expected women to transmit traditional values and culture through motherhood; nationalists were not concerned with women's legal or political equality. As British nationalist writer Elizabeth Sloan-Chesser explained in her book *Perfect Health for Women and Children* (1912), the home was "the cradle of the race . . . the Empire's first line of defense."[33]

The protection of national interests led to increased militarism and a heightening of political tensions. Britain and Germany vied for control of the ocean. France plotted to regain Alsace-Lorraine, territory lost to the Germans in the Franco-Prussian War, and squabbled with Italy over territory in northern Africa. Politicians often linked militarism with masculinity. Many conservatives, such as German political theorist Heinrich von Treitschke (1834–1896), believed that enfranchising women would weaken the country and destroy the family. In 1912, a group of professional men founded the League for the Prevention of the Emancipation of Women, known as the Anti-League. It argued that as Germany faced more hostility outside its borders, it had to heal divisions within. The women's movement turned women against men, and because it was international in focus, it was not patriotic. Italian political theorist Filippo Tommaso Marinetti (1876–1944) espoused a political doctrine called Futurism that advocated the triumph of society over nature. In 1909, he wrote a Futurist manifesto that explicitly connected militarism and antifeminism. He believed that a military buildup would cure what he saw as the growing feminization of modern society.

> We will glorify war—the world's only hygiene—militarism, patriotism, the destructive gesture of freedom-bringers, beautiful ideas worth dying for, and scorn for women. We will destroy the museums, libraries, academies of every kind, [we] will fight moralism, feminism, [and] every opportunistic or utilitarian cowardice.[34]

Only with the destruction of the feminine elements of society would nations retain their masculinity and virility. From this perspective, the feminist goals of peace, compassion, and humane values inhibited national greatness.

In the east, Russians, Austrians, and Greeks competed for influence in the Balkans, as the Ottoman Empire lost its hold on its European territories. Russia not only wanted access to the Mediterranean via the Dardanelles, it also supported self-determination for Slavs living under Ottoman and Austrian rule. Russia's support of the nationalist Pan-Slavic movement increased tensions between Russia and Austria. Female activists, whether they were socialists, feminists, or suffragists, felt torn between their desire for peace and social revolution and the relationship between nationalism and potential citizenship. Many women hoped that support of nationalist goals would lead to political rights. Socialists

believed that capitalism drove nationalist agendas and, just as socialists needed to fight capitalism, they should fight militarism in the service of nationalism.

The military buildup and the inevitability of war divided women over national and international issues. Many socialists, including Clara Zetkin, Rosa Luxemburg, and Russian feminist Alexandra Kollontai (1872–1952), who would play a role in the Russian Revolution of 1917 and the Bolshevik government, strongly opposed militarization and broke with their parties over the issue. In Britain, Sylvia Pankhurst disagreed with her mother and sister. Emmeline and Christabel believed that if they supported the war, the British government would repay their loyalty with women's suffrage. At the outbreak of World War I in 1914, both the WSPU and the NUWSS stopped their activities and joined with the war effort. Emmeline Pankhurst moved from demanding the right to vote to demanding the right to work for the war effort.

Female activists pressed for better working conditions and demanded the right to vote. While some women preferred mainstream politics, socialist agitators and militant suffragists shocked the public by defying authorities and risking their lives for their causes. However, opposition to women's equality remained strong, and as international tensions grew, many women's attention turned from the ballot box to the battlefield.

## WOMEN AND THE GREAT WAR

World War I was unlike any war the world had ever seen. Many historians describe it as the fulfillment of the Industrial Revolution, as technological innovations dehumanized the conflict and alienated men from its goals. It was a total war; no aspect of life—from consumption, to fashion, to gender roles—escaped its influence. In particular, the relationship between citizens and the state changed as nations dedicated their energies to the war. The expansion of social services led to the development of welfare states. With millions of men on the battlefield, unprecedented numbers of women entered the workplace to support themselves and their families and to help with the war effort. Those who opposed the war challenged their governments' growing intervention in their lives and sought international solutions to the expanding conflict.

## Women in the Military and at the Front

With nationalist tensions running high across Europe, the assassination of Archduke Franz Ferdinand (1863–1914), the heir to the Austrian throne, by a Serbian nationalist in Sarajevo, Serbia, on June 28, 1914, set off World War I. In the days that followed, the tangled network of European alliances led to the mobilization of most of the Continent. The Serbian government had not sponsored the assassination, yet it felt compelled to defend its national interests and prevented Austrian authorities from investigating the crime. As a consequence, Austria declared war on Serbia. Russia then declared war on Austria, bringing Germany into the war on Austria's side. France hoped that the Serbian conflict would distract Germany and allow France to mobilize and retake Alsace-Lorraine. To stage a preemptive attack on France, Germany invaded France through neutral Belgium, pulling Great Britain into the war on France's side. The two dominant alliances, the Triple Entente (France, Britain, Russia, and later the United States) and the Central Powers (Germany and the Austrian Empire), pulled smaller nations into the conflict, and within two months, nearly all of Europe was at war (see Map 12.1).

World War I had two major fronts. The Western Front ran through the flat lands of Belgium and northern France and involved soldiers in protracted trench warfare. In the five-month Battle of the Somme, more than a million French, British, and German soldiers died or were injured. With soldiers mired in miles of trenches, neither side gained an advantage. This new type of warfare grew out of the increased use of the machine gun, which turned traditional infantry assaults into bloody massacres. In addition, weapons manufacturers in Germany experimented with chemical weapons, particularly poison gases such as Vesicant or mustard gas. Poison gas bombs cleared trenches and made easy targets of men gasping for breath. Although most gas poisoning, which burned soldiers' skin and lungs,

could be treated, it inspired terror and incapacitated soldiers for months at a time.

The Eastern Front stretched from Estonia in the Baltic to Albania in southern Europe. German soldiers fought in the Balkans and occupied Romania. On this front, poor weather, rugged terrain, and tenuous supply lines posed bigger threats than trench warfare. As the war spread, belligerent countries drew in soldiers from their colonies, and fighting spread into the Ottoman Empire, Africa, and the Middle East. In 1917, Russia pulled out of the war, while attacks on American ships by German submarines brought the United States into the war on the side of Britain and France.

The first women caught in the fighting lived in Belgium and northern France. Despite Belgium's neutrality, the Germans invaded on August 3, 1914. Thousands of civilians fled to Britain, France, or the neutral Netherlands. The invasion separated families, leaving women to fend for themselves. The Germans needed them to work as cooks, cleaners, and laundresses and the women needed the income. Yet women who worked for the Germans faced accusations of collaboration and sexual misbehavior. The choice between survival and social ostracism only added to Belgian women's misery. During Easter week of 1916, the Germans deported hundreds of young women from the northern French towns of Lille, Roubaix, and Tourcoing to work in German factories.

Many Belgian women worked in the Belgian resistance movement. They smuggled Allied soldiers out of the country, nursed wounded soldiers, spread Allied propaganda, gathered military information, and committed acts of sabotage. The most organized group was *La Dame Blanche* (The White Lady), which was allied with the British War Office. Organized along military lines, the members received salaries, military ranks, and after the war, medals. They took oaths of loyalty and submitted to military discipline; those who betrayed the group faced postwar court-martials. The Germans considered them spies, but the personnel of La Dame Blanche saw themselves as soldiers or intelligence agents. Women made up about a third of the members of La Dame Blanche.[35] Members ranged in age from sixteen to eighty-one, although most were unmarried or widowed women between twenty and forty-two.

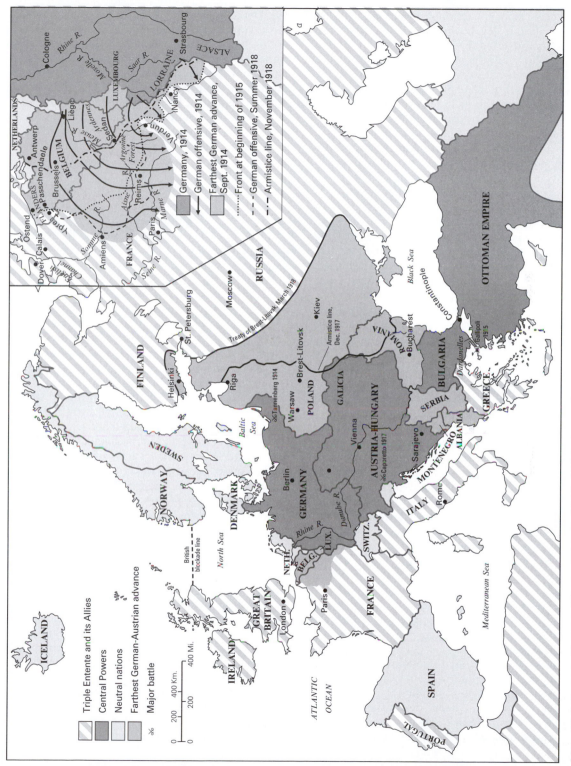

**Map 12.1** EUROPE DURING WORLD WAR I, 1914–1918. A complex system of alliances and an arms race led to World War I, a war of unprecedented scope.

They came from a wide range of occupations and socioeconomic levels. For example, when the Germans converted the convent at Chimay into a military hospital, the nuns gathered information from the wounded soldiers and passed it on to the Allies. A schoolteacher, Laure Tandel, ran Battalion III, which included the important railway linking the industrial cities of Brussels, Malines, Mons, and Charleroi. She supervised some 190 agents. A Belgian aristocrat and her daughters ran Platoon 49 out of their chateau.[36] Survivors remembered with pride their sense of purpose in working for Belgium's liberation.

Life in La Dame Blanche was dangerous. Vicomtesse Gabrielle de Monge operated an escape service for fugitive Allied soldiers from 1914 to 1916. The Germans arrested her and sentenced her to hard labor. The prison at Siegburg in Germany held at least three hundred members of La Dame Blanche. When inmates refused to do munitions work, the Germans put them in solitary confinement with little food and no heat. The women held out and prison authorities ultimately gave them other work. Many other women, such as Oxford-educated Gabrielle Petit (1893–1916), were executed. Petit used her linguistic skills in code breaking and writing. Her execution made her a national heroine and martyr.

Female nurses and doctors also entered combat zones. The high number of casualties from the Western Front required a continual supply of medical personnel. At first, governments resisted putting women close to the fighting or sending female doctors who would have to supervise men. The unwillingness of Allied governments to "endanger" female medical workers meant that women working near combat areas went on their own initiatives. Dr. Elsie Inglis (1865–1917), founder of the Scottish Women's Hospitals (SWH) and a leading Scottish suffragist, opened a number of hospitals in France, Serbia, and Russia. Women from all over the British Empire worked for the SWH as surgeons, orderlies, nurses, and ambulance drivers.

Nurses were crucial to soldiers' survival. In Britain, professional nurses could join a variety of military nursing services including the Royal Army Medical Corps and Queen Alexandra's Imperial Military Nursing Service. Volunteers received nursing training when they joined the Voluntary Aid Detachments (VADs). In Germany, most nurses volunteered through the Red Cross or came from religious orders. Although German nurses found themselves working with the wounded on both fronts, those on the Western Front had a much more difficult time, as outbreaks of malaria and typhus added to the number of wounded. When the United States joined the war, it sent over nurses as part of the Army Nurse Corps (ANC). At the war's end a year later, more than twenty-one thousand U.S. women were serving in military hospitals around the globe.[37] Queen Marie of Romania (1875–1938) promoted nursing as a form of women's patriotism by working as a nurse and by only being photographed in her nursing uniform. In the occupied zones, Romanian women served as nurses in the POW camps where they not only provided medical care but also tried to boost morale by writing letters to soldiers' families. In one hospital, the nurses also helped 162 wounded soldiers escape to Moldavia.[38]

Despite governments' desires to keep women out of combat areas, women often found themselves close to the line of fire, working in difficult and dangerous conditions. For example, Edith Cavell (1867–1915), a British nurse who had lived and worked in Belgium before the war, hid Allied soldiers and helped them escape. In 1915, the Germans arrested and executed her as a spy. Her martyrdom became an international cause célèbre and further elevated the status of nurses in the public's mind. Most nurses, however, faced different kinds of dangers. The memoirs of nurses from World War I, such as Vera Brittain's *Testament of Youth* (1933), have left us with some of the most haunting images of the war, and in particular, the brutality of trench warfare. Even the most thoroughly trained nurses were unprepared for the horror of military hospitals: long hours, limited supplies, and endless patients with missing limbs or damaged faces (see **Sources from the Past:** Letters from a Canadian Nurse in France). Army nurses received a great deal of admiration and praise for their skill, commitment, and compassion, but they did not earn military rank or veterans' benefits when the war ended.

Modern war also required armies of clerks, and with so many men at the front, the military lacked the personnel to keep track of its supplies, requisitions, and transport schedules. In 1916, the British military created a women's auxiliary corps in order to free men to fight. The first of these groups was the Women's Army Auxiliary Corps (WAACs), followed by the Women's Royal Naval Service and the Women's Royal Air Force Service. By 1920, forty-one thousand women had served as WAACs.[39] To attract women, the military offered competitive wages, which was a controversial move. The military targeted single women because of their lack of family obligations. Parents objected and the WAACs imposed many rules to ease parents' worries about their daughters' reputations. There was an eight o'clock curfew; hotels, bars, and cafés were off-limits; and men were not allowed in their common rooms or dormitories. France and Germany set up no such auxiliary services, believing that women's service should be focused on their families. Even when women worked in some military desk jobs, they remained civilians. The U.S. government established women's branches of the navy and the marines. These women received military ranks, observed military discipline, and received veterans' benefits when the war ended. Women serving in the U.S. Navy, known as "yeomen (F)," provided a variety of clerical and managerial services. Recognizing that women in uniform would provide publicity for the war effort, yeomen (F) participated in war bond drives, rallies, troop sendoffs, and recruitment drives. Using the slogan "Free Men to Fight," the navy recruited more than eleven thousand women. Four months before the war ended in 1918, the U.S. Marines began recruiting women. Most women working in the military remained in the United States, although female telephone operators, or "Hello Girls," went to France to staff the military phone system. When the Army Signal Corp created a new communications system, they recruited 450 civilian women fluent in French, of whom 223 traveled to Europe. Hello Girls worked with codes, kept secrets, and maintained communications between fighting units and their commanders. Some worked close to the front, facilitating communications during the last phases of the war.[40]

The British and U.S. women who joined the military or women's auxiliary joined out of a sense of patriotism, a desire for adventure, and sometimes revenge for the death of loved ones. One British woman recalled, "the advertisements said release a man for the firing line, which we thought was very heroic, and of course things were going very badly for us. . . . Everyday there were casualty lists in the papers and we'd look down them for someone we knew."[41] Women who served in World War I remembered their service with pleasure and pride. They celebrated their abilities, commitment, and the camaraderie they found with other men and women. An anonymous American poem from the time expresses some of these sentiments:

> My dear old uniform of blue, I hate to lay
> you by
> And merely be a citizen when the blue-clad
> boys march by
> For you won me a place in the ranks of men;
> a chance to do my bit
> And now to go back to be "merely a girl,"
> I hate to think of it.[42]

Relatively few women saw actual combat. However, Russian newspapers report instances of women dressing like men and joining their husbands' regiments. At the end of the war, Maria Bochareva (1889–ca. post 1936), a Siberian peasant, joined the Twenty-fifth Reserve Battalion, where her bravery and courage overcame male resentment and derision. In 1917, after the tsar had abdicated, she convinced the provisional government to form an all-women's battalion. According to some reports, she had two thousand women under her command.[43] The "Battalion of Death" was "to serve as an example to the army and lead men into battle . . . to shame the men in the trenches by having the women go over the top first."[44] After three months of fighting on the frontlines, only 250 women were still alive. Although the Battalion of Death was the most notable example of women in combat, individual women also fought on the frontlines. Russian princess Eugenie Shakhovskaia (b. 1889) reportedly flew reconnaissance flights over Germany and received a medal for her service. In Romania, Ecaterina Teodoroiu (1894–1917) volunteered as a nurse. When her two brothers died fighting, she volunteered to fight in their battalion. The Germans captured her in November of 1916, but she escaped. She went back to the front and was killed in September of 1917. Her bravery earned a great deal of praise, and many likened her to Joan of Arc.[45] As brave

# Letters from a Canadian Nurse in France

*When Canada entered World War I in August 1914, Canadians united behind the war, and thousands of men and women answered the prime minister's call to serve. These letters from a Canadian nurse stationed in France describe the physical and emotional difficulty that nurses had serving so close to the front. They also bring a human dimension to the scale of the conflict.*

DIVONNE-LES-BAINS, FRANCE,

August 2, 1914.

Dear Mother:

The awful war we have all been dreading is upon us—*France is Mobilizing.* At five o'clock yesterday morning the tocsin [bells] sounded from the Marie [village hall] and men, women, and children, all flocked to hear the proclamation which the Mayor of the village read. It called upon all of military age—between twenty years and fifty years—to march at once, and inside of twenty-four hours five hundred men had gone, they knew not where. The bravery of these villagers—men and women—is remarkable, and not to be forgotten. No murmuring, no complaining,—just, "Ma Patrie," tying up the little bundle—so little—and going; none left but old men, women and children.

We have started teaching the women and girls to make bandages, sponges, etc., for the hospital which will be needed here.

DIVONNE-LES-BAINS, FRANCE,

August 23, 1914.

Your letter came yesterday—twenty days on the way—but I was fortunate to get it at all; so many of these poor people, whose nearest and dearest have gone to fight for their country, have had no word from them since they marched away, and they do not know where they are. . . .

I am filled with admiration and respect for these people. The courage of both the men and women is remarkable. There is no hesitation, and no grumbling, and everyone tries to do whatever he or she can to help the cause.

I do not know if I told you, in my last letter, of the poor lady who walked all night through the dark and storm to see her son who was leaving the next morning. All the horses and motors had been taken by the Government for the army, so she started at eleven o'clock at night, all by herself, and got here about five in the morning—her son left at seven, so she had two hours with him. There are many such stories I might tell you, but I have not the time.

The Red Cross has started a branch hospital here, and I have been helping them to get it in order. It is just about ready now, and we may get soldiers any day.

I have classes every morning and find many of the women very quick to learn the rudiments of nursing. Every one in the place is making supplies and our sitting room is a sort of depot where they come for work.

PARIS,

about February 15, 1915.

I have seen quite a number of operations, and as X-ray pictures are taken of all the cases there is no time wasted in hunting for a bullet; they get the bullet out in about two minutes. They are using Dr. Criles' anaesthetic—nitrous oxide gas and oxygen—it has no bad effects whatever. The patients come out of it at once as soon as the mask is taken off, and there is no nausea or illness at all; and most of them go off laughing, for they cannot believe that it is all over,—they feel so well; but oh, mother, it is awful to see the sad things that have happened. In some cases there are only pieces of men left. One young chap, twenty-one years old, has lost both legs. At first he did not want to live, but now he is beginning to take an interest in things and is being fitted for wooden legs.

The dental department have done wonderful work. They build up the framework of the face and jaws and then the surgeons finish the work by making new noses and lips and eyelids.

I thought I had seen a good many wonderful things, but I did not believe it possible to make any thing human out of some of the pieces of faces that were left, and in some of the cases they even get rid of the scars. Photos are taken when they first come in, and then in the various stages of recovery. One of the worst cases I saw the last day I was out. He has to have one more operation to fill in a small hole in one side of his nose and then he will be all right. . . .

I must tell you about the wonderful dog that is at the American Ambulance. . . . His master came from Algeria, and of course did not expect to take his dog with him, but when the ship left the wharf the dog jumped into the sea and swam after it, so they put off a boat and hauled him on board, and he has been with his master all through the war. He was in the trenches with him, and one day a German shell burst in the trench and killed all of his companions and buried this man in the mud and dirt as well as injuring him terribly. Strange to say the dog was not hurt at all, and the first thing the man remembered was the dog digging the mud off his face. As soon as he realized his master was alive he ran off for help, and when they were brought into the Ambulance together there were not many dry eyes about. After he was sure his master was being taken care of he consented to go and be fed, and now he is having the time of his life. He is the most important person in the place. He has a beautiful new collar and medal, lives in the diet kitchen, and is taken out to walk by the nurses, and best of all is allowed to see his master every day. I will send a photo of him to you. His master has lost one leg, the other is terribly crushed, and one hand also, but Doctor B—thinks he can save them. . . .

January 1, 1917.

The men had a wonderful Christmas day. They were like a happy lot of children. We deco-rated the wards with flags, holly, mistletoe, and paper flowers that the men made, and a tree in each ward. You cannot imagine how pretty they were. Each patient began the day with a sock that was hung to the foot of their bed by the night nurses. In each was an orange, a small bag of sweets, nuts and raisins, a handkerchief, pencil, tooth brush, pocket comb and a small toy that pleased them almost more than anything else, and which they at once passed on to their children. They had a fine dinner: jam, stewed rabbit, peas, plum pudding, fruit, nuts, raisins and sweets. The plum puddings were sent by the sister of one of the nurses.

In the afternoon the trees were lighted and we had the official visit of the medicine chef and all the staff. After the festivities were over we began preparing for the tree for the refugee children. We had thought that we would have enough left over to manage for fifty children, but the list grew to one hundred and twenty-five. The mayor of the village let us have a large room in his house, as the first place we had chosen was too small. We had the tree on Sunday afternoon and three hundred and thirty-one children arrived. Fortunately we had some extra things so there was enough of something to go around. They had a lovely time, each one got a small toy, a biscuit, and most of them a small bag of sweets and an orange. The oranges and sweets gave out, but there was enough biscuits and toys, but there was nothing left.

We are all dead tired, for we worked like nail-ers for the past two weeks; but it was worth while, for we were able to make a great many people happy, and now we are sending off packages to the trenches—things that came too late for Christmas.

. . . It is hard to believe that another year of war has begun.

Source: http://www.ku.edu/carrie/specoll/medical/canadian/ cnurse.htm; originally published as *My Beloved Polius* (St. John, N.B.: Barnes & Co., Limited, Publishers, 1917).

and admired as many of these women were, their combat experience made them unusual.

## Women at Home: Inventing the Home Front

The fear of invasion and subversion at home led governments to think of the war as having a "home front" in addition to the battlefront. Fighting the war at home brought profound changes to civilians' daily lives. Governments monitored residents' movements, their correspondence, their food consumption, and their speech. For the first time, governments began issuing passports and registering resident aliens. Many accepted these limitations on their civil liberties as necessary for the war effort, but they also came to expect greater support from their governments in the form of medical care and military pensions. For women living in occupied areas, there was no home front; they lived in the midst of the war and felt its violence on a daily basis.

Patriotism inspired many women to volunteer. They knitted socks, assembled first-aid kits, and sent care packages to the front. In France, one charitable organization facilitated the adoption of soldiers without families. These *marraine de guerre* (godmothers for the war) wrote to soldiers, sent care packages, and provided moral inspiration. In Germany, the BDF promoted a "women's year of service." Feminists wanted a year of compulsory service for women to educate them in social work and prove that women made important contributions to the states and, therefore, deserved the vote. The National Women's Service worked with the Department of the Interior looking after dislocated families, publishing job openings for women, and setting up hospitals and soup kitchens. Jewish women hoped that their contributions would prove their German identities and loyalty. They joined the Red Cross, the National Women's Service, and the League of Jewish Women. Increased interaction between Jewish and Christian women in support of the war effort led to some new friendships, but it did not end anti-Semitism or the common misperception that Jewish men evaded the draft.

One of the most significant changes in governments' relationships with their citizens was the introduction of separation pay. The mobilization of large numbers of men left many women and families without economic support. As the war wore on, soldiers' wives demanded financial support from their governments. All governments eventually created separation payment schemes for the dependents of soldiers. Some countries, such as Great Britain, considered the number of children in a family when disbursing the payments. Others, like Romania, set up flat rates that were rarely enough to provide for a family. Germany established its separation scheme at the very beginning of the war in hopes of increasing recruits, and these separation payments provoked controversy. Many Germans felt that soldiers' families benefited from the war while others endured intense hardship. Yet, separation payments potentially gave some women economic independence. In Austria and Germany, the pay gave some housewives control of family budgets for the first time.[46]

The demand for separation pay highlights the difficult conditions of women on the home front. Life in Britain and much of France was not as difficult, however, as in the occupied areas of France, Belgium, or Romania. Conditions also quickly deteriorated in Germany after Britain established a blockade of the North Sea and Baltic in 1915 that prevented Germany from importing food. Yet with all countries depending to some degree on imports and with poor harvests in the United States in 1916 and 1917, food became scarce everywhere. As early as February 1915, women in London and Berlin protested the rising cost of food, and in early 1917 women in Boston, New York, and Philadelphia attacked pushcart vendors and grocery stores and fought with police over the cost of provisions.

In addition to the problem of poor harvests, food was also scarce and expensive because there were fewer people to plant and harvest grain. Russia's entry into World War I mobilized more than five million troops in the first five months of war. Three years later, Russia had nearly fifteen million troops, 36 percent of the male population, most of whom had been either factory or agricultural workers. Nearly 66 percent of Russian flour mills lay dormant due to lack of fuel or grain to grind.[47] In Austria, the government conscripted 60 percent of the male population between the ages of eighteen and fifty-three. One Austrian man recalled how his mother had to thresh grain in a pillowcase using a rolling pin because she could not buy flour.[48]

In response to shortages, governments set up food rationing programs that equated food allocation with patriotism. The slogan of one British poster declared "The kitchen is the key to victory: eat less bread."[49] Even with coupons, food was difficult to come by. Survival required standing in long lines for food and fuel. In Austria, the problem was exacerbated because most food came from Hungary, which cut food shipments and refused to release information on grain production. The Austrian government limited workers in heavy industry to 1,292 calories a day, down from a normal consumption of 3,900. An Austrian woman remembered waiting in line for potatoes all day during the winter. Another woman had to beg for milk for her infant brother. Urban families with rural relatives relied on them for extra food and fuel.[50] The urban standard of living in Germany suffered a serious decline. Meat consumption declined by 40 percent and potato consumption increased by 300 percent.[51] The fight over food and rationing raised questions about who contributed the most to the war effort. Working women bore the brunt of the effects of rationing; men in the police force received more rations than working-class women. Many urban women felt that the food rationing system favored rural families. As the war progressed, bread riots broke out. A police report described one violent outbreak: "several women left the market for the city hall to demand bread and potatoes. . . . They asked where they could buy bread. . . . Then they went down the street to the baker and violently took thirty breads without paying for them."[52] Police were unable or unwilling to arrest these women. They may have been sympathetic to their complaints about the unequal food distribution. The German government never solved these problems, and more than seven hundred thousand Germans died of malnutrition by the end of the war.[53]

Governments' failures to control black markets or boost food production highlighted class divisions and created massive social unrest, especially in Germany and Russia. As the war dragged on, it became clear that Russia had no means to care for the enormous numbers of refugees, war orphans, and casualties. Refugees fleeing the war set up

**AUSTRIAN BREAD LINE IN WORLD WAR I.** During World War I, governments instituted strict food rationing, which left women and children in Germany and Austria without enough to eat. Black markets and the governments' failures to provide enough food exacerbated class tensions and social unrest. *(Hulton-Deutsch Collection/Corbis.)*

housekeeping in train stations, abandoned factories, or public squares. Orphaned or abandoned children roamed cities in gangs, committing crimes and harassing the population. One women's journal complained, "We are raising a whole generation of criminals."[54] On the other end of the social spectrum, the rich lived as if nothing had changed. They threw lavish parties, went to the races, and wore clothing made from yards of luxurious cloth. Journals that catered to wealthy women printed recipes with exotic ingredients such as pineapples. Ostentatious public displays of wealth in the face of starvation and displacement outraged many, and the popular press poked fun at the idle rich. By the end of the war, working-class women in

Russian and German cities regularly protested the governments' inability to care for them and their children. The obvious inequities in the distribution of necessities led to calls for revolution in both countries.

Government involvement in its citizens' daily lives also came in the form of increased surveillance. In an effort to maintain security, England passed the Defense of the Realm Act (DORA) in 1914, expanding the government's ability to monitor its citizens' behavior and movements. Single women received special scrutiny, because they had more disposable income and were out in public more. DORA restricted women's drinking in bars and established earlier curfews for women than men. Before the war, many single women from the European continent had come to Britain to work, mostly as domestics or governesses. By January 1915, nearly seven thousand single women of foreign birth had either voluntarily left Britain or were deported. Until deportation, the government held them in women's prisons, such as Holoway Prison in London, or lock hospitals, medical prisons for women with venereal diseases. Moreover, naturalization did not protect citizens from the force of DORA. The government expelled celebrated writer D. H. Lawrence (1885–1930) and his German-born wife, Frieda von Richthofen (1879–1956), from their home on the southern coast because of its proximity to shipping. Naturalized women were especially problematic for the government because women's citizenship automatically changed when they married men from other countries, regardless of their personal loyalties. In 1918, sixty-eight-year-old Martha Earle received a sentence of one year in prison for passing secret information to her sister in Germany. Earle had lived in Britain as the wife of a British schoolmaster since 1908. Her so-called secret information was of no military value and she received no payment from the German government. The government arrested her after reading her mail, another intrusion allowed by DORA.[55]

When the United States joined the war in 1917, the government passed the Espionage Act and a year later the Sedition Act, which banned all organizing against the war. In 1919, the U.S. Supreme Court upheld limits on the freedom of speech to protect national security. Working with patriotic groups such as the National Security League, the Justice Department spied on potential dissidents and subversives. Officials particularly targeted trade unions because of their links to socialism and anarchism.

Mass mobilization led many factories to replace their lost male workforce with women. Women worked on railroads, in factories and mines, and as truck drivers. Often wives replaced their husbands on the job; for example, 20 percent of women working on German streetcars were replacing their husbands.[56] In Russia, the proportion of women in industry expanded from 1914 to 1917, from 26.6 percent to 43.2.[57] In Britain and France, the war shifted the nature of women's work away from domestic service and toward industry. By 1918, nearly a million British women worked in munitions factories alone.[58] Munitions work earned good wages, but the job was dangerous. There were frequent explosions and the TNT poisoned workers and turned their skin yellow, earning them the name "canary girls." The numbers of married women working outside the home also increased. Although some wanted to contribute to the war effort, most also needed to put food on the table and keep a roof over their heads. Despite deprivation and difficulties, many remembered this as an exhilarating time of their lives.

Although World War I brought more European women into the workforce, work outside the home remained a difficult option for many. They faced shortages of basic goods, lack of childcare and medical care, little training, and resistance from men who felt they should stay home. In the end, most German women did not work outside the home during the war.[59] Munitions factories hired more women, but they took them from other industrial jobs. Moreover, male unions prevented factory women from earning equal pay or taking over men's jobs permanently. In Romania, where industrialization was limited, women did not take up men's work. Most Romanians still lived in the countryside and felt that women should stay home and care for children and the household. The popular press portrayed western European women as unwomanly, even traitorous to their sex, for working in war industries because the weapons they made destroyed families. As a consequence, Romania suffered from labor shortages, which hurt both the military and the home front. When

**BRITISH WOMEN CARPENTERS (1917).** To put as many men as possible on the front, women took over jobs traditionally held by men. Many women enjoyed the freedom and comradeship that came with their new positions. *(Corbis.)*

Germany occupied parts of Romania in the last two years of the war, conditions worsened, and those women who sought work for the Germans, usually as domestics, were condemned as traitors.

## Antiwar Activism

Many women opposed the war, asserting that feminism and pacifism were inseparable. They initiated many international conferences to promote peace. In March 1915, socialist women, led by Clara Zetkin, met in neutral Switzerland. The congress passed a series of resolutions that reasserted the common socialist position that capitalism and oppression of the working classes were their common enemies. In addition, participants argued that because the conflict took men away from political action, women were obligated to speak out against the war on men's behalf. A larger gathering of women opposed to the war assembled at The Hague in the Netherlands a month later. Physician Aletta Jacobs (1854–1929) convened a meeting for all women who supported women's suffrage and peaceful resolutions to international conflicts

(see **Women's Lives:** Aletta Jacobs, Physician, Suffragist, Pacifist). Jane Addams, who led forty-nine American delegates, agreed to chair the congress, and the gathering gave rise to the International Committee of Women for Permanent Peace (later to become the Women's International League for Peace and Freedom). Although the French, Russian, and German governments prevented many women from attending, the congress drew women from both sides of the conflict into a productive dialogue and participants agreed to meet with their governments to press for peace negotiations. Afterward, Addams met with President Woodrow Wilson (1913–1921). Anita Augspurg, who led the German delegation, returned to Germany and founded the German Women's Committee for Lasting Peace.

Participants also worked locally to support women affected by the war. Pacifists associated with the Women's Suffrage League in Stuttgart, Germany, telegraphed the kaiser to stop the war. In Hamburg they protested Germany's invasion of Belgium. German peace activists also tried to educate teachers who would in turn educate their

## Aletta Jacobs, Physician, Suffragist, Pacifist

Aletta Jacobs's career reflects both the lifestyle of a new woman and the close connections among the women's reform movements. Jacobs was a pioneer in education, women's health care, and political reform. Her training as a medical doctor and subsequent work with poor women led her to connect women's lack of legal, sexual, and political rights to their poverty. She devoted her life to trying to improve women's lives throughout the world.

Aletta Jacobs was born to a Dutch-Jewish family. Her father, a physician, inspired her to become a physician as well. Although she was the first woman admitted to the University of Groningen, her professors and fellow students accepted her. After completing her studies in 1879, she opened a medical practice in Amsterdam, where she treated poor and sick women. Having witnessed the brutal treatment of prostitutes undergoing forced medical exams, she joined the crusade against the regulation of prostitutes. She also waged a campaign on behalf of female store clerks who had to stand for up to sixteen hours a day. She believed that such working conditions caused lifelong gynecological problems.

Jacobs also came to believe that much of women's poverty derived from their inability to control their fertility. From 1882 to 1894, she ran a free medical clinic for working women where she dispensed the newly invented cervical caps. Her frank public discussions about birth control and the relationship between women's poor health and multiple pregnancies created a furor. Many doctors equated birth control with abortion, and newspaper editorials denounced her for indecency. Nonetheless, Jacobs found that women across the country wanted information on how to limit their families' size.

Jacobs's advocacy of women's rights shaped her personal life. In 1892, she married Carel Victor Gerritsen (1850–1905), a freethinker, liberal politician, and longtime friend. The couple maintained separate finances and separate apartments within the same house, and Aletta kept her last name. Carel shared her feminism and the belief that women should be treated equally in law, politics, and society.

The cause that most inspired Jacobs was women's suffrage. She believed that if women had the right to vote, militarism would be less of a political problem and that women would compel governments to provide social services for the poor. Between 1903 and 1919, she was the chair of the Dutch Association for Women's Suffrage and spoke and wrote on behalf of the International Women's Suffrage Alliance. In 1908, she organized the International Woman Suffrage Alliance Conference in Amsterdam. She went on speaking engagements all over the world and collaborated with other suffrage leaders, including Carrie Chapman Catt, the head of the U.S. National Women's Suffrage Association. Jacobs and Catt toured the world together between 1911 and 1912, speaking about women's rights.

At the start of World War I, Aletta Jacobs convened the International Congress of Women at The Hague, where she and Jane Addams promoted a peaceful end to international conflict. She met with U.S. president Woodrow Wilson in an effort to convince him to broker a peaceful settlement, but quickly realized that his limited powers as president and limited knowledge of European politics made him an ineffective peace advocate. At the end of World War I, Aletta worked to reform the Treaty of Versailles, believing it was grounded in hatred and revenge and would only bring more war.

In 1919, Dutch women gained the right to vote, and Jacobs turned her attention to reforming citizenship laws. Women who married men from another country automatically lost citizenship in their countries of birth.

The last ten years of her life were marked by ill health and declining finances. Jacobs had given up her practice in 1904 to devote herself to her activism. In 1924, she published her memoirs and received national acclaim for her service to women and the Netherlands. She died on August 10, 1929.

---

Source: Aletta Jacobs, *Memories: My Life as an International Leader in Health, Suffrage, and Peace*, trans. Annie Wright (New York: Feminist Press, 1996).

students about peace. In Glasgow, Scotland, activists supported rent strikes by military families who could not afford increases in their rent. In response to these strikes the British government passed the Rent Restriction Act for the whole nation, limiting rent increases for the duration of the war. In the United States, Emma Goldman founded the No-Conscription League in 1917. In public speeches she urged men to resist the draft. The group was popular among immigrants in New York City who had fled conscription in their native countries only to be forced into service in the United States.

Many felt threatened by the critiques of female activists. Nationalist women's societies, suffrage groups such as the Pankhursts' WSPU, and many of France's mainstream feminist organizations denounced the meeting at The Hague as antithetical to their nations' interests. The French police maintained a list of pacifists, which included not only feminists but also trade unionists opposed to the war. In 1917, French feminist schoolteacher Hélène Brion (1882–1962) was arrested for the new crime of "defeatism." Defeatists advocated a negotiated settlement rather than a fight to victory. At her trial, the prosecution criticized her for her politics, her influence on children, and her mannish clothing. By framing the case in this way, the prosecution linked radicalism with deviant sexuality.[60] Brion's defense focused on the hypocrisy of a government that would try her for a political crime when as a woman she had no political rights. In Britain, Nellie Best, an associate of Sylvia Pankhurst, received six months in prison for interfering with military recruitment. In the United States, Kate Richards O'Hare (1877–1948), a socialist lecturer, was indicted under the Espionage Act in 1917 for claiming that "war corrupted motherhood."[61] She received a sentence of five years in prison, which President Wilson commuted after the war. Emma Goldman's antidraft rallies grew violent when police raided them. The police dramatically arrested Goldman, brought her to trial, and convicted her of defying the Selective Service Act. She received a two-year prison sentence. In Germany, the government harassed Augspurg and her committee but stopped short of arresting her lest she become a martyr. Clearly, governments took these women's messages seriously.

As the war dragged on, morale declined in much of Europe, and many outside the antiwar movement began to talk about ending the war. When the United States entered the war, the Germans countered declining morale at home by creating the Woman's Home Army. The women were instructed to listen in on conversations on streetcars and other public places. If they heard defeatist talk, they were to demand identification and turn the speaker over to authorities. In music halls, they were to request that musicians play patriotic music. In front of food stores, they were to counter criticism of food rationing and "shame the parties concerned."[62]

World War I endangered women as never before. Millions fought hunger, government scrutiny, and violence. During these difficult times, many women learned new independence as they struggled to maintain their families. Despite the high stakes, Western society did not willingly relinquish traditional gender roles even as it compelled women to defy them on behalf of the war effort.

## The World Turned Upside Down: Gender and World War I

The war brought dramatic changes to society. Large numbers of women entered the workplace and lived independently. At the same time, the war left millions of wounded men unable to care for themselves. These changes often inverted gender roles and accentuated tensions between the generations. Older men and women criticized the move away from Victorian standards of behavior, while the younger generation, who worked and fought in the war, felt alienated and resentful of the demands and the criticisms they endured.

From the outbreak of the war, concerns about women's roles on the home front filled propaganda. Drawing on the Victorian ideology of the domestic angel, recruitment posters emphasized women's domesticity and identities as mothers. One popular British poster showed a mother and her two children watching a regiment of soldiers march by. The caption reads, "Women of Britain say 'Go!'"[63] Posters such as these promoted the idea that men were fighting to protect their families. After the German air raids on the British seaside town of Scarborough in 1915, posters showed ruined buildings and homeless women and children. One poster reminded viewers that the air raids had killed 78 women and children and wounded 228 more. Headlining the posters was the question, "Men of Britain! Will you stand this?"[64] By invoking the idea that attacks on women and children compromised men's masculinity, recruiters hoped to inspire more men to enlist.

Women's sexual vulnerability filled the images that came out of Belgium after the German invasion. Newspaper articles, recruitment posters, and newsreels deployed the metaphor of rape to describe the German invasion of neutral Belgium. This propaganda turned Germans into brutal and bloodthirsty Huns. Depictions of Edith Cavell's execution as a spy also defined German barbarism in terms of women's sexual vulnerability. Although forty-eight years old when she died, postcards and posters routinely portrayed Cavell as a young virginal woman brutally murdered by hypermasculinized Germans. While Allied propaganda emphasized gender and sexuality, German officials countered with explanations that they treated all spies the same, regardless of sex.[65]

At the beginning of the war, British women participated in this gendering of war duties with the white-feather campaign. The white feather was a symbol of cowardice. During this campaign, women passed out white feathers to men they believed were avoiding military service. One poster asked women, "If your best boy does not think that you and your country are worth fighting for—do you think he is WORTHY of you?"[66] Ultimately, the campaign backfired, when women inadvertently handed out feathers to soldiers out of uniform while on leave or men wounded in the war and no longer able to fight. Recruitment efforts in all countries relied on the belief that the war was to preserve not only national security but also a way of life in which women were mothers in need of male protection.

In the context of the war, women's actions and sexuality threatened many deeply held beliefs and highlighted society's ambivalence toward women's war contributions. In France, officials worried simultaneously about the declining birthrate and a rise in illegitimate babies. France's rate of illegitimacy rose from 8.4 percent before World War I to 14.2 percent in 1917.[67] Many of these babies were the product of liaisons between women and soldiers, either native French or occupying Germans. The existence of "Boche babies" (*Boche* is a derogatory term for Germans) created a complicated controversy over the babies' nationalities. Many argued

that Frenchwomen pregnant from rape should have access to abortions, then illegal in France. Yet those who worried about declining populations resisted this solution. The Catholic Church and pronatalist officials joined forces arguing that motherhood was a service to France. Advocates of legal abortion, inspired by eugenic theories, worried that these babies would inherit their German fathers' aggressive and brutal natures. Critics countered that French maternal love would triumph and create good French citizens. The infanticide case of Josephine Barthélemy, who claimed that a German raped her in November of 1915, vividly expressed these fears. Barthélemy claimed that the child had been born dead, although her defense lawyers engaged in a lengthy debate about the meaning of motherhood in cases of rape. The court ultimately acquitted Barthélemy early in 1917. However, pronatalist beliefs and religious and cultural beliefs about women's primary duty to motherhood prevented the legalization of abortion, even in the case of rape.

Women pregnant out of wedlock, but not from rape, provoked different concerns. While many of these women claimed that their impending motherhood was war service, their uncontrolled sexual behavior shocked traditionalists. The fathers of many of these children were soldiers and their absence or death created obstacles to their children's eventual legitimacy. In response, French legislators legalized marriage by proxy and posthumous legitimization of children whose fathers had died fighting for France. These provisions expired after the war. In Britain, Parliament did not seek governmental solutions to the problems of illegitimacy. Instead, the country debated whether to provide financial support for these women and their children, many of whom were the products of long-term relationships. Advocates of financial support argued that these women and children gave up their men and needed separation pay, just as married women did. Critics countered that government support condoned women's sexual misbehavior.

Women's freedom of movement and its association with sexuality also raised fears that women's sexuality would hinder the war effort. In England, DORA reinstated the Contagious Diseases Act because officials worried about the increase in venereal disease among soldiers. Governments also linked women's sexuality to spying. By far the most notorious case of spying and sexual influence was the case of Mata Hari, born Margaretha Geertruida Zelle (1876–1917). A native of the Netherlands, she married a colonial officer and moved to the Dutch East Indies. In 1902, she left her husband and daughter for the life of an exotic dancer in Paris. Drawing on her familiarity with Indonesian culture, she created nude dances that attracted large audiences. Meanwhile, she had a number of sexual relationships with politicians and military men. Her travel, lavish lifestyle, and sexual relations with many men made the French and British governments suspicious. The specifics of her espionage career remain unclear, but she accepted money from the French government to spy for them, traveling to Spain and Belgium on its behalf. There is some evidence that the Germans recruited her to spy for them as well. In 1917, the French arrested and tried her for spying for Germany, although she never passed on any information. After her conviction, she was executed. In life, Mata Hari did no real damage to any countries' war efforts, but in death she became notorious as a seductress who sent thousands of young men to their deaths in the trenches.[68] Her growing reputation contributed to suspicions about women's loyalty and anxieties over female sexuality.

Efforts to control female sexuality faced repeated challenges not only from women who relished their newfound freedom but also from situations created by the war itself. In Germany, the government asked women to cut their hair in order to use it to make belts because hemp was in short supply. A poster of a woman in front of a cross holding out her hair emphasized the sacrifice she was making.[69] Although short hair became patriotic, German society was slow to adjust its definition of femininity, as short hair had been considered "mannish." Similarly, limited supplies of cloth raised hemlines, revealing women's legs.

Soldiers were not immune from the heightened concerns with gender roles. Trench warfare brought on a new medical condition called shell shock, which in many people's minds, effeminized its victims. Men exhibited a variety of symptoms from nervous twitching to paralysis, hallucinations, and nightmares. Physicians commented on shell shock's similarities to women's hysteria. Films such as the 1916 *The Battle of the Somme* contributed to effeminate images of wounded soldiers by describing German prisoners of war, sick with shell shock, as "nerve-shattered."[70] World War I was the first war in which mental breakdown played a significant role. By 1916, as many as 40 percent of casualties in all the combat zones suffered from shell shock. In 1918, in Britain alone, more than twenty military hospitals were devoted to their care, treating a total of eighty thousand cases by the end of the war.[71] Although initially doctors had difficulty understanding shell shock, as the war progressed, doctors came to understand it as an emotional or mental disturbance produced by the war itself. For the most part, treatment of shell shock involved attempts to remasculinize the soldier so that he could return to the front as quickly as possible.

The large numbers of wounded men requiring continual care by women also contributed to the reversal of gender roles. One Red Cross poster showed a large nurse cradling a wounded soldier on a stretcher in her arms. The out-of-proportion nurse and her patient stand over the caption "The Greatest Mother in the World."[72] While valorizing the work of Red Cross nurses, the poster infantilized the soldier. The real and perceived exuberance of women working for the war effort added to men's war crises. Women took men's jobs, and when wounded men returned home, they could not resume their places as heads of the household. This tension between home front and military front found its way into war literature. For example, D. H. Lawrence's poem "Eloi, Eloi, Lama Sabacthani" (1915) asks,

> *Why do the women follow us, satisfied / Feed on our wounds like bread, receive our blood / Like glittering seed upon them for fulfillment?*"[73]

Women become insatiable furies in need of men's blood.

The emasculation of the wounded soldier became complete during recovery in military hospitals. Recuperation required the care of physical and occupational therapists, many of whom were female volunteers. The underlying idea was to restore health and physical coordination and to provide activities for the men. However, "reconstruction aides" often taught basket weaving, knitting, and other handwork identified with women.[74] Although these activities sought to reinvigorate men, they nonetheless contributed to the sense of wounded men becoming like women.

The totality of World War I changed everything. In order to win the war, countries asked their women to break out of some traditional roles, while remaining in others. The contradictions inherent in these demands created anxiety for societies confronted with a rising number of independent, wage-earning women. At the same time, the realities of trench war changed men, breaking their bodies and minds so that they could not return to their prewar roles as breadwinners and heads of families. Although roles changed during the war, the underlying belief in traditional gender roles did not disappear. Even as women took on men's roles, society came to view and value their contributions as secondary and thus maintained the gender hierarchy.

## New States, New Citizens

By 1917, the death toll both at home and on the fronts wore down the European population, and governments faced increased opposition to the war. A worldwide flu epidemic further taxed exhausted medical staff, government resources, and war-ravished families. Finally, the end of the war on November 11, 1918, brought victory for the Allies. The peace settlement introduced lofty political ideals of self-determination and international cooperation. However, many working-class men and women, particularly in Germany, remained resentful and alienated by their wartime experiences. Women across Europe returned to their demands for suffrage, arguing that they had proven their loyalty and deserved full political participation. Instead of peace and prosperity, Europe faced unrest, as socialists, communists, women, and nationalists rejected the political system that brought them war and denied them political involvement. Women gained the vote in some countries, but in others, opponents continued to assert that women belonged at home, not in politics. Just as the violence came to an end in most of Europe, socialists seized power in Russia, establishing a new state determined to end class and gender inequality.

### The Great Influenza Epidemic

Influenza accompanied U.S. troops across the Atlantic, creating a worldwide pandemic that would kill more people than the war. The "Spanish Flu," as many called it, added new horrors and tragedy to those trying to cope with the war. The flu appeared almost simultaneously in Massachusetts, West Africa, and France. In August of 1918, Camp Devens, an army base some thirty miles west of Boston, Massachusetts, was overcrowded with forty-five thousand men; it proved to be an ideal breeding ground for disease. Over the next ten months, the disease spread across the United States Europe, Africa, and Asia. Scandinavia suffered a second bout in 1920. Ports and cities suffered the worst, as dense populations and limited social services made it difficult to quarantine victims.[75] Among those worst hit were the poor and in the United States, immigrants, who lived in crowded conditions, with little access to effective medical care. Globally scholars estimated that fifty million people may have died.[76] In Europe, the highest death tolls were in Spain and Italy. About 200,000 people died in Britain and Wales, and the United States lost 675,000 to the disease. One of the most striking aspects of the epidemic was its heavy toll on young adults. Both parents of American novelist and social critic Mary McCarthy (1912–1989) were killed in the epidemic. In her autobiography *Memories of a Catholic Girlhood* (1957), she described her embarrassment about the gratitude she was supposed to show her grandfather for raising her and the pity heaped on her as an orphan.

Autopsies on victims revealed bluish lungs filled with mucus, causing the victim to drown in his or her own bodily fluids. About 20 percent of those infected quickly recovered, but the rest either died or suffered a long convalescence as their lungs healed. The rapidity and severity of the epidemic mystified medical experts and taxed medical staff. As the disease spread to Europe, it added to the burdens already facing military hospitals.

A shortage of nurses would be a constant problem in trying to address the epidemic. In Camp Devens, ninety out of the three hundred regular nurses, nearly one-third, became sick and could not attend to the sick soldiers.[77] As the disease moved into the rest of the United States in the autumn of 1918, terrible nurse shortages appeared in its wake. In Philadelphia, the Lebanon Hospital had only 3 nurses for 125 flu patients. To cope with the crisis the Emergency Aid Nursing Committee and the Visiting Nurses

Association took charge of the city nurses.[78] Medical and nursing students were pressed into service and retired doctors called out of retirement. In an effort to stem the disease, municipal authorities shut down schools and encouraged teachers to volunteer in hospitals. In San Francisco, an advertisement urged women to help out, explaining that work in hospitals was just as important as war work: "Women of San Francisco. We Beseech Your Help. You Can Save as Many Lives Today in San Francisco as You Could in France. The Afflicted—Children, Men, Women, The Bread-Winners of the Family—Are Calling for Your Merciful Ministrations."[79]

As workers became sick, basic services, such as the telephone system, which depended on operators, faltered. Philadelphia did not have enough people to embalm corpses or build coffins, and the stacks of bodies began to mount.[80] Theaters and restaurants also closed, and public health officials required people to wear masks in public. When some women in San Francisco tried to exchange masks for heavy veils, because they were better looking and less cumbersome, the Board of Health declared them illegal. Resistance to masks became widespread, and journalists even photographed the San Francisco mayor, a Supreme Court judge, a congressman, and a rear admiral at a boxing match without masks.[81] In Spain, where eight million were sick, including the king, many government agencies shut down as did public transportation.[82]

Despite its terrible devastation, the flu epidemic of 1918 has received relatively little attention by writers and scholars. Katherine Anne Porter's (1890–1980) short story "Pale Horse, Pale Rider" (1939) remains one of the few literary treatments of the epidemic. A journalist in Denver, she nearly died of the flu in 1919. She was so sick that her newspaper had already written her obituary. While Porter recovered, her fiancé an army lieutenant died in the epidemic and she chronicled the dislocation and pain of this loss in her later work.

## The End of the War

The U.S. entry into the war added two million men to the Allies' side and turned the tide of the war. As conditions deteriorated for Germany, the government faced considerable unrest at home as civilians, particularly women, lost faith in the war and the government. Working-class women faced starvation from the failed food-rationing system and rioted over the lack of food. German sailors weary of the destruction and horror mutinied.

Unrest remained strongest in Germany but spread among women in other countries as well. Many distanced themselves from the goals of the war and their governments, as they realized that even though their governments expected their support and obedience, they refused to give them a voice in politics. Female munitions workers in Germany and France struck for better wages, Sundays off, and an end to the war. Even in non-belligerent countries such as Spain, food and fuel became increasingly scarce and living standards declined. In January of 1918, working women in Barcelona struck, and housewives joined them in protesting living conditions. Their protest was so strong that the government had to use military force to end the demonstrations.

Recognizing the potential of this widespread unrest, Rosa Luxemburg and Karl Liebknecht (1874–1919), the founders of the radical Spartacus League, began distributing antiwar and prorevolutionary literature throughout Germany. Luxemburg had spent much of the war in prison for her opposition to it. Now with the end in sight, she demanded greater internationalism and political power for workers and women and denounced socialists who had supported the war. By early 1918, many shared her opinions; in September of that year, demonstrations and strikes paralyzed the German capital of Berlin. On November 3, the Austro-Hungarian Empire surrendered and, under pressure from nationalists within the empire and the Allies, dissolved into separate independent states. Revolution erupted in Germany on November 7, when soldiers and sailors left their posts and joined workers and housewives in the streets. The kaiser abdicated two days later and a German republic was declared. On November 11, an armistice ending combat went into effect.

The peace talks that followed the armistice opened on an optimistic note. Negotiators hoped to create a settlement that would guarantee perpetual peace and end state-sponsored aggression. Yet divisions and disagreements quickly emerged. Germany was not allowed to participate, and Russia, occupied with its own revolution, did not engage in the talks. U.S. president Woodrow Wilson worked to create the League of Nations as a forum for international grievances; however,

France and Britain were more interested in revenge on Germany, and the U.S. Congress wanted to return to a policy of isolation. The Treaty of Versailles established the League of Nations, but without the participation of Germany, the new Soviet Union, and the United States. As a result, the organization was weak and ineffective. The Treaty also created a new European order (see Map 12.2). Out of the Habsburg Empire came the new states of Austria, Hungary, and Czechoslovakia. Poland gained territory from both Germany and the Habsburg Empire. Serbia united with the southern Slavs of the former empire to form a united Slavic country called the Kingdom of the Serbs, Croats, and Slovenes (renamed Yugoslavia in 1929). However, many national groups felt their own concerns and interests trampled in the face of the overwhelming power of Britain, France, and the United States. The Treaty also mandated that Germany pay unlimited war payments to France for its aggression and damage to the country. The new map of Europe that emerged from the Versailles Treaty solved some problems, but it created many more that would haunt the next decades of the twentieth century.

Looming over the negotiations were the memories of the dead and the tragic faces of the survivors. The mortality rates of World War I were staggering. An estimated 723,000 British and Irish men, 1,327,000 Frenchmen, and 1,811,000 Russians died. Nearly 5.5 million died on the Allied side, and the Central Powers lost more than 4 million.[83] The mortality of men left hundreds of thousands of war widows: 600,000 in France, 500,000 in Germany, and 200,000 each in Italy and Britain.[84]

## Postwar Politics

The numbers of widows, orphans, and wounded men and the experience of a home front changed many people's relationships with government. They expected their governments to alleviate their suffering. New government programs provided some relief, but it was usually not enough. For example, the new German republic's inability to please the wide spectrum of political interests led to civil unrest. Socialists like Rosa Luxemburg wanted a full-scale revolution, and other groups demanded increased worker rights and democ-racy, but not at the cost of nationalizing all industries. Clashes between socialist factions broke out and the Social Democrats, who played a strong role in the new government, called in the military to put down the revolt. They arrested members of the Spartacus League, including Luxemburg and Liebknecht. While in police custody, they were killed. Street violence continued and social and political reforms stalled.

Socialist violence in Germany and Russia fueled a "Red Scare" in the United States. As the U.S. Congress grew increasingly isolationist, it feared foreign agitators. Relying on legislation passed during the war to regulate speech and public behavior, U.S. attorney general A. Mitchell Palmer (1872–1936) went looking for communists. His officers from the judicial department raided immigrant associations and trade unions such as the Union of Russian Workers. In what became known as the Palmer Raids, they arrested hundreds of immigrants and union organizers and harassed pacifist women such as Jane Addams and Carrie Chapman Catt. In 1919, the government deported 250 immigrants to the Soviet Union, including Emma Goldman, who had recently been released from prison. As the violence and excess of the Palmer raids escalated, public support for the anti-red campaign declined, but distrust of foreigners and involvement in foreign affairs remained.

After the war, many women expected to be rewarded for their wartime support with suffrage. The creation of new states in eastern Europe raised the question of women's suffrage, and the new constitutions in the Soviet Union (1917), Czechoslovakia (1918), Germany (1919), Austria (1920), Poland (1921), and Hungary (1925) all enfranchised women.

In Britain, voting reform began as the war ended. Suffragist organizations, such as the NUWSS, which had stopped its activities during the war, resumed demands for the right to vote. Britain still based suffrage on sex and wealth, and politicians wanted to make sure that all returning soldiers could vote. However, suffragists insisted women be included in these reforms. In 1917, the Representation of the People Bill passed the House of Commons, and a year later passed the House of Lords. It gave women over thirty the right to vote. Many acknowledged that this bill was a compromise that ignored the women who

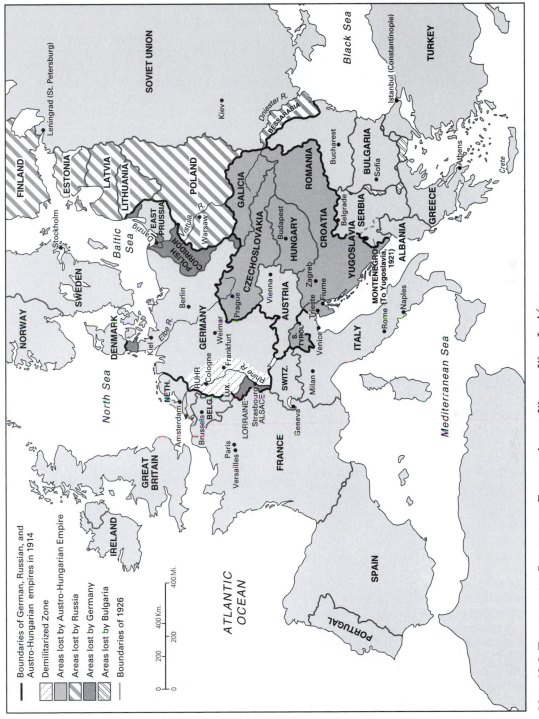

***Map 12.2*** **TERRITORIAL CHANGES IN EUROPE AFTER WORLD WAR I.** After World War I, the victors redrew the map of Europe, hoping to avert future conflicts.

had worked most directly in the war. Millicent Garrett Fawcett (1847–1929), leader of the NUWSS, admitted that women had achieved not full enfranchisement, but a "motherhood franchise," meaning that most women of voting age were generally mothers, not single women.[85]

In the United States, Alice Paul and the NWP protested throughout the war for women's suffrage. Picketing and chaining herself to the White House fence, Paul and her colleagues likened women's second-class citizenship to Germany's oppression and barbarism. Congress finally passed the Twenty-first Amendment in June of 1919, and the next year, enough states ratified the Nineteenth Amendment to grant suffrage to all women, except Native American women living on reservations. This last group did not gain suffrage until 1924, when the United States extended suffrage to all Native Americans. Moreover, women's suffrage was virtually meaningless to African American women, who faced discriminations when trying to register to vote.

Suffrage faced stiff opposition in other parts of Europe. After extended debates, Romania's new constitution of 1923 denied women equal civil and political rights, despite the government's claim that it was a liberal democracy. In France, the postwar government debated suffrage, and a suffrage bill passed one of the two houses of the government; however, unable to pass the conservative Senate, the bill was defeated in November 1922.

## Gender and the Russian Revolution

Russia's entry into World War I was disastrous for the tsarist regime. Russia also experienced the horrors and dislocation of the war, but the autocratic government proved incapable of relieving the suffering. In the short term, mobilization gave women more responsibilities at home and opened up more jobs for them, but the government's lack of preparedness to deal with the influx of casualties and the crumbling economy made life intolerable. When food riots broke out in 1917, the government collapsed and nearly a century of underground revolutionary work came to fruition. As in previous movements, female revolutionaries not only held important leadership roles, they lived nontraditional lives, disavowing traditional expectations for women and bringing new gender ideals to the revolution.

Although Russians initially supported the war, repeated defeats and continuing deprivation caused many to question their country's participation. Moreover, distrustful of its citizens and their initiatives, the tsar repeatedly refused to allow civilians to participate in the war effort. Because of their previous criticisms of the government's social policies, the tsar prevented many doctors from working with wounded soldiers or setting up much needed hospitals. By 1917, Russians were starving and conditions were worse on the front. Short of food, ammunition, and competent leadership, soldiers began deserting in large numbers. On International Woman's Day, March 8, 1917, angry mobs of working-class women assembled in Saint Petersburg demanding bread and peace. Over the next few days, thousands of men and women joined them. The soldiers guarding the palace refused to fire on them, and the revolution started. On March 15, Tsar Nicholas abdicated.

The tsarist government fell quickly and a provisional government, led by Alexander Kerensky (1881–1970), came to power. Largely dominated by liberal democrats, Russia remained in the war. Many elite women supported the provisional government. They had not suffered as a result of the war and even enjoyed their new roles as nurses and war volunteers. They were completely alienated from the masses of working-class women who had marched on the Winter Palace in March.

Tensions within the socialist movement led to continued political instability. At the turn of the century, Russian socialists had split over how to implement revolution. The Mensheviks favored working with the liberals and gradually introducing socialism through a process of worker education. Revolution would be the spontaneous result of these efforts. The Bolsheviks, led by Vladimir Ilyich Lenin (1870–1923), believed that a small elite vanguard of revolutionaries with secret and wide-ranging powers must impose revolution. The Mensheviks' support of the war led Alexandra Kollontai (1873–1952) and others to join Lenin, despite their reservations about his revolutionary theories.

Exiled Bolsheviks, including Lenin and Kollontai, returned to Russia after the tsar's abdication. They gathered support for their revolutionary agenda by promising bread and peace. At the same time, the provisional government was further weakened by continual strikes, demonstrations, and violence. Female factory workers, laundresses, and soldiers' wives protested against the government. On November 7–8, 1917, the Bolsheviks overthrew the provisional government.

The coup gave the Bolsheviks control of Saint Petersburg and then Moscow. However, their control in the provinces was far from complete. Although most provinces had workers councils, or soviets, they did not automatically join the Bolsheviks, despite Lenin's slogan of "All power to the soviets." With control of the capitals, the Bolsheviks quickly sued for peace, and the Treaty of Brest-Litovsk (1918) ended Russia's participation in World War I. Not all Bolsheviks agreed with Lenin's strategies. Even some of his closest supporters, including Alexandra Kollontai, felt that he had conceded too much territory and that he should have negotiated with the German workers and not the government. This conflict among the Bolsheviks would fester for several more years as pragmatists and idealists struggled to establish a government.

Russia's exit from World War I left the nation embroiled in a massive civil war. The Bolsheviks finally declared victory in 1920, but the experience profoundly influenced the character of their government. Military opposition and a continual need for food and supplies militarized the Bolshevik government. The anti-Bolshevik or "White" forces, a disunited group of armies more loyal to individual military leaders than to political ideologies, opposed the Bolsheviks and their Red Army. Several European nations and the United States invaded in attempts to aid the Whites. To fight the opposition and rebuild Russia's shattered economy, the Bolsheviks resorted to authoritarianism. The government compelled peasants to give up most of their harvests and resorted to conscripted labor. Opponents received beatings, imprisonment, and executions. The Bolsheviks justified their authoritarian policies as necessary to root out opposition, to abolish private property, and to establish a socialist state. However, the strategy marked a change from the egalitarian ideology that many socialists had promoted and expected. In the end, the authoritarian government distrusted all who questioned it.[86]

The pressing need for soldiers to fight the civil war made building an army the Bolsheviks' primary focus in the early years of their rule. Women, who joined the Red Army in large numbers, composed about 2 percent of the forces, although most did not serve in combat positions. Most of the sixty-six thousand women worked as clerks or nurses. A few notable women also served as propagandists, rallying the troops to support the Bolsheviks and educating the soldiers about socialism. Among the new female recruits, 14 percent served as spies for the Red Army, reporting on troop movements and supply depots, maintaining local socialist organizations, and working to convince deserting White soldiers to join the revolution.[87] Women's visibility drew comment and controversy. Many women reported difficulties getting male soldiers to take them seriously and follow their orders.

Women who became successful military leaders, such as Evgeniia Bosh (1879–1925) and Rozaliia Zemliachka (1875–1947), exhibited the quality of *tverdost*, or "hardness," cultivated by prerevolutionary female Bolsheviks. Tverdost encompassed a variety of characteristics, including ideological purity, steadfastness, and ruthlessness.[88] Zemliachka dressed in men's clothes and reveled in the growing authoritarianism of the Bolsheviks. Because of her uncompromising loyalty and military skills, she was put in charge of rooting out White opposition in the Crimea. She interpreted her orders as a license for mass murder. Bosh could be similarly ruthless, but she disagreed with the authoritarian direction of the party. Her inability to adhere to the new party line ended her military career despite several notable successes in the field.[89] Alienated from the revolution, she committed suicide in 1925.

The years of the civil war were marked by frightful loss of life and destruction of property. Epidemics of cholera, typhus, and scarlet fever raged through the country. In 1918–1919, typhus alone killed one and a half million people. The combination of war, disease, and famine killed sixteen million Russians between 1914 and 1921, leaving millions of orphaned children. By 1921, there were 540,000 children in orphanages, and probably nearly that many homeless. The Bolsheviks could not provide basic social services such as food, clothes, or shelter.[90]

Although the Revolution of 1917 had succeeded, many challenges lay ahead. The new government would not only have to alleviate the tragic consequences of World War I and civil war, but it would also have to create a new society out of the ashes of the old regime. In this new society, the goal of gender equality would fall victim to other, more pressing priorities.

The end of World War I was fraught with crisis. The flu epidemic killed millions, and food shortages taxed governments' abilities to maintain order among civilians. Unable to cope, the tsar abdicated in Russia, and in the ensuing civil war, socialists took over and tried to build a society based on class and gender equality. When the war finally ended, the victors set about redrawing the map of Europe, and women expected to be rewarded for their war service with suffrage. Although some countries granted universal suffrage, many governments balked at granting women the vote. Suffragists again took to the streets, but with mixed results.

## CONCLUSION

The twentieth century opened with both new opportunities for women and increased consciousness of their political marginalization. In an effort to gain a political voice, women joined political movements and some used violence to achieve their goals. Their activism made many uncomfortable because they perceived it as attacking family life and traditional values. The optimism of the belle époque quickly deteriorated in the face of total war. Advances in military technology brought war to every facet of life and created a new society in which traditional gender norms no longer seemed to apply. Hopeful that their wartime service would be rewarded, women stepped up the demands for suffrage and equal rights when the war ended. However, even in the new socialist Soviet Union, women found it difficult to cast off old associations of submission and domesticity in order to achieve a more gender-equal society.

## NOTES

1. Teresa Davy, "'A Cissy Job for Men; A Nice Job for Girls': Women Shorthand Typists in London, 1900–1939," in *Our Work, Our Lives, Our Words*, ed. Leonore Davidoff and Belinda Westover (Totowa, NJ: Barnes and Noble Books, 1986), 127.

2. Davy, 129.

3. Joan Scott, "The Woman Worker," in *A History of Women in the West: Emerging Feminism from Revolution to World War*, ed. Genevieve Fraisse and Michelle Perrot (Cambridge, MA: Harvard University Press, 1993), 407.

4. Anne T. Quartararo, *Women Teachers and Popular Education in Nineteenth-Century France: Social Values and Corporate Identity at the Normal School Institution* (Newark, NJ: University of Delaware Press, 1995), 161.

5. Sarah Deustch, *Women and the City: Gender, Space, and Power in Boston, 1870–1940* (Oxford: Oxford University Press, 2000), 91.

6. Viv Gardner, *The New Woman and Her Sisters: Feminism and the Theatre, 1850–1914* (Ann Arbor: University of Michigan Press, 1992), 2, 5.

7. Maureen E. Montgomery, *Displaying Women: Spectacles of Leisure in Edith Wharton's New York* (New York: Routledge, 1998), 104.

8. *New York Times,* March 17, 1895, 1, 14.

9. Marjorie Rosen, *Popcorn Venus: Women, Movies, and the American Dream* (New York: Coward, McCann, and Goeghegan, 1973), 38.

10. Rosen, 60.

11. Mary Louise Roberts, *Disruptive Acts: The New Woman in Fin-de-Siécle France* (Chicago: University of Chicago Press, 2002), 90.

12. Quoted in Roberts, 49.

13. Whitney Chadwick, *Women, Art, and Society* (London: Thames and Hudson, 1990), 228.

14. Jane A. Sharp, "Redrawing the Margins of Russian Vanguard Art: Natalia Goncharova's Trial for Pornography in 1910," in *Sexuality and the Body in Russian Culture*, ed. Jane T. Costlow, Stephanie Sandler, and Judith Vowles (Stanford, CA: Stanford University Press, 1993), 98.

15. Louise McReynolds, *Russia at Play: Leisure Activities at the End of the Tsarist Era* (Ithaca, NY: Cornell University Press, 2003), 1.

16. Christine Ruane, "Vestal Virgins of St. Petersburg: School Teachers and the 1897 Marriage Ban, *The Russian Review* 50 (1991): 167.

17. Ruane, 171.

18. Quoted in McReynolds, 5.

19. Quoted in Barbara Franzoi, *At the Very Least She Pays the Rent: Women and German Industrialization, 1871–1914* (Westport, CT: Greenwood Press, 1985), 144–145.

20. Rose L. Glickman, *Russian Factory Women: Workplace and Society, 1880–1914* (Berkeley: University of California Press, 1984), 186.

21. Glickman, 192.

22. Glickman, 194.

23. Amy Knight, "Female Terrorists in the Russian Socialist Revolutionary Party," *Russian Review* 38:2 (1979): 146.

24. Quoted in Linda H. Edmondson, *Feminism in Russia, 1900–1917* (Stanford, CA: Stanford University Press, 1984), 35, 37.

25. Barbara Alpern Engel, *Women in Russia, 1700–2000* (Cambridge: Cambridge University Press, 2004), 119.

26. Edmonson, 36–37.

27. Susan Kingsley Kent, *Sex and Suffrage in Britain: 1860–1914* (Princeton, NJ: Princeton University Press, 1987), 197.

28. Quoted in Kent, 205.

29. Thomas Jablonsky, "Female Opposition: The Anti-Suffrage Campaign," in *Votes for Women: The Struggle for Suffrage Revisited*, ed. Jean H. Baker (Oxford: Oxford University Press, 2002), 120–121.

30. Richard J. Evans, *The Feminist Movement in Germany, 1894–1933* (London: Sage, 1976), 79–80.

31. Evans, 93.

32. Jacqueline Jones, Peter H. Wood, Thomas Borstelmann, Elaine Tyler May, and Vicki L. Ruiz, *Created Equal: A Social and Political History of the United States*, vol. 2 (New York: Longman, 2003), 662.

33. Quoted in Neil MacMaster, *Racism in Europe* (New York: Palgrave Macmillan, 2001), 47.

34. Filippo Tommaso Marinetti, "The Futurist Manifesto," in *Marinetti: Selected Writings*, ed. R. W. Flint, trans. R. W. Flint and Arthur A. Coppotelli (New York: Farrar, Strauss and Giroux, 1972), 42.

35. Tammy M. Proctor, *Female Intelligence: Women and Espionage in the First World War* (New York: New York University Press, 2003), 79.

36. Proctor, 81–83.

37. Lettie Gavin, *American Women in World War I: They Also Served* (Niwot: University Press of Colorado, 1997), 45.

38. Maria Bucar, "Between the Mother of the Wounded and the Virgin of Jiu: Romanian Woman and the Gender of Heroism During the Great War," *Journal of Women's History* 12:2 (2000): 38.

39. Elizabeth Crosthwait, "'The Girl Behind the Man Behind the Gun': The Women's Army Auxiliary Corps, 1914–1918," in *Our Work, Our Lives*, 165.

40. Gavin, 3, 15, 79.

41. Quoted in Crosthwait, 171.

42. Quoted in Jean Ebbert and Marie-Beth Hall, *The First Few, the Forgotten: Navy and Marine Corps Women in World War I* (Annapolis, MD: Naval Institute Press, 2002), 37.

43. Richard Abraham, "Mariia L. Bochkareva and the Russian Amazons of 1917," in *Women and Society in Russia and the Soviet Union*, ed. Linda Edmondson (Cambridge: Cambridge University Press, 1992), 124–144.

44. Quoted in Reina Pennington, *Wings, Women, and War: Soviet Airwomen in World War II Combat* (Lawrence: University of Kansas, 2001), 5.

45. Bucar, 48.

46. Susan R. Grayzel, *Women and the First World War* (New York: Longman, 2002), 22–24.

47. Alfred G. Meyer, "The Impact of World War I on Russian Women's Lives," in *Russia's Women: Accomodations, Resistance and Transformation* ed. Barbara Clements Evans (Berkeley: University of California Press, 1991), 210–211, 216–217.

48. Reinhard Sieder, "Working-Class Family Life in Wartime Vienna," in *The Upheaval of War: Family, Work, and Welfare in Europe, 1914–1918*, ed. Richard Wall and Jay Winter (Cambridge: Cambridge University Press, 1988), 113, 115.

49. Quoted in Grayzel, *Women and the First World War*, 14.

50. Sieder, 112, 120–122.

51. Armin Triebel, "Variations in Consumption Patterns in Germany," in *The Upheaval of War*, 169.

52. Quoted in Belinda Davis, *Home Fires Burning: Food Politics and Everyday Life in World War I Berlin* (Chapel Hill: University of North Carolina Press, 2000), 211.

53. Davis, 185.

54. Quoted in Meyer, 216.

55. Proctor, 49.

56. Ute Daniel, *The War from Within: German Working-Class Women in the First World War*, trans. Margaret Ries (Oxford: Berg, 1997), 55.

57. Meyer, 214.

58. Crosthwait, 162.

59. Daniel, 278.

60. Susan R. Grayzel, *Women's Identities at War: Gender, Motherhood, and Politics in Britain and France During*

*the First World War* (Chapel Hill: University of North Carolina, 1999), 165–186.

61. Grayzel, *Women and the First World War*, 87.

62. Quoted in David Welch, *Germany, Propaganda and Total War, 1914–1918: The Sins of Omission* (London: Athlone Press, 2000), 235.

63. Quoted in Grayzel, *Women's Identities at War*, 88.

64. Quoted in Grayzel, *Women's Identities at War*, 47.

65. Proctor, 102–106.

66. Quoted in Grayzel, *Women and the First World War*, 20.

67. Grayzel, *Women's Identities*, 261, n. 3.

68. Proctor, 127–131.

69. Welch, 157.

70. Nicholas Reeves, "Film Propaganda and Its Audience: The Example of Britain's Official Films During the First World War," *Journal of Contemporary History* 18 (1983): 469.

71. Elaine Showalter, "Rivers and Sassoon: the Inscription of Male Gender Anxieties," in *Behind the Lines: Gender and the Two World Wars*, ed. Margaret Randolph Higonnet, Jane Jenson, Sonya Michel, and Margaret Collins Weitz (New Haven, CT: Yale University Press, 1987), 62, 63.

72. Quoted in Sandra M. Gilbert, "Soldier's Heart: Literary Men, Literary Women, and the Great War" in *Behind the Lines,* 213.

73. The title comes from the New Testament, it is the phrase uttered by Jesus before he died (*Matt.* 27:45).

74. Gavin, 26.

75. Niall P. A. S. Johnson and Juergen Mueller, "Updating the Accounts: Global Mortality of the 1918–1920 'Spanish' Influenza Pandemic," *Bulletin of the History of Medicine* 76 (2002): 113, 111.

76. Johnson and Mueller, 105.

77. Alfred W. Crosby, *Epidemic and Peace, 1918* (Westport, CT: Greenwood Press, 1976), 7.

78. Crosby, 80.

79. Crosby, 97.

80. Crosby, 81.

81. Crosby, 105.

82. Gina Kolata, *Flu: The Story of the Great Influenza Pandemic* (New York: Farrar, Straus, and Giroux, 1999), 9.

83. J. M. Winter, *The Great War and the British People* (Cambridge, MA: Harvard University Press, 1986), 75.

84. Grayzel, *Women and the First World War*, 115.

85. Quoted in Grayzel, *Women and the First World War*, 103.

86. Barbara Evans Clements, *Bolshevik Women* (Cambridge: Cambridge University Press, 1997), 193.

87. Clements, 172–175.

88. Clements, 58–65.

89. Clements, 182–184.

90. Wendy Z. Goldman, *Women, the State, and Revolution: Soviet Family Policy, and Social Life, 1917–1936* (Cambridge: Cambridge University Press, 1993), 60–67.

## SUGGESTED READINGS

Clements, Barbara Evans. *Bolshevik Women.* Cambridge: Cambridge University Press, 1997. A study of the women who worked for the Russian Revolution, placing the famous women in a larger context of women's participation.

Daniel, Ute. *The War from Within: German Working-Class Women in the First World War*, trans. Margaret Ries. Oxford: Berg, 1997. A study of the class tensions that built up in Germany and their impact on women.

Davis, Belinda J. *Home Fires Burning: Food Politics and Everyday Life in World War I Berlin.* Chapel Hill: University of North Carolina Press, 2000. A detailed study of the implementation and effect of food rationing in Berlin.

Grayzel, Susan R. *Women's Identities at War: Gender, Motherhood, and Politics in Britain and France during the First World War.* Chapel Hill: University of North Carolina, 1999.

Roberts, Mary Louise, *Disruptive Acts: The New Woman in Fin-de-Siècle France.* Chicago: University of Chicago Press, 2002. A study of the image of the new woman, and those women who tried to live out this ideal.

Wall, Richard and Jay Winter, eds. *The Upheaval of War: Family, Work, and Welfare in Europe, 1914–1918.* Cambridge: Cambridge University Press, 1988. A collection of essays that looks particularly at the demographic impact of WWI.

# Chapter 13

# The Modern Woman Between the Wars, 1920–1939

*Fanny Rosenfeld in the 1928 Olympics.* The athleticism of the modern woman made many people uncomfortable. Many believed that such activity endangered women's health and compromised their femininity. Nevertheless, the Olympics introduced women's track and field at the 1928 games in Amsterdam. Rosenfeld (Canada) won the silver medal at the first women's 100 meters. Betty Robinson (United States) won the gold. *(National Archives of Canada.)*

■ **A Modern Society**  450

  *The Modern Woman*  450
  *Gender and Consumer Culture*  453
  *Birth Control*  454
  *Modern Relationships*  455

■ **Women and Work**  457

  *The Interwar Workplace*  457
  *Women and Trade Unionism*  459
  *New Careers*  460

■ **Women in Postwar Democracies**  462

  *Suffrage and Its Impact*  462
  *After the Vote*  463
  *New Relations Between Women and the State*  465

■ **Women Under Authoritarian Rule**  468

  *Nationalizing Women in Mussolini's Italy*  468
  *Fascism and Its Opponents in Spain*  470
  *Other Authoritarian Regimes*  473

■ **Women Under the Soviet State**  473

  *Women and Early Soviet Society: Theory Versus Reality*  473
  *Economic Revolutions*  475
  *Soviet Regulation of the Family*  476
  *Politics*  477

■ **Gender and New Forms of Expression**  479

  *The Avant-Garde*  479
  *New Forms of Entertainment*  481

World War I transformed the lives of those who survived. As Europeans grappled with the tragic legacy of the Great War, many found relief and excitement in new ideas of modernity. Women wore new styles and engaged in new relationships. However, modernity did not always mean progress. As they pushed for full legal rights, governments came to expect that women would fulfill their citizen duties as mothers, not as voters and candidates. The emphasis on motherhood became even more central in authoritarian regimes, where women had few legal rights. Across Europe, most of the political and legal gains women made immediately after the war were quickly forgotten. As political instability and the economic depression of the 1930s intensified, many Europeans sought a return to a more conservative way of life. Soon, these tensions between traditional and modern led Europe again to the brink of war.

## A MODERN SOCIETY

Traumatized by the devastating loss of life in the Great War, Europeans looked to all things modern to erase the war's painful memories. For women with money and education, modernity meant a life less determined by rigid social expectations. Middle- and upper-class women in northern Europe and the United States flaunted their modernity with new shocking fashions, new technologies, and new relationships.

### The Modern Woman

The most visible expression of this enthusiasm for modernity was the 1920s figure of the modern woman, who had much in common with the new woman who had made prewar society so uncomfortable. However, the modern woman became a much broader cultural phenomenon. She was independent, somewhat androgynous, and definitely not bound by Victorian conventions. She was usually a socially and sexually liberated professional, student, or an artist. This modern woman, known as the flapper in America, the bachelor girl in Britain, and *la garçonne* in France, brought a fresh new face to Western society as she challenged traditional ideas of sex and gender.

# Chapter 13 ❖ Chronology

| | |
|---|---|
| **1918** | Lenin's law code on Marriage, Family, and Guardianship |
| **1919** | Jessie Redmon Fauset becomes literary editor of *The Crisis* |
| | Lady Astor the first woman to take a seat in the British House of Commons |
| **1920** | League of Nations established |
| | Oxford awards first full degrees to women |
| **1921** | Famine kills millions of Russians |
| | Sheppard Towner Maternity and Infancy Act (U.S.) |
| **1922** | Mussolini takes power in Italy |
| | Victor Margueritte writes *La Garçonne* |
| **1923** | Introduction of the Equal Rights Amendment in the US |
| | Release of *Maisie's Marriage* |
| **1924** | Stalin becomes head of Soviet Union |
| **1925** | Josephine Baker and *La Revue Negre* arrive in Paris |
| **1926** | Six Point Group puts forward international equal rights treaty |
| | Stalin's Family Code |
| **1928** | Trial of Radclyff Hall for obscenity |
| | Full female suffrage, Great Britain |
| **1930** | Stalin liquidates Zhenodtel |
| **1931** | Jane Addams wins Nobel Peace Prize |
| | Spanish women win the right to vote |
| **1936** | Aviator Maryse Bastié crosses South Atlantic alone |
| | Great Terror begins in Soviet Union |
| | Spanish Civil War begins |
| **1939** | French Family Code provides allowances for children |

Fashion was one of the key identifiers of the modern woman. Unlike the formfitting and modest fashions of the nineteenth century, the new fashions reconfigured the female body. The sporty, boxy styles of designers like Coco Chanel (1883–1971) had no waistlines and shorter skirts that daringly revealed most of the lower leg. The commercial production of rayon meant that more women could wear provocative flesh-colored stockings. Underneath, fashionable women scandalized the more conservative set by refusing to wear traditional undergarments.

The new look also blurred traditional gender expectations. Chanel and other designers looked to men's clothing for inspiration, using pajamas, trousers, ties, and men's cut jackets to fashion new designs for women that removed the obvious distinctions between men's and women's wear. The new fashions promoted boyish bodies that women achieved through dieting rather than constrictive clothing.

Among the new looks, the most controversy swirled around the short bobbed haircut. For centuries, long hair had symbolized modesty, femininity, and lack of vanity. In contrast, short hair revealed more of a woman's body, was sexually ambiguous, and highly stylized. Much like the masculine clothing styles, for the women who adopted it, the bob conferred upon the wearer a sense of virility and independence. To those who opposed it, short hair challenged traditional notions of gender difference and patriarchal authority. Stories abound of daughters who defied their fathers' authority by cutting their hair and of fathers who sued hairdressers or even killed their daughters for doing so.[1] Cartoonists regularly ridiculed the new look, claiming that between the short hair and the masculine styles, one could no longer distinguish women from men.

Modern women not only dressed and cut their hair like men but also adopted many activities that had been exclusively male. Before the war, smoking had only been associated with female sexual deviance: prostitutes and "unnaturally masculine" women were the only acknowledged female smokers. However, during the twenties, growing numbers of upper-class women began to smoke as an indication of their newfound social freedom and their desire for equality with men. Similarly, women began to drive automobiles more often and more publicly. In fact, automobile advertisers marketed directly to women, making the explicit connection between driving, female mobility, and freedom.

Books and cinema promoted both the modern woman's look and her independent, vivacious ways as the newest rage. In 1922, Victor Margueritte's novel *La Garçonne* became an instant bestseller in Paris. Actress Clara Bow (1906–1965) brought the young, single working girl with sex appeal to the big screen in her 1927 movie *It*. A myriad of other motion pictures featured assertive, sexual, single women, including Marlene Dietrich's 1930 classic *Morocco* and Norma Shearer's *The Divorcee* (1930). Actress and celebrity Louise Brooks (1906–1985) is often

**TWO FLAPPERS LISTENING TO THE RADIO (1932).** The modern woman of the interwar period not only dressed in the latest fashions, but was comfortable with new technologies including radio and film. These new media brought the world into women's homes, giving them information on international events and connecting them to the newest trends. *(Bettmann/Corbis.)*

considered the quintessential flapper. Her hair and clothing were the epitome of modern style, and her social circle included the most important and fashionable intellectuals and artists of the period.

The modern woman also created the first female athletic superstars. Probably the most legendary of this new breed of female athletes was the French tennis player Suzanne Lenglen (1899–1938). Known as "the Goddess," Lenglen became famous both for her talent and for her outrageous, revealing clothing on the court. She played in short (just below her knees), very stylish pleated skirts instead of the traditional long skirt. From 1920, she had her own clothing designer and was the first female player to play in full makeup and sport a tan. As a teenager, she dominated the sport, winning her first world hard court tennis title in 1914 at the age of fifteen. From 1919 to 1926, Lenglen lost only one match and became one of first tennis players to turn professional. Although she cultivated more of an all-American girl persona, Helen Wills Moody (1905–1998), Lenglen's great rival, won nineteen singles titles at the French and U.S. Opens and Wimbledon.

Female athletes attracted public attention off the court as well. In 1926, Gertrude Ederle (1906–2003) set a new record for swimming the English Channel and two million people cheered her feat during a ticker tape parade in New York City. In contrast, track-and-field events for women proved to be quite controversial. The first international women's track-and-field meet was held in Paris in 1922, and women's track-and-field events and team gymnastics were added to the 1928 Olympics despite considerable opposition from groups, including the Vatican. When a number of women collapsed at the end of the women's 1,000 meters race, opponents of female participation felt dramatically vindicated and argued against the inclusion of women's track and field in the 1932 Olympics. However, the International Olympic Committee eventually relented and added track and field to the list of women's events that already included tennis, ice skating, and golf. Without a doubt, the star of the 1932 Olympics was American Babe Didrikson Zaharias (1913–1956). Often considered one of the greatest overall athletes of the century, she set records in the javelin throw and the 80 meter hurdles. Zaharias also played professional basketball, and between 1936 and 1954, she won every major women's golf championship. No longer mere curiosities, female athletes captured the public's imagination as they publicly competed in arenas formerly reserved for men.

## Gender and Consumer Culture

The expansion of mass production and mass media brought the image of the modern woman and the products that adorned her to a wide audience. In particular, the great female-run cosmetics empires created by entrepreneurs Helena Rubenstein (1870–1965) and Elizabeth Arden (ca. 1878–1966) stood at the forefront of mass marketing aimed at women. The manufacture of affordable cosmetics and their promotion through mass-media advertising meant that all women could aspire to modern standards of beauty. In the

process, the cosmetics industry promoted specific notions of beauty to a broad spectrum of consumers. In the United States, cosmetics allowed immigrant women to signal their Americanization by toning down their "ethnic" looks. Similarly, cosmetics and hair products aimed at African American women promoted light skin and straight hair. Pressure to conform to certain standards of beauty created tensions within immigrant and black families and communities as lighter-skinned women more often conformed to the Anglo-American ideal.[2]

Advertisers not only directed growing attention to women's physical appearance, they also sought to reconfigure women's domestic life through the introduction of timesaving appliances. The innovations in household technology began with the electric iron, followed by the vacuum cleaner, and later the washer, the water heater, and the refrigerator. At first, few women could take advantage of these products, as most European households did not have electricity until the 1930s. However, class, rather than access to the new technology, was the most important factor in the adoption of electrical appliances. Despite increased electrification (in Britain, only 30 percent of homes were wired for electricity in 1932, but by 1938, 65 percent were) working-class women showed little interest in the new appliances. Forced out of the workplace at the end of the war, they could not afford such items and had time to do the work themselves. Moreover, even when working-class women could afford electric appliances, they preferred to spend their money on leisure items such as radios, household furnishings, clothing, restaurants, and movies.[3]

In contrast, middle-class women enthusiastically invested in appliances. Gas or electric stoves and refrigerators saved some money for women who had relied on servants, and women who did not have servants no longer dedicated hours each day to maintaining adequate stores of firewood and ice. However, middle-class women also fell victim to increased pressure from advertisers to use electric appliances to keep a better, cleaner house. Women's magazines like *Good Housekeeping* (founded in 1900) promoted the image of the modern middle-class housewife dedicated to cleanliness. In addition, the domestic science movement renewed its emphasis on housework as an occupation. Thus, ironically, although such appliances were supposed to save time, they probably caused women to spend more time on housework as the accompanying advertising raised the bar on cleanliness.[4]

## Birth Control

For some women, modernity also translated into freedom to choose their sexual partners and control their fertility. Women in England and the United States had the easiest access to birth control during the interwar years. In these countries, men and women could choose among a variety of contraceptives. Condoms had long been available to male consumers, cervical caps date from the 1830s, and the rubber diaphragm was invented in 1882. In addition, at the turn of the century, companies began to market contraceptive jellies, antiseptic douches, and vaginal foaming tablets at affordable prices. Unfortunately, many of these items were neither safe nor effective, and no agencies regulated either the claims or the quality of such products, many of which were sold as "feminine hygiene products," a term advertisers coined so that manufacturers could evade restrictions on the sale of contraceptives. Manufacturers could also avoid inquiries into the reliability of their products for birth control. Neither their ineffectiveness nor the potential dangers slowed sales. Increasingly, department stores dedicated special aisles to these "feminine hygiene products" staffed exclusively by female salesclerks. Other companies employed women to sell products door-to-door, so that interested women could purchase "feminine hygiene" products in the privacy of their own homes. By the late 1930s, female contraceptives outsold condoms five to one in the United States.[5]

Most poor women could not afford contraceptives, and Margaret Sanger (1883–1966) led a vigorous campaign to make birth control (a term that she coined), especially the diaphragm, more accessible. Her actions caused controversy, and authorities arrested Sanger in 1916 for opening a birth control clinic in Brooklyn for immigrant women. State officials prohibited her from opening clinics in many states and used antiobscenity laws to bar physicians from obtaining contraceptives by mail. Even the American Medical Association opposed making birth control a part of medical practice

until 1937. However, Sanger was undeterred and continued to work for the health and reproductive freedom of women. Dr. Marie Stopes (1880–1956) led a similar campaign to facilitate access to birth control and fitted poor women with cervical caps at her clinics across England. Among poor women, access to birth control was an important alternative to illegal and self-induced abortion, which was commonly used to limit family size. In working-class England, between 16 and 20 percent of all pregnancies may have ended in abortion, a figure that may have been even higher in some industrial centers.[6] The desire to make contraception available to all women had its negative side as well. Eugenics (see Chapter 9) underwent a rebirth in the 1930s, and many social reformers advocated the voluntary sterilization of poor women.

However modern they felt, women in the rest of Europe had little access to contraceptives. Catholic countries such as Spain and Italy forbade birth control, and in France and Germany, World War I weighed heavily on official attitudes toward fertility. Many believed that the loss of millions of young men in the war exacerbated the supposed surplus of women that had persisted since the nineteenth century, and in France, many politicians and other intellectuals were obsessed with the idea that unless fertility rose, the nation would be vulnerable to another war with Germany. These pronatalist critics described modern women as egoistic, frivolous, and unwilling to do their patriotic duty to bear children in order to replace the war losses. Indeed, the French government equated war heroism and maternity by awarding medals to women who produced five or more children.

In fact, women who refused to bear children were seen as threatening from many perspectives. They denied their biological duty, they compromised national power, and they emasculated war veterans who needed to prove their virility. Thus, in 1920, French legislation imposed stiff penalties on those who supported or provided contraception and abortion. Merely placing advertisements in papers for contraceptives, giving lectures promoting them, or distributing such literature could be penalized with one to six months in prison and serious fines. Advocates of abortion might face six months to three years in prison in addition to fines. Despite the dramatic rhetoric about fertility decline, the French birthrate actually rose in the years immediately after World War I. Between 1920 and 1925, the birthrate increased from 19.7/1,000 inhabitants from a prewar birthrate of only 18.2/1,000. It was not until after 1925 that the French birthrate began to fall, declining to 14.8/1,000 by the mid 1930s.[7]

With the lowest fertility rate in Europe except for Austria, Germans were even more concerned about population growth. The fertility rate had been declining steadily and was half what it had been at the turn of the century. Here, too, the government emphasized the need to replace war losses. While state-sponsored marriage counseling centers advised couples on how to increase their fertility, German women eagerly sought out birth control. With financial and intellectual support from Margaret Sanger, activists established private birth control clinics to provide German men and women with affordable contraception.[8]

Across Europe, by the end of the 1930s, most women were restricting their fertility whether or not they had access to formal birth control. Although it is difficult for scholars to know exactly why women began to limit the size of their families, better female education, the pressures of economic depression, and access to birth control all influenced women's choices and created smaller, modern families.

## Modern Relationships

Armed with the ability to prevent pregnancy, the modern woman no longer viewed marriage as the ultimate goal of her relationships with men. More often, couples became friends without declaring any preexisting intention to marry. Sometimes these couples never married, an outcome that was often considered shameful in previous eras.

One factor in the reconfiguration of relationships during the interwar years was the tremendous loss of life among young men in the war, which had accentuated the "surplus" of women. In 1921, in both England and France, there were 20 percent more marriageable-age women than men in both populations.[9] For many, the "lost generation" included women who had lost the opportunity to marry because their fiancés, both real and potential, had died during the war. Politicians and the media decried the society-wide

crisis that forced thousands of women into the dangerous state of spinsterhood. Single women were denigrated as unhappy, selfish, lesbians, and temptresses.

The supposed crisis had little basis in reality. Marriage rates rose considerably in 1919 and 1920. By 1924, the proportion of the population who married was not much different than it had been before the war. Among the English, casualty rates were highest among the officer corps, many of whom had been students at Cambridge and Oxford, so that middle and upper-class women would have faced the most serious dearth of men. However, across the population, most women found husbands by choosing spouses who were closer to them in age and from different social classes.[10]

Moreover, interviews with those women who remained single indicate that many of them drew upon the belief that they would never marry in order to carve out careers and live independently or care for family members. In doing so, they created an identity as war spinsters that allowed them to remain unmarried without the negative connotations of lifelong singleness.[11]

The war was not the only factor to alter people's expectations of relationships during the 1920s. Not only did sexologists and their theories attract more attention from a wider audience, but sexual topics appeared more frequently in books, magazines, and even the movies. In general, the new discussions about sexual interactions promoted the importance of sexual pleasure and eroticism over modesty and restraint. Advertising encouraged women to be sexually expressive in order to attract men. For some radical feminists, healthy sexuality even became a precondition for public life. Janet Chance (1885–1953), a founding member of the Abortion Law Reform Association in England, even asserted that nonorgasmic women could not adequately represent the rest of the population in politics.[12]

Women's interactions with men also changed as society came to accept dating as an early stage in the creation of a new relationship. Young people dedicated Saturday and Sunday nights to going out with members of the opposite sex. Boys and girls congregated in the growing numbers of dance halls and movie theaters, often without chaperones, and British society accepted the presence of women in pubs and other previously male sites without compromising their reputations.[13] However, even with the freer social norms, "good girls" did not go out in public alone. Like their counterparts across Europe, Danish women relied heavily on their female friends for companionship, for safety, and for protection of their sexual reputations.[14]

There are clear indications that, as in previous eras, premarital sex was common. One English report from 1939 noted that nearly 30 percent of mothers conceived their first child out of wedlock; however, official illegitimacy rates remained low as most of these children were born after the wedding.[15] Across Europe, illegitimacy rates varied widely. In Austria, more than one-fifth of children were born out of wedlock, while in most of the rest of Europe between 5 and 15 percent of all births were illegitimate.[16]

Even notions about married relationships began to change as social reformers and sexologists emphasized the importance of companionate marriage, in which men and women shared emotional and sexual intimacy, cooperated in birth control, and worked together for strong relationships. However, many married couples knew little about sex until 1918 when Marie Stopes published her groundbreaking work, *Married Love: A New Contribution to the Solution of Sex Difficulties*. Believing that sex was a critical part of a good relationship, *Married Love* provided clear instructions about how to have a mutually satisfying sexual relationship and emphasized the need for women to be aroused before penetration and to achieve orgasm. It was an immediate success, selling half a million copies by 1925. Her ideas reached an even larger audience with the release of a controversial film, *Maisie's Marriage* (1923), which Stopes cowrote. The film reiterated the connection between sexual satisfaction, birth control, and marital happiness. A prolific writer, Stopes's next two works supported birth control for lower-class women as well as upper-class women, whom she instructed to insert a cervical cap "while dressing for dinner."[17]

Scientists also showed renewed interest in female sexuality. In the early twenties, Katherine Bement Davis (1860–1935) conducted a study of the sexual behaviors of more than twenty-two hundred women. Fifty percent of the respondents reported having "intense emotional relations with women," and nearly 10 percent admitted to having had physical relations with another woman.[18] Their candidness on her surveys is remarkable considering that women who loved other women were largely unable to express those feelings in public.

In the 1930s, anthropologists Ruth Benedict (1887–1948) and Margaret Mead (1901–1978) transformed the study of sexuality and culture. The two women met while students at Columbia, becoming lovers for a time, and formed a lifelong friendship. Benedict's *Patterns of Culture* (1934), based on her fieldwork among Native American tribes, and Mead's studies of New Guinea demonstrated that gender roles and sexual identities were not the same across cultures. Deviant behavior in one society was unproblematic in another. Mead's examinations of male and female homosexuality and heterosexuality showed that such notions were cultural constructions rather than static categories based in biology.

During the interwar years, it became increasingly common for intellectuals and artists to engage openly in same-sex relationships and, for some, bisexual experimentation became quite fashionable. Wealthy New York lesbians and bisexuals often took their lovers to Harlem's clubs, where they felt free to cross-dress and express their affections in public.[19] However, outside of these clearly defined venues, lesbians tended to act in public as if they were heterosexual. Most were able to avoid marriage and find partners who kept their relationship secret from the public. Discretion was critical. Relationships with closeted gay men often provided a cover that allowed lesbians to fully integrate into their communities. Many lesbians never discussed their sexuality in private, let alone in public. Others married under pressure from their families or to deflect criticism of their seemingly reclusive lifestyles.[20]

Lesbians also appeared more frequently in literature, most notably in Virginia Woolf's (1882–1941) *Orlando* (1928) and Djuna Barnes's (1892–1982) novel *Nightwood* (1936) that portrayed her love affair with American sculptor Thelma Wood (1901–1970). While few outside of intellectual circles read works describing love and romance between women, the portrayal of lesbian relationships in literature attracted the public's attention during the English trial of novelist Radclyff Hall (1880–1943) over her book *The*

*Well of Loneliness* (1928), which recounts a love affair between two female ambulance drivers. By the time *The Well of Loneliness* reached the reading public, Hall was already a well-known novelist. Initial reviews of the book were favorable and it quickly went into a second printing. However, a conservative journalist attacked the book and used his influence to have Hall charged with obscenity. She was convicted and the book was withdrawn from the English market and the third printing cancelled. The media frenzy that ensued made the book a bestseller in the United States.

The modern woman was the reflection of post–World War I enthusiasms and anxieties. Her ability to control her own fertility and engage in a wide variety of relationships gave her unprecedented freedoms, opportunities, and responsibilities. However, few women had the economic wherewithal to be modern. Tennis lessons, tobacco, automobiles, and designer clothing all cost money, and many families struggled to make ends meet after years of wartime dearth and without male breadwinners. Moreover, not all women were enthused by the changing trends. What some saw as liberation, others viewed as decadence. Some viewed the modern woman as unnatural and dangerously masculine. For the large numbers of European women who remained outside the growing influence of movies, radio, and magazines, traditional gender norms persisted.

## WOMEN AND WORK

Well into the twentieth century, most women did more or less the same work as their mothers and grandmothers had, working in agriculture, bearing children, and tending the house. Although World War I caused unprecedented numbers of women to enter the workplace, at the end of the war, they were either encouraged to return home or fired in order to provide work for the recently discharged soldiers. The reemployment of men was critical to reassert what many believed was the natural gendered division of labor: men in the workplace and women at home. Pressure to move women out of wage labor increased after the U.S. stock market crashed in October 1929. Unemployment skyrocketed, banks failed, and inflation spiraled out of control around the world. Many, including weakened trade unions, believed that women were unfairly taking jobs away from men. As a result, most women who had to work to support their families were forced into low paid, unstable work.

## The Interwar Workplace

Although many critics viewed women workers as another negative consequence of modernity, most women who continued to work after the war did so because they had to, not to fulfill career aspirations. At the end of the war, most English working-class families lived in poverty. Under these conditions, families could not rely solely on husband's incomes even if they were engaged in full-time employment. In order for the family to survive, a woman might work in the formal sector, in assembly-line industries like automobile production, or she might work in the informal sector, catering, sewing, or taking in laundry.

Working-class girls could expect to enter the workforce around age fourteen, at which point they left school. Many women who came of age during that period expressed their desire to continue their schooling; however, for young men and women of the period, family needs outweighed personal ambition. Working-class parents often believed that school did little to advance their children's futures and prevented them from aiding their families financially.

Industries and tasks were nearly always sex segregated. For example, the Spanish cigar making industry employed twelve women for every man.[21] Even in the new industrialized workplace, men rarely engaged in work designated as female or vice versa. As a result, despite assertions to the contrary, women rarely displaced men as they entered the workforce, and men and women were rarely in competition for promotions. Instead, women often took low-paying, unstable jobs that men did not want or jobs in new industries. In Germany, where more than three-quarters of the jobs created between 1925 and 1933 went to men, women worked in the emergent electronics industry, where they made light bulbs, telephone equipment, and radios.[22]

To fulfill the societal expectation that they would raise a proper family, most women left full-

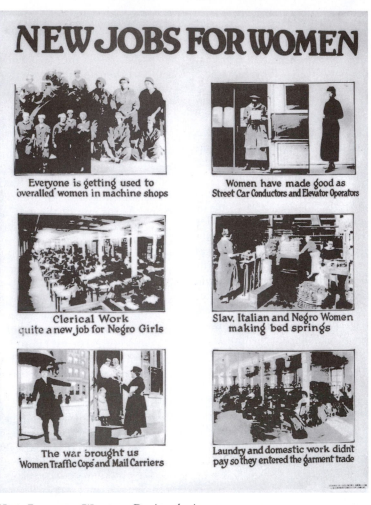

NEW JOBS FOR WOMEN

Everyone is getting used to
'overalled' women in machine shops

Women have made good as
Street Car Conductors and Elevator Operators

Clerical Work
quite a new job for Negro Girls

Slav, Italian and Negro Women
making bed springs

The war brought us
Women Traffic Cops and Mail Carriers

Laundry and domestic work didn't
pay so they entered the garment trade

**NEW JOBS FOR WOMEN.** During the interwar years, changes in the economy and technological advances led to increased job opportunities for women. This poster put out by the U.S. Department of Labor reveals both the diversity of women's employment and the increasing diversity of the female labor force. *(National Archives.)*

time work at least temporarily when they married; however, despite low pay and workplace hostility, large numbers of married women remained in the workforce. In Germany in 1925, 29 percent of married women worked, and by 1939, 34 percent did. In the United States, nearly 30 percent of the female workforce in 1930 was married, although legislators made numerous attempts to prohibit them from working.[23]

The official numbers of working married women in Great Britain and France were much lower. There, legislation and social convention barred married women from many occupations and nearly all government jobs. Women were often frustrated by the marriage ban. After physician Dr. Isabel Hutton was rejected for a government position because of her marital status, she replied, "it was a pity I had disclosed this heinous crime of marriage . . . better . . . would it have been to live in sin and then all the posts would have been open."[24] However, such laws did not prevent women from working; they only forced married women into lower-paid sectors of the economy.

Although many governments provided some type of unemployment compensation for men, few women were eligible for government benefits when they lost their jobs. In England, married women and women in occupations like domestic service received no unemployment benefits, and governments never invested the same time and energy in their attempts to relieve female unemployment as they did for male workers. During the Depression, Eleanor Roosevelt (1884–1962), the wife of U.S. president Franklin Delano Roosevelt (1933–1945), had to remind the head of the Works Progress Administration (WPA), "I hope in some way you will impress on state administrators that the women's programs are as important as the men's. They are so apt to forget us." In fact, the WPA had a difficult time creating employment for women. While major construction projects employed large numbers of men, projects aimed at women's employment tended to be smaller, service oriented, and shorter term.[25] As a result, women were less likely to work in the 1930s than at the turn of the century.

## Women and Trade Unionism

Working women found little support from labor unions and the postwar depression and rising unemployment led to significant declines in both male and female union membership. Between 1920 and 1933, male membership in English trade unions declined by 48 percent and female membership by 46 percent. The same was true in France and Germany. Due to the decline in membership, a number of women's unions merged with men's. Although such mergers may have helped keep unions alive, men held all the leadership posts, sexism pervaded the ranks, and women workers rarely had the experience of public speaking and organizing that their male counterparts had. Even in largely female occupations, women's labor activism declined. In England, women's membership in textile unions fell from 163,000 in 1918 to only 45,000 in 1939.[26] Only in rare cases, such as the emerging automobile industry, was there an increase in unionized women.

Women regularly found themselves at odds with the unions that were supposed to represent them. In France, new collective bargaining agreements reached in 1936 set women's wages at 13 to 15 percent below men's.[27] In the United States, the American Federation of Labor argued against married women working in order to keep male wages higher. When union organizer Ann Washington Craton (1891–1968) attempted to organize women in New Jersey, a union official first told them to go work for the YWCA and then complained, "Why don't you forget all this business and leave the labor movement to men? It's too rough for women. Why don't you get married?" Craton and her colleague answered, "Perhaps we are married . . . we still want to organize women into unions in Newark." As the union official left, he told the women that women would not be organized for another twenty-five or fifty years: "The trouble with you two is that you are ahead of your time."[28] This attitude was so pervasive that when employers laid off large numbers of female workers, unions generally took no action on their behalf.

Women's unions struck more frequently than men's. Spanish workers regularly struck against employers over issues from the right to organize to sexual harassment.[29] In the United States, black and white women mill workers walked out frequently in the 1920s and early 1930s. In 1936, a wave of strikes hit France after the Popular Front won the election. Women made up significant percentages of the employees in the most affected sectors of the economy from food processing to garment workers to department store clerks and were critical to the strikes' effectiveness. In Denmark when the larger Union of Unskilled Women Workers failed to gain desired concessions in collective bargaining, a small group of workers formed the Working Women's Association in 1925. This new organization supported a strike by women in the iron industry in 1930 in which its leaders demanded equal pay for equal work, a seven-hour workday, and maternity leave.[30] Even in countries where unions were weak or prohibited by authoritarian regimes, women workers defended themselves against rapacious owners and forced employers to make improvements in the workplace. During the late 1920s and early 1930s in Italy, female textile workers, rice weeders, cigar makers, and sardine packers frequently struck to protest their deteriorating working conditions.[31] The fact that both the Communist and the Socialist Parties that had supported them had been outlawed did not deter them from engaging in labor militancy. Time and time again, male employers and trade unionists underestimated women's willingness to defend their rights as workers.

Although unionization proved to be problematic for women workers, it is also important to remember that many female occupations remained nonunionized, in particular domestic service. Although there were sporadic attempts to form such unions, the circumstances of domestic service made unionization difficult. There were also short-lived attempts to unionize housewives. Influenced by the domestic science movement, many women began to see themselves as part of a potentially powerful group of workers who faced many of the same problems as their peers in manufacturing. These conservative organizations combined some of the rhetoric and tools of labor organizing with traditional gender expectations. For instance, while extolling the virtues of motherhood, the French Professional Union of Housewives (1935) demanded wages for housework. At one point, the German housewives' associations issued a call to action, proclaiming that "No man can, in the final analysis, grasp the professional needs of the housewife to the extent that he will intercede for them unequivocally. Housewives themselves must find their voices."[32] In Denmark, the Federation of Danish Housewives' Associations had more than ten thousand members in 1925.[33] Although these advocates of domesticity worked to educate women and modernize housework, they rejected other aspects of feminism, including suffrage.

## New Careers

In the postwar years, women entered a variety of new occupations beyond the assembly lines. In fact, the expansion of the service sector, especially retail, was built on the low paid labor of women. As the number of department stores grew, thousands of women joined the corps of saleswomen. In the United States in 1890, fewer than one in fifty working women was a salesperson, but by 1940 one in sixteen was. Retail sales work provided an excellent opportunity for social mobility for many young women. Sales positions required little or no education, yet allowed women to work in healthier circumstances than in industry, and the work was steadier. However, there were serious obstacles to advancement, and women rarely moved into management positions. Although the majority of salesclerks were women, they earned less than their male counterparts whose base salary was higher. In addition, men more often worked in departments where wages were based on sales commissions, like appliances, rugs, and sporting goods.[34]

As colleges and universities opened their doors to women, more women entered traditionally male professions. In 1920, Oxford University first awarded full degrees to women, and by the 1920s, women made up more than 40 percent of college students in the United States.[35] As a result, the numbers of female doctors and lawyers increased dramatically during the interwar years. In 1932, slightly more than 10 percent of Berlin's physicians were female.[36] Yet, despite the growth in absolute numbers, female professionals faced extensive discrimination. In both Germany and France, most female doctors were forced to work in public clinics and other public health services as private practice remained a bastion of male privilege. Similarly, female lawyers faced serious employment discrimination. In the United States and elsewhere, few law firms would hire qualified women.

Probably the most substantial change in women's employment was the large-scale movement of women into clerical work. Traditionally, secretarial work had been men's work, an opportunity for men to learn the business and move into management. However, by the 1920s, those jobs had been redefined as women's work. As office organization became more complex, men moved into supervisory positions and women were hired to fill the less desirable positions that offered little chance for promotion. Historians have referred to the feminization of clerical work as the "pinking" of the job, as women's pink-collared shirts replaced the traditional white collars of men's suits. Secretarial work came to have some degree of prestige among women's occupations, as it allowed women with some education the opportunity to move out of manual labor. By 1930, one-fifth of the female labor force was engaged in office work. The pinking of white-collar work also reconfigured the office hierarchy. Rather than potential coworkers and managers, male bosses came to prefer young, less-educated women as their secretaries. "Girl" had become a synonym for clerical worker.[37]

In education, women's progress varied. Although women made up one-third of all teachers in interwar Germany, this was not an increase over the prewar years, and fear of the feminization of education meant that few women headed schools. A Prussian law even required that one-third of the teachers in girls' schools be men, and a 1922 court decision required female teachers to be paid less than men because, "men teachers were contributing to the material restoration of Germany by training workmen, whereas the women were only making housewives."[38] The marriage ban in England prevented married women from working in the classroom. Although the numbers of female teachers in the United States doubled during the 1920s, during the Great Depression of the 1930s communities laid off large numbers of female schoolteachers. By 1940, only 13 percent of communities would hire married women as teachers, and only 30 percent would retain female teachers who got married.[39]

Although teaching was an attractive career for single women, life could be difficult for those who taught in rural villages. Their morality was often suspect as Émilie Carles (1900–1979) remembered during her first winter as a single teacher in 1924. After planning a successful evening of entertainment for the villagers, the local priest spread scandalous rumors about the performances and denied absolution to any villager who let their daughter consort with "the loose woman." Despite her personal discretion, she quickly realized that the priest was referring to her.[40]

A few courageous women took advantage of new technologies despite the social and physical risks involved. Early aviation held great promise for women, and after the war, women pursued flying with great enthusiasm. Female aviators became glamorous and the subject of intense media attention. Certainly, Amelia Earhart (1898–1937) became a household name in the United States. Her dramatic solo flights across both the Atlantic and the Pacific set records and gripped the imaginations of people around the world. She disappeared during an attempt to circumnavigate the globe in 1937. However, Earhart was far from alone. The possibilities of flight attracted other women. The Frenchwoman Maryse Bastié (1898–1952) made her name crossing the South Atlantic alone in 1936. In the Soviet Union, female pilots became symbols of modernity, technological innovation, and gender equality. When three female Russian pilots crashed in Siberia after attempting to set a new distance record in 1938, Stalin nevertheless hailed them as heroes.[41] Unfortunately, women who hoped to make flying a career faced nearly insurmountable obstacles. Legal constraints prohibited women from obtaining the license necessary to fly passengers. Industry officials tried to discourage women from flying because of the perceived risk, and the influence of the masculine armed forces in the development of the aviation industry further hindered women flyers. As a result, the field of aviation aggressively excluded female aviators and forced them into the more media-friendly and sensational aspects of flying, such as setting speed and distance records.[42]

Women were also eager to bring the political, economic, and social disruptions of the interwar period to broader audiences in both pictures and words. Margaret Bourke White (1904–1971), one of the most celebrated photojournalists of her day, became the first staff photographer for *Fortune* magazine in 1929. A year later, she was the first Western photographer allowed into the Soviet Union after the Russian Revolution. Like many other women, Nancy Cunard (1896–1965), the heir to the British shipping line, became a freelance correspondent in Spain during its civil war (see below). As the Great Depression brought millions of Americans to the brink of starvation, Dorothea Lange's (1895–1965) emotional photographs documented the plight of migrant women and children. Such women brought a sharp, new eye to journalism and photography, vividly reporting the violence and human suffering in the world around them.

During the interwar years, women faced contradictions in the workplace. On the one hand, women needed to work to support their families, and changes in the workplace meant more jobs for women. On the other hand, governments, employers, and unions were often uncomfortable with working women. In particular, the perception that women took jobs from men kept women in unstable, low-paying work. Nevertheless, women pushed for workers' rights and a place at the top of new professions.

## WOMEN IN POSTWAR DEMOCRACIES

Women's political organizations also faced new challenges in the postwar world. Prior to the war, most women's organizations had focused on suffrage, and by the end of the war, many nations had granted women the right to vote. However, suffrage did not bring the widespread changes that many women had hoped. Women often voted against the very parties that had supported their right to the franchise. In addition, after suffrage, many organizations rededicated themselves to other causes, dividing women's energies among a variety of domestic and international concerns. However, women's concerns did not fall by the wayside. As postwar governments created some of the first welfare programs, women and women's issues came to the forefront of domestic policy debates.

### Suffrage and Its Impact

After the war, supporters of suffrage pushed the remaining democratic governments to reward women's wartime patriotism and service with the vote, but class issues and political differences continued to hinder the campaign for full female suffrage in England. Under the 1918 Representation of the People Act, the majority of Englishwomen still could not cast a ballot. Although few English legislators publicly opposed equal suffrage, none of the major political parties believed that granting the vote to all women would be beneficial to their political interests. However, in time, the Conservative Party, which had opposed suffrage, changed tactics. The Conservatives believed that the five million working-class men who had been enfranchised in 1918 would support the Labour Party. They hoped to counteract those Labour votes with the votes of women, whom they believed would vote conserva-

tively. In addition, the Conservative Party faced pressure from within its own ranks. Lady Astor (1879–1964), the American-born wife of a British politician, led the Conservative Party's agitation for suffrage. Her husband had served in Parliament for years until he inherited his noble title and vacated his seat. Ambitious in her own right, Lady Astor ran for his seat and in 1919 became the first woman to take an elected seat in the House of Commons (Constance Markievicz had been the first woman elected to Parliament in 1918; see Chapter 11). Conservative support put pressure on the Labour Party to attend to the issue. When the Equal Franchise Act finally passed in 1928, it gave five and a half million Englishwomen the vote.

After suffrage, women had a difficult time entering the inner circle of any of the major political parties. Although both the Conservative and the Labour parties created women's branches and reserved candidacies for women at all levels, women rarely held leadership positions and frequently complained that their views remained unheard. Moreover, the parties voiced their disdain for feminist activism. At the Labour Party women's conferences of 1918 and 1920, party leaders urged women not to join feminist organizations for fear that "they would be in danger of getting their political opinions muddled."[43]

Despite these obstacles, a few women ran for office. Between 1918 and 1935, 323 women ran for the House of Commons, but only 36 won. Most of the female candidates lost because the parties tended to run women candidates in jurisdictions safely held by another party. In fact, fewer than 7 percent of the women were nominated in constituencies in which they might be expected to win.[44] Once in Parliament, female legislators were constrained by traditional gender expectations. Party leaders pushed women into domestic issues like welfare and education and excluded them from traditional male domains like foreign policy.

Similarly, in the United States, both the Republican and Democratic parties hesitated to nominate women to stand for office. In 1916, Jeannette Rankin (1880–1968) from Montana became the first woman elected to the U.S. Congress. Following in her footsteps, between 1917 and 1940, twenty-three women served in the House of Representatives. However, eight of those women were appointed or elected to finish the term of a deceased spouse and did not stand for reelection. Even at the state level, few women successfully ran for office. In 1926, only 2 percent of state legislators were female. Those numbers would not change significantly for another fifty years.

Female candidates fared better in other nations. In Finland during the interwar years, women made up nearly 10 percent of the parliament, the highest rate of female representation in western Europe. The majority of female members of Parliament (MPs) were working-class women from the Socialist Party, many of whom were feminists and labor activists.[45]

The establishment of the Weimar Republic in Germany at the end of the Great War seemed to offer great political opportunities for women. The new constitution assured women the same rights as men, including the vote, and women voted for the first time in 1918. We can analyze the role of gender in this critical election because men's and women's votes were cast and counted separately. In 1919, nearly 80 percent of eligible women cast ballots, slightly higher than that of male voters. Women tended to vote conservatively, showing no preference for either female candidates or candidates supporting feminist programs. Nevertheless, from 1919 to 1932, women made up between 7 and 10 percent of the German parliament, the Reichstag, one of the highest proportions of female representatives in Europe. Unfortunately, women's enthusiasm for electoral politics did not last long. From the outset, the Weimar government was weak, and over the course of the 1920s, political instability and extraordinarily high inflation left Germans with little confidence in their new government. In response, fewer women voted in each successive election, and fewer women ran for office. Moreover, German women did not tend to favor the parties that had supported their right to vote. In fact, the women's vote in the 1928 Reichstag elections increased the number of members of right-leaning parties by twenty-three and decreased those on the left by fourteen.[46] German women's turn to the right would have serious implications in the coming decade.

French suffragists emerged from World War I confident that the government would reward women's support of the war effort with the franchise. Leaders of the suffrage movement like Maria Vérone (1874–1938) fought hard against

antisuffrage legislators like Alexandre Bérard (1859–1923) who capitalized on France's demographic concerns. According to Bérard,

> *Nearly two million men would be missing from the ballot box if an election were held tomorrow. They would be replaced by women, which would dangerously upset the balance. If the female electorate were to be established, there would be two million more women voters than men. According to a phrase in our ancient law and contrary to its wise and prudent principles, "France would fall to the distaff."*[47]

Even more so than in England, suffrage fell victim to the machinations of politicians. In 1919, France's lower house, the Chamber of Deputies, voted overwhelmingly for woman suffrage; however, the Senate remained an obstacle. Historians speculate that many in the Chamber voted for suffrage knowing that it would never pass the Senate. In 1922, using tactics of parliamentary delays and debates, the Senate resolution in support of suffrage failed without ever coming to a vote. Regular attempts by socialists, communists, and various centrist parties to revive the legislation kept the issue on the table throughout the interwar period, but without any progress. It would be 1945 before Frenchwomen would vote in their first election.

## After the Vote

For decades, feminist activists had dedicated their attentions and even their lives to obtaining the vote, believing that suffrage would bring social transformation. Once engaged as full citizens, women would be in a position to end a wide variety of social ills from prostitution to war. However, as we have seen, the vote was not the panacea that many had anticipated. Moreover, once governments extended the franchise to women, divisions among women quickly emerged. Many organizations suffered a crisis of identity, overwhelmed by the sense that they had achieved their goal and stymied by the notion that feminism was now unnecessary. Even author Virginia Woolf noted, "What more fitting than to destroy an old word, a vicious and corrupt word that has done much harm in its day and is now obsolete? The word 'feminist' is the word indicated. That word, according to the dictionary, means 'one who champions the rights of women'. Since the only right, the right to earn a living, has been won, the word no longer has a meaning."[48] By the 1930s, some activist women even refused to use the word *feminism*. Dedicated activists felt betrayed by the new generation. Feminist Ray Strachey (1887–1940), in the preface to her 1936 work *Our Freedom and Its Results*, remarked on young women's failure to acknowledge their place in the evolution of women's rights:

> *Modern young women know amazingly little of what life was like before the war, and show a strong hostility to the word "feminism" and all which they imagine it to connote. They are, nevertheless, themselves the products of the women's movement and the difficult and confusing conditions in which they live are partly due to the fact that it is in their generation that the change-over from the old to the new conception of the place of women in society is taking place.*[49]

Even outside of intellectual circles, women lost interest in feminism. Energized by the possibilities of the new republic, many German women saw feminism as old-fashioned. Satisfied with the equality guaranteed by the Weimar constitution, they believed that gender struggles had become passé.[50] In the United States, the National Women's Party, which had thirty-five thousand members in 1920, lost steam after the passage of the Nineteenth Amendment and never became a force in U.S. politics.

Many organizations redirected their energies toward other domestic and international issues that affected women. As we saw in Chapters 11 and 12, women were deeply involved in the temperance movement. Energized by the successful passage of the Eighteenth Amendment to the U.S. Constitution prohibiting the manufacture and sale of alcohol in 1917, temperance organizations in Europe pushed for similar restrictions. Iceland, which had banned alcohol sales since 1915, was soon joined by Finland (1918) and Norway (1919). Most Canadian provinces outlawed alcohol, and groups made numerous attempts to do so in the Australian provinces. However, these attempts to regulate people's consumption were never very effective, and illegal production and sales continued unabated. Most governments repealed prohibition legislation by the early 1930s.

Alice Paul and other leaders of the National Women's Party pursued an Equal Rights Amendment to the U.S. Constitution. Introduced in Congress in 1923, the amendment stated, "Men and women shall have equal rights throughout the United States and every place subject to its jurisdiction." It was a highly controversial piece of legislation, even among feminists, as many feared that its language would invalidate any protective legislation aimed specifically at women, including labor reform laws. Opposition to the proposed amendment came from a wide variety of social and political organizations, including the League of Women Voters, and it failed to gain the necessary two-thirds majority in the U.S. Congress. Supporters introduced the amendment in every session of Congress until 1972.

The ongoing controversy about abortion rights also divided women's organizations, although the focus of the debate differed from country to country. In Germany, where abortion had been illegal since the nineteenth century, sex reformers and feminists worked to rescind legislation that punished both the mother and the person who assisted in the abortion. However, the power of the Catholic Center Party and opposition from Catholic women's groups stymied their efforts. In England, the Abortion Law Reform Association formed in 1936 to push for legalized abortion. Two years later, a prominent gynecologist tested the law, performing an abortion for a fourteen-year-old rape victim. His acquittal led to an intense debate about the law, but legalization found few supporters in Parliament despite the very high numbers of illegal abortions sought by working-class women.

Horrified by the violence of World War I, many feminist activists dedicated themselves to the expanding pacifist and disarmament movements. Participants in these movements believed that war was the realm of men and that peace was the realm of morally superior women, and their hopes for international influence were buoyed by the formation of the League of Nations in 1920. The League seemed to offer a new platform for women's rights advocates, particularly for women from nations like France where they had not yet obtained suffrage. However, few nations appointed female delegates, and those who did encouraged them to stick to "women's issues" like maternal care and education. Only Sweden, Norway, and Denmark regularly sent female delegates to the League. Even Anna Bugge Wicksell (1862–1928), who served as a full general assembly delegate from Sweden, was frequently called upon to speak for women and on issues pertaining to women and children. However, feminist activists did attempt to use the League to put forward new internationalist legislation focused on women. In 1926, the English women's rights organization the Six Point Group sought out American Alice Paul to draft a treaty that would guarantee equal rights to men and women. English pacifist Vera Brittain (1893–1970) spoke for many feminists when she said, "the time has now come to move from the national to the international sphere, and to endeavor to obtain by international agreement what national legislation has failed to accomplish."[51] Indeed, feminists from all parts of Europe and the United States hoped that the treaty could help counter the increasingly conservative tides of legislation at home. However, the treaty faltered as the opposition asserted that biological differences necessitated some legal distinctions, especially in labor legislation.

Other organizations fared considerably better. The International Council of Women and the Women's International League for Peace and Freedom (WILPF) brought women from the United States, across Europe, and as far away as China together for regular international congresses (see **Sources from the Past:** Resolutions of the Women's International League for Peace and Freedom, 1926 and 1932). The WILPF lobbied for peace, and at its 1924 congress, Swiss biochemist Gertrud Woker (1878–1968) and others formed the International Committee against Scientific Warfare to educate the public and lobby against chemical warfare. The WILPF took an active role in international conflicts. In 1926, it sent a delegation led by Emily Greene Balch (1867–1961), who would win the Noble Peace Prize in 1946, to Haiti to investigate the U.S. occupation. Jane Addams, who won the Nobel Prize for Peace for her peace activism in 1931, was a

founding member. These internationalist organizations were critical in promoting the formation of a feminist identity that transcended national borders and urging women to reach beyond traditional women's issues.

## New Relations Between Women and the State

Suffrage was not the only issue that brought women into politics during the interwar period. As postwar governments rebuilt their devastated societies, they created and expanded state welfare programs to compensate disabled soldiers, war widows, and war orphans. In addition, they used welfare programs to promote maternity in order to replace the millions killed during the war. However, not everyone believed that government intervention in maternity was a positive step. Many argued that maternity was a private responsibility, not a public one. Yet, the notion that reproduction was women's natural and patriotic duty and thus should be supported by the state won the day in much of Europe.

In Weimar Germany, female legislators from all seven major parties drafted a bill that made the wartime allowance granted to mothers permanent. This legislation was one of the first demonstrations of women's newly acquired political status. The Reichstag regularly extended the law and later incorporated a breastfeeding allowance and an additional benefit for needy mothers.[52]

In France, government propaganda vigorously asserted the parallel between reproduction and military duty. Just as men received allowances for doing their military duty, women received them for bearing children. As mentioned earlier, women who gave birth to five or more children were awarded medals by the French government. To make this duty financially feasible, the 1939 Family Code provided an allowance to every woman at the birth of her first child (if the child was born within the first two years of marriage). That allowance increased to 10 percent of the average wage for the second child and 20 percent of the average wage for each additional child. However, those payments almost always went to the father, thereby accentuating the father's role as the primary provider for the family.

# Resolutions of the Women's International League for Peace and Freedom, 1926 and 1932

*The Women's International League for Peace and Freedom was a critical force in antiwar activism. At their international conferences held in Dublin in 1926 and Grenoble in 1932, the membership passed the following resolutions.*

## Women's International League for Peace and Freedom Fifth Congress, Dublin July 8–15, 1926

### I. MIGRATION

Believing that all restriction of the free and peaceful migration of peoples contradicts the fundamental principles of peace and freedom and impressed by the menace to morality to which the present restrictions of emigration lead through the frequent enforced separation of families:

This Congress asks the Economic Commission to deal with this question as one of vital importance.

### II. ANTISEMITISM

This Congress convinced that the Antisemitic movement is a constant menace, expresses the need of contending against Antisemitism amongst the youth in schools and universities.

### III. EQUALITY OF SEXES

Whereas women of the world are today denied full equality although it is of vital importance that they have power to direct with authority their own lives and equally with men to direct the affairs of the world:

Be it resolved: that this Congress affirms its belief in the political, social and economic equality of the sexes, and in the right of women to equal opportunity and recognition in the industrial field.

### IV. IMPERIALISTIC CONTROL

Resolved: that, the WILPF being opposed in principle to the forcible control of one people by another;

This Congress supports the intention of the United Sates Section to work for the evacuation of Haiti and the independence of the Philippines.

### V. PASSPORTS

In the interest of free intercourse among the peoples of the world,

This Congress protests against the continuation of passport requirements between nations, and particularly against the secrecy of the archives collected by the secret service departments of all governments and used by them as a basis for the refusal of passports and visas and the circulation

---

The tensions surrounding government support of maternity came to the fore in the United States with the first federal welfare law, the Sheppard-Towner Maternity and Infancy Act of 1921, which subsidized health care for mothers and infants. This legislation demonstrated the new political clout of the Women's Joint Congressional Committee, but support for such government intervention quickly declined. After the next election, legislators called the act communistic and failed to renew it in 1928. However, the intense poverty brought about by the Depression increased maternal and infant mortality rates and forced yet another reversal in attitudes. Politicians revived the idea and reintroduced the program in 1935 as a part of President Franklin Delano Roosevelt's New Deal reforms. Over the next few years, more social welfare legislation was enacted under the guidance of Frances Perkins (1882–1965), the secretary of labor from 1933 to 1945 and the first female cabinet member, and first lady Eleanor Roosevelt. However, the focus had changed. Like the French programs, most New Deal programs supported male breadwinners and only secondarily provided for the care of women and children. Moreover, New Deal programs excluded domestic and agricultural workers, thereby denying government benefits to nearly all African American women and Latinas.

of unproved charges against innocent citizens, who are thus condemned without a hearing.

## VI. POLITICAL PRISONERS AND CONSCIENTIOUS OBJECTORS

Resolved: that this Congress demands general amnesty for political prisoners in all countries and sends greetings and sympathy to those men who on account of conscientious objections are now in prison for refusing military service.

### Seventh Congress, Grenoble
### May 15–19th, 1932

#### KELLOGG PACT

Considering that in general the existing constitutions are not in conformity with the obligations of the Briand-Kellogg Pact, the Women's Inter-national League for Peace and Freedom urges its National Sections to demand from their Governments and Parliaments revision of their respective Constitutions in order effectively to outlaw war as an instrument of national policy.

#### PRINCIPLES OF THE W.I.L.P.F.

In the anxious days when the fate of the world seems to hang in the balance and violence is growing in many directions throughout the world, this VIIth Congress assembled in Grenoble desires to re-affirm the stand of the Women's International League for Peace and Freedom and all its National Groups and Sections, against violence and oppression of every kind; whether employed between different nations, classes or individuals and whether under the influence of Fascism or Communism or any other system of government.

It declares the League to have no financial affiliation with nor to be under the domination of any political party, national or international or any government whatsoever.

The W.I.L.P.F. aims at uniting women in all countries who are opposed to every kind of war, exploitation and oppression and who work for universal disarmament and for the solution of conflicts by the recognition of human solidarity, by conciliation and arbitration, by world co-operation, and by the establishment of social, political and economic justice for all, without distinction of sex, race, class or creed. The work of all National Sections is based upon the statements adopted and the Resolutions passed by the International Congresses of the League.

Sources: http://www.wilpf.int.ch/statements/1926.htm and http://www.wilpf.int.ch/statements/1932.htm.

Women's groups were often split on the desirability of welfare tied to maternity. Some feminists viewed privileges for mothers and working women as incompatible with pure equality. Others like Eleanor Rathbone (1872–1946), a leader in the English suffrage movement and a member of Parliament, believed that women could only become economically independent with the aid of government programs. She and others argued for a family allowance that would provide the equivalent of a wage for mothers and help alleviate child poverty. The idea found broad support in England. Male workers and trade unions supported the idea of a family allowance, hoping that it would allow women to leave the workplace, thereby freeing jobs for men and increasing wages. Employers also supported such allowances, believing that working-class women who had multiple pregnancies were more expensive to employ than men. Certainly, family allowances reinforced traditional gender norms, presenting men as the primary wage earners and women as childbearers. However, anxiety about government intervention and the cost of the program slowed progress, and Parliament did not pass the measure until 1945.

During the interwar years, European nations extended a number of other rights to women. In

England, women were finally allowed to sue for divorce on the basis of adultery, and divorced women could seek custody of their children. In France, feminists won a small legislative victory when the parliament altered the law on women's nationality. Under the earlier code, a woman who married a foreigner lost her right to French nationality even if the couple resided in France. Thus, a woman's citizenship status was completely dependent on that of her husband. The new law, although still restrictive, allowed such women to keep their French citizenship under certain circumstances. A similar act passed in the United States in 1922.

Scandinavian legislators passed the most dramatic legal reforms. Based on the recommendations of an all-male commission, new laws made divorce easier and clearly delineated spouses' mutual obligations in cases of separation and divorce. Later legislation established complete legal equality between spouses. It also recognized the importance of housework, noting that both spouses were to contribute economically to the household, "through activity in the home, or in other ways."[53] Women in the rest of Europe would have to wait until the 1970s for legislators to even consider the possibility of such equality under the law.

After the war, women's political action changed course. In nations where women could vote, they struggled to find a place in party politics. Many suffrage organizations refocused their energies on other domestic and international issues. Indeed, the debate over women's relationship to the state continued as postwar governments used welfare programs to try to reestablish the traditional gender order.

## WOMEN UNDER AUTHORITARIAN RULE

The 1920s proved difficult for the fragile democracies of southern and eastern Europe. Although many nations made the transition from monarchy to democracy during the first decade of the twentieth century or immediately after World War I, intense economic problems and fears of socialism and communism led to the emergence of many authoritarian governments. Fascism, which pro-

moted an authoritarian, centralized state based on a strong national identity, found many supporters. These regimes were profoundly antifeminist in their assertion that women should be confined to "*Kinder, Küche, Kirche*" (children, kitchen, church).

## Nationalizing Women in Mussolini's Italy

Despite its support of the Allied cause and the Allies' ultimate victory in World War I, Italy did not fare well at the peace negotiations at Versailles. Economically devastated, Italians felt as though their war efforts had been wasted. In addition, postwar inflation, high national debt, and unemployment led to increased political instability and worker unrest that neither the weak king, Victor Emmanuel III (r. 1900–1946), nor the weak parliament could effectively control. In this environment, Benito Mussolini (1883–1945) and his National Fascist Party capitalized on fears of a communist revolution, gaining support from both the wealthy and the working class. Using angry rhetoric and the Black Shirt paramilitary, he became a powerful force in Italian politics. Finally, in 1922, the king gave into pressure and appointed Mussolini to the position of prime minister. Within months, Mussolini had consolidated his authority and became a dictator known as *Il Duce*, the Leader.

Under Mussolini, the state was closely connected to the Catholic Church and regulated all aspects of social, political, and economic life. Women were no exception. Before the war, the Italian government had largely ignored women and they had few legal rights; they had to take their husbands' surnames and could not undertake most legal or contractual acts, even writing checks, without their husbands' permission. They could not even be the guardians of their own minor children. Italian women had only been allowed to vote once, in the administrative elections of 1925.

Mussolini gave women prominence by constructing a new vision of the Italian woman who would fulfill her duties as wife and mother for the benefit of the state. Mussolini vividly asserted the relationship between women and the state in 1935, when after invading Ethiopia, he encouraged women to give him their gold wedding rings to be melted down in support of the colonial war.

The fascist government needed women, but it needed them only to produce children. Mussolini encouraged women to be self-sacrificing in support of the state. Mussolini's celebration of Mother's Day brought the country's most fertile women to Rome for a national rally. As they paraded by, the announcer called out not their names, but the number of live children that each had given birth to.[54] However, in accordance with Catholic doctrine, officials did not count illegitimate children, and couples married in civil ceremonies could not participate.

Mussolini pursued pronatalist policies similar to those put forward by the French and German governments, despite the fact that Italy faced such serious overpopulation that thousands emigrated to the United States and South America every year. In addition to maternity allowances, he gave tax exemptions to fathers and implored men to procreate by proclaiming that, "He who is not a father is not a man." Indeed, after 1937, men's careers in government depended on marriage and numbers of children. While on the one hand, these policies made a wide array of public health services available to women and made maternity central to Italian politics, on the other hand, such policies further burdened women, especially poor women, during a period when economic growth was limited, and they reasserted the traditional gender hierarchy. Moreover, the state punished those who refused to procreate, taxing men who remained single and declaring homosexuality illegal. Reinforced by papal decrees against abortion and contraception, Italy's penal code made even encouraging contraception a "crime against the integrity and health of the race."[55] Among urban and educated women, Mussolini's pleas for more children went largely unheeded. Far from increasing family size, the criminalization of birth control led to an increase in illegal abortions and an increased reliance on coitus interruptus. The birthrate dropped from 30.8/1,000 in 1920 to 23.4/1,000 in 1935, despite the fact that rural women continued to have nearly twice as many children as their urban counterparts.[56]

Fascist organizations reflected Mussolini's emphasis on the biological differences between men and women. Women could not be full members of the Fascist Party, but instead joined a separate women's organization, the *Fasci Femminili*. The party used these groups to channel women's energies into state-approved activities. Separate associations formed for rural housewives and women workers. A few young women even engaged in violent agitation alongside the Black Shirt paramilitarists. By the mid 1930s, more than three million women and girls had joined fascist organizations.[57] In truth, Mussolini's influence was even greater, as his close association with the Catholic Church meant that thousands of small Catholic women's organizations cooperated with the regime. Fascism's promise of a return to social order, its emphasis on maternity, and its rhetoric of national pride appealed to Italian women from many walks of life.

Mussolini's emphasis on maternity as women's primary contribution to the state often conflicted with his need for an expanded workforce as he attempted to modernize the Italian economy. Although fascist rhetoric discouraged women from engaging in paid labor, the government expanded benefits for working mothers in many sectors of the economy. Many women received two months paid leave, job protection for up to three months after childbirth, and guaranteed work breaks for breastfeeding.[58]

However, by the mid 1930s, the regime decided to focus solely on male employment. Women should only work until they married in order to maintain traditional gender norms and protect Italian masculinity. According to Mussolini:

> *With work a woman becomes like a man; she causes man's unemployment; she develops an independence and a fashion that is contrary to the process of childbirth, and lowers the demographic curve; man is deprived of work and dignity; he is castrated in every sense because the machine deprives him either of his woman or of his virility.*[59]

The state sometimes specifically required certain sectors of the economy to reduce their female workforce. To make it worthwhile not to hire women, the state lowered men's wages so that they were roughly the same as women's and created hiring quotas that favored men.[60]

Overall, Mussolini's attempts to modernize Italy did not include women. The modern woman was rare, partly because most Italians did not have access to electricity, film, and radio, technologies that spread new fashions and ideas. In addition, few women could read and write. Poverty, family priorities, and the authority of the Catholic Church further restricted women's lives. Mussolini completely repressed any feminist opposition. By the late 1930s, Mussolini had completed the nationalization and subjugation of Italian women.

## Fascism and Its Opponents in Spain

Fascism took root in Spain under circumstances quite similar to those in postwar Italy. Spain emerged from its neutrality in World War I in political chaos. Between 1918 and 1923, the First Republic faced four general elections and eleven coalition governments. Frustrated by the political instability, General Miguel Primo de Rivera (r. 1923–1929) overthrew the parliamentary system in a coup d'etat in 1923, and promising an end to corruption and a return to order, he maintained dictatorial control for six years. However, Primo de Rivera resigned in 1930 in the face of increased opposition and a deterioration of the economy. The next year, a republican-socialist coalition triumphed over monarchist parties, forcing King Alfonso XIII's (r. 1886–1931) abdication and the creation of the Second Republic. Unfortunately, Spain's Second Republic was every bit as unstable as the First.

Most Spanish women knew little about the modern woman. Rural and poor, Spanish women focused on their identities as wives and mothers. Most women's organizations were tied to the Catholic Church and thus reinforced traditional gender roles. Nevertheless, during the early 1930s, women did experience some gains. The 1931 parliament passed laws allowing for no-fault divorce, civil marriage, and legal rights for illegitimate children, and educational reform brought female illiteracy down to 39 percent by 1936.

One of the quirks of the Second Republic's constitution was that women could stand for election to Parliament despite the fact that women did not yet have the right to vote. Three women won election to the legislature in 1931: the feminist suffragist lawyer Clara Campoamor (1888–1972) from the Radical Party, lawyer Victoria Kent (ca. 1892–1987) from the Radical Socialist Party, and

Margarita Nelken (1896–1968), a journalist and art critic from the Socialist Party. In response to these electoral successes, the National Association of Spanish Women (1918–1936) attempted to create a feminist political party and sponsor its own candidate in the 1936 elections. Yet, many of the most politically active Spanish women were not as enthusiastic about the possibilities of suffrage. Kent advocated postponing woman suffrage, fearing that Spanish women were not educated enough to vote and thus would vote conservatively. She even proposed that women be required to vote in two municipal elections before gaining the right to vote in national elections. Nelken's radical politics also made her wary of the female vote. Despite their concerns, the 1931 parliament granted Spanish women the right to vote. The decision to enfranchise women affected each of the three female legislators quite differently. Nelken, the most radical of the three, retained her seat in all three parliaments. Kent was initially defeated by conservative voters but regained her seat through election on a coalition ballot. Clara Campoamor's career came to a rapid end, as she was rejected by voters on the right for her leftist politics and by her own party for her outspoken feminism.[61]

None of these women could have imagined how quickly Spanish democracy would disintegrate. In July 1936, a group of generals led by Francisco Franco (1892–1975) attempted to seize power from the coalition government; however, a variety of political parties, mostly from the left and center, joined in defense of the Second Republic and the coup was not immediately successful. Civil war broke out between the military and members of the fascist Falange Party on one side and republicans, socialists, communists, trade unionists, and anarchists on the other side. The level of violence was unprecedented. Republicans and anarchist revolutionaries killed thousands of clergy and sacked churches. Members of right-wing groups massacred unionists, non-Catholics, and members of leftist parties.

The civil war mobilized women on all sides. In the first days of fighting and sporadically after that, women took up arms against the fascists. The bravery of these militia fighters took the men at the front by surprise. Of course, the most politicized women were most likely to head to the front,

**WOMEN'S MILITIA IN THE SPANISH CIVIL WAR.** Like many other twentieth century conflicts, the Spanish Civil War drew women into the conflict both as combatants and as civilians. This women's militia was photographed setting off from Barcelona to the Aragonese front in the early days of the war. *(Agusti Centelles, Barcelona.)*

enlisting alongside friends, husbands, and fiancés. The intense hatred of fascism even led some mothers to follow their sons into battle.[62] When they got to the front, many women were seriously disappointed by the gender segregation that male fighters imposed on them. Women, eager to fight, reported being forced to cook, clean, and do laundry for the men. One militiawoman complained, "I have not come to the front in order to die with a kitchen cloth in my hand."[63] Despite their courage, attitudes toward female fighters quickly changed. Within weeks, official propaganda encouraged women to stay at home. However, with opposing forces battling for key cities and pillaging the countryside, home was not necessarily safer. The violence followed many women into their fields, shops, and living rooms.

Eager to focus women's activities against fascism, prominent women's organizations united into the *Agrupación de Mujeres Antifascistas*, the Association of Antifascist Women (AMA). The AMA included women from a diverse array of center and leftist political parties dedicated to defeating the fascists. AMA national committee member and dynamic communist leader Dolores Ibárruri, "La Pasionaria," (1895–1989) became the chief propagandist for the republican cause. Her radio speeches inspired men on the battlefield and war widows at home to overcome their losses and forge ahead against the fascist onslaught. At its height, the AMA's sixty-five thousand members undertook a wide variety of support services, including gathering supplies for men at the front, visiting the wounded, creating orphanages, and organizing aid for women workers in war industries.[64] Through its programs, AMA also educated and empowered thousands of rural women. However, the AMA's energies were not directed at women's issues. Indeed, even La Pasionaria emphatically denied that she was a feminist. Her work and that of the AMA focused solely on defeating the fascist insurgency, not promoting women's issues.

Early in the war, Spain's anarchist women actively fought fascism. Anarchism had a long history in Spain, particularly among trade unionists, and had considerable political clout. Just before the war broke out, anarchist leader Federica Montseny (1905–1994) had become the first female government minister in Spain when she was appointed minister of health and social assistance in 1936; in that position she allowed Spanish women access to abortion for the first time. However, female anarchists faced many of the same problems that communist and socialist women experienced. Like other leftist ideologies, anarchism denied the importance of gender differences. Instead, anarchists asserted that they could achieve a completely egalitarian society by destroying hierarchies and the institutions that created them. It was unclear to most anarchists exactly how women's roles would be reconfigured in this new society, and female anarchists often found that their male counterparts refused to treat them like equals. In response, anarchofeminists founded the *Asociación de Mujeres Libres* (the Association of Free Women) in 1936. The Mujeres Libres stressed that although it was not a feminist organization, it actively opposed the subjugation of women as both women and as workers. The organization's stated purpose was to "emancipate [women] from the triple enslavement to which they have been, and continue to be, subject, the enslavement of ignorance, enslavement as a woman, and enslavement as a worker." Most of the Mujeres Libres's twenty thousand members came from the working class, and the group attempted to help relieve the misery of its membership. Its programs focused on literacy, job training, consciousness raising, and empowerment, and it created a network of centers that provided medical, economic, psychological, educational support, and work training for former prostitutes.[65] With Franco's victory in 1939, the organization was forced to disband, and most of its members went into exile.

Lured by the romantic hope of defeating fascism, the republican opposition attracted liberals from around the world. Between 1936 and 1939, forty to fifty thousand men and women came to fight in the International Brigades. The American unit, known as the Abraham Lincoln Brigade, brought idealistic men and women like Salaria Kea (1917–1990) to the Spanish front. Kea, a politically active African American nurse from Akron, Ohio, had offered her services to the Red Cross during disastrous floods, but they declined her help because of her race. Then, a friend suggested that she join the Abraham Lincoln Brigade. After nursing antifascist soldiers under the most horrific conditions, she was captured by Franco's troops and forced to witness the massacre of civilians. She escaped seven weeks later and was wounded working in a U.S. field hospital before returning to the United States. French philosopher Simone Weil (1909–1943) became a camp cook for the International Brigade. Hundreds of women from the United States and Europe similarly risked their lives on behalf of the republican cause.

With Franco's victory in 1939, he created his "New State" on Catholic ideals. Like Mussolini, he reinforced a very traditional gender hierarchy, which extolled courage and military values for men, and maternity and devotion to family for women. Birth control was prohibited, as was abortion. To promote fertility, the state provided special concessions for large families, including tax exemptions, school grants, and housing assistance. Like his counterparts in France and Italy, Franco gave prizes to the largest families in each province and paid family allowances to successfully reproducing male heads of household. Despite these pronatalist policies, the birthrate dropped from 27.7/1,000 in 1933 to 22.9/1,000 in 1943.[66]

Under Franco, the women's section of the Falange Party, the *Sección Feminina* (Women's Section), became the dominant influence over Spanish women for the next forty years. Founded by Pilar Primo de Rivera (1912–1990), this organization appealed to "true Catholic womanhood." Franco, through the Sección Feminina, promoted maternity as women's sole duty. Spanish women were expected to find comfort and identity as "angels of the home," submissive to men and self-sacrificing on behalf of both their families and the nation. In interviews, former members have argued that their goal was to promote women in all aspects of Spanish society.[67] However, Pilar Primo de Rivera, belied their progressive rhetoric when she declared, "Our goal is that women find [in the home] all their purpose in life and find in men all their comfort."[68]

## Other Authoritarian Regimes

Authoritarianism also nullified the social and political achievements of women in Portugal and much of eastern Europe. After World War I, Portugal's unstable First Republic was overthrown by the military in 1926, and under the military dictatorship, a young economist, Antonio de Oliveira Salazar (1889–1970), was given broad powers to reform the economy. Salazar acquired tremendous personal power, becoming president in 1932. Salazar's Estado Novo, or New State, shied away from the militaristic fascism that overtook Spain and Italy, but remained a one-party, Catholic state. The conservative, religious nature of the Estado Novo was clearly expressed in the 1933 constitution. While it supposedly granted equal rights to all citizens, it also stated that "women's differences result from their nature and from the good of the family." However, Salazar's policies never made motherhood a priority. Under his regime, the government cut maternity leave in half and made maternity allowances optional. In terms of political participation, widows, university-educated women, divorced women, and women whose husbands were absent overseas had been granted the right to vote under the military dictatorship. Although Salazar did not deny them that right, under the one-party system it became meaningless. An officially recognized women's group provided health and educational programs to rural women, and a youth organization whose goal was to train "Christian Portuguese women" was obligatory for school-age girls until age fourteen. However, Catholic organizations continued to be the centers of female activity, and Salazar never felt the need to mobilize women to the same degree as occurred in Spain and Italy.[69]

The Allies' defeat of the Austro-Hungarian Empire during World War I led to the creation of a number of new nations in eastern Europe, including Czechoslovakia, Hungary, and Yugoslavia. Women gained the right to vote in each of these newly established democracies, but most of these governments were unstable. With the exception of Czechoslovakia and Austria, all returned to authoritarian governments that soon either revoked women's right to vote or made it ineffective.

Despite their rhetoric of revitalization and progress, the spread of authoritarian governments in the interwar years stymied women's social and political progress. The most powerful authoritarian government came to power in Germany during the interwar years; however, we will discuss the lives of women living under National Socialism in the next chapter.

## WOMEN UNDER THE SOVIET STATE

The supposed transformation in gender relations that would accompany the Russian Revolution inspired female members of the Communist Party in both the United States and Europe. Under Lenin, Russian women gained citizenship and the promise of economic and political equality. However, from the outset, the notion that women's needs might differ from men's conflicted with official communist ideology that promoted class interests over gender interests.

## Women and Early Soviet Society: Theory Versus Reality

As the Bolsheviks worked toward a classless society, feminism and its goals remained outside party priorities. The Bolsheviks believed that the way to sexual equality was through the abolition of class divisions and the private sphere, which was traditionally dominated by women. In Lenin's view, housework and child-rearing prevented women from earning wages and gaining equality. He described the housewife as "wast[ing] her labor on barbarously unproductive, petty, nerve wracking, and stultifying drudgery."[70] Women would be emancipated as the state took control of domestic tasks. Although the Bolsheviks diminished the importance of the private sphere and made it easier for women to earn wages, they did not end the age-old association of women with home and traditional gender expectations in Soviet society.

The centerpiece of Lenin's social policy was the 1918 law code on Marriage, Family, and Guardianship. The code aimed to free women from traditional religious marriage that placed them under their husbands' control. Marriage became a matter of individual choice. Men and women would choose their partners based on love and respect, not family politics or the need for financial support. Couples could choose to register their marriages but did not have to, and divorce was easily available. Parents had responsibility for their children regardless of their marital status, making the distinctions between legitimate and illegitimate children meaningless. The code assumed that both husband and wife would work and, therefore, marriage did not create any community or family property.

Women within Lenin's inner circle, such as his wife, Nadezhda Krupskaia (1869–1939), Alexandra Kollontai (1872–1952), and his one-time lover Inessa Armand (1874–1920), argued that women needed special attention; in response, Lenin established the Department for Work Among Women, known as the *Zhenotdel*, headed by Armand. Under her leadership, the Zhenotdel organized local chapters, published literature helpful to women, planned periodic conferences, and sent fieldworkers to educate women. Armand worked hard to mitigate concerns that the Zhenotdel was a separatist association, but after her death in 1920, the organization took a more radical turn under the leadership of Alexandra Kollontai.

Kollontai's blend of feminism and socialism made the Zhenotdel more controversial. Prior to the Revolution of 1917, she had written extensively on the role of sex in keeping women oppressed. For Kollontai, economic and political equality was not enough. As she argued in her work, *The Social Basis of the Woman Question* (1909), women's sexual relationships drove them into emotional dependence and physical submission. Once women changed that behavior, they could be equal partners in sexual relationships and thus achieve social equality.[71] However, despite her strong advocacy of women's rights, Kollontai saw herself first and foremost as a socialist and believed that feminists and feminism

were bourgeois and needed to be overcome as much as capitalism.

Nevertheless, Kollontai repeatedly decried the lack of female delegates to local and national soviets and protested women's exclusion from union leadership positions. She also believed that the Zhenotdel should take the lead in initiatives to abolish the family. Cooking, cleaning, and childcare would be replaced by state-run dinning halls, dormitories, and childcare facilities staffed by wage workers. Kollontai used her position in the Zhenotdel to criticize the increased authoritarianism of the government. Her criticisms led Lenin to remove her from the Zhenotdel in 1922.

Members of the Zhenotdel also fought distrust and hostility in the provinces. Male workers were openly hostile to attempts to educate women. Zhenotdel workers also struggled against deeply entrenched local traditions, especially in the Caucasus and Central Asian provinces, where Muslim populations dictated that women wear veils and marry young and allowed for polygynous marriage. After the government outlawed veils and child marriage, the Zhenotdel organized and educated Muslim women in Soviet ways and established medical clinics and legal aid societies. In the late 1920s, Muslim men rioted in defense of their patriarchal privilege. The conflict became deadly for many Muslim women who rejected their veils and refused to ally with their fathers and husbands. Between March 1927 and December 1928, eight hundred female activists and rebels were murdered.[72]

Gender tensions were especially apparent in the Young Communist League, known as the *Komsomol*. The Komsomol was created to educate and acculturate its members in Soviet values. However, the ideal image of a young communist—a male Red Army soldier dressed in boots, pants, and a big leather coat—coupled with traditional Russian gender expectations made it difficult to integrate young women into the organization. The male leadership of the organization remained indifferent to women's issues and asserted that women were politically backward. Moreover, parents often refused to allow daughters to join because they feared that Komsomol meetings would encourage their daughters to be promiscuous and they expected their daughters to care for younger siblings and help with the housework. Furthermore, many parents associated the organization with hooliganism, urban licentiousness, and antireligious behavior. Popular novels for young people, such as *The First Girl in the Komsomol*, perpetuated these gender expectations. The book's main character, Sania, had fought bravely for the revolution. After the war, she joined the Komsomol and began having sex with its members. Eventually she caught venereal disease. Angered by her sickness and her promiscuity, the young men in her Komsomol prepared to publicly humiliate her. However, her best friend killed her to spare her this punishment and save the local Komsomol from further degradation.[73] Because of these attitudes, women remained only a minority of the membership.

## Economic Revolutions

The Bolshevik victory presented the new government with the challenge of restoring the economy. The violence of the revolution and the ensuing civil war had devastated the Russian countryside. The deaths of millions of men left women alone working family plots and struggling to provide for their families. The scope of the human disaster multiplied with the famine of 1921, in which hunger and disease killed 90 to 95 percent of children under three in some areas. Lenin responded with the New Economic Plan (NEP) in 1921.

The NEP attempted to rebuild the economy, end the peasant revolutions that plagued the countryside, and halt the starvation faced by millions of urbanites. The plan replaced grain requisitioning with a tax in kind and a series of other measures affected budgeting, production, and wages. Lenin also allowed peasants to sell their surplus crops for cash, and small business owners and factory owners could operate and earn profits.

For a few elite members of the Soviet hierarchy, the economic improvements led to a significant rise in the standard of living. Well-dressed Soviet officials and their wives dined in restaurants and danced to the newest music from western Europe. Many young women dressed as flappers, eschewing the austere clothing and hairstyles of the revolution. In this atmosphere, artists, architects, and filmmakers celebrated the Soviet state and the worker in new avant-garde art. However, for critics, the concessions to bourgeois values

undermined all the goals for which the Red Army had fought.

Beginning in 1921, Lenin suffered a series of strokes and his declining health took him away from politics. After his death in 1924, a power struggle within Lenin's small circle ensued, and Josef Stalin (1879–1953) took over leadership of the Communist Party.

Stalin attempted an extensive overhaul of the Soviet economy. In 1928, he presented the first of two five-year plans that would completely transform Russia's agricultural and industrial sectors. He attempted to restructure agriculture through the collectivization of farming, which placed private farms, livestock, and farm equipment under state control. Stalin hoped that collectivization would resolve the persistent food shortages and that once the state effectively controlled the food supply, the agricultural surplus could fund rapid industrialization. Moreover, collectivization would ease the abolition of private property.

Collectivization proved to be disastrous. Peasants refused to give up their lands and enter the collective farms. In response, the government killed or deported hundreds of thousands of peasants. In particular, Stalin attempted to liquidate the class of wealthier, landowning peasants known as *kulaks*. Officials often blamed kulaks, for among other things, encouraging women to resist collectivization. However, women's grievances were real, as tending farm animals was generally women's responsibility and collectivization struck at the heart of their identity. In the Ukraine, crowds of women armed with clubs attacked party representatives demanding that their animals be returned. Women burned collective stables, stole seeds, and destroyed farm equipment. Some, but not all, of these revolts were successful. In 1933, a women's revolt successfully broke into the government's grain store and got the grain, but not before the women were fired upon by police. Many women died and the survivors were all deported.[74] Through coercion and terror, Stalin succeeded in collectivizing more than 90 percent of Soviet farms; however, agricultural production dropped precipitously, causing widespread famine. The violence and hunger killed between four and six million Russian men, women, and children.

The second part of Stalin's economic reforms focused on rapid industrialization. Beginning in

1928, millions of Russian women entered the workplace as a part of Stalin's industrialization plans. He desperately needed women's labor, and due to the overall declines in wages, women needed the work. In 1929, women made up 27 percent of the paid workforce, but by 1935 that number had risen to 33 percent. Most of the expansion of the female labor force took place by recruiting women who had not previously been in the workforce, such as unskilled urban women or women who had recently moved to urban areas. Thirty percent of the women who entered industrial work during this period were former housewives.[75] Under Stalin's second five-year plan, more women moved into heavy industry, especially mining and machine building. Despite this expansion, millions of rural women remained unemployed.

Like their western European counterparts, women in the Soviet Union who entered the workplace both increased their incomes and compounded their burden. Running water and electricity were still rare in the Soviet Union, so domestic tasks like keeping fires lit and washing clothes took hours. Moreover, food shortages under Stalin meant long waits in shops for basic foodstuffs. In urban areas, many women lived far from family networks that would have helped them cope with the additional work.

As Stalin implemented his economic plans, the Soviet government sometimes emphasized the equality of men and women and at other times asserted that women required special labor laws to aid and protect them in the workplace. As a result of official studies on the impact of labor on menstruation and fertility, the government proposed that employers offer menstrual leave: two to three paid days off each month to ensure that menstruation did not have a negative impact on productivity and that work did not decrease female fertility. Concerns about fertility also influenced the creation of workforce rules for women in certain occupations, especially those in which workers dealt extensively with toxic chemicals like the printing, tobacco, and oil industries.[76]

To train women for industrial and professional work, the government increased women's access to education. The results were dramatic. Female literacy rates rose from 42.7 percent in 1926 to 81.6 percent in 1939. The numbers of women in higher education institutions also increased dramatically from 31 percent in 1926 to 58 percent in 1940. During the same period, the percentage of women in Russia's industrial institutes increased from a meager 7 percent to 40 percent.[77] Greater access to education and more occupational opportunities meant that during the 1930s many women were able to move from the peasantry to become professionals and government bureaucrats. However, few women entered the almost exclusively masculine Soviet hierarchy.

## Soviet Regulation of the Family

The Soviet state was highly ambivalent toward the family. According to Marxist-Leninist thought, with the complete transformation of daily life, the family would gradually "wither away." However, until the family withered away, the state would have to regulate all aspects of family life and establish institutions that would perform the work done by the traditional family.

The focus of Stalin's family regulation was the 1926 Family Code. Provisions of the new laws altered traditional relationships by recognizing de facto marriage, establishing joint property, allowing for adoption, and simplifying divorce. The most controversial of these reforms was the recognition of de facto marriage, defined as a marriage based on cohabitation, mutual upbringing of children, and third-party recognition of the relationship. Russians complained that it would be difficult to determine the validity of marriages and that the law would complicate the enforcement of traditional inheritance rights. Many Russian women opposed the reform of divorce laws, believing that stricter divorce laws protected the family from male irresponsibility. Women's fears were confirmed, especially in Soviet cities. Across the European part of the Soviet Union, divorce rates doubled or tripled within a year. In 1927 in Moscow, three-fourths of marriages ended in divorce and in Leningrad, two-thirds. In Moscow, there was nearly one divorce for every two marriages. In addition, although the new law confirmed divorced women's right to alimony, it only granted disabled spouses one year of support and six months for unemployed spouses. Women complained that men took shameless advantage of the new laws, marrying one woman after another, abandoning them, and failing to pay child support for their offspring.[78]

Abortion provides an excellent example of the changing tides in policies aimed at women. In 1920, the Bolsheviks legalized abortion in order to prevent dangerous and deadly illegal abortions. With that legislation, the Soviet Union became the first Western country to give women access to legal, publicly funded abortion. However, this legislation included important provisions that limited both who could perform abortions and who could receive them. For instance, although doctors could perform abortions, midwives, who performed abortions in large numbers, could not. Scarce resources also forced the state to prioritize potential recipients. Women with medical problems were given first priority, followed by healthy women with social insurance (most white- and blue-collar workers). The system also gave preference to single working women with at least one child and married women with three or more children. Uninsured women, which included peasants, students, servants, and artists, followed. Ironically, the women who were least able to care for additional children were last on the priority list.[79]

With contraceptives largely unavailable, many poor and rural women resorted to abortions to end unwanted pregnancies. In a 1927 survey of more than a thousand peasant women, one in four women admitted to a legal or illegal abortion, making it the second most common form of birth control. In the cities, the numbers were even higher. Twentysomething white-collar employees and urban workers made up the majority of women receiving abortions. Most cited poverty as the reason.[80] Under Stalin, the conditions of urban life were very difficult. Families crowded into tiny apartments. Almost half of the women who sought abortions in 1924 lived with a family of four or more people in one room. By 1932, the government allotted only 4.6 square meters per person in towns.[81] Many other women simply stated that they did not want to have a child. They struggled without male breadwinners, and additional children often sent them from poverty to desperation. During the interwar years, the birthrate dropped from 44.7/1,000 in 1925 to 30.1/1,000 in 1940.[82]

Stalin liquidated the Zhenodtel in 1930, proclaiming that gender equality had been achieved.

This move foreshadowed the government's change in attitude towards women. By the mid 1930s, Stalin's pronatalist policies dominated the social agenda. A 1936 law outlawed abortion, which the Soviet government asserted was no longer necessary. With the improving economy, every Soviet woman could now "realize her right to be a mother."[83] Doctors who performed abortions could be sentenced to jail and women who got abortions could be fined. Women who bore children received extra stipends and women who bore more than seven children were eligible for bonuses. The new law also provided for four months of pregnancy leave, made it illegal to refuse to hire a pregnant woman, and allowed pregnant women to perform less strenuous work at her former pay. The 1936 law also made divorce more difficult and expensive to obtain and set new levels for child support. As a result, the divorce rate dropped precipitously, and in one year, abortions in Moscow decreased by a factor of fifteen.[84] In less than twenty years, Russian women had made the transition from worker to mother, all in the name of the Soviet state.

## Politics

In the first two decades after the Revolution of 1917, government officials encouraged women to participate in the façade of democracy that existed alongside the increasing totalitarianism of the Soviet state. Indeed, in the early years, Soviet women eagerly stepped up to the ballot box. In elections for deputies to the local, regional, and national soviets (councils elected by workers), women voted in large numbers, and those numbers rose steadily until 1934, when 89.7 percent of urban women and 80.3 percent of village women cast ballots. Women also increasingly stood for election as deputies. In 1934, women made up 27 percent of deputies in rural local soviets and 32 percent of urban soviets. However, their numbers did not translate into political influence because these governing bodies met rarely and had little influence in policy. Most true political power was concentrated in the hands of Communist Party members. Membership in the Communist Party was required for political careers and most upper-level positions in the state bureaucracy. Yet, throughout the interwar period, women remained only about 15 percent

**SOVIET WOMEN AT THE ALL UNION CONGRESS OF SOVIETS (1924).** The creation of the Soviet Union gave Russian women new opportunities for political participation. This group of women delegates to the All Union Congress of Soviets represented their local worker's councils. *(Tass/Sovfoto.)*

of the party's membership. There were even fewer women in the party's leadership. No more than a handful of women ever served on the Central Committee, and many years there were no women on the Committee. Thus, women were largely absent from the decision-making process.[85]

Politics directly affected most women (and men) during the Great Terror of 1936–1939. The government suddenly became interested in the political opinions of peasants and workers during this campaign against the "enemies of the people," which began after the assassination of a party leader in December 1934. This massive repression sent at least three million Russians to prisons and forced labor camps.[86] Many were common criminals caught in a crackdown on crime, but officials accused many others of being "counterrevolutionaries" for their opposition to government policies, especially collectivization. Women made up only a small percentage of the prisoners in forced labor camps, only 5.9 percent in 1934 and 8.1 percent in 1940; however, by 1939, there were more than one hundred thousand women in Soviet prison camps.

Many of these female prisoners were charged under a section of the Criminal Code that made wives and relatives of "enemies of the people" into criminals if they did not denounce and completely reject any association with the accused. After 1937, government officials arrested wives for the actions of their spouses and sent them to prisons known as "The Special Camps for Wives of Traitors to the Motherland." Conditions in the camps were squalid. Despite the fact that many of the camps were located in Siberia and other frigid regions, the women were not issued adequate food or clothing. They faced sexual abuse by guards, and mortality rates were ten times that of the civilian population. Millions died and even more suffered for years in these dismal prisons.[87]

Despite the violence that the government inflicted on its people, Soviet political propaganda capitalized on both the responsibilities and the successes of Russian women. Posters, stamps, movies, and other official propaganda featured the woman worker as emblematic of the potential for the Soviet state. However, the strong, youthful images of women enthusiastically working on behalf of the state were more the product of the artists' imaginations than the reality of Soviet women's lives.

As the Soviet Union emerged from the revolution and civil war, many women were enticed by the new jobs and educational opportunities offered by the regime. Initially, Stalin's reforms even considered women's special needs as workers. However, by the 1930s, women's interests fell victim to an increasingly authoritarian state that viewed them as hindrances rather than helpers on the Soviet road to progress.

## GENDER AND NEW FORMS OF EXPRESSION

During the interwar years, many artists were eager to move beyond traditional forms of expression to better depict the changes in European society that resulted from World War I. In Berlin, New York, and Paris, artists, writers, and performers sought modern ways to express their anger, their fears, their distrust, and at times, even their optimism about the world around them.

### The Avant-Garde

The art of the interwar years reflected the social and gender tensions of the period. Female artists were often forced into secondary roles, as even the most progressive male artists had a difficult time rejecting traditional gender expectations.

When Walter Gropius (1883–1969) founded his art school, the Bauhaus, in 1919, it quickly became a center for the production of avant-garde art. Gropius believed in the functionality of art and that the best way to achieve that functionality was through workshops that combined fine arts with the best craft skills. The Bauhaus attracted some of the greatest abstract artists of the time.

Although ostensibly egalitarian, the large numbers of female applicants to his workshops surprised Gropius and exposed his gender prejudices. Neither Gropius nor the other workshop masters were comfortable with women in most of the craft workshops. Quickly, he directed women only to the weaving, bookbinding, and pottery workshops, no matter what their original field of interest had been. However, the master artist of the pottery workshop refused to accept women, and the bookbinding workshop quickly closed. In the end, the only workshop to include women was the weaving workshop, almost completely segregating women from the rest of the school. Although the weavers workshop was the longest lasting workshop at the Bauhaus and the women produced some of the finest examples of abstract art of the period, they faced constant derision from their male colleagues. Gunta Stöltz (1897–1983), the head of the weavers workshop, became the only female Bauhaus master.[88]

Reacting to the trauma of World War I, a number of artists found expression in Dada, an antiart movement centered in Zürich, Berlin, and later in Paris. Dadaists believed that European culture had become bereft of meaning. While some products of the movement were meant to shock and scandalize, it also attempted to break down the barriers between art and daily life. Dada artists worked in new media, refusing to be constrained by traditional forms such as sculpture and painting. The only woman at the center of Berlin's Dadaist circle was Hannah Höch (1889–1978). In her photomontages, she sought to portray the modern woman of Weimar Germany in innovative ways, juxtaposing pictures of women from the German mass media with fragments of photographs. Her productions are often shockingly violent, with dismembered body parts positioned over and under new technologies and machine parts. Many of her montages critiqued traditional gender ideologies, showing women as mannequin-like beings, while other compositions dealt with the intersections of race, gender, and sexuality. Other female artists associated with Dada found the fullest expression of their ideals in textiles. Sonia Terk Delaunay (1884–1979), a Russian painter who lost her family wealth in the revolution, turned from painting to fashion and textile design after the war. Her geometric designs and bold colors transformed bodies and interiors into works of art.

Surrealism also captured the imagination of many artists seeking to reconfigure the postwar reality. Based on the manifestos of André Breton (1896–1966), the surrealists understood women not as artists but only as muses to spark men's creativity. Indeed, until recently, scholars studied women in the surrealist circle only as the spouses and lovers of male artists. However, a few women were attracted to surrealism. Meret Oppenheim (1916–1986) came to Paris in 1932 at age eighteen. Among her most famous works, her "Fur-Lined Teacup" transformed an object of daily life into something strange and useless. Gisèle Prassinos (b. 1920), a poet, also joined the surrealist circle as a young woman and was quickly anointed the "embodiment of *femme-enfant*," the woman-child who could best evoke men's creative sensibilities.[89] Their emphasis on women as muse meant that women had to leave the surrealist circle in order to become artists. Many other female artists, including Mexican artist Frida Kahlo (1910–1954), sometimes exhibited with the surrealists but emphatically denied any relationship to the movement and indeed detested surrealism.

Drawn to Paris's cosmopolitan culture, a remarkable group of American expatriate writers established their own social and artistic subculture on the Left Bank. As mostly wealthy foreigners, these women were not subject to the social constraints placed on Frenchwomen. This cultural cocoon also became a haven for lesbians and bisexual women. Natalie Barney (1876–1972), an American heiress, whose writing and scandalous love affairs became the talk of the town, created a vibrant salon in her Paris home that attracted the great artists of the period. Gertrude Stein (1874–1946) came to Paris to live with her brother. She collected cubist art and wrote in an abstract style that reflected her love of the avant-garde. She and her lover, Alice B. Toklas (1877–1967), also entertained the literary artistic innovators of the period.

New York's Harlem neighborhood became the center of an artistic renaissance for African Americans. Encouraged by Alain Locke (1886–1954) and W. E. B. Du Bois (1868–1963), African American writers, artists, and musicians rejected the simplistic contemporary portrayals of African Americans as inferior, primitive, and erotic. Instead, their works explored the dynamism of African American culture, the emergence of new racial identity, and the racial tensions that beset American life. With the "New Negro Movement," Locke and others hoped that artistic distinction would promote social and political progress. In 1919, Jessie Redmon Fauset became the literary editor of *The Crisis*, a new journal that published the most innovative writings by African Americans (see **Women's Lives:** Jesse Redmon Fauset, Writer of the Harlem Renaissance). The Harlem Renaissance produced many great female writers, among them Zora Neale Hurston (1891–1960). Trained as an anthropologist at Barnard College, she studied African American folkways. In addition to her scholarly work, between 1931 and 1943 she published six major novels. Her works were very controversial among African American writers because Hurston focused on poor, rural culture and wrote in dialect, rather than portraying the middle-class African Americans that many writers preferred.

Augusta Savage (1892–1961) was one of the Harlem Renaissance's great female sculptors. After her initial training in the United States, Savage was determined to study abroad, and in 1923, she won a fellowship to study in France; however, the sponsors withdrew the fellowship when they discovered that she was black. Undeterred, Savage eventually reached Paris in 1929, when she was awarded a series of other fellowships. In her very modern pieces, she depicted African women's bodies in provocative new ways. She was the first African American woman elected to the National Association of Women Painters and Sculptors, but her work was often perceived as too modern to please the public.

Unlike their male counterparts, many of whom became prominent professors, politicians, and activists, most of the women of the Harlem Renaissance retired from public life. Constrained by both race discrimination and gender expectations, most had ended their artistic production by 1950. When they died, their books were out of print and their artworks forgotten. They would not gain recognition for their work until the 1970s.

Women were also at the forefront of avant-garde music. In Paris, Nadia Boulanger (1887–1979) helped train and launch the careers of some of America's great composers, including Aaron Copeland (1900–1990). In fact, Copeland was the first student to enroll in Boulanger's class at the American Conservatory of Music in Fontainebleau (France). In addition to cultivating some of the most progressive composers of the period, her conducting skills were highly regarded, and she became the first woman to conduct major symphony orchestras including the Royal Philharmonic, the New York Philharmonic, and the Philadelphia Orchestra. In New York, Ruth Crawford-Seeger (1901–1953) became one of the few women to gain fame as an ultramodern composer, defying gender stereotypes with the publication of her renowned String Quartet of 1931.

Women's patronage of the arts underwent a revival in the 1920s. In part, this revival was because most avant-garde artists were determinedly anticommercial and thus had to rely on patrons for financial support and publicity. Gertrude Vanderbilt Whitney (1875–1942), the benefactor of the so-called ultramodern composers, was one of a number of prominent American women who fostered the movement. However, these women were the subject of intense criticism from both the male artists they patronized and music critics more generally. While these women saw themselves as modern, active participants in the creative process, the male composers feared the "feminization" of music and often spoke of female patrons with disdain.[90]

## New Forms of Entertainment

In both Europe and America, the innovative rhythms of jazz attracted young audiences. They flocked to dance halls to hear the moving vocals of Billie Holliday (1915–1959) and dance to all-women bands like Bobbie Howell's American Syncopators. Although the public often viewed these bands as novelty acts, the musicians were some of the finest performers in the business. Offstage, women also had a powerful presence in the music business. Mary Lou Williams (1910–1981) arranged music and wrote scores for the great bandleaders of the era.

Jazz also brought growing numbers of African Americans to Paris. Many African American musicians felt more comfortable in France where they were not confined by segregation and overt racial prejudice. Most famously, Josephine Baker (1906–1975) and her act, *La Revue Negre*, arrived in 1925, shocking and exciting Parisian audiences.

During the interwar years, people began to realize the potential of radio and film. At times, governments used these media to reinforce traditional gender norms. For instance, in 1924, German radio began programming specifically directed at women. Solidly middle class in tone, these shows tended to deal with recipes and home management. However, they also created educational programming for women. Critics quickly decried radio as a feminizing force in society, arguing that it encouraged men to sit around the house rather than participate in public life.[91] Radio became a critical component of women's lives as it brought the latest news and information from the outside world into their kitchens and living rooms.

From the beginning, women shaped the emergent film industry. In the early days, when filmmaking was cheap and had little social prestige, women had easy access to careers on both sides of the camera. Director Alice Guy-Blaché (1873–1968) was working as a secretary in a photographic business in Paris when her office received a camera. When no one else in the office showed any interest, she asked if she might make films. She went on to make hundreds of films and became the first person to direct a sound motion picture. Guy-Blaché then moved to the United States, where she became the first woman to establish her own movie studio. According to many scholars, she was the first director, male or female, to bring a narrative film to the screen. Her career set the stage for other women. Between 1913 and 1923, at least twenty-six women directors were active in Hollywood.

Among the other innovations women brought to film, Germaine Dulac (1882–1942), a French film director, made the first surrealist films from an unabashedly female perspective. In 1915, she started her own film production company and in 1923 made her most well-known film, *The Smiling Madame Beudet*, about a woman trapped in a loveless marriage. Dulac used pioneering cinematic techniques to move from the main narrative to reveal the main character's thoughts. Director Lois Weber (1882–1939) used film to advance her feminist views, with films that advocated birth control and explored other controversial topics. Despite the fact that some of her films were censored and even banned, Universal Studios built her a studio. She later pioneered the use of film in classrooms.

# Women's Lives

## Jessie Redmon Fauset, Writer of the Harlem Renaissance

Jessie Redmon Fauset, one the leaders of the Harlem Renaissance, epitomized the opportunities and obstacles African American women faced in the interwar years. Raised by her widowed father, Fauset had a brilliant and challenging academic career. Despite the snubs of her wealthy white classmates, she was the only "colored" girl to graduate in her class from the prestigious Philadelphia High School for girls. Bryn Mawr College in Pennsylvania rejected her application because she was black. Indeed, the president of Bryn Mawr, M. Carey Thomas (see the **Women's Lives** box in Chapter 9), may have paid for Jessie Fauset's tuition at Cornell University in order to avoid having her enroll at her institution.[1] Possibly the first African American to attend Cornell, she was not welcomed in the dormitories and instead lived with a professor's family. In 1905, she graduated Phi Beta Kappa with a major in classical languages. Although Phi Beta Kappa records do not indicate race, she may have been the first black woman to receive this honor.

Like many other African American women, upon graduation, Fauset found that she had few professional opportunities. She taught Latin and French, first in Baltimore and then at Washington, D.C.'s renowned Dunbar High School for fourteen years. She continued her education with courses at the Sorbonne in Paris and completed a master's degree in French at the University of Pennsylvania.

In 1918, Fauset began writing a column for *The Crisis*, the official publication of the National Association for the Advancement of Colored People, the NAACP. Originally founded by W. E. B. Du Bois as a national African American newspaper, *The Crisis* quickly became a literary journal focused on issues of race. Fauset's columns emphasized the contributions of African Americans to the war effort in an era when they were often targeted as unpatriotic or Socialist. At the same time, many of her columns noted the irony in sending African American men to fight for freedom and democracy overseas, while their rights as citizens were limited.[2]

As literary editor of *The Crisis*, Fauset achieved her status as one of the "midwives" of the Harlem Renaissance. She was the first to publish works by poet Langston Hughes (1902–1967) and encouraged many others, including Countee Cullen (1903–1946), Jean Toomer (1894–1967), and Anne Spencer (1882–1975). At the same time, as the managing editor of *The Brownie's Book*, a publication for African American children, Fauset cultivated the work of female writers and illustrators, many of whom went on to brilliant careers.[3]

At the height of the Harlem Renaissance, Fauset wrote four novels in ten years and unlike many of her male counterparts, she wrote without the financial backing of a wealthy patron. Her works chronicle the struggles of the black middle class, of blacks passing as white, and of interracial couples. However, they were not well received. Many African American critics found her works too conservative and too melodramatic.[4]

Like many women of the Harlem Renaissance, Jessie Fauset retired from public life at the peak of her career. She continued to teach but withdrew from all but local affairs until she died in Philadelphia in 1961.

In some ways, Jessie Redmon Fauset was the typical modern woman of the interwar years. She was well educated, well traveled, economically independent, political, and single until midlife. However, as an African American woman, her choices were constantly constrained by the racial politics of her time.

---

[1] Cheryl Wall, *Women of the Harlem Renaissance* (Bloomington: Indiana University Press, 1995), 40, n. 14.

[2] Carol J. Batker, *Reforming Fictions: Native, African, and Jewish American Women's Literature and Journalism in the Progressive Era* (New York: Columbia University Press, 2000), 57–58.

[3] Wall, 54.

[4] Wall, 36, 38.

Sources: Carol J. Batker, *Reforming Fictions: Native, African, and Jewish American Women's Literature and Journalism in the Progressive Era* (New York: Columbia University Press, 2000); and Cheryl Wall, *Women of the Harlem Renaissance* (Bloomington: Indiana University Press, 1995).

During the interwar years, women found exciting new ways to express both the vibrancy and the angst of the period. The new, gendered perspective that women brought to artistic production, whether it was in textiles, via music, or on film, made the most innovative art movements of the 1920s truly modern.

## CONCLUSION

European women experienced the tensions of a changing society during the interwar years. Some women felt the thrill of being modern with its loosening of gender and sexual norms. They drove cars, voted in elections, and danced to jazz. However, millions of other women struggled to earn livings on farms and in low-paying industrial jobs. Authoritarian regimes from the Soviet Union to Portugal extolled the virtues of motherhood while denying women political and social rights. Even Europe's democracies were hesitant to extend full equality to women. Those unresolved tensions would have serious implications for European society. By the end of the 1930s, gender tensions would be a key component of both domestic and international conflicts.

## NOTES

1. Mary Louise Roberts, *Civilization Without Sexes: Reconstructing Gender in Postwar France, 1917–1927* (Chicago: University of Chicago Press, 1994), 63–64.

2. Kathy Peiss, *Hope in Jar: The Making of America's Beauty Culture* (New York: Henry Holt, 1999), esp. 188–190 and chap. 7.

3. Sue Bowden and Avner Offer, "The Technological Revolution That Never Was: Gender, Class, and the Diffusion of Household Appliances in Interwar England," in *The Sex of Things: Gender and Consumption in Historical Perspective*, ed. Victoria de Grazia and Ellen Furlough (Berkeley: University of California Press, 1996), 250, 261.

4. Bowden and Offer, 262.

5. Andrea Tone, *Devices and Desires: A History of Contraceptives in America* (New York: Hill and Wang, 2001), 152, 164–165.

6. Jane Lewis, "In Search of Real Equality: Women Between the Wars," in *Class, Culture, and Social Change: A New View of the 1930s*, ed. Frank Gloversmith (Brighton, England: Harvester Press, 1980), 227.

7. Roberts, 123, 263.

8. Atina Grossmann, *Reforming Sex: The German Movement for Birth Control and Abortion Reform, 1920–1950* (New York: Oxford University Press, 1995), 39, 53.

9. B. R. Mitchell, *European Historical Statistics, 1750–1970* (New York: Columbia University Press, 1975), 36, 52.

10. Jay Winter, "The European Family and the Two World Wars," in *The History of the European Family*, vol. 3, *Family Life in the Twentieth Century*, ed. David I. Kertzer and Marzio Barbagli (New Haven, CT: Yale University Press, 2003), 160.

11. Katherine Holden, "Imaginary Widows: Spinsters, Marriage and the 'Lost Generation' in Britain After the Great War," *Journal of Family History* 30:4 (October 2005): 398.

12. Barbara Caine, *English Feminism, 1780–1980* (Oxford: Oxford University Press, 1997), 186.

13. John R. Gillis, *For Better, For Worse: British Marriages, 1600 to the Present* (New York: Oxford University Press, 1985), 271–274.

14. Birgitte Søland, *Becoming Modern: Young Women and the Reconstruction of Womanhood in the 1920s* (Princeton: Princeton University Press, 2000), 76.

15. Lesley A. Hall, *Sex, Gender, and Social Change in Britain Since 1880* (New York: St. Martin's Press, 2000), 122.

16. Shirley Forster Hartley, *Illegitimacy* (Berkeley: University of California Press, 1975), 36–39.

17. Hall, 98.

18. Vern L. Bullough, *Science in the Bedroom: A History of Sex Research* (New York: Basic Books, 1994), 115–116.

19. Lilian Faderman, "Lesbian Chic: Experimentation and Repression in the 1920s," in *The Gender and Consumer Culture Reader*, ed. Jennifer Scanlon (New York: New York University Press, 2000), 161.

20. Elizabeth Lapovsky Kennedy, "'But We Would Never Talk About It': The Structures of Lesbian Discretion in South Dakota, 1928–1933," in *Unequal Sisters: A Multicultural Reader in U.S. Women's History*, ed. Vicki L. Ruiz and Ellen Carol DuBois (New York: Routledge, 2000), 409–425.

21. Rosa María Capel Martínez, "Life and Work in the Tobacco Factories: Female Industrial Workers in the Early Twentieth Century," in *Constructing Spanish Womanhood: Female Identity in Modern Spain*, ed. Victoria Lorée Enders and Pamela Beth Radcliff (Albany, NY: SUNY Press, 1999), 135.

22. Renate Bridenthal and Claudia Koonz, "Beyond *Kinder, Küche, Kirche*: Weimar Women in Politics and Work," in *When Biology Became Destiny: Women in Weimar and Nazi Germany*, ed. Renate Bridenthal, Atina Grossman, and Marion Kaplan (New York: Monthly Review Press, 1984), 49.

23. For Germany, Gisela Bock, *Women in European History* (Malden, MA: Blackwell, 2002), 176; For the United States, Alice Kessler-Harris, *Out to Work: A History of Wage Earning Women in the United States* (New York: Oxford University Press, 1982), 229.

24. Quoted in Hall, 100.

25. Quoted in Susan Ware, *Beyond Suffrage: Women in the New Deal* (Cambridge, MA: Harvard University Press, 1981), 105, 109.

26. Sheila Rowbotham, *A Century of Women: The History of Women in Britain and the United States in the Twentieth Century* (New York: Penguin, 1997), 179; Elizabeth Roberts, *Women's Work, 1840–1940* (Cambridge: Cambridge University Press, 1995), 62.

27. Helmut Gruber, "French Women in the Crossfire of Class, Sex, Maternity, and Citizenship," in *Women and Socialism, Socialism and Women: Europe Between the Two World Wars*, ed. Helmut Gruber and Pamela Graves (New York: Berghahn Books, 1998), 289.

28. Ann Washington Craton, "Working the Women Workers," *The Nation* 124:3220 (March 23, 1927): 313.

29. Mary Nash, "'Ideas of Redemption': Socialism and Women on the Left in Spain," in *Women and Socialism, Socialism and Women*, 362–363.

30. Hilda Romer Christensen, "Socialist Feminists and Feminist Socialists in Denmark, 1920–1940," in *Women and Socialism, Socialism and Women*, 489.

31. Mary Gibson, "Women and the Left in the Shadow of Fascism in Interwar Italy," in *Women and Socialism, Socialism and Women*, 402.

32. Renate Bridenthal, "'Professional' Housewives: Stepsisters of the Women's Movement," in *When Biology Became Destiny*, 157.

33. Søland, 148.

34. Susan Porter Benson, *Counter Cultures: Saleswomen, Managers, and Customers in American Department Stores, 1890–1940* (Urbana: University of Illinois Press, 1988), 178, 180.

35. Sarah Jane Deutsch, "From Ballots to Breadlines, 1920–1940," in *No Small Courage: A History of Women in the United States*, ed. Nancy F. Cott (Oxford: Oxford University Press, 2000), 429.

36. Grossmann, 49.

37. Deutsch, 428.

38. Quoted in Bridenthal and Koonz, "Beyond *Kinder, Küche, Kirche*," 53.

39. Deutsch, 453.

40. Émilie Carles, *A Life of Her Own: The Transformation of a Countrywoman in Twentieth-Century France*, trans. Avriel H. Goldberger (New York: Penguin, 1991), 99.

41. Alison Rowley, "Ready for Work and Defense: Visual Propaganda and Soviet Women's Military Preparedness in the 1930s," *Minerva: Quarterly Report on Women and the Military* (Fall–Winter 2000), 7–8.

42. Sian Reynolds, *France Between the Wars: Gender and Politics* (London: Routledge, 1996), 66–70.

43. Quoted in Harold L. Smith, *The British Women's Suffrage Campaign, 1866–1928* (New York: Longman, 1998), 73.

44. Martin Pugh, *Women and the Women's Movement in Britain*, 2nd ed. (New York: St. Martin's, 2000), 160.

45. Elina Haavio-Mannila, "Finland," in *The Politics of the Second Electorate: Women and Political Participation, Britain, USA, Canada, Australia, France, Spain, West Germany, Italy, Sweden, Finland, Eastern Europe, USSR, Japan*, ed. Joni Lovenduski and Jill Hills (London: Routledge, 1981), 241.

46. Bridenthal and Koonz, "Beyond *Kinder, Küche, Kirche*," 36–37.

47. Quoted in Paul Smith, *Feminism and the Third Republic: Women's Political and Civil Rights in France, 1918–1945* (Oxford: Clarendon, 1996), 108–109.

48. Virginia Woolf, *Three Guineas* (New York: Harcourt, Brace, 1938), 154–155.

49. Ray Strachey, ed., *Our Freedom and Its Results* (London: Hogarth Press, 1936), 10.

50. Nancy R. Reagin, *A German Women's Movement: Class and Gender in Hanover, 1880–1933* (Chapel Hill: University of North Carolina Press, 1995), 216.

51. Quoted in Carol Miller, "'Geneva—the Key to Equality': Inter-war Feminists and the League of Nations," *Women's History Review* 3:2 (1994): 221.

52. Irene Stoehr, "Housework and Motherhood: Debates and Policies in the Women's Movement in Imperial Germany and the Weimar Republic," in *Maternity and Gender Policies: Women and the Rise of the European Welfare States, 1880–1950s*, ed. Gisela Bock and Pat Thane (New York: Routledge, 1991), 227.

53. Søland, 121.

54. Victoria de Grazia, *How Fascism Ruled Women: Italy, 1922–1945* (Berkeley: University of California Press, 1992), 71.

55. Quotes from de Grazia, *How Fascism Ruled Women*, 43, 55.

56. Mitchell, 117; de Grazia, *How Fascism Ruled Women*, 47.

57. Victoria de Grazia, "How Mussolini Ruled Italian Women," in *A History of Women in the West: Toward a Cultural Identity in the Twentieth Century*, vol. 5, ed. Françoise Thébaud (Cambridge: Belknap, 1994), 142.

58. de Grazia, *How Fascism Ruled Women*, 178.

59. Quoted in Mariolina Graziosi, "Gender Struggle and the Social Manipulation and Ideological Use of Gender Identity in the Interwar Years," in *Mothers of Invention: Women, Italian Fascism, and Culture*, ed. Robin Pickering-Iazzi (Minneapolis: University of Minnesota Press, 1995), 40.

60. de Grazia, *How Fascism Ruled Women*, 179.

61. Judith Keene, "'Into the Clear Air of the Plaza': Spanish Women Achieve the Vote in 1931," in *Constructing Spanish Womanhood*, 341.

62. Mary Nash, *Defying Male Civilization: Women in the Spanish Civil War* (Denver: Arden Press, 1995), 50, 107.

63. *The Visual Front: Posters of the Spanish Civil War* from UCSD's Southworth Collection; http://orpheus.ucsd.edu/speccoll/visfront/acusamos.html.

64. Nash, *Defying*, 71.

65. Quoted in Martha Ackelsberg, *Free Women of Spain: Anarchism and the Struggle for the Emancipation of Women* (Bloomington: Indiana University Press, 1991), 115, 136.

66. Mitchell, 119.

67. Victoria Loreé Enders, "Problematic Portraits: The Ambiguous Historical Role of the Sección Feminina of the Falange," in *Constructing Spanish Womanhood*, 387.

68. Quoted in Aurora G. Morcillo, *True Catholic Womanhood: Gender Ideology in Franco's Spain* (DeKalb: Northern Illinois University Press, 2000), 101.

69. Anne Cova and António Costa Pinto, "Women Under Salazar's Dictatorship," *Portuguese Journal of Social Science* 1:2 (2002): 129–144.

70. Quoted in Wendy Goldman, *Women, the State, and Revolution: Soviet Family Policy and Social Life, 1917–1936* (Cambridge: Cambridge University Press, 1993), 5.

71. Barbara Evans Clements, *Bolshevik Feminist: The Life of Aleksandra Kollontai* (Bloomington: Indiana University Press, 1979), 69–74.

72. Barbara Alpern Engel, "Transformation Versus Tradition," in *Russia's Women: Accommodation, Resistance, Transformation*, ed. Barbara Evans Clements, Barbara Alpern Engel, and Christine D. Worobec (Berkeley: University of California Press, 1991), 146.

73. Anne E. Gorsuch, *Youth in Revolutionary Russia: Enthusiasts, Bohemians, Delinquents* (Bloomington: Indiana University Press, 2000), 108.

74. Robert Conquest, *Harvest of Sorrow: Soviet Collectivization and the Terror Famine* (New York: Oxford University Press, 1986), 158.

75. Melanic Ilič, *Women Workers in the Soviet Interwar Economy: From 'Protection' to 'Equality'* (New York: St. Martin's Press, 1999), Appendix 4, 37.

76. Ilič, *Women Workers*, 135–136.

77. Gail Lapidus, *Women in Soviet Society: Equality, Development and Social Change* (Berkeley: University of California Press, 1978), 136,149.

78. Goldman, *Women, the State, and Revolution*, 108–109.

79. Wendy Goldman, "Women, Abortion, and the State, 1917–1936," in *Russia's Women*, 248.

80. Goldman, "Women, Abortion, and the State," 246, 254.

81. Goldman, *Women, the State, and Revolution*, 275.

82. Mitchell, 119.

83. Goldman, "Women, Abortion, and the State," 244.

84. Françoise Navailh, "The Soviet Model," in *A History of Women in the West*, 245.

85. Lapidus, 204, 210.

86. J. Arch Getty, Gábor T. Rittersporn, and Viktor N. Zemskov, "Victims of the Soviet Penal System in the Pre-War Years: A First Approach on the Basis of Archival Evidence," *American Historical Review* 98:4 (October 1993): 1023–1026.

87. Emma Mason, "Women in the Gulag in the 1930s," in *Women in the Stalin Era*, ed. Melanic Ilič (New York: Palgrave, 2001), 132, 134–140.

88. Sigrid Weltge-Wortmann, *Women's Work: Textile Art from the Bauhaus* (San Francisco: Chronicle Books, 1993), 41–49.

89. Whitney Chadwick, *Women Artists and the Surrealist Movement* (New York: Thames and Hudson, 1992), 43.

90. Carole J. Oja, "Women Patrons and Activists for Modernist Music: New York in the 1920s," *Modernism/Modernity* 4:1 (1997): 144.

91. Kate Lacey, *Feminine Frequencies: Gender, German Radio, and the Public Sphere, 1923–1945* (Ann Arbor: University of Michigan Press, 1996), 39–40.

## SUGGESTED READINGS

Benstock, Shari. *Women of the Left Bank: Paris, 1900–1940.* Austin: University of Texas Press, 1986. Benstock's work looks at the literary culture created by the expatriate women living in interwar Paris.

Chadwick, Whitney. *Women Artists and the Surrealist Movement.* New York: Thames and Hudson, 1992.

De Grazia, Victoria. *How Fascism Ruled Women: Italy, 1922–1945.* Berkeley: University of California Press, 1992. This important study examines the relationships between Mussolini's fascist state and Italian women.

Goldman, Wendy Z. *Women at the Gates: Gender and Industry in Stalin's Russia.* London: Cambridge University Press, 2002. Goldman explores the impact of Stalin's economic plans on Russian women.

Nash, Mary. *Defying Male Civilization: Women in the Spanish Civil War.* Denver: Arden Press, 1995.

Roberts, Mary Louise. *Civilization Without Sexes: Reconstructing Gender in Postwar France, 1917–1927.* Chicago: University of Chicago Press, 1994. Roberts provides a fascinating analysis of gender tensions during the interwar period.

Rupp, Leila. *Worlds of Women: The Making of an International Women's Movement.* Princeton: Princeton University Press, 1997.

## Chapter 14

# New Possibilities, New Perils: Women in World War II, 1939–1945

*Shaved Women Selected for Forced Labor.* Women suffered through innumerable physical humiliations and horrific working conditions in Nazi labor camps. As the war progressed, the Nazis transferred most of the prisoners who survived to extermination camps where they were eventually killed. (Yad Vashem.)

■ **Race, Sex, and the National Socialist Agenda**   488

    *Nazi Racism*   489

    *Nazism, Sex, and the Family*   491

    *Nazi Women's Organizations*   492

■ **Women at War**   493

    *Reactions to War*   495

    *Women in Uniform*   497

    *The Resistance*   500

    *Female POWs*   501

■ **On the Home Front**   504

    *Women and Wartime Work*   504

    *The Kitchen Front*   506

    *Other Pressures at Home*   508

    *The Home Front in Germany*   510

■ **The Holocaust**   511

    *Life in the Ghetto*   511

    *Labor and Extermination Camps*   512

■ **The End of the War**   514

    *Occupation and Liberation*   515

    *Returning to "Normal"*   518

    *Out of the Service*   520

During the late 1930s, Europeans grew increasingly uneasy as Germany's international conflicts and growing economic instability contributed to the rise of the National Socialists, a racist, fascist political party. Once in power, the Nazis manipulated women's reproductive ability and instigated the systematic extermination of millions of people in order to fulfill their desire for racial purification. At the same time, unchecked German aggression led to a world war of unprecedented size and violence. From the outset, women were part of every aspect of the war, from wartime propaganda to fighting on the battlefield. At home, the war tested women's emotional strength and wartime industries relied heavily on their labor. When the war finally ended, women took on the backbreaking labor of rebuilding Europe, as they remade their relationships, reconstructed their homes, and began the process of restructuring their nations in the aftermath of the devastation.

## RACE, SEX, AND THE NATIONAL SOCIALIST AGENDA

Many historians believe that World War II had its origins in World War I. The seeds of National Socialism were sown in the battlefields of the Great War, as many Germans could not accept the humiliating terms of the Versailles Treaty (1919). Political discontent and instability plagued the Weimar Republic. During the late 1930s, as the depression intensified, increasing numbers of Germans looked for radical solutions to their nation's problems. In this highly charged atmosphere, some Germans were attracted to the ideas of Adolf Hitler (1889–1945), the head of the National Socialist German Workers Party (the Nazi Party). With the disintegration of Germany's ruling centrist coalition, Hitler and his party garnered 37 percent of the votes in the elections of 1932 and the German president appointed Adolf Hitler as chancellor of Germany. Quickly, Hitler consolidated power and transformed the republic into an authoritarian state. Hitler drew upon all available resources to implement his nationalistic program, using women's bodies to create a racially pure German nation.

## Chapter 14 ❖ Chronology

| | |
|---|---|
| **1933** | Hitler becomes chancellor of Germany |
| **1938** | Kristallnacht |
| **1939** | Hitler invades Poland |
| **1940** | Germans invade France |
| | Battle of Britain |
| **1941** | British women to register for wartime service |
| | United States enters the war |
| | Nazis begin operating extermination camps |
| **1942** | United States establishes women's auxiliaries for all branches of the armed services |
| | Soviet Union mobilizes childless women and women not already engaged in wartime work |
| **1943** | Hitler orders large-scale deportation of Jews to concentration camps |
| | Warsaw Ghetto uprising |
| **1944** | D-Day invasion of Normandy |
| **1945** | Germany surrenders |
| | United States drops atomic bombs on Japan; Japan surrenders |

## Nazi Racism

Racial purity was at the center of Hitler's political and social ideology. As we saw in the previous chapter, interest in eugenics surged during the interwar period, as supporters argued that such a program would help to remedy the perceived political, economic, and social decline that plagued the West after World War I. However, Hitler took eugenics further, promoting the purification of the "Aryan" race, which he defined as white Christian northern Europeans, by systematically ridding the country of all non-Aryans, a diverse group of "undesirables" that included Jews, Slavs, Roma and Sinti (Gypsies), and the physically and mentally handicapped.

Beginning in 1934, Hitler required the sterilization of people whom he deemed "unfit." The use of sterilization was not unique to Nazis; forced sterilization was legal in the United States and some other northern European countries. However, the scope of Nazi sterilizations was unparalleled. Between 1934 and 1939, the German government sterilized 320,000 people, 0.5 percent of the population. Women were two-thirds of the sterilization victims.[1]

Most of the people subjected to compulsory sterilization were Germans, especially the mentally retarded, schizophrenics, people with manic depression, those with other serious mental illnesses, hereditary blindness or deafness, epilepsy, and people with many types of physical deformities. Inmates of mental institutions had to be sterilized before being discharged. Doctors operated on people whom the government deemed "asocial" or "habitual delinquents," including prostitutes.

Germany's small black population, most of whom had immigrated from Germany's African colonies, were also subject to sterilization.

Local officials urged employers and clergy to suggest possible candidates for sterilization. Women assisted in this process, making up 15 percent of the medical officers who put candidates forward for sterilization.[2] Once selected, a citizen could protest the decision to sterilize him or her in special sterilization courts. For instance, the husband of a woman named Olga tried to stop her sterilization: "My wife and I will not consent to sterilization. I also cannot understand why my wife would even be considered for sterilization, since in my opinion she is not feeble-minded." Her boss at the factory where she worked also believed that she was "normal," but the local priest declared her entire family "easily distracted, bad-tempered, and obdurate." She had also failed a year of school. Like thousands of others, Olga was sterilized against her and her family's will in 1936.[3]

During sterilization, Nazi doctors removed men's gonads and performed complete ovarectomies on women. Some women were sterilized by high doses of x-rays.[4] As a consequence, many women suffered serious medical problems. Others suffered depression, feeling useless in a society that valued motherhood as the only meaningful role for women. Tragically, between 1934 and 1937, eighty men and four hundred women died from the operations.[5]

The Nazis not only believed that some people should reproduce, they also categorized others as "lives unworthy of life." Between 1939 and 1941, the Nazis murdered more than seventy thousand mentally and physically handicapped adults and long-term inmates of psychiatric hospitals as well as fifty-two hundred "deformed" children in a project known as "Aktion T-4." This secret "euthanasia" project took place at six asylums, where Nazi doctors gassed selected patients and cremated their bodies. Officials told their parents and relatives that their family members had died of sudden illnesses.[6]

The Nazis aimed most of their race policy at ridding the German state of its non-Aryan inhabitants. During the Weimar Republic, Roma and Sinti peoples (Gypsies) had been subject to a variety of discriminatory laws, but under Hitler, the oppression worsened. The state sterilized more than two thousand Roma and Sinti, and in 1936, with the creation of an office to "Combat the Gypsy Nuisance," Berlin police imprisoned six hundred Gypsies in a special internment camp to keep them out of the city during the summer Olympics. The camp had only three water pumps and two toilets and disease was rampant. In time, the Nazis erected other Roma internment camps across Germany, and later, they would deport thousands of Roma to concentration camps for extermination.

Germany's large and thriving Jewish population bore the brunt of Hitler's pursuit of racial purity. Hitler defined Judaism as a racial category, not as a religion. Anyone with at least three Jewish grandparents was a Jew even if that person was not religious or if his or her parents had converted to Christianity. The first discriminatory acts against Jews were social and economic. Hitler's regime encouraged Germans to publicly insult Jews or completely ignore them on streetcars and other public places. Even at home, the center of Jewish women's lives, Jews felt unsafe. The Nazi Secret Police, the *Gestapo*, randomly searched and ransacked Jewish homes, and many Jewish families faced eviction from German landlords. Beginning in 1933, the Nazi government outlawed kosher butchering, which made it impossible for Jewish women to maintain the dietary laws. Boycotts and legislation forced Jewish shops to close, and officials pressured non-Jewish employers to fire Jewish employees. The government also required all German professional and social organizations to expel their Jewish members. Beginning in 1935, the Nuremberg laws restricted citizenship to Aryans. As a result, Jews lost their rights as citizens to vote or hold public office. As Claire Bachrach Dratch recalled many years later, "Friends no longer wanted to walk down the street with me. They no longer wished to sit next to me on the train, eventually they did not wish to be seen with me at all . . . I was the same Claire Bacharach—but I was Jewish . . . I had become a non-person."[7]

The Nazi government also attempted to end relationships between Jews and Aryans. German authorities paraded women accused of having Jewish lovers through the streets of their hometowns with signs around their necks that said,

"I have committed racial treason" or "I fornicate with Jews." Marriages between Jews and non-Jews became illegal in 1935. However, although Aryan wives sometimes divorced their Jewish husbands, few Aryan men divorced their Jewish wives. These women seem to have been protected by their marriages and subject to less harassment as their husbands helped them hide their religious identities.[8]

Anti-Semitic activity came to a head on November 9, 1938, when, under Nazi orders, Germans looted, set fire to, and destroyed Jewish synagogues, businesses, schools, and homes. The night known as *Kristallnacht,* the "night of the broken glass," led to the beating, arrest, and removal to concentration camps of thirty thousand Jewish men. Fearful of more violence, during the next year, 112,000 Jews left for other parts of Europe and the United States. Many of the immigrants were the wives and children of men arrested by the Nazis. The decision to leave was difficult, as families pressured many women to remain and care for elderly relatives and/or work for their husbands' releases.[9] To protect their children, thousands of Jewish women put approximately ten thousand children on the *Kindertransporte* trains to England, where caring strangers took them in. The fate of most of Germany's remaining Jewish population would be decided in ghettos and extermination camps, where millions of men, women, and children would suffer the violence of Hitler's racial extermination policies.

## Nazism, Sex, and the Family

As the Nazis worked to prevent non-Aryan women from reproducing, they made marriage and motherhood the focus of Aryan women's lives. Although Hitler only married at the end of his life, he promoted early marriage as a means to control adolescent sexuality and encouraged women to bear more children. Of course, the Nazis did not approve of all marriages. Beginning in 1935, prospective couples had to obtain the approval of the Nazi bureaucracy by applying for a "certificate of fitness to marry." The Reich even changed divorce laws to reflect the emphasis on permanent marriage and procreation. For the most part, a couple could only divorce if one spouse was unable or unwilling to reproduce, although occasionally, judges accepted the "irretrievable breakdown" of a marriage as a reason for divorce because people who could not live together could not successfully bear children.[10]

Hitler was particularly concerned about the drop in the German birthrate during World War I and the interwar years. By 1933, the German birthrate had fallen to only 14.7/1,000, nearly half what it had been in 1910.[11] Like many other European nations, the government provided incentives for people to marry and have as many children as possible. In 1933, Hitler introduced a system through which an Aryan couple could get a loan of one thousand reichsmarks (about one-fifth the average German annual take-home pay) in the form of vouchers for household goods if the woman gave up work at marriage and became a mother. The government paid the vouchers directly to the husband. At first, the plan was quite successful. Many couples who had delayed marriage during the depression took the opportunity to tie the knot and begin families. The cost of the loan was tied to the couple's fertility and was reduced by one-fourth at the birth of each child. In fact, the government encouraged families to have four children in order to achieve a *Kinderreich,* a nation rich in children. Hitler also offered tax breaks so that parents of six children paid no personal income tax. For a while, women who bore five children could choose a famous man as the godfather, but when women chose Paul von Hindenburg (1847–1934), the president of the Reich, more often than himself, Hitler ended the program.[12]

As a part of his promotion of motherhood, Hitler encouraged public celebrations of "German womanhood." Mother's Day gained special status, and the date was changed to Hitler's mother's birthday. Officials encouraged ministers to deliver sermons on mothers and motherhood and theaters to put on appropriate plays. Starting in 1939, the government began awarding "Mother's Honor Crosses." Three million women, most of whom were older with four or more children, received the title "Mothers of the Reich." There were three types of crosses: bronze for mothers of four children, silver for mothers of six children, and gold for mothers of eight or more. In addition to recognition from the government, Mothers of the Reich could cut in line in shops and received extra ration cards during the war.[13] Of course, the government only awarded crosses to women of German blood. The Nazis excluded women who had prison convictions, who had abortions, who had "defiled" the race by bearing children with physical or mental illnesses, or who were deemed "asocial." Untidy housekeepers, alcoholics, and women termed "uneconomical" because they used their child allowances to buy luxury goods were also ineligible.[14] The Nazi regime discouraged these and non-Aryan mothers from having children if not already prevented from doing so by sterilization.

The Nazi regime officially promoted the view that sex was for procreation only. Thus, Nazi propaganda discouraged women from wearing makeup and referred to sex appeal as "Jewish cosmopolitanism." In fact, in 1933, the Nazis set up a German Fashion Bureau to design clothing appropriate for German women, with folk-inspired dirndl skirts for rural women and stylish uniforms for urban working women.[15]

However, Nazism was far from prudish, and scholars have noted the erotic nature of Nazi propaganda. Nazi youth groups provided adolescents with opportunities for interactions with youth of the opposite sex and described sex as a part of a healthy life. Even schoolchildren were indoctrinated with the basics of Nazi sex ideology as they memorized the "Ten Commandments for Choosing a Partner":

1. *Remember you are a German!*
2. *Remain pure in mind and spirit!*
3. *Keep your body pure!*
4. *If hereditarily fit, do not remain single!*
5. *Marry only for love.*
6. *Being a German, choose only a spouse of similar or related blood!*
7. *When choosing your spouse, inquire into his or her forebears!*
8. *Health is essential to outward beauty as well!*
9. *Seek a companion in marriage, not a playmate!*
10. *Hope for as many children as possible!*[16]

Since the goal of sex was the production of children, the Nazi government quickly closed the birth control centers that activists had established during the Weimar Republic. Abortion was already illegal, but even after the government increased punishments for abortionists (except for abortions performed on prostitutes and Jews), German women sought abortions in large numbers. In fact, more children were aborted during this period than were born to couples who received marriage loans to promote their fertility.[17] Heinrich Himmler (1900–1945), head of the SS, the Nazi paramilitary, designed his *Lebensborn* program to encourage single pregnant Aryan women to carry their pregnancies to term and put their children up for adoption.

As he believed that sex was for procreation only, Hitler did not tolerate homosexuality. Homosexuality had been illegal in Germany since the late nineteenth century, but during the interwar years, Berlin had been home to a vibrant homosexual community. Upon coming to power, the Nazis quickly closed down the city's gay bars and nightclubs. In addition, they destroyed institutions like the Institute for Sex Science run by Max Hirschfeld (1868–1935), which promoted homosexual rights and studied transsexuals. Lesbianism was never against the law because, as one Nazi official pointed out, "women who indulge in unnatural sexual relations are not lost forever as procreative factors in the same way that homosexual men are, for experience shows that they later often resume normal relations."[18] However, lesbians who would not conform to the ideals of German womanhood may have been prosecuted for other crimes, such as being "asocial." In fact, the Nazis made the distinction between male and female homosexuality clear when homosexuals were later deported to concentration camps. Lesbians wore the black triangles of "asocials" or red triangles of "political" prisoners while gay men wore pink triangles. During the war, the Nazis sent fifty thousand male homosexuals and ten thousand to fifteenth thousand lesbians to concentration camps.

## Nazi Women's Organizations

Initially, the Nazis did not mobilize women as right-wing parties had in Italy and Spain (see Chapter 13), because they did not believe that women should participate in politics. Nevertheless, many women supported the Nazis from early on for many of the same reasons that fascism appealed to women in Spain and Italy. The Nazi emphasis on maternity, and the promise of social order and a more stable, stronger nation led some right-wing women to form their own National Socialist organizations. Initially, these groups had extensive autonomy and worked hard to win Hitler's favor. However, in 1931, the Nazi Party ordered that all women's groups disband. In their place, the party established the National Socialist Women's League (NSF). The Nazi leadership appointed Elsbeth Zander (1888–1963) as the head of NSF, but male officials found her too independent. Indeed, within a year, no women leaders held any major office in the Nazi organization.[19] Even women who enthusiastically supported the Nazis before 1933 were removed from positions of authority and replaced with more compliant women who expressed no desire for autonomy. Gertrud Scholtz-Klink (b. 1902), who was administratively capable but willing to work under the watchful eye of the Nazi hierarchy, then took over the NSF.

Under Scholtz-Klink, the NSF encouraged "valuable" German women to work for their communities and subordinate their own goals and desires to those of the Nazis. They should have pride in their racial identity and fulfill all Nazi expectations for being good Aryan wives. The NSF encouraged women to attend courses in housekeeping and cooking, and the government discouraged women from purchasing new appliances that would save them time, in order to ensure that housework was their main activity. Women who did not conform to these values were branded "asocial" and faced imprisonment and possible sterilization. Most members of the NSF were middle-class housewives. Rural women were encouraged to join the rural workers' association, and working women joined the DAF, the German Labor Front. Although German working-class women labored full-time in Germany's factories and their workload increased as war became imminent, the DAF encouraged them to fulfill the same housekeeping expectations as housewives, holding courses on cooking, sewing, and other household work at the factories.[20]

The process of indoctrinating women into Nazi culture began with school-age girls who joined the *Bund Deutscher Mädel* (BDM). This group of "valuable Aryan" girls was associated with the Hitler Youth movement, and by 1939, membership was compulsory for girls ten to fourteen years old. The organization taught girls to aspire to be "heroine mothers" and to be beautiful.[21] Group activities stressed sports, hiking, and camping in order to maintain excellent physical health. Girls did some volunteer work in their communities, but they could only help those who were declared "socially valuable," hardworking, but poor Aryans.

By 1939, the Nazis had fully implemented their policies concerning sex and womanhood. Unworthy women were sterilized or socially marginalized and Aryan women were praised for their contributions as mothers. Participation in Nazi girls' and women's organizations constantly reaffirmed Nazi values and created frameworks to regulate women's activities. However, while German women struggled to meet Nazi standards of cleanliness and motherhood, their husbands were preparing for war.

## WOMEN AT WAR

Proceeding with his plan to extend his pure Aryan nation beyond Germany's borders, on September 1, 1939, Hitler invaded and quickly occupied neighboring Poland after signing a nonaggression pact with the Soviet Union. Two days later Britain and France declared war on Germany and World War II began (see Map 14.1). Hitler's successes came rapidly. In the spring of 1940, German forces invaded Norway, Denmark, the neutral Low Countries (Netherlands, Belgium, and Luxembourg), and France. Within a month, France had signed an armistice with Germany, which provided for the German occupation of the northern part of the country and the establishment of a collaborating regime in the south with its capital in Vichy. The Soviet Union occupied the Baltic States (Lithuania, Latvia, and Estonia) in June 1940, and Mussolini announced that Italy would enter the war on the German side. Hitler then began an intensive air war against England. British forces successfully defended against a German victory, and then Hitler attacked Yugoslavia and Greece. On June 22, 1941, Hitler broke his nonaggression pact with Soviet leader Joseph Stalin and invaded the Soviet Union. Stalin had no choice but to switch to the Allied cause. The United States, which had stayed out of the conflict, entered the

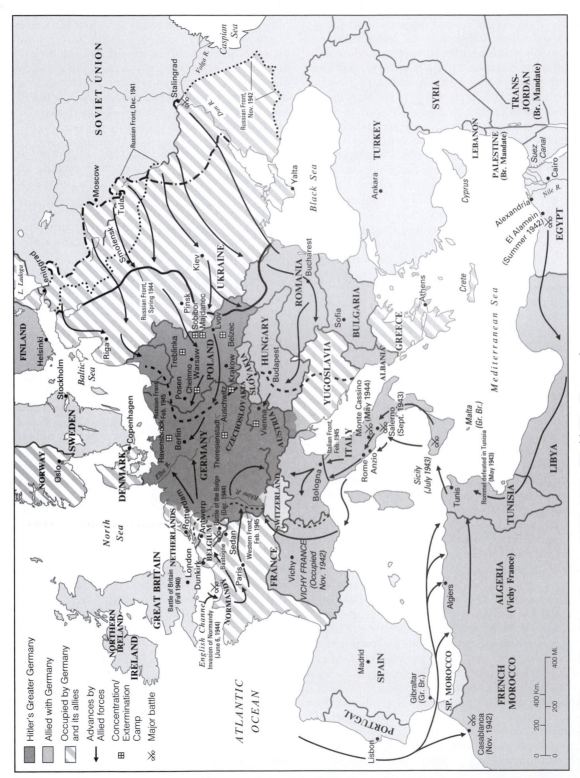

*Map 14.1* **World War II in Europe, 1939–1945.** World War II created hardship for millions of European women and led to the deaths of millions more.

war when Japan, a German ally, bombed Pearl Harbor, Hawaii, on December 7, 1941 (see Map 14.2). In retaliation, Germany and Italy declared war on the United States. For women around the world, the war would be a defining moment in their lives. Millions of women died both in military service and as civilians. Six years of brutal warfare would change the way a generation of women worked, ate, socialized, and thought about peace and war.

## Reactions to War

During the interwar years, international women's organizations had invested most of their energies in preventing another world war. They campaigned against chemical weapons and fought to strengthen the League of Nations. However, by the late 1930s, it was difficult for many organizations to respond to the threat of war, because the depression had seriously depleted their funds and limited their visibility. Nazism also created a philosophical dilemma for women's groups. For instance, the International Woman Suffrage Alliance (IWSA) met in Copenhagen, Demark, in July 1939, just as Hitler was preparing to invade Poland. For nearly two decades, they had lobbied for international cooperation, but their disgust with Hitler's ideology made many uneasy about seeking peace. After the Nazi invasion of Poland, the IWSA, the International Council of Women, and other groups had to accept the uncomfortable truth. They had to support war in order to support democracy, a reality that was especially true by June of 1940, when Great Britain was the only European democracy that had not fallen to Hitler.[22]

After 1940, with German soldiers occupying European villages and bombs destroying their homes, most European women did not have the luxury of deciding whether or not to support the war. However, women in the United States vigorously debated the possibility of U.S. entry into the European conflict. Officially, the United States had declared its nonengagement in the Neutrality Acts of the 1930s that forbade the sale of arms to either side in "foreign" wars. As the war progressed, the U.S. Congress amended the acts to allow Allied governments at war to buy U.S. arms and supplies, but they had to pay cash and transport the goods in their own ships. After the Nazi occupa-

tion of France and the bombing of Britain, Allied forces could no longer comply with those provisions. In late 1940, President Franklin Delano Roosevelt (1932–1945) proposed the Lend-Lease Act, which would allow the United States to provide Britain, the Soviet Union, and other countries with arms without payment. Initially, internationalist organizations such as the League of Women Voters pushed for international cooperation. However, as the war in Europe intensified, many women's groups came to believe that the Lend-Lease Act was the best way to ensure that U.S. allies would be ultimately victorious without making U.S. entry into the war inevitable.

On the other end of the political spectrum, the far right Mothers' Movement was vehemently isolationist and opposed to the war and communism. This loose confederation of fifty to one hundred women's groups claimed to have ten million members in the early 1940s, but they probably had closer to five to six million members. The National Legion of Mothers of America, the largest of these groups, was composed of white, middle-aged, middle-class women who had draft-age sons. These women held a wide array of right-wing ideas. Many of the groups supported Hitler, believing that his anticommunism was the most important part of his ideology. Most of the groups were virulently anti-Semitic, a view many Americans shared. In polls taken in the late 1930s, 60 percent of Americans said that they thought that Jews had "objectionable qualities," and 20 percent would be sympathetic to an anti-Semitic campaign.[23] Some groups were also anti-black and/or anti-Catholic. Elizabeth Dilling (1894–1966), a vocal leader of the Mothers' Movement, published a series of books and worked closely with male leaders of the far right, including the infamous anti-Semite Father Charles Coughlin (1891–1979).

Lyrl Clark Van Hyning led the group We the Mothers Mobilize for America, which claimed to have 150,000 members. She believed that Jews had plotted Lincoln's assassination, that they planned to introduce free love so that Christian families would be weakened, and that General Eisenhower (1890–1969), the leader of U.S. forces, was a Swedish Jew. Many female leaders of the far right vociferously opposed President Roosevelt and his New Deal and created conspiracy theories in

**Map 14.2** WORLD WAR II IN THE PACIFIC, 1941–1945. As the war in the Pacific expanded, many European and American nurses and civilians were captured and held in Japanese prison camps.

which he and other government officials played central roles.[24] These women organized protests in major U.S. cities and shouted their hate across the airwaves. However, all the angry words became moot with the bombing of Pearl Harbor. The United States entered the war and women of all political persuasions focused on other issues for the next four years.

## Women in Uniform

Although Western nations still viewed war as a masculine pursuit, the scope of World War II drew women into military service in large numbers for the first time in history. Despite the fact that their governments badly needed their help in the war effort, the idea of women in uniform provoked a wide array of gender conflicts in the military and in society more broadly.

By early 1941, appeals for volunteers had proven ineffective, and the British government, led by Winston Churchill (prime minister 1940–1945), faced an acute labor shortage. Churchill ordered all women between the ages of nineteen and forty to register for essential wartime work. More than five hundred thousand women enlisted in the different branches of Britain's military and volunteer services. The Auxiliary Territorial Service (ATS) placed women into a variety of support tasks from clerical work to drivers, military police, butchers, and bakers. The Women's Voluntary Services (WVS), established in 1938, helped with evacuations and cared for victims of air raids, and the Women's Land Army worked on the nation's farms, harvesting crops, caring for livestock, and even running sawmills. In the Air Transport Auxiliary (ATA), female pilots like Pauline Gower (ca. 1910–1947) ferried planes from factories to airfields.

The British military generally welcomed women's assistance, hoping to free as many adult men as possible for combat. Englishwomen worked in antiaircraft units, armed bomber and fighter planes, and maintained and repaired military equipment. The decision to deploy women from the ATS in anti-aircraft units allowed women to officially participate in combat operations for the first time. All but the most traditional officers recognized that the women performed admirably.

The commanding officer of the first mixed-sex battery to bring down a German bomber said, "I say without hesitation I would take the mixed battery. The girls cannot be beaten in action, and in my opinion they are definitely better than the men on the instruments they are manning . . . they are quite as steady if not steadier than the men." However, according to military policy, women were only allowed to use range finders to direct, but not to fire, guns. In fact, near the end of the war, the British military did not even allow women in anti-aircraft batteries to shoot at pilotless missiles. Nevertheless, many women found the experience exhilarating. Vera Robinson, a member of the ATS, noted, "the girls, might I say, were all very proud, because we were treated exactly like the men, and that's how we wanted it." At the same time, other women reported that their male peers treated them more like daughters and sisters than equals. Indeed, the Auxiliary forces were not integrated into the regular military structure until after World War II.[25]

The Women's Auxiliary Air Force (WAAF), which had 180,000 members by 1943, was unique in that it was not a separate service but was integrated into the Royal Air Force. WAAFs lived and worked alongside men and officers assigned duties not according to gender, but availability. However, the WAAF challenged gender boundaries in ways that often made men uncomfortable. The press regularly sexualized WAAFs in their descriptions, and one press headline even promoted the WAAF as a beauty aid, declaring, "WAAF service helps the figure."[26] Moreover, despite the gender equity in job distribution, the hierarchy of the WAAF always described women as "behind" the armed forces, "assisting" men who were giving their lives in battle. The clearest evidence of their lack of equality was that no members of the WAAF were allowed to fly aircraft.

Military service gave women confidence and allowed them to make important contributions to the war effort. However, it also introduced them to frank sexuality in ways that surprised many proper middle-class Englishwomen. They had to dress and shower in front of other women and they met lesbians for the first time. Critics accused servicewomen of being either too manly or too feminine. Allegations abounded that servicewomen were sexually promiscuous. Such charges were frequently aimed at the large numbers of working-class women who made up the ATS.[27]

Women's military experience in the Soviet Union could not have been more different. By 1942, the Soviet government had mobilized all childless women and women not engaged in critical industrial or government work. By 1943, more than eight hundred thousand female volunteers served in the military, about 8 percent of the Soviet forces. Soviet women not only fired weapons, but they were the only European servicewomen to fight outside their native country.[28] Women served as pilots, machine gunners, in tank crews, as well as all variety of communications troops. A few female officers even led battalions of men into battle.[29]

In addition to the women in the trenches, the Soviet Union had one thousand female aviators who were trained as fighter and military transport pilots. Initially, the Soviet military did not conscript female aviators, and women were not allowed to enlist in aviation units. So, female pilots voluntarily formed Aviation Group 122 in 1941. Within a year, the Soviet Union's most famous female aviator, Marina Raskova (1912–1943), had organized three regiments of skilled female pilots—the 586th Fighter Aviation Regiment, the 587th Bomber Aviation Regiment, and the 588th Night Bomber Aviation Regiment. These women were assigned to the battlefront in the spring of 1942. There was no difference in numbers or types of missions flown by the female and male regiments; one woman logged more than a thousand combat flights. The Soviet government decorated personnel of all three regiments and awarded at least thirty-three female pilots and navigators the title of Heroes of the Soviet Union. Liliia Litviak (d. 1943), a pilot in a mostly male unit, wrote to her mother, "I am completely absorbed in combat life. I can't seem to think of anything but the fighting."[30] When her plane went down in 1943, she had completed 268 combat flights and was the first woman in history to shoot down an enemy bomber.

Because the Soviet government had made no special provisions for female service members, life on the front was often exceptionally difficult. Initially, the military provided no uniforms for the women; they wore men's clothing, including underwear and shoes. There were no bras, and women later described fashioning them out of

scraps.[31] It was difficult for women to urinate during long marches, so male soldiers used their coats to provide some privacy. Without feminine hygiene products, many women were relieved to stop menstruating due to stress and poor nutrition.

With women and men together in the trenches, there was considerable opportunity for sexual interactions, but female fighters noted that early on in the war, ordinary soldiers began using the term "little sister" to refer to women of all ranks. Although somewhat patronizing, the use of the term created a sexual taboo between the men and the women, and women believed that it helped prevent rape by their peers.[32] Women also noted that they suffered less sexual harassment from ordinary soldiers than from officers and Soviet party officials. A few women, known as "mobile field wives," formed relationships with male soldiers. Those relationships brought both companionship and privileges such as better rations. However, if a woman became pregnant, she had to continue to serve until her seventh month.

Approximately 280,000 women served in all branches of the U.S. military, although they never officially participated in combat. At the beginning of the war, many women, including Eleanor Roosevelt, had to fight for women's right to serve their country as full citizens and to have that service recognized, unlike their predecessors in World War I. When Congresswoman Edith Nourse Rogers (1881–1960) introduced the bill to establish the Women's Army Auxiliary Corps (WAAC) in 1941, resistance was strong. One senator retorted, "A women's army to defend the United States of America! Think of the humiliation. What has become of the manhood of America, that we have to call on our women to do what has ever been the duty of men." Despite the support of the Roosevelt administration and the War Department, the bill languished even after Pearl Harbor. The ensuing congressional debate centered not on military readiness, but on the implications of women's military service for American masculinity and femininity.[33]

In 1942, the U.S. Congress finally approved the formation of women's auxiliaries for each branch of the military. Like their British counterparts, these women deciphered coded messages, worked as telephone and radio operators, rigged parachutes, and repaired planes and trucks. Female scientists provided technical information for the military, and many others served in the Office of Strategic Services (OSS), the U.S. intelligence service. Although women were indispensable to the military effort, the WAACs remained outside the military hierarchy, supervised by a separate director, Oveta Culp Hobby (1905–1995). Even when they were reconfigured as the Women's Army Corps (WAC) in 1943, they were not equal to servicemen. The WAC did not automatically grant members allowances for spouses or children, female officers could not give orders to men, and women were prohibited from engaging in combat.[34]

The one hundred thousand WACs were almost exclusively white and single, and most came from farms and small towns.[35] Women with children under fourteen years old were not permitted to enlist. The military recruited some Asian American women to serve as translators and in other technical positions, and four thousand African American women served in the WAC, but racism kept them in low-level jobs and few were sent overseas.

Military officials, both male and female, feared that military service compromised femininity and encouraged lesbianism. Regulations excluded women with "rough or coarse" manners, whose build was "stocky or shapeless," and women whose demeanor, including dress and "voice type" was "masculine" from officer training. To get away from any perceptions of mannishness and lesbianism, the WACs tried to create a "feminine" look for female soldiers, including scarves and gloves. Officials even worked with Elizabeth Arden salons to develop an appropriately feminine hairstyle that maintained military standards. Concerns about femininity were so serious that although women served near the European front where it was cold and in the Pacific front where insects threatened women's health, the military refused to allow them to wear trousers.[36]

In two years, the 1,074 female pilots who joined the WASPs (Women Airforce Service Pilots) flew a total of sixty million miles, delivering more than twelve thousand planes to bases around the country. However, male pilots found the women's presence threatening and some military officials took advantage of the gender tensions. Officers tried to cajole men into flying planes that they were unsure of by having female pilots fly them first, including the B-29, the plane used to drop the atomic bomb on Hiroshima.[37] Flying new planes was not the most dangerous task that women accepted, however. Female pilots also towed targets for gunnery practice, placing them directly in the line of fire of male pilots.

The Army and Navy Nurse Corps, who administered medical care to American servicemen from the Philippines to Italy, were the only U.S. women to serve in combat zones. Despite their hard work and bravery, they rarely received the respect that they deserved. Military nurses were poorly paid, and their reputations were often suspect because most were single and their work entailed close unsupervised interactions with men. Of the 30,000 nurses who volunteered and served in combat zones, hundreds of nurses became prisoners of war and 201 died.[38]

However, most American women showed little enthusiasm for these volunteer services. In May 1942, an admiral told the secretary of the navy that "there seems to be a tendency on the part of male members of the family to discourage females from joining the armed services. This includes all branches."[39] The widely held perception that servicewomen were sexually promiscuous and, just as important, not tending to their proper household duties kept most American women at home.

With its emphasis on traditional femininity, Germany did not enlist any women in its armed forces, although 450,000 women served in auxiliary units in addition to those who were military nurses.[40] Even toward the end of the war, Nazi officials resisted drafting women. However, they did allow women to test new models of aircraft, probably to spare the lives of male fighter pilots. Hannah Reitsch (1912–1979) was a German test pilot during the war. She was the only pilot that Hitler and his inner circle trusted to fly them into Berlin into enemy fire in 1944–45 and the only woman ever awarded the Iron Cross and Luftwaffe Diamond Clasp.[41]

Women served bravely, but rarely as equals. Their nations could not overcome the idea that combat was for men, even when women fired weapons on enemy forces. Their governments, their commanding officers, and society in general considered women's diligence and loyalty secondary to men's. Whether they were caring for victims in evacuation hospitals in France, ferrying airplanes to bases in Canada, or deciphering code in offices in Washington, D.C., few recognized the extent of servicewomen's sacrifices.

## The Resistance

In Axis-controlled areas, men and women joined the underground movements known as the Resistance to fight the occupying forces. These forces engaged in sabotage, assassination, code breaking, and other subversive activities, and women distinguished themselves as both leaders and participants in Resistance movements around Europe.

After the Germans invaded in April 1941, Yugoslavia became a fascist state under German supervision and Italy, Bulgaria, and Hungary occupied large parts of the country. Approximately two million Yugoslav women fought the occupation, one hundred thousand as Resistance fighters, or *partisans*. Nearly two thousand women, including Danica Milosavljevic who commanded the First Battalion of the Second Proletarian Brigade, achieved officer rank in those units. Yugoslav partisans were mostly young women, 70 percent under twenty years of age. Large numbers of women also aided the Resistance through the Anti-Fascist Front of Women (AFZ), providing supplies, propaganda, medical care, refugee aid, and childcare.[42]

Women figured prominently in nearly all aspects of the French Resistance. Berthie Albrecht (1910–1943) helped to found and lead Combat, France's most important Resistance movement. She initiated and produced the movement's newsletter, *Combat,* which became the major clandestine newspaper in the south of France with a circulation of more than two hundred thousand by 1944 and provided supporters with information on the occupation and the Resistance. The great French writer and philosopher Simone de Beauvoir (1908–1986) acknowledged many years later that she had written the accounts of the liberation of Paris that had appeared in *Combat* under Jean-Paul Sartre's (1905–1980) name. Under the pseudonym of Emma, Simone Michel-Lévy (1906–1945) organized a Resistance network in the Post and Telecommunications Service. In 1943, she was captured by Germans and later deported to Ravensbrück (see below), tortured, and hanged for sabotage. The French government posthumously awarded Michel-Lévy the honor of *Compagnon de la Libération*, one of only six women to receive that award. Marie-Madeleine (Méric) Fourcade (1909–1989) headed an intelligence network of more than three thousand agents, and Georgette (Claude) Gérard (b. 1914) headed a *maquis*, a Resistance fighting unit (see **Women's Lives:** Marie-Madeleine Fourcade, Resistance Fighter). Gérard organized Combat's Secret Army in Dordogne and then led all partisan combat units in southwestern France, with several thousand men under her command.[43]

Like their male counterparts, some female resisters took on new identities and went underground to fight the Germans. Many of these women joined along with parents and siblings, but others sacrificed those relationships, so as not to jeopardize the lives of their loved ones. When working above ground, women used their identities as mothers and housewives and the facilities at their workplaces on behalf of the Resistance. They hid secret documents under maternity dresses and took resisters into their homes, where they fed and clothed them. Many resisters credited women with providing them with emotional support when they were tired, afraid, or discouraged. Building supervisors became informants and accomplices. Henriette Labarbe, a Parisian concierge, hid partisans in the tunnels of her buildings during the battle for the liberation of Paris.[44] Secretaries used office typewriters to help provide false papers. Still other women were complicit with the Resistance without publicly professing their support. In interviews, many female resisters cited the importance of neighbors and relatives who took care of the children of resisters without asking questions. Women also contributed to the Resistance through the *Service Social,* a section of *Combat* staffed entirely by women. It and similar groups provided care and assistance to families of resisters, political prisoners, and children whose parents had been arrested or killed.

Despite their willingness to participate in dangerous activities, women faced discrimination from their male colleagues in the Resistance. Male members of fighting units feared that women compromised the legitimacy of rural combat groups because they gossiped and got involved with men. As a result, French explosives expert Jeanne Bohec (b. 1919) had to fight to work with a maquis unit. Having escaped to England just prior to the war, she eagerly volunteered when French Resistance leader Charles De Gaulle (1890–1970) formed the women's volunteer corps in 1940. Despite her extensive scientific training, she was made a nurse and had to insist on work that made better use of her scientific skills. Even then, she recalled that when she and six men secretly parachuted into France, the maquis member that met her was unpleasantly surprised to see a young woman. Over the course of the war, she blew up a major rail line and worked as a decoder.[45]

Communist opposition to Mussolini's regime formed the basis of the Italian Resistance. However, the thirty-five thousand female partisan fighters and twenty thousand "patriots" were largely young and without official party affiliations. Some women gradually became resisters because of the activities of their husbands and brothers. Leda Orlandi Bastia told an interviewer, "I found myself joining the resistance gradually, almost without understanding, working at the side of my husband Mario." Other women joined out of passionate political beliefs, and still others saw it as a pragmatic way to confront the daily hardship that they faced during the war. Many women became couriers between Resistance units. Although some women took part in fighting, Resistance brigades remained ambivalent about their presence, and women had to assert themselves to get weapons. Elsa Oliva told her brigade commander in 1944, "I am not here to find a lover. I am here to fight and I will remain here if I am given a weapon and placed in the sector of those who do guard duty and take action." Paola Del Din, a recent Italian university graduate, trained as a parachutist and took part in eleven air missions bringing information to the Allies.[46]

After German troops invaded Denmark in April 1940, women engaged in both passive and active resistance. When Hitler ordered the deportation of all Danish Jews in September 1943, Danes began hiding their Jewish neighbors and securing their escape to Sweden. Mrs. Ellen Nielsen, a widow with six children, was a fishmonger who hid more than one hundred refugees. She and her children fed and cared for them, and her sons helped guide them to the fishing boats that would take them to Sweden. After the Jews were safe, she hid saboteurs for the underground. With help from ordinary women like Mrs.

Nielsen, Danes saved seventy-two hundred of their nation's seventy-five hundred Jews. She was arrested in 1944 and sent to Ravensbrück concentration camp (see below), where she escaped the gas chambers on three separate occasions.[47]

Women also served in Resistance groups in eastern Europe and the Soviet Union. In western Byelorussia, escapees from Jewish ghettos met with Soviet partisans and struggled against the German invaders. Although only a few official participants were women, they struggled against difficult odds. Most Jewish partisans had no experience living in the dense forests of Byelorussia. Jewish women who fought with Russian resisters faced double discrimination as both women and Jews, as many partisans were vocally anti-Semitic. This was especially true toward the end of the war when Nazi collaborators switched sides to avoid punishment. Women fared better in Jewish-led partisan groups but still only achieved influence through men with whom they were sexually involved.[48]

Sexuality was an important tool of the Resistance. In Belgium, fifteen to twenty Austrian young women, both Jews and political exiles, became known as *Mädelgruppe,* girls who flirted with German soldiers hoping to win them over to the Allied cause. Women engaged in similar resistance work in France. Consorting with German soldiers was quite dangerous, and Germans arrested many female resisters and sent them to concentration camps.

## Female POWs

As the Japanese quickly conquered much of East Asia, they captured thousands of prisoners. Although some civilian prisoners were put on ships and torpedoed by the Japanese, others were held in internment camps. The Japanese also captured hundreds of nurses, including Lieutenant Frances Nash and sixty-six others, at Corregidor (Philippines) in 1941–42. Warned that they might be taken prisoner as U.S. troops pulled out of the area, nurses hid morphine tablets in their hairpieces so that they could commit suicide rather than submit to more violent death by Japanese captors. Nash and her fellow nurses remained POWs for the rest of the war.[49]

Conditions in the camps were horrible. Prisoners received little food and endured regular

## Marie-Madeleine (Meric) Fourcade, Resistance Fighter

Although rarely remembered in histories of the war, women were active in the Resistance. Many worked in intelligence gathering and often coordinated the work of radio operators, couriers, and agents. At the height of the war, Marie-Madeleine Meric was the chief of *Alliance*—the largest espionage network and a critical force in the Resistance against the Nazis.

A divorced mother of two, Meric found a job as the general secretary of a publishing company headed by Commandant Georges Loustanau-Lacau (1894–1955), a military intelligence specialist. Officially, Loustanau-Lacau led a veterans' organization for the Vichy government, but behind the scenes he formed the Alliance and coordinated undercover intelligence work for the Resistance.

To protect his cover, Loustanau-Lacau asked Meric to help coordinate the underground work of agents whom he recruited. Then, when the Vichy police arrested him in 1941, she took over command of the Alliance. The Alliance provided information to the British secret intelligence service, the SIS, and Meric worried that they would not respect her because of her sex. So she used the code name POZ/55 to disguise her identity until she had proven her ability to lead.

Meric organized information collected by intelligence sectors across France and sent it to England. Women were an important part of the intelligence network. Approximately one-sixth of the Alliance membership was female, and 9 percent gave their lives for the cause. Meric always bragged that the women in her organization never broke under torture. During the war, the Alliance provided critical intelligence, among them a fifty-five-foot-long detailed map of German defenses in Normandy and information on German secret weapons.

She was always quick thinking during times of crisis. At one point, her mother and some of her compatriots were arrested, and Meric was forced to flee over the Pyrenees, doubled up in a mail bag for more than nine hours. After an English radio operator with fascist sympathies betrayed some Alliance members, she quickly reorganized the operation, giving all her agents new pseudonyms, the names of animals. Meric became known as Hedgehog and other operatives became mastiff, hyena, vicuna, and so on. The Germans came to refer to the group as Noah's Ark.

To prevent her capture by the Gestapo, the British insisted she come to London for protection. During her stay in England, she continued to run her intelligence network from a home in Chelsea. Meric desperately wanted to return to France, but the British refused to allow it, certain that she would be immediately arrested. Soon after D-Day, in July 1944, Meric did return to France and was quickly captured by the Gestapo in Aix-en-Provence. She immediately planned her escape. First, she got the soldier who was guarding her to let her go to the bathroom so she could get a sense of the prison. Certain that there was no other means of escape, she then assessed the bars on the window. After the guards changed and fell asleep, she took off her clothes, held her dress and some money in her teeth, and painfully squeezed through the bars of her cell. She then made her way into the countryside. When she spotted German soldiers setting up roadblocks, she joined a group of peasant women gleaning until she could move on.

After the war, Marie-Madeleine was awarded the highest honors: the Legion of Honor, the Medal of the Resistance with Rosette, and the Croix de Guerre. She married Hubert Fourcade in 1947 and chronicled her experiences in her autobiography, *Noah's Ark,* which was first published in French in 1968. Marie-Madeleine (Meric) Fourcade valiantly risked her life to save her nation.

---

Sources: Marie-Madeleine Fourcade, *Noah's Ark* (New York: E. P. Dutton, 1974); and Margaret L. Rossiter, *Women in the Resistance* (New York: Praeger, 1986), 126–129.

physical abuse. The Japanese separated civilian men from women and children. When sons turned eleven, the Japanese transferred them to the men's camp, a traumatic separation for both the young boys and their mothers. The Japanese internment camp in Sumatra housed Western women from all walks of life—Australian nurses, Catholic nuns, Protestant missionaries, English and Dutch colonists. One way women maintained their morale and showed their defiance of their Japanese captors was through music. Although slowly starving to death, female POWs in Sumatra formed a choir. Because they spoke so many different languages, they did not sing the words but hummed instead. Their heroic struggle was chronicled in the film *Paradise Road* (1996).

After the Japanese invasion of Singapore in 1942, approximately twenty-five hundred mostly British civilians were interned in Changi Prison. By mid 1944, that number had grown to almost four thousand, of which nearly one-quarter were women and children. In an attempt to both express themselves and connect with the men in the other camp, female prisoners embroidered patchwork quilts. Their designs included conciliatory messages to their Japanese captors as well as symbols of home. Most important, by "putting something of themselves" in each of the squares, the quilts indicated who was still alive when the quilts arrived in the men's camp.[50]

Australian nurses on the Malaya Peninsula found themselves victims of military and diplomatic confusion when Japanese forces approached. In February 1942, members of the Australian Army Nursing Service (AANS), some civilians, and sick and wounded soldiers were not evacuated until the last moment because the major-general in charge did not want to lower civilian morale. Finally, six AANS nurses and 120 of their ill charges boarded the *Wah Sui*, a convalescent ship. Fifty-nine nurses and nearly two thousand other passengers boarded the SS *Empire Star*, and another sixty-five nursing sisters and two hundred civilians sailed on the SS *Vyner Brooke*. The Japanese attacked the *Empire Star* from the air, killing many, but the ship eventually reached Australia safely. The Japanese sunk the *Vyner Brooke* and then massacred twenty-two survivors who made it to Bangka Island. Only Vivian Bullwinkle survived, feigning death and hiding

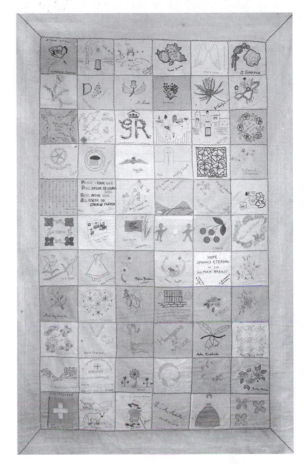

**QUILT MADE BY FEMALE POWS AT CHANGI PRISONER OF WAR CAMP (1944).** By 1944, the Japanese had taken nearly 1000 women and children prisoner and held them at Changi Prison in Singapore. Women interned in the camps used handmade quilts to communicate with both their Japanese captors and their loved ones in the adjacent men's camp. *(Museum & Archives, BRCS: British Red Cross Society. Copyright © British Red Cross Museum.)*

from the Japanese in the thick island forests. The Japanese took the other thirty-two survivors prisoner and held them in the internment camp in Sumatra. Eight more died before the end of the war.

Women played critical roles both in combat and in support services during the war. Although traditional gender expectations often prevented them from firing weapons or even traveling overseas, many stood bravely in the face of enemy fire and endured the traumas of war. Despite their valor, gender stereotypes prevailed, and their contributions on the battlefront, behind desks, and in the forests were quickly forgotten.

## ON THE HOME FRONT

Although most women did not join the military or volunteer services, the war touched nearly all aspects of their lives. Of course, women who lived in war zones experienced the war differently than women whose homes and farms escaped the fighting. To keep their countries running and the military supplied, millions of women entered the paid workforce. Governments also relied on women to cope with the rationing of food and basic supplies. Women with husbands away at war had the additional burden of caring for traumatized children during air raids and evacuations. Despite their diligent work in a time of crisis, governments, militaries, and even neighbors became uncomfortable with the large numbers of women managing on their own.

### Women and Wartime Work

The war transformed the economies of Europe and the United States, as nations dedicated every available resource to the war effort. Like World War I, World War II brought millions of women into the workplace. They filled jobs left by men mobilized into combat and took up new positions created by the wartime economy. Women worked as lawyers, accountants, doctors, and agricultural workers, as well as in machine shops, munitions factories, and construction sites. Although there was no doubt that governments and employers needed women's labor to maintain war production, workplace and government policies revealed their long-term intentions to protect maternity and domesticity during the crisis and to prevent women from becoming a permanent part of the workforce.

In Great Britain, nine of ten single women and eight of ten married women between eighteen and forty-nine years old worked in either the armed

**TAMPAX AD (1944).** During World War II, advertisers focused their attentions on the masses of women workers. Many advertisements, like this one for tampons, connected their products to women's critical place in the wartime workplace. *(Duke University.)*

forces or in industry. The rest looked after children or worked part-time. Not all women entering the wartime workplace were new to work. Many returned to jobs that they had held as single women before the war. Although most women moved into white-collar jobs, opportunities for women in traditionally male positions increased dramatically. At the peak of the war, women made up half of the workforce of explosives and chemicals industries in Britain.[51]

Female employment provoked considerable debate about the relationship between government and the family. For instance, although the

British government needed low- and middle-class women to work, many could not because they had no one to care for their children. The Ministry of Labour wanted to provide childcare as a part of a work program while the Ministry of Health wanted to push women to make their own arrangements as a part of encouraging self-help and mutual aid.[52] Because the government could not agree on a course of action, the problem of childcare remained unresolved during the war.

In the United States, the growth in women's employment did not come until after 1942. In the first few months of the war, employers looked to hire men, and federal agencies counseled against hiring women until all male breadwinners had found employment. Nevertheless, by 1944, 48 percent of women had spent some part of the year in the workforce. Many women entered occupations that had been almost exclusively male, such as grocery clerks and bank tellers. Before the war, only 230,000 women worked in steel, machinery, shipbuilding, aircraft, and automobile factories. During the war, that number rose to 1.7 million.[53] The powerful image of Rosie the Riveter glamorized industrial work and encouraged women to see such labor as compatible with their femininity.

Not surprisingly, gender stereotypes dominated the workplace. Studies of auto factories and the electrical industry show that women were clustered into a few jobs that were labeled "female." In a meeting of the National Association of Manufacturers in 1942, participants decided that "jobs of a particularly 'dirty' character, jobs that subject women to heat process or are of a 'wet' nature should not be filled by women . . . despite the fact that women could, if required, perform them." Instead, employers assigned women monotonous work because of their supposedly patient natures and delicate handiwork because of their nimbleness. Both the government and the press connected domestic tasks to wartime jobs. One 1943 newsreel proclaimed, "Instead of cutting the lines of a dress, this woman cuts the pattern of aircraft parts. Instead of baking cake, this woman is cooking gears to reduce the tension in gears after use."[54] Such propaganda also helped to assure the American public that wartime work was temporary and that women would easily return to domestic life.

In addition to new types of jobs, the war changed the type of woman in the workforce. By the end of the war, more married women and women over thirty-five were in the workforce than women who were unmarried and under thirty-five.[55] African American women only slowly moved out of domestic service and agriculture and into manufacturing jobs, as the defense industry proved reticent to hire African American women despite Executive Order 8802 that prohibited discriminatory hiring practices by defense contractors. In 1943, racial tensions erupted into riots in Harlem, Detroit, and twenty-five other cities.[56] Many Mexican American women entered the workforce for the first time, and others negotiated higher wages and benefits when they took jobs in defense plants. Their new working conditions affected economics and gender relations in the Mexican American community. According to one Chicana from Albuquerque, New Mexico, "Through earning our own wages, we had a taste of independence that we hadn't known before the war. . . . The women of my neighborhood had changed as much as the men who went to war. We developed a feeling of self-confidence and a sense of worth."[57]

Working conditions did not necessarily improve despite the increase in female workers. In 1942, the National War Labor Board decreed that women should receive equal pay for "work of the same quality and quantity," but employers frequently ignored this mandate. Between lower wages and the concentration of women in lower-paying jobs that offered fewer promotions, the average weekly wage for women in manufacturing jobs in 1944 was $31, while men earned nearly double that ($55).[58] A survey of industrial plants in 1943 showed that more than half had no intention of promoting women.[59] In addition to low pay, female workers faced resentment, sexual harassment, and allegations of sexual impropriety. Women workers reported that some male coworkers even sabotaged equipment despite the dangers involved.

The problems of low pay and workplace discrimination led women to join trade unions, even those that had been predominantly male before the war. Across occupations, female union membership grew from 9.4 percent in 1940 to 21.8 percent in 1944. The United Auto Workers (UAW) and the United Electrical (UE) workers, both dominant unions in industries central to the war economy, increased their female membership during the war, paid attention to women's concerns, and even offered women some leadership positions. By 1945, each union had a quarter million women members, 28 percent of the UAW and 40 percent of the UE.[60]

Female journalists brought the war to American's living rooms as 127 women became accredited war correspondents. Many, including Clare Boothe Luce (1903–1987), reported from the battlefronts where they bravely dodged enemy fire. Therese Bonney (1894–1978) revealed the horror of war through her photo essays. Others remained at home, providing the British and American publics with the latest information and shaping their opinions about the war. Before the war, conservative journalist Dorothy Thompson (1893–1961) headed the Berlin bureau of the *New York Post*. After the Nazis expelled her from Germany for her negative reporting on Hitler in 1936, the wife of the publisher of the *New York Herald Tribune* asked Thompson to write "a column about politics, wars, and domestic and international problems written so that women could understand it and would not always be seeking information from their husbands." Her weekly column reached an audience of eight to ten million readers.[61]

Soviet women had already entered the industrial workforce in large numbers before the war; however, as the government drafted most adult males, 70 percent of the agricultural workforce became female. Women also dominated industry, especially near the front. By February 1943, women were 84 percent of Leningrad's industrial workers. Although the number of women in the workforce had been steadily increasing since the 1930s, it rose to 53 percent of the workforce in 1943–44 in both light and heavy industries. In 1942, one-half of all turbine operators in power stations were women.[62] As the war intensified, working conditions deteriorated, and in cities near the front, workers faced enemy fire. Despite the dangers, the Soviet media worked to normalize and even heroicize women in male jobs. For example, a popular women's magazine profiled eighteen-year-old Dina Mikheicheva whose "masculine" job in a foundry led to her promotion as head of the shop laboratory.[63]

**THERESE BONNEY (1894–1978).** A number of women braved the dangers of the battlefield as journalists and photographers to tell the story of the war firsthand. Photographer Therese Bonney's compelling images of displaced adults and children brought the impact of the war on civilians home to millions of readers. *(Library of Congress.)*

Despite their massive mobilization for the war economy, governments and employers worked to ensure that women would willingly leave the workplace once the war ended. Although women acquired new skills, employers often relegated them to jobs that did not challenge traditional gender expectations and wartime propaganda reassured the public that even women in heavy industry did not lose their femininity. Moreover, as we will see, rather than a great transition in women's work, most gains that women made were quickly lost after the war.

## The Kitchen Front

The war was a dramatically different experience for women on the home front depending on their

**SOVIET WOMEN MUNITIONS WORKERS (CA. 1942).** By 1942, nearly all Russian women had been mobilized as a part of the war effort. Women undertook all types of industrial labor, including putting grease on shells at this munitions plant. *(Hulton Deutsch Collection/Corbis.)*

proximity to enemy fire. Women in and around combat zones constantly struggled to survive and to maintain some sense of normalcy amid air raids and evacuations. Even for the most fortunate, the war caused emotional stress and some privation. Yet, from Los Angeles to Moscow, most women altered their eating habits because of food rationing and managed their families and family businesses while their husbands were away at war.

In most homes, elaborate and extensive food rationing created "the Kitchen Front." Governments issued ration tickets, either separately or in books, that allotted each person a certain amount of a product over a period of time, as long as it was available. Rationing made feeding a family an onerous task. After waiting in line to obtain her family's ration tickets, a woman stood in other long lines to get her allotment of food or other scarce supplies. In Great Britain, bread, potatoes, vegetables, fruit, and fish were not rationed, but eggs, butter, cheese, sugar, and ham were. At the peak of rationing in

August 1942, every citizen got approximately one pound of meat per week. Over an eight-week period, adult ration books allowed each person one packet of dried eggs, which equaled twelve fresh eggs. Children under six got two packets.[64] The U.S. government rationed rubber supplies and gasoline because they were necessary to the war effort, along with canned goods, since the military used tin in weapons production. The government also rationed meat, sugar, coffee, butter, and other staples.[65] Rationing disproportionately affected urban women, as rural women produced more of their own food.

Both the British and the U.S. governments attempted to keep families happy and healthy despite the limits on their diets. The British Broadcasting Corporation radio (BBC) aired "Kitchen Front," a program that gave advice on how to make new recipes with available products, every morning at 8:15. In the United States, the government created an entire bureaucracy around rationing. The Committee on Food Habits, led by anthropologist Margaret Mead, helped determine the government's food policy, and the National Victory Garden Institute urged Americans to grow and eat their own produce.[66] In addition, women's magazines and government booklets taught women how to can their own fruits and vegetables, make recipes with day-old bread, salvage fats, and make pleasing desserts with little or no sugar. In 1943, Betty Crocker came out with a well-timed cookbook entitled *How to Prepare Appetizing, Healthful Meals with Foods Available Today.*

The rapid fall of France to the Nazis changed Frenchwomen's lives nearly overnight. In northern parts of France, women lived under Nazi occupation, and in southern France, they were governed by a Nazi supportive government led by Marshall Philippe Pétain (1856–1951). With the collapse of the French government in 1940, Germans took 1.8 million French male prisoners; 57 percent were married and 39 percent were fathers.[67] Most were taken to labor camps in Germany. In addition, the Germans had already killed ninety-two thousand Frenchmen by 1940.

During the war, Frenchwomen faced some of the most severe shortages and rationing in Europe. Malnutrition was rampant in major cities and parts of the south. Many people lived on only a thousand calories per day.[68] The meat ration in 1942 was twenty grams a day (less than one ounce).[69] Frustrated by the lack of food, women set up People's Committees that initiated housewives' demonstrations to force the government to release stockpiled foods in the spring of 1942.[70]

With a government allowance, a French mother could do little more than feed her family. One week's worth of basic food (no fresh fruits or vegetables) at official (not black market) prices was 93.90 francs, leaving 46.10 francs for everything else, including housing and heating costs. The government fixed clothing prices; a dress cost one month's allowance and a shirt nearly a week's allowance. In addition, POW wives sent regular packages to their husbands, hoping to keep them healthy during their imprisonment. The Germans did not always provide their prisoners with clothing, so women sent whatever they could scrounge although they received no additional rations for that purpose. To supplement their government allowances, some women took in sewing and laundry; others ran family businesses and farms. Many replaced their husbands at work. One employer asked a POW's wife to learn to drive so that she could take over her husband's job delivering goods, which she did for five years. As many as 10 percent of POW's wives became prostitutes in order to survive.[71]

## Other Pressures at Home

Women who lived under the threat of bombings and evacuation faced much more serious problems. Beginning in 1939, the British government evacuated approximately 3.5 million people from cities, such as London and Liverpool, to the countryside.[72] This massive movement of people involved nearly one-third of the population, 1.5 million mothers and children. The government placed them temporarily in country homes, whose owners were not always welcoming. Air raids meant nights in underground shelters and living for extended periods with no water or power. Many lost their homes. The Germans bombarded London for seventy-six straight nights in the fall of 1940. Nearly sixty thousand British civilians died, and tens of thousands were wounded.

In the midst of the bombing, media campaigns sent mixed messages to women. Although the British government urged women to "make do and mend," advertisers urged women to show their patriotism by looking good. Without enough money for clothes, women turned to elaborate hats and hairdos to keep in style.[73] The image of a stylish but frugal homemaker defined women's wartime patriotism and reassured the public that women would remain appropriately feminine despite the war.

Life under the Vichy government proved difficult for women in a number of different ways. As it worked to establish a Catholic, family-oriented society in a program known as the National Revolution, the government promoted motherhood, made divorce more difficult, and intensively prosecuted abortionists. Between 1942 and 1944, authorities convicted an average of four thousand people annually under antiabortion laws and guillotined one female abortionist in 1943.[74]

Wives of French POWs faced other challenges. Until 1942, women could not get loans without their husbands' consent even though their husbands were captives in Germany. Rural women found it difficult to maintain family farms without enough laborers to sow and harvest. Moreover, the Germans requisitioned most livestock, trucks, and cars for the war effort.[75]

The Vichy government attempted to alleviate the despair by granting families of POWs tax immunity and ordering landlords to lower rents by 75 percent. The government also sent up an emergency fund for wives of POWs. Beyond the government, the *Fédération des Associations de Femmes de Prisonniers* and *Service des Femmes de Prisonniers* helped raise money for POW families and provide other basic social services.[76]

The Germans held nearly all French prisoners for the entire war. POWs could write two letters per month of twenty-seven lines each and two postcards of seven lines each and wives sneaked messages in code to husbands in packages and in cigarettes. One woman even had her secret notes to her husband baked into a loaf of bread, but the Germans discovered it. However, these brief communications with their loved ones did little to mitigate women's anguish. In addition to general anxiety about the war, women feared for their husbands' lives. Many were concerned that they might be arrested purely because their husbands had been. Anxious about the length of the war, many young women feared that they would never have children.[77]

Compounding these difficulties, POW wives faced extreme pressure to be sexually faithful to husbands and fiancés. Although there is no evidence that adultery increased during the war, suspicions ran high. POWs received letters from friends, neighbors, and even anonymous letters repeating gossip about their wives' sexual activity. Fearful that adultery might lead to divorce and thus a decline in the birthrate, the Vichy government passed a law that punished adultery with a prisoner's wife with jail terms and fines.[78]

Women in the United States did not live under the same constraints. After Pearl Harbor, no fighting took place on U.S. territory, and no American homes were bombed. More than one-quarter of American servicemen remained in the United States during the war, and only one in eight saw combat.[79] Seven out of eight women who were homemakers in 1941 remained so in 1944.[80] For many, the war was very far away. Nevertheless, women found socially acceptable ways to support the war effort. Middle- and upper-middle-class women often volunteered to work for support organizations like the Red Cross and the United Service Organizations for National Defense (USO). At monthly dances, junior hostesses, usually young single women, talked to and danced with servicemen, while senior hostesses, usually married women over thirty-five, mended shirts, baked cookies, and provided emotional support to young servicemen. Relying on traditional notions of female nurturing, senior hostesses cultivated the image of "asexual moms" who patiently listened to servicemen's problems. Unaccustomed to the idea of women in the military, USO clubs neglected the needs of servicewomen. At one canteen in Washington, D.C., USO staff gave servicewomen tours of the facilities and then asked them to leave. Canteen workers forbade servicewomen from sitting at the tables, eating, or dancing in the building.[81]

The media sent contradictory messages about the interactions between young women and servicemen. An advertisement for perfume that featured a woman in a sexy dress told women to "Sell it to the Marines" and pinup posters of movie stars like Rita Hayworth (1918–1969) reminded young men of the sexy women they were fighting to protect. In the United States, some magazines encouraged women to "meet their patriotic obligation" by being "the thrill in his furlough" and making "the wounded wiggle." However, other magazines criticized promiscuous girls whom they nicknamed, "Khaki-wackies," "Victory Girls," and "Good time Charlottes" for their relationships with servicemen.[82] In England, where one million American GIs were posted by 1944, critics ridiculed "good-time" girls who were supposedly willing to be sexual partners to lonely soldiers. Not surprisingly, the criticism was aimed at the behavior of the girls, not the sexual assertiveness of the men, and tied sexual morality to good citizenship in both Great Britain and the United States.[83] Race further complicated these interactions. Hoping to mitigate racial tensions, the U.S. military forbade the media from printing photographs of African American men dancing with white women.

As war raged around the world, it exacerbated racial tensions in the United States. As mentioned earlier, African American women faced regular discrimination in the workplace and in housing as they relocated for war work. In Los Angeles, anti-Latino sentiments erupted in 1943 in the Zoot Suit Riots when white servicemen attacked Mexican American youths and rampaged through Mexican American barrios. However, racial prejudice found its worst manifestation against Japanese Americans. After Pearl Harbor, Japanese American women's groups attempted to demonstrate their loyalty by working for the Red Cross and joining in fundraising efforts. However, three months later President Roosevelt ordered the evacuation and internment of all Americans with at least one-sixteenth Japanese blood living on the West Coast. Seventy thousand Japanese Americans had three weeks to arrange their affairs and property. In the ten camps, families often lived in appallingly filthy conditions with few bathrooms and no privacy. The atmosphere was prisonlike. A few German American and Italian American families were also interned, classified as dangerous by the U.S. government.

## The Home Front in Germany

Although during the first two years of the war Germany was largely unscathed by the war, after 1942, life there became quite dangerous. The Nazi regime mobilized nearly one-quarter of the German population, twenty million people, mostly men between eighteen and forty, for military or related service. As a result, women, children, and the elderly made up the bulk of the urban population. As the Allied campaign intensified, German civilians suffered through constant air-raid sirens and bombing raids. Women and children survived Allied bombings by hiding in shelters and cellars. In one week, Allied bombs destroyed 55 to 60 percent of the city of Hamburg, leaving seven hundred and fifty thousand homeless. By the end of the war, as many as fourteen million Germans had lost their homes and six hundred thousand had died in air raids. Many families found themselves constantly searching for safety. Beginning in 1943, the Nazi government evacuated ten million people, mainly women and children, from German cities. Employed women remained to work despite enemy fire. The story of Frau F. reveals the compounding horrors of the war. Frau F., her two small children, and her mother spent many nights in a bomb shelter in 1944. One night, a bomb struck their shelter and set fire to her one-year-old son's clothes. While she put out the flames, her three-year-old daughter disappeared and was never found. Mother and son eventually found her sister-in-law, who was also homeless. The trio spent the next three days in open air and nights in an air shelter. Eventually, Frau F. left her son with her mother in the countryside, and she and her sister-in-law headed back to Darmstadt to return to work. Her obligations to the Nazi regime continued despite her personal loss and the constant danger.[84]

Despite the Nazi emphasis on motherhood, the labor shortage was serious enough that the government encouraged or forced many middle- and lower-class women to work in the munitions industry. Women could get exemptions from work if they had young children, and many women became pregnant in order to leave their jobs.[85] Many other women found that the pensions that the government handed out to military wives were generous enough to let them leave their jobs. Not surprisingly, middle-class women often got exemptions from the labor draft while working-class women with children did not.[86] To fill that vacuum, in 1944 the Nazis relied on 1.9 million Soviet and eastern European forced laborers and concentration camp prisoners (see below). Nevertheless, German women's wartime participation in the labor force always exceeded that of women in the United States.[87]

The Nazis hesitated to force women to work in industry, preferring instead to recognize women's roles as caretakers of the millions of mobilized men. Nazi ideology strongly asserted women's importance not only for cooking and cleaning, but emotional support as well. The regime also feared that forcing women to work and/or separating them from their husbands during evacuations would lead to marital breakup.[88]

Women's participation in the Nazi regime has provoked considerable debate. Some scholars have seen women's participation as merely one aspect of their motherly duties. Others have viewed them as victims of the Nazi patriarchy. A few scholars have even argued that German women experienced a degree of liberation through their participation in the Third Reich. Most German women complied with the regime either as followers or bystanders, going about their daily lives without voicing any opposition. A few actively participated in racist and genocidal policies just like men, and a minority were victims, resisters, or rescuers.[89] Actively or passively, Nazi success relied on women.

World War II did not just take place on the battlefield. It also affected people's homes and relationships. Both the Allies and the Axis powers relied on women's labor, despite the fact that working women challenged traditional notions of masculinity and femininity. However, governments did little to lessen the burden on women who not only built the airplanes and tended family businesses but were expected to come home at the end of the shift and cook and clean as usual. Daily life was a series of battles for women on the home front.

## THE HOLOCAUST

Nazi racial policy culminated in the imprisonment and extermination of all non-Aryans living under German occupation. In this process, the Nazis deported millions of Jews—as well as thousands of Gypsies, Poles, Slavs, socialists, communists, and homosexuals—to labor and extermination camps across German-occupied Europe. As the Germans advanced, Jews across Europe went into hiding. Some took refuge in attics, as Anne Frank (1929–1945), a thirteen-year-old Dutch Jew, chronicled in her diary. Others found temporary havens in the barns and closets of Christian neighbors and even strangers. For most Jews, these hideouts would provide only temporary safety. Beginning in 1942, the Nazis deported French, Belgian, Norwegian, and Dutch Jews to concentration camps such as Auschwitz. Some Jews were arrested and taken in trains directly to extermination camps. Other Jews began their imprisonment in a ghetto, after which the Nazis moved them to labor camps, and then finally to extermination camps. This horrifying and unpredictable situation tested women's physical and emotional endurance as they struggled to keep themselves and their families alive.

### Life in the Ghetto

With the German invasion of Poland, Nazi authorities decreed that Poland's Jewish population must be concentrated in large cities near major railroad lines to facilitate their deportation.[90] In these cities, as well as in Czechoslovakia, the Soviet Union, and Luxembourg, the German government confined all Jews to defined areas known as ghettos. The formation of the ghettos was the last of series of discriminatory actions. Most Polish Jews had already been deprived of their jobs and possessions and had suffered physical violence from beatings to rape.

Two of the largest ghettos were in Lódz, with a population of 160,000 Jews, and Warsaw, with 450,000. The Lódz ghetto was completely cut off from the surrounding city. The Warsaw ghetto remained somewhat connected to the rest of the city until November 1941 when authorities sealed the ghetto and required the death penalty for any Jews found outside. However, even the ghetto was not impermeable, and smuggling helped to provide basic supplies during most of the ghetto's existence.

The Nazis administered the ghetto through the *Judenrat*, a council of Jewish men appointed by the Germans. The Nazis expected the Judenrat to force Jewish residents to comply with German orders and to provide municipal services from health care to postal services. With only meager resources, it was an impossible task. Food rationing in the Warsaw ghetto in 1941 allotted each Jewish resident a mere 184 calories per day.[91] Food became an obsession. One woman in the ghetto at Theresienstadt in Czechoslovakia reported that, "the main topic of conversation was food, the most beautiful recipes that anybody could think of, and also a hot bath as soon as the war was over."[92] Even at the beginning, the Warsaw ghetto was very overcrowded, with an average of 7.2 persons per room.[93] Living conditions were terrible, and most people lived without running water, sewers, or electricity. Outbreaks of disease added to the death rate. Approximately 20 percent of the combined population of the Lódz and Warsaw ghettos died in 1941–42. Most died from starvation and exhaustion.[94]

There were more women than men in the Lódz ghetto. The Nazis had captured and killed some men early in the invasion, and another third of the male Jewish population left before the Nazis sealed the ghetto, believing that the Germans would not harm women and children. Moreover, women made up the majority of those transported to the ghetto and most Jews deported from the ghettos to the labor camps were men. Men also suffered very high mortality rates. During the most difficult periods in the ghetto, between May 1940 and July 1942, men were 60 percent of those who died. By 1944, among the twenty- to thirty-four-year-olds, women outnumbered men nearly two to one.[95]

Beginning in 1940, local German authorities organized many of the ghettos for production. Some ghetto factories made textiles for German military authorities. As the ghettos turned into labor camps, the Germans considered anyone not working to be expendable; therefore, work became key to survival. Working conditions were harsh, especially because of the hunger that most Jews suffered. By 1943, workers toiled for ten hours each day with an hour break to eat a thin watery soup. Workers were "paid" in small wages and some rations (the only way to obtain them). Mothers brought children to workplaces and shared soup with them. Even in the ghetto, men were paid more than women.[96]

In addition to large numbers of women, the Warsaw ghetto housed one hundred thousand children under fifteen years old. Most suffered from malnutrition. Some children begged for food, while others became involved in smuggling gangs. Polish police often forced young smugglers to crawl through barbed wire until they bled or crawl through sewers full of waste to punish them.[97]

Jewish residents attempted to maintain some degree of normalcy whenever possible. Musicians held concerts, theaters produced plays, and whenever possible children went to school. In Theresienstadt, there was a coffeehouse where Käthe Breslauer remembered being able to "sit on proper chairs at tables with flowers and be able to forget our misery for a while."[98] Self-help organizations formed soup kitchens and tried to help the elderly and the ill with the basics of life. Nevertheless, life was reduced to an ongoing struggle for survival. Malnutrition curtailed fertility so that few children were born in the ghettos and very few newborns survived

The situation became even more desperate in the summer of 1942 when the Germans deported at least three hundred thousand from the Warsaw ghetto to death camps. Jewish underground organizations took action when it became clear that the last sixty thousand Jews would also be exterminated. Many young women were actively involved in the Jewish underground. Zivia Lubetkin (1914–1978) was one of the founding members of the major Resistance movement, the Jewish Fighting Organization. On April 19, 1943, when the Germans began the deportations, the Resistance began an armed uprising and Lubetkin was one of the central figures. The fighting lasted only a few days, but the resisters held out for more than a month. Then, the German commander began burning the ghetto to force Jews out of hiding. By May 16, the uprising was over and bodies were piled in the streets. One survivor told of finding a little girl alive in the pile of bodies with her dead mother on top of her. The girl had miraculously survived because her mother had taught her to fall on the ground and lay still when she heard shooting.[99] Although the Nazis deported the remaining Jews to death camps, the Warsaw ghetto uprising was symbolically important as the first urban uprising against Nazi atrocities.

In 1942, the Germans began liquidating most ghettos. Sixty-two percent of those taken to the extermination camp at Chelmno (Poland) were women. Women between the ages of twenty and forty were deported in numbers double and even more than triple that of men, largely because welfare recipients, the unemployed, and families of men who were not inside the ghetto were deported first.[100] The Nazis packed men, women, and children into trains and forced them to pay for their own transit to death camps.

## Labor and Extermination Camps

Although some Jews lived in ghettos for at least part of the war, the Nazis transported most Jews to forced labor camps in eastern Europe. These camps, many of which were in Poland, helped Germany control its occupied population while simultaneously providing for the war effort. There were at least 437 forced labor camps in Poland, mostly for Jews. In these camps, women worked under the most deplorable conditions.

Work in the labor camps varied according to the task. In an ammunitions plant in Poland, women worked in the shell department. In each ten-hour shift, women shell cleaners carried eighteen hundred shells, each weighing nine pounds, to polishing machines. Women also manufactured light ammunition for the German infantry and finished and inspected ammunition parts. In the most dangerous department, workers packed underwater mines with toxic substances. In the department where the shell cases were filled, women stirred the boiling TNT, with two seconds per stir; 1,800 stirs per hour; and 21,600 in a twelve-hour shift all without sitting. Some women used bribery to get better assignments in the kitchen or in other food-related duties. Not only were their working conditions somewhat better, but they were able to pilfer food to improve their diets and sell to other inmates.[101]

Twice a day, workers received three-fourths liter of watery soup flavored with dried potato flakes, two hundred grams of bread made with the same potato flakes, something coffeelike, and sometimes a bit of jam. Twice a week they got a spoonful of sugar in the soup. They slept in bunks with no mattresses or blankets. Once a month, each inmate received a hot shower and clothing disinfection.[102] In addition to these appalling physical conditions, failure to keep pace with the quotas could result in whippings, and anti-Semitic Polish workers often harassed and ridiculed Jews during their shifts.

Many other enemies of the Nazi regime were taken to concentration camps. The concentration camp experience differed depending on the inmate and the camp. Five thousand Jehovah's Witnesses were arrested because they refused to give the raised arm salute, take an oath to Hitler, or join any Nazi organizations or the army. Unlike other prisoners, Jehovah's Witnesses were given the opportunity to be freed. All one had to do was sign a document recanting his or her beliefs. Few did.

The camps fostered little solidarity among female prisoners. Many Jews felt that they had nothing in common with Roma or Polish socialists and vice versa. Most survivors reported shunning the prostitutes and other criminals housed with them. Not surprisingly, there was not much interaction between female camp guards and female inmates. Approximately 10 percent of the camp guards were women, most of whom were single, lower-class women attracted by promises of better pay. Few women served on extermination squads and none at the death camps.[103]

The concentration camp at Ravensbrück in Germany was the only camp almost exclusively for women and children, although a women's camp was established at Bergen-Belsen in 1944. About 130,000 women and children and about 20,000 men passed through there between 1939 and 1945. Officially, Ravensbrück was a work camp, and much of the running of the camp was in the prisoners' hands. Nazis recruited most of the female overseers. Anna David was working at a factory in Berlin when a Nazi policeman ordered her to choose between her low-paying job there and training to become an overseer. The female overseers were expected to be brutal, and many were promoted for their violent acts, including whipping, kicking, and unleashing dogs on prisoners even for small offenses.[104]

When inmates arrived, German authorities stripped them and took their possessions. Many women had their vaginas searched for hidden valuables, and the doctors used the same instruments on all women without disinfecting them.[105] After being inspected for lice, prisoners were shaven, including their pubic area, often by other inmates, and made to parade naked in front of male doctors and soldiers. Lily Malnick, imprisoned in Auschwitz at age sixteen, remembered, "when they told us to undress, . . . they made us feel like animals. The men were walking around and laughing and looking at us. . . . I wanted the ground to open and I should go in it."[106] Humiliation was a critical part of Nazi tactics. Similarly, Gypsy men were forced to violate their community's taboos by parading naked in front of their wives and children.[107]

In addition to Jews and Jehovah's Witnesses, criminals and "asocial" women were imprisoned in Ravensbrück. Mariechen Schneeman was arrested for "malicious behavior" in 1941 for wearing a Hitler Youth badge without being a member. After serving time in jail for this offense, she supposedly contracted syphilis and was jailed for not seeing a doctor. She was sent to Ravensbrück as an asocial in 1943 and was never heard from again. The Nazis deported many adolescent girls to the camps because they had venereal diseases. A number of Roma were also held at Ravensbrück. At the beginning of 1945, Nazi officials offered to release the Roma women if they would be sterilized. Between 120 and 140 agreed. Many had chemical solution sprayed into their uteruses or had electrodes placed in vaginas and on ovaries. Some died; none were ever released.[108]

Life in the camps forced women to utilize all their survival skills. According to Rudolf Höss (1900–1947), the commandant of Auschwitz, "general living conditions in the women's camp were incomparably worse [than in the men's camp]. They were far more tightly packed in and the sanitary and hygienic conditions were notably inferior."[109] They refashioned clothing from rags and created meals and medicines from meager rations. Still thousands died of exhaustion and starvation. To make matters worse, some women worked in camp brothels under orders from Nazi guards. Although they were disgusted by their situation, they had furnished rooms, clean clothes, and could wash regularly. For some, the time bought in the brothels was just enough to survive the war.[110]

The Germans began operating extermination camps in 1941. The first was at Chelmno, and the other deaths camps were Belzec, Sobibór, Treblinka, Majdanek, and Birkenau (Auschwitz II), all in Poland. The victims were mostly Jews, but also thousands of Gypsies, Poles, homosexuals, and Soviet POWs. Upon arriving at the camps, guards targeted women because of their reproductive abilities. Women with small children or those who were visibly pregnant were marked for immediate execution. Mothers were sent to the crematoria with their children because according to Josef Mengele (1911–1979?), the ruthless and sadistic Nazi doctor at Auschwitz, "it would not be humanitarian to send a child to the ovens without permitting the mother to be there to witness the child's death. That is why I send the mother and the child to the gas ovens together."[111] Guards stripped all prisoners of their belongings before sending them to be gassed, collecting prisoners' shoes, rings, hair, and teeth. Gold teeth were melted down; hair was used to stuff mattresses and make socks for submarine crews and railroad workers.[112] Human ashes from the crematoria became fertilizer. The Nazis chose some prisoners to work before killing them. In addition to being shaved, they had numbers tattooed on their arms and were given prison pajamas and wooden clogs. Each day, concentration camp officials selected more inmates for extermination. At Auschwitz, doctors also experimented on prisoners. Women had their ovaries burned by electrodes or irradiated with x-rays. Mengele subjected Gypsy children, dwarfs, and twins to a horrifying array of experiments. Those who did not die from the experiments were then killed.

Survival in the death camps was a matter of luck. In addition to the daily selections, the inmates constantly fought typhus, tuberculosis, and fungal diseases. Many women got urinary tract infections. Most stopped menstruating because of malnutrition, which was in some ways better because no sanitary napkins were available.[113] Many died of hunger and exhaustion; others committed suicide rather than wait to die (see **Sources from the Past: A Woman's Story of the Holocaust**).

In Chelmno, most Jews were gassed in hermetically sealed trucks. Fifty to seventy people were loaded in and the exhaust pipe was connected to the compartment. The Nazis murdered at least 320,000 Jews there. At the other camps, the Nazis killed 1.7 million using carbon monoxide gas from engines or Zyklon B, an insecticide that could kill two thousand people in thirty minutes. At Auschwitz-Birkenau, the largest labor and extermination camp, more than 1.1 million died in four gas chambers, which pumped hydrocyanic acid through shower plumbing. At the height of the exterminations, the Nazis gassed as many as twelve thousand Jews in one day.[114]

Not all Jews died in camps and ghettos. The Nazis also executed thousands with mobile killing units that rounded up Jewish men, women, and children; forced them to dig ditches; and then shot them. About 1.5 million Jews were massacred between June and December 1941, mostly in the Baltic nations and the Ukraine.[115]

In ghettos in eastern Europe, the Nazis forced Jews to live in the most humiliating and painful circumstances. Gradually, the Nazis transported most of Europe's Jewish population to labor and extermination camps. Known as the "Final Solution," within three years, the Nazis murdered six million Jews, as well as tens of thousands of Poles, Slavs, homosexuals, and members of the political opposition.

## THE END OF THE WAR

The fighting during the last two years of World War II was some of the most deadly and most destructive. Beginning with the D-Day invasion on June 6, 1944, Allied forces pressured the Axis powers on three battlefronts: northwestern Europe, the Soviet Union, and southern France. Within months, the Allies had forced Hitler out of France and began an intensive air campaign against German cities. Soviet victories in the east and American and British penetration into Germany spelled the end of the Nazi regime. Hitler, his wife, Eva Braun (1912–1945), and other Nazi officials committed suicide, and Germany surrendered on May 8, 1945. With the end of the war in Europe, the United States and the British were able to focus on the Pacific front. In a controversial decision, on August 6, 1945, U.S. president Harry S. Truman (1945–1953) dropped an atomic bomb on the Japanese city of Hiroshima. Two days later, the United States destroyed the city of Nagasaki with a second atomic weapon. The scope of the tragedy was immense. Eighty thousand inhabitants of Hiroshima and fifty thousand inhabitants of Nagasaki died instantly. Tens of thousands died of radiation poisoning soon after. The Japanese surrendered on August 15, 1945, ending World War II.

The end of the war revealed the extent of the damage. Both in human and economic terms, it had been the most expensive war in history. Three-quarters of the world's population had taken part. In addition to the six million Jews who died in the Holocaust, fifty-five million others died in the fighting—twenty-five million military personnel and thirty million civilians. The economic costs were also staggering. The Soviet Union may have lost 30 percent of its national wealth. Much of Continental Europe was completely destroyed. Many European cities, especially in eastern Europe, were still in rubble in 1947. For the women who survived, the immediate postwar period brought new dangers and challenges.

## Occupation and Liberation

With the German surrender, Allied troops divided Germany and Austria into four occupation zones. However, the violence against women did not end with the Allied victory. American, Canadian, French, and English soldiers raped German women and looted German homes. The worst vio-lence occurred when the Soviet army secured Berlin in April 1945. Between April 24 and May 5, Soviet soldiers raped German women en masse as they emerged from cellars and shelters to scrounge for food. It is difficult to know exactly how many women were raped, but estimates vary from twenty thousand to one million; as many as one in three Berlin women, and perhaps as many as ten thousand, died as a result. In addition, soldiers spread venereal disease and thousands of women became pregnant. Women had to request permission to get an abortion from British and American officials. To do so, they had to describe their ordeals in painful detail. One woman wrote, "On the way to work on the second Easter holiday I was raped by a Mongol [Russian soldier]. The abuse can be seen on my body. . . . Now I am pregnant by this person, [I] can think of this only with disgust and ask for help. Since I would not even consider carrying this child to term, both my children would lose their mother. With kind greetings." Another woman described her despair in her plea for an abortion, "Since I am single, my mother dead for fifteen years, my father a half-Jew from who I have had no sign of life for six years, it is impossible for me to set a child into the world under these conditions."[116] The situation for German women did not improve after the occupation ended because the postwar German government refused to recognize rape as a wartime injury worthy of compensation and refused to help support the children produced by wartime and occupation-era rapes.[117]

The Allied soldiers who arrived at the labor and concentration camps discovered the most unimaginable horrors. They found tens of thousands of unburied bodies and the surviving inmates shrunken from malnutrition. Most described them as walking skeletons. Marie Ellifritz, a nurse with the 130th Evacuation Hospital was dispatched to care for victims of Mauthausen concentration camp in Austria. She recalled that it was difficult to talk to the survivors because of their weakness and the language barrier. Nevertheless, she found a way to communicate with them. Many died within days of liberation, having used the last of their energy to die free.[118]

Some concentration camp survivors straggled back to the ghettos that had once been their homes. Some came by train, while other emaciated

## A Woman's Story of the Holocaust

*In 1946, psychologist David Boder undertook the first oral history of Holocaust survivors. He interviewed 109 survivors in displaced persons camps across Europe. These are excerpts from his interview with Nechama E., a twenty-three-year-old survivor from Warsaw. During the war, she had escaped Warsaw, jumped from a train taking Jews to a death camp, was recaptured, become ill at Auschwitz, and spent time in Bergen-Belsen. At the time of the interview, Nechama was recently married, pregnant, and waiting to emigrate to Palestine. Boder's questions are italicized.*

[Nechama describes the deportation train from Warsaw in September 1942.]

Two hundred persons were packed into one railroad car. . . . Everybody wanted to catch air. One lay suffocating on top of another. We were in that railroad car a whole night. We grew very thirsty. It became terribly hot. Everybody undressed. There were small children who began to cry terribly, "Water!" So we started banging on the doors, screaming. So they began to shoot inside, from all four sides, while traveling. They were sitting on the roofs, on the steps. Very many people died. I was sitting and looking at one taking a bullet, another taking a bullet. I, too, expected to get hit in a moment. And I saved myself by hiding under the dead. The blood of the killed was flowing over me.

A little girl of four years lay there. "Give me a little bit of water. Save me." And I could do nothing. Mothers were giving the children urine to drink. . . .

I lived in that [Miedzyrzec] ghetto eight months, in deathly fear. . . . And from there all the Jews were being sent to Treblinka. There I lived through three terrible deportations. During the first deportation I hid in an open attic and lay there for four weeks. I lived on just raw beets.

I did not have anything to drink. The first snow fell then, so I made a hole in the roof and pulled in a little snow by hand. And this I licked. . . .

[Nechama was then taken to Majdanek concentration camp.]

*Did you work there?*

Yes. We were sent to do garden work. We were sent to carry the shit which . . . there were no toilets there, so we carried it in buckets. We were given nothing to eat. They were hitting over the legs. They were beating over the heads. The food consisted of 200 grams [7 ounces] of bread a day, and a little soup of water with nettles. The hunger was so great that when a cauldron of food was brought, we could not wait for it to be distributed, but we threw ourselves on the food, and that food would spill on the ground, and we ate it with the mud. . . .

I was taken away to Auschwitz. The conditions were then already a little better. Fewer were being packed into a railroad car. They were putting sixty into a wagon. [After] arriving at Auschwitz, we were led into a large hall before taking us to be bathed. All the women had their hair cut off. For the first time in Auschwitz. In Majdanek I was not shorn, just in Auschwitz. And they tattooed numbers on us. And a little triangle. We had very great anguish because we had our hair cut off. How can women live without hair? And we were dressed in trousers and in blouses. We were terribly hungry. We went to work in a detail called the "Death Detail." Why? We went to work, the 600 women from Majdanek. It took a month, and there remained no more than 450. We died out of hunger. We worked carrying large stones on barrows, building a highway. They gave us nothing to eat. We were beaten terribly. There were German women who were also prisoners [i.e., prisoner trustees]. They were imprisoned for prostitution. They said that every day they must kill three, four Jews. . . .

*Could the crematorium be seen burning?*

Of course! When we went out at night we saw the entire sky red, the glow of the fire. Blood was pouring on the sky. We saw everything. We knew. When we went to the shower hall, we recognized the clothing of the people who had left and returned no more. In the warehouses where we were issued clothing we recognized the clothing of the people who had been taken away. Sometimes, when we would go out at night to relieve ourselves, we saw how transports were brought with mothers and children. The children were calling to the mothers. . . .

We were led into a freight car, which is used for transporting cattle. Among us were many ethnic German women,[1] who had also been imprisoned there in the camp. They were [there] for prostitution. . . .

After we had been in Majdanek for eight months, an order came: the 300 women survivors of the action must go to Auschwitz. And we, the thirteen tattooed women [i.e., the ones who had come from Auschwitz], of whom eleven remained, were to go someplace else. And we began to cry very much. "Why aren't we being taken with them? We are Jews, too." She [the SS woman] answered, "You have seen too much and know too much to be able to go with those women." So [we] saw our death coming.

Two days later we were taken away to Plaszow. They added another 300 women from Radom. There were little children, too. In Plaszow they took away the small children [and] the pregnant women. There was a famous hill. They were taken to the top and undressed. There were no crematoria. They were shot, and afterward we carried boards and made a fire, and they were all burned. . . .

[Nechama describes her liberation from the ghetto at Theresienstadt.]

There was very little food. And the Germans prepared a large crematorium, but they did not have enough time to do it. One fine day they called all the Jews together. A German came and said that if he would be escorted to Switzerland, [extermination] would not be carried out. The Swiss Red Cross would take us over, and all of us would be saved.[2]

Two hours before the entry of the Russians the Germans drove through, the SS men with tanks, with weapons, and began to fire on the whole camp. All of us were hiding. We thought, "This is the end." But two hours passed. We heard the Russian tanks were there. And we didn't believe it. We went out, whoever was able. There were a lot of sick who couldn't go. We went out with great joy, with much crying. We had lived to see the moment of liberation.

But then a real death began! The Russians had opened all the German storehouses, and they said, "Take whatever you want." And the people began to eat, too much, greedily. And that was harmful for them. There was a great epidemic. Hundreds of people fell a day. In about a month half of the camp had fallen. There were stables full of dead people. People crawled over the dead. It stank terribly. There was a severe typhus raging. And I, too, got sick. I lay in the hospital four weeks. I had spotted typhus. All night I lay and cried, "What will I do now? What did I survive for?" But my fate had not been completely lost. I still had hope.

---

[1] "Ethnic Germans" were residents of eastern European countries who identified themselves, and were accepted by Nazi authorities, as racially German.

[2] Theresienstadt's commander, SS Major Karl Rahm, hoped to save his neck by striking a deal that would have turned the ghetto over to Swiss officials. Already twelve hundred of Theresienstadt's Jews had been transferred to Switzerland in February 1945. Rahm was hanged as a war criminal in 1947.

Source: Donald L. Niewyk, *Fresh Wounds: Early Narratives of Holocaust Survival* (Chapel Hill: University of North Carolina Press, 1998), 94–107.

skeletons walked hundreds of miles. They were weak and covered in lice and open sores. Most wore only rags. Even then, their struggle was not over. Two of Edith Kramer's four roommates in the refugee camp committed suicide, unable to face the battle for survival that lay before them.[119]

At the end of the war, perhaps as many as twenty million people attempted to relocate. Forced laborers, soldiers, concentration camp inmates, and millions of displaced families set out for home. Between May and September 1945, four million to six million people were repatriated. Most of the residents of France, Holland, Luxembourg, and Belgium chose to return home. However, more than 1.2 million displaced people, including approximately three hundred thousand Jewish refugees, remained in displaced persons camps in the U.S. and British zones of occupation. Many survivors were physically ill and depressed, and some were the sole survivors of their families. The camps were horrible; they had little food and poor sanitation. One American official reported to President Truman, "We [the United States] appear to be treating the Jews as the Nazis treated them, except that we do not exterminate them."[120]

Despite the ongoing traumas, Jewish displaced persons married in high numbers and recorded the highest birthrate in the world, a remarkable 35.8/1,000.[121] Some were lonely and in search of companionship and hope for the future; others were enthralled with a new zest for life. Rabbis were lenient in their interpretation of a Jewish tradition that required that a widow could not remarry unless witnesses had seen her spouse dead, as most women could not present such testimony.[122] Women who had stopped menstruating in the camps enthusiastically reclaimed their roles as wives and mothers.[123] Moreover, the refugee baby boom was an important part of the Jewish process of becoming more than merely victims of the Holocaust. These babies were symbols of both revenge on the Nazis and the future of the Jewish people.

Soviet citizens were the largest group of refugees, when as many as 7.2 million forced laborers and POWs were returned to the USSR, some against their wills. However, the Soviet occupation of Eastern Europe left many displaced persons unwilling to return home. Ukrainians refused to return home because of the Russian occupation of their lands. Citizens of the Baltic nations were exempted from repatriation because of the Soviet occupation. Many Poles could not return because Russians had taken their homes, and others were fearful of the unstable political situation in their homeland. Some Polish Jews resettled in their hometown of Kielce only to be killed by their Polish neighbors in a pogrom in 1946. More than one hundred thousand Soviet and eastern European Jews fled into occupied Germany seeking asylum from continued anti-Semitism. By the end of 1946, more than nine hundred thousand people remained in displaced persons camps.

Most of the Jewish displaced persons wanted to emigrate to Palestine, but British officials refused to allow such a massive influx of people. In the hope of providing refuge for some of the displaced women, Great Britain and Canada established programs to allow them to migrate and serve as domestic servants. Canadians expressed a great need for domestics, as many women had left this employment to work in war industries. One government official lamented that those same women, "would rather loaf and starve than to go back to housework."[124] However, most Canadians did not want Jewish servants, preferring women from the Baltic States. In the end, these programs were both quite small, each taking only a few thousand carefully chosen single women. Interestingly, authorities in Ottawa decided to redefine *single* for purposes of the program, allowing women who did not know the whereabouts of their husbands to apply. Finally, under international pressure, the British allowed for the creation of the state of Israel in 1948, as a home for hundreds of thousands of displaced European Jews.

At the same time, the United States was hesitant to take large numbers of refugees as the wartime economy began to contract. Although Congress reluctantly increased immigration quotas with the passage of the Displaced Persons Act of 1948, the United States admitted fewer than one hundred thousand Jews before the closing of the last displaced persons camp in 1952.

## Returning to "Normal"

Across Europe, women worked to rebuild their lives, often from nothing. Millions of husbands and family members were dead or missing in the waves of refugees. They tried to recreate normalcy in cities without running water or electricity. They settled down to replant farms and restore families with limited resources, as five years of warfare had destroyed most of Europe's infrastructure. In France, food shortages lasted until 1949.

Despite women's importance to the wartime workplace, government policies quickly reverted to prewar promarriage and pronatalist policies. In the Soviet Union, where as many as twenty-five million people died, women made up 57 percent of the postwar population. Stalin's policies pressed women to marry and reproduce in order to replace the dead. The New Family Code of 1944 made divorce more difficult, although divorces rose consistently from 1945 to 1953.[125] The government heavily taxed single people and those with fewer than three children and awarded motherhood medals to those with five or more children; those with ten or more received the honor of "heroine mother."[126] Other restrictions ended common law marriage and prohibited single mothers from filing paternity suits.[127] At the same time, the Soviet government made no attempt to send women home from the workplace. Women had to work to survive, and the Soviet Union needed them to continue to work during reconstruction. In fact, during the postwar period, Soviet propaganda emphasized the image of the woman as a dedicated productive worker and enticed women with promises of career advancement. However, managerial opportunities did not exist for women, so few received promotions. A 1949 article in *Pravda*, the Communist Party newspaper, blamed women, stating that "women were not as dedicated to socialist competition as they should be."[128] Faced with these contradictions, most Soviet women focused on their home lives and dealt with postwar life as best as possible.

Germany was in shambles. Among young adults, there were 1,700 women for every 1,000 men. Millions of Germans were homeless and hungry. The official ration was only 1,275 calories per day in 1946, and many received even less. By November 1947, the average weight for an adult woman was 93.4 pounds, for men, 92.3 pounds.[129] To survive, German women made bread out of acorns and soap out of ash. They stole coal and used whatever money they could find to buy food on the black market. American troops traded food and cigarettes for sex.[130] Despite their poor health and difficulty in making ends meet, the occupation government called upon women to help clear the rubble of Germany's cities. Lured by extra ration cards, "women of the rubble" made up 5–10 percent of employed women in Berlin and were a symbol of immediate postwar Germany. Dressed in rags, during the day they cleared bricks from German streets; at night they worked to feed their families.[131] Women's work allowed Germany to emerge from the war.

Officially, Allied governments forbade troops from fraternizing with local women, but such policies were not well enforced. For instance, the U.S. military prohibited American troops from marrying Austrian women until January 1946 and German women until December 1946. It also tried to prevent all mixed-race marriages. Nevertheless, men and women entered into both casual and long-lasting relationships, angering local men who were already demoralized by their defeat. In retaliation, German and Austrian men publicly cut the hair of girls who fraternized with American GIs.[132]

Approximately 115,000 European women, the majority of whom were British, became the war brides of American servicemen. Another forty-eight thousand war brides went to Canada. Most of these women were young (around eighteen years old) working-class and middle-class girls who had not finished high school. Their GI husbands were from the same economic class and education levels, but were slightly older, on average around twenty-three.[133] Some women who had married African American GIs were surprised to find out that their marriages were illegal in fifteen states. However, most created new families and new lives in North America, far from the devastation of their homelands.

Across Europe, the end of the war put family relationships to the test. Soldiers returned from war physically injured and mentally traumatized. Many had acquired venereal diseases. Some men returned home to find that their wives had taken up with other men. Many couples felt the strains of rebuilding. Women had become accustomed to managing without their husbands and husbands felt powerless. Such feelings of impotence were even greater among the defeated Axis troops.

Allied forces liberated France in September 1944. With the thrill of freedom, Frenchwomen had to deal with the two million Frenchmen who returned from Germany between March and July 1945. For women whose husbands came home, the trauma of war was far from over. In addition to long-term physical and mental health problems, the fact that Resistance fighters had helped liberate France while POWs waited in camps meant that French society did not praise the returnees as heroes. Moreover, the horrifying images of the Jews liberated from concentration camps overshadowed their own suffering in the POW camps and the deprivations that their families had suffered.[134] Not all families survived. The number of divorces increased substantially between 1945 and 1957.[135]

The new government headed by General Charles de Gaulle demonstrated little interest in undoing interwar and wartime policies that disadvantaged women. Prior to the war, only husbands could be heads of households and they were solely responsible for decisions affecting the family. A husband could even veto his wife's desire to work. The postwar government revived these laws in 1945 as "public order statutes," which remained in effect until 1965. Husbands remained the only legal heads of the family until 1970. Through such legislation, the French state protected the masculinity of its male citizens.[136]

## Out of the Service

Many women were disappointed to discover that their governments intended to ignore their contributions to the war effort. In the Soviet Union, wartime propaganda had focused almost exclusively on women on the home front. There were no posters of Soviet women on the front, and films portrayed women as loyal wives waiting patiently at home. At the end of the war, although the Soviet government had decorated one hundred thousand women for their brave defense of their nation, there were no monuments to their bravery or sacrifice. Official government histories made no mention of women's service. The government and the media branded the women who had fought on the front as "camp followers," and the Soviet public came to assume that they had all been prostitutes. Women veterans who wore their medals and uniforms in public remembered being accosted by

passers-by and called whores.[137] In a victory parade in Great Britain, women protested after the Women's Land Army was forced to march behind the Boy Scouts.[138] Gender stereotypes almost completely erased women's contribution to the war.

In the United States, the government began pushing women out of the military even before the war ended, disbanding the WASPs in 1944. After the war, the military demobilized servicewomen and urged them to go home and retake their traditional domestic roles without providing them any veterans' benefits. Most of them did not consider themselves veterans and neither did the government. The government also discouraged army nurses from taking advantage of military benefits like the GI bill, and Veterans Administration (VA) officials kept haphazard records, so that when women married and took their husbands' surnames, they disappeared from the bureaucracy. Moreover, VA hospitals were completely unprepared for female veterans. They had no gynecologists on staff, no women's wards, no designated women's bathrooms for inpatients, not even hospital pajamas for women.[139] Nevertheless, military experience benefited many women. After the war, they found new jobs that used the skills that they learned in the service. One-third went to college or made plans to attend school. Former WAC Laura Frank described her experience as "wonderful," an opportunity to "find myself, be independent. I like it because it was my choice."[140]

For many women, the end of the war brought a complex array of emotions: sadness, exhilaration, fear, hope. Mies Boissevain-van Lennep (1896–1965), a prominent feminist, member of the Dutch Resistance, and survivor of Ravensbrück, worked tirelessly to heal Dutch society. The Nazis killed both of her sons, and her husband died in a concentration camp. In the fall of 1945, only six months after the liberation of the Netherlands, Boissevain encouraged Dutch women to wear homemade patchwork skirts. The patchwork skirt, a uniquely female form of political expression, symbolized how an otherwise loosely connected Dutch society might come together again after the trauma of the Nazi occupation and the war. Each woman would make her own skirt from her own used materials, but women would share their experience by wearing them at public and private celebrations. Women embroidered moments of their wartime experience into the skirts: arrests, concentration camps, the desire for chocolate. The skirts gave women an outlet for coming to grips with their horrific past and passing their war memories on to their daughters.[141]

## CONCLUSION

World War II was the transformative event in the lives of women during the middle of the twentieth century. Wartime politics focused on women's reproductive and emotional roles. Wartime economies relied on women's labor, and women were the center of any home life that remained. At the same time, women's military service challenged traditional gender expectations, forcing nations to reconsider how and when women could serve their countries. Governments bombarded women with mixed messages. They were expected to work and stay home, be sexy and be asexual. Of course, for Jewish and millions of other non-Aryan women, the war brought the specter of death and genocide on a scale previously unknown to Western civilization. The courage of those who gave their lives and those who survived serves as a testament to women's strength.

## NOTES

1. Gisela Bock, "Racism and Sexism in Nazi Germany: Motherhood, Compulsory Sterilization, and the State," in *When Biology Became Destiny: Women in Weimar and Nazi Germany*, ed. Renate Bridenthal, Atina Grossmann, and Marion Kaplan (New York: Monthly Review Press, 1984), 279; Lisa Pine, *Nazi Family Policy, 1933–1945* (Oxford: Berg, 1997), 13.

2. Gisela Bock, *Women in European History*, trans. Allison Brown (Oxford: Blackwell Publishers, 2002), 211.

3. Matthew Stibbe, *Women in the Third Reich* (London: Arnold, 2003), 73.

4. Bock, "Racism and Sexism," 277.

5. Stibbe, 60, 72.

6. Stibbe, 74.

7. Quoted in Pine, 153.

8. Stibbe, 68–69.

9. Stibbe, 66.

10. Pine, 18.

11. Jill Stephenson, *Women in Nazi Germany* (London: Longman, 2001), 24.

12. Claudia Koonz, *Mothers in the Fatherland: Women, the Family, and Nazi Politics* (New York: St. Martin's Press, 1987), 186.

13. Stibbe, 41–42.

14. Pine, 128–129.

15. Irene Guenther, *Nazi Chic? Fashioning Women in the Third Reich* (Oxford: Berg, 2004), esp. chap. 4.

16. Koonz, *Mothers in the Fatherland*, 189.

17. Koonz, *Mothers in the Fatherland*, 187.

18. Quoted in Stephenson, 151–152.

19. Claudia Koonz, "The Competition for a Women's *Lebensraum*," in *When Biology Became Destiny*, 226.

20. Stephenson, 89, 60.

21. Stephenson, 78, 163.

22. Karen Offen, *European Feminisms, 1700–1950: A Political History* (Stanford, CA: Stanford University Press, 2000), 368.

23. Michael Berenbaum, *The World Must Know: The History of the Holocaust as Told in the United States Holocaust Memorial Museum* (Boston: Little, Brown, 1993), 57.

24. Glen Jeansonne, *Women of the Far Right: The Mothers' Movement and World War II* (Chicago: University of Chicago Press, 1996), 8, 51.

25. Gerard J. De Groot, "'I Love the Scent of Cordite in Your Hair': Gender Dynamics in Mixed Anti-Aircraft Batteries During the Second World War," *History* 82:265 (1997): esp. 74, 75, 83, 77.

26. Tessa Stone, "Creating a (Gendered?) Military Identity: The Women's Auxiliary Air Force in Great Britain in the Second World War," *Women's History Review* 8:4 (1999): 617.

27. De Groot, 79.

28. Reina Pennington, *Wings, Women, and War: Soviet Airwomen in World War II Combat* (Lawrence: University of Kansas Press, 2001), 56.

29. K. Jean Cottam, "Soviet Women in Combat in World War II: The Ground Forces and the Navy," *International Journal of Women's Studies* 3:4 (1980): 345.

30. Pennington, 161, 162, 170, 141.

31. Barbara Alpern Engel, "The Womanly Face of War: Soviet Women Remember World War II," in *Women and War in the Twentieth Century: Enlisted With or Without Consent*, ed. Nicole Ann Dombrowski (New York: Garland, 1999), 142.

32. Engel, 143.

33. Quoted in Leisa D. Meyer, *Creating GI Jane: Sexuality and Power in the Women's Army Corps During World War II* (New York: Columbia University Press, 1996), 13, 19.

34. John W. Jeffries, *Wartime America: The World War II Home Front* (Chicago: Ivan R. Dee, 1996), 100.

35. Meyer, *Creating GI Jane*, 73.

36. Leisa D. Meyer, "The Lesbian Threat: Within the World War II Women's Army Corps," in *Women and War in the Twentieth Century*, 191–193.

37. Molly Merryman, *Clipped Wings: The Rise and Fall of the Women Airforce Service Pilots (WASPs) of World War II* (New York: New York University Press, 1998), 26.

38. Evelyn M. Monahan and Rosemary Neidel-Greenlee, *And If I Perish: Frontline U.S. Army Nurses in World War II* (New York: Alfred A. Knopf, 2003), 9, 13–14, 458.

39. Quoted in Kathleen Broome Williams, *Improbable Warriors: Women Scientists and the U.S. Navy in World War II* (Annapolis: Naval Institute Press, 2001), 7.

40. D'Ann Campbell, "Women in Combat: The World War II Experience in the United States, Great Britain, and the Soviet Union," *The Journal of Military History* 57 (April 1993): 314.

41. Koonz, *Mothers in the Fatherland*, 395.

42. Barbara Jancar-Webster, *Women and Revolution in Yugoslavia, 1941–1945* (Denver: Arden Press, 1990), 48, 139.

43. Margaret Collins Weitz, *Sisters in the Resistance: How Women Fought to Free France, 1940–1945* (New York: John Wiley and Sons, 1995), 3, 65, 15, 150.

44. Paula Schwartz, "Redefining Resistance: Women's Activism in Wartime France," in *Behind the Lines: Gender and the Two World Wars*, ed. Margaret Randolph Higonnet, Jane Jenson, Sonya Michel, and Margaret Weitz (New Haven: Yale University Press, 1987), 145.

45. Weitz, 66, 148–149.

46. Jane Slaughter, *Women and the Italian Resistance, 1943–1945* (Denver: Arden Press, 1997), 33, 41, 43, 59, 60.

47. Emily E. Werner, *A Conspiracy of Decency: The Rescue of the Danish Jews During World War II* (Boulder, CO: Westview Press, 2002), 57.

48. Nechama Tec, "Women Among the Forest Partisans," in *Women in the Holocaust*, ed. Dalia Ofer and Lenore J. Weitzman (New Haven: Yale University Press, 1998), 226 and 231.

49. Monahan and Neidel-Greenlee, 16, 19.

50. Bernice Archer, "A Patchwork of Internment," *History Today* 47:7 (July 1997): 11–19.

51. Angus Calder, *The People's War: Britain, 1939–1945* (New York: Pantheon Books, 1969), 334.

52. Sheila Rowbotham, *A Century of Women: The History of Women in Britain and the United States in the Twentieth Century* (New York: Penguin, 1997), 234.

53. Jeffries, 94–95, 98.

54. Ruth Milkman, "Gender at Work: The Sexual Division of Labor During World War II," in *Women's America: Refocusing the Past*, ed. Linda K. Kerber and Jane Sherron De Hart (New York: Oxford University Press, 2004), 469–470.

55. Jeffries, 98.

56. Rowbotham, 262.

57. Quoted in Vicki L. Ruiz, *From Out of the Shadows: Mexican Women in Twentieth-Century America* (New York: Oxford University Press, 1998), 82.

58. Jeffries, 96.

59. Susan M. Hartmann, *The Home Front and Beyond: American Women in the 1940s* (Boston: Twayne, 1982), 62.

60. Ruth Milkman, "American Women and Industrial Unionism During World War II," in *Behind the Lines*, 169.

61. Margaret Paton-Walsh, *Our War Too: American Women Against the Axis* (Lawrence: University Press of Kansas, 2002), 2.

62. John Barber and Mark Harrison, *The Soviet Homefront, 1941–1945: A Social and Economic History of the USSR in World War II* (London: Longman, 1991), 98.

63. Greta Bucher, "Struggling to Survive: Soviet Women in the Postwar Years," *Journal of Women's History* 12:1 (Spring 2000): 141.

64. Calder, 381.

65. Jeffries, 30.

66. Amy Bentley, *Eating for Victory: Food Rationing and the Politics of Domesticity* (Urbana: University of Illinois Press, 1998), 25, 114.

67. Sarah Fishman, "Waiting for the Captive Sons of France: Prisoner of War Wives, 1940–1945," in *Behind the Lines*, 182.

68. Sarah Fishman, *We Will Wait: Wives of French Prisoners of War, 1940–1945* (New Haven: Yale University Press, 1991), 60.

69. Fishman, "Waiting for the Captive Sons," 183, n. 3.

70. Hélène Eck, "French Women Under Vichy," in *A History of Women in the West: Toward a Cultural Identity in the Twentieth Century*, vol. 5, ed. Françoise Thébaud (Cambridge: Belknap, 1994), 218.

71. Fishman, *We Will Wait*, 49, 59, 58.

72. Calder, 35.

73. Calder, 377–378.

74. Eck, 200.

75. Fishman, *We Will Wait*, 62.

76. Fishman, in *Behind the Lines*, 186, 188.

77. Fishman, *We Will Wait*, 66, 67.

78. Fishman, in *Behind the Lines*, 187.

79. Hartmann, 4.

80. Jeffries, 102.

81. Meghan K. Winchell, "'To Make the Boys Feel at Home': USO Senior Hostesses and Gendered Citizenship," *Frontiers* 25:1 (2004): 201, 197.

82. Marilyn E. Hegarty, "Patriot or Prostitute?: Sexual Discourses, Print Media, and American Women During World War II," *Journal of Women's History* 10:2 (Summer 1998): 115, 122.

83. Sonya O. Rose, "Sex, Citizenship, and the Nation in World War II Britain," *American Historical Review* 103:4 (October 1998): 1164, 1167.

84. Elizabeth Heineman, "The Hour of the Woman: Memories of Germany's 'Crisis Years' and West German National Identity," *American Historical Review* 101:2 (April 1996): 362–363.

85. Bock, "Racism and Sexism," 278.

86. Elizabeth D. Heineman, "Whose Mothers? Generational Difference, War, and the Nazi Cult of Mother," *Journal of Women's History* 12:4 (Winter 2001): 142–143.

87. Leila J. Rupp, *Mobilizing Women for War: German and American Propaganda, 1939–1945* (Princeton: Princeton University Press, 1978), 185.

88. Heineman, "Whose Mothers," 145.

89. Gisela Bock, "Ordinary Women in Nazi Germany: Perpetrators, Victims, Followers, and Bystanders," in *Women in the Holocaust*, 91–94.

90. Dalia Ofer and Lenore J. Weitzman, *Women in the Holocaust,* 103.

91. Ofer and Weitzman, 103.

92. In Ruth Schwertfeger, *Women of Theresienstadt: Voices from a Concentration Camp* (Oxford: Berg, 1989), 38.

93. Charles G. Roland, *Courage Under Siege: Starvation, Disease, and Death in the Warsaw Ghetto* (New York: Oxford University Press, 1992), 27.

94. Ofer and Weitzman, 104.

95. Michal Unger, "The Status and Plight of Women in the Lódz Ghetto," in *Women in the Holocaust*, 123–125.

96. Unger, 129–133.

97. Roland, 174–175.

98. Quoted in Schwertfeger, 82.

99. Israel Gutman, *Resistance: The Warsaw Ghetto Uprising* (Boston: Houghton Mifflin, 1994), 245–246.

100. Unger, 126.

101. Felicja Karay, "Women in the Forced-Labor Camps," in *Women in the Holocaust*, 287–288.

102. Karay, 289.

103. Bock, "Ordinary Women in Nazi Germany," 89.

104. Jack G. Morrison, *Ravensbrück: Everyday Life in a Women's Concentration Camp, 1939–1945* (Princeton: Markus Wiener, 2000), 23–26.

105. Morrison, 34.

106. Quoted in Berenbaum, 149.

107. Elizabeth D. Heineman, "Sexuality and Nazism: The Doubly Unspeakable?" *Journal of the History of Sexuality* 11:1/2 (January/April 2002): 60.

108. Morrison, 43, 53.

109. Rudolf Höss, Pery Broad, Johann Paul Kremer, Jadwiga Bezwinska, Danuta Czech, *KL Auschwitz Seen by the SS: Höss, Broad, Kremer* (New York: Howard Fertig, 1984), 75.

110. Heineman, "Sexuality and Nazism," 57.

111. Sara Nomberg-Przytyk, *Auschwitz: True Tales from a Grotesque Land*, trans. Roslyn Hirsch (Chapel Hill: University of North Carolina Press, 1985), 69.

112. Berenbaum, 149.

113. Magda Herzberger, "God Saved Me for a Purpose," in *Sisters in Sorrow: Voices of Care in the Holocaust*, ed. Roger A. Ritvo and Diane M. Plotkin (College Station: Texas A&M University Press, 1998), 213.

114. Berenbaum, 123.

115. Ofer and Weitzman, 105.

116. Atina Grossmann, "A Question of Silence: The Rape of German Women by Soviet Occupation Soldiers," in *Women and War in the Twentieth Century*, esp. 174–175.

117. Heineman, "The Hour," 372.

118. Marie Ellifritz, "My Sorrow Is Continuously Before Me," in *Sisters in Sorrow,* 239.

119. Schwertfeger, 104, 114.

120. Quoted in Berenbaum, 206.

121. Atina Grossman, "Victims, Villains, and Survivors: Gendered Perceptions and Self-Perceptions of Jewish Displaced Persons in Occupied Postwar Germany," *Journal of the History of Sexuality* 11/1–2 (January–April 2002): 307.

122. Berenbaum, 208.

123. Grossman, "Victims," 308–309.

124. Christiane Harzig, "MacNamara's DP Domestics: Immigration Policy Makers Negotiate Class, Race, and Gender in the Aftermath of World War II," *Social*

*Politics: International Studies in Gender, State, and Society* 10:1 (Spring 2003): 31.

125. Bucher, 145.

126. Engel, 149.

127. Françoise Navailh, "The Soviet Model," in *A History of Women in the West*, 248.

128. Quoted in Bucher, 143.

129. Heineman, "The Hour," 374.

130. Perry Biddiscombe, "Dangerous Liaisons: The Anti-Fraternization Movement in the U.S. Occupation Zones of Germany and Austria, 1945–1948," *Journal of Social History* 34:3 (2001): 615–616.

131. Heineman, "The Hour," 375.

132. Biddiscombe, 616, 619–620.

133. Jenel Virden, *Good-bye Piccadilly: British War Brides in America* (Urbana: University of Illinois Press, 1996), 2.

134. Fishman, *We Will Wait*, 154–155.

135. Eck, 208.

136. Eck, 200.

137. Engel, 150.

138. Rowbotham, 228.

139. Monahan and Neidel-Greenlee, 457–460.

140. Quoted in Meyer, *Creating GI Jane*, 182.

141. Jolande Withius, "Patchwork Politics in the Netherlands, 1946–1950: Women, Gender and the World War II Trauma," *Women's History Review* 3:3 (1994): 293–313.

## SUGGESTED READINGS

Dombrowski, Nicole Ann, ed. *Women and War in the Twentieth Century: Enlisted With or Without Consent*. New York: Garland, 1999.

Fishman, Sarah. *We Will Wait: Wives of French Prisoners of War, 1940–1945*. New Haven: Yale University Press, 1991. A comprehensive examination of the lives of French women living under the most dire circumstances.

Higonnet, Margaret, Jane Jenson, Sonya Michel, and Margaret Weitz, *Behind the Lines: Gender and the Two World Wars*. New Haven: Yale University Press, 1987. Many of these essays have become classics in the field.

Koonz, Claudia. *Mothers in the Fatherland: Women, the Family, and Nazi Politics*. New York: St.

Martin's Press, 1987. This monumental study includes Koonz's engrossing description of her interview with Gertrud Scholtz-Klink.

Meyer, Leisa D. *Creating GI Jane: Sexuality and Power in the Women's Army Corps During World War II*. New York: Columbia University Press, 1996.

Ofer, Dalia and Lenore J. Weitzman, eds. *Women in the Holocaust*. New Haven: Yale University Press, 1998. This collection of essays explores the experience of the Holocaust through the lives of many different types of women.

Pennington, Reina. *Wings, Women, and War: Soviet Airwomen in World War II Combat*. Lawrence: University of Kansas Press, 2001.

# Women and the Postwar Generation, 1945–1970

*German Women Building Airstrip During Berlin Airlift.* To prevent the Soviets from taking over Berlin and the citizens from starving, British and American planes flew in all necessary supplies for eleven months. The airlift required Berliners to build new landing strips to accommodate the air traffic, in addition to rebuilding their city. (Bettmann/Corbis.)

■ **Gender and the Cold War**  528

   *The Creation of the
      United Nations*  528
   *Women and International Conflict
      in the Cold War*  530
   *Anti-Communist Hysteria in the
      United States*  531
   *Dividing German Women*  531

■ **Postwar Society**  533

   *The Postwar Family*  533
   *Women and the European Welfare
      State*  534
   *Women and the Postwar
      Economy*  535

■ **Gender Behind the Iron
   Curtain**  537

   *Women and Politics in the Soviet
      Union*  537
   *Communism, the Family, and the
      State*  538
   *Gender, Production, and the Soviet
      Economic System*  539
   *Women Against the Regime*  541

■ **Women and Decolonization**  543

   *Native Women and Nationalist
      Movements*  543
   *Gender and the Wars of
      Independence*  545
   *Postcolonial Repercussions*  546

■ **Agitating for Change**  548

   *The Antinuclear and
      Environmental Movements*  548
   *The Pill and the Sexual
      Revolution*  551
   *Social Protest Movements*  554
   *A New Woman's Movement*  556

■ **Gender and Postwar Culture**  558

   *The Transformation of the Modern
      Home*  558
   *Creating an Image: Women in Film
      and Television*  559
   *The Rise of Rock 'n' Roll*  560

# *Chapter 15* ❖ Chronology

| | |
|---|---|
| **1946** | UN Commission of Women |
| | Norway launches its welfare state |
| **1947** | Marshall Plan |
| **1949** | Simone de Beauvoir publishes *The Second Sex* |
| **1950** | U.S. Senator Joseph McCarthy starts his anti-communist hearings |
| **1953** | Alfred Kinsey publishes his *Sexual Behavior in the Human Female* |
| **1954** | French pull out of Vietnam after their defeat at Dien Bien Phu |
| | U.S. Supreme Court declares segregation illegal in *Brown v. the Board of Education* |
| **1956** | Khrushchev initiates de-Stalinization |
| | Hungarian Uprising |
| **1960** | Gregory Pincus invents the birth control pill |
| **1961** | Berlin Wall built |
| | Tanzania independence |
| **1962** | Algerian independence from France |
| | Rachael Carson publishes *Silent Spring* |
| | Beatles cut their first single "Love Me Do" |
| **1963** | Kenyan independence |
| | Betty Friedan publishes *The Feminine Mystique* |
| **1964** | U.S. President Johnson signs the Civil Rights Act |
| **1968** | Student uprisings in United States and Europe |
| | Prague Spring |

The West emerged from World War II divided. The United States enjoyed a period of economic prosperity and international power that influenced postwar culture around the world, while the Soviet Union struggled to overcome the devastation and population loss of the war. Europe was also split in two. Eastern Europe fell under the ideological influence and control of the Soviet Union, while Western Europe rebuilt under the watchful eye and gen- erosity of the United States. The cold war, the ongoing conflict between Western capitalism and Soviet communism, permeated society from a military buildup to the promotion of traditional gender roles. The United States and the Soviet Union battled physically and ideologically to win the hearts and minds of the world. Cold war gender expectations pressured women to remain at home and bear children whenever possible, and governments intervened to make this happen. In the

Soviet Union, leaders relied on women to rebuild the economy, but the totalitarian regime quashed their critiques of the system. In the United States, frustration with government policies and social norms erupted into widespread social protest. Postwar culture reflected these tensions as the young tried to live the freedom their mothers and fathers fought for in World War II.

## GENDER AND THE COLD WAR

The division of Europe into Eastern and Western blocs began at the end of World War II. Relations between the United States and the Soviets soured when Soviet leader Josef Stalin (1879–1953) rejected American president Harry Truman's (1945–1953) demand for free elections in Eastern Europe. The animosity grew as the United States supported the rebuilding of Western Europe with grants of money and supplies under the Marshall Plan (1947) and Stalin rejected U.S. aid for both the Soviet Union and Eastern Europe. In 1949, twelve Western European nations and the United States formed the North Atlantic Treaty Organization (NATO) to defend against Soviet expansion. In 1955, the Soviet Union created its own alliance of seven Eastern European nations, the Warsaw Pact. An "iron curtain" divided Europe (see Map 15.1).

The cold war that resulted from these ideological differences drew women on both sides into political action. Some women worked to promote peace while others took to the battlefield, hoping for a better future. The battle over communism pitted some American women against their own government. For women in the two Germanys, the ultimate manifestation of the cold war, the Berlin Wall, would define their lives for the next thirty years.

### The Creation of the United Nations

Horrified by the destruction of World War II, the Allies set up the United Nations (UN) as a new transnational institution aimed at settling international disputes. The goals were lofty; the UN would "save succeeding generations from the scourge of war—to reaffirm faith in fundamental human rights—to promote social progress and better standards of life in larger freedoms." Women's organizations like the Women's International League of

Peace and Freedom (see Chapter 13) saw promise in the institution and actively promoted its creation. In addition to supporting international peace, many women hoped that the UN would present new opportunities for feminist action. However, many Western delegations, including the United States and Great Britain, opposed the inclusion of a statement of women's equality in the UN charter. Nevertheless, pressure from female activists and delegates resulted in a UN charter that "reaffirm[ed] faith in fundamental human rights, in the dignity and worth of the human person, in the equal rights of men and women and of nations large and small."[1]

The inclusion of gender equity among the UN's goals led to a tense debate about the relationship between women's rights and human rights. In particular, some delegates asserted that women's issues should not be separated from human rights issues. However, feminists felt victorious when the UN created the Commission on Women to "promote implementation of the principle that men and women shall have equal rights" in 1946.[2]

Beyond bringing women's issues to the forefront of the UN's agenda, women energetically pressed for a broad statement on human rights. As the chairperson of the UN Commission on Human Rights, Eleanor Roosevelt (1884–1962) negotiated tremendous political and cultural differences to champion the creation of the Universal Declaration of Human Rights in 1948. For Roosevelt, human rights were fundamental to all aspects of life:

> Where, after all, do universal human rights begin? In small places, close to home—so close and so small that they cannot be seen on any maps of the world. Yet they are the world of the individual person; the neighborhood he lives in; the school or college he attends; the factory, farm, or office where he works. Such are the places where every man, woman, and child seeks equal justice, equal opportunity, equal dignity without discrimination. Unless these rights have meaning there, they have little meaning anywhere. Without concerted citizen action to uphold them close to home, we shall look in vain for progress in the larger world.[3]

The Universal Declaration of Human Rights did not ignore gender. It asserted that freedom

**Map 15.1 COLD WAR EUROPE, 1949–1989.** After World War II, Europe split
into two rival spheres, each with its own economic and gender assumptions.

from gender discrimination was a basic human
right. However, when the body approved the
Declaration in 1948, only four women were among
the signers: Minerva Bernardino (1907–1998)
from the Dominican Republic, Bertha Lutz
(1894–1976) of Brazil, Virginia Gildersleeves

(1877–1965) from the United States, and Wu Yi-
Tang of China. In 1953, Roosevelt went on to
help create the Draft Convention on the Political
Rights of Women, which pressed for both
women's voting rights and their inclusion in
policymaking.

## Women and International Conflict in the Cold War

The first cold war confrontation, the Greek civil war, dimmed any hope for a permanent postwar peace. In 1943, disagreements between communists and other Resistance fighters working to end the Nazi occupation of Greece erupted into civil war. The *Ethniko Apeleftherotiko Metopo* (EAM), the communist liberation front, strongly advocated for women's emancipation and brought many working-class women into the Communist Party. However, at the end of World War II, the government in Athens dismantled these leftist groups. It arrested their members, put them in concentration camps, and relocated entire villages in order to sever ties between villagers and communist guerillas. Nevertheless, the communists remained popular. Scholars estimate that between 20 and 25 percent of partisan fighters were women.[4] One woman explained that, "Any woman who happened to be passing by could get beaten [by soldiers in the right-wing paramilitary]. We got up and left. What else could we do? We joined the GDA [communist-led Greek Democratic Army]. I joined my husband. I believed in their cause."[5] The Communist Panhellenic Democratic Union of Women (PDEG) was particularly important in mobilizing women to join the GDA. During World War II, women's lives in unoccupied Greece had improved under the communists. Local courts had given illiterate peasant women some protections, the EAM had provided literacy education, and women had gained legal equality and voting rights. They were willing to risk their lives to regain those opportunities.

The United States saw the communists' popularity in Greece as a threat to democracy. In a speech asking the U.S. Congress to appropriate funds to help defeat the communists, President Truman articulated his doctrine for the containment of communism, the Truman Doctrine. By the time the civil war ended in 1949 with the defeat of the communists, it had displaced thousands of people and killed nearly eighty thousand more.[6]

The civil war divided Greeks for the next two decades and led to the overthrow of the democratic government by a military coup in 1967. The repressive dictatorship tolerated no opposition. It placed Eleni Vlachou (1911–1995), the owner of an influential newspaper, under house arrest in Athens. Using false papers, she escaped and spoke out against the military government. Lady Amalia Fleming (née Koutsouri-Voureka; 1909–1986), a bacteriologist and the widow of Alexander Fleming (1881–1955) who discovered penicillin, was imprisoned for her criticism of the regime. An international campaign finally gained her release. Thousands of others, mostly students, suffered beatings and imprisonment.

Cold war divisions also influenced conflicts outside of Europe. The 1949 triumph of Chinese communists sparked American fears of a worldwide communist conspiracy. Tensions heightened when the Soviets backed a communist invasion of South Korea by North Korea in 1950. The United Nations, led by American troops, intervened in defense of the South Koreans. Twenty-three nations contributed personnel to the war effort. However, despite cold war rhetoric, the United States had a difficult time generating support for the Korean War (1950–1953) at home. It was particularly difficult to recruit women. In 1948, the Women's Armed Services Integration Act gave enlisted women full military status but limited the number of women who could serve in the military to 2 percent of the total forces in each branch. The military still failed to meet established quotas, and in response, called up women reservists and prohibited the WAVES (Women Accepted for Volunteer Emergency Service) from resigning when they got married. Like their predecessors in World War II, women worked in clerical, supply, or communications units to free men for fighting, and many nurses working in the Mobile Army Surgical Hospitals (MASH units) served close to the front. These brave women had their work cut out for them; many would die on cold war battlefields in the coming decades.

The United States and USSR also fought their ideological battle in scientific laboratories, as the cold war arms race created a hypermasculinized scientific culture in which teams of scientists competed to advance nuclear technology and conquer space travel. In the sixties, women were 92 percent of the clerical staff and only 2 percent of the scientists and engineers at NASA's Jet Propulsion Laboratory. Many scientists believed that menstruating women would destroy the delicate equipment.[7] In 1961, the Soviets launched the first man into space, and two years later, they sent the first woman, Valentina Vladimirovna Tereshkova (b. 1937). The United States responded by promising to put a "man on the moon" and poured millions of dollars into scientific education to make it happen.

## Anti-Communist Hysteria in the United States

Worried about the spread of communism at home, many American politicians suspected their own citizens of having communist sympathies. In 1950, Joseph McCarthy (1908–1957), a senator from Wisconsin, claimed to have a secret list of two hundred communists employed by the State Department and convened hearings before the Senate to expose them and their supporters. He was aided by the Internal Security, or McCarran, Act (1950) that required all organizations labeled as "communist fronts" to register with the Subversive Activities Control Board. At the same time, the House Committee on Un-American Activities (HUAC) also looked for communists, especially in the movie industry. These hearings devastated families and careers and created a climate of fear. The government encouraged friends, families, and colleagues to testify against each other, bringing women into conflict with the U.S. government.

Accused of leftist sympathies, many prominent artists, movie stars, and writers had their works banned, went to prison for refusing to testify before Congress, or were forced underground. For example, when called to testify, playwright Lillian Hellman (1905–1984) refused to provide the names of communists whom she knew. She told HUAC,

> I do not like subversion or disloyalty in any form and if I had ever seen any I would have considered it my duty to have reported it to the proper authorities. But to hurt innocent people whom I knew many years ago in order to save myself is, to me, inhuman and indecent and dishonorable. I cannot and will not cut my conscience to fit this year's fashions, even though I long ago came to the conclusion that I was not a political person and could have no comfortable place in any political group.[8]

As a result, she was blacklisted and unable to work. Her partner, writer Dashiell Hammett (1894–1961), went to prison for six months for his political beliefs, and Hellman had to sell her home to pay her bills. Dozens of others faced the same humiliation for joining organizations that were legal under U.S. law.

FBI agents used women to get at suspected men, by tailing the wives and children of suspected and known communists. Defiantly, the wives of the defendants formed the Families Committee to raise money for food, bail, and even summer camp for the children of the victims of HUAC's investigations.[9] Not surprisingly, the Families Committee found itself on the list of subversive organizations in 1956. The government also targeted gays and lesbians, arguing that their lifestyle was un-American and that their sexuality made them more susceptible to communist indoctrination. A pamphlet published by HUAC even warned that schoolteachers might be subversives. According to the pamphlet, because most female schoolteachers were single, their sexual frustration might make them amenable to communism.

McCarthy's "witch-hunt" expanded until 1954 when he accused the army of favoring communists. Millions watched televised hearings and saw McCarthy confronted by Joseph Welch (1890–1960), the lead council for the army. McCarthy's erratic and aggressive behavior alienated viewers. The Senate then charged McCarthy with blackmailing the military and began investigating him. Several months later, the Senate voted to censure him and McCarthyism gradually diminished.

## Dividing German Women

Concerns about the spread of communism were much more immediate in postwar Germany. At the end of World War II, the Allied powers divided a devastated Germany into occupation zones, and Berlin, which was in the Soviet zone, was governed by all four occupying nations. By 1948, relations between the Soviets and the Western powers had soured. Confrontation came after the Western powers reformed the worthless currency in use in their sectors, setting Germany on a path toward a free-market economy. In retaliation, the Soviet Union withdrew from the alliance and blockaded

Berlin. For the next eleven months, the Western powers airlifted supplies into the city. Finally, the Soviets lifted the blockade, and subsequent negotiations divided Germany into the Federal Republic of Germany in the West controlled by the Allies and the German Democratic Republic (GDR) in the East controlled by the Soviets.

During the 1950s, Berlin was a gateway for East Germans fleeing their new communist government. As an open city, it was easy to take the train out of Berlin and into West Germany. Beginning on August 13, 1961, Berliners watched as the East German government built a barrier of barbed wire, concrete, and bricks through the middle of the city, creating a visible barrier, the Berlin Wall, between communist and capitalist Europe. For the next thirty years, German women would be defined by the political ideology under which they lived.

In East Germany, the communist government transformed the lives of its citizens according to the Soviet model. To ensure conformity with communist ideology, secret police watched for dissent, and schools inculcated students with Marxist-Leninist ideals. The government centralized the economy and collectivized agriculture.

The new economy needed workers, so to bring women into the economy, as early as 1946, the government guaranteed that women and men would receive equal pay in many sectors of the economy. To help integrate women into the socialist economy, the government created the Democratic Women's Union of Germany (DFD) to represent women and women's issues. The DFD had two main goals: to encourage non-working women to join the workforce and to counter deeply held prejudices against working mothers. The communist state also provided extensive support for working mothers, including childcare, abortion on demand, and generous maternity leave at full pay. In many ways, this campaign was successful. By 1957, 65 percent of women were engaged in paid labor. However, for the most part, women were concentrated in low-paying, low-prestige jobs. With its mission accomplished, and concerned about the political power of a women's organization, the state gradually diminished the DFD's authority. After 1963, the government refocused its mission to social work.

East German women often had a difficult time providing for their families. Although food rationing ended in 1959, prices for many goods and services were considerably higher than in the West, and wages remained low. The government-controlled economy dictated production levels and prices, and basic goods such as underwear, meat, shoes, and laundry detergent became scarce. When the government lifted some price controls in the early 1960s, many products became too expensive for most East Germans. Moreover, East German consumers never had the array of consumer choices that their West German counterparts had. From a communist perspective, the goal was standardization rather than individuality. Why make three models of refrigerators, when one would do? One model of refrigerator better reflected communist goals of the needs of society over the needs of the individual.

West German women faced a very different set of circumstances. As politicians drafted the constitution of the new republic, feminist activists worked tirelessly to ensure that the document included a simple statement of women's rights. Elizabeth Selbert (1896–1986), a prominent lawyer and member of the Social Democratic Party, led the fight. She stated: "I took it for granted that after two world wars and the experiences that we women had in those decades, equal rights for women would make it through the political process without struggle and with no further ado."[10] However, many politicians argued that such a statement denied the sexual differences between men and women that allowed for special treatment for women. After considerable debate, Selbert and her supporters won. The West German Basic Law of 1949 declared that "men and women have the same rights." Nevertheless, social and legal changes came slowly. During the 1950s, the government focused on protecting women's place as wives and mothers, not their access to education, divorce, or equal pay. In 1961, a German court asserted that "in light of the present-day understanding of the character of the German marriage, the wife is to be the lifelong helper of her husband."[11]

Although many women might have accepted the idea they were to be mothers not workers, the reality was very different. Because of the devastation of World War II, in 1950, women headed one in three West German households.[12] Women had to work to survive. Whereas the government provided pensions for war widows and assumed the role of father for their children so that war widows would not have to work, unmarried women with children received no such help. Their plight was caught up in an effort to distance West Germany from its Nazi past. Both the government and churches argued that the Nazis had encouraged sexual immorality and promiscuity, thus unwed mothers became a painful reminder of the war.[13] Regardless of marital status, life in West Germany during the early 1950s remained difficult. Very few homes had modern appliances, and even those appliances that were available were too expensive for most families. However, a boost from the Marshall Plan combined with Germany's own economic policies of a free market with strong social welfare policies improved the German economy by the early 1960s. Families saw the benefits of modernization, and more women with young children worked outside the home.

The creation of the United Nations expressed the hope for a permanent peace and gender equity. However, these hopes were dashed as the United States and Soviet Union battled for ideological supremacy around the world. Women from Korea to Kansas were called on to defend themselves and their beliefs. The impact of the cold war was most evident in Germany. In East Germany, the government imposed gender equality with little input from women. In West Germany, where women might have had input in the democratic process, they opted for domesticity over politics. The Berlin Wall not only separated families, it formed a political and ideological barrier between women.

## POSTWAR SOCIETY

The United States' drive to contain communism led Americans to embrace domesticity as an antidote to cold war tensions. Preservation of the postwar family, which included traditional gender roles, became a cold war goal.[14] The United States' leadership in the rebuilding of Europe spread this message across the Atlantic. Women

were encouraged to raise large families, and the new welfare states of Western Europe reflected this emphasis on motherhood. However, despite the rhetoric of domesticity that pervaded Western culture, economic necessity and a boom economy brought increasing numbers of women into the workforce.

## The Postwar Family

After the war, Western Europeans and Americans settled in at home, focusing on marriage, child-rearing, and domesticity. Between 1945 and 1964, the population in Western Europe grew as more women married, married at earlier ages, and had more children. The increase in marriage rates was dramatic. Although nearly 20 percent of British women did not marry before World War II, after the war, that number fell to around 5 percent. The average age at marriage also fell from the mid-twenties to the low twenties. These younger couples had more children, creating a postwar baby boom. Among European industrialized nations, Italy had one of the highest birthrates in the 1950s and 1960s. Italian women bore on average 2.7 children in 1963, up from 2.35 in 1954.[15] From 1946 to 1959, Norwegian women averaged 2.63 children, a figure that rose to 2.93 by the early 1960s.[16] The baby boom was even more evident in the United States, where U.S. college-educated and middle-class white women married around age twenty and bore an average of three children each.[17] The baby boom ended by the early 1960s due in part to the introduction of the birth control pill (see below).

The Marshall Plan transmitted gender expectations and shared conceptions of the postwar family to Europe through American goods and mass media. In the first twenty years after the war, women increasingly came to believe that they needed to defer or give up career expectations for marriage and family. They also wanted the romance and companionship portrayed in the popular media; however, men retained traditional notions of marriage. British men in the 1950s considered good housekeeping skills as the most important trait in a wife. Aware of these trends, the media encouraged women to stay home with their children and at the same time campaigned for fathers to be more interested in their children, thus minimizing the impact of mothering, which they asserted could make boys soft, or "sissies," a code for homosexuality.

The new Western family also focused more on children. Dr. Benjamin Spock's (1903–1998) *The Common Sense Book of Baby and Child Care* taught parents to trust their own instincts about raising their children rather than rely on professionals. First published in the United States in 1946, the book came to Britain in 1955 and was an immediate bestseller. In addition, the combination of economic prosperity and child-labor laws meant that children stayed in school in record numbers after the war. After school, rather than work, they played and did homework. Marketers of consumer goods saw a new source of revenue in the vast numbers of children. New baby products emerged to help mothers take care of their children. As children aged, they enjoyed changing clothing styles, as well as a burgeoning market in children's books, toys, and television shows directed at their entertainment. Teenagers emerged as the biggest market. The new youth culture taught girls how to attract husbands by putting on makeup and wearing the newest styles of clothing and hairstyles. At the same time, the media also led them to expect to stay in school and go to college. Although many girls and women did not live out these fantasies, these cultural expectations were a pervasive force in postwar culture and family life.

## Women and the European Welfare State

After World War II, the governments of Great Britain, France, West Germany, and the Scandinavian countries confronted the problem of bringing equality to women workers while recognizing their role as child bearers. These issues became even more important when the baby boom ended and the birthrate declined. Governments wanted women to have more and healthier babies. Consequently, governments devoted considerable resources to mothers and children through state-funded nutrition and hygiene programs, medical care, daycare, education, and public housing.

The 1934 book *Crisis in the Population Question*, by Swedish economists Alva (1902–1986) and Gunnar (1898–1987) Myrdal, influenced the expansion of welfare states across Europe. The Myrdals argued that social conditions needed to improve to make it easier to have children. They documented a lack of housing and good nutrition throughout Sweden and showed that having children lowered a couple's standard of living. The Myrdals did not advocate direct government payments to families, but rather programs such as school lunches, free health care, subsidized food, and daycare. They believed that such programs would increase production and consumption and strengthen the economy.

Norway ushered in the postwar welfare state in 1946 with the passage of family allowances to every Norwegian family with more than one child, without regard to income level. Child-rearing became a matter of public concern.[18] Many of the richer cities in the south also created pensions for widows and single women. In 1957, the government began providing health care for children with unemployed parents, and the following year, the state began paying child support to abandoned mothers. As the result of pressure from women's groups, the government expanded this right to widows and unwed mothers in 1964. Norway's welfare state would become one of the most extensive in the world.

Welfare states expressed different assumptions about women's roles in society. France's welfare state reflected both continued concerns about its declining population and pressure for women's rights, which increased after Frenchwomen obtained the vote in 1944. At the end of the war, French president Charles de Gaulle (1890–1970) admonished Frenchwomen to produce "in ten years, 12 million beautiful babies for France." Thus, much of the French welfare system focused on increasing female fertility, regardless of a woman's marital status. In addition to extensive childcare services, such as early education and after-school programs, women received the same pensions, health care, and other job-related benefits as men regardless of marital status. The founder of Britain's welfare program, William Beveridge (1879–1960), strongly supported the man as the family breadwinner and believed that women's most important contribution was motherhood. Thus, he wanted family allowances to go to fathers; however, female members of Parliament pressured the government to make family payments a wage for motherhood and to provide allowances for children so that women and children could be free from undependable husbands and fathers. In 1948, the British government complemented these payments with the launch of the National Health Service, which provided comprehensive health care for all Britons from cradle to grave.

By the 1960s, the United States was the only developed country without a universal family support system. In keeping with strong capitalist and classic liberal ideology, the government preferred that employers provide benefits, rather than the government. Nonetheless, in 1954, Congress approved tax deductions for childcare expenses, in an effort to help more women enter the workforce. Women also benefited from a wide array of social reforms implemented during Lyndon Johnson's (1963–1968) administration. Known as the Great Society, these programs expanded health-care coverage to the poor and elderly, aided women and children in poverty, and created programs to fight crime and illiteracy.

## Women and the Postwar Economy

After World War II ended, governments and businesses encouraged women to leave their wartime work and return home. However, many women did not have the financial support to become homemakers. Thus, the number of women working outside the home grew throughout the postwar period. In Great Britain, nearly all single women worked, and by 1951, nearly 20 percent of married women were employed.[19] Rising divorce rates at the end of the 1950s forced more women to support themselves. In 1961, 48.6 percent of divorced Belgian women worked outside the home compared with only 20.5 percent of married women.[20] By 1970, there were more Western European women in the labor force than in the 1940s.[21] Major changes occurred in the structure of women's work. Domestic service all but disappeared as a source of women's employment, paid agricultural work became less important, and increased mechanization in the textile industry moved women out of cloth production. At the same time, new products created manufacturing jobs, and the bureaucracy of the welfare state employed thousands of women as clerks and social workers.

Many women did not want to work after marriage. For them, equality meant husbands and wives doing different tasks to support the family. One Frenchwoman explained that work was "a necessary evil, to be endured until marriage might allow them to abandon it."[22] According to the Italian Feminine Center, which polled more than one hundred thousand housewives in 1949, women preferred housework because it was in keeping with the will of God. At the same time, growing corporatism moved many men into rigid nine-to-five jobs where they had little autonomy. Contemporary observers often felt that men were the oppressed segment of society.[23]

Women working outside the home faced a number of challenges. By 1960, U.S. women earned just under sixty cents for every dollar earned by a man. Throughout the 1950s, many countries still discouraged or legally prevented married women from entering the workplace. In Austria, the constitutional convention of 1950 prohibited night work for women, except in health, sanitation, education, entertainment, and tourism industries. This policy effectively kept women out of high-paying jobs in industry but allowed them to remain in poor-paying fields traditionally dominated by women. In the Ruhr Valley, an industrial part of West Germany, companies routinely fired women the day they got married. One woman explained, "the employers think it is enough if the husband is earning."[24]

In addition, few women had the education to pursue careers. Although most universities admitted women, many educators still felt it was inappropriate for women to pursue the same curriculum as men; such education was thought to be wasted on women because they would just get married. Supervisors used the same rational to deny women promotions. Women heard the message. In 1963 in Britain, only 7 percent of women went on to higher education.[25]

Other factors also made it difficult for women to work. Most European stores kept the same hours as offices and factories, making it hard for women to do their marketing. Although state-funded daycare centers in Scandinavia and the creation of public kindergartens in Italy in 1963 freed some women to enter the workplace, most countries offered women no assistance with childcare. As a result, some mothers opted for part-time work, but these jobs were low paying and did not provide benefits.

Women entering the job market in the sixties were concentrated in the service sector, elementary and secondary education, nursing, and clerical work. The growth of welfare states created a huge number of jobs for social workers and civil servants. In West Germany, the number of women working in the civil service increased two and a half times between 1950 and 1980, employing 55.9 percent of all women workers. In 1954, Frenchwomen filled 52.8 percent of all clerical positions, a number that rose to 60.8 percent by 1968. Despite the increase in numbers, clerical employment remained segregated. Male clerks dominated manufacturing while female clerks worked in the textile industry.[26]

Industry remained a large employer of women, yet the growth of mechanization in the postwar period shifted patterns of women's employment.

By the 1950s, nearly 40 percent of Belgian and British working women were in industry, compared with around 25 percent in France, Germany, and Italy. Most women worked in light industry, such as printing and shoe making, where mechanization reduced wages and factory owners hired more women. In the French metallurgical industry of the 1960s, women worked at less complex and more repetitive tasks than men. It goes without saying that women held few supervisory positions, and men held most better-paying jobs in heavy industry, such as assembly of cars, airplanes, and heavy machinery.

Rural life and work also changed after World War II. Agriculture became mechanized and economic prosperity ended rural isolation. In Norway, small family farms gave way to part-time farms, as men took jobs in nearby cities and towns. For women, farm work became an extension of housework. The tractor aided some West

**WOMEN CLERICAL WORKERS IN A BRITISH BANK, CA. 1955.** The postwar economy required thousands of clerical workers, most of whom were women. Yet women found it difficult to move out of clerical pools and into management. *(Hulton-Deutsch Collection/Corbis.)*

German farmwomen, but others complained of the tension brought on by noisy tractors, the isolation of working alone, and the loss of old work rhythms.[27] In the fishing communities of northern Europe, women continued to work as net-makers, but mechanization and increased demand centralized fishing so that it ceased to be a family venture. Factories took over fish processing, with women concentrated in gutting and packing units.

In Puerto Rico, Mexico, and in the rural American South, mechanization allowed employers to replace farm workers with poorly paid migrant workers. Many African Americans left cotton-picking jobs and migrated to northern cities. By 1960, more than a third of all African Americans lived outside of the South, and three-fifths lived in towns or cities. Although most African American women had fewer employment opportunities than white women, more black women than white women worked outside the home. By 1950, 30 percent of black wives worked compared with 19 percent of white wives.[28] The National Council of Negro Women, led by Dorothy Height (b. 1912), argued that discrimination and poor economic conditions forced African American women into the labor market to support their families.

In the conservative atmosphere of postwar society, women opted for marriage and child-rearing in unprecedented numbers. Welfare states, eager to increase their populations, provided them with economic assistance. Yet, by the early sixties, women were returning to the workforce to either support themselves or help their families afford the new consumer items produced by the booming postwar economy.

# GENDER BEHIND THE IRON CURTAIN

Soviet and Soviet bloc women experienced the postwar period very differently from their Western European counterparts. Millions had died during the war and the economy was in ruins. Material deprivation made daily life difficult. As a result, Soviet society experienced neither a baby boom nor a significant rise in the standard of living. When Stalin died in 1953, his successor, Nikita Khrushchev (1894–1971), tried to meet some of the demands of the Soviet people. He reassessed women's role in Soviet society and attempted to bring more women into politics. However, the combination of Soviet totalitarianism and a weak economy led many women to agitate against the government.

## Women and Politics in the Soviet Union

Stalin's death in 1953 brought major changes to the USSR. After a power struggle, Nikita Khrushchev emerged as the new leader in 1955 and began a process of de-Stalinization. In 1956, Khrushchev revealed Stalin's crimes against Soviet citizens in a secret speech at the Party Congress. He denounced Stalin's cult of personality and his extensive powers at the expense of local soviets and the collective will. De-Stalinization was, in its own way, revolutionary.

De-Stalinization emphasized rationality and citizen action, goals that directly targeted women. Khrushchev abandoned the use of overt state terror, promised to end state corruption, and returned power to the unions and local-level soviets. He admonished citizens to work for the betterment of society and to give up personal ambition, greed, and selfishness. Khrushchev wanted women to play an equal role in bringing about true communism through activism in their local unions and housing committees. In practice, Khrushchev's policies only addressed women's lack of political participation in fits and starts. By 1961, party officials acknowledged that women's heavy domestic responsibilities caused their lack of political participation.[29] Women called for wide-ranging solutions from more daycare centers and household appliances to changing laws and gender quotas.

To encourage women's political participation, Khrushchev promoted women's organizations called *zhhensovety*. The zhhensovety were part of a new differentiated approach to politics. Supporters now viewed women's groups as analogous to groups educating young people or pensioners instead of a manifestation of bourgeois feminism. Through the zhhensovety, women worked with other women, sharing experiences, gaining political education, or enhancing mothering skills. No central plan governed zhhensovety; instead, they reacted to local interests and needs. Some worked closely with trade unions; others held seminars on science and culture. However, all had to meet governmentally approved goals. The zhhensovety's successes are difficult to measure. There were modest increases in the number of women participating in local government, but not at the highest levels or in party membership. Overall, the zhhensovety legitimized women's political issues and validated their claims that housework took up time they would have used for other activities.[30]

Khrushchev's promotion of rationality included an antireligious campaign that often targeted women. Stalin had persecuted the clergy and shut down many churches. However, during the war, he tolerated organized religion and reopened a number of churches. With so many priests in prison, women had assumed responsibility for churches, cleaning them, singing in choirs, and raising money. Throughout the thirties and forties, three-quarters of women identified themselves as believers, while less than half of men did, and women went to church more often than men.[31] Khrushchev believed that religion prevented citizens from reaching their full creative potential. According to Khrushchev, religious celebrations encouraged drunkenness, the irresponsible uses of resources, and a breakdown in work discipline.[32] His antireligious campaign produced publications specifically for women, whom he saw as an obstacle to progress because of their association with religion.

Many of Khrushchev's reforms focused on agriculture. For example, his Virgin Lands program attempted to turn the steppes of Kazakhstan into productive agricultural land by voluntarily relocating thousands of Russians, Ukrainians, and Byelorussians. He asked women to volunteer for the program in 1954 and 1958, believing that they would provide stability by marrying the men and working on farms. Many women volunteered in order to leave the terrible conditions of postwar cities. However, conditions were hard on the new farms; they lacked sufficient food and other resources. Moreover, cultural differences between the urban settlers and the rural inhabitants subjected women settlers to accusations of sexual promiscuity, and lack of police control left many vulnerable to sexual violence. Ecologically the project was a disaster, and many returned home disillusioned. However, the women who remained spoke of their pride in overcoming difficulty, creating families, and helping Soviet society.[33]

Khrushchev accomplished many reforms and involved more women in government. But this so-called thaw in Soviet society did not abolish the secret police, or labor camps, nor did it create more time for working mothers. The state continued to limit the information available to ordinary citizens and their ability to travel. The changes in the Soviet system were often difficult to detect.

## Communism, the Family, and the State

In an effort to replace its devastated population, the Soviet state changed its family policies several times in the two decades following World War II. These changes reflect communism's continuing ambivalence toward the nuclear family. In 1944, Stalin's regime revised the Family Code, and the following year, he imposed it on Eastern Europe. He wanted to homogenize socialist societies, increase the population, and rectify the gender imbalance caused by the war. The 1959 census showed that women were 55 percent of the population and for every 1,000 women between the ages of thirty-five and forty-four there were only 633 men of the same age.[34] Under these conditions, many women were not having children. The Family Code made it difficult for couples to get divorces and illegal for women to get abortions. The Code also distinguished between legitimate and illegitimate children and no longer recognized unregistered marriages. Soviet women also married later than their Western counterparts, which meant that they had fewer children.[35] The number of children Soviet women bore dropped from 3.05 in 1949 to 2.85 in the 1950s to 2.67 by 1964.[36] By the early 1970s, the population no longer replaced itself.

Changing attitudes toward women and their roles as mothers and workers are also apparent in changes to abortion laws. In 1956, the Soviets decriminalized abortion. Although the government justified this change on the grounds that women had the absolute freedom to choose if and when they became mothers, the change actually reflected concerns for women's health. Too many women were dying from botched illegal abortions.[37] Bulgaria and Hungary quickly passed similar laws and Poland allowed abortions in cases of rape or incest. However, birth control remained difficult to obtain and women relied on abortions as a means of controlling their fertility. More than 50 percent of Soviet women had three or more abortions.[38] Faced with continuing population declines in the mid 1960s, pronatalist forces eventually won out. Many Soviet bloc countries, including Hungary and Romania, again restricted access to abortions.

The Soviet government also discouraged divorce, stating that it created instability, reflected individual emotionalism, and was, therefore, bad for the state. However, in the early fifties, jurists, legal scholars, and judges called for a liberalization of divorce laws. Although actual reform was slow, judges became more lenient in granting divorces, and between 1955 and 1965, the divorce rate in the Soviet Union rose 270 percent.[39] By the mid 1960s, divorce again became more difficult, especially in Soviet bloc states such as Poland and Romania. Romania also promoted marriage by taxing single people.

Lack of housing often hampered the creation of families. Wartime dislocation and devastation, especially in Stalingrad, exacerbated an already serious housing crisis. Families crowded together, as sometimes two and three generations lived in two small rooms. The state tried to meet the need for more housing by building apartment complexes on a massive scale. However, these buildings were poorly maintained and far from public transportation. Residents complained that the complexes were too big, bleak, and alienating. Many inhabitants believed that their stark surroundings contributed to vandalism and hooliganism.

The government countered that austere houses were important for broader social and economic reform. Khrushchev believed that he could liberate women from housework by returning to Lenin's plans for communal living. Communist ideology and the lack of consumer goods combined to promote an aesthetic of home furnishing that emphasized simplicity and functionality and minimized domesticity. Rationalizing domestic space became women's responsibility and their success reflected their ability to de-Stalinize. Stalin

became associated with lavish furnishings, clutter, and superfluous goods. Popular magazines such as *Ogonek* published photographs and gave advice on how to achieve the new look. These magazines argued that women should embrace communal living as the fulfillment of communist goals for the family. In reality, Soviet women resisted throwing out their family's old possessions. Both because they had emotional meaning and because consumer items remained scarce, Soviet houses and apartments remained filled with family heirlooms, items acquired on the black market, and newly produced goods of dubious quality.[40]

As the Soviet government promoted population growth, it vacillated between promoting the family and recognizing women's individual rights to control their fertility and living arrangements. It also showed continued ambivalence over the role of the family in Soviet society. In the end, women were both unable and unwilling to produce a baby boom for the Soviet state.

## Gender, Production, and the Soviet Economic System

In the decades following World War II, the Soviet Union and Eastern Europe continued to industrialize. As men returned home from the war, the proportion of women in the workforce dropped to 45 percent of paid workers. Khrushchev's reorganization of the economy increased the numbers of women workers, so that by 1964 women made up nearly half of the paid workforce and were a significant proportion of every industry. Most women worked in light industries, such as textiles, clothing manufacturing, and food preparation. They also dominated public services areas such as education, low-level scientific work, and the civil service. The increase of women in clerical and service sector jobs was the result of an overall increase in women's access to higher education. At the end of the war, most women entered the workforce between the ages of sixteen and nineteen, but under Khrushchev, more women attended university. In 1958, women were 75 percent of physicians, and by 1964, women were 63 percent of students seeking specialized higher education.[41]

Despite women's educational and professional gains, they still faced discrimination. As with nineteenth-century Western industrialization, women

**GOOD AND BAD TASTE IN SOVIET HOME FUR-
NISHINGS.** Interior decorations and home furnishings
became an ideological battleground in the Soviet
Union. Khrushchev wanted women to adopt minimal-
ist and functionalist styles (bottom), as opposed to the
cultured "old fashioned" look popular in Stalin's time
(top); lack of consumer goods made this plan unrealis-
tic for most families. *(Illustration from Podruga, 1959
reproduced courtesy of Susan E. Reid, "Cold War in
the Kitchen: Gender and the De-Stalinization of
Consumer Taste in the Soviet Union under Khrushchev,"* Slavic Review 61 [2002], 248.)

were frequently consigned to low-skill jobs while
management jobs went to men. Women also made
up the majority of unskilled and semiskilled labor
pools. These two factors kept women's wages lower
than men's and shaped their expectations of work.
Few chose their jobs for personal satisfaction or
opportunities for advancement; rather, most women
in industry based their choices on working hours
and proximity to home. Women also received less
recognition for their industrial productivity.[42]

In the countryside, Khrushchev initiated a
series of agricultural reforms. After seeing the
massive corn and wheat fields of the American
Midwest, he wanted to establish corn as a staple

crop and mechanize agriculture to increase food production. In many parts of the Soviet Union, peasants resisted government-imposed mechanization as another form of state-sponsored harassment. Many men believed that women could not operate the new machinery and refused to train them. In Romania, collectivization between 1949 and 1962 drew more heavily on women's labor, so that by 1978 they were the majority of the rural workforce; however, they held a minority of supervisory positions.[43] Inefficiencies in the Soviet system also affected women's agricultural work. Machines remained in short supply throughout the Soviet bloc, and the state gave men first priority for available ones. As a result, women continued to perform traditional and highly repetitive tasks in addition to their work at home and caring for livestock. In popular magazines such as *Rabotnitsa*, women complained about the government's emphasis on mechanizing agriculture, and not improving livestock production, where most women worked.[44]

Between 1949 and 1969, Hungary industrialized and the labor force expanded, but the government vacillated between policies that encouraged women to work and those that promoted motherhood. The 1949 Hungarian constitution declared that women had the right to the same work as men under the same working conditions; however, traditional notions of gendered work prevailed. Between 1949 and 1951, the government undertook a concerted campaign to push women into the workplace, and in 1951, it established minimum quotas for women workers. However, fearing that women working outside the home compromised their ability to be mothers, in 1952 the government passed protective labor legislation that banned women from many physically challenging jobs and extended maternity leave up to twenty weeks. After the Soviets repressed the 1956 revolution (see below), the new government made a half-hearted attempt to increase the number of working women. It encouraged the promotion of women, and party officials handpicked and promoted token women to positions of authority, but did not reestablish sex quotas. By 1965, amid general concern for the population's failure to grow, the government reintroduced restrictions on what jobs women could do and extended maternity leave for up to three years.[45]

Women remained disadvantaged by the planned economy of the Soviet Union. Their needs rarely dictated production. Housekeeping and food shopping included foraging for necessary but scarce items. Women complained about the lack of toilet paper, tampons, and nylon stockings. Even ordinary food items such as sugar were often difficult to purchase. Women learned to buy large quantities of anything that unexpectedly appeared in shops. The string shopping bag became an unofficial symbol for women because it was easy to carry but could expand to carry large quantities of goods and food.[46]

## Women Against the Regime

During his regime, Stalin persecuted millions of people for real and imagined crimes against the state and held them in an elaborate network of prisons in Siberia, called gulags. Prisoners earned their keep through forced labor, building railroads, digging canals, mining coal, and digging oil wells. The government claimed that these camps were economical and self-supporting. In truth, they were not only cruel and dehumanizing, they were also a financial drain on the economy. Although the rate of persecution in Stalin's last years was not as high as during the purges in the late thirties, thousands of men and women were arrested and imprisoned for unknown crimes. According to official records, women made up 22 percent of those sent to the gulags in 1948, although those numbers declined to 17 percent by 1950 and 1951. Approximately 1,775,000 women lived in forced labor camps at the time of Stalin's death.[47]

When Khrushchev came to power, he freed thousands of prisoners and promised to investigate the convictions of thousands more. Frustrated by the slow pace of releases, violent rebellions broke out in 1953 in several gulags. They took months to pacify. One witness recalled that during the revolt, Ukrainian women dressed in their finest embroidered blouses and faced army tanks with linked arms. "We thought the tanks would halt before the serried [crowded] ranks of these defenseless women. But no, they only accelerated."[48] The women were crushed.

De-Stalinization inspired many Eastern Europeans to demand freedom from Soviet domination. Revolts spread across Poland and Hungary. Although Poland escaped violent repression,

Hungary found its rebellion brutally suppressed in 1956. Communist leader Imre Nagy (1896–1958), with the support of workers and students, tried to loosen the Soviet's hold on the country. Hungarian university students organized armed resistance around the student-run non-communist league, the MEFESZ. One seventeen-year-old girl studying electrical engineering in Budapest explained her involvement, "We only wanted to better the lot of students. No one thought it would end in revolution."[49] Anticipated or not, the Soviet government ignored Hungary's wishes and brought more troops into Hungary. Women's issues were not included in the political demands, but women demonstrated and fought both as workers and as students. They also provided food and hid revolutionaries from the police. The revolutionaries broadcasted news of their actions and the Soviet invasion to the West, begging for help. However, unwilling to upset the balance in the cold war, the West did not respond. In the resulting crackdown, thousands of Hungarian men and women died in the fighting or, as was the case with Nagy, were executed by the government. Another two hundred thousand fled to the West.[50]

Khrushchev's release of thousands of prisoners without increasing freedom of expression created what some scholars have called the "era of dissidents." Many returning prisoners did not know what crimes they had been accused of, but felt compelled to write about their gulag experiences. Evgeniya Ginzburg's (1906–1977) two memoirs, *Journey into the Whirlwind* and *Within the Whirlwind*, describe her arrest in 1937 and imprisonment until 1954. Ginzburg was a journalist, professor, and loyal party member before her arrest, and her memoirs chronicle her moral awakening as she came to value individual thought over party loyalty.

Khrushchev faced resistance to his reforms from within the government and was forced from power in 1964. His successor, Leonid Brezhnev (1906–1982), rehabilitated Stalin and began persecuting writers, artists, and those who wrote about their prison experiences. The new wave of persecution began with the 1964 trial of poet Joseph Brodsky (1940–1996) for "parasitism" or eating without working. The court found him guilty and sentenced him to forced labor. Brodsky's trial and those that followed set off a wave of literary protests. Observers of the trials made clandestine transcripts, which they then shared with secret networks of supporters. Secret publication had a long tradition in Russia as a way of defying censorship. Many works were circulated through *samizdat*, hand-to-hand circulation, in which a person who received a manuscript made carbon copies on a typewriter or hand-copied material and passed it along to sympathetic readers. Nadezhda Mandelstam (1899–1980), the widow of dissident poet Osip Mandelstam (1891–ca. 1939), saved his works by memorizing and copying them. Novels, poetry, and short stories, as well as smuggled reports of daily life and death in the prison camps, news from the West, and political commentary appeared as samizdat. Samizdat gave life to the works of deceased dissident writers and spread the memoirs of survivors of the gulags, making the experiences of earlier dissidents central to postwar criticism of the government.[51]

Poet Anna Akhmatova (1889–1966) composed a long cycle poem about Stalin's terror called *Requiem*, which earned her a devoted following in the samizdat world. She wrote *Requiem* between 1935 and 1940, adding an afterword in 1957 when government persecution of writers increased. *Requiem* chronicled her despair at the loss of two husbands and a son to the gulags and her own censorship and harassment by the secret police. Its publication in West Germany in 1963 exposed her to more government persecution. It only appeared legally in the USSR in 1987. Akhmatova's experiences gave her great moral authority in the dissident community. Her prose introduction explains the power of writers in Soviet society and the reasons the government had to fear them:

> *In the fearful years of the Yezhov terror[52] I spent seventeen months waiting in prison queues in Leningrad. One day somebody "identified" me. Beside me in the queue; there was a woman with blue lips, she had, of course, never heard of me; but she suddenly came out of that trance so common to us all and whispered in my ear (everyone spoke in whispers there): "Can you describe this?" And I said: "Yes, I can." Then something like the shadow of a smile crossed what had once been her face.[53]*

The writings of those who survived the purges and the gulags provided evidence of the Soviet government's moral corruption. Women who found themselves denounced as dissidents provided valuable witness to the sufferings of others.

Soviet and Soviet bloc women faced very different experiences from their Western counterparts. They had fewer children and suffered physical deprivation and political persecution. Under Khrushchev, conditions improved as he made more goods available and curtailed the power of the secret police. Khrushchev also increased the role women played in public life by making it easier for women to gain an education and advancement in employment. Yet despite Khrushchev's rhetoric, Soviet society continued to associate women with childbearing and housewifery. The communist ideal of communal living to relieve women of their double burden remained elusive, and their protests did little to relieve their misery.

## WOMEN AND DECOLONIZATION

During the nineteenth century, Europeans colonized most of Africa and portions of Asia (see Chapter 11). However, by the 1930s, nationalist movements began to demand self-rule or outright independence, and these movements accelerated during the postwar era. The reach of the international women's movement was vividly demonstrated as native women joined these nationalist groups in large numbers, hoping to forge new noncolonial identities based on sexual equality. When women's rights and nationalist aspirations coincided, nationalists embraced them as a means of undermining colonial domination. However, after independence, it became clear that gender equality would come at the expense of male power. Legislatures were reluctant to grant outright equality, often arguing that it defied local traditions.

## Native Women and Nationalist Movements

In the wake of World War II, African and Asian nationalists increased their demands for independence. Many nationalist leaders had European

educations and, having learned about socialism, liberal democracy, and self-determination, wanted the same options for their own people. Although many Europeans continued to believe that their colonial subjects were not ready for self-rule, as the costs of maintaining colonial rule grew and violence escalated, European governments addressed the possibility of independence.

Prior to World War II, Indian nationalists moved from advocating self-rule to demanding independence. The major figure in Indian nationalism was Mohandas K. Gandhi (1869–1948). Despite his European education, he adopted the lifestyle of an Indian ascetic and brought the nationalist movement to the lower castes. Gandhi preached nonviolent resistance, launching a series of noncooperation campaigns, or *Satyagraha*.

In 1930, he announced a civil disobedience campaign. In response, the British declared the Indian National Congress an illegal organization and arrested Gandhi and the other leaders of the Indian National Congress. While in prison women kept the campaign alive. Indian leader Jawaharlal Nehru (1889–1964) recalled,

> *Our women came to the front and took charge of the struggle. Women had always been there, of course, but now there was an avalanche of them, which took not only the British government but their men folk by surprise. Here were these women, women of the upper or middle classes, leading sheltered lives in their homes, peasant women, working class women, rich women, poor women, pouring out in the tens of thousands in defiance of government order.*[54]

Gandhi was happy to encourage women's participation as long as their demands fit nationalists' aims. He needed women to grow his movement, but he wanted to control their behavior and define the limits and extent of their involvement. He approved of their boycotting liquor stores and picketing cloth shops, but when he organized his Salt March in 1930, he refused to let women join. The goal was to make illegal salt from the ocean to protest a hated salt tax. However, women refused to be excluded. The poet and social reformer Sarojini Naidu (1879–1949) led the protest until her arrest.

The relationship between feminism and Indian nationalism was complex. Gandhi retained many traditional ideas about women. He wanted to bring women out of seclusion and end caste oppression, but he continued to believe that women were more suited to sacrifice than protest. Not all nationalist women expressed a feminist agenda. Moreover, many of the women involved in Indian nationalism came from the upper castes who had been influenced by their relationships with British women or educated in British mission schools. They wanted property rights, access to divorce, widow remarriage, and an end to dowry and polygyny.[55] Among others, feminist and nationalist activist Kamaladevi Chattopadhyay (1903–1988) was inspired by her interactions with British and Irish feminists including Annie Besant (see Chapter 11) and Margaret Cousins (1878–1954).[56]

Independence leaders in French Indochina also attempted to use feminism to their advantage. During World War II, the Japanese occupied Vietnam and threatened India. The pro-Axis French government based in Vichy negotiated the Japanese occupation of Vietnam but maintained its colonial administration. Faced with two unpopular colonial powers, the Vietnamese supported the communists, or Viet Minh, led by Ho Chi Minh (1890–1969). The Viet Minh attracted a strong base of support among the peasants who suffered under both French and Japanese rule. In an effort to increase his support, Ho Chi Minh created popular coalitions of teachers, petty bureaucrats, and students to fight French domination. Women belonged to all of these groups. Ho Chi Minh saw women's rights as a means of expanding his power and uniting all women. He argued that bourgeois feminism was only a partial liberation for women, but that communism would free all classes of women. The communists enjoyed mixed success in bringing about their professed equality for Vietnamese women. After the surrender of Japan in 1945, Ho Chi Minh rode a wave of nationalist and anticolonial fervor, taking control of Hanoi. In 1946, he extended his political revolution to culture with the "New Life Movement." It introduced simpler clothing for women, promoted women's health care, abolished religious customs detrimental to women, and ended concubinage. The party's platform put winning equal rights for women ninth on the list of "Ten Essential Tasks of the Revolution." Yet until 1960, women held only 10 of the 403 seats in the National Assembly.[57]

The East African colonies of Tanganyika and Kenya provide a powerful comparison of women's roles in the drive for independence. Racial, ethnic, class, and religious differences complicated relations between Africans and colonial governments and among Africans themselves. Initially a German colony, Tanganyika came under British control under the guidance of the United Nations after Germany's defeat in World War I. Kenya had been a British colony since the nineteenth century. Tanganyika faced fewer obstacles to state building than Kenya. Although both colonies had ethnically, racially, and religiously diverse populations, Tanganyika had no dominant ethnic or racial group. In Kenya, the Kikuyu constituted a majority of the population, but they were deeply divided by wealth, education, and proximity to colonial power. Divisions among native Africans also ran along ethnic groups, urban and rural lines, and between pastoralists and settled agriculturalists. While Tanganyika had no unified European settler community and little wealth, Kenya had an entrenched white minority that constituted about 2 percent of the population. White settlers violently resisted government attempts to weaken their political power and African attempts to retake their lands. These differences meant that Tanganyika achieved independence with far less violence than Kenya.

Tanganyika's main nationalist group, TANU (Tanganyika African National Union), drew heavily upon Muslim women's independence and strong social and economic networks to spread their message. Muslim women spent most of their teenage years in seclusion, either in their natal homes or married to much older men. Many of these marriages ended in divorce, and women emerged from seclusion to run their own lives. In the capital city of Dar es Salaam, women made up 11.2 percent of heads of households in 1956, and among some ethnic groups this percentage was as high as 45 percent.[58] Muslim women tended to share kitchens and courtyards. This closeness created opportunities for sharing grievances and politicization. In contrast, the minority Christian population lived in nuclear families. Women were subservient to either their fathers or husbands. They did not share housekeeping with other women, nor did they have much contact with other women. As a result, they joined TANU in much smaller numbers.

TANU promoted a platform of equality for all regardless of sex, race, religion, or class. TANU women hoped for both educational and economic opportunities for themselves and their daughters that they did not have under British rule. Female TANU members often risked social censure for their fundraising, recruiting, and public speaking. The most prominent female activist was Bibi Titi Mohamed (b. 1926), who traveled throughout the country giving speeches, explaining TANU's mission for independence, and recruiting members. She worked closely with TANU's leader, Julius Nyerere (1922–1999), who would become the first prime minister of independent Tanzania.

Britain's longer history in Kenya meant that colonialism had a deeper impact on Kenyan women. Women lost land to white settlers and suffered great poverty. Women worked as migrant laborers on coffee plantations, making up to 60 percent of the seasonal labor force.[59] Colonial taxes directly affected women. As we saw in Chapter 11, missionaries advocated social changes such as an end to bridewealth (the payment by the groom's family to the bride's family at marriage), prohibitions against widow remarriage, and female circumcision (a puberty right among the Kikuyu). Kenyan women led labor strikes in the thirties and forties and became politicized earlier than Tanganyikan women. Women joined nationalist groups such as the Kenya African Union (KAU) and the Kikuyu Central Association (KCA) in large numbers before the government shut down their activities.

## Gender and the Wars of Independence

Many independence movements became violent during the 1950s, and as European nations recovered from World War II, they were better equipped to undertake military action against nationalist forces. France, with support from the United States, tried unsuccessfully to reestablish its hold on Vietnam. Its defeat at Dien Bien Phu in 1954 led to a French pullout and the division of Vietnam along the seventeenth parallel between the communists in the North and a pro-West puppet regime in the South. Eager to contain communism, the United States escalated its involvement in Vietnam, turning it into an American war by the mid 1960s. Women fought on both sides of this cold war battlefield. Inspired by both communist ideology and Vietnamese legends of women who had fought Chinese invaders in the first and third centuries, Vietnamese women worked as soldiers, nurses, couriers, laundresses, and cooks for the communists. Duc Hoan (ca. 1938–2004) an artillery woman and entertainer, and following the war an actress and director, consciously rejected European models such as Joan of Arc, "Our heroines were not always successful in the long run— but they weren't sad crazy figures like Joan of Arc!"[60] Women served in some of the most dangerous areas, such as the Ho Chi Minh Trail, a jungle supply line to the communists. It came under constant attack by the Americans and was subject to deforestation with Agent Orange. Some estimate that nearly 70 percent of the people working on the Trail were women.[61]

As U.S. involvement increased, eleven thousand American women served in Vietnam, most as nurses. As the war continued, protests in the United States escalated. Ultimately the United States withdrew from Vietnam in 1972. Soon afterward, South Vietnam fell to the communists.

France also faced violent resistance from nationalists in its North African colony of Algeria. The most visible resistance group in Algeria was as the FLN (National Liberation Front). The FLN was an affiliation of Muslim groups united in their opposition to France but divided among themselves by competing ideologies, such as socialism or level of adherence to Islam. Women were important to the FLN's success, but they held no leadership roles. Worried about adding to divisions among the FLN, leaders accepted female members but only vaguely addressed their rights and concerns. During the ensuing war, the FLN blamed women's lack of equality on colonialism and argued that fighting would essentially free women. The FLN's unwillingness to confront women's issues highlights the complicated relationship between colonialism, Islam, nationalism, and feminism. Although colonial leaders viewed Muslim women's veiling as a sign of their oppression, many Algerian women saw the veil as a nationalist statement. By wearing the veil, they promoted Algerian and Islamic culture and rejected colonialism and colonial culture.[62] In this war of clothing and symbols, women were central to the propaganda of both sides. The ability to put on and take off the veil gave women freedom of movement. Much of the fighting involved urban guerilla warfare, and women worked as couriers, hiding weapons and supplies under their robes and passing information to the FLN that they gleaned from moving about the city. They helped to keep isolated units in the countryside connected and provided food and needed supplies. Much of their work seemed mundane but was necessary to the survival of the resistance.

Fighting began in 1954, and by 1958, the French wanted to negotiate a settlement. Fearful of defeat, the white settlers and the French soldiers attempted a coup to prevent the French government from negotiating with the FLN. The coup failed, but it brought an end to the Fourth Republic. Charles de Gaulle agreed to form a new government, providing that the new constitution gave him the necessary powers to deal with Algeria. Violence continued through 1962. Accounts of human rights abuses filled the left-wing press and diminished enthusiasm for the war. Accounts of the arrest, torture, and rape by French interrogators of the Algerian rebel Djamila Boupacha (b. c. 1947) became a cause célèbre in France. Philosophers Jean Paul Sartre (1905–1980) and Simone de Beauvoir (1905–1986) protested French brutality and the lack of human rights in Algeria. The accusations that Boupacha planted a bomb at the University of Algiers were never proven. The French and Algerians finally reached a peace settlement in 1962.

Elsewhere in Africa, the nationalist movement in Kenya led to the Mau Mau revolt of the mid 1950s. Kikuyu participants in Mau Mau swore religious oaths of loyalty and common action. Having sworn an oath, participants bound themselves into a secret community whose stated goal was the removal of the British from Kenya. The revolt was not only a nationalist effort but also a civil war among the Kikuyu, as members of the Mau Mau attacked both whites and Kikuyu loyalists. The politicization of women under colonialism meant that probably as many women as men joined the Mau Mau. As in the FLN, Mau Mau

women smuggled arms, food, and medicine to the guerilla army hiding in the forests. They acted as couriers of information and as lookouts. Many families divided membership in Mau Mau. Women openly aided the Mau Mau, while their husbands remained loyal to the colonial governments. It may have seemed safer for women to support the Mau Mau because, if caught, the impact on the family was less serious.[63]

The British may not have understood women's motivations for joining the Mau Mau, but they took their participation seriously. A total of 34,147 Kenyan women received prison terms for defying the colonial government. Prison conditions were horrible. Women suffered beatings, rape, forced work, and starvation. Their poor treatment created a scandal in Britain when a former prison staff member, Eileen Fletcher, revealed to British Parliament the appalling prison conditions that women and children endured. Before being released, women underwent a reeducation program. Colonial authorities hoped that by getting women to disavow their Mau Mau oaths and learn new skills, they could defuse future nationalist violence. The British also tried to end the uprising through a relocation program of Kikuyu villages that lasted from 1954 to 1958. The so-called villagization programs uprooted the entire Kikuyu population of three districts and forced them into new villages behind barbed wire and with armed guards. Relocation cut off contacts between Mau Mau members and outside supporters. In the rest of Kenya, the colonial government established a state of emergency, suspending civil rights and giving extraordinary police powers to the military that remained in effect until 1960.

During the 1950s, European powers actively countered colonial independence movements. Harsh measures from Western governments and increased violence among colonized peoples took thousands of lives and hindered women's demands for freedom and equality.

## Postcolonial Repercussions

As former colonies achieved independence, women worked to ensure that the new constitutions granted them equal rights with men. However, many men believed that equality meant a loss of family control and that they had to preserve local

**KIKUYU WOMEN FORMING A HOME GUARD AGAINST THE MAU MAU.** The Mau Mau insurgency was both a Kikuyu civil war and an anti-colonial movement that attracted large numbers of women. The woman in the black shawl, Esther Wanyui, was a former member of the Mau Mau. *(Bettmann/Corbis.)*

gender expectations and local traditions. For instance, in Algeria, the new constitution of September 1962 gave women the right to vote. Leaders and politicians struggled to reconcile traditional notions of women's subservience with the constitution. With only a limited tradition of women's public participation, Algerian women were as constrained by Islamic custom as they had been before independence. After independence, some eleven thousand women registered as veterans of the war, probably far less than the number of women who actually served. Registration required some level of literacy and familiarity with the bureaucracy, and most women had neither

skill. The government attempted educational reforms that targeted women. However, textbooks and the curricula emphasized women's traditional roles within the family. For Algerian women, modernization meant housekeeping with electrical appliances. Although the FLN created the National Union of Algerian Women (UNFA), this organization had only limited ability to lobby for changes to women's lives.[64]

Independence came to Tanganyika in 1961 under the name Tanzania. As TANU won more local council elections, the move to independence seemed inevitable. On several state occasions, Bibi Titi shared the public platform with Nyerere and promoted women's equality. In 1962, she helped found the All Africa Women's Congress (AAWC) and traveled throughout Africa speaking about the problems facing African women in obtaining education, health care, childcare, and economic development. The AAWC held numerous conferences throughout the 1960s. Bibi Titi also encouraged greater political involvement for women. In 1965, she ran for political office in the first election since independence and lost. Meanwhile, Nyerere advocated the merging of all women's groups into the UWT (*Umoja wa Wanawake wa Tanganyika*), which was largely run by educated women. Bibi Titi, who had only limited education, found these changes difficult but nevertheless assumed leadership of the UWT until 1967. She eventually disagreed with Nyerere over the direction of the government. In 1969, she was implicated in a plot to overthrow him, convicted of treason, and sentenced to life in prison. The evidence for her involvement remains limited, and in 1972 Nyerere pardoned her.

After Kenyan independence in 1963, the government, led by the Kenya African National Union (KANU), advocated a classless society where individuals regardless of race or sex could fully develop their potential, and where women's role in nation building was "equal to men's in every respect."[65] However, life after independence did not change very much for women. Politicians treated the women's section of the KANU as a "ladies auxiliary" that would mobilize male votes. The abolition of the Affiliation Act in 1969, which had given single mothers and their children legal protections, was even more detrimental to women. Women who demanded equal rights were often frustrated by the lack of change after independence. Both the colonial and postcolonial governments tried to mitigate tribal rivalries by severing the connection between masculinity and warrior behavior. However, women experienced no such shift in identity. Their domestic roles were largely unchanged.

Kenyan women, especially those in cities, agitated for change through traditional women's voluntary associations, cooperatives, and conferences, many of which dated back to the colonial period. Groups such as the Federation of University Women and the Kenya National Council for Women promoted women's education, health, and development. Women could also choose lifestyles associated with modernization and social progress, such as monogamous marriages to men they chose, hospital deliveries of their babies, and divorces by civil courts rather than tribal custom. Both urban and rural women also sent their daughters to school in increasing numbers. Rural women participated in church groups and economic cooperatives that addressed their economic and educational needs.

Decolonization raised profound questions about the relationships between colonialism and gender expectations and nationalism and women's rights. On the one hand, colonial governments educated women and encouraged them to participate in politics. On the other hand, those same governments brutally repressed political activism aimed at independence. Women's participation in nationalist movements expanded their traditional roles and raised expectations, not all of which were realized at independence.

## AGITATING FOR CHANGE

Although historians often present the fifties and early sixties as conservative and complacent, at the time, many men and women expressed concerns about postwar society's goals and values. Cold war tensions led to heightened concerns about nuclear warfare and the environment. Students, workers, and mothers took to the streets to protest the policies of both communist and democratic governments. Empowered by increased access to contraception and less rigid sexual norms, women began to question their secondary status. Rarely tranquil, these two decades demonstrate the tensions that dominated postwar society.

### The Antinuclear and Environmental Movements

Cold war tensions increased fears that nuclear war was imminent. In response, women joined new groups such as the European-based Campaign for Nuclear Disarmament (CND) and the U.S. National Committee for a Sane Nuclear Policy (SANE) dedicated to ending nuclear proliferation (see **Women's Lives:** Dorothy Crowfoot Hodgkin,

Scientist and Peace Activist). In 1955, forty-three Swedish women's groups petitioned the UN for an end to nuclear testing. They also lobbied the Swedish government not to develop its own nuclear weapons. Although many of these groups attracted old leftist and longtime peace activists such as Vera Brittain (see Chapter 12), they also attracted new support among middle-class mothers worried about their children's futures. The head of the Canadian Voice of Women (VOW), Helen Tucker, argued that "maternal urges to feed, protect, and to love characteristics of creation not destruction" drove women to environmental and antinuclear activism.[66]

Many antinuclear activists such as Peggy Duff (1910–1981), a leader of the British wing of the CND, were openly skeptical of feminism; however, nuclear proliferation challenged even conservative gender identities. In the event of nuclear attack, women could not protect their children and men could not guarantee their safety through military service.[67] Thus, both men and women felt compelled to take public action against their governments to ensure the safety of their loved ones. The campaign enjoyed some success. Between 1958 and 1961, the atomic powers—the Soviet Union, the United States, and Britain—all agreed to a moratorium on testing.

The destruction of World War II also invigorated the European and North American environmental movements. Increasingly, citizens looked to their governments to protect nature from such devastation and ensure that postwar rebuilding included environmental planning. In 1949, the British government established the Nature Conservancy. Dutch, Italian, and Belgian conservation groups also emerged as a part of the new political milieu. In 1960, West German organizations formed the German Nature Protection Ring to unite the diverse conservation lobby, and a year later, British conservationists formed the World Wildlife Fund.

Concern for the health and well-being of both humans and the earth pushed many women into public action. Margaret (Mardy) Murie (1902–2003), often called the grandmother of the conservation movement, spent much of her life in Alaska and chronicled her honeymoon in Alaska's Brooks Range in *Two in the Far North* (1962). She and her husband, Olaus (d. 1963), lobbied for the creation of the Arctic National Wildlife Refuge

(ANWR) in 1960. She was also instrumental in convincing Congress to pass the Wilderness Act in 1964, which designated portions of national forests as protected wilderness. In 1998, President Clinton (1993–2001) awarded her the Presidential Medal of Freedom, the highest honor for a civilian, for her preservation work.

Also in 1960, the Richardson-Merrell pharmaceutical company of Cincinnati requested FDA approval to market the drug thalidomide as an anti–morning sickness drug. Thousands of women in Europe and Canada took the drug. A young medical officer named Frances Oldham Kelsey (b. 1914) felt there was insufficient study on the drug's long-term effects and held up the application despite a great deal of pressure. By 1961, it was evident that the drug, which was legal in Europe and Canada, caused serious birth defects. Called the "Heroine of the FDA," Kelsey received a gold medal from the president.

One of the most passionate environmental activists was Rachel Carson (1907–1964). Scientists had developed DDT during World War II to kill lice and insects that carried diseases to soldiers. Despite few tests of its safety, the U.S. Department of Agriculture, with the consent of the army, released the Du Pont Company's stockpiles for civilian use. Many scientists and naturalists warned that there had not been enough testing. In *Silent Spring* (1962), Carson, who was already dying of cancer, explained the threats that DDT posed to wildlife, challenging the gospel of social progress and the integrity of the chemical industry. Carson lucidly explained the interconnectedness of nature and likened the threat posed to nature to nuclear fallout. Unable to refute Carson's charges, the chemical industry attacked Carson's lack of academic background (she only had a master's degree) and her sex, demanding to know why a single woman cared about future generations. Despite these attacks, the public noticed. Her eloquent writing attracted readers, and she tapped into the general unease that many felt about the growing materialism of postwar society. In May of 1963, the President's Science Advisory Committee confirmed most of Carson's evidence. Nevertheless, the government did not ban the pesticide until 1972.

After the success of *Silent Spring,* the U.S. government gradually began to address other envi-

## Dorothy Crowfoot Hodgkin, Scientist and Peace Activist

Dorothy Crowfoot Hodgkin won the Nobel Prize for Chemistry in 1964, the third woman to do so. (The first two were Madame Curie in 1911 and her daughter, Irene Joliet-Curie, in 1935.) The prize honored her work in crystallography, which allowed her to identify the structures of penicillin and vitamin $B_{12}$, the vitamin that prevents pernicious anemia. Her achievements show how much progress women had made in science and her peace activism captured her humanistic desire to make the world a healthier and safer place.

Dorothy Crowfoot was born in Cairo in 1910. Her father was an archaeologist in Britain's colonial service. Her mother was an amateur archaeologist and an expert on Egyptian textiles and botany. Her family inspired Dorothy to an early interest in both archaeology and chemistry. She worked for a season at an archaeological dig in Jerash, now in modern-day Jordan, analyzing the chemical components of the glass pieces (tesserae) in the Roman mosaics.

From 1928 to 1932, she attended Somerville College, one of the two women's colleges at Oxford University. While at university, she became interested in crystallography. She discovered that if she exposed crystals to x-rays, the crystals would diffract them. Interpreting the diffraction patterns, a process that required mathematics and physics, made it possible to identify the crystal's molecular or atomic structure. She then applied this process to proteins, which also contain crystals, to identify their structures. Scientists used knowledge of a protein's structure to formulate chemical compounds to perform specific functions, or imitate ones found in the natural world. The process is very important for designing new drugs.

Hodgkin transferred to Cambridge University for graduate school and then returned to Somerville in 1934 to teach chemistry and to study crystallography. She received her Ph.D. in 1937. Despite her status as a faculty member, the faculty chemistry club initially barred her from their research meetings because she was a woman.

In 1947, she published her work on the structure of penicillin. Although penicillin was a well-known and frequently used antibiotic, World War II increased demand for it. Doctors wanted to be able to make the drug, rather than use natural penicillin, which was difficult and time-consuming to purify. Hodgkin pioneered the use of one IBM's first analog computers to help with the computations. She won the Nobel Prize for her discovery of the structure of vitamin $B_{12}$. She also identified the structures of other bio-compounds such as cholesterol and insulin. Her students, who included Margaret Thatcher (prime minister of Great Britain in the 1970s and 1980s), remembered her for the productive and cheerful environment in her lab, and her support of new scientists.

Hodgkin was also heavily involved in social and peace activism. In 1970, she was elected chancellor of Bristol University. In honor of her late husband, a specialist in African politics, she established the Hodgkin Scholarship for students from third world countries and founded Hodgkin House to help house students. Although officially retired in 1977, she was chair of the Pugwash movement from 1976 to 1988. The Pugwash movement started as a series of scientific conferences focused on limiting nuclear proliferation. The first meeting was held in Pugwash, Nova Scotia, Canada, in 1957. During the height of the cold war, it was one of the few ways that scientists on both sides of the Iron Curtain could communicate. For her work with Pugwash and easing cold war tensions, Hodgkin received the Lenin Peace Prize in 1987. From 1972 to 1978, she was also president of the International Union of Crystallography. As president she insisted on including Soviet and Soviet bloc crystallographers in conferences. Because of her activism, the U.S. government refused to grant her a travel visa to visit the United States until 1990. She died in 1994.

Sources: Georgina Ferry, *Dorothy Hodgkin: A Life* (London: Granta, 1998); and Sharon Bertsch McGrayne, *Nobel Prize Women in Science* (Secaucus, NJ: Carol Publishing Group, 1993).

ronmental concerns. In 1963, the Clean Air Act appropriated funds for federal efforts to clean up air pollution. Carson's work also spurred environmental action in Europe, and by the late 1960s, major environmental disasters heightened activism. In 1967, a supertanker ran aground in the English Channel and spilled millions of gallons of crude oil into the sea. The disaster destroyed birds and sea life. In 1969, toxins leaked into the Rhine River, poisoning drinking water and killing fish. The environmental movement would become a critical part of international politics and grassroots activism in the coming decades.

## The Pill and the Sexual Revolution

The study of both sexual behavior and the science of reproduction in the 1950s challenged cold war sexual norms and laid the groundwork for dramatic changes in Western sexuality. Western governments cast fear of the Soviets in terms of sexual predation. Loose women and deviant sexuality made the West vulnerable to communism. Sex, like communism, had to be contained. The rhetoric seemed to work. According to British sociological studies during the 1950s, most women believed that premarital sex was wrong and that sex was not an important criterion for marital happiness. In addition, most women had only general ideas about how to achieve orgasm. More Frenchwomen acknowledged having premarital sex than British women, but French society still believed that sexual permissiveness was for men only.

Then, in 1953, Alfred Kinsey, a biologist at Indiana University, published *Sexual Behavior in the Human Female* (see **Sources from the Past:** The Kinsey Report). He found that American women did not adhere to the conservative sexual norms of the time. Fifty percent of American women had premarital sex and an equally high number masturbated, experimented with homosexual sex, and engaged in "petting." He argued that the vaginal orgasm was a myth because the vagina had few nerves, whereas the clitoris had millions, making it the locus of women's sexual pleasure. The so-called Kinsey Report shocked many, but it became a bestseller and transformed Western notions of female sexuality.[68]

Kinsey also asserted that homosexuality was a natural part of human sexuality, and his conclu-

sions helped lesbians and gay men come out of the closet. In 1955, San Francisco residents Del Martin (b. 1921) and Phyllis Lyon (b. 1924) formed the Daughters of Bilitis (DOB) as a social club, although it evolved into a civil rights society for lesbians. Martin and Lyon wanted to end the "conspiracy of silence" that trapped lesbians in dangerous stereotypes and left them vulnerable to harassment. To this end, the DOB published a monthly newsletter, *The Ladder,* in 1956. Circulated nationally, it eventually appeared in London. The DOB hosted public lectures and encouraged members to participate in scientific studies of homosexuality to help demystify lesbianism.[69]

While Kinsey's work revealed important information about female sexuality, male heterosexuality found a ready outlet in a resurgence of men's magazines, the most popular of which was *Playboy*, started by Hugh Hefner (b. 1926) in 1953. Aimed at middle-class readers, it promoted a new "sophisticated" and "educated" masculinity. *Playboy* connected heterosexual masculinity with a consumer culture that was removed from domesticity and family. Playboys were modern, familiar with the latest technology, artistic, and musical styles, and comfortable hosting their own parties, whether it was a "guy's" night of poker, an intimate dinner with a woman, or a large all-night bash. Although *Playboy* included photographs of naked women as one of its main attractions, Hefner believed that his magazine was more than pornography. He published articles by leading writers of the day and argued that sex was only part of the well-rounded playboy life.

The arrival of oral contraceptives helped women to make sexual demands of their own without fear of pregnancy. Before the pill, women's most effective birth control options were diaphragms used in conjunction with spermicidal jelly and condoms, which were both inconvenient and unreliable if used incorrectly. As concerns about overpopulation emerged, research on a scientific method of family planning accelerated. Margaret Sanger (1883–1966) (see Chapter 13), a longtime advocate of family planning, called for scientists to develop a birth control pill. In 1960, after feverish competition among drug companies, the U.S. Food and Drug Administration approved such a drug. Developed by Gregory Goodwin

# The Kinsey Report

*The publication of the Kinsey Report in 1953 sent shock waves through Western society. Far from the demure, submissive women praised in postwar propaganda, women were more sexually active than anyone had anticipated. This excerpt reveals some of the key findings of Kinsey's research.*

## *"Occurrence of Orgasm in the Female"*

### INCIDENCE OF FEMALE ORGASM

About 36 per cent of the married females in the sample never experienced orgasm from any source prior to marriage. In their early adolescent years, when 95 per cent of the boys of corresponding age were experiencing orgasm with average frequencies of 2.3 per week, only 22 per cent of the girls in the sample were reaching orgasm in any sort of activity, either solitary, heterosexual, or homosexual. In the later teens, when over 99 per cent of the males were responding sexually to orgasm with average (median) frequencies of over 2.2 per week if they were single, and 3.2 per week if they were married—at a period when the average male was at the peak of his sexual capacity and activity—, there was still nearly half (47 per cent) of the females who had not had their first orgasm. With this relatively limited background of experience and limited understanding of the nature and significance and desirability of orgasm, it is not surprising to find that a goodly number of the married females never or rarely reach orgasm in their marital coitus.

The failure of a female to be aroused or to reach orgasm during coitus is commonly identified in the popular and technical literature as "sexual frigidity." We dislike the term, for it has come to connote either an unwillingness or an incapacity to function sexually. In most circumstances neither of these implications is correct. It is doubtful whether there is ever a complete lack of capacity, although individuals do appear to differ in their levels of response.

In general, females and males appear to be equally responsive to the whole range of physical stimuli which may initiate erotic reactions (Chapters 14–15), and the specific data show that the average female is no slower in response than the average male when she is sufficiently stimulated and when she is not inhibited in her activity. Females may not be often aroused by psychological stimuli (Chapter 16); but if there is any sufficient physical stimulation, it is probable that all females are physiologically capable of responding to the point of orgasm.

While there are many cases of quite unresponsive females reported in the literature, and while we have found such cases in the present study, we do not find evidence in any of them that the individual, rid of her inhibitions, would not be capable of response. We have histories of women who had been married to a single husband for many years, in some instances for as long as twenty-eight years, before they ever reached their first orgasm. We have histories of females who had been married and divorced two or three or four times before they finally effected a marriage in which they were able to reach orgasm in their coitus. Anyone examining the histories of such women before they had ever responded would have pronounced them frigid and probably incapable of response; but their subsequent performance proved that they were not basically incapable. In fact, in some of these cases, the formerly unresponsive females developed patterns of response which included orgasm and even multiple orgasm whenever they engaged in coitus. It should be added, however, that many unresponsive individuals need clinical help to overcome the psychologic blockages and considerable inhibitions which are the sources of their difficulties.

There has, of course, been widespread interest in discovering what proportion of the coitus of the average female does lead to orgasm, and in discovering some of the factors which account for such success or failure in coitus. Unfortunately, it is not a statistically simple matter to calculate what percentage of the copulations in any particular sample leads to orgasm. Before adding together the data on any series of females, one must take into account the age of each individual, the age at which she married, the number of years that she has been married, the frequencies of her coital relationships, the techniques that have been employed in the coitus, and changes in the incidences of orgasm at various periods in the history. No significant correlations can be demonstrated unless the data are considered from all of these angles.

Taking these several factors into account, we find that the average (median) female in the sample had reached orgasm in something between 70 and 77 per cent of her marital coitus. The percentages had varied considerably in different periods of the marriage. In the earliest years of marriage, not more than 63 per cent of the coitus of the average age (median) female had resulted in orgasm, but the percentage had increased as the marriages became more extended. The data, calculated from Table 112, are as follows:

In the first year 63% of coitus resulted in orgasm

By the fifth year 71% of coitus resulted in orgasm

By the tenth year 77% of coitus resulted in orgasm

By the fifteenth year 81% of coitus resulted in orgasm

By the twentieth year 85% of coitus resulted in orgasm

This means that something between 36 and 44 per cent of the females in the sample had responded to orgasm in a part but not in all of their coitus in marriage. About one-third of those females had responded only a small part of the time, another third had responded more or less half of the time, and the other third had responded a major portion of the time, even though it was not a hundred per cent of the time.

## MULTIPLE ORGASM

There were some 14 per cent of the females in the sample who had regularly responded with multiple orgasm. This, interestingly enough, was true not only of the females who responded every time they had coitus, but also of some of the females who had responded to orgasm only part of the time. In either event the female may have had two or three or even as many as a dozen or more orgasms in a relationship in which her husband had ejaculated only once.

Among the younger males, some 8 to 15 per cent in the sample had been capable of multiple orgasm, but the capacity had decreased among the older males. The accidents of mating in human marriages had rarely brought together two individuals who were equally capable of multiple orgasm; and whether it was the female or the male who had been most capable, it had often been difficult for a couple to work out satisfactory coital techniques when one but only one of them was accustomed to having several orgasms in each contact. Many males are incapable of maintaining an erection and continuing coitus after they have reached orgasm, and many males become so hypersensitive that it is painful and sometime excruciatingly painful for them to continue movement after orgasm. If the female has not yet reached orgasm, or if she is capable of multiple orgasm and is not yet satisfied sexually, the male who is incapable of proceeding may leave his wife much disturbed. Some males, therefore, regularly carry their wives to orgasm by manually or orally manipulating their genitalia. More expert males have learned to bring their wives to a number of orgasms in their coitus, before they allow themselves to ejaculate for the first time.

Source: Alfred C. Kinsey et al., *Sexual Behavior in the Human Female* (Philadelphia: W. B. Saunders, 1953), 373–376.

Pincus (1903–1967) of the Worcester Foundation for Experimental Biology in Shrewsbury, Massachusetts, the pill was 95 percent effective. Within five years, 6.5 million married women and hundreds of thousands of single women in the United States were "on the pill."[70] The pill was also widely available in Europe. However, it met with a harsh reception from the Catholic Church. In 1968, Pope Paul VI (r. 1963–1978) affirmed the Church's long-standing opposition to any artificial birth control in his encyclical *Humanae Vitae*. As a result, the pill was largely unavailable in Catholic countries such as Ireland, Italy, and Spain. In France, the French Movement for Family Planning (MFPF) in 1956 formed to pressure politicians to revoke the 1920 law that made it criminal to provide any information on contraception or abortion. The MFPF defied the law by opening family planning centers in Grenoble and Paris in 1961. These centers proliferated, but contraceptives had to be brought in from outside the country until 1967, when the French parliament finally abolished the prohibition on the sale of contraceptives. In West Germany, Catholic women protested the pill as another attack on the family. However, some young women saw it differently, arguing that sexual repression, not promiscuity, had led to Nazism, and that West Germany needed to embrace sexual freedom. One poster declared "We're not talking about 'the pill,' we're taking it."[71]

By the mid 1960s, evidence of the pill's side effects generated concerns among women. The early pill had high doses of hormones, and women experienced a range of mild to severe side effects. Many women linked the pill to the increasing medicalization of women's health care. Moreover, the pill required a prescription, which made it difficult for women without medical care to obtain, and physicians often refused to prescribe it to single women. Increasingly, women challenged the rights of their physicians to withhold information about their health and birth control options.

Female sexual freedom had implications beyond the bedroom. In Great Britain, the publication of D. H. Lawrence's previously banned work, *Lady Chatterley's Lover* (1928), brought female sexuality to the forefront of British politics. The British government prosecuted Penguin Books for obscenity, but the publisher was acquitted and the trial initiated a new era of literary freedom. In 1962, Helen Gurley Brown (b. 1922) published *Sex and the Single Girl*, which offered a female counterpart to *Playboy*. Brown made being single sexy and exciting. However, although she rejected the marriage ideals of the fifties and advocated for women's equality in the bedroom, she did not write a feminist manifesto. Behind Brown's message was the desire to please men and overt advice on how to be attractive and successful as a single girl. Buoyed by newfound sexual confidence, young women wore miniskirts and bikini swimsuits.

The ability to enjoy sex and not worry about a cooperative sexual partner or pregnancy put women in the position of advocating new sexual standards. Freedom to control their fertility and engage in sex for pleasure gave Western women new insights into their roles in society. Women took to the streets to express their anger and frustration and demand new rights.

## Social Protest Movements

The political protests of the 1960s had their roots in postwar changes. When African American men returned from World War II, they began to demand equal opportunity. Having risked their lives for democracy, they were profoundly disappointed to return to social and legal inequality at home. Segregation was still legal, and southern blacks were relegated to inferior schools and unable to vote because of intimidation by whites. Then, in 1954, the American Supreme Court ruled in *Brown v. the Board of Education of Topeka, Kansas* that segregation based on race was illegal. The next year, Rosa Parks (1913–2005), a seamstress in Montgomery, Alabama, and an officer in the NAACP refused to give up her seat on the bus to a white man. These two actions galvanized the civil rights movement. Although the national leadership, led by Dr. Martin Luther King, (1929–1968), was almost exclusively male, black women were important organizers and participants at the local level. They organized boycotts of white businesses, registered black voters, and committed acts of civil disobedience to bring attention to discrimination. Daisy Bates (ca. 1914–1999), the president of the Little Rock, Arkansas, NAACP, led local efforts to desegregate the schools. Diane Nash (b. 1938), a student at Fisk University in Nashville, Tennessee, led a boycott of white businesses. For her, these acts were "applied religion."[72]

Resistance to the civil rights movement brought violence to the South, but civil rights activists were undeterred. In 1964, U.S. president Lyndon Johnson signed into law the Civil Rights Act, and the next year, he signed the Voting Rights Act. Together these two pieces of legislation protected black voting rights and provided for the integration of public spaces.

While African Americans and sympathetic whites took to the streets of the United States, university students came to understand how their education was going to perpetuate a world they found intolerable. Students protested university systems and government policies, which they saw as archaic and indefensible. Student movements in Italy, France, Germany, Czechoslovakia, and the United States expressed the frustration of a generation of young people who felt that they lacked social freedoms and economic opportunities and were frustrated by imperialism and U.S. involvement in Vietnam.

Many protests focused on the need for changes in higher education. In France, Italy, and Germany, the postwar baby boom not only increased the number of students, but more students came from working-class families and were women. For example, in Italy, women were one-third of all students by 1968.[73] However, European universities had not adapted to these changes. Classrooms were overcrowded, resources limited, and living conditions squalid. Students wanted fewer regulations on their behavior. Student newspapers, such as the Italian school magazine *La Zanzara* (*Mosquito*) ran articles on female students' ideas about sex to highlight the differences between students and administrators. Class issues also rankled higher education. For working-class students, a university education was supposed to lead to a better life; they had little tolerance for elitist university traditions and found university curricula outdated and irrelevant.

Meanwhile, Czech students demanded more democracy and an end to Soviet domination. Student groups in Prague worked with the new communist government led by reform-minded Alexander Dubček (1921–1992) to ease censorship and increase citizen participation in govern-

ment. The movement, which became known as the Prague Spring, included few women leaders, although Irena Dubská (b. 1924), among others, was important in the debates that led to the reformist government and student protests. Their activism in the political tumult reflected a new stage in women's political participation. Czech and Slovak women's political voices had only recently been restored with the reestablishment of the official party women's organization, the Union of Czechoslovak Women in 1967. The government had disbanded the group in 1950, with a proclamation that gender equality had been achieved.

In 1968, student protests turned violent. In Prague, Soviet tanks moved in and put an end to the Prague Spring. In the Soviet Union, dissidents opposed the suppression of the Czech uprising. Larisa Daniel (1929–2004) and six others unfurled a handmade banner in Red Square to protest the Soviet invasion of Czechoslovakia. The KGB promptly arrested them. At her trial, Larisa defended her actions, saying that "staying silent would have meant for me sharing in the general approval of actions which I did not approve. Staying silent would have meant lying."[74] She was exiled to Siberia. At the same time, a coalition of French students and workers nearly brought down the French government in May 1968. In the United States and Italy, students battled with armed police and the military. Across Europe and the United States, student movements galvanized young people, both male and female, to become politically involved and take risks for what they believed.

Antiwar protests also politicized new groups. In the United States, Women's Strike for Peace (WSP) stands out as one of the most visible organizations of women activists protesting the war. Many women came to this group as concerned mothers worried about nuclear proliferation. In 1963, WSP began protesting deaths in the Vietnam War. The members waged a letter writing campaign to the White House and joined with the WILPF to protest the use of napalm. By the end of the decade, the WSP had over one hundred thousand members in twenty-five states.[75] Because the focus of most activism was on resisting the draft, antiwar activism had a masculine focus. One popular antidraft slogan proclaimed that "Girls Say Yes to Guys Who Say No."[76] Traditional gender roles pervaded most antiwar groups, such as Students for a Democratic Society (SDS) and Student Nonviolent Coordinating Committee (SNCC). Women distributed pamphlets, cooked, and even cleaned organization headquarters. They rarely set policy or led demonstrations.

By 1965, dissatisfied with both the left and the right, students looked for new political ideologies grounded in individual freedom of expression. Integral to these emerging ideologies was the practice of "free love." Student leaders were all male, but they surrounded themselves with women, who saw themselves as the lovers of heroic male figures.[77] Although female students enjoyed more freedoms than their mothers and grandmothers, within these movements, they assumed supporting roles and were often discouraged by their relationships with male leaders.

These social protest movements included women, but did not typically focus on women's concerns, and women were not equally involved in policymaking or leadership. Recognition that many male leaders just wanted women for support and sex led women to turn their activism toward demands for equality. As we will see, Second Wave Feminism had its roots in these experiences.

## A New Women's Movement

In 1949, existentialist philosopher and novelist Simone de Beauvoir (1908–1986) published the first of her two-volume discussion of women, *The Second Sex*. The book was notable for its philosophical position that women were the "other." Patriarchy and the role of caregiver and nurturer denied women the individuality or "selfhood" that men had. Although Beauvior had close relationships with women, some of them sexual, she did not celebrate these relationships as a source of women's creativity; rather, she believed they constrained and oppressed women's sense of self. *The Second Sex* was wide-ranging, discussing biology, history, and literature. The first volume sold well and received good reviews. The second volume, appearing late in 1949 and including discussions of sexual initiation and lesbians, caused a sensation. The Catholic Church put it on the list of forbidden books. The American publisher Alfred A. Knopf published an abridged English translation

in 1953. It received a great deal of attention in the United States and Britain, although some critics charged Beauvoir with creating a false sense of universalism regarding women and the causes of their secondary status.[78] These criticisms notwithstanding, the book became one of the foundational texts of Second Wave Feminism.

Outside of intellectual circles, women were also beginning to question their status. In the United States, a network of politically active women convinced newly-elected president John Kennedy (1961–1963) that he owed his narrow victory in part to women and that he should return their support by advocating equal rights for women. In 1961, he established the Presidential Commission on the Status of Women and selected Eleanor Roosevelt as its chair. In 1963, the Commission issued its report calling for equal pay for comparable work, rather than equal pay for equal work, in order to resolve pay problems caused by sex segregation in the workplace. The Commission also called for childcare and paid maternity leave. That same year, Betty Friedan's (1921–2006) *The Feminine Mystique* argued that the American dream was a nightmare for women. Although Friedan's book only addressed white, college-educated women, she tapped into the unhappiness of this affluent group and provided the vocabulary to describe their sense of loss and disempowerment.

In Europe, where the welfare state provided many women with the social and workplace protections demanded by women in the United States, feminists were slower to organize. In 1966, the radical feminist group DEMAU (the Group for the Demystification of Authoritarianism) appeared in Milan, Italy. This tiny group published a manifesto demanding an end to the sexual division of labor and compulsory domesticity for women, an exploration of the underlying patriarchal assumptions of family and Italian society, and the establishment of programs to educate women to an awareness of their history and value to society.[79] Compared to American feminists, this was a more tentative program, because leaders of DEMAU appeared less certain of the causes of women's inferiority.

Until the 1970s, feminist activism was sporadic and localized. During the student protests at Columbia University in New York City, participants in the occupation of Fayerweather Hall claimed "girls . . . were not expected to do the kitchen work alone, for this was a 'liberated' area, and boys had to help."[80] One of the most publicized feminist actions was the 1968 protest of the Miss America Pageant in Atlantic City, New Jersey. Women engaged in street theater that emphasized how the pageant reduced women to sexual objects for men's consumption. They crowned a sheep as Miss America and set up a "freedom trash-can" where women could throw away symbols of femininity such as high-heel shoes, bras, women's magazines, curlers, and "other instruments of torture to women." Later accounts claimed that women burned their bras, and this became a symbol for how outrageous feminists were. In fact, there was

no bra burning at the protest. The media gave this event a great deal of attention, using it to show feminists as crazy, ugly women, with no sense of humor. They also emphasized divisions among feminists, some of whom saw the protests as unfairly targeting beautiful women and nonfeminists. The media's coverage indirectly added to the education of women by highlighting the demands of feminists. In the next decade, this activism would pay off in the large-scale expansion of the women's movement.

Despite their reputation for conservatism and conformity, the two decades after the end of World War II reflected the tensions in Western society. As

**MISS AMERICA PROTEST (1968).** When journalists began to investigate women's concerns, they found endless examples of inequality and secondary treatment of women. Feminists called attention to the objectification and degradation of women in American society. *(AP/Wide World.)*

governments pursued an arms race, women sought to ease nuclear tensions and protect the environment. Although welfare states promoted family and fertility, a new generation of women challenged conservative sexual norms after the introduction of the pill. Confident in their ability to control their own lives, they took to the streets to protest against government policies and promote causes about which they cared passionately.

## GENDER AND POSTWAR CULTURE

With the aid of the Marshall Plan, Europe rebuilt its houses and public spaces, and the U.S. population expanded into the suburbs. The new structures improved the overall quality of housing and diminished class differences. In the countryside, houses acquired electricity, running water, and central heat. In many ways, home life lost its diversity. Postwar film and television taught women to relish that homogeneity, but audiences frequently rejected those ideals in favor of more assertive and engaged images of women.

### The Transformation of the Modern Home

Rebuilding Europe after World War II represented an opportunity to destroy unhealthy slums and engineer productive and healthy family settings. The war had destroyed nearly a quarter of the housing stock, and many urban families aspired to move out of apartments and into new houses. Some European developers incorporated American notions of suburbia with lawns, gardens, and even garages, although far fewer Europeans than Americans owned cars. Modernist architects and city planners put their beliefs in social equality and the value of communal living into practice. Between 1947 and 1953, Le Corbusier (born Charles-Edouard Jeanneret-Gris, 1887–1965) built his *Unite d'habitation* in Marseilles, France, for working-class families. His design promoted a self-contained, classless community that boasted educational, leisure, and social amenities. However, his combination of public and private spaces grew out of middle-class notions of space. Le Corbusier arranged family life around dining and living rooms, where middle-class families gathered. Working-class families rebelled and put tables in their tiny kitchens, where they felt more at home.[81]

Throughout the 1950s, magazines extolled housekeeping as a worthwhile career for women of all classes. In Italy, housekeeping took on an added twist, as both social theorists and advertisers distanced housewifery from women's roles under fascism. Housekeeping became associated with social peace, order, and family tranquility. Men's work outside the home complemented women's work inside the home, as reciprocal family obligations were defined by gender. The housewife's sacrifice replaced the prewar notion of the housewife as manager and the fascist idea of the house as factory. By the 1960s, the position of housewife was the only female profession on the rise in Italy.[82]

New appliances transformed the postwar American home and were supposed to make the housewife's life easier. While women worked in the kitchen with dishwashers and blenders, men took care of backyard barbecues and the lawn, which also required new specialized appliances. The booming economy made appliances more affordable for Europeans, although consumerism remained slower in Europe than in the United States. Between 1955 and 1965, the proportion of British families owning televisions, refrigerators, vacuum cleaners, and washing machines doubled. As the economy expanded, West German families invested in new consumer goods until the majority owned radios, vacuum cleaners, and TVs. In 1958, 84 percent of Italian families still did not own large appliances such as washing machines, but by the 1970s they were almost universal.[83]

Appliances changed, but did not lessen, housework. While washing machines made it easier to do laundry, they raised the standards of cleanliness. With clothes easier to clean, housewives did laundry more often. Wall-to-wall carpeting covered floors, but also raised fears of disease, making the washing of wall-to-wall carpeting a new task for the postwar housewife. Vacuum sealing, refrigeration, and pasteurization changed women's cooking habits but did not free them from the kitchen. They spent less time preserving food, but now learned from women's magazines that their meals needed to be more elaborate. Italian cookbooks of the period encouraged women to make elaborate sauces and decorate their food. UNESCO, a United Nations agency, produced a report that stated, "there is little sign . . . that the gains from an abundant labour saving technology receive much translation into leisure. Variations in time devoted to household obligations . . . are not spectacularly large." Changing expectations of cleanliness affected women of all classes. Whereas in the 1930s, working-class women did about half the housework of middle-class women, by 1961 the difference was negligible.[84]

The postwar home created a complex relationship between science and technology in the service of efficiency and femininity. These forces came together in the rise of Tupperware, invented in 1942 by Earl Tupper (1907–1983). His flexible and durable plastic containers transformed American housekeeping. This transformation was more than their stylish design, but the way in which he sold them. In 1951, Tupper started selling his products through the "home party plan." He appointed Brownie Wise (1913–1992), a divorced mother from Detroit, to oversee the party distribution network. Wise created a corporate culture that celebrated femininity. Although men ran the corporation, publicity always showed Wise in charge. She even had herself photographed with male executives offering her gifts on bended knee. The control Brownie Wise held over Tupperware rankled Tupper, who fired her in 1958, ending the heyday of this product.

Furnishing the postwar home became a source of contention between the West and the Soviet bloc. As we have seen, the planned economy of the Soviets and their satellites failed to produce many of the basic items families wanted and needed for daily life. Vice President Richard Nixon (1953–1960) used this consumer gap as evidence of U.S. superiority. In the so-called kitchen debate in 1959, Nixon equated American superiority with a secure and abundant family life rooted in the suburbs.[85] Newly built and boasting large garages and expansive lawns, the suburbs became showcases of postwar success.

## Creating an Image: Women in Film and Television

Movies and television became critical media for the transmission of gender norms in the postwar period. During the 1950s, television sitcoms and Hollywood movies promoted ideal wives, mothers, and blond bombshells. However, by the early 1960s, audiences craved female characters who spoke more to the realities of their lives.

Many 1950s Hollywood movie plots revolved around finding happiness through marriage. Marriage could solve a wide array of women's problems. The successful 1954 movie musical *Seven Brides for Seven Brothers*, a comic retelling of Rape of the Sabine Women (see Chapter 3), recounts the abduction of six young women to become the brides of six brothers in the Oregon Territory. All live happily ever after. The German film industry also encouraged marriage and domesticity. A series of romantic melodramas such as *The Private Secretary* (1953), *Love Without Illusion* (1955), and *Without You All Is Darkness* (1956) all featured independent career women who learned that their sexual and emotional independence was a shallow existence compared to marriage and housekeeping for a man who loves them.

The movie industry was also taken with what one film critic called "the mammary madness" of the 1950s.[86] Katharine Hepburn's (1907–2003) lean and athletic build, so popular in the 1940s, gave way to large-breasted actresses, most notably Marilyn Monroe (1926–1962). Her sex appeal, vulnerability, and blond luminescence defined women's beauty for nearly a decade. For many feminists, Monroe's tragic life symbolizes Hollywood's manipulation of women and their bodies. Rising to stardom in 1953 with the movie *Gentlemen Prefer Blondes*, she was torn between her need for male approval and her desire for intellectually challenging roles. She died of a drug overdose in 1962. Monroe would spawn several imitators, including French actress Brigitte Bardot (b. 1934) who took the image of the sex kitten into the sexual revolution.

The sexual revolution introduced the pregnancy melodrama, in which the loss of virginity did not disgrace the heroine. Movies like *A Summer Place* (1959), *Susan Slade* (1961), and *Love with the Proper Stranger* (1963) acknowledged what Kinsey found: that women liked sex, and that many women had sex before they were married. The plots usually pitted a virginal but vibrant young heroine against her frigid and emotionally and sexually dead mother. The young woman's pregnancy showed the hero as sensitive and caring, and the couple always married in the end. By the mid 1960s, audiences found this plotline cloying. Two British films, *Darling* (1965) and *Georgy Girl* (1966), challenged the happily-ever-after narrative of the pregnancy melodrama. In both films, the women have multiple sexual partners and do not end up happily married. The popularity of these films indicates that women craved something more reflective of their real-life experiences.

French New Wave cinema dealt with many of the same issues as Hollywood, but in much less conventional ways. Many of the films by young directors Jean-Luc Godard (b. 1930), Francois Truffaut (1932–1984), and Agnés Varda (b. 1928) addressed issues facing young people, but New Wave films had none of the predictability of Hollywood. The characters were often marginalized, young, immoral loners. Although not necessarily political, the characters often expressed cynical views about social norms and politics. In Varda's *Cléo de 5 á 7* (1961), a young pop singer wanders around waiting for the results of medical tests to see if she has cancer. During her ninety-minute odyssey, the protagonist discovers herself as she faces the possibility of death. Like *Cléo de 5 á 7*, New Wave films were more personal, less smooth, and rarely had tidy endings.

Television promoted some of the same images as Hollywood. Scholar Susan Douglas has described the women in American sitcoms, such as *Father Knows Best, The Adventures of Ozzie and Harriet, Leave It to Beaver,* and *The Donna Reed Show,* as "benevolent, self-effacing, pearl-clad moms who loved to vacuum in high heels."[87] The television brought those same gender expectations into European living rooms. In France, *Le Magazine Feminin (The Woman's Journal)* gave practical homemaking and fashion advice to French housewives, teaching women to be happy, successful home managers. Other programs urged rural women to take on more responsibility for family farms in addition to their domestic tasks. However, not all programs promoted such conservative views. The 1963 French drama *What Do You Think About It? The Grain of Sand* presented a young pregnant medical student who refused to marry the father of her child.[88] Starting in 1960, British women were drawn to *Coronation Street,* a realistic soap opera about working-class families with strong female characters.

## The Rise of Rock 'n' Roll

America's racial and cultural diversity had a profound impact on postwar music both at home and across the Atlantic. Gospel, folk, blues, jazz, and country all drew large followings, and female performers attracted large audiences. The fusion of these musical styles led to the emergence of rock 'n' roll, in which women were important innovators and consumers.

The American music scene reflected the nation's cultural mix. Gospel music sung by women like Willie Mae "Big Mama" Thornton (1926–1984) influenced later rock 'n' rollers like Elvis Presley (1935–1977), who recorded her song "Hound Dog," taking it to number one in the country. Patsy Cline (1932–1963) surprised audiences as she reached beyond traditional country music fans with her haunting melodies. The folk revival of the early 1960s introduced political messages and social responsibility to the music scene. In 1959, Joan Baez (b. 1941) made her debut at the Newport Folk Festival, and by 1962, she had sold more records than any female folk singer. In 1967, when the Daughters of the American Revolution denied Baez permission to perform in Constitution Hall because of her anti-war politics, she drew ten times the audience by performing at the Washington Monument.[89]

Rock 'n' roll emerged as an aggressively masculine music form. Elvis Presley dressed like a hoodlum and moved in sexually suggestive ways. He attracted both male and female followers with his controversial style. West Germans struggling to redefine their sense of national and cultural identity saw Elvis as introducing dangerous changes in gender roles. The popular press likened Elvis's movements to a striptease act and understood his sensuality as distinctly feminine. The press condemned his female fans for their sexual aggression. One commentator likened their dancing to "wild barbarians in ecstasy."[90] However, female fans liked him because they believed he was more understanding and open than German men.

In December of 1960, the song "Will You Still Love me Tomorrow?" by the Shirelles, a black all-female group, hit number one on the record charts. The Shirelles were the first girl group to achieve this kind of success. The lyrics outlined the sexual dilemma facing many girls: if they slept with their boyfriends, would they lose both their virginity and their respectability?

One of the most powerful forces in postwar music came from England. The Beatles cut their first record "Love Me Do," in 1962, and within a year, they were a huge success. By December 1963, American radio stations were playing the Beatles, and by January 1964, sales of "I Want to Hold Your Hand" had reached 1.5 million. Their fans were overwhelmingly young women, whose wild response to the band caused parental concern and media condescension. Although reporters often described fans as empty-headed bimbos caught up in mass hysteria, "Beatlemania" was, in the words of Barbara Ehrenreich, Elizabeth Hess, and Gloria Jacobs, "the first mass outburst of the sixties to feature women—in this case girls."[91]

Female singers put their own experiences of sexuality and sexual longing into song. They became tremendously popular among a wide range of young women trying to negotiate the conflicting messages of 1950s and 1960s society. Even the Beatles highlighted women as consumers of a popular culture directed at their entertainment.

In many ways, postwar culture tried to ease cold war anxiety by emphasizing the safety and confidence of homogeneity and gender order. Postwar construction and new consumer items made one home much like another, and television and film taught women to find contentment at home. However, those ideas had limited appeal, and women came to prefer characters and performers who challenged the idealistic portrayals of the suburban housewife.

## CONCLUSION

At the end of World War II, Western society focused on rebuilding nations, homes, and families. Although the cold war divided women in Eastern and Western Europe, communist governments and democratic regimes promoted equally conservative gender norms. Yet, better educated, in control of their own sexuality, and more socially aware, the postwar generation of women was not necessarily willing or able to conform to such conventional views of womanhood.

## NOTES

1. http://www.un.org/aboutun/charter/preamble.htm.

2. http://www.un.org/womenwatch/daw/csw/index.html.

3. Eleanor Roosevelt at the presentation of "IN YOUR HANDS: A Guide for Community Action for the Tenth Anniversary of the Universal Declaration of Human Rights," Thursday, March 27, 1958: http://www.udhr.org/history/inyour.htm.

4. Margaret Poulos, "Gender, Civil War and National Identity: Women Partisans During the Greek Civil War, 1946–1949," *Australian Journal of Politics and History* 46: 3 (2000): 421.

5. Quoted in Poulos, 422.

6. Richard Clogg, *Modern Greece* (Cambridge: Cambridge University Press, 1979), 164.

7. M. G. Lord, *Astro Turf: the Private Life of Rocket Science* (New York: Walker, 2005), 130, 200.

8. Lillian Hellman, "Letter to HUAC," May 19, 1952, at http://historymatters.gmu.edu/d/6454/.

9. Deborah A. Gerson, "'Is Family Devotion Now Subversive?' Familialism Against McCarthyism," in *Not June Cleaver*, ed. Joanne Meyerowitz (Philadelphia: Temple University Press, 1994), 151–176.

10. Quoted in Robert G. Moeller, *Protecting Motherhood: Women and the Family in the Politics of Post-War West Germany* (Berkeley: University of California Press, 1993), 40.

11. Renate Jaeger, "The Federal Constitutional Court: Fifty Years of the Struggle for Gender Equality," *German Law Journal* 9 (June 1, 2001), at http://www.germanlawjournal.com/article.php?id=35.

12. Elizabeth Heineman, "Complete Families, Half Families, No Families at All: Female-Headed Households and the Reconstruction of the Family in the Early Federal Republic," *Central European History* 29 (1996): 19–20.

13. Dagmar Herzog, "'Pleasure, Sex, and Politics Belong Together': Post-Holocaust Memory and the Sexual Revolution in West Germany," *Critical Inquiry* 24 (1998): 397.

14. Elaine Tyler May, *Homeward Bound: American Families in the Cold War Era* (New York: Basic Books, 1988), 3–4.

15. Luisa Tasca, "The 'Average Housewife' in Post–World War II Italy," trans. Stuart Hilwig, *Journal of Women's History* 16:2 (2004): 108.

16. Marzio Barbagli and David I. Kertzer, "Introduction," in *Family Life in the Twentieth Century*, ed. David I. Kertzer and Marzio Barbagli (New Haven: Yale University Press, 2003), xxii.

17. May, 6, 137.

18. Anne-Lise Seip and Hilde Ibsen, "Family Welfare, Which Policy? Norway's Road to Child Allowances," in *Maternity and Gender Policies: Women and the Rise of European Welfare States, 1880s–1950s*, ed. Gisela Bock and Pat Thane (London: Routledge, 1991), 40.

19. Louise A. Tilly and Joan W. Scott, *Women, Work, and Family* (New York: Holt, Rinehart and Winston, 1978), 214.

20. Deborah Simonton, *A History of European Women's Work: 1700 to the Present* (London: Routledge, 1998), 194.

21. Simonton, 183.

22. Quoted in Simonton, 227.

23. May, 20.

24. Quoted in Simonton, 188.

25. Simonton, 241.

26. Simonton, 240–241.

27. Simonton, 211.

28. Nancy Woloch, *Women and the American Experience*, 3rd ed. (New York: McGraw-Hill, 2000), 523–524.

29. Mary Buckley, *Women and Ideology in the Soviet Union* (Ann Arbor: University of Michigan Press, 1989), 144.

30. Buckley, 147.

31. Irina Paert, "Demystifying the Heavens: Women, Religion, and Khrushchev's Anti-Religious Campaign, 1954–64," in *Women in the Khrushchev Era*, ed. Melanie Ilič, Susan E. Reid, and Lynne Attwood (Basingstoke, England: Palgrave Macmillan, 2004), 205.

32. Joan Delaney Grossman, "Khrushchev's Anti-Religious Policy and the Campaign of 1954," *Soviet Studies* 24:2 (1973): 375.

33. Michaela Pohl, "Women and Girls in the Virgin Lands," in *Women in the Khrushchev Era*, 72.

34. Melanie Ilič, "Women in the Khrushchev Era: An Overview," in *Women in the Khrushchev Era*, 7; Geoffrey Hosking, *The First Socialist Society: A History of the Soviet Union from Within*, 2nd ed. (Cambridge, MA: Harvard University Press, 1985), 296.

35. Alain Blum, "Socialist Families?" in *Family Life in the Twentieth Century*, 217.

36. Kertzer and Barbagli, xxii.

37. Buckley, 156.

38. Barbara A. Anderson, "The Life Course of Soviet Women Born 1905–1960," in *Politics, Work and Daily Life in the USSR: A Survey of Former Soviet Citizens*, ed. James R. Millar (Cambridge: Cambridge University Press, 1987), 213.

39. Deborah A. Field, "Irreconcilable Differences: Divorce and Conceptions of Private Life in the Khrushchev Era," *The Russian Review* 57 (1988): 599.

40. Susan E. Reid, "Cold War in the Kitchen: Gender and the De-Stalinization of Consumer Taste in the Soviet Union Under Khrushchev," *Slavic Review* 61:2 (2002): 246, 249.

41. Ilič, "Introduction," 8.

42. Ilič, "Introduction," 8; Donald Filtzer, "Women Workers in the Khruschev Era," in *Women in the Khrushchev Era*, 38.

43. Simonton, 210.

44. Ilič, "Introduction," 15.

45. Éva Fodor, *Working Difference: Women's Working Lives in Hungary and Austria, 1945–1980* (Durham, NC: Duke University Press, 2003), 170–171.

46. Reid, 211.

47. Anne Applebaum, *Gulag: A History* (New York: Anchor Books, 2003), 311, 579.

48. Quoted in Hosking, *The First Socialist Society*, 331.

49. Quoted in Richard Lettis and William Morris, *The Hungarian Revolt* (New York: Charles Scribner's Sons, 1961), 71.

50. Robert O. Paxton, *Europe in the Twentieth Century*, 4th ed. (Belmont, CA: Thomson Wadsworth, 2005), 528.

51. Marshall S. Shatz, *Soviet Dissent in Historical Perspective* (Cambridge: Cambridge University Press, 1980), 154–155.

52. Nikolai Yezhov (1895–c. 1939) was director of internal security under Stalin and oversaw the purges of 1937–38.

53. Anna Akhmatova, *Requiem and Poem Without a Hero*, trans. D. M. Thomas (London: Elek, 1976), 23.

54. Quoted in Janna Liddle and Rama Joshi, *Daughters of Independence: Gender, Caste and Class in India* (London: Zed Books, 1986), 34.

55. Liddle and Joshi, 21.

56. Aparna Basu, "Feminism and Nationalism in India, 1917–1947," *Journal of Women's History* 7:4 (Winter 1996): 103, and Catherine Candy, "Relating Feminisms, Nationalisms and Imperialisms: Ireland, India, and Margaret Cousins's Sexual Politics," *Women's History Review* 3:4 (1994): 588.

57. William S. Turley, "Women in the Communist Revolution in Vietnam," *Asian Survey* 12:9 (1975): 797.

58. Susan Geiger, *TANU Women: Gender and Culture in the Making of Tanganyikan Nationalism, 1955–1965* (Portsmouth, NH: Heinemann, 1997), 37.

59. Cora Ann Presley, "The Mau Mau Rebellion, Kikuyu Women, and Social Change," *Canadian Journal of African Studies* 22:3 (1988): 506.

60. Quoted in Karen Turner, "Soldiers and Symbols: North Vietnamese Women and the American War," in *A Soldier and a Woman: Sexual Integration in the Military*, ed. Gerard J. DeGroot and Corinna Peniston-Bird (London: Longman, 2000), 189–190.

61. Turner, 193.

62. Nicole F. Ladewig, "Between Worlds: Algerian Women in Conflict," in *A Soldier and a Woman*, 245.

63. Presley, 503.

64. Ladewig, 247.

65. Audrey Wipper, "Equal Rights for Women in Kenya?" *The Journal of Modern African Studies*, 9:3 (1971): 431.

66. Quoted in Lawrence S. Wittner, "Gender Roles and Nuclear Disarmament Activism, 1954–1965," *Gender and History* 12:1(2000): 204.

67. Wittner, "Gender Roles and Nuclear Disarmament Activism," 214.

68. May, 101.

69. Nan Alamilla Boyd, *Wide Open Town: A History of Queer San Francisco to 1965* (Berkeley: University of California Press, 2003), 159–193.

70. Elizabeth Siegel Watkins, *On the Pill: A Social History of Oral Contraceptives, 1950–1970* (Baltimore: The Johns Hopkins University Press, 1998), 34.

71. Quoted in Herzog, 418.

72. Quoted in James Farrell, *The Spirit of the Sixties: The Making of Post-War Radicalism* (London: Routledge, 1997), 96.

73. Arthur Marwick, *The Sixties: Cultural Revolution in Britain, France, Italy and the United States, c.* 1958–1974 (Oxford: Oxford University Press, 1998), 548.

74. Quoted in Shatz, 127.

75. Farrell, 175.

76. Quoted in Woloch, 531.

77. Marwick, 631.

78. Jo-Ann Pilardi, "The Changing Critical Fortunes of The Second Sex," *History and Theory* 32:2 (1993): 59.

79. Marwick, 683.

80. Quoted in Marwick, 661.

81. Denise Lawrence-Zúñiga, "Material Conditions of Family Life," in *Family Life in the Twentieth Century*, 24–25.

82. Tasca, 96, 99.

83. Simonton, 199–200.

84. Simonton, 198–199.

85. May, 16–17.

86. Marjorie Rosen, *Popcorn Venus: Women, Movies and the American Dream* (New York: Coward, McCann, and Geoghegan, 1973), 267–282.

87. Susan Douglas, *Where the Girls Are: Growing Up Female with the Mass Media* (New York: Random House, 1994), 36.

88. Marie-Francoise Levy, "Television, Family, and Society in France, 1949–1968," *Historical Journal of Film, Radio and Television* 18:2 (June 1998): 208.

89. S. Kay Hoke, "American Popular Music," in *Women and Music: A History*, ed. Karin Pendle (Bloomington: Indiana University Press, 2001), 400–401.

90. Uta G. Poiger, "Rock 'n' Roll, Female Sexuality, and the Cold War Battle Over German Identities," *Journal of Modern History* 68 (1996): 577–616, quote 594.

91. Barbara Ehrenreich, Elizabeth Hess, and Gloria Jacobs, *Re-making Love: The Feminization of Sex* (Garden City, NY: Anchor Press, Doubleday, 1986), 11.

## SUGGESTED READINGS

Bock, Gisela and Pat Thane, eds. *Maternity and Gender Policies: Women and the Rise of the European Welfare States, 1880s–1950s*. London: Routledge, 1991.

Clarke, Alison J. *Tupperware: The Promise of Plastic in 1950s America*. Washington, DC: Smithsonian Institution Press, 1999. A cultural study of how Tupperware was marketed and how it changed American kitchens.

Frevert, Ute. *Women in German History: From Bourgeois Emancipation to Sexual Liberation*. Oxford: Berg, 1990.

Geiger, Susan. *TANU Women: Gender and Culture in the Making of Tanganyikan Nationalism, 1955–1965*. Portsmouth, NH: Heinemann, 1997.

Ilič, Melanie, Susan E. Reid, and Lynne Attwood, eds. *Women in the Khrushchev Era*. Basingstoke,

Hampshire: Palgrave Macmillan, 2004. A collection of essays on the life and culture of women living in Soviet Union during the Khrushchev era.

May, Elaine Tyler. *Homeward Bound: American Families in the Cold War Era*. New York: Basic Books, 1988. A study of the impact of cold war ideology on white middle-class families.

Presley, Cora Ann. "The Mau Mau Rebellion, Kikuyu Women, and Social Change." *Canadian Journal of African Studies* 22:3 (1988): 502–527.

Key article that looks at why so many women joined the Mau Mau.

Rupp, Leila J. *Worlds of Women: The Making of an International Women's Movement*. Princeton: Princeton University Press, 1997.

Watkins, Elizabeth Siegel. *On the Pill: A Social History of Oral Contraceptives, 1950–1970*. Baltimore: The Johns Hopkins University Press, 1998.

# Chapter 16

# Gender at the Turn of the Millennium

*The German Women's Soccer Team Wins the World Cup (2003). The popularity of women's sports has increased dramatically as schools developed athletic programs for girls and young women. International sporting events such as the Women's World Cup attract the best female athletes and large crowds. (Corbis.)*

■ **Feminist Action**  567

   *Women's Liberation and Second
      Wave Feminism*  568
   *The Push for Reproductive
      Rights*  569
   *Ending Violence Against
      Women*  570
   *Lesbian Rights*  571

■ **Political Transformations**  572

   *Women and the Democratic
      Transition in Southern
      Europe*  573
   *Violent Reactions*  574
   *Transformations in the Soviet
      Union*  575
   *The Limits of Progress in Eastern
      Europe*  576
   *German Unification: Hope and
      Disappointment*  578
   *The Fall of the Soviet Union*  580

■ **Recent Trends in Gender and
   Politics**  581

   *Electoral Quotas and Women's
      Representation*  581
   *Women at the Helm*  582
   *Women in Radical Politics*  583

■ **Gender Politics Beyond
   Nations**  585

   *The UN and the
      Internationalization of the
      Women's Movement*  585
   *Gender Politics in the European
      Union*  586
   *Nongovernmental Activism*  588

■ **Changes in the Family and at
   Work**  590

   *A New Demographic Regime*  590
   *New Relationships*  591
   *Aging*  592

   *New Opportunities*  593
   *Gender Equity in the
      Workplace*  593

■ **Women and Culture**  595

   *Women's Studies and Feminist
      Theory*  595
   *Feminist Culture*  596
   *Women in Mainstream
      Culture*  600

# *Chapter 16* ❖ Chronology

| | |
|---|---|
| **1966** | National Organization for Women (NOW) founded in United States |
| **1969** | Stonewall Riots in New York |
| | London Women's Liberation Workshop founded |
| **1970** | First Women's Studies Department created at San Diego State University |
| **1972** | U.S. Senate passes the Equal Rights Amendment |
| | *Ms. Magazine* and *Spare Rib* magazine founded |
| **1975** | United Nations International Year of the Woman |
| **1978** | Red Brigade assassinates former Italian prime minister Aldo Moro |
| **1985** | Gorbachev begins reforms in Soviet Union |
| **1989** | Fall of the Berlin Wall, democratic revolutions in much of Eastern Europe |
| **1990** | Mary Robinson elected prime minister of Ireland |
| **1992** | Maastricht Treaty creates European Union |
| **1999** | French Civil Solidarity Pact |
| **2001** | Netherlands legalizes gay marriage |
| | International Criminal Tribunal on the former Yugoslavia convicts three Serbian men of sexual enslavement and rape |
| **2003** | Valentina Matvienko elected governor of Saint Petersburg, Russia |
| **2004** | Austrian Elfriede Jelinek wins Nobel Prize for Literature |
| **2005** | Angela Merkel becomes first woman chancellor of Germany |

*I*n the last quarter of the twentieth century, feminism emerged as the single most important force for changing women's lives. An expanded and more visible feminist movement energized women, giving them a sense of identity and motivating them to demand equality in all aspects of life. As millions of European women entered the democratic process, either through the creation of new democratic nations or through changes in traditional politics, feminists worked for the inclusion of women at all levels of government. In addition, the growth of international governmental structures offered new forums for women's voices. Women's struggle for equality led to monumental changes in the family, education, and the workforce. By the beginning of the twenty-first century, women were vibrant, powerful actors in both public and private life.

## FEMINIST ACTION

By the late 1960s, many women were frustrated by the lack of attention that women's issues received from activist trade unions, socialist parties, and student movements. In response, they created their own groups focused on the struggle to end discrimination against women. The women's liberation movement had diverse memberships, ideologies, and strategies. Whether they worked within the political system or outside of it, these new dynamic organizations gave voice to women's hopes and frustrations and galvanized women in the struggle against sexism in its many forms.

## Women's Liberation and Second Wave Feminism

A new phase in the fight for women's equality began in the late 1960s with Second Wave Feminism. (First Wave Feminism was associated with the nineteenth and early twentieth-century women's rights and suffrage movements.) The largest of these new Second Wave feminist organizations was the National Organization for Women (NOW) founded in the United States by Betty Friedan, Betty Furness (1916–1994), and twenty-six others at the Third National Conference of the Commission on the Status of Women in 1966. Ambitiously, NOW would take "action to bring women into full participation in the mainstream of American society now, assuming all the privileges and responsibilities thereof in truly equal partnership with men."[1] European feminists also formed broad-based organizations. In 1969, the London Women's Liberation Workshop (LWLW) became the largest umbrella organization for British feminist groups, sponsoring Britain's first major women's rights conference in Oxford a year later. Similarly in France, feminist writer Christine Delphy (b. 1941) and others formed the Women's Liberation Movement. These organizations proclaimed that "the personal is political," women's personal issues were political issues and women's lives were not merely the product of personal choices but were subject to political, economic, and social forces beyond an individual woman's control. Thus, the only way to improve women's lives was through political action.

In the United States, feminist organizations renewed their call for constitutionally guaranteed equality. NOW and other women's groups supported a new version of the Equal Rights Amendment (ERA) that decreed, "Equality of rights under the law shall not be denied or abridged by the United States or by any state on account of sex." Despite intense public debate, in 1972, the momentum for legal change was so strong that the U.S. Senate passed the amendment and within a year, twenty-two of the necessary thirty-five states had approved the measure. Although ultimately the amendment failed to achieve the necessary two-thirds majority of the states, the ERA helped publicize the concerns of the women's liberation movement and demonstrated the possibilities for ending legal discrimination.

Second Wave feminists pressed for an end to sexism in all aspects of women's lives. In the workplace, feminists encouraged the formation of women's business and professional networks to counteract the influence of the "old boy network." They boycotted employers who discriminated against women and lobbied for legislation to end discriminatory practices. In 1970, a group of women engaged in a sit-in at the *Ladies Home Journal* magazine to protest both its treatment of female employees and the magazine's content.

Feminists formed consciousness-raising groups to encourage women to discuss problems and work together toward resolving them. Although often belittled, such groups were particularly important to women from cultures that expected them to suffer silently rather than acknowledge emotional or other troubles. These groups taught women that their experiences were not unique and that they could benefit from sharing common problems. Many of these groups met in the growing numbers of women's centers that emerged. These centers provided feminist education to a broad spectrum of women and a place for local activists to gather.

Feminist organizations kept their members informed and enthused through a growing array of magazines and newsletters. By 1970, women published more than five hundred feminist periodicals in the United States, although most had only small readerships.[2] However, the feminist media changed dramatically in 1972, when Gloria Steinem (b. 1934) founded *Ms. Magazine*, the first feminist magazine aimed at a popular audience. With its glossy format, it was attractive to mainstream women and became an important forum for readers to exchange ideas. In Great Britain, *Spare Rib*, a glossy British feminist magazine also founded in 1972, brought feminist ideas to the British public, while in Germany, tens of thousands of readers kept up with women's issues by reading journals such as *Courage* and *Emma*. In addition to connecting feminists to the movement, these periodicals promoted the works of feminist artists, singers, and songwriters.

From the outset, Second Wave Feminism faced criticism from many sides. Conservative Catholic organizations railed against feminists in Europe, proclaiming the breakdown of traditional values. During the 1970s, American activist Phyllis Schafly (b. 1924) led a vociferous campaign against the ERA and feminism. She and others argued that feminists were radical lesbians and socialists who

**GLORIA STEINEM (1975).** Since the early 1970s, Gloria Steinem has been one of the most visible leaders of the Women's Movement in the United States. In this picture, she shakes hands with demonstrators in New York City prior to the start of the International Women's Day March. *(Bettmann/Corbis.)*

rejected family, motherhood, and men; in response, conservative women formed their own organizations, including Concerned Women for America. Even some feminists criticized the movement for being elitist and racist. In the United States, African American women, Latinas, and other women of color formed their own feminist organizations, such as the National Center for Lesbian Rights and the Mexican American Women's National Association (MANA). Lesbians often clashed with mainstream feminist groups. Betty Friedan, the president of NOW, supposedly once referred to lesbians as the "lavender menace."[3] In France, lesbians and heterosexual feminists also argued over strategies and priorities.

Recently, young feminists in the United States developed Third Wave Feminism, which focuses on organizing young women and emphasizes the intersections between race, class, sexual orientation, and gender. Third Wave feminists Rebecca Walker (b. 1969) and Amy Richards (b. 1970) have emphasized their connections to some Second Wave feminist ideas, while asserting that young feminists must cope with a range of issues unfamiliar to an older generation of women. Despite their differences, all these organizations worked toward the same goal—an end to sexism—and their diverse voices would indelibly alter the political landscape at the turn of the millennium.

## The Push for Reproductive Rights

Many women were drawn to the women's movement because of its focus on sexual liberation and reproductive rights. Second Wave feminists argued that a woman's right to choose her sexual partners and control her own fertility were central to her physical health, her mental well-being, and political and economic equality. All women deserve equal access to contraception, sex education, and abortion.

Although by 1970 millions of Western women relied on the birth control pill for contraception, it remained unavailable to many more. In Spain, Italy, and other Catholic countries, the Catholic Church successfully prevented the sale of contraceptives, while in others, many women simply could not afford them. In the United States, as late as 1970, some states denied single women access to birth control. Finally, in 1972, the Supreme Court heard the case of William Baird, who had been convicted of exhibiting contraceptive products during a lecture on contraception to a group of students at Boston University and of giving a young woman a package of vaginal foam at the end of the lecture. In a landmark decision, the Supreme Court struck down the Massachusetts statute that barred the distribution of contraceptives to unmarried people, recognizing "the right of the *individual,* married or single, to be free from unwarranted governmental intrusion into matters so fundamentally affecting a person as the decision whether to bear or beget a child."[4]

Women's organizations also pressed for better sex education in schools and the expansion of contraceptive and women's health clinics. In the United States, the Boston Women's Health Collective publication of *Our Bodies, Our Selves* in 1970 gave women clear, easy-to-understand information about menstruation, fertility, mental health issues, and menopause. In Germany and Norway, women's organizations also published guides to abortion and contraception. Written for the general public, these publications promoted women's participation in their own health care rather than strict reliance on the male-dominated health-care systems. Moreover, they helped transcend class and cultural differences by giving women from many backgrounds and educational levels access to the same basic knowledge about their bodies and reproduction.

Feminists mobilized around the issue of abortion rights. They argued that access to legal and safe abortion was critical to a woman's control of her own body and integral to a woman's health. In 1971 in West Germany, where both obtaining and performing abortions was illegal, the popular magazine *Der Stern* published a letter from 374 well-known women stating that they had had abortions. At the same time, in the publication *Der Spiegel,* 329 doctors signed a letter stating that they had performed abortions.[5] These letters sparked controversy and mass demonstrations across Germany. In France, Simone de Beauvoir and 342 other women signed the "*manifeste des 343*" stating that they also had had abortions, a move that intensified the debate about abortion rights in that country. By showing that many respected women and men were criminals in the eyes of the law, these protests highlighted the widespread failure of antiabortion laws.

Italian women's groups working to reform abortion laws made little headway until 1974, when authorities prosecuted 263 Italian women from the city of Trento for having undergone abortions. The next year, police raided and closed an illegal abortion clinic in Florence. The outcry against the prosecutions was intense. Finally, in 1978 under pressure from feminist organizations, Italy legalized abortion, although only under certain conditions.[6] Similarly, in the Netherlands, abortion rights brought feminist organizations together in common cause. In 1974, a national committee, We Women Demand, formed to press for the decriminalization of abortion and access to abortion through the National Health Service. The coalition of women's groups held large demonstrations and sit-ins and occupied an abortion clinic when police threatened to shut it down. However, the Dutch legislature did not legalize abortion until 1980, and even that legislation required women to first consult with a physician and then wait five days before undergoing the procedure.[7]

By the first decade of the twenty-first century, most women in Europe and the United States had some access to abortion. Abortion rates were highest in Russia and Romania and lowest in Ireland and the Netherlands. Ireland has the strictest abortion laws, limiting access to only women whose lives are in danger. In Spain, Portugal, Poland, and Switzerland, a woman must demonstrate that her physical or mental health is in jeopardy before authorities allow her to have an abortion. In the United States, some states have few or no doctors who will provide abortions, and poor women often cannot afford the procedure. Recently, the campaign for abortion rights has been reinvigorated, as opposition organizations, many of which are closely tied to the Catholic Church and evangelical Protestant churches, work to restrict access to abortion or recriminalize it altogether.

## Ending Violence Against Women

Women's rights groups have also focused on ending violence against women. The extent of this violence is staggering. In the United States, murder is the number one cause of death among pregnant women, and half of all women murdered are killed by their husbands or partners. The Council of Europe has stated that domestic violence is the major cause of death and disability for women aged sixteen to forty-four and accounts for more death and ill-health than cancer or traffic accidents. In 2000, 60 percent of divorced women in Poland reported that their ex-husbands had struck them at least once. In 1999, 42 percent of all married and cohabiting women in Lithuania reported that their present partner had either assaulted them or threatened them with physical or sexual violence. In Austria, physical violence is the primary cause of divorces initiated by women, and only 20 percent of reported rape cases ended in convictions in the 1990s. In Ireland, a 2003 report noted that 20 percent of women have reported sexual assault as adults.[8]

Despite the scope of the problem, governments rarely provided services for victims. In 1971, Erin Pizzey (b. 1939) established the Women's Aid Centre, the first shelter for female victims of violence, in Chiswick, England (outside of London). The same year, the Red Stockings, a Danish women's liberation organization, opened a shelter in Copenhagen. Yet, activists knew that caring for the victims of violence was only part of their goal. Women held the first Take Back the Night March in Germany in 1973. Since then, annual marches have supported victims of violence while bringing national attention to the issue. Antiviolence activism culminated with the first International Tribunal on Crimes Against Women in Brussels, Belgium, in 1976. More than two thousand women from forty countries gathered to listen to women's experiences of victimization and to denounce all forms of violence.

Canada was one of the first nations to adopt a broad-based approach to protect women against violence. In 1967, the government worked closely with women's groups to establish the Royal Commission on the Status of Women. This partnership produced a series of reports that outlined the severity of the problem and recommended responses, including special training for the Royal Canadian Mounted Police, funding for shelters, and programs to raise awareness. During the 1990s, women's groups pressured the government to expand its programs into Canada's Native American, immigrant, and minority communities.

Other nations have been slower to respond. In Italy, the first shelter for victims of violence

opened only in 1990. Until 1996 Italian law defined sexual violence as a crime against morality, rather than a crime against a person, and few perpetrators received serious punishment. As recently as 2004, the Spanish Bishops Conference declared that domestic violence was the "bitter fruit" of sexual liberation.

Violence against women has also mobilized profeminist men. In 1989, Mark Lepine murdered fourteen women at the University of Montreal before committing suicide. Before shooting his victims, he shouted, "I hate feminists." Horrified by the Montreal Massacre, Canadians created December 6 as a national day of remembrance for Canadian victims of violence against women. The tragedy also galvanized thousands of men to support antiviolence campaigns. For one week in December 1991, Canadian men wore white ribbons in opposition to violence against women. In the ensuing decades, the White Ribbon campaign has spread to the United States and Europe.

These and other antiviolence organizations have successfully changed societal attitudes. A 1999 survey of Europeans found that although nearly half of all Europeans believed that violence against women was "fairly common," less than 3 percent found it acceptable and many nations have passed strong antiviolence laws.[9] Nevertheless, legal barriers still prevent women, particularly recent immigrants, from leaving violent relationships. In the Netherlands, an immigrant woman must live with her partner for five years or face deportation; in Britain, she must live with him for one year. Thus, immigrant women must often endure abuse to obtain legal residence.[10] Antiviolence organizations continue to work for a world in which all women can live without the threat of violence.

## Lesbian Rights

The same desire for fair treatment and equal opportunity that fueled the feminist movement inspired the lesbian rights movement. In Belgium, France, and some other northern European nations, homosexuality had not been illegal for centuries. However, in many countries, sodomy laws prevented lesbians from living openly. Gay and lesbian activists successfully lobbied for the decriminalization of homosexuality in the United Kingdom in 1967, Germany in 1969, and Austria in 1971. After the 1969 Stonewall Riots in New York, gay and lesbian activists in the United States pressed for antidiscrimination laws at the municipal and state levels. However, many states retained antisodomy laws until the Supreme Court ruled them unconstitutional in 2003.

Most lesbian and gay liberation organizations arose during the political tumult of the early 1970s. In West Germany, the screening of Rosa von Praunheim's film *Nicht der Homosexuelle ist pervers, sondern die Situation in der er lebt* (*It Is Not the Homosexual Who Is Perverse, But the Situation in Which He Lives*) at the Berlin Film Festival in 1971 spawned the formation of the Homosexual Interest Group. In 1972, lesbians in West Berlin formed the "women's section" of the gay and lesbian group Homosexual Action Westberlin, and in 1973 they organized a demonstration to protest against a series of anti-lesbian articles that had appeared in the German press.

In France, the gay liberation movement had its roots in the *Front Homosexuel Action Révolutionnaire* (FHAR). In 1971, FHAR worked with the radical left-wing review *Tout* (*Everything*) to publish a special issue on gay politics that brought homosexual issues to national attention. However, lesbian activists were not always comfortable working in an organization increasingly dominated by gay men. Gradually, they left the organization to form smaller lesbian groups. Despite these divisions, lesbians and gay men marched together in the first French Gay Pride Day on June 25, 1977.[11]

Activists demanded equal recognition for same-sex relationships and access to the rights afforded to heterosexual couples, but even socially progressive countries were slow to respond. In Finland, although legislators first proposed legal recognition of same-sex partnerships in 1974 in the charter of the Finnish Organization for Sexual Equality, the Finnish Parliament would not take up the issue of gay and lesbian civil unions for another twenty years. After a number of defeats, Finland's parliament finally passed the same-sex partnership bill in 2001.

The European Union (see below) took an early stand against discrimination based on sexual orientation. The European Court of Human Rights ruled in 1981 that laws against same-sex relationships violated the European Convention on Human Rights. As a result, over the next two decades, many European nations altered their legal codes to include same-sex relationships. In September 2003, the European Parliament recommended that gay and lesbian Europeans be allowed to marry and adopt children and that these recommendations be forwarded to the Council for immediate consideration. By 2004, all European countries except Great Britain, Ireland, Italy, and Greece recognized some form of same-sex civil partnerships. The Netherlands legalized gay marriage in 2001, and Belgium and Canada followed two years later. In 2004, Sweden's parliament was considering making its marriage laws gender neutral, replacing same-sex civil unions with marriage. Spanish legislators approved same-sex marriage in 2005.

Buoyed by recent successes, gay and lesbian activists have galvanized large numbers of supports in their fight for equal treatment in the workplace and as parents. Other activists work for equal rights for bisexuals and transsexuals. Many of these campaigns have met with strong opposition from conservative religious groups. Nevertheless, the campaigns for sexual and reproductive rights have transformed traditional notions of family, sexuality, and individual rights.

In the 1970s, the women's liberation movement became the voice of millions of women who wanted legal and sexual equality, reproductive rights, and freedom from violence. Although the movement is diverse in both membership and strategies, it has successfully mobilized women for political action and brought feminist issues to public attention.

## POLITICAL TRANSFORMATIONS

Through the women's liberation movement, women gained a sense of collective identity and acquired the confidence to press for legal and political change. Feminists determinedly fought for equal rights, as the last of Western Europe's authoritarian governments gave way to democracy. Even the tightly controlled Soviet Union witnessed a rebirth of feminist activity that would be critical during the dramatic changes of the coming decades. However, change did not always mean progress for women. By the late 1980s, as political and economic revolution swept over Eastern Europe and the Soviet Union, many women paid a high price during the transition to democratic governments and free-market economies.

## Women and the Democratic Transition in Southern Europe

Francisco Franco's death in 1975 paved the way for Spain's return to democracy and the reintegration of women into the political system. As Spain's leaders moved toward the creation of parliamentary monarchy, feminists secretly met in Madrid to discuss strategies and priorities. Within months of Franco's death, female activists formed the Women's Liberation Front, and more than four thousand women attended a women's conference in Barcelona.

Defying gender expectations in Spain's religiously conservative society, a number of women, mostly from socialist, communist, and other leftist parties, entered the political arena when the government legalized political parties in advance of the first elections in 1977. Despite their lack of political experience, 13 percent of the candidates for the Spanish parliament's Congress of Deputies were female. However, with little party or popular support, these candidates did not fare very well. Women made up only 6 percent of the newly elected deputies and only 2.4 percent of senators. In an attempt to counter male-dominated politics, feminist Lidia Falcón (b. 1935) and others established the Feminist Party in 1979, although the party never achieved much electoral success.

Women's limited education and exclusion from politics under Franco led many feminists to believe that female voters would prefer conservative candidates; however, their concerns proved to be unfounded. In the first few democratic elections, women tended to vote for the centrist UCD (Union of the Democratic Center) rather than for either left- or right-wing parties.[12] At the regional level, where radical parties were gaining visibility, women also consistently preferred moderate parties.

With such limited representation, women had little influence on the formulation of Spain's new constitution, and feminists were disappointed that it did not deal with many critical issues, including divorce, abortion, access to contraception, and patriarchal authority. However, the constitution significantly altered women's legal status, establishing equality of the sexes and prohibiting discrimination within marriage or employment. Subsequent reforms of the civil code gave women equality in property administration and authority over their children.

Moreover, change came quickly over the next decade. Parliament granted women access to birth control in 1978 and introduced civil marriage and divorce in 1981. In 1983, the governing socialist party, the *Partido Socialista Obrero Español* (PSOE), created the Institute for Women to develop policies to improve women's lives and to subsidize the expansion of women's groups. Within a decade after Franco's death, Spanish women had benefited from remarkable legal and political changes.

Greece also returned to parliamentary government in 1974 after seven years of military rule. However, Greek politics remained dominated by "old-boy" relationships, and politicians demonstrated little interest in women's issues. Thus, Greek women had to create other opportunities for political participation. In 1975, a group of political activists formed the nonpartisan Movement of Democratic Women to ensure women's inclusion in democratic processes and women became quite visible in leftist parties. Maria Damanaki (b. 1952) headed the KKE, the Greek Communist Party, and Margaret Papandreou (b. 1923), the American-born wife of Andreas Papandreou (1919–1996), the head of PASOK, the socialist-leaning party that ruled through the 1980s, was an active proponent of women's issues while her husband led the government.

Legal equality came slowly. Greek family law gave fathers complete control over their children until age twenty-one and allowed women only limited property rights. There was no civil marriage or divorce and married women had to adopt their husbands' surnames. Finally, under pressure from women's groups, Parliament passed reforms in 1983 giving both parents authority over their children, abolishing dowry, introducing civil marriage, and making provisions for divorce and child custody.

Millions of women across southern Europe experienced the dramatic transition from authoritarian governments to democracy during the mid 1970s (Portugal also returned to democracy in 1974). In 1970, they had few rights and were almost completely excluded from formal politics. During the transition, they pushed for constitutional equality and bravely defied traditional gender expectations by standing for office in the first free elections. By the early 1980s, Spanish, Greek, and Portuguese women were critical players in government and had made remarkable progress toward legal equality.

## Violent Reactions

Feminism also spurred many women to challenge their national governments through radical political action. Many intellectuals and working-class women had been exposed to revolutionary politics during the trade union and student protests of 1968–1969 and were attracted by their calls to end class divisions and overthrow the current political system, which frequently excluded women. They believed that the violent political change advocated by these groups would also end sexism.

Although right-wing and neofascist groups also proliferated, radical women overwhelmingly joined left-wing organizations. In Italy and other nations between 1970 and 1984, women made up nearly one-quarter of the membership of left-wing terrorist organizations, but less than 10 percent of the membership of neofascist organizations.[13] According to former members, male members of leftist terrorist groups generally welcomed their female comrades, praising them for their practicality, their single-mindedness, and their coolness under pressure.

In Italy, the Red Brigades, a Marxist-Leninist group, believed that social and political change could only come through the violent overthrow of the existing political system. In their attempt to disrupt Italian political and economic life, they terrorized Italians with a violent campaign that included bombings, abductions, and assassinations. Female members came from many walks of life. Most had been students or teachers, but more than one-quarter had been white-collar workers before they became involved. Former members regularly note that feminism was a driving force behind their decisions to join the movement.[14]

At its height, women made up 36 percent of the Red Brigades' leadership,[15] and former members have emphasized the group's gender egalitarianism. Former member Vincenza Fioroni told an interviewer that, "the group was very democratic because roles were decided upon on the basis on one's ability, not one's sex."[16] Indeed, female members eagerly defied traditional gender expectations by learning to use firearms and kill in cold blood. In February 1975, Mara Cagol, one of the founders of the Red Brigades, planned and executed the escape of her husband from prison, but she was killed a few months later in a shootout with police.[17] Other women participated in the killing of Italian businessmen and politicians, including former prime minister Aldo Moro (1916–1978). However, despite the prominence of women in the organization, the Red Brigades never supported feminism per se.

In Germany, the anticapitalist and antidemocratic Red Army Faction (RAF) carried out a campaign of violence during the 1970s. One subgroup of the RAF, led by Andreas Baader (1947–1977) and his girlfriend, Gudrun Ensslin (1940–1977), assassinated high-profile Germans. After Ulrike Meinhof (1934–1976) joined in the late 1960s and helped Baader escape from prison, the group was dubbed the Baader-Meinhof Gang. Meinhof spent the next two years on the run, robbing banks and bombing buildings, before being captured in 1973. She died under mysterious circumstances in prison, awaiting trial for four murders, fifty-four attempted murders, and for forming a criminal association. Other female members served time for a car bomb attack that killed three U.S. soldiers in 1972 and a series of attacks on U.S. installations in 1981. By the mid 1980s, women made up a majority of the RAF's core activists and about half of the membership. Of the twenty-two terrorists sought by German police in 1991, thirteen were women.[18]

Because women were so visible in the RAF, many Germans associated them with radical feminism, despite the fact that captured members generally disassociated themselves from feminist politics. Radical German feminists, however, formed their own exclusively female terrorist organization, Red Zora. Red Zora attacked companies that it saw as patriarchal and sexist, such as pornographers. In 1987, Red Zora planted incendiary bombs in eight branches of the Adler Corporation, one of West

Germany's largest clothing chains, to protest its exploitation of South Korean female labor. They also took action against pharmaceutical companies that engaged in genetic research.

Although these radical organizations were small, their unpredictable violence thrust them into the media spotlight. Europeans were unaccustomed to seeing women's faces on television associated with bombings and assassinations. For many, the brutality of the violence seemed even more serious because of their sex.

## Transformations in the Soviet Union

While opportunities for women in the other parts of Europe expanded in the 1970s and 1980s, life in the Soviet Union grew increasingly difficult. Bureaucratic inefficiency and poor planning by the Soviet state hindered growth, and women bore the brunt of the economic slowdown. As unemployment increased, the Soviet government pushed women out of the workplace in order to maintain jobs for men. In 1981, the government published a new list of 460 occupations that were closed to women ostensibly to protect them from dangerous working conditions. However, those same jobs were immediately opened to men. The government also attempted to keep women at home through a series of pronatalist policies, including extending maternity benefits and instigating a propaganda campaign to encourage women in non-Asian areas to identify primarily as mothers not workers.[19] By the late 1980s, the Soviet economy particularly disadvantaged women. Although nearly 90 percent of women worked outside the home, employers segregated women in low-paying jobs and often denied them promotions. In addition, women did almost all household labor. Their double burden increased as shortages of goods increased and women spent hours in long lines at state stores.

As the economy faltered, Soviet citizens suffered. Average life expectancy fell from 69.3 years in 1969–70 to 67.7 years in 1979–80.[20] Poor nutrition and medical services led to an increase in infant mortality rates. In 1979, 11.6 percent of the adult population of Leningrad was arrested for drunkenness, and alcoholism was a major cause of divorce. With birth control in short supply, the Soviet Union had one of the world's highest abortion rates. In 1980, there were 7 million registered abortions to 4.9 million births. The total number was no doubt greater because in many rural areas women only had access to illegal abortions.

As the social crisis grew, feminism provided an outlet for a few women to express their discontent. Under the communist regime, the Soviet Women's Committee was the only legal women's group. Nevertheless, in 1979, a small group of feminists in Leningrad published a women's journal, *An Almanac: Women and Russia*. The journal's editors hoped that "by pooling our efforts we can rekindle support for the forgotten cause of women's liberation and give women a new courage."[21] However, the government banned the publication, and the KGB (the Soviet secret service) repeatedly interrogated and intimidated the authors and their families. Eventually, authorities forced four of the women into exile.[22] The crackdown was only a temporary setback for the emergent feminist movement. Within a matter of months, other women, including prominent feminist Tatyana Mamonova (b. 1943), risked further harassment and arrest by publishing two new feminist journals.

While Soviet citizens struggled to make ends meet, the cold war provoked international anxiety about the possibility of nuclear war between the superpowers. In response, beginning in the early 1970s, Russian leader Leonid Brezhnev (1964–1982) and U.S. president Richard Nixon (1969–1974) adopted a policy to permanently relax cold war tensions known as *détente*. The two nations supported détente with ongoing talks to reduce nuclear arms and visits by Nixon to Moscow in 1972 and 1974 and Brezhnev to the United States in 1973. However, the policy was seriously tested during the late 1970s with the Soviet invasion of Afghanistan and a series of crises in the Middle East. Ultimately, U.S. president Ronald Reagan (1980–1988) rejected détente and urged the defeat of the Soviet Union and communism. At the same time, changes within the Soviet Union quickly turned the government's focus inward and away from international politics.

Mikhail Gorbachev (b. 1931), who became the head of the Communist Party in 1985, initiated a series of reforms that changed the course of Soviet history. With *perestroika*, his economic restructuring, Gorbachev eased government control of the economy and allowed for some private enterprise. His policy of *glasnost*, openness, meant less government censorship of the media and public opinion. Gorbachev also pursued a policy of improved relations with both Western Europe and the United States. In 1989, Gorbachev permitted the first free elections to the Soviet Congress since 1917. Although he and the Communist Party retained control of the government, his policies of openness increased the scope of political debate.

Gorbachev's economic policies were intended to slowly introduce a market economy. Among other reforms, he ended price and wage regulations and many state benefits, including childcare. The reforms shocked the Soviet economy. Inflation soared and wages remained low. As state-owned companies gave way to private firms, they laid off thousands of workers, most of whom were women. By the end of 1991, women made up 80 percent of the unemployed.[23] In addition to the increased unemployment, Soviet families could no longer rely on state benefits to prevent them from falling into extreme poverty.

Glasnost both created new opportunities for women and brought new challenges. On the one hand, by the late 1980s, the new openness allowed women to form consciousness-raising groups and other organizations. Groups for single mothers, lesbian groups, anti-domestic-violence advocates, and educational and cultural organizations like the Petersburg Centre for Gender Issues sprang up across the country. By 1994, Russia had over three hundred registered women's groups, although most were centered in Moscow.[24] For the first time in decades, Russian feminists could openly criticize Soviet government and society without fear of recrimination. On the other hand, with the opening of the press, hyperfeminine and highly sexualized images replaced more somber Soviet portrayals of strong working women. The entry of new consumer goods onto the market also promoted Western ideas of beauty. Suddenly, the media bombarded Soviet women with ads for skin care products, makeup, and diets. Just as Soviet women were able to move beyond traditional Soviet ideas of womanhood, they were assaulted with traditional Western ideas of femininity.

## The Limits of Progress in Eastern Europe

The economic crisis that strained the Soviet Union also took its toll on Eastern Europe. Disheartened by economic stagnation and encouraged by new Soviet policies of openness, millions of dissatisfied citizens in Eastern Europe challenged communism. As early as 1980, the ongoing economic crises in Poland led to the formation of Solidarity, the first independent trade union in the communist bloc. With more than nine million members, Solidarity successfully united Polish workers against the communist government. Although it had been declared illegal in 1983, the union led by Lech Walesa (b. 1943) crippled the Polish economy with a wave of new strikes in 1988 and forced the government to reorganize the legislature and guarantee limited free elections in 1989. Despite the fact that the government reserved some seats for the Communist Party, Solidarity's victory was dramatic. It won all of the open seats, including ninety-nine of one hundred seats in the Polish Senate. In free elections the next year, Poles chose Walesa as their first noncommunist president.

Women played little role in the transition to democracy. Neither the government nor the opposition (Solidarity) had any female negotiators. Women were active in labor and other organizations, but no autonomous women's movement emerged. Polish women generally distrusted feminism, viewing it as a foreign idea imported by Westernized elites. Moreover, Polish women believed that the Solidarity movement sincerely worked to alleviate their concerns. Although women were poorly represented in the leadership of the movement (only 8 percent of delegates to the Solidarity Congress), Solidarity gained concessions on issues important to them, including maternity leave and daycare.[25]

Despite women's marginalization from the new government, their bodies became the focus of intense political debate. With the expansion of leftist and feminist organizations, the Catholic Church pushed to make abortion, which had been widely available under communism, illegal. Polish legislators gradually limited access to abortions. In 1990, a woman had to consult three physicians and a psychologist before she could end a pregnancy. In 1993, Parliament passed a restrictive abortion law that prohibited doctors in private practice from performing abortions, forbade abortions for nonmedical reasons, and mandated two years imprisonment for women who aborted.[26] The election of Hanna Suchocka (b. 1946) as prime minister in 1993 did little to improve women's access to abortion, as she worked with the Vatican to further restrict the procedure.[27] Although the parliament again liberalized abortion laws in 1996, Polish politics continue to be shaped by the ongoing social conflict over abortion.[28] For many Poles, the abortion debate exemplifies the uncertainties about the important role of the Catholic Church in Polish society and discomfort with changing gender roles and expectations.

Women in the former Czechoslovakia (now the Czech Republic and Slovakia), Hungary, Bulgaria, and Romania faced similar issues during the transition from communism to democracy. For instance, after the Czechoslovakia's "Velvet Revolution" of late 1989, the leader of the new government, Vaclav Havel (b. 1936), appointed several women to important offices, including the Czech ambassador to the United States. However, these women were exceptions to the rule. There were few female ministers or women in other leadership positions, and with the end of electoral quotas, female representation in the legislature declined from approximately 25 percent to 10 percent. In fact, there were no women in the Czech government formed after the 1996 elections. Although the numbers of women's organizations has expanded considerably, most denied any feminist affiliation. Even the Party of Women and Mothers, established in 1990, never attracted many voters.[29] Economically, although the transition to a market economy brought new opportunities for female entrepreneurs, the new governments could not ensure the continued provision of benefits such as maternity leave, equal pay, and childcare leave. As a result, women in the Czech Republic and Slovakia face considerable political and economic challenges.

Women in the former Yugoslavia have suffered through some of the most tragic transitions from communist rule. After the death of longtime leader Josef Tito in 1980, his ineffective successors plunged the nation into crisis. Gradually, economic and political tensions among the Yugoslav states led to the slow and violent disintegration of the multiethnic and multireligious nation.

After a brief, but costly war, women in the new nation of Slovenia experienced a dramatic decline in political representation. With the first multiparty elections in 1990, the number of women in the Slovenian parliament dropped by half, a trend that continued throughout the decade. As new political parties formed, Slovenian political leaders made no attempt to include women, and many were vocally antifeminist. The few women who entered politics distanced themselves from feminism in order to prevent being stigmatized by opponents.[30]

In other parts of the former Yugoslavia, women have endured great suffering. In Croatia, the ruling party has promoted a highly rigid, hypermasculine national identity that equates success and power with men only.[31] Beginning in 1991, the new nation of Serbia and Montenegro, which voted to retain communist rule under the authoritarian rule of ethnic nationalist Slobodan Milošević (b. 1941–2006), attacked neighboring Croatia and Bosnia-Herzegovina. During that conflict, members of the Serbian military and paramilitaries assaulted civilians. Soldiers raped Muslim women to promote ethnic cleansing, the targeting of certain ethnic groups for elimination, and to hasten the genocide of Bosnian Muslims. Soldiers repeatedly asserted that they intended to force Bosnian women to bear Serbian children. In addition to the physical violence, women suffered from the shame that rape brought on them and their families. These fears forced many victims to remain silent. One woman told an interviewer that a Serbian neighbor raped her repeatedly: "He raped me. I told nobody because I didn't want to cause panic. Not even my husband. I am afraid of blood revenge. That must not happen."[32] Soldiers victimized women both physically and psychologically. According to one news report, Bosnian Serb soldiers cut a cross in the head of a Muslim woman after a gang rape.[33] Estimates of numbers of raped women range from twenty thousand to sixty thousand. Similar violence took place in Kosovo, where ethnic Albanians also suffered from Serbian aggression.

International attempts to pressure Serbia to end the conflict also negatively affected women. When the United Nations sanctioned Serbia, the economic isolation forced half of the Serbian population into poverty and caused an increase in infant mortality from 12 percent in 1992 to 16 percent in 1996.[34] However, international intervention may bring long-term benefits. In February 1993, the United Nations Security Council created an international tribunal to investigate war crimes in the former Yugoslavia. In February 2001, the International Criminal Tribunal on the former Yugoslavia convicted three Serbian men of sexual

**BOSNIAN WOMEN AT MEMORIAL FOR SREBRENICA MASSACRE (2005).** These women weeping at a memorial marking the 1995 massacre of 7,000 Bosnian Muslim men by Serbs are poignant reminders of the trauma that women faced during and after the violent conflicts in the former Yugoslavia. *(Reuters/Landov.)*

enslavement and rape. The ongoing prosecution of Serbian officials by the war crimes tribunal has focused extensively on the violence that Serbian men inflicted on women and brought worldwide attention to the use of rape as a war crime.

## German Unification: Hope and Disappointment

The same social and economic forces that brought down the governments of Eastern Europe put pressure on the communist regime in East Germany. In 1989, Hungary opened its border to Austria and within six months, 220,000 East Germans had traveled through Hungary to freedom in the West. At the same time, East Germans intensified their protests, pushing for a democratic, but still socialist government. Women's groups, including the Lila Offensive, used the opportunity to demand women's equality in addition to political freedoms.[35] In an attempt to maintain power, the East German government opened the Berlin Wall, which had symbolized the division of Eastern and Western Europe for nearly thirty years, in November 1989. Overcome with emotion, people literally tore down this potent symbol of the cold war and forced the hard-line communists from power (see Map 16.1).

As East Germany collapsed and Chancellor Helmut Kohl (1982–1998) began the reunification of Germany, feminists from both countries worked to ensure that their issues would take center stage at the negotiating table. However, feminism had evolved in radically different ways on each side of the Berlin Wall. Because traditional politics and political parties had excluded them, West German feminism was more autonomous and militant—they were unaccustomed to "working within the system." In sharp contrast, East German feminists were closely tied to the socialist state system. Change came quickly. Within one month of the collapse of the Wall, East German feminists created a national feminist organization, the Independent Women's League, a coalition of newly formed and rapidly expanding women's groups whose slogan was "Without women there is no state."[36]

At the almost exclusively male reunification negotiations, the issue of abortion nearly derailed German unification. East German women had unrestricted access to abortion for the first twelve weeks of pregnancy, while West German women could only obtain abortions in cases of fetal deformity, rape, when the health of the mother was threatened, or because of social hardship. After tense negotiations, the two sides agreed that each state would retain its own abortion law until a united German parliament could pass a new law.[37] After unification in 1990, the debate continued in the courts and Parliament. In 1995, Parliament finally passed legislation that permitted abortion

*Map 16.1* DEMOCRATIC MOVEMENTS IN EASTERN EUROPE, 1989. From the Velvet Revolution in Czechoslovakia to the dismantling of the Berlin Wall, women were central actors in the protests that led to the fall of communism in Eastern Europe.

during the first trimester only if the woman received counseling aimed at convincing her to continue her pregnancy.

After the celebrations of the fall of the Berlin Wall ended, East German women saw the full picture of unification. They gained some political and civil liberties but forfeited reproductive rights. Moreover, increased unemployment due to the decline of the East German economy meant a severe loss of economic independence. The eco-

nomic crisis led to a dramatic decrease in the birthrate, which dropped by two-thirds between 1988 and 1993.[38]

Feminists on both sides of the Wall had expected a renegotiation of gender relations upon unification, but that did not happen. Even the expected merger of feminist movements never occurred. East German feminists remained connected to the state while West German feminists pursued strategies outside of traditional political structures. Women's relationship to East Germany's communist state or West Germany's market economy proved more important for their identity than either their German ethnicity or their feminism. Thus, the two Germanys united but German feminists did not.[39]

## The Fall of the Soviet Union

Gorbachev's policies of openness and increased political participation also set the stage for political revolution at home. In 1990, the Soviet Communist Party was defeated in local elections, and Gorbachev presented Soviet citizens with a new constitution that abolished Communist Party rule. Boris Yeltsin (b. 1931), the newly elected president of what was then known as the Russian Federation, and other reformers then outlawed the Communist Party, wrestled authority from Gorbachev, and declared Russian independence. The rest of the former Soviet states followed soon after, declaring their independence and forming the short-lived Commonwealth of Independent States. Eventually, most of the former Soviet states became independent nations.

Not surprisingly, the end of the Communist monopoly on politics and the abolition of its quotas for female candidates led to a decline in female representation in government. During the 1970s and 1980s, 35 percent of people's deputies in republic-level supreme soviets were women. With free elections, that number fell to 5.4 percent, as most new political parties put few or no women on their candidate lists in 1993. Women made the most gains through the former Soviet Women's Committee (SWC). The SWC, which had been an arm of the Communist Party, renamed itself the Union of Women of Russia; in 1993, it joined forces with other women's organizations and fielded thirty-six candidates in elections under the movement Women of Russia. The party won 8.1 percent of the vote (twenty-three seats) in the Soviet parliament, the Duma, drawing the majority (82 percent) of its support from women. In 1994–95, Women of Russia deputy Alevtina Fedulova (b. ca. 1940) was elected to the high-profile position of deputy chair of the Duma. Politically, Women of Russia representatives declared themselves uncompromisingly centrist. Emphasizing consensus building, Women of Russia candidates asserted that this was not a

"political" organization and that they were more interested in getting work done than in engaging in partisan politics. However, their failure to affiliate with stronger political parties hindered their success. In the 1995 elections, the party ran eighty candidates, but won only 4.6 percent of the vote, seating only three deputies. Their campaign suffered from limited funds for television ads, and some candidates did not even have enough money to print posters. Moreover, during the campaign, candidates from other parties regularly asserted that women belonged at home, not in politics.[40]

The gender gap in Russian politics has persisted. By 1999, women constituted only 7 percent of the Duma's members, and many regional and local legislatures had no women representatives. However, the future looks somewhat brighter. In 2003, female politicians gained new visibility when voters elected Valentina Matvienko (b. 1949) governor of Saint Petersburg.

The transition to a market economy also hurt Soviet women. The economic crisis quickly worsened, and by 1993, one-third of the population, mostly women and children, lived below the poverty level.[41] As unemployment increased, Gorbachev supported female layoffs, saying that women should return to their "purely female mission."[42] Boris Yeltsin also promoted a more traditional view of women as mothers not workers, in part to ease tensions surrounding high female unemployment. On International Women's Day in 1998, President Yeltsin asserted that "Women's nature is built thus, to think of peace and your children's future, which means the future of our country and just because of this we must satisfy your whims today."[43] Not surprisingly, neither leader devoted much effort to halting the decline in female employment or the resulting economic crisis for women.

Although a few well-educated women have prospered in the new economy, most women in post-Soviet Russia face a myriad of obstacles. Ethnic conflict in Central Asia has produced extensive internal migration, and at least half of those migrants are women.[44] Persistent poverty has pushed birthrates to the lowest levels since World War II.[45] Abortion rates have remained very high. In 1996–97, there were two abortions for every birth.[46] With little political representation and a stagnant economy, the future for many women in the former Soviet Union seems dim.

Feminism brought women into politics by the millions in the 1970s and 1980s. As women in southern Europe experienced democracy for the first time in decades, feminists pressed the new governments for greater inclusion of women and equal rights. Not all the political transformations of the period were as generous to women. During the 1980s and 1990s, the transition to democracy in Eastern Europe, and the Soviet Union offered hope to millions of women, but the reality has often been disappointing. New political parties and governments failed to include women or address their concerns. The end of state-sponsored welfare systems disproportionately affected women and children, and in the worst cases, violence in postcommunist nations increased the pain and suffering of millions. As a result, many women have been unable to take advantage of the freedoms of democratic society.

## RECENT TRENDS IN GENDER AND POLITICS

Even in the West's oldest and most stable democracies, women have only recently begun to overcome the obstacles presented by male-dominated politics. The implementation of electoral quotas has been critical to increasing women's representation. Indeed, a few women have even succeeded in becoming heads of state. However, those success stories have not satisfied everyone. Dissatisfied with mainstream politics, women continue to join radical political organizations on both the left and the right.

### Electoral Quotas and Women's Representation

Feminists have argued that the lack of representation in legislative bodies compromises women's citizenship. To counteract centuries of political discrimination, European political parties instituted quotas that reserve a certain percentage of candidacies and positions for women. Initially, the quotas were voluntary. In France, beginning in 1974, the Socialist Party required that the proportion of women on internal governing bodies match the proportion of women in the membership. Although those quotas were rarely respected, the idea gained momentum and in the mid 1990s, many European governments passed reforms that required all parties to reserve candidacies for women. In 1994, Belgium guaranteed that one-third of candidates would be women, beginning with the elections of 1999. That same year, France passed a law that required equal numbers of men and women stand for office. The results were dramatic. In French municipal elections in 2001, the first election under the new law, the percentage of women in office rose from 22 percent to 47.5 percent. Similarly, because of a 2002 quota law, Greek women more than doubled their representation, making up 14 percent of Parliament in 2004. That same year, Anna Psarouda-Benaki (b. 1934) became the first woman elected as the Speaker of the Greek parliament.[47]

Although political quotas has been quite controversial, they have proven to be quite successful. In Denmark, some leftist parties ended the quota system once women's representation of 40 percent became common. The Danish have also expanded quotas to other parts of government. In 1985, the Danish parliament mandated that any organization represented on a committee had to nominate both a woman and a man for each position, and it would then be up to the minister responsible to select among the candidates in a manner that would achieve a gender balance. In 1991, legislatures extended the pursuit of gender parity to all government institutions and state bodies. Similarly, a 1995 Finnish law requires at least a 60–40 gender ratio on all consultative councils, committees, and other decision-making bodies.

With or without quotas, women do not tend to vote for female candidates merely because they are women. Studies of women's political affiliation and voting patterns have shown that piety, ethnicity, income level, marital status, education, participation in the labor force, and national political issues all influence women's electoral choices just as they influence men's. In the early 1970s, women in Europe tended to identify themselves as slightly more conservative than their male counterparts; however, the size of the gender gap varied considerably. In Italy and Germany, women were much less likely to support leftist parties than men, while in the Netherlands, they were only slightly less likely to do so. In the United States, women were actually more likely to support leftist parties than men. By 1981, the gender gap had closed considerably so that, in much of Europe, women were just as likely to vote for leftist candidates as men were, and by 1990, European women had moved to the left of men except in Spain and Ireland. The traditional gender gap, in which women are more conservative than men, persists among elderly voters, while the "modern" gender gap, in which women's voting varies little from men's, is most visible among younger voters.[48]

## Women at the Helm

Outside of quotas, few women have been able to rise to leadership positions in male-dominated political parties. In the United States, where individuals, not parties, run for office, both the Republican and the Democratic parties have each had a number of women run for president in the past forty years. However, most of their candidacies were short-lived, and many withdrew before the nominating convention. The most prominent female candidates for the U.S. presidency have been Senator Margaret Chase Smith (in 1964) and former labor secretary Elizabeth Dole (in 2000), both of whom ran unsuccessfully for the nomination of the Republican Party, and African American congresswoman Shirley Chisholm (1972) and Congresswoman Patricia Schroeder (1988) who ran for the Democratic nomination. When Chisholm chose Frances "Sissy" Farenthold as her running mate, they became the only female ticket to run for the nomination of a major party. Congresswoman Geraldine Ferraro (b. 1935), chosen by Democratic presidential nominee Walter Mondale (b. 1928) in 1984 as his vice-presidential candidate, is the only woman to have received the nomination of a major party. Although they receive little press coverage, women have regularly run for president from smaller parties. Native American Winona LaDuke (b. 1959) ran for vice president from the Green Party in 1996 and 2000. In 1988 and 1992, Dr. Leonora B. Fulani (b. 1950) was the first woman and first African American to appear on the presidential ballot in all fifty states as a National Alliance Party candidate. Among others, the Socialist Party and the Workers' World Party have also fielded female candidates. Although few Americans would recognize their names, more than thirty women have run for president since 1964.

The European political system has allowed more women to rise to leadership positions (see **Women's Lives:** Gro Harlem Brundtland: Politician and Women's Rights Activist). In parliamentary systems, the leader of the party that wins a majority of legislative seats heads the government as the prime minister. Margaret Thatcher (b. 1925) became the leader of Great Britain's Conservative Party in 1975. When the party won a majority in the House of Commons in 1979, she became prime minister and was the longest-serving prime minister in English history. Often referred to as the "Iron Lady," Thatcher was widely disliked by feminists because she denied the contribution of the women's movement to her career, asserting that her success was due solely to her own hard work. In addition, her conservative economic policies were at odds with the priorities of many female activists. She privatized much of the state-owned industry, which led to high unemployment, and dismantled parts of the state welfare system increasing poverty across the country. In 2005, Angela Merkel became the first female chancellor of Germany, representing the conservative Christian Democratic party. She also has demonstrated little interest in women's rights or feminist issues.

However, most female heads of state have represented center or leftist parties that had closer ties to women and gender issues. Mary Robinson (b. 1944) of the Irish Labour Party was elected president of Ireland in 1990. Her campaign included an extensive grassroots effort and mobilized the support of women across the political spectrum. Ireland also has the distinction of being the only country in which a woman succeeded another when, in 1997, Mary McAleese (b. 1951) became the new president of Ireland. She won reelection in 2004.

Finland is the only country that has had a woman president and prime minister at the same time. Tarja Halonen (b. 1943) became Finland's first female president in 2000, and in 2003, Anneli Jaatteenmaki (b. 1955) came to power as the prime minister. Jaatteenmaki's cabinet, which was half female, demonstrated her dedication to gender equity. However, Jaatteenmaki was forced to resign after only two months in office due to a scandal over her use of secret documents during the election. These women leaders benefited from an increased acceptance of female leadership in European society as well as changes in electoral laws.

Whether or not female leaders view themselves as feminists, they have a dramatic impact on the gender ideologies of their nations. Men in politics become accustomed to working for women. Male and female citizens see women working in positions of authority, respected internationally, and guiding their nations' policies on everything from childcare to nuclear weapons.

## Women in Radical Politics

In the past two decades, women's increased visibility in electoral politics has not dissuaded a few women from joining radical political organizations on both the left and the right. In fact, women in these groups may have benefited from the success of their mainstream peers. For nearly forty years, ETA, *Basque Homeland and Freedom*, has carried out a bloody campaign for Basque independence from Spain. ETA's bombings and assassinations have killed more than 850 people since 1968. Although for most of its history, men dominated the organization, authorities believe that in recent years, ETA has been recruiting more women into its ranks and more women have appeared in positions of authority. In 2002, arrests of women associated with ETA rose by 30 percent. For example, Spanish authorities charged Nerea Bengoa with disrupting the EU conference in Barcelona in 2002 and planning the assassination of politicians, police officers, and journalists. Spanish judges sentenced Idoia López Riaño, known as "The Tigress," to more than twenty years in jail for her role in dozens of killings. The increase in female activity may be connected to increased radical activism by a younger generation of women, or it may be because many of the male leaders of the group are currently in prison.

Since 1980, Europe has also witnessed the growth of right-wing radical parties. They tend to be highly nationalistic and xenophobic, opposed to European integration, and supportive of traditional gender roles for women. Between 1984 and 1997, Jean-Marie Le Pen's (b. 1928) National Front in France won at least 10 percent of the vote in national elections and over 15 percent in the 1995 presidential election. The National Front's nationalist rhetoric calls for stricter immigration policies, less state intervention, and the defense of French identity against outsiders, including Muslim immigrants and institutions such as the European Union. As many as one-third of French voters have voiced their agreement with the party's ideas.[49] Although the National Front has found more support among men than among women, it has put forward a number of female candidates, although nearly all have run in place of imprisoned or deceased husbands. Ironically, in the 2002 election, the National Front put forward more female candidates (49 percent) than any of the major parties despite its message that women are better suited for domestic work than for politics.[50]

Austria came to international attention when the far right Freedom Party won enough seats to become a member of the ruling coalition in 2000. Under the leadership of Jörg Haider (b. 1950), the Freedom Party promotes a platform similar to that of the National Front in France. Haider first appointed his personal secretary, Susanne Riess-Passer (b. 1961), as Austria's first woman vice chancellor. When he later resigned as head of the party, she was his hand-picked successor. Herbert Haupt (b. 1947), the Freedom Party's minister of Women's Affairs in 2001, declared that women's liberation had ended sexism and that men were the primary victims of discrimination. He abolished the separate women's ministry and set up a new department dedicated to "men's issues" that would work with existing organizations and advice centers for oppressed Austrian males. Austrian novelist and playwright Elfriede Jelinek (b. 1946), winner of the 2004 Nobel Prize for Literature, has been an outspoken opponent of the Freedom Party. In 2000, she withheld performances of her plays from all Austrian theaters as long as Haider's party was part of the government.

Both France's National Front and Austria's Freedom Party promote maternalist policies as means to counter perceived immigration problems and have encouraged anti-immigrant and anti-Semitic activity. Supporters have desecrated Jewish graves and vandalized public spaces with racist graffiti. They have used violence to intimidate immigrant women and their families. Although

## Gro Harlem Brundtland, Politician and Human Rights Activist

Gro Harlem Brundtland's international activism began when she was still a child in Norway. Her father, a physician and activist, encouraged her to join the Children's section of the Norwegian Labor Movement.

Gro pursued a career in medicine, first obtaining a medical degree from the University of Oslo in 1963 and then a master's in public health from Harvard University in 1965. She then returned to Oslo to work for the Ministry of Health for nine years, focusing on children's health issues. At the same time, she raised her four young children.

Brundtland's emphasis on public service and longtime political activism quickly led to a second career as a leader in Norway's leftist Labour Party. During the early 1970s, she developed both an international reputation as a public health specialist and garnered considerable political support at home. In 1974, when the Labour Party came to power, she was named minister of the environment.

In 1981, Brundtland became Norway's first female and youngest prime minister at the age of forty-one. Over the next fifteen years, she served as prime minister twice more, in 1986–1989 and 1990–1996. During her terms, Brundtland demonstrated her commitment to placing women in leadership positions, naming women to eight of eighteen cabinet positions. Her political influence continued even when she was not in power, as the Conservative Party maintained significant numbers of women in cabinet positions.

In 1983, United Nations secretary general Javier de Perez de Cuellar asked Brundtland to form and chair the World Commission on the Environment and Development, which became known as the Brundtland Commission. Under her leadership, the Brundtland Commission was critical in formulating the idea of sustainable development. Sustainable development works to help people, particularly in developing nations, meet their needs without compromising the quality of life of future generations. The Commission emphasized the interconnectedness of environmental issues, social justice, and economic development. Its recommendations led to the Earth Summit held in Rio de Janeiro in 1992.

Brundtland has also been a powerful activist for women's rights and a vocal proponent of efforts to improve women's social and economic status around the world. In her closing address to the United Nation's Conference on Women in Beijing in 1994, she rallied the participants with her proclamation that, "We now need a tidal change—Women will no longer accept the role as second-rate citizens."[1]

Brundtland resigned as prime minister in 1996, and two years later was elected the first female director general of the World Health Organization (WHO) headquartered in Geneva. At the helm of the largest international health organization, Brundtland emphasized violence and poverty as public health issues. She worked to improve women's health around the world, halt the spread of tuberculosis and AIDS, and increase awareness of the dangers of tobacco.

Brundtland made extensive reforms within the organization. When she reorganized the administration, she appointed women as five of the nine executive directors. Her hard work has been widely applauded and she has received numerous awards. In 2003, the journal *Scientific American* recognized Brundtland as its Policy Leader of the Year for coordinating a rapid worldwide response to stem outbreaks of SARS in Asia.

Despite the accolades, Brundtland served only one term at WHO. Since 2003 she has continued her public service, speaking out on behalf of women, the environment, and the health of men, women, and children around the world.

---

[1] www.un.org/esa/gopher-data/conf/fwcw/conf/gov/950915135459.txt

Source: Gro Harlem Brundtland, *Madam Prime Minister: A Life in Power and Politics* (New York: Farrar, Strauss, and Giroux, 2002).

they promote traditional values, those values apply only to members of the white majority.

Until the 1990s, women could not translate their right to vote into equal political representation. However, in the past decade, electoral quotas have done much to rectify the gender gap in national politics. Indeed, a few women have transcended traditional gender expectations as leaders of their nations. While women have made great strides in the political arena, on the edges of the political spectrum, a tiny minority of women have resorted to violence and a rhetoric of hate to express their dissatisfaction with the political status quo.

# GENDER POLITICS BEYOND NATIONS

In addition to engaging in politics at home, feminist activists have taken advantage of the high-visibility forums provided by the European Union and the United Nations. These institutions have allowed women to move beyond the constraints of national politics and have brought gender issues to international attention. Women have also become prominent in an expanding array of nongovernmental organizations (NGOs), which offer women the opportunity to develop unique approaches to issues affecting their lives and the lives of women around the world.

## The UN and the Internationalization of the Women's Movement

In the past forty years, the United Nations has focused extensive attention on women's issues and has been a key force in bringing together women from around the world. The UN began its women's activism by declaring 1975 the International Year of the Woman and the decade 1975–1985 as the Decade of Women. Subsequently, the UN has actively pursued improvements in women's standards of living and women's rights around the world.

The International Year of the Woman began with the first UN-sponsored international women's conference in Mexico City. Officials chose Helvi Sipilä (b. 1915), a Finnish lawyer and representative to the UN Commission on the Status of Women (CSW) since 1960, as assistant secretary general for Social Development and Humanitarian Affairs to head the UN's programs for the year. The conference themes were equality, development, and peace. Five thousand representatives attended the conference from 133 nations and hundreds of NGOs. Representatives from developed and developing nations debated the best approaches to achieving equality.

Despite ongoing conflicts between rich and poor nations and ideological rifts between the Soviet Union and the United States, attendees adopted a fourteen-point plan for attaining equality for women, and they drafted and adopted the UN Convention on Eliminating Discrimination Against Women. Signatory nations agreed to provide legal equality for women, prohibit sex discrimination, and establish institutions to protect women against discrimination. During the opening ceremony of the second UN conference held in 1980 in Copenhagen, sixty-four nations signed the document, and by December 1981 it had the twenty ratifications necessary to give the Convention force as a treaty. The treaty's ratification occurred faster than any previous human rights convention. As of 2004, 177 countries had ratified or acceded to the treaty; the United States is the only Western nation that has not approved it.

Successive UN conferences in Nairobi, Kenya (1985), and Beijing, China (1995), emphasized the problem of violence against women and economic concerns. In December 1993, the UN adopted the Declaration on the Elimination of Violence Against Women, which outlined actions that governments and communities should take to prevent such violence, and a year later, the UN appointed a Special Rapporteur on Violence Against Women, who seeks and receives information on violence against women, its causes, and its consequences. The Rapporteur recommends ways to eliminate the violence and reports to the UN Commission on Human Rights. In addition, since the late 1970s, the UN has worked with foreign aid donor nations to establish Women in Development (WID) offices to help focus money, attention, and energy on the specific needs of women in developing nations.

Although no woman has ever been the general secretary of the United Nations, in recent years, women have held high-profile positions in the organization. Mary Robinson, the former president of Ireland, became the UN Chief High Commissioner on Human Rights in 1997. During her five years in the position, Robinson worked to end human rights violations around the world, including East Timor and Afghanistan. Canadian lawyer Louise Arbour (b. 1947) was appointed to the same position in 2004.

Women have also played critical roles in the International Criminal Court in the Netherlands, which hears cases of human rights violations from around the world. Women's prominence is largely due to the Women's Caucus for Gender Justice, an international feminist organization that successfully pushed for the tribunal to define a broad array of sexual crimes as war crimes, including sexual exploitation, rape, murder, and female genital mutilation, and for the tribunal to include female judges. In 1996, Louise Arbour became the chief prosecutor of war crimes for Rwanda and the former Yugoslavia at the tribunal. She was replaced in 1999 by Italian lawyer Carla del Ponte (b. 1947). Del Ponte is responsible for bringing former Serbian leader Slobodan Milošević to trial for war crimes as well as for prosecuting Rwandan leaders for genocide.

## Gender Politics in the European Union

In the first two decades after World War II, European nations cooperated in a variety of transnational organizations and agreements to strengthen European unity and economic power. By the late 1960s, those efforts had coalesced into two major organizations, the European Communities and the European Parliament. In 1992, the Maastricht Treaty officially created the European Union (EU), and by 2004, the EU had twenty-five member states with nearly five hundred million citizens, making it a powerful economic and political institution (see Map 16.2).

The EU is governed by an executive body, the European Commission (EC), and a legislative body, the European Parliament. The presidency of the EC rotates among member nations and the other members of the Commission are nominated for five-year terms by member governments.

Originally, national legislatures chose members of the European Parliament (MEPs), but since 1979, they have been chosen through direct elections held in each member nation. The EU has developed policies and passed legislation on a wide range of issues from agriculture and trade to culture. On January 1, 2002, twelve of fifteen member nations adopted a common currency, the euro.

The EU has a mixed record on gender issues. Since the 1970s the EU has promoted gender equality by requiring member nations to pass provisions enforcing equal pay, equal employment, and equality in social security. In 1997, with the adoption of the Treaty of Amsterdam, the EU rejected all forms of discrimination; however, although the treaty empowers the EC to take action to combat discrimination in member nations, it does not oblige it to do so, and any action requires a unanimous vote. Thus, although gender equity and equal protection are implicit in the European constitution, the EC has little ability to enforce antidiscrimination policies.[51] Indeed, the EU has only partially attained its goals for gender equity in hiring and promotion within its own staff, and in 2005, only seven women served on the twenty-five member EC

In contrast, women have broad representation in the European Parliament. Not only have women stood as candidates to the EP in greater numbers than in national parliaments, but they have also won more seats. In the first direct elections in 1979, women made up 17 percent of MEPs and that number doubled by 1999. In the EP, women's rights activists have benefited from the opportunity to bypass restrictive national bureaucracies, laws, and cultures. One French female MEP said, "Here at the European level, it has always been relatively easy because there have always been a relatively large number of women. . . . I think that this Parliament provides the least misogynistic surroundings that I have ever experienced during my time in politics."[52] Many women see the EP as a positive setting for the discussion of women's issues.

However, many political scientists assert that parties may encourage the candidacies of women to the EP because they do not see it as an effective center of power. Parties thus get the political benefits of endorsing female candidates without placing them in positions of authority. Moreover, the

*Map 16.2* **Contemporary Europe.** At peace and free of cold war divisions, Europe in the twenty-first century is working to transcend national boundaries with the expansion of the European Union.

EP may not be as gender equitable as many avow. Female MEPs face serious personal challenges. They have to travel regularly to Brussels as well as to other locations. Thus, women cannot stand as candidates unless they are wealthy enough to afford full-time childcare or fortunate enough to have the strong cooperation of their spouses. Parliamentary provisions include nothing about maternity leave. Female MEPs have to delay bearing children or feel pressure to resign if they become pregnant during their terms.[53]

Despite the high numbers of female representatives, European women have shown limited support for the EU. According to a 2000 poll, only 47 percent of women favor their country's membership in EU in contrast to 55 percent of men. Moreover, women are less likely than men to vote in EU elections and have been very active in campaigns against European unification.[54]

## Nongovernmental Activism

The EU and the UN are only part of women's international political activity. In the past thirty years, non-governmental organizations (NGOs) have proven to be important means of organizing for women. In particular, women have played prominent roles in nongovernmental activism in the environmental and disarmament movements. Women often joined together to take aggressive action to resolve local environmental problems. In 1971, women in Swansea, Wales, blocked the entrance to a factory that had been polluting a nearby canal with industrial waste. Similarly, in 1976, Lois Gibbs and her neighbors formed the Love Canal Homeowners Association when they realized that their homes in New York had been built atop a toxic waste dump. Her work led to the creation of the Superfund, a U.S. government program to clean up toxic waste. Such local action developed into *ecofeminism,* a movement that emphasizes the connection between the oppression of women and human domination of nature. One prominent ecofeminist organization is the Netherlands-based Women in Europe for a Common Future (WECF), which has worked on a diverse array of projects, including nuclear contamination in Russia and Central Asia, sanitation and safe water in Romania, and prenatal care in Armenia. Grassroots organizations have become a

critical part of women's democratic participation, as they allow women to transcend and manipulate ideas of feminist and nonfeminist, public and private, to suit their political goals.[55]

Women have also been active in international attempts to end the proliferation of nuclear weapons. One of the most ardent members of the disarmament movement was Alva Myrdal (1902–1986), a Swedish diplomat. She worked for twelve years as the only female delegate to negotiations in Geneva, Switzerland, to end the spread of nuclear weapons. Her best-selling book *The Game of Disarmament: How the United States and the Soviet Union Run the Arms Race* (1976) decried the irrationality of the arms race. In 1982, Myrdal received the Nobel Peace Prize for her work. Her work influenced many women to get involved in antinuclear campaigns. In 1981, Ann Petitt organized British women to protesting the North Atlantic Treaty Organization's (NATO) decision to house cruise missiles at Greenham Common military base near Newbury, Berkshire. Protesters formed a permanent Peace Camp that became home to hundreds of women. Eventually, the United States housed nearly one hundred nuclear weapons at the site. Although they failed to prevent the placement of the weapons, the women at Greenham Common were not dissuaded. In December 1982, thirty thousand women joined hands to "embrace the base" in one of the largest antinuclear protests of its time. Greenham Common became the site of regular protests and arrests. Finally, the women's determination and the end of the cold war brought the removal of the cruise missiles. In 1987, U.S. president Reagan and Soviet president Gorbachev signed the Intermediate-range Nuclear Forces (INF) Treaty, which reduced both powers' nuclear arsenals, and the United States removed its missiles from Greenham Common in 1991. Women remained at the Peace Camp until 2000 in continued protest against nuclear arms.

In 1991, American Jodi Williams (b. 1950) began a vigorous campaign against the deployment of antipersonnel land mines, which kill and maim thousands of innocent civilians each year. Williams and her International Campaign to Ban Land Mines (ICBL) worked with veterans' organizations, victims, and more than eleven hundred NGOs from around the world to promote a

**DEMONSTRATORS AT GREENHAM COMMON (1983).** Female demonstrators blocked the gates of the Greenham Common Airbase, England. They tied themselves together with string to protest the decision to house nuclear weapons at the base. The anti-nuclear protest at the base was largely women led and continued until 2000. *(Bettmann/Corbis)*

comprehensive ban on the weapons. Activists, including Princess Diana of Great Britain (1961–1997), brought the issue to worldwide attention. In September 1997, representatives from 121 nations convened for more than two weeks to negotiate a comprehensive international land mine treaty. Known as the Ottawa Treaty, the ban prohibits the production, transfer, stockpiling, and use of antipersonnel land mines of any sort around the world. Williams was awarded the 1997 Nobel Peace Prize for her efforts, and by 2004, 137 nations had signed the treaty.

Women have also taken independent grassroots action to resolve ongoing conflicts in Europe. For decades, Catholics and Protestants have waged violent and destructive civil war in British-ruled Northern Ireland. Catholics want to be united with the Republic of Ireland, while Protestants hope to remain affiliated with the United Kingdom. Since the late 1960s violence between the Irish Republican Army and Protestant Unionists has left more than three thousand dead and displaced more than thirty thousand. In Belfast, Protestants and Catholics live in clearly designated and visibly secured sections of the city. The violence has hindered economic growth, leaving women and children in poverty, and made it very difficult to accomplish daily activities like taking children to school. Despite the immediate impact on their lives, women have been almost completely absent from decades of negotiations to end the conflict. However, in recent years, activist women have formed the Women's Support Network, an alliance of Catholic and Protestant women, to pressure political parties to take women's political action and needs seriously and to bridge divisions among women.[56]

Women have become increasingly important to the resolution of international conflicts. In 2000, the UN Security Council passed resolution 1325 reaffirming, "the important role of women in the prevention and resolution of conflicts and in peace-building, and stressing the importance of their equal participation and full involvement in all efforts for the maintenance and promotion of peace and security, and the need to increase their role in decision-making with regard to conflict prevention and resolution." From pollution to war, women's grassroots organizing has dramatically changed the world of international politics.

Women's political participation has been transformed at both local and international levels. The EU and the UN have provided women with new forums for political action and powerful institutions to deal with women's issues. Closer to home, women have become key actors in the expansion of NGOs and grassroots organizations. They have devoted time, energy, and money to ending conflict in war-torn regions, improving the environment, and lessening the threat of nuclear destruction.

## CHANGES IN THE FAMILY AND AT WORK

The feminist movement's push for reproductive rights and legal equality has had dramatic implications for Western families and women's economic activity. Women bear fewer children and marry later. At the same time, demands for equal treatment have opened new opportunities in higher education and in the workplace. More women spend more years living and working independently than ever before.

### A New Demographic Regime

Since 1970 the most dramatic changes in women's lives have arisen from their ability to control their own fertility. Although in 1970 most women bore their first child around age twenty-three, by 2000 most European and many American women

waited until they were nearly thirty years old. In the Netherlands, Spain, and Italy, half of all births were to women over thirty.[57]

Better access to contraception has played a key role in delaying women's fertility. Across Europe, more than 70 percent of married women use some form of contraception. However, other factors have also influenced fertility patterns. In wealthier nations, many women delay childbearing in order to pursue educational and career opportunities. Lagging economies and high rates of female unemployment and underemployment have made it difficult for women in southern and eastern Europe to afford children. As a result, birthrates have declined substantially. In 1970, a European woman had an average of 2.38 children. By 2004, that number had fallen to 1.48, but in Italy, Greece, and Spain, countries where women have gained access to contraceptives relatively recently, birthrates are even lower; women have an average of only 1.25 children each. European fertility rates have been below replacement level (more people die than children are born) since 1974.[58]

Women who remain permanently childless are a small but growing part of the population. Childlessness among Irish and English women who were born in 1960 was nearly double that of women born two decades earlier. The majority of childless women are not professional women, as is often the stereotype, but instead women in middle- and lower-level jobs. Moreover, childless women in high-status jobs do not identify their career aspirations as the main reason that they did not have children.[59]

While many women have chosen to limit their fertility, medical advances have allowed many couples with fertility problems to bear children. In 1978, using in vitro fertilization (IVF), Lesley Brown gave birth to her daughter Louise, the first test tube baby. Doctors removed an egg from Lesley's ovary, fertilized it with her husband's sperm, and reinserted it into Lesley's womb. In recent years, children have been born from frozen embryos and sperm, including the embryos and sperm of deceased parents. These fertility procedures have forced legal systems to reconsider the legal definitions of fatherhood and motherhood and have led societies to reassess their expectations about maternity and paternity. Surrogate motherhood has engendered custody battles over children born from the egg of one woman but gestated in the body of another. Divorcing couples have sued over the rights to eggs preserved for IVF. Nations are wrangling over the expansion of anonymous sperm and egg donation, unsure about issues of kinship, responsibility, and rights. Recently, some menopausal and postmenopausal women have provoked controversy by employing these technologies to extend their fertility beyond their bodies' natural limits.

Women's organizations across Europe and the United States have been active in lobbying for and against state regulation of these and other new reproductive technologies. Many are concerned about potential abuses, include cloning and trafficking in human eggs and sperm. In 2003, concerns over medical abuses and pressure from the Catholic Church led the Italian parliament to limit access to medically-assisted procreation. The law only allows heterosexual and married couples access to artificial insemination. The law also bans surrogate motherhood and the use of semen or ova from third parties or for single people or same-sex couples. Women's and lesbian rights organizations have protested this very restrictive and discriminatory legislation.

## New Relationships

In addition to bearing fewer children, since 1970 more women have chosen to marry later or not to marry at all. In 1970, women's mean age at first marriage in Europe was twenty-three years old; by 2000 that average had risen to nearly twenty-eight years old. In Switzerland and the Scandinavian countries, the mean age at first marriage is more than thirty. Consequently, in 2000, fewer than half of women aged twenty-five to twenty-nine were married (except in the United States and Belgium).[60] Late marriage has meant that many women are economically independent for at least part of their lives and, as mentioned above, this development has led to a substantial decrease in fertility rates.

Overall, nearly 10 percent of women in western Europe never marry. Some women have found that their career goals and/or educational level have made it difficult to find a desirable partner. A small percentage of women have entered lesbian relationships, but the majority of single women have chosen cohabitation over marriage (see below).

There has also been an increase in the numbers of women bearing children outside of marriage. In 1980, more than 90 percent of children in the EU were born to married couples; however, by 1997, one-quarter of births took place outside of marriage. In Sweden and Iceland, more than half of births occur outside marriage, and in Denmark and Finland, more than 40 percent.[61] Unmarried women bear children because, among other reasons, changing attitudes have made nonmarital sex more acceptable. Society is also more tolerant of motherhood outside of marriage than in the past. As few countries retain any discrimination against children born outside of wedlock, pregnant single women feel less pressure to hide their pregnancies and give their children up for adoption. Moreover, medically-assisted reproduction allows lesbians and well-to-do women who have not yet found partners to bear children without male intervention. Finally, as more women remain single longer, more women are engaged in relationships that produce children but do not culminate in marriage.

Since 1980 young European couples have preferred cohabitation (also known as consensual unions) over marriage. In many cases, cohabitation is a transitional relationship between singleness and marriage, while in others, couples cohabit without intending to marry. In the United Kingdom, cohabitation rates jumped from 16 to 32 percent between 1985 and 2001.[62] In most of Europe, the majority of couples between the ages of twenty and twenty-four cohabit. However, Europeans' preference for cohabitation has not caused a decline in marriage rates, as most cohabitating couples eventually marry. In the Netherlands, about 70 percent of cohabitating couples marry at some point in their relationships.[63] However, in Scandinavia and eastern Europe (especially the Czech Republic, Latvia, Bulgaria, and many of the former Soviet republics), the number of marriages contracted annually has declined substantially in recent years.

Western governments have begun to recognize these nonmarital relationships, creating or expanding the legal rights granted to heterosexual partnerships. Although nearly all European nations have some type of domestic partnership arrangement, the legal status of couples in such relationships varies considerably. In Belgium, cohabiting couples can register with authorities and sign a cohabitation contract that provides for mutual maintenance and other issues relating to the illness or death of a partner. The law includes provisions both for mutual dissolution of the relationship and for court intervention should a couple decide to separate. In France, the 1999 Civil Solidarity Pact removed legal distinctions between married and unmarried couples regardless of gender, granting homosexual couples and unmarried heterosexual couples the same rights as married couples.

Changes in attitudes toward divorce have also affected millions of women's relationships. In 1965, almost half of all Dutch people were opposed to divorce, but by 1977, that number had declined to 11.5 percent.[64] Moreover, before the mid 1970s, divorce was difficult to obtain. In Spain and Italy, the Catholic Church allowed for divorce only in limited circumstances. Although most other countries allowed for divorce, they restricted women's rights to marital property, their ability to remarry, and/or their custody over their children. As a result, many women felt forced to remain in unhappy or even dangerous marriages. However, since the mid 1970s family law reforms across Europe have made divorce easier for women. For instance, in 1978, Austrian legislators finally granted women the right to property acquired during the marriage. Many countries have made ending a marriage easier by adopting no-fault divorce, in which the spouse does not have to prove that the other spouse was to blame for the end of the marriage. Even predominately Catholic countries have reformed their civil codes to allow for civil divorce. Many nations have added welfare programs that help recently divorced women care for children and make the transition to economic independence.

As a result of these changes in legal norms and social attitudes, at least 40 percent of marriages in the United Kingdom and Switzerland end in divorce. In Sweden and the United States, half of all marriages end in divorce. A rise in divorce rates has even become evident in southern and eastern Europe.[65] The increase in divorces has led to an increase in remarriages. In Denmark and the United Kingdom, almost 30 percent of marriages are second marriages for at least one partner.[66] However, many women do not remarry after divorce, preferring instead to cohabit in successive relationships. With increases in women's education and participation in the labor force (see below), more divorced women are able to support themselves.

Across Europe, women head slightly less than 30 percent of households, but in Slovenia, Denmark, and Finland more than 40 percent of households are headed by women.[67] In many nations, these single-parent households are at great risk of falling into poverty, as single women are more likely to be unemployed and because nations tie many social security benefits, including childcare, to employment. Ironically, despite social pressure for mothers to remain at home, the children of stay-at-home mothers often receive fewer benefits than children of working mothers.[68]

## Aging

These changes in fertility and families have serious consequences for women. As birthrates decline and life spans increase, the European population is growing older. Nearly half of all Spaniards are over forty years old. Women are often responsible for caring for elderly relatives, as few European countries have sufficient programs for their aging populations or aiding caregivers. A woman in western Europe can expect to live to be eighty years old and is likely to outlive her husband or partner by at least five years. Thus, more women spend more of their adult lives either single, divorced, or widowed, and elderly women frequently suffer economic and social discrimination.

Women still typically spend fewer years in the workforce than men, earn less than men, and combine paid and unpaid work for much of their lives. Therefore, their pensions are significant lower than men's. Moreover, women generally spend longer in old age than men, unable to work and surviving on smaller pensions. Finally, many state pension and welfare systems discriminate against women. As a result, many older women live in poverty. The United States has the highest rates of poverty among elderly women in the developed world, and in Poland, women seventy years and older and living alone have a poverty rate more than twice as high as those living in households headed by men of the same age.[69] Only Norway has worked to mitigate the discrimination against older women. Since 1992 at-home parents of either sex responsible for children under age seven, adults in need of care, and the mentally handicapped receive three pension points a year. Thus, full-time caregivers (both male and female) will receive an adequate pension despite the fact that they have not been earning wages. However, Norway is the exception, and as the Western population ages, older women will increasingly fall into poverty.

## New Opportunities

With smaller families and longer life spans, women now spend less of their adult lives caring for children and devote more time to education and careers. The expansion of educational opportunities for women has been key to women's economic successes. Compulsory education through high school has led to almost 100 percent literacy across western Europe. Some nations have made enormous strides. As recently as 1981, 24 percent of Greek women were illiterate and only 3.5 percent attended university.[70] By 2000, female illiteracy had fallen to 4 percent and women made up 50 percent of Greek university students.[71] Until 1970 many major U.S. universities did not allow women to enroll, including Columbia University in New York, Harvard University, and the University of Virginia, and certain academic programs did not admit married women. In a famous incident, Luci Baines Johnson (b. 1947), the daughter of President Lyndon Johnson (1963–1968) was refused readmission to Georgetown University's nursing program after she got married. Other programs refused to grant financial aid to married women. Into the 1970s, Stanford University admitted only one woman for every three men.[72]

During the early 1970s, the U.S. Congress passed a flurry of legislative reforms, including Title IX of the Higher Education Act, which prohibited sex discrimination in education. In addition to forcing changes in many universities' admissions policies, one of the most important results of this statute was increased funding for women's athletics at every level of education. As a result, women's participation in sports expanded tremendously. European nations have also increased women's enrollment, and by 2000, women outnumbered men in universities across the United States and Europe (except Switzerland). Indeed, women make up 60 percent or more of university students in places as diverse as the United States, Albania, and Iceland.[73] Increasingly, women make up more than half of law and medical students in European and American universities.

## Gender Equity in the Workplace

Late ages at marriage and women's ability to control their own fertility made it both easier and necessary for women to work. Women spend fewer years caring for children than ever before. Whereas the average woman in 1900 could expect to spend half her life in her role as mother, by 2000, she would spend less than one-quarter of her lifetime raising children.[74] Since 1970 millions of women have entered the paid workforce, and by 1998, women made up slightly more than half of all workers.

Changes in the workplace have contributed to the increases in female employment. By 1980, the majority of jobs were in services and industry, and fewer people were employed in agriculture. The proportion of self-employed workers also fell considerably. The decline in agriculture and family-owned businesses significantly decreased the numbers of women engaged in unpaid labor and both freed and forced women into paid work.

In the United Kingdom, women's organizations successfully pushed for the passage of the Equal Pay Act in 1970, the Sex Discrimination Act (1975), and a new law that granted homemakers full pension rights. The Employment Protection Act (1975) made maternity leave a right, prohibited dismissal for pregnancy, and preserved women's jobs for twenty-nine weeks after giving birth. Similar changes in employment laws took place in other parts of Europe. However, equal pay laws do not always apply to all occupations, and discrimination still hinders women at work.

The characteristics of working women have also changed. Whereas traditionally young single women made up the majority of the female workforce, since 1970 few young women leave school for work and most spend more years in school than ever before. Indeed, the single largest change in the workplace has been the increase in working married women and mothers. In Canada, the United States, and in much of the EU, more than 50 percent of mothers with children under three are employed.[75] Moreover, fewer women leave the workforce permanently to bear children. In the Netherlands in the early 1980s, only one-quarter of women continued working after bearing their first child. In the next ten years, that number doubled.[76]

Under pressure from women's rights organizations, many welfare states and businesses have begun to reform their policies to facilitate married women's employment; however, the results are mixed. Many offer extended maternity and paternity leaves, although most are unpaid. Only the Scandinavian countries offered parental leave with reasonable pay. Flexible work hours and opportunities for telecommuting have eased the stress of many working mothers, but few nations provide any childcare facilities for young children and infants.[77] In response, women increasingly rely on low-paid part-time work and short-term contracts to ease the conflict between work and family. The lack of childcare has also led to high rates of unemployment among single mothers. Too often, childcare costs are such a high percentage of their income that women cannot afford to work outside the home. Recently, European researchers have demonstrated that although parenthood has little effect on men's earnings and employment rates, it is a key factor in women's lower pay and lower levels of employment. The more children a woman has, the less likely she is to work outside the home and the more likely she is to suffer a decline in earnings if she continues to work there.[78]

Male employers often discriminate against women as they attempt to rise through the professional hierarchy. In many professions, women hit "the glass ceiling," a point in their organization beyond which women are not promoted. In 2003, only eight Fortune 500 companies had female chief executive officers (CEOs). Even high-profile CEOs like Carly Fiorina (b. 1954), the former head of Hewlett Packard, made substantially less than their male peers. A *Business Week* survey of 825 U.S. companies found that for the twenty highest-paid male executives, total compensation averaged $138.5 million, while the twenty best-paid females made an average of $11.2 million

apiece.[79] In Australia in 2002, only one of the top two hundred companies had a female CEO.[80] The transition to capitalism has meant that the glass ceiling is less evident in eastern Europe and Russia; a recent survey noted that 89 percent of Russian companies had women in senior management roles compared with only 75 percent in the United States.[81]

Women's increased participation in the workforce initially improved women's wage rates in comparison with men's, but recently that trend has been reversed. In the United Kingdom, women's wages were only 65.4 percent of men's in 1970 but rose to 75.7 percent of men's in 1977. However, women's wages began to decline after that.[82] In the United States in 1970, women made only 60 cents for every dollar men earned. By 2002, the gap had closed dramatically—women made 75 cents for every dollar earned by men—but in 2003, that number declined to 72 cents.[83] Interestingly, Portugal has the most egalitarian wage structure in the West. In 2003, women made 95 cents for every dollar made by a man.[84]

Women's wages have remained low not only because of the increasing numbers of women engaged in part-time work but also because women remained segregated into low-paying work, including retail, secretarial work, social service provision, and education. Women make up 77 percent of low-wage workers in the EU and 59 percent in the United States. At less than eight dollars per hour, 16 percent of low-wage women in the United States live in poverty.[85]

Finally, across both Europe and North America, attitudes toward women, work, and domestic work have changed somewhat. By 1983, Europeans generally believed that, ideally, men and women should share household tasks, and according to a recent study, almost one-quarter of Europeans believed that sharing household tasks was the most important way to end gender inequality. However, that arrangement was not the reality in most homes. Women continued to do the majority of household tasks and devoted the most time to childcare. Traditional gender norms also continue to influence the workplace. Both men and women expected women to subordinate their careers to the needs of their families or the demands of their husbands' careers. Indeed in 1996, twice as many women as men would consider taking unpaid leave to care for children, and a majority of Europeans believed that when jobs are scarce, men should have the priority over women.[86]

Both at home and at work, women's opportunities have expanded greatly. Access to birth control and changing ideas about marriage have increased women's options in terms of families and relationships. Changes in legal codes and societal attitudes have opened up new opportunities for women in education and at work. Although complete gender equality is still in the future, the pace of change in the past forty years has been unprecedented.

# WOMEN AND CULTURE

The women's movement has transformed all aspects of Western culture from philosophy to garage bands. Innovative scholars have formulated new theoretical perspectives through which we can study women and their place in society, and feminists have employed a wide range of cultural media to create a culture that challenges the male-dominated Western tradition. These works of scholarship and art give voice to women's views on politics, society, and their bodies. At the same time, women have become more visible and more influential in mainstream culture, sometimes promoting feminist ideas and sometimes defying them.

## Women's Studies and Feminist Theory

Feminist activists' desire to make gender analysis central to both learning and intellectual inquiry led to the establishment of the first women's studies program in the United States in 1970 at San Diego State University. Both men and women recognized the importance of integrating gender into academic life, and by the late 1990s, 70 percent of U.S. colleges and universities offered women's studies classes. Women's studies came to European universities somewhat later. The United Kingdom and Finland already had well-established programs by 1995, but women in Germany, Spain, and France still had to rely on individuals

working on women's topics rather than institutionalized degree programs.[87] Women's studies programs created an intellectual space for both students and faculty to focus on women's issues in individual disciplines and through interdisciplinary study. By increasing the academic acceptance of such study, women's studies helped cultivate women's history, women's literature, and feminist art history (among others) as legitimate scholarly topics that brought new visibility to women's contributions as scholars as well as women's contributions throughout history.

Feminist theory has provided the intellectual framework for understanding the relationship between sex, gender, culture, society, and ideas of sexual difference. Although it has had many influences, Freudian psychoanalysis has been central to the creation of modern feminist theory. Many American Second Wave feminist thinkers such as Kate Millet (b. 1934) in *Sexual Politics* (1970) and Shulamith Firestone (b. 1945) in *The Dialectic of Sex* (1970) criticized the biological determinism of Freudian thought. However, French feminists, including Heléne Cixous (b. 1937), reworked Freud using the critical linguistic ideas of Jacques Lacan (1901–1981). Lacan was influenced by Freud and psychoanalysis, but reinterpreted Freud's work using linguistic and anthropological analysis. Thinkers influenced by Lacan emphasized the symbolic over the material, especially in terms of sexuality. Cixous also became famous for developing the idea of "écriture feminine," a method of writing from the perspective of a woman that challenges the way that women are constructed through language and culture. Other French theorists known as Psych et Po (*Psychanalyse et Politics*) asserted the need to integrate Lacan's thought into a political movement. French writers Julia Kristeva (b. 1941) and Luce Irigaray (b. 1930) have also responded to Lacan's ideas about the relationship between psychoanalysis and women. Kristeva has argued that "woman" is not a biological entity but is instead a "position" created by patriarchy. In her 1977 work, *The Sex That Is Not One*, Irigaray asserted that reason and language are constructed as male in the Western philosophical tradition and thus do not adequately represent women. From another perspective, based on the work of Michel Foucault (1926–1984), Judith Butler (b. 1956) argued in

*Gender Trouble* (1990) that gender is not based in biological sex but is a performance of social and cultural norms.

Many feminist thinkers have used Marxist ideas about capitalism and subordination to explain gender oppression. In particular, German theorist Maria Mies (b. 1931) has criticized classical Marxism's failure to acknowledge the particular ways that the capitalist-patriarchal system affects women through its exploitation of female labor.

Although highly controversial, Carol Gilligan (b. 1936) transformed feminist scholarship with her groundbreaking work *In a Different Voice* (1982). Gilligan asserted that women are essentially different from men and have different moral reasoning than men. "Difference feminists" sharply disagree with ideas of "equality feminists" that emphasize that women and men are alike in nearly all ways (except menstruation, lactation, and reproduction) and therefore deserving of the same rights as men.

In addition to providing new theories that focus on women's place in society and philosophy, feminist scholarship has changed nearly all intellectual fields. Sandra Harding (b. 1935), Donna Haraway (b. 1944), and Evelyn Fox Keller (b. 1936) have pushed for the reexamination of the gender bias inherent in most scientific inquiry. From agriculture to zoology, feminist scholars have asked new questions about the relationship between sex and gender, women's place in society, and the ways that gender influences the world.

## Feminist Culture

From the outset, feminist culture offered a critique of traditional expectations of women and artistic expression. Many feminist artists hope to change society through their performances and artworks. Feminist art is intensely political, often focusing on the oppression of women and women's bodies.

Although it has often been difficult for female actors, directors, and playwrights to find opportunities in the professional theater, feminist and alternative theaters have created new forums for their work. In the United States, beginning in the mid 1970s, the At the Foot of the Mountain theater company in Minneapolis and Spiderwoman Theater, founded by three Native American sisters in New York, brought issues of race, sex, and gender to the stage. Heléne Cixous collaborated with Ariane Mnouchkine (b. 1939) at the Théâtre du Soleil in Paris to stage politically charged and groundbreaking feminist productions. Mary Ann "Buzz" Goodbody (1947–1975), the first female director at the Royal Shakespeare Company, was the founder and first artistic director of The Other Place, Stratford's studio theater, where she produced many experimental productions.

Female artists have made sexuality and the female body central to their artistic expression. Since the 1970s Yugoslav performance artist Marina Abramovic (b. 1946) has tested her body's limits in order to renegotiate the relationship between performer, body, and audience. Ana Mendieta (1948–1985) became famous for her *Siluetas* (silhouettes), in which she left imprints of her own body in a variety of settings. Ann Hamilton (b. 1956) has used a variety of media, including toothpicks and recorded soundtracks, to reconceptualize the body by substituting one sense organ for another. At the 1999 Venice Biennale, she combined walls embossed with Braille text with a fuchsia-colored powder that sifted slowly down the walls to explore issues of violence and democracy. Pipolotti Rist (b. 1962), a Swiss video and installation artist, employs video imaging to examine the objectification of women.

These artists have often stirred debate as they pushed the limits of what has been considered socially acceptable. In a famous incident, lesbian feminist Holly Hughes (b. 1955) became the center of controversy when her one-woman performance piece, *Clitnotes* (1990), was condemned by the American right as obscene and she was denied a grant from the National Endowment for the Arts (NEA). Hughes, performance artist Karen Finley (b. 1956), and two male artists unsuccessfully sued to have their grants reinstated.

Feminist playwrights have brought contemporary experiences to the stage in compelling new ways. In the United Kingdom, playwright Caryl Churchill (b. 1938) has turned ideas of gender and class upside down in productions like *Owners* (1972) and *Top Girls* (1982). Anna Deavere Smith (b. 1950) deftly defies American notions of race, religion, and ethnicity in her one-woman performance pieces in which she portrays characters of different, races, sexes, and backgrounds. She developed her piece *Fires in the Mirror* from interviews with people involved in the conflict that ensued in Crown Heights, New York, after the deaths of a rabbinical student and an African American boy in 1991. Eve Ensler (b. 1953) created her *Vagina Monologues* based on interviews with women about their vaginas. She has taken a once taboo topic and made it funny, poignant, and approachable. The performance company Split Britches has been a leader in lesbian feminist theater, traveling throughout Europe and the United States for more than forty years.

Feminist filmmakers have refocused plots around women and used film to explore sexuality and femininity. In German filmmaker Margerethe Von Trotta's (b. 1942) *The Second Awakening of Christa Klages* (1978), a young woman robs a bank when the funding for the daycare center she runs is cut, challenging the law, gender expectations, and societal priorities. French filmmakers have been at the forefront of feminist innovation and in challenging masculine film traditions. Catherine Breillat's (b. 1948) explicit images of female sexuality have led countries to censor or even ban her films. France's most famous feminist filmmaker is probably Agnés Varda (b. 1928). In *Vagabond* (1985), Varda constructed a portrait of a drifter named Mona, exploring Mona's femininity through the people that she meets during her wanderings.

Many feminist filmmakers have made audiences uncomfortable with their depictions of women who fail to conform to social expectations. Dutch director Marleen Gorris brought women's anger and violence to the screen in *A Question of Silence* (1984). In the film, after a group of women spontaneously and brutally beat a man, they display no remorse for their violent act. Gorris became only the second female director ever to win an Academy Award when she was honored for her film *Antonia's Line* (1995). Jane Campion's 1989 film *Sweetie* also examined a woman who failed to conform to societal norms and the relationship between "madness," gender, and nonconformity.

Few artists have been able to break into the male-dominated world of art galleries, museums, and exhibitions. Beginning in 1970, female artists began to protest their exclusion and push for exhibitions of women's works. The Women's Liberation Art Group formed in London and mounted a large-scale exhibition of female British artists including the works of Margaret Harrison (b. 1940). Harrison went on to have one of the first one-woman feminist exhibitions in London. Her portrait of Hugh Hefner, *Bunny Girl with Bunny Penis*, created so much controversy that police closed the gallery. In New York, Ann Sutherland Harris (b. 1937) and Linda Nochlin's (b. 1931) exhibition *Women Artists, 1550–1950* brought many previous unheralded female artists to public attention and transformed our understanding of women's exclusion from the artistic canon (see **Sources from the Past:** Why Have There Been No Great Women Artists?).

Judy Chicago (b. 1939) was a central figure in the development of the feminist art movement. She was one of the first women to teach a feminist art course and helped to develop a feminist art program in California. Her work *The Dinner Party* (1974–1979), now housed in the Brooklyn Museum of Art, has proven to be very controversial among feminists. Created as an enormous three-dimensional testament to women's contributions, it is a table with thirty-nine place settings reminiscent of female genitalia dedicated to prominent women and 999 names of other women inscribed on the floor.

Although female artists have made considerable strides, they continue to face discrimination in the art world. Since 1985 a group of art activists known as the Guerilla Girls have protested museums' and art critics' failures to promote the works of women artists. As art prices skyrocketed in the 1980s, women artists were conspicuously absent from exhibitions and auctions. Wearing gorilla masks, the Guerilla Girls plastered New York walls with posters decrying discrimination and gave public presentations about the role of gender in the art world. In recent years, the Guerilla Girls have expanded their protests to Hollywood, giving visibility to the dearth of female directors and to racism in the arts.

A number of musicians have cultivated feminism as a critical part of their image and work. In the early 1990s, the Riot Grrrls movement, led by all-female bands like Bikini Kill and Bratmobile, brought feminist lyrics to a new generation of young women and made opposition to sexism

## Why Have There Been No Great Women Artists?

*In 1971, Linda Nochlin, a member of the Vassar College Art History Faculty, composed this essay sharply criticizing the traditional perception of artistic genius as exclusively male and the systematic discrimination that prevented women from achieving such status in the art world. The essay is a fundamental text in feminist art history.*

"Why have there been no great women artists?" The question tolls reproachfully in the background of most discussions of the so-called woman problem. But like so many other so-called questions involved in the feminist "controversy," it falsifies the nature of the issue at the same time that it insidiously supplies its own answer: "There are no great women artists because women are incapable of greatness."

The assumptions behind such a question are varied in range and sophistication, running anywhere from "scientifically proven" demonstrations of the inability of human beings with wombs rather than penises to create anything significant, to relatively open minded wonderment that women, despite so many years of near equality and after all, a lot of men have had their disadvantages too have still not achieved anything of exceptional significance in the visual arts.

The feminist's first reaction is to swallow the bait, hook, line and sinker, and to attempt to answer the question as it is put: that is, to dig up examples of worthy or insufficiently appreciated women artists throughout history; to rehabilitate rather modest, if interesting and productive careers; to "rediscover" forgotten flower painters or David followers and make out a case for them; to demonstrate that Berthe Morisot was really less dependent upon Manet than one had been led to think—in other words, to engage in the normal activity of the specialist scholar who makes a case for the importance of his very own neglected or minor master. Such attempts, whether undertaken from a feminist point of view, like the ambitious article on women artists which appeared in the 1858 *Westminster Review*, or more recent scholarly studies on such artists as Angelica Kauffmann and Artemisia Gentileschi, are certainly worth the effort, both in adding to our knowledge of women's achievement and of art history generally. But they do nothing to question the assumptions lying behind the question "Why have there been no great women artists?" On the contrary, by attempting to answer it, they tacitly reinforce its negative implications.

Another attempt to answer the question involves shifting the ground slightly and asserting, as some contemporary feminists do, that there is a different kind of "greatness" for women's art than for men's, thereby postulating the existence of a distinctive and recognizable feminine style, different both in its formal and its expressive qualities and based on the special character of women's situation and experience.

This, on the surface of it, seems reasonable enough: in general, women's experience and situation in society, and hence as artists, is different from men's, and certainly the art produced by a group of consciously united and purposefully articulate women intent on bodying forth a group consciousness of feminine experience might indeed be stylistically identifiable as feminist, if not feminine, art. Unfortunately, though this remains within the realm of possibility it has so far not occurred. While the members of the Danube School, the followers of Caravaggio, the painters gathered around Gauguin at Pont-Aven, the Blue Rider, or the Cubists may be recognized by certain clearly defined stylistic or expressive qualities, no such common qualities of "femininity" would seem to link the styles of women artists generally, any more than such qualities can be said to link women writers, a case brilliantly argued, against the most devastating, and mutually contradictory, masculine critical cliches, by Mary Ellmann in her *Thinking about Women*. No subtle essence of femininity would seem to link the work of

Artemesia Gentileschi, Mine Vigee-Lebrun, Angelica Kauffmann, Rosa Bonheur, Berthe Morlsot, Suzanne Valadon, Kathe Kollwitz, Barbara Hepworth, Georgia O'Keeffe, Sophie Taeuber-Arp, Helen Frankenthaler, Bridget Riley, Lee Bontecou, or Louise Nevelson, any more than that of Sappho, Marie de France, Jane Austen, Emily Bronte, George Sand, George Eliot, Virginia Woolf, Gertrude Stein, Anais Nin, Emily Dickinson, Sylvia Plath, and Susan Sontag. In every instance, women artists and writers would seem to be closer to other artists and writers of their own period and outlook than they are to each other. . . .

Underlying the question about woman as artist, then, we find the myth of the Great Artist—subject of a hundred monographs, unique, godlike—bearing within his person since birth a mysterious essence, rather like the golden nugget in Mrs. Grass's chicken soup, called Genius or Talent, which, like murder, must always out, no matter how unlikely or unpromising the circumstances. . . .

What is stressed in all these stories is the apparently miraculous, nondetermined, and asocial nature of artistic achievement; this semireligious conception of the artist's role is elevated to hagiography in the nineteenth century, when art historians, critics, and, not least, some of the artists themselves tended to elevate the making of art into a substitute religion, the last bulwark of higher values in a materialistic world. The artist, in the nineteenth-century Saints' Legend, struggles against the most determined parental and social opposition, suffering the slings and arrows of social opprobrium like any Christian martyr, and ultimately succeeds against all odds generally, alas, after his death—because from deep within himself radiates that mysterious, holy effulgence: Genius. Here we have the mad van Gogh, spinning out sunflowers despite epileptic seizures and near-starvation; Cezanne, braving paternal rejection and public scorn in order to revolutionize painting; Gauguin throwing away respectability and financial security with a single existential gesture to pursue his calling in the tropics; or Toulouse-Lautrec, dwarfed, crippled, and alcoholic, sacrificing his aristocratic birthright in favor of the squalid surroundings that provided him with inspiration.

Now no serious contemporary art historian takes such obvious fairy tales at their face value. Yet it is this sort of mythology about artistic achievement and its concomitants which forms the unconscious or unquestioned assumptions of scholars, no matter how many crumbs are thrown to social influences, ideas of the times, economic crises, and so on. Behind the most sophisticated investigations of great artists—more specifically, the art-historical monograph, which accepts the notion of the great artist as primary, and the social and institutional structures within which he lived and worked as mere secondary "influences" or "background"—lurks the golden-nugget theory of genius and the free-enterprise conception of individual achievement. On this basis, women's lack of major achievement in art may be formulated as a syllogism: If women had the golden nugget of artistic genius then it would reveal itself. But it has never revealed itself. Q.E.D. Women do not have the golden nugget theory of artistic genius. If Giotto, the obscure shepherd boy, and van Gogh with his fits could make it, why not women? . . .

The question "Why have there been no great women artists?" has led us to the conclusion, so far, that art is not a free, autonomous activity of a super-endowed individual, "influenced" by previous artists, and, more vaguely and superficially, by "social forces," but rather, that the total situation of art making, both in terms of the development of the art maker and in the nature and quality of the work of art itself, occur in a social situation, are integral elements of this social structure, and are mediated and determined by specific and definable social institutions, be they art academies, systems of patronage, mythologies of the divine creator, artist as he-man or social outcast.

Source: Excerpted from Linda Nochlin, *Women, Art and Power and Other Essays* (New York: Harper and Row, 1988), 147–158.

**GUERRILLA GIRLS POSTER (1989).** Despite the remarkable gains made by women in arts, women are still seriously underrepresented in museums and other exhibit spaces. The lack of exhibition has kept the price of women's artwork low and hinders female artists' ability to get commissions. The Guerilla Girls shocked New Yorkers when this poster appeared on city buses; ironically, bus company officials later refused to run the advertisement, calling it too suggestive. *(Courtesy of www.guerrillagirls.com.)*

central to their performances. Ironically, although Riot Grrl bands emerged from the punk rock scene and expounded a political message, because of their popularity, the media quickly herded them into the mainstream and trivialized their feminist message.

## Women in Mainstream Culture

A number of women have also become superstars in mainstream culture. The United States' domination of media around the world has meant that many of the most recognizable names in popular culture have been Americans. Few women have gained as much international fame as Madonna (b. 1958). A star in both Europe and the United States, Madonna has become known for her challenges to traditional gender expectations and her explicit sexuality. In the United States, talk-show host Oprah Winfrey (b. 1954) has become one of the wealthiest and powerful women in the entertainment business. However, few female stars command salaries as large as their male peers, and they complain that they constantly battle media standards that demand youth and thinness in celebrities.

Television has become the prime medium of communication in the past thirty years and as such, it has been influential in the transmission of gender norms. Women have made great inroads in broadcast news, and new networks in both Europe and the United States are devoted to "women's" programming. These networks have addressed issues important to women, including breast cancer, abortion, and domestic violence; and they also have proven to be important advocates for women's issues. However, commercial networks are less comfortable with highly politicized women and rarely present feminist views.

Indeed, gender stereotypes pervade television in regular programming and commercials. Women are rarely depicted in positions of authority. One study found that women were the voiceover conveying information about the product only 26 percent of the time in British, Italian, and U.S. commercials. Across Europe and the United States, commercials generally portray women as young and men as middle-aged, and in the majority of advertisements, men act as the authorities while women are the consumers.[88]

Women's magazines and fashion models also present contradictory notions of women. Many times, magazines juxtapose articles on pleasing husbands and fashion layouts with models wearing sexy dresses with articles on dealing with difficult bosses. Magazine articles encourage women to both love their bodies *and* diet, purchase makeup, and undergo plastic surgery to change their bodies.

Finally, women's professional sports leagues have expanded in Europe and the United States, and superstar athletes are icons in popular culture. Female athletes have been critical in transforming gender expectations and demonstrating the tremendous benefits of equal opportunity. In 1971, the fastest female marathoner ran nearly 38 minutes slower than her male counterpart. By 2003, that gap was only 11 minutes. Although female athletes earn less than their male counterparts, such successes belie arguments about the importance of biological difference and are emblematic of the cultural changes that women have experienced over the past 35 years.

Feminist culture has been criticized as being overly separatist and thus replicating the exclusivity of male-dominated culture; however, it has also provided models for women's creative activity, brought attention to women whose work would have otherwise remained obscure, and provided an artistic forum for women's issues. Women's growing power in mainstream culture today is due in large part to the determination of feminist thinkers, writers, athletes, and performers.

## CONCLUSION

Since 1970 the women's movement and feminism have become formidable players in Western society and politics. As women have struggled for legal and social equality, their determination has created new opportunities at work, at home, and in all aspects of public life. Although not all women in the West have benefited equally from these changes, feminism and feminist action have been critical in ensuring that women can look forward to a better, more equal future.

## NOTES

1. http://www.NOW.org.

2. Amy Erdman Farrell, *Yours in Sisterhood: Ms. Magazine and the Promise of Popular Feminism* (Chapel Hill: University of North Carolina Press, 1998), 24.

3. Although many have credited her with coining the term, Friedan has always denied that she said it. See for instance, Michele Kort, "Portrait of a Feminist as an Old Woman," in *Interviews with Betty Friedan*, ed. Janann Sherman (Jackson: University of Mississippi Press, 2002), 127–128.

4. *Eisenstadt v. Baird*, 405 U.S. 438, 453 (1972).

5. Gisela Kaplan, *Contemporary Western European Feminism* (New York: New York University Press, 1992), 114.

6. Kaplan, *Contemporary Western European Feminism*, 245–247.

7. Monique Leijenaar and Kees Niemöller, "Political Participation of Women: The Netherlands," in *Women and Politics Worldwide*, ed. Barbara J.Nelson and Najma Chowdhury (New Haven: Yale University Press, 1994), 500.

8. All data from http://web.amnesty.org/library/index/ENGACT770362004.

9. "Europeans and Their Views on Domestic Violence Against Women," *Eurobarometer* 51.0 (1999); http://europa.eu.int/comm/public_opinion/archives/eb/ebs_127_en.p 7.

10. R. Amy Elman, "Testing the Limits of European Citizenship: Ethnic Hatred and Male Violence," *National Association of Women's Studies Journal* 13:3 (2001): 60–61.

11. Ursula Tidd, "Visible Subjects: Lesbians in Contemporary France," in *Women in Contemporary France*, ed. Abigail Gregory and Ursula Tidd (Oxford: Berg, 2000), 177.

12. Gerard Alexander, "Women and Men at the Ballot Box: Voting in Spain's Two Democracies," in *Constructing Spanish Womanhood: Female Identity in Modern Spain*, ed. Victoria Lorée Enders and Pamela Beth Radcliff (Albany, NY: SUNY Press, 1999), 363.

13. Leonard Weinberg and William Lee Eubank, "Neo-Fascist and Far Left Terrorists in Italy: Some Biographical Observations," *The British Journal of Political Science* 18:4 (1988): 538, 548.

14. Alison Jamieson, "Mafiosi and Terrorists: Italian Women in Violent Organizations," *Sais Review* (Summer–Fall 2000): 54–55.

15. Luisella de Cataldo Neuburger and Tiziana Valentini, *Women and Terrorism*, trans. Leo Michael Hughes (New York: St. Martin's Press, 1996), 8

16. Cataldo Neuburger and Valentini, 80.

17. Jamieson, 55.

18. Rex A. Hudson, "The Sociology and Psychology of Terrorism: Who Becomes a Terrorist and Why?" A report prepared for the Library of Congress, September 1999, http://www.loc.gov/rr/frd/pdf-files/Soc_Psych_of_Terrorism.pdf, 54.

19. Sue Bridger, Rebecca Kay, and Kathryn Pinnick, *No More Heroines? Russia, Women and the Market* (London: Routledge, 1996), 22–23.

20. John L. Keep, *A History of the Soviet Union, 1945–1991: Last of the Empires* (Oxford: Oxford University Press, 1995), 264, 265, 266, 268.

21. Quoted in Alix Holt, "The First Soviet Feminists" in *Soviet Sisterhood*, ed. Barbara Holland (Bloomington: Indiana University Press, 1985), 237.

22. Valerie Sperling, *Organizing Women in Contemporary Russia: Engendering Transition* (Cambridge: Cambridge University Press, 1999), 18.

23. Linda Racioppi and Katherine O'Sullivan See, "Engendering the Democratic Transition in Russia: Women, Politics, and Civil Society," http://www3.isp.msu.edu/cers/Racioppi%20See.htm, 6.

24. Sperling, 21.

25. Lisa Baldez, "Women's Movements and Democratic Transition in Chile, Brazil, East Germany, and Poland," *Comparative Politics* (April 2003): 266–267.

26. Eleonora Zielińska, "Between Ideology, Politics, and Common Sense: The Discourse of Reproductive Rights in Poland," in *Reproducing Gender: Politics, Publics, and Everyday Life After Socialism*, ed. Susan Gal and Gail Klingman (Princeton: Princeton University Press, 2000), 29, 31.

27. Peggy Simpson, "An Update of the Polish Election: What Did It Mean for Women?" *Journal of Women's History* 6:1 (1994): 68.

28. Zielińska, 52.

29. Sharon L. Wolchik, "Women and the Politics of Transition in the Czech and Slovak Republics," in *Women in the Politics of Post-Communist Eastern Europe*, ed. Marilyn Rueschemeyer (Armonk, NY: M. E. Sharpe, 1998), 120, 131.

30. Vlasta Jalušič, "Women in Post-Socialist Slovenia: Socially Adapted, Politically Marginalized," in *Gender Politics in the Western Balkans: Women and Society in Yugoslavia and the Yugoslav Successor States*, ed. Sabrina P. Ramet (University Park: Pennsylvania State University Press, 1999), 125.

31. Tatjana Pavlović, "Women in Croatia: Feminists, Nationalists, and Homosexuals," in *Gender Politics in the Western Balkans*, 133.

32. Julie A. Mertus, *War's Offensive on Women: The Humanitarian Challenge in Bosnia, Kosovo, and Afghanistan* (Bloomfield, CT: Kumarian Press, 2000), 24.

33. "Investigators Compile Mass Rape Allegations," *USA Today*; http://www.usatoday.com/news/index/bosnia/jan96/nbos141.htm (accessed February 14, 1996).

34. Žarana Papić, "Women in Serbia: Post-Communism, War, and Nationalist Mutations," in *Gender Politics in the Western Balkans*, 164.

35. Baldez, 265.

36. Baldez, 265.

37. Brigitte Young, *Triumph of the Fatherland: German Unification and the Marginalization of Women* (Ann Arbor: University of Michigan Press, 1999), 6–7.

38. Young, 199.

39. Young, 213.

40. Mary Buckley, "Adaptation of the Soviet Women's Committee: Deputies' Voices from 'Women of Russia'," in *Post-Soviet Women: From the Baltic to Central Asia*, ed. Mary Buckley (Cambridge: Cambridge University Press, 1997), 158–177.

41. Bridger, Kay, and Pinnick, 61.

42. Sarah Ashwin and Elain Bowers, "Do Russian Women Want to Work," in *Post-Soviet Women*, 22.

43. "Yeltsin Extols Virtues of Russia's Women," BBC.com (March 8, 1998); http://news.bbc.co.uk/1/hi/world/monitoring/63182.stm.

44. Hilary Pilkington, "'For the Sake of the Children': Gender and Migration in the Former Soviet Union," in *Post-Soviet Women*, 121.

45. Rebecca Kay, "Images of an Ideal Woman: Perceptions of Russian Womanhood Through the Media, Education, and Women's Own Eyes," in *Post-Soviet Women*, 88.

46. The United Nations, *The World's Women 2000 Trends and Statistics* (New York: The United Nations, 2000), 34.

47. For France, see "Women in Politics in the Council of Europe Member States," http://www.coe.int/T/E/Human_Rights/Equality/PDF_EG(2002)6_E.pdf, 62; for Greece, *Global Database of Quotas for Women*, at http://www.quotaproject.org.

48. Ronald Inglehart and Pippa Norris, *The Rising Tide: Gender Equality and Cultural Change Around the World* (Cambridge: Cambridge University Press, 2003).

49. Nonna Mayer, "The French National Front," in *The New Politics of the Right: Neo-Populist Parties and*

*Movements in Established Democracies*, ed. Hans-Georg Betz and Stefan Immerfall (New York: St. Martin's Press, 1998), 16–17.

50. Raylene L. Ramsey, *French Women in Politics: Writing Power, Paternal Legitimization, and Maternal Legacies* (New York: Bergham Books, 2003), 91.

51. Elman, 54–55.

52. Quoted in Jane Freedman, "Women in the European Parliament," *Parliamentary Affairs* 55 (2002): 184.

53. Freedman, 179, 183.

54. Elman, 57.

55. Temma Kaplan, *Crazy for Democracy: Women in Grassroots Movements* (New York: Routledge, 1997).

56. Cynthia Cockburn, *The Space Between Us: Negotiating Gender and National Identities in Conflict* (London: Zed Books, 1998), esp. 20, 21, 76.

57. United Nations Economic Commission for Europe Gender Statistics Database, http://w3.unece.org/stat/gender.asp.

58. "Family and Fertility Issues in an Enlarged Europe," http://www.eurofound.eu.int/publications/files/EF03115 EN.pdf, 7.

59. Dr. Catherine Hakim, "Childlessness in Europe," summary of findings at http://www.esrcsocietytoday.ac.uk/ESRCInfoCentre/Plain_English_Summaries/LLH/lifecourse/index498.aspx; and JaneMaree Maher, M. Dever, J. Curtin, and A. Singleton, "What Women (and Men) Want: Births, Policies, and Choices," Monash University (2004): http://www.arts.monash.edu.au/ws/research/projects/what-women-want-report.pdf, 20.

60. The United Nations, 24.

61. United Nations, 36.

62. Council of Europe: http://www.coe.int/T/E/Social_Cohesion/Population/Demographic_Year_Book/2003_Edition/04%20Country%20Data/Member%20States/United%20Kingdom/UK%20General%20Page.asp.

63. David Coleman and Joop Garssen, "The Netherlands: Paradigm or Exception in Western Europe's Demography?" *Demographic Research* 7:12 (September 2002): http://www.demographic-research.org/volumes/vol7/12/7-12.pdf, 454.

64. Kaplan, *Crazy for Democracy,* 176.

65. United Nations, 28.

66. United Nations, 29.

67. United Nations, 42, 49.

68. Chiara Saraceno, "Social and Family Policy," in *Family Life in the Twentieth Century*, vol. 3, *The History of the European Family*, ed. David I. Kertzer and Marzio Barbagli (New Haven: Yale University Press, 2003), 264.

69. For the United States, Janet C. Gornick, "Women's Economic Outcomes, Gender Inequality, and Public Policy: Findings from the Luxembourg Income Study," *SocioEconomic Review* 2 (2004): 227; for Poland, see World Bank Group, "Pension Systems Challenged," http://www.worldbank.bg/WBSITE/EXTERNAL/COUNTRIES/ECAEXT/BULGARIAEXTN/0, content MDK:20035049~menuPK: 305460~pagePK:141137~piPK: 141127~theSitePK:305439,00.html.

70. Kaplan, *Crazy for Democracy*, 223.

71. United Nations Economic Commission for Europe: Trends in Europe, Highlights on Education, "Illiteracy Rate (population older than 15) 2000" and "Percentage of Female University students, Selected Fields of Study, Latest Year," http://www.unece.org/stats/trends/#ch2.

72. National Women's Law Center, "Discrimination Against Women and Girls in Education: Why Affirmative Action Remains Essential"; http://www.nwlc.org/details. cfm?id=94&section=education.

73. United Nations Economic Commission for Europe, "Trends in Europe, Highlights on Education Percentage of Female University Students, Selected Fields of Study, Latest Year"; http://www. unece.org/stats/trends/#ch2.

74. Angélique Janssens, "Economic Transformation, Women's Work, and Family Life," in *Family Life in the Twentieth Century*, 89.

75. United Nations, 37.

76. Jill Rubery, Mark Smith, and Colette Fagan, *Women's Employment in Europe: Trends and Perspectives* (London: Routledge, 1999), 83.

77. Rubery, Smith, and Fagan, 163.

78. Gornick, "Women's Economic Outcomes," 215.

79. Louis Lavelle, "For Female CEOs, It's Stingy at the Top," *Business Week Online* (April 23, 2001).

80. "Breaking Through the Glass Ceiling: Women in Management," International Labor Office, Geneva, Switzerland (Update 2004), http://www.ilo.org/dyn/gender/docs/RES/292/F267981337/Breaking%20Glass%20PDF%20English.pdf, 26.

81. Nick Easen, "Russia Tops Women Management Survey," CNN.com (March 6, 2004).

82. Sheila Rowbotham, *A Century of Women: The History of Women in Britain and the United States in the Twentieth Century* (New York: Penguin, 1997), 413.

83. National Committee on Pay Equity, "The Wage Gap Over Time: In Real Dollars, Women See a Continuing Gap," http://www.pay-equity.org/info-time.html.

84. "The Social Situation in the European Union 2003 in Brief," http://europa.eu.int/comm/employment_social/news/2003/sep/2003_in_brief_en.pdf, 32.

85. Elman, 50; and Marlene Kim, "Women Paid Low Wages: Who They Are and Where They Work," Bureau of Labor Statistics, *Monthly Labor Review* (September 2000); http://www.bls. gov/opub/mlr/2000/09/art3full. pdf, 1.

86. "Equal Opportunities for Women and Men in Europe?" *Eurobarometer* 44.3 (1996): 67, 46, 26.

87. Gabriele Griffen and Rosi Braidotti, "Introduction: Configuring European Women's Studies," in *Thinking Differently: A Reader in European Women's Studies*, ed. Gabriele Griffen and Rosi Braidotti (London: Zed Books, 2002), 3–4.

88. Adrian Furnham, Matte Babitzkow, and Smerelda Ugguccioni, "Gender Stereotyping in Television Advertisements: A Study of French and Danish Television," *Genetic, Social, and General Psychology Monographs* 126:1 (2000): 82, 97, 101.

## SUGGESTED READINGS

Inglehart, Ronald and Pippa Norris. *Rising Tide: Gender Inequality and Cultural Change around the World.* Cambridge: Cambridge University Press, 2003. A study of women's voting patterns and the changing gender gap in voting.

Mertus, Julie A. *War's Offensive on Women: The Humanitarian Challenge in Bosnia, Kosovo, and Afghanistan.* Bloomfield, CT: Kumarian Press, 2000. A dramatic analysis of the impact of violence on women.

Ramet, Sabrina P., ed. *Gender Politics in the Western Balkans: Women and Society in Yugoslavia and the Yugoslav Successor States.* University Park: Pennsylvania State University Press, 1999.

Sperling, Valerie. *Organizing Women in Contemporary Russia: Engendering Transition.* Cambridge: Cambridge University Press, 1999. An excellent discussion of the transformation of women's groups during Russian democratization.

Young, Brigitte. *Triumph of the Fatherland: German Unification and the Marginalization of Women.* Ann Arbor: University of Michigan Press, 1999.

# Index

Abolitionist movements: activities of, 276; campaign material and, 336; organizations of, 335, 336; Society of the Friends of Blacks, 276, 277. *See also* Slaves and slavery

Abortions: Abortion Law Reform Association, 464; access to, 318; anarchist publications and, 419; birth control and, 454; countries and number of, 570; division about, 464; failure of laws on, 570; France and antiabortion laws, 508; issue of rights to, 570; Italy and illegal, 469; Nazi government and, 492; rape and, 438; Russia and legalized, 477; Soviet Union and outlawing of, 477; in Spain, 472; USSR and, 538, 539

Abraham, Karl, 317

Abraham Lincoln Brigade, 472

Abramovic, Marina, 596

*Académie de Saint-Luc,* 272

Academy of Sciences, 271

Academy of the Study of the Russian Language, 271

Activists and activism: after suffrage, 464; antiwar, 435–437; Christianity and, 353; in defense of prostitutes, 352, 353; deviant sexuality and radical, 437; League of Nations and, 464, 465; Netherlands and, 355; political parties and, 462; politics and, 352, 418, 419; Pugwash Movement, 550; Quakers as, 335; reforms of liberals and, 356–360, 361; Republican, 365; women and newspapers, 346; women's rights and, 355

Adams, Abigail, 278

Adams, John, 277

Addams, Jane, 323, 397, 404, 424, 435, 442, 465

*The Adulateur* (Warren), 277

Advertisements: consumerism and, 306; of housework and cleanliness, 453, 454; propaganda posters as, 437, 438; reversal of gender roles and, 439; Rosie the Riveter and, 505; sexuality during World War II and, 509; wartime patriotism and, 508; women and automobile, 452; women and mass media, 453

Afghanistan, 575

Africa: Catholic missionaries in, 383–384; colonial government conflicts and, 544; European nations and, 373; infant mortality and, 392; interracial relationships and, 379; Mau Mau revolt in, 546; mixed marriages and, 380; Muslim migration to, 234; native missionaries in, 384, 386; Portugal and colonies in, 246; practice of clitoridectomy and, 382; slave trade and, 276

African Americans: anti-black groups and, 495; anti-slavery campaign and, 335; cosmetics and hair products for, 453; Crimean War nurse and, 323; discrimination and suffrage, 444; discrimination in war work, 510; Harlem Renaissance and, 480, 482; jazz and, 481; manufacturing jobs and, 505; migration to the North, 537; "New Negro Movement" of, 480; Owenites and, 339, 340; Philadelphia Anti-Slavery Society and, 335; political candidates and, 528; postwar and male, 554; racial tension and interactions of, 509;

Salaria Kea, 472; settlement houses and, 323; "special mission" of, 386; WAC and, 499; war brides and, 519; work and women, 537

Aging, 592, 593

Agnesi, Maria Gaetana, 261

Agriculture: crop innovations and, 275; East Germany collectivized, 532; food inventions and, 299; food shortages and, 432, 433; Free Economic Society and, 271; indigo and economy of, 275; industrialization of, 299, 302; mechanized, 536; technological innovations of, 299; USSR and, 540, 541

Agrippa von Nettesheim, Heinrich, 240

Agrupación de Mujeres Antifascistas (AMA), 471, 472

AIDS, 584

Air Transport Auxiliary (ATA), 497

Akhmatova, Anna, 542

Alaska, 270

Albrecht, Berthie, 500

Alcohol and alcoholism: Eighteenth Amendment and, 464; prostitutes and, 308; suffrage movements and, 398; temperance movements and, 322

Alexander II (tsar of Russia), 299, 367, 369

Alexander III (tsar of Russia), 369

Alfonso XIII (king of Spain), 470

Algeria, 347, 398, 431, 545, 546, 547

All Africa Women's Congress (AAWC), 548

All-Russian Union of Equal Rights for Women (SRZh), 421

Amar y Borbón, Josefa, 265

Amendment(s): Eighteenth, 464; Nineteenth, 399, 444, 464; Twenty-first, 444

American Anti-Slavery Society (AASS), 335

American Board of Commissioners for Foreign Missions (ABCFM), 385, 386

American Federation of Labor, 405, 459

American Medical Association, 454

American Peace Society, 354

American Revolution, 277, 278

American Temperance Society, 322

American Temperance Union, 322

Anabaptists, 223, 224

Anglican Church: Catholic Church and the, 224; during Civil War, 238; papacy vs, 224; Protestantism and, 224, 225

Anguissola, Sofonisba, 241

Anna (ruler of Russia), 270

Anne (queen of England), 239

Anthony, Susan B., 340, 349

Anti-League, 425

Antinuclear campaigns, 548, 588

Antis, 423

Anti-slavery. *See* Abolitionist movements

Anti-Slavery Society, 334

Anti-war protest movements, 555, 556

*A Poem on the Inhumanity of the Slave Trade* (Yearsley), 276

Aragón: Ferdinand of, 232; Muslims and, 234; witchcraft accusations of men in, 231

Arbour, Louise, 586

Arctic National Widlife Refuge (ANWR), 549

Arden, Elizabeth, 453, 499

Arenal, Concepción, 349, 355

Armand, Inessa, 474

Army Nurse Corps (ANC), 428

*The Arraignment of Lewd, Idle, Forward and Unconstant Women* (Swetnam), 240

Artisans and crafts: Arts and Crafts Movement and, 416; French Revolution and, 280; gender prejudices and, 479; masculinity and skills of, 296; paintings and china patterns for, 272; workshops of, 479

Artists and art: abstract, 479; academy and exclusion of women, 272; Adélaïde Labille-Guiard, 272; Agostino Tassi, 241; Ana Mendieta,

596; André Breton, 479; Angelica Kauffmann, 272, 599; Ann Hamilton, 596; Artemesia Gentileschi, 241, 598, 599; artistic academies and, 271, 272; avant-garde of, 479–480, 481; Barbara Hepworth, 599; Bertha Morisot, 415, 416, 599; Bridget Riley, 599; *Bunny Girl with Bunny Penis,* 597; Clara Peeters, 241; Dada and, 479; *The Dinner Party,* 597; Elisabeth-Louise Vigée-Lebrun, 262, 599; Enlightenment themes of, 272; feminist culture and, 596–599, 600; Frida Kahlo, 480; "Fur-Lined Teacup," 480; Georgia O'Keefe, 599; Gian Paolo Zappi, 241; Giorgio Vasari, 241; Guerrilla Girls and, 597; Gunta Stöltz, 479; Hannah Höch, 479; Helen Frankenthauler, 599; hierarchy of painting genres in, 272; Holly Hughes, 596; impressionism and, 415, 416; Judy Chicago, 597; Kathe Kollwitz, 599; Karen Finley, 596; Lavinia Fontana, 241; Lee Bontecou, 599; Margaret Harrison, 597; Maria van Oosterwyck, 241; Meret Oppenheim, 480; minor arts and, 272; modernist and abstract, 416; modesty and, 244; motherhood and domesticity in, 272; nationalism and, 351; new woman and belle époque, 415, 416; nude paintings and, 416; Orazio Gentileschi, 241; overcoming obstacles as, 241, 244; photographs in, 479; Pipolotti Rist, 596; Rachel Ruysch, 241; Rosalba Carriera, 272; salons and, 264; School of Fine Arts for Women, 324; Sofonisba Anguissola, 241; Sonia Terk Delaunay, 479; still life and flowers as, 241; surrealism and, 479, 480; Sophie Taeuber-Arp, 599; Suzanne Valadon, 599; textiles in, 479; Walter Gropius, 479; *Women Artists,* 597; Women's Liberation Art Group and, 597; women travelers and, 401

Arts and Crafts Movement, 416

Asian Americans: WAC and, 499

Asile Maternel, 322

Askew, Anne, 224

Asociación de Mujeres Libres (Association of Free Women), 472

Assembly of Russian Factory Workers, 419, 420

Association for Married Women's Property Rights, 361

Association of Antifascist Women (AMA), 471, 472

Association of Peace and Disarmament by Women, 354

Aston, Louise, 317

Astor, Lady Nancy, 462

Athletes and athletics: Babe Didrikson Zaharias, 453; Gertrude Ederle, 453; Helen Wills Moody, 453; Olympics, 453; Suzanne Lenglen (the Goddess), 452, 453; swimming, 453; tennis, 452, 453; track and field, 453; female professional, 601

Auclert, Hubertine, 355, 397

Augspurg, Anita, 423, 435, 437

Augusta, Sophia Frederika, 271

*Aus dem Leben einer Frau* (*About the Life of a Wife*) (Aston), 317

Austen, Jane, 274, 317, 599

Australia: immigration to, 390–391; Malaya Peninsula and nurses of, 503; move to 390–391; prohibition of alcohol in, 464; temperance movement in, 398; vote for European women in, 398

Austria: abolition of serfs and, 299; diversity of empire of, 344; female miners in, 310; Freedom Party and, 583; German Confederation and, 342; government opposition and, 344; legal limitations of married working women in, 310; Napoleon and, 286; night work and women of, 535; revolutions and, 347; women voters in, 473; World War I and, 426

Auxiliary Territorial Service (ATS), 497

Aviation: career obstacles of, 461; women pilots and dangerous tasks in, 499; Women's Auxiliary Air Force (WAAF) and, 497

Baader, Andreas, 574

Ba'al Shem Tov, 321

Baez, Joan, 560

Bagley, Sarah, 297

Bailey, Henrietta, 386

Bajer, Mathilde, 361

Baker, Josephine, 481

Balch, Emily Greene, 465

Bara, Theda, 414

Barbauld, Anna Laetitia, 276

Bardot, Brigitte, 559
Barnes, Djuna, 456
Barnett, Samuel and Henrietta, 323
Barney, Natalie, 480
Barry, Leonora, 298
Barthélemy, Josephine, 438
Bassi, Laura, 261
Bastia, Leda Orlandi, 501
Bastié, Maryse, 461
Bastille Day, 281
Bates, Daisy, 554
Bazán, Emilia Pardo, 349, 352
The Beatles, 561
Beauvoir, Simone de, 500, 546, 556, 570
Bebel, August, 359
Beccari, Gaulberta Alaide, 365
Beeton, Isabella Mary, 300–301, 313
Behn, Aphra, 244
Belgium: environmental movement and, 549; female miners and, 308–309, 310; French expansion and, 285; Germany's invasion of, 493; World War I and women in, 426, 428
Bell, Acton, 349
Benedict, Ruth, 456
Benevskaia, Mariia, 420
Béquet deVienne, Marie, 322
Berkman, Alexander, 419
Bernardino, Minerva, 529
Berry, Marguerite, 355
Besant, Annie, 393, 395, 544
Best, Nellie, 437
Beveridge, William, 534
Bieber-Böhm, Hanne, 353
Bikini Kill, 597
Binzer, Ina Sofie Amalie von, 389
Birkett, Mary, 276
Birmingham Ladies Society for the Relief of Negro Slaves, 335
Birth control: Aletta Jacobs and, 436; anarchist publications and, 419; cervical cap, 436; fertility and, 454, 455, 590, 591; Italy's penal code and, 469; Nazi government and clinics of, 492; the "pill" as, 533, 551, 554; reproductive rights and, 569, 570; Russia and, 477; Sanger and, 454; Stope's and, 456; women and effects of, 454, 455
Bismarck, Otto von, 359, 361, 362
Blacks. *See* African Americans
Blackwell, Antoinette Brown, 314
Blackwell, Elizabeth, 327
Blackwell, Henry, 360

Blavatsky, Helena, 393
Blixen, Karen, 392
Bloom, Ursula, 304
Bluestockings, 265, 276
Bochareva, Maria, 429
Bockelszoon, Jan, 223
Bohec, Jeanne, 500
Bohemia: expulsion of Jews from, 268; Habsburg monarchy and, 267, 268; law code and Maria Theresa of, 268; "Mother of the Country" and, 268; peasant revolt in, 259; peasants and famine in, 259; War of the Austrian Succession, 267
Boissevain-van Lennep, Mies, 520
Bokova-Sechenova, Maria, 326–327
Boldyreva, Anna, 420
Boleyn, Anne, 224
Bolsheviks, 444, 445, 473
Bonaparte, Joseph, 288
Bonaparte, Napoleon. *See* Napoleon
Bon Marché Department Store, 306
Bonheur, Rosa, 599
Bonney, Therese, 506
Bontecou, Lee, 599
*Book of Common Prayer,* 225
Bora, Katherine von, 219
Bordoni, Faustina (Hasse), 273
Bosh, Evgeniia, 445
Boston Female Anti-Slavery Society, 335
Botanical Society of America, 326
Boulanger, Nadia, 480
Buonarroti, Michelangelo, 241
Boupacha, Djamila, 546
Bourgeois, Louise, 245
Bow, Clara, 452
Bratmobile, 597
Brauchitsch, Margaretha von, 416
Braun, Eva, 515
Brazil: convents in, 250; "orphans of the king" and, 246
Breillat, Catherine, 597
Bremer, Fredrika, 349, 353, 400
Brent, Margaret, 249
Breslauer, Käthe, 512
Breton, André, 479
Breuer, Josef, 316
Brezhnev, Leonid, 542, 575
Briand-Kellogg Pact, 467
Brilliant, Dora, 420
Brion, Hélène, 437
British America. *See* Colonies and colonization

British and Foreign Anti-Slavery Society (BFASS), 336
British Education Dispatch of 1854, 382
British Women's Emigration Association (BWEA), 388
British Women's Temperance Association, 398
Brittain, Vera, 428, 465, 549
Broder, David, 516
Britton, Elizabeth Knight, 326
Brodsky, Joseph, 542
Brontë, Anne, 349
Brontë, Charlotte, 349
Brontë, Emily, 599
Brooks, Louise, 452
Brown, Helen Gurley, 554
Brown, Isaac Baker, 315
Brown, Lesley, 590
*Browne's Book,* 482
Brundtland Commission, 584
Brundtland, Gro Harlem, 584
*El Buen Gusto,* 279
Bulgaria, 539
Bullinger, Henry, 240
Bullwinkle, Vivian, 503
Bülow, Frieda von, 395
Bund Deutscher Frauenvereine (BDF) (German Women's Association), 423
Bund Deutscher Mädel (BDM), 493
Burns, Lucy, 423
Business: "cottage industry" and, 259; production process and, 258, 259; in Spanish America, 278, 279; tea imports and, 260, 276; women and domestic service as a, 260
Butler, Eleanor, 317
Butler, Josephine, 352
Butler, Judith, 595, 596

Caccini, Francesca, 244
Caccini, Giulio, 244
Cagol, Mara, 574
Calcar, Elise van, 355
Calvin, John, 221–222, 223
Calvinism: Huguenots and, 222; Madaleine Mailly and, 237; women and, 222
Campaign for Nuclear Disarmament (CND), 548
Campion, Jane, 597
Campoamor, Clara, 470
Canada: Americanized, 394; colonial expansion of England, 275; convent and Native Americans of, 250; Jews

Canada (cont.)
  and migrant programs of, 518;
  Montreal Massacre and, 571; nurses,
  430–431; prohibition of alcohol in,
  464; Pugwash, Nova Scotia, 550;
  war brides and, 519; World War I,
  430–431
Canadian Methodist Women's
  Missionary Society, 385
Canadian Voice of Women (VOW), 549
Careers: in aviation, 461; families and
  husbands', 594, 595; female profes-
  sionals and, 460; in housekeeping,
  558; in retail sales work, 460;
  Russian women and, 476; in secre-
  tarial work, 460, 461; women and
  "the glass ceiling" of, 594; women's
  image in films and, 559
Carles, Émilie, 461
Carolina (queen of Naples), 272
Caroline (queen of England), 336, 337
Carriera, Rosalba, 272
Carson, Rachel, 549
Carter, Elizabeth, 265
Cartmell, Martha, 385
Cassatt, Mary, 415, 416
Castrati, 273
Castration anxiety, 317
Catherine I (Russian consort), 270, 271
Catherine II "the Great" (empress of
  Russia), 271, 272
Catherine of Aragón, 224
Catholic Church: abortion and the,
  438; African girls and concubinage,
  379; Anabaptists, 223, 224;
  Anglican Church and the, 224; Anne
  Hutchinson and the, 250; anti-
  Catholic groups and the, 495; birth
  control and the, 454; Calvinism and
  the, 222; convent music and the,
  244; Council of Trent and the, 225,
  226, 228; crypto-Jews and the, 232,
  233; decrease power of the, 268; forbidden books and the, 556; French
  National Assembly and the, 281;
  Habsburgs and the, 268; Huguenots
  and the, 222; Inquisition and the,
  227, 228; "loose woman" and the, 461;
  Martin Luther and the, 218, 219;
  missionaries and the, 382; Mussolini
  and the, 468, 469; new nuns and the,
  319–320; Papal States and the, 363;
  the pill and the, 554; Poland and the,
  576, 577; Protestant clergy and the, 268;
  Protestant reformations and the,

218–224, 225; reformation of the,
  225–228, 229; Saint Bartholomew's
  Day Massacre, 222; Swedish law and
  the, 237; witches and witchcraft and
  the, 231; women's organizations and
  the, 365; Women's Support Network
  in, 589, 590. *See also* Christianity
Catholic missionaries, 381, 383–384
Catholic Reformation, 225–228, 229
Catt, Carrie Chapman, 398, 423, 442,
  436
Cavell, Edith, 428, 438
Cavour, Camillo Benso di (Sardinia),
  363
Cecil, Robert, 236
Celibacy. *See* Christianity; Sex and
  Sexuality
Central Park, 304
*Cercle Social,* 281
Chaikovskii Circle, 368
Champseix, Léodile Bera, 354
Chandler, Elizabeth, 335
Chanel, Coco, 451
Chaplin, Charlie, 423
Chapman, Maria Weston, 335
Charity: philanthropic organizations
  and, 321–323; as public duty,
  310–311; settlement houses and,
  323; work and German women,
  363
Charles I (king of England), 238, 239
Charles II (king of England), 239
Charles V (Holy Roman Emperor),
  233, 234, 237
Charles VI (Habsburg emperor), 267
Charles IX (king of France), 236
Charles X (king of France), 342
Chartist movement, 337
Châtelet, Emilie du, 261
Châtelet, Marquis du, 261
Chattopadhyay, Kamaladevi, 544
Chauvin, Jeanne, 415
Chelmsford Ladies' Anti-Slavery
  Society, 335
Chicago, Judy, 597
Child, Lydia Maria, 336
Childbirth: aristocracy and, 257; birth
  control and, 318; birth control dur-
  ing Enlightenment, 258; dissemina-
  tion of birth control, 395; midwives
  and, 245; Nazis incentives for, 491;
  as patriotic duty of France, 286;
  thalidomide and, 549; USSR and,
  539; in vitro fertilization (IVF) and,
  590

Children: abandoned, 322; abandoned
  mixed race, 380; for adoption and
  Aryan women, 492; baby boomers
  and, 533; birthday parties and, 313;
  birth decline and, 258, 418, 438;
  childcare and, 322, 535; colonies
  and orphanages of, 246; Europe and
  African, 276; as factory workers,
  296; France and custody of, 339;
  France and economic support of,
  285; French orphanages and, 311;
  high mortality rate and, 259; illegitimacy rates of, 260, 438, 456; illegitimacy reforms and, 310; mixed-race,
  380, 381, 387; and motherhood during Enlightenment, 257, 258; music
  conservatories and, 273; Napoleonic
  Code and, 286; non-European men
  and, 376; nuns and aid for, 319–320;
  outside of marriage, 591; Poor Laws
  and, 310, 311; sexual trauma and,
  316, 317; Switzerland and unpaid
  maternity leave for, 310; Ursulines
  and abandoned, 229; women and
  bonuses for, 477; women's sexual
  behavior and, 438; working conditions and, 308–309; working mothers and daycare, 504, 505
China: convent and marriages in, 249;
  description of men from, 376; missionaries in, 383; Portugal and
  colonies in, 246; U.N. international
  women's conference in, 585
China Inland Mission, 385
Chisholm, Shirley, 582
Christianity: charitable organizations
  and, 321–322; and converts of Islam,
  234; cultural identity and, 252; first
  U.S. ordained woman minister, 314;
  French Revolution and, 284; Jewish
  salon women and, 265; Jews conversion to, 232; Martin Luther and,
  219; missionaries and, 382; mixed
  race children and, 380; Moriscas
  and, 234; Pocahontas and, 252;
  women activists and, 353
Christina (queen of Sweden), 237
Churchill, Caryl, 596
Churchill, Winston, 497
Church of England. *See* Anglican
  Church
Cinema. *See* Films and film industry
Cities. *See* Urban life
Citizenship: democracy and French,
  281; France's "public utility" and,

281; French women and, 468; individual states and women's, 278, 436; mixed race children and, 380; Napoleon's view of, 286

Civil rights movement: Civil Rights and Voting Rights Acts and the, 555; start of, 554

Cixous, Heléne, 595, 596

Clark, Edward, 325

Clement VII, Pope, 224

Cleveland, Frances Folsom, 423

Cline, Patsy, 560

Clinton, William, 549

Clothing: adoption of native, 249, 351; Anita Garibaldi and men's, 363; British preoccupation with, 387; Christina of Sweden and men's, 238; colonial women and, 249; in concentration camps, 514; Cromwell and prohibitions on, 239; dressed in male, 352, 393, 401, 445; *Encyclopédie* and, 264; European women wearing native, 392; female miners and, 308–309, 310; George Sand and, 341; Hasidic, 321; miniskirts and bikinis as, 554; mobility and, 304; modern woman and men's, 451, 452; Muslim women's veil and, 545, 546; National Guard uniform and Michel, 357; Native Americans and French, 250; native women and European, 383; nihilism and mannish, 367, 368; nonelite women and fashionable, 259; pink-collared shirts and, 460; rational, 414; Reform Dress Movement and, 416; Russia and Western-style, 270; Soviet women and military, 498; styles during World War I, 439; Thomas Hall controversy and, 249, 250; Vietnamese women and, 544; women's and men's, 238. *See also* Fashion

Coffeehouses, 260

Colbert, Jean-Baptiste, 275

Coligny, Gaspar de, 236

Colette, 317

Colonial Nursing Association (CNA), 389

Colonies and colonization: boycotts by, 277; concubinage and, 378; economies of the, 275, 276; European women working in, 248, 388–393, 394; female domesticity expectations in, 394, 395; feminine terms and, 376; "going native" in,

392–393, 394; Gothic novels and, 274; Kenya women and, 545; lifestyle change in the, 388; medical practitioners and, 389; native women and, 251–252; postcolonial governments of, 545–547, 548; re-creating society of middle class in, 387; representation in Parliament, 277; slave trade and, 276; native men and women in, 376; taxes and the, 277; Victorian femininity and, 389; white Europeanized children of, 387; wives of colonial officials in the, 386–388, 389; women's importance to, 246–252

Columbus, Christopher, 246

*Combat* (newsletter), 500

Committee on the Rights of Women, 346

*The Common Sense Book of Baby and Child Care* (Spock), 534

Communication services: radio and film, 481; women and employment in, 414; World War I and women in, 429

*Communist Manifesto* (Marx and Engels), 358

Communist Panhellenic Democratic Union of Women (PDEG), 530

Communists: Vietnam and, 544; women and Greek, 530

Compagnon de la Libération, 500

*The Complete Indian Housekeeper and Cook* (Steel), 388

Computers, 550

Concentration camps: for "asocials," 513; Auschwitz, 514, 516; Bergen-Belsen, 513; Chelmno, 514; Jehovah Witnesses in, 513; liberation and, 515; living conditions in, 514; Majdanek, 514, 516; Ravensbrück, 500, 501, 513; survivors, 516; treatment of women in, 513; Sobibor, 514; Treblinka, 514; for women and children, 513. *See also* Ghettos; Labor camps

Concerned Women for America, 569

Concubinage: Colonial life and, 378; European bloodlines and, 387; European men and, 378; interracial relationships and, 379; treatment of women in, 379; Vietnam and end of, 544

Congregation of Missionary Sisters of Our Lady of Africa, 383

Congress of Vienna, 289

The Consistory, 222

Constantinople, 233

Consumerism: advertisements and, 306; baby products and, 534; department stores and, 305, 306, 460; male reaction to, 306; new appliances and postwar, 558; in the Soviet Union, 576; women and, 453, 454

Contagious Diseases Acts, 395

Convents. *See* Nuns and convents

Conversas, 233

Copeland, Aaron, 480

Corbin, Margaret, 278

Le Corbusier, 558

Corday, Charlotte, 285

Cordeliers Club, 281

*Corinne* (de Staël), 288

Cortés, Hernán, 246, 251

Cosmetics and cosmetic industry: Elizabeth Arden, 453; Helena Rubenstein, 453; modern woman and, 452; Nazis and, 492

Coughlin, Charles, 495

Council of the Indies, 248

Council of Trent, 225, 226, 228

Counter Reformation. *See* Catholic Church

Cousins, Margaret, 544

Craton, Ann Washington, 459

Crawford-Seeger, Ruth, 481

Cremer, William, 397

Crimes: abandoned children and, 433; defeatism as French, 437; gulags and, 541; urban problems and, 306–307

*The Crisis*, 480, 482

*Crisis in the Population Question* (Myrdal), 534

Cromwell, Oliver, 239

Cross of the Order of the Legion of Honor, 401

Crypto-Jews, 233

Crystallography, 550

Cuba, 374

Countee, Cullen, 482

Cultures: gender roles and sexual identities in, 456; Russia's counter, 367; women and mainstream, 600, 601

Cumann na mBan, 397

Cunard, Nancy, 461

Cunitz, Maria, 245

Curie, Marie, 550

Curzon, George, 397

Czechoslovakia: ghetto in, 511; Union of Czechoslovak Women, 555; Velvet Revolution in, 577; women and politics in, 555; women voters in, 473

Czech Republic: women and the, 577

Dalai Lama, 393

d'Albret, Jeanne, 237

d'Alembert, Jean Le Rond, 264

Damanaki, Maria, 573

La Dame Blanche (The White Lady), 426, 428

Dance: folk, 351; Mata Hari and, 439; new woman and changes to, 417

Daniel, Larisa, 555

Danish Women's Association, 361

d'Arconville, Marie Thiroux, 262

Darnley, Lord, 236

Darwin, Charles, 314

Daughters of Bilitis (DOB), 551

Daughters of Charity, 229

Daughters of the American Revolution, 560

David, Anna, 513

David-Neél, Alexandra, 393

Davies, Emily, 325

Davis, Katherine Bement, 456

Davison, Emily Wilding, 422

Death: Africa and infant mortality, 392; camp procedures by Nazis, 514; in the ghettos, 511, 512; pandemic and, 440; textile workers and highest rate of, 404; World War II and number of, 515; World War I number of, 442

*Declaration of the Rights of Man and Citizen*, 280

*Declaration of the Rights of Woman and Female Citizen* (Gouge), 284, 285

Defense of the Realm Act (DORA), 434

de Gaulle, Charles, 501, 520, 534, 546

*Dei Waffen Nieder (Lay Down Your Arms)* (Suttner), 354

Delaunay, Sonia Terk, 479

*Delphine* (de Staël), 288

de Marillac, Louise, 229

DEMAU (Demystification of Authoritarianism group), 556

Demands of the Radical Hungarian Women (1848), 350–351

Democracy: communism and threat to, 530; Europe and, 572–580, 581; of

Great Britain and Hitler, 495; women and, 588

Democratic Women's Union of Germany (DFD), 532

Demonic possession, 232

Denmark: dairy workers and, 299; deportation of Jews and, 501; enfranchised women and, 421; Germany's invasion of, 493; Henrik Ibsen and, 317; housewives and unions in, 460; laws and women's status in, 360, 361; Margaret of, 235; Red Stockings in, 571; Resistance in, 501; U.N. international women's conference in, 585; witchcraft in, 231; women's unions in, 459

Department Stores: clerks, 306, 436; rise of 305–306

de Paul, Vincent, 229

Deroin, Jeanne, 338, 340, 341, 346, 347

Descartes, René, 245, 262

*Descent of Man* (Darwin), 314

de Staël, Germaine, 288

Détente, 575

*The Dialectic of Sex* (Firestone), 595

Diana, Princess (Great Britain), 589

Dickens, Charles, 306

Dickenson, Emily, 599

Diderot, Denis, 264, 271

Dietrich, Marlene, 452

Dieulafoy, Jane, 401

Digby, Jane, 392

Dilling, Elizabeth, 495

Dinesen, Isak, 392

Discrimination: of African Americans in war work, 510; art world and, 597; black sculptor and, 480; black women and, 554, 555; of black women and suffrage, 444; ERA and, 568; EU and gender, 586; female professionals and, 460; feminist organizations and, 569; Hitler's laws and, 490; immigrants and, 405; men and victim of, 583; Nazi ghettos and, 511, 512; New Deal welfare programs and, 466; Red Cross and, 472; the Resistance and, 500; Soviet Union Resistance and Jewish partisans, 501; striking women and, 297; Title IX and, 593; trade unions and, 505, 506; United Nations and, 585; United States and racial, 424; USSR

women and, 539, 540; of women and Commune, 357; of women and work, 297–298; of women in military services, 499; women of color and, 322; women's organizations and, 495; women's rights and, 336; women's wages and, 594

Diseases: of colonial prostitutes, 379; DDT and, 549; in the death camps, 514; European conquests and, 246; influenza and, 440, 441; native women and, 251; prostitutes and, 311–312; Russia and epidemics of, 445; venereal, 438, 439

*The Disenchantments of Love* (Zayas), 244

d'Istria, Dora, 349

Dittmar, Louise, 320

Divorce: Anabaptists women and, 223; the Consistory and, 222; in England, 468; France and, 339; French National Assembly and, 281; increase in 520; legal norms and social attitudes of, 592; Muslim women and, 544; Napoleonic Code and, 286; Nazism and, 491; Queen Caroline and, 336; in Russia, 474; Soviet Union and, 477

Dmietrieff, Elizabeth, 357

Dodge, Josephine, 423

Dole, Elizabeth, 582

*A Doll's House* (Ibsen), 317

Domesticity: celebratory occasions and, 313; cleanliness and, 313, 453; cult of, 312, 313; missionaries and, 382, 383; and motherhood in art, 272; non-European women and middle class, 386; propaganda and, 437; in Russia, 476

Domestic service movement, 453, 460

Domestic work: factory work *versus*, 298; governesses and, 396; impact of technological innovations on, 299; industry jobs and, 434; middle class employers and, 298, 300, 351; socioeconomic hierarchy of, 389; unionization and, 460; women and, 260, 390–391

*Domostroi*, 240

*La Donna (Woman)* (Beccari), 365

d'Orleans, Philippe Duc (regent of France), 258

Douglass, Frederick, 340

Dowries: colonial businesses and, 246; French incentives and, 246;

orphaned girls and, 273; single women and, 258
Draft. *See* Military
Droz, Gustave, 317
Duarte, Leonora, 233
Dubcek, Alexander, 555
Du Bois, W. E. B., 480
Dubská, Irena, 555
Duff, Peggy, 549
Duke, Anne, 289
Dulac, Germaine, 481
Duncan, Isadora, 417
Dupin, Aurore, 341
Du Pont Company, 549
Durand, Marguerite, 415
Dustin, Hannah, 249
Dutch East Indies Company (VOC), 378
Dyer, Martha, 250

Earhart, Amelia, 461
Earle, Martha, 434
Earth Summit, 584
East Africa. *See* Africa
East Germany. *See* Germany, East
East India Company, 275, 276
Eberhardt, Isabelle, 393
Ecofeminism, 588
Economic Society of Madrid, 265
Economy: agricultural, 275; of Germany and 1873 crisis, 361, 362, 363; Germany and free-market, 531, 532; Mussolini and Italy's, 469; Napoleonic Code and, 286; Poor Laws and the, 310; Prussian taxation and the, 268; revolutions and, 347, 348; single women and the, 296; slave trade and, 276; widows and the, 260; women and postwar, 535–536, 537; women investors and, 275; working-class women and urban, 260; working conditions and, 346
Eddy, Mary Baker, 320
Ederle, Gertrude, 453
Edict of Amboise, 237
Edison, Thomas, 414, 423
Education: bluestockings and, 265; boarding schools and, 350, 389; Catherine II and, 271; Catholic holdings and, 268; colonial subjects and missionary, 383; Enlightenment and, 258, 266; equal rights and, 244; European, 270; exclusion of women from art academies, 272; feminist art movement and, 597; Finland and coeducational schools, 365, 366; of girls and physical and mental development, 392; Henry VIII's policies and, 224; high school, 482; Institutes of the Blessed Virgin: Mary and, 229; interwar years with teachers and, 461; Jesuits and, 268; Jewish children and, 321; Lutheran, 221; mathematical sciences and, 261; men and limitation of women's, 261; men's *versus* women's, 263; missionaries and, 382; Moriscas and, 234; nationalism and, 351; orphaned boys and, 273; purpose of, 383; reforms of, 320, 324–325, 326, 482; revolutions and, 347, 348; Russian women and, 476; sciences and graduate, 326–328; Sephardic women and, 233; sex, 570; social status and teaching in, 414; Spain and women's, 265; Title IX and, 593; use of film in classroom, 481; women and, 535, 593; women's movements and, 339. *See also* Teachers; Universities and colleges
*The Education of a Christian Woman:* (Vives), 240
Edward VI (king of England), 224
Egerton, Sarah Fyge, 242
Egypt: archaeology in 550; missionaries and education in, 382; women's rights in, 398
Ehrenreich, Barbara, 561
Eisenhower, Dwight D., 495
Eliezer, Israel ben, 321
Eliot, George, 599
Elizabeth (empress of Russia), 257, 270
Elizabeth I (queen of England), 225, 235, 236
Elizabeth (princess of Bohemia), 245
Ellifritz, Marie, 515
Ellis, Havelock, 316, 317
Ellis, Sarah Stickney, 313
Ellmann, Mary, 598
"Eloi, Eloi, Lama Sabachthani" (Lawrence), 439
*Embassy Letters* (Montague), 266
Emergency Aid Nursing Committee, 440
*Emile* (Rousseau), 258
Employers and employment: clerical work and, 460, 461; crimes and lack of, 306–307; expansion of communication services, 414; governesses and, 389; increase in female, 593; industry as, 536; male jobs during World War I and, 434; manufacturing and domestic, 404; metropoles and rising unemployment, 388; Mussolini and male, 469; service section and, 536; unemployment compensation and, 459; of women during World War II, 505
*Encyclopédie*, 264
Enfantin, Prosper, 338
Engels, Freidrich, 356, 358
England: abolitionist movement and, 276; Abortion Law Reform Association in, 464; Act of Succession and, 235; Biblical defenses of women and, 241; bluestockings of, 265; Catholic Mary Ward and, 229; Civil War and, 238; colonial expansion of, 275; colonial taxes and, 277; color fashion advertisements in, 259; divorce in, 468; East India Company, 275; government surveillance and, 434; House of Commons candidates in, 462; Huguenots and, 222; legislation limitation on women, 224; mercantilist policies and, 275; papacy vs Anglican Church, 224; Royal Academy of Arts, 272; Royal Society of London, 261; Seven Years' War and, 275; Six Point Group in, 465; society and people of India, 275; tea and, 276, 277; white women and colonies of, 249; widows of, 260; witchcraft in, 230, 231; women and Civil War in, 238; women and the political system of, 238; working wives in, 260
English Society for Promoting the Employment of Women, 389
Enlightenment: art and themes of, 272; birth decline during, 258; chronology of, 257; class distinctions and gender norms of, 270; class tensions during the, 256; *Encyclopédie* project of, 264; in Europe and Russia, 267–270; European economic growth and, 276; French Revolution and, 279–289; Gothic novels and, 274; ideas about women, 262–266; illegitimate births and, 260; marriage during the, 258; motherhood during the, 257, 258; natural science debates during, 261; Newtonian and Cartesian thinkers, 261; peasants during, 258, 259; roles of men and

Enlightenment (cont.)
women, 263, 266; the salon and ideas of, 264; Scotland and, 265; slavery and, 276; Spanish America and, 278, 279; women's education during, 261; women's goals during, 258

Ensler, Eve, 597

Ensslin, Gudrun, 574

Entertainers and entertainment: Cromwell and prohibitions on, 239; La Revue Negre and Josephine Baker, 481; Madonna as, 600; Oprah Winfrey as, 600; radio, 481. *See also* Dance; Films and film industry; Television and television industry

Environment: Clean Air Act and, 551; DDT and, 549; ecofeminism and, 588; Europe and North America movements and, 549, 551

Equal rights: after the American Revolution, 278; Agrippa's views on, 240; Amendment and, 464; classes of women and, 365; education and, 244; ERA and, 568; during the French Revolution, 285; German Free Churches and, 320; human basic rights as, 262, 263; Levellers and, 238; Prussia and, 270; right to work as, 310; Scandinavian reforms of, 468; Social Darwinism and impact on, 314–315; teacher's pay and, 414; U.N. treaty and, 585; United Nations and, 528; Vietnam and, 544

Equal Rights Amendment (ERA), 464, 568

Erasmus, Desiderius, 225

Erauso, Catalina de, 248

Erik of Pomerania, 235

Espionage Act, 434, 437

Estonia, 231

ETA (Basque Homeland and Freedom), 583

Ethniko Apeleftherotiko Metopo (EAM), 530

Eugenics, 315, 438, 454, 489

European Parliament (EP), 586, 588

European Union: formation of the, 586; sexual orientation discrimination and, 572

Evolution. *See* Sciences

Evreinova, Anna, 421

Extermination camps, 514. *See also* Concentration Camps

Factories: British Parliament laws and, 308; children as workers in, 296; fish processing and, 537; gendering work in, 296–297, 298; reform of, 339, 368; working conditions of, 297

Falcón, Lidia, 573

Families: allowances to, 465; aristocracy and, 257; cult of domesticity and, 312–313; cultural expectations of, 534; end of war and relationships of, 519; Enlightenment art and, 272; French patriarchal, 281; Maria Theresa (Habsburg) and her, 268; modernization and West German, 533; Napoleonic Code and, 286; New York's Central Park and, 304; postwar, 533, 534; Royal Pragmatic and, 279; Russia and abolishment of, 474; Russia's 1926 Family Code and, 476, 477; slave, 276; USSR housing and, 539; working-class, 296

Families Committee, 531

Farenthold, Frances "Sissy," 582

Farmers and farming: Muslims and, 234; Enlightenment and new techniques of, 258; new crops and, 258; potato cultivation, 268

Fasci Femminili, 469

Fascists and fascism, 468–472, 473

Fashion: advertised in France and Italy, 259; color and advertisements in England, 259; German Fashion Bureau and, 492; modern woman and, 451; nationalist, 351; tennis court, 452

Fauset, Jessie Redmon, 480, 482

Fawcett, Millicent Garrett, 444

Federal Bureau of Investigations (FBI), 531

Federal Republic of Germany. *See* Germany, West

Federation of Danish Housewives' Associations, 460

Federation of University Women, 548

Fedulova, Alevtina, 580

Fell, Margaret, 238

The Female Advocate (Egerton), 242–243

Female Association, 321

Female Labor Reform Association, 297

Female Middle Class Emigration Society, 389

Female Society for Birmingham, 335

*The Feminine Mystique* (Friedan), 556

Feminist Anti-Imperialism, 395–396, 397

Feminists and feminism: after suffrage, 463, 464; definition of, 464; French Indochina and, 544; goal of organizations, 569; home party plan and, 559; imperialism and, 394; Indian nationalism and, 544; *La Fronde* and, 415; movements in Europe, 572–580, 581; Mussolini and repression of, 468–469, 470; organizations, 568–571, 572; pacifism and, 435, 437; Second Wave, 556, 568, 569, 595; socialism and integration of, 418, 419; theory, 595, 596; Third Wave, 569; United Nations and, 528

Femme-enfant, 480

Ferdinand, Franz, 426

Ferdinand II (Holy Roman Emperor), 237

Ferdinand (king of Aragón), 232, 235

Ferraro, Geraldine, 582

Ferry, Jules, 414

Fertility: control of, 590, 591; immigrants and high, 405; malnutrition and, 512; Nazis loans and, 491; post–World War I and, 454, 455; women and limiting of, 318

Fifth Monarchists, 239

Films and film industry: *An Arcadian Maid*, 414; *Antonia's Line*, 597; *The Battle of the Somme*, 439; *Birth of a Nation*, 424; *A Busy Day*, 423; careers in, 481; *Cléo de 5 á 7*, 560; *Darling*, 560; *Deti veka (Children of the Age)*, 417; *The Divorcee*, 452; feminist filmmakers in the, 597; *A Fool There Was*, 414; *Gentlemen Prefer Blondes*, 559; *Georgy Girl*, 560; HUAC hearings and the, 531; *It*, 452; *The Little Princess*, 414; *Little Red Riding Hood*, 414; *Love without Illusion*, 559; *Love With the Proper Stranger*, 559; *Maisie's Marriage*, 456; *Militant Suffragette*, 423; *80 Million Women Want——?*, 423; *Morocco*, 452; narrative, 481; New Wave, 560; new woman and the, 414, 415; *Nicht der Homosexuelle ist pervers*, 572; *Paradise Road*, 503; *The Private Secretary*, 559; *Question of Silence*, 597; *The Second Awakening of Christa Klages*, 597; *Seven Brides for Seven Brothers*, 559; *The Smiling Madame*

*Beudet*, 481; *In the Sultan's Garden*, 414; *Summer Place*, 559; surrealist, 481; *Susan Slade*, 559; *Sweetie*, 597; *Vagabond*, 597; *Votes for Women*, 423; *Without You All Is Darkness*, 559

Finland: independence and, 365; mother-educators in, 365; nationalist movement an, 365; Parliament and female representation in, 463; Russia and independence for, 366; same-sex partnership bill in, 572; socialism and, 365; temperance organizations in, 464; witchcraft in, 231; women politicians in, 582, 583

Finley, Karen, 596

Fiorina, Carly, 594

Firestone, Shulamith, 595

*The First Girl in the Komsomol*, 475

Flammarion, Sylvie, 354

Fleming, Alexander, 530

Fleming, Amalia, 530

Fletcher, Eileen, 546

FLN (National Liberation Front), 545, 546

Flynn, Elizabeth Gurley, 405

Fontana, Lavinia, 241

Fonte, Moderata da, 240

Foucault, Michel, 595

Fourcade, Marie-Madeleine (Méric), 500, 502

Fourier, Charles, 338

Fox Studios, 414

France: abandoned children in, 311; abolishment of slavery and, 346; abortion rights in, 570; advertised fashions in, 259; "Amazons of the Seine," 356; antiabortion laws, 508; aristocracy sold and, 258; aristocratic children of, 257; Bastille prison and, 280; Battle of Waterloo, 289; birth control and, 554; "Boche babies" and, 438; brothels in, 308; Catherine de Médicis, 235; citizenship and women of, 468; Civil Solidarity Pact and, 592; *Combat* and, 500; Committee of Public Safety and, 285; Commune and, 357, 358; Congress of Vienna and, 289; coup d'état in, 356; Crimean War and, 299; Daughters of Charity and, 229; day-care centers and, 311; declaration of war by, 493; denial of rights in, 444; Directory and, 285;

domestic servants and, 298; dowries as incentives and, 246; Edict of Nantes and, 222; Family Code and, 465; female athletes and, 452; female miners and, 310; fertility and, 454, 455; FLN and, 546; food rationing in, 508; Franco-Prussian War, 356; French revolutionaries role and, 281, 284–285; French Royal Academy of Painting: and Sculpture, 271; la garçonne in, 450; gay liberation movement in, 572; Germany's invasion of, 493; government allowances and, 508; housework wages and, 460; Huguenots and, 222; Indochina and, 373; Inquisition and homosexuality, 228; International Exposition in, 355; jazz and African Americans in, 481; journalists in, 415; "June Days" and, 347; lesbian subcultures and, 317; liberation of, 520; Maria Theresa and, 267; motherhood and patriotic duty of, 286; the mother of, 236; Napoleon and "consul for life" of, 285; Napoleonic Code, 286; National Assembly and, 280, 281; National Convention and, 285; National Front and, 583, 585; National Revolution, 508; natural science debates in, 261; Nazis occupation in, 508; New Wave cinema, 560; non-Europeans and mission of, 398; opposition to Napoleon and, 288–289; Parisian Royal Academy of Science, 261; postwar welfare state and, 534; pragmatic sanction and, 267; "public order statutes," 520; "public utility" and citizenship of, 281; Reign of Terror and, 285; Revolution of 1848 in, 345–346, 347; Royal Academy, 272; salons and, 265; Second French Republic and, 346; strikes in, 296–297; student movements in, 555; suffrage and politics in, 463; Théâtre du Soleil, 596; Ultras and, 342; urban radical revolutionaries of, 281; Vichy Government, 502; Vietnam and U.S. relations with, 545; war and pacifists in, 354; Wars of Religion, 237; witch-hunting in, 231; wives of POWs in, 508, 509; women activities in, 347; women and the Resistance, 500, 502; women's equal rights and, 534; women's rights movements and, 285; women's unions in, 459;

Workers of Northern France, 297; World's Fair, 305; World War I and women in, 426, 430–431

France, Marie de, 599

Francis I (king of France), 237

Francis II (king of France), 236

Franco, Francisco, 470, 573

Franco, Veronica, 244

Frank, Anne, 511

Frankenthaler, Helen, 599

Frederick, the Duke of Saxony, 219

Frederick II (king of Prussia), 268

Frederick William I (king of Prussia), 268

Frederick William IV (king of Prussia), 342, 343

Fredrika Bremer Society, 361

Free Economic Society, 271

Free Evangelical Church, 320

French Guiana, 392

French Movement for Family Planning (MFPF), 554

French Professional Union of Housewives, 460

French Revolution, 279–286

French Royal Academy of Painting and Sculpture, 271

French Section of the Workers International (SFIO), 419

French Society for the Emigration of Women to the Colonies, 388

Freud, Sigmund, 316, 595

Frick, Henry Clay, 419

Friedan, Betty, 556, 568, 569

*From Man to Man* (Schreiner), 396

Frondeuses, 415

Front Homosexual Action Révolutionnaire (FHAR), 572

Fulani, Leonora B., 582

Furness, Betty, 568

Futurism, 425

Galien, Blanche, 415

Galton, Sir Francis, 315

*The Game of Disarmament* (Myrdal), 588

Gandhi, Mohandas K., 543, 544

*La Garçonne* (Margueritte), 452

Garibaldi, Anita, 363

Garett, Mary, 320

Garibaldi, Giuseppe, 363

Garrison, William Lloyd, 335

Gaspar de Coligny, 236

Gay, Désirée, 346

Geiger, Abraham, 320

Gel'fman, Gesia, 369
Gender Complementarity, 263
*Gender Trouble* (Butler), 595, 596
Gentileschi, Artemesia, 241
Gentileschi, Orazio, 241
Geoffrin, Marie-Thérèse Rodet, 264
George III (king of England), 261, 262, 266, 336
George IV (king of England), 336
George (regent of England), 336
*Georgia Journal of Medicine and Surgery,* 304
Gérard, Georgette (Claude), 500
German Americans: internment of, 510
German Democratic Republic (GDR). *See* Germany, East
German Free Church, 320
German Labor Front (DAF), 493
German National Women's League, 395
German Social Democratic Women's Movement, 359
German's Women's Committee for Lasting Peace, 435
German Union for Women's Suffrage, 423
Germany: abortion rights in, 570; Africa and, 373; air raids in, 510; Anabaptists and, 223; Aryan race, 489; Baader-Meinhof Gang and, 574; black population and, 490; boycotts in, 348; brothels in, 308; Calvinism and the, 223; compulsory sterilization and, 489; divided, 531, 532; domestic servants and, 298; effects of war on, 510; and expansion of Aryan nation, 493; female miners in, 310; fertility and, 454, 455; food prices and immigrants from, 403; free-market economy and, 531, 532; gay and lesbian organizations in, 572; Hitler and racially pure, 488–490, 491; Huguenots and, 222; inequities and class division in, 433, 434; Japan and, 495; labor draft, 510; Lutheranism and, 221; military suppression in, 348; mixed marriages and, 380; Mother's Day in, 491; Mother's Honor Crosses and, 491, 492; Mussolini and, 493; Poland and, 493; political activities and, 362, 363; political opportunities in, 463; propaganda about, 438; prosti-

tutes and, 352, 353; raped women of, 515; Ravensbrück, 513; Red Army Faction (RAF) in, 574; Red Zora in, 574, 575; religious congregations in, 320; revolutions and, 347; Royal Society of Sciences, 261; salons and, 265; *Schweizer Frauenheim,* 313; suffrage in, 423, 424; Tanzania and, 373; "undesirables" and, 489; Weimar Republic, 488; Woman's Home Army, 437; women and postwar, 519; women and the spinning industry in, 260; women of, 532; "women's carnival" of, 227; women's charity organizations and, 321–322; World War I and women in, 426, 428. *See also* Nazi Party
Germany, East: Berlin Wall and, 532, 578; collapse of, 578; collectivized agriculture in, 532; Independent Women's League in, 578; socialist economy and, 532; Soviet communist model and, 532; women and, 532
Germany, West: Basic Law of 1949 and, 532; feminists in, 578; gay and lesbian organizations in, 572; German Nature Protection Ring and, 549; Take Back the Night March in, 571; women and marriage, 535; women's rights in, 532, 533
Germany (unified), 578, 579, 580
Gerritsen, Carel Victor, 436
Gestapo, 490, 502
Ghettos: gender discrimination and wages in, 512; living conditions in, 511, 512; Lódz, Poland, 511; music in the, 512; organized production in the, 512; Theresienstadt, Czechoslovakia, 511; Warsaw, Poland, 511
Ghika, Helen, 349
Gibbs, Lois, 588
Gibson, Isabella, 390–391
Gildersleeves, Virginia, 529
Gilligan, Carol, 596
Gilman, Charlotte Perkins, 314
Ginzburg, Evgeniya, 542
Gish, Lillian, 424
Glasnost, 575, 576
Godard, Jean-Luc, 560
Goegg, Marie, 354, 355
Goldman, Emma, 419, 437, 442
Goncharova, Natalia, 416

Goodbody, Mary Ann "Buzz," 596
Goodman, Dena, 264
Gorbachev, Mikhail, 575, 576, 580, 588
Gordon, Anna, 323
Gorris, Marleen, 597
Gouge, Olympe de, 284, 285
Gower, Pauline, 497
Graffigny, Françoise, 274
Granada, 234, 235
Great Britain: African countries and, 373, 544, 545; air raids in, 508; atomic testing and the, 549; aviation and, 497; bachelor girl in, 450; Contagious Diseases Acts and, 352; Crimean War and, 299; Crystal Palace and, 305; declaration of war by, 493; democracy and Hitler, 495; Divorce Act and, 360; domestic servants and, 298; Duke of Wellington and, 289; East India Company and, 373; Emancipation Act and, 335; environmental movement and, 549; Equal Franchise Act and, 462; equal rights laws and the, 593; India and, 543, 544; Indian Rebellion of 1857, 380; international exhibitions and, 305; Jews and migrant programs of, 518; law of coverture and, 359; London police department and, 306–307; Majesty Theatre in, 304; Married Women's Property Act, 360; Mau Mau revolt and, 546; military auxiliary corps and, 429; military combat operations and, 497; "Mud March" and, 421; National Health Service and, 535; opposition to Napoleon and, 289; politics and women's rights, 337; rent restriction and, 437; Royal Shakespeare Company and, 596; slave trade and, 333; Taunton commission in, 325; "the Kitchen Front" in, 507, 508; volunteer services and, 497; voting reform after World War I, 442, 444; war brides and Americans, 519; welfare program and, 534; women and political candidates in, 582; World Wildlife Fund, 549
Greece: civil war in, 530; Germany's attack on, 493; legal equality in, 573; Movement of Democratic Women in, 573; women and Communist Party of, 530
Greek Democratic Army (GDA), 530

Griffith, D. W., 424
Grimké, Sarah and Angelina, 335
Gripenberg, Aleksandra, 366
Gropius, Walter, 478
Grumbach, Argula von, 221
Grundy, Sydney, 417
Guerrilla Girls, 597
Guérin de Tencin, Claudine-Alexandrine, 258, 264
Guérin de Tencin, Pierre, 258
Guilds, 260, 279
Gulags, 541
Gustav II Adolf (king of Sweden), 237
Guy-Blaché, Alice, 481
Gypsies, 511, 513, 514

Haakon VI (king of Norway), 235
Habsburg monarchy: first female rule and the, 267; pragmatic sanction and the, 267; queen regents and the, 237; Salic law and the, 267; serfs and the, 237
Haider, Jörg, 583
Hair styles: Austrian women and, 519; bobbed haircut, 452; military standard, 499; short hair, 248, 368, 439
Haiti, 373
Hall, Radclyff, 456, 457
Hall, Thomas, 249, 250
Halonen, Tarja, 582
Hamilton, Ann, 596
Hammett, Dashiell, 531
Handel, Frederic, 273
Hanum, Djavidan, 393
Haraway, Donna, 596
Harding, Sandra, 596
Harems, 266
*Harem Life* (Hanum), 393
Harlem Renaissance, 480, 482
Harris, Ann Sutherland, 597
Harrison, Margaret, 597
Hartwell, Emily, 383
Hasidim, 321
*Haskalah* (Jewish Enlightenment), 265
Hasse, Johan Adolph, 273
Haupt, Herbert, 583
Haussman, Baron von, 304
Havel, Vaclav, 577
Hawaiian Islands: missionaries in, 385; Nineteenth Amendment and women of, 399; suffrage and the, 399
Hawaiian Patriotic League, 399
Haydn, Franz Josef, 273
Haymarket Riots, 419

Hayworth, Rita, 509
Hefner, Hugh, 551, 597
Height, Dorothy, 537
Hellman, Lillian, 531
Henry III (king of France), 236
Henry IV (king of France), 222
Henry VIII (king of England), 224, 235
Hepburn, Katharine, 559
Hepworth, Barbara, 599
Herschel, Caroline, 261, 262
*Hertha, or the Story of a Soul* (Bremer), 349
Hess, Elizabeth, 561
Hevelius, Johannes, 245
Heyman, Lida Gustava, 353
Heyrick, Elizabeth, 334
Hiller, Johann Adam, 273
Himmler, Heinrich, 492
Hindenburg, Paul von, 491
Hirsch, Jenny, 355
Hirsch, Samson Raphael, 320–321
Hirschfeld, Max, 492
*The History of Mary Prince* (Strickland), 336
Hitler, Adolf, 488, 515. *See also* Germany, Nazi Party
Hoan, Duc, 545
Hobby, Oveta Culp, 499
Höch, Hannah, 479
Ho Chi Minh, 544
Hodgkin, Dorothy Crowfoot, 550
Holliday, Billie, 481
Holloway, Thomas, 325
Holocaust, 511–513, 514, 516–517
Home front, 432–434
Home Rule Bill, 397
Home Rule for India League, 395
Homosexual Action West Berlin, 572
Homosexual Interest Group, 572
Homosexuals and homosexuality: cultural construction and, 456; in death camps, 514; decriminalization of, 571, 572; Europe and, 317; French Inquisition and, 228; inborn and learned, 316; Italy and illegality of, 469; Kinsey Report and, 551; Nazis and, 492; sissies as, 534. *See also* Sex and sexuality
Höss, Rudolf, 514
House Committee on Un-American Activites (HUAC), 531
Hughes, Holly, 596
Hughes, Langston, 482
Huguenots, 222, 236
Hull House, 323

*Humanae Vitae* (Pope Paul VI), 554
Humanists and humanism: Heinrich Agrippa von Nettesheim, 240; John Calvin and, 221; Marguerite of Navarre, 237
Human rights: European Court of, 572; Universal Declaration of, 528, 529; women's rights and, 528
Hume, David, 265
Hungary: abortions and, 539; authoritarianism and, 473; Calvinism and the, 223; de-Stalinization and, 541, 542; families and land in, 256; Habsburg monarchy and, 267; language of 351; military suppression in, 348; revolutions and, 347; witchcraft in, 231, 232; women and workforce in, 541
Hurston, Zora Neale, 480
Hutchinson, Anne, 250

Ibárruri, Dolores, 471
Ibsen, Henrik, 317
Iceland: enfranchised women and, 421; temperance organizations in, 464; witchcraft in, 231
Il Duce, 468
*Il Risorgimento*, 363
*Immediate Not Gradual Abolition* (Heyrick), 334
Immigrants and immigration: birth control clinic and, 454; conscription into the military and, 437; cosmetics and, 453; deportation of, 434, 442; discrimination of, 405; Europeans and, 403–407; Palmer Raids and, 442; reasons for, 403; recruitment efforts of women and, 388, 389; traditions by, 405; violence against women and, 571
Imperial feminism, 395
Imperialism: feminism and, 394; new, 397; opposition to, 395–396, 397; South American women and, 397
*In a Different Voice* (Gilligan), 596
*In Bamboo Lands* (Baxter), 401
India: colonial expansion of England, 275; dowries and, 246, 249; East India Company and, 275, 276; English single women in, 275; Ilbert Bill and, 376; independence and, 543, 544; Indian National Congress, 395; Indian Rebellion of 1857, 380; marriage and, 378; memsahibs in, 387; missionaries and cultures of,

India (cont.)
382; "orphans of the king" and,
246; people and English society, 275;
Portugal and colonies in, 246; Salt
March in, 543; self-government
movements in, 395; "the fishing
fleet" and, 275; widows and funeral
pyres, 382; women and Ghandi's,
543, 544
*Indiana* (Sand), 341
Indigo, 275
Indochina: France and, 373; marriages
and, 378
Indonesia, 223
Indulgences, 219
Industrialization: of agriculture, 299,
302; better wages and, 403; cult of
domesticity and, 312–313; social
critic of, 338
Industrial revolution, 294–328
Influenza epidemic, 440
Inger of Austråt, 244
Inglis, Elsie, 428
Inquisition: Catholic Church and the,
227, 228; crypto-Jews and the, 233;
Old Christian women and the, 227;
witchcraft and the, 230, 232
Institutes of the Blessed Virgin Mary,
229
*The Institutes of the Christian: Reli-
gion* (Calvin), 222
Intellectual revolution. *See* Enlight-
enment
Intermediate-range Nuclear Forces
Treaty (INF), 588
Internal Security Act, 531
International Abolitionist Federation,
353
International Association of Women,
354, 355
International Brigades, 472
International Campaign to Ban Land
Mines (ICBL), 588, 589
International Committee Against
Scientific Warfare, 465
International Committee of Women for
Permanent Peace, 435
International Council of Women, 354,
465, 495
International Exposition, 355
International Ladies' Garment Workers
Union, 404
International League of Peace and
Liberty, 354
International Olympic Committee, 453

International Peace Bureau, 354
International Proletarian Women's Day,
359
International Red Cross, 363, 430,
472, 509, 516
International Socialist Women's
Secretariat, 359
International Theosophical Society,
393
International Woman Suffrage
Alliance, 398, 436
International Woman Suffrage Alliance
(IWSA), 495
International Workers of the World,
405
International Year of the Woman, 585
Ireland: abolitionist speakers and, 276;
Catholic rebellion in, 238; Easter
rebellion, 397; England and, 395,
397; famine and immigrants from,
403; women politicians in, 582;
Women's Support Network in, 589,
590
Irigaray, Luce, 595
Irish Home Rule, 394
Irish Sisters of Charity, 320
Isabella II (queen of Spain), 354
Isabel of Portugal (regent of Spain),
237
Isabel (queen of Spain), 227, 232, 235
Islam: Algerian women and, 457;
Christianity and converts of, 234;
conversion to, 393; European expul-
sion and, 234; FLN and, 545;
Granada and, 234; Ramadan and,
234; rape of women of, 577; Tangan-
yika and, 544; Zhenotdel and tradi-
tions of, 474
Israel: Great Britain and state of, 518;
Zionism and, 405
Italian Americans: internment of, 510
Italian Socialist Party, 419
Italian Union of Catholic Women,
365
Italy: abortion rights in, 570; advertised fashions in, 259; birth control
and, 454; brothels in, 308; *Critica
Sociale (Social Criticism)*, 419; environmental movement and, 549; family controlled peasants and, 256,
257; fascist government of, 469;
women and agricultural labor, 299;
Germany and Mussolini's, 493; Red
Brigades and, 574; the Resistance in,
501; United States and, 495

Jaatteenmaki, Anneli, 582, 583
Jacobi, Mary Putnam, 327
Jacobs, Aletta, 318, 398, 435, 436
Jacobs, Gloria, 561
James II (king of England), 239
James VI (king of Scotland), 236
*Jane Eyre* (Brontë), 349
Japan: Hiroshima and Nagasaki, 515;
missionaries in, 385; Pearl Harbor
and, 495; prisoners of war camps,
501, 503
Japanese Americans: internment of,
510
Javouhey, Anne-Marie, 383
Jayawardena, Kumari, 386
Jehovah's Witnesses, 513
Jelinek, Elfriede, 583
*Jenny* (Undset), 416, 417
Jesuits, 229, 268
Jet Propulsion Laboratory, 530
Jewish Colonization Association,
405
Jewish Fighting Organization, 512
Jews: anti-Semitic Americans and, 495;
consequences of German, 490, 491;
conversion to Christianity, 232;
Denmark and deportation of, 501;
displaced, 518; Dutch, 436; economic status of, 405; executed con-
verted, 233; expulsion from Spain
and, 232; Freedom Party and, 583;
ghetto, 516; Hadassah and, 405;
Hasidic, 321; *Haskalah* (Jewish
Enlightenment), 265; and the Holo-
caust, 511–513, 514, 516; immigration of, 405; marriage and births
after the war, 518; National Front
and, 583; as New Christians, 233;
Poland and the, 234; prostitution
and, 406; racial purity and, 490;
salons and, 265; Social Revolutionary Party and, 420; during
World War I, 432
Jodin, Marie-Madeleine, 281, 282–283
Johnson, Luci Baines, 593
Johnson, Lyndon, 535, 555, 593
Johnson, Samuel, 265
Joliet-Curie, Irene, 550
Joseph II (emperor of Austria), 268,
272
Joshi, Anandibai, 392
Journalists: in France, 415; war corre-
spondents, 506
*Journey into the Whirlwind*
(Ginzburg), 542

*Joys and Sorrows of a School Teacher in Brazil* (Binzer), 389
Judaism: Gracia Mendes Nasi and, 233; Hasidism and, 321; Kabbalah and, 321; Orthodox, 321; as racial category, 490; reform movement and, 320–321
Judenrat, 511
*Judith Decapitating Holofernes* (Gentileschi, A.), 241
Jugan, Jeanne, 320
Junkers, 268

Kahlo, Frida, 480
Kandinsky, Wassily, 416
Kareline, Vera, 419
Kauffmann, Angelica, 272
KAU (Kenya African Union), 545
KCA (Kikuyu Central Association), 545
Kea, Salaria, 472
Keller, Evelyn Fox, 596
Kelsey, Frances Oldham, 549
Kennedy, John, 556
Kent, Victoria, 470
Kenya, 544, 545, 548, 585
Kenya African National Union (KANU), 548
Kenya National Council for Women, 548
Kerber, Linda, 278
Kerensky, Alexander, 444
Kettering, Sharon, 237
Khrushchev, Nikita, 537
Kikuyu Central Association, 545, 546
Kinderreich, 491
King, Martin Luther, 554
Kingsley, Mary, 401
Kinkel, Johanna, 348
Kinsey, Alfred, 551–553
The Kinsey Report, 552–553
Knight, Anne, 335
Knights of Labor, 297
Knox, John, 222, 235
Kobryns'ka, Natalie Ozarkevych, 367
Kohl, Helmut, 578
Kollontai, Alexandra, 425, 444, 445, 474
Kollwitz, Kathe, 599
Komsomol, 474, 475
Koopman, Elizabeth, 245
Korea and the Korean War, 530
Koutsouri-Voureka, Amalia, 530
Kovalevskaia, Sofia, 327

Kozeluch, Leopold, 273
Krafft-Ebing, Richard von, 315–316
Kramer, Edith, 518
Kramer, Heinrich, 230
Kristeva, Julia, 595
Krupskaia, Nadezhda, 474
Ku Klux Klan, 424
Kulaks, 475
Kuliscioff, Anna, 419

Labarbe, Henriette, 500
Labille-Guiard, Adélaïde, 272
Labor camps, 512, 513. *See also* concentration camps
Labor union(s): discrimination of, 297; Female Labor Reform Association, 297; first women and black members of a, 298; immigrant workers and, 404, 405; Knights of Labor, 297; membership in, 418; Owenites and, 339; reasons for joining, 505, 506; sexism and, 459; Working Woman's Protective Union, 340
Lacan, Jacques, 595
*Ladies' Diary,* 261
Ladies National Association (LNA), 352
LaDuke, Winona, 582
*Lady Anne Lee Embroidering* (Read), 272
Ladybug Society, 348
*Lady Chatterley's Lover* (Lawrence), 554
*The Lady's Magazine,* 259
Land and Liberty, 369
Lange, Dorothea, 461
Larymore, Constance, 387
Latin America: beneficent societies and, 405
Lawrence, D. H., 434, 439, 554
League for the Defense of Women's Interests, 365
League for the Prevention of the Emancipation of Women, 425
League for the Protection of Black Children, 389, 392
League of German Patriotic Women's Societies, 363
League of Jewish Women, 432
League of Nations, 441, 464, 465
League of Women's Equality, 421
League of Women Voters, 464, 495
League to Promote the Interests of Women, 363
Leavitt, Mary Clement, 323

Lebensborn, 492
Le Brun, Eugenie, 393
Legal rights: Anabaptists women and, 223; class distinction and, 268; Continental Congress and women's, 278; economic independence and women's, 361; female honor and, 240; "Jim Crow" law and, 424; Napoleon and women's, 286; Scandinavian confederation and women's, 360, 361; Virginia women and, 249; widows and prevention of, 260; witchcraft trials and, 230, 231
Leith-Ross, Sylvia, 387
Lemire, Madame, 324
Lenglen, Suzanane, 452
Lenin, Vladimir Ilyich, 444, 445, 474, 475
Leó, André, 354, 357
Léon, Pauline, 281
Leonarda, Isabella, 244
Leo XIII, Pope, 365
Le Pen, Jean-Marie, 583
Lepine, Mark, 571
Lesbians and lesbianism: accusations of 266; British military and, 497; as fashionable, 456; Daughters of Bilitis (DOB), 551; Kinsey Report and, 551; "lavender menace" and, 569; male temperament and, 316; National Center for Lesbian Rights, 569; Nazis and, 492; nude paintings and, 416; Paris' Left Bank and, 480; reclusive lifestyle of, 456; reproductive techniques and, 591; rights of, 571, 572; sexual behavior study and, 456; Split Britches and, 597; subcultures, 317. *See also* Sex and sexuality
Lespinasse, Julie de, 264
*Letters from a Peruvian Woman:* (Montesquieu), 274
Levellers, 238
*La liberazione di Ruggiero dall'isola d'Alcina* (Caccini), 244
Liebknecht, Karl, 441, 442
Lieder, 273
l'Incarnation, Marie de, 250
Literature: antislavery, 276, 277; children, 313; debates in 239–241, 266; female novelists and, 274, 416, 417; Germaine de Staël and, 288; Gothic novels, 274; lending libraries and, 273; lesbians in, 456; the salon and writers of, 264; travel, 400; war, 439. *See also* Poets and poetry

Lithuania, 321
Little Sisters of the Poor, 320
Litviak, Liliia, 498
*Lives of the Painters* (Vasari), 241
Locke, Alain, 480
Locke, John, 262
Lockwood, Belva, 354
Locust Street Social Settlement, 323
Lombardini, Maddalena, 273
*London Journal* (Tristan), 339
London Missionary Society, 385, 396
London Women's Liberation
   Workshop (LWLW), 568
Louis-Philippe I (king of France), 342
Louis-Philippe (king of France), 345,
   346
Louis XIV (king of France), 222
Louis XV (king of France), 258, 272
Louis XVI (king of France), 268, 280,
   281, 285
Louis XVIII (king of France), 289, 342
Loustanau-Lacau, Georges, 502
Loyola, Ignatius, 229
Lubetkin, Zivia, 512
Luce, Clare Boothe, 506
Luther, Martin, 218–219, 221
Lutheranism, 221, 228
Lutz, Bertha, 529
Luxembourg, 493
Luxemburg, Rosa, 418, 441, 442
Lyon, Phyllis, 551

Mack, Phyllis, 238
Mädelgruppe, 501
Madonna, 600
Mailly, Madaleine, 237
Maleficia, 229
*Malleus Malificarum* (Kramer and
   Sprengler), 230
Malnick, Lily, 513
Mamonova, Tatyana, 575
*Man and Woman* (Ellis), 316
Mandelstam, Nadezhda, 542
Mandelstam, Osip, 542
Mangakahia, Meri, 398
Manufacturers and manufacturing:
   feminine hygiene products and, 454;
   guild, 260; new techniques and, 259,
   260; technological innovations and,
   276; women workers in, 505; during
   World War I, 434, 435
Maquis, 500, 501
Marat, Jean-Paul, 285
Margaret of Austria, 237
Margaret (queen of Denmark), 235

Margaret (queen of Norway), 235
Margaret (queen of Sweden), 235
Marguerite of Navarre, 237
Margueritte, Victor, 452
María (Habsburg empress), 237
Maria Josepha (archduchess of
   Austria), 257
Maria Theresa of Austria, 261, 267,
   268
Marie Antoinette (queen of France),
   258, 268, 272, 280, 284, 285
Marie (queen of Romania), 428
Marina, Doña, 251
Marinetti, Filippo Tommaso, 425
Mario, Jesse White, 363, 365
Markham, Violet, 395
Markievicz, Constance, 397, 462
Marquis of Condorcet, 263
Marriage: Agrippa's view on, 240;
   alliances and, 268; aristocracy and,
   257; bans on, 417; "Boston," 317;
   Catholic Church and ceremonies of,
   226; the Consistory and, 222; education and Brazilian, 250; emigration
   and, 403; employment and, 417,
   458; during Enlightenment, 258;
   equals in, 339; eugenics and, 315;
   films and women's image in, 559;
   German-Catholic Church and, 320;
   Henry VIII and, 224; hierarchy
   within, 262; husbands' careers and,
   387; immigration and, 403; increase
   in, 533; Indian child, 378; interracial,
   279; interracial/interreligious, 379;
   later ages and, 591, 592; legally constituted, 359; legitimate Christian,
   380; manual for a subservient
   wife and, 240; Martin Luther and
   view of, 220, 221; Muslim women
   and, 544; Mussolini and, 469;
   Napoleonic Code and, 286; native
   men and European women in, 393;
   Nazis and, 491; Owenites and
   racially mixed, 339; postwar gender
   expectations of, 533, 534; in Russia,
   474; Russia and de facto, 476;
   Russia's white, 367; Russia's working women and, 417; social standing
   and, 268, 270; in Spanish America,
   279; teachers and, 461; working
   women and, 296
*Married Love* (Stopes), 456
Marshall Plan, 558
Martin, Del, 551
Martineau, Harriet, 310, 340, 352

Marx, Eleanor, 396
Marx, Karl, 356, 358, 396, 418, 596
Maryknoll Sisters of Saint Dominic,
   383, 384
Mary of Hungary, 237
Mary (queen of England), 224, 225
Mata Hari, 439
Maternity: France and allowances for,
   465; government support of, 466;
   leave and Switzerland, 310;
   Mussolini and, 469
Matoaka, 252
Matthys, Jan, 223
Matvienko, Valentina, 580
Mau Mau, 546
Mauthausen, 515
Maximilian II (Holy Roman Emperor),
   237
Mazuchelli, Elizabeth Sarah, 401
McAleese, Mary, 582
McCarthy, Joseph, 531
McCarthy, Mary, 440
McLaughlin, Mary Louis, 416
Mead, Margaret, 456, 508
Médicis, Catherine de, 235, 236, 237
Médicis, Marie de, 245
Medicine and medical care: birth control
   pill, 551, 554; charitable organiza-
   tions and, 321–322; colonial outposts
   and, 389; gender complementarity
   and, 263; in concentration camps,
   513; Daughters of Charity and, 229;
   hypnosis and, 316; Mary Baker Eddy
   and, 320; Nazi doctors and extreme
   use of, 490; Nazi procedures and,
   514; Nightingale Nurses and, 322;
   nurses and combat zones of, 428,
   499; nurturing of patients and, 327;
   *Our Bodies, Our Selves,* 570; penicillin and, 530; promiscuity and
   nurses of, 389; removal of women
   from, 245; shell shock and, 439;
   thalidomide, 549; Wasserman test
   and, 312; witchcraft and, 231, 232;
   women and, 326; women in Veterans
   Administration Hospitals and, 520;
   World War I, 430; women's sexuality
   and, 315, 316. *See also* Nurses
MEFESZ, 542
Meinhof, Ulrike, 574
Meir, Golda, 403
Meisel, Hanna, 406
*Memories of a Bachelor* (Bazán), 352
*Memories of a Catholic Girlhood*
   (McCarthy), 440

Memsahibs, 387
Mendelssohn, Moses, 265
Mendez, Francisco, 233
Mendieta, Ana, 596
Mengele, Josef, 514
Mensheviks, 444
Mercantilism, 275
Merian, Maria Sibylla, 261
Merici, Angela, 228, 229
Mérida, María Magdalena de, 279
Merkel, Angela, 582
Mestizos, 250, 252
*Metamorphosis Insectorum Surinamensium* (Merian), 261
Methodism, 313
Metternich, Prince (Austria), 344
Mexican Americans: women in the workforce, 505; Zoot Suit Riot, 510
Mexican American Women's National Association (MANA), 569
Mexico: convents and, 250; Doña Marina and, 252; female settlers of, 246; Frida Kahlo, 480; Pershing Expedition and, 379; U.N. international women's conference in, 585
Meysenbug, Malwida von, 320
Michel, Louise, 354, 357, 358, 392
Michel-Lévy, Simone (Emma), 500
Middle class: attack on family of, 336; and equality, 363; new woman and, 412, 414; pacifist groups and the, 354; politics and the, 345; re-creating society of, 387; Russian women of, 367; timesaving appliances and the, 453, 454; values and new woman, 417; women at home and, 362; working-class women and, 337
Mies, Maria, 596
Migrant workers, 537
Mikheicheva, Dina, 506
Military: Florence Nightingale and the, 322; French conscription in the, 286, 288; Great Britain and mixed-sex, 497; immigrants and conscription into the, 437; lotteries and British, 288; masculine culture and the Prussian, 268; masculinity and the, 378; Napoleon and French, 285, 286; Napoleonic Code and, 286; "selling of wives" and the, 289; Vietnam and the draft in the, 555, 556; war brides and, 519; white feather campaign and the, 438; women and full status, 530; women

and Russia's Red Army, 445; women disguised in the, 278; women in the, 426–431, 429; women's auxiliary corps and, 429; women's femininity and the, 499; World War I and nurses in the, 428
Mill, Harriet Taylor, 340
Mill, John Stuart, 359, 360
Mille, Pierre, 376, 387
Millet, Kate, 595
Milosavljevic, Danica, 500
Milosevic, Slobodan, 577, 578, 586
Mink, Paule, 310
Mirovich, Zinaida, 421
Missionaries: African girls and concubinage, 379, 380; challenges of, 385, 386; gender order and, 383; multiple goals of, 382; native dress and China, 393; native peoples and women, 381; native traditions and, 382, 383; teachers or nurses as, 385; values of, 382
Mitchell, Maria, 326
Mnouchkine, Ariane, 596
Modern woman, 450–457
Mohamed, Bibi Titi, 545, 547, 548
Monarchies: abdication and Sweden, 237, 238; absolutist, 262; Catherine II and absolute, 271; collapse of French constitutional, 285; Cromwell and restoration of, 239; Enlightenment and legitimacy of, 261; Europe's most conservative, 268; France's constitutional, 281; gender expectations of, 236–237, 238; Habsburg's absolute, 267; legitimacy of French, 284; marriage regulations by Spanish, 279; powerful female, 235–237, 238; Puritan Commonwealth and, 239; queen regents and, 237, 238; reassertion of absolute, 342; Russian hereditary rule and, 271; Salic laws of inheritance and, 236; the salon and, 264; use of femininity and Habsburg, 267
Mondale, Walter, 582
Monge, Gabrielle de, 428
Monks and monasteries: closure of, 268; Henry VIII policies and, 224; Jesuits as, 229; Martin Luther and, 219. *See also* Nuns and convents
Monroe, Marilyn, 559
*Monsieur, Madame, et Bébé* (Droz), 317
Montague, Elizabeth, 265

Montague, Lady Mary Wortley, 266
Montesquieu, Baron de. *See* Secondat, Charles-Louis de
Montseny, Federica, 472
Moody, Helen Wills, 453
More, Hannah, 265, 273, 276
Moriscas, 234
Morisot, Berthe, 415, 416, 598, 599
Moro, Aldo, 574
Morris, William, 416
Mosher, Clelia, 318
Motherhood: during Enlightenment, 257, 258; franchise, 444; as French patriotic duty, 286; Hitler and, 491; non-Aryan, 492; nuclear weapons and, 549; Republican, 278; surrogate, 590, 591; welfare states and, 534, 535
Mother Kevin (Franciscan nun), 384
Mothers' Movement, 495
Mott, Lucretia, 335, 336, 340, 354
Mozart, Wolfgang Amadeus, 273
Mozzoni, Anna Maria, 353, 363
*Mrs. Beeton's Book of Household Management* (Beeton), 300–301
Münter, Gabriele, 416
Murie, Margaret (Mardy), 549
Musicians and music: Aaron Copeland, 480; American Syncopators, 481; Antonio Vivaldi, 273; Bikini Kill, 597; Bobbie Howell, 481; Bratmobile, 597; choral, 273; convent music, 244; Duarte family, 233; feminism and, 597, 600; Franz Josef Haydn, 273; Frederic Handel, 273; in the ghettos, 512; jazz, 481; Johan Adolph Hasse, 273; Kinkel, Johanna, 348; Leopold Kozeluch, 273; Maria Theresia von Paradis, 273; Mary Lou Williams, 481; Nadia Boulanger, 480; nationalist, 351; opera, 273; Pietà, Anna Maria della, 273; popular secular, 272, 273; in prisoners of war camps, 503; religious piety and, 244; Riot Grrrls and, 597; rock 'n' roll as, 560, 561; Ruth Crawford-Seeger, 481; secular music, 244; sonata and, 244; "the new music," 244; Wolfgang Amadeus Mozart, 273; women as, 273; World War I and patriotic, 437. *See also* Singers
Muslim. *See* Islam
Mussolini, Benito, 468
Myrdal, Alva, 534, 588

Myrdal, Gunnar, 534
Mystics, 228

NAACP, 424
Na Fianna Eireann, 397
Nagy, Imre, 542
Naidu, Sarojini, 543
Napoleon, 285–289, 304
Napoleon, Louis, 356
Napoleonic Code, 286, 365
Napoleon III (emperor of France), 356
NASA, 530
Nash, Diane, 554, 555
Nash, Frances, 501
Nasi, Gracia Mendes, 233
Nation, Carrie, 323
National Aeronautics and Space
     Administration (NASA), 530
National Association for the
     Advancement of Colored People
     (NAACP), 424, 482
National Association of
     Manufacturers, 505
National Association of Spanish
     Women, 470
National Association of Women
     Painters and Sculptors, 480
National Association Opposed to
     Woman Suffrage (NAOWS), 423
*The National Bordello Under the:
     Auspices of the Queen,* 284
National Center for Lesbian Rights,
     569
National Council of Jewish Women,
     405
National Council of Negro Women, 537
National Council of Women, 354
National Fascist Party, 468
Nationalism: Europe and, 424, 425;
     patriotic mothers and, 365; racism
     and, 395; Russia and, 365–369
National Legion of Mothers of
     America, 495
National Liberation Front, 545, 546
National Organization for Women
     (NOW), 568
National Security League, 434
National Socialist German Workers
     Party. *See* Nazi Party
National Socialist Women's League
     (NSF), 493
National Union of Algerian Women
     (UNA), 457
National Union of Women's Suffrage
     Societies (NUWSS), 421, 444

National Victory Garden Institute,
     508
National Women's Party (NWP), 423,
     444, 464
National Women's Service, 432
National Women's Suffrage
     Association (NWSA), 423
Native Americans: diseases and, 246;
     experiences of conquest, 250–252
Nature Conservancy, 549
Nazi Party: "asocial" women and the,
     493; concentration camps and
     deportation, 511; concentration
     camps and the, 513; death camps
     and the, 512–514; family and the,
     491, 492; Gestapo and the, 490;
     Hitler and the, 488; ideology and
     women's role, 510, 511; indoctrina-
     tion into, 493; labor, concentration,
     and death camps of, 511–513, 514;
     non-Aryan population and, 511;
     race policy and the, 490; sex and the,
     492; women's groups and the, 493
Nechama E. (Holocaust survivor), 516
Necker, Suzanne, 264
Nehru, Jawaharlal, 543
Nelken, Margarita, 470
Netherlands: abortion rights in, 570;
     Anabaptists and the, 223, 224; birth
     control clinic in, 318; Calvinism and
     the, 223; environmental movement
     and, 549; French expansion and the,
     285; Germany's invasion of, 493;
     Habsburg monarchy and, 267; legal
     limitations of married working
     women, 310; Mata Hari and the,
     439; New World insects and, 261;
     Sephardic Jewish culture and the,
     233; women activists in, 355;
     women and International Criminal
     Court in the, 586; women and the
     East India Company, 275; Women in
     Europe for a Common Future
     (WECF), 588
New Caledonia: prison camp in, 358;
     prison colonies and, 392
Newspapers and magazines: activist
     women and, 346; *Almanack des
     femmes (The Women's Almanac),*
     341; *An Almanac: Women and
     Russia,* 575; *Business Week,* 594;
     *The Christian Science Journal,* 320;
     *The Christian Science Monitor,* 320;
     *La Citoyenne,* 397; *Combat,* 500;
     *Common Cause,* 397; contradic-

tory messages in, 509, 600, 601;
     *Courage,* 569; *Daily News,* 352; *Der
     Spiegel,* 570; *Die Gleicheit (Equal-
     ity),* 359; *Emma,* 569; *The Family
     Magazine,* 274; feminist, 568, 569;
     *La Femme Libre (Free Woman),*
     338; founding of popular, 273, 274;
     *Frauenzeitung (The Women's News-
     paper),* 347; French Revolution and,
     347; *La Fronde,* 415; *Genius of
     Universal Emancipation,* 335; *Good
     Housekeeping,* 453; *Il Monitore,*
     274; *Ladies Home Journal,* 568; *The
     Liberator,* 335; *l'Opinion de femmes
     (The Opinion of Women),* 347; *Le
     Magazine Feminin (The Woman's
     Journal),* 560; *Ms. Magazine,* 568;
     *National Anti-Slavery Standard,*
     336; *New Bonn Newspaper,* 348;
     *New York Herald Tribune,* 506;
     *New York Post,* 506; *New York
     Times,* 404; *The Northern Star,* 337,
     338; *Ogonek,* 539; *Pesti Dvatlap
     (Pest Fashion Magazine),* 348; *Play-
     boy,* 551; *Pravda,* 519; *Rabotnitsa,*
     541; recipes with rations, 508; *Spare
     Rib,* 568; *Swiss Womanhood,* 313;
     *The Times,* 394; *Times of London,*
     353; *Tout (Everything),* 572;
     *The Westminster Review,* 340,
     598
*The New Woman* (Grundy), 417
New Zealand: enfranchisement of
     native women in, 398; scientific
     views of gender differences and, 392;
     Sisters of Saint Joseph in, 384; tem-
     perance movement in, 398
NGOs (non-governmental organiza-
     tions), 585, 588–589, 590
Nicholas, Maria Longworth (Storer),
     416
Nicholas II (tsar of Russia), 420,
     444
Nielsen, Ellen, 501
Nielsen, Hanne, 299
Nigeria, 394
Nightingale, Florence, 322, 352
*Nightwood* (Barnes), 456
Nihilism, 367
Nineteenth Amendment, 399, 464
Nixon, Richard, 559, 575
*Noah's Ark* (Meric), 502
Nobel Prize: Chemistry, 550;
     Literature, 417, 583; Peace, 354,
     465, 588, 589

Nochlin, Linda, 597–599
No-Conscription League, 437
Non-governmental organizations (NGOs), 585, 588–589, 590
North, Marianne, 401
North Africa. *See* Africa
North Atlantic Treaty Organization (NATO), 528, 588
Norway: conservative party of, 584; Germany's invasion of, 493; laws and women's status in, 360; pacifist groups in, 354; part-time farms in, 536; postwar welfare state and, 534; prime minister of 584; temperance organizations in, 464
Novels: antiwar, 354; as connection with women, 349; in the form of letters, 274; of opposition to Napoleon, 288; Russian gender expectations in, 475. *See also* Books
Nuns and convents: Agrippa's view on, 240; cloistered, 228; Empress María and, 237; Henry VIII policies and, 224; Mexico and, 250; as missionaries and hospitals, 383; music and, 244; native women and, 384; Protestantism's impact on, 221; reassertion of, 319–320; two-tiered system of, 250; World War I hospital and, 428
Nurses: Army and Navy Nurse Corps, 499; epidemic and shortage of, 440, 441; Florence Nightingale, 322, 352; fundraisers during warfare and, 363; in Malaya Peninsula, 503; as missionaries, 385; Nightingale Nurses as, 322; promiscuity and, 389; Russian elite women as, 444; Salaria Kea, 472; Vietnam War and, 545; World War I and women as, 428, 430-431; World War II and German, 499; *See also* Medicine and medical care
Nyerere, Julius, 545, 547, 548

Odynets, Kamilla, 310
Oedipus conflict, 317
*Of the Nobilitie and excellencye of: woman kynde* (Agrippa), 240
O'Hare, Kate Richards, 437
O'Keefe, Georgia, 599
Oliva, Elsa, 501
*Oliver Twist* (Dickens), 306
Olmsted, Frederick Law, 304
Olympics: arenas of competition in the, 453; Babe Didrikson Zaharias, 453;

oppositions to women and, 453. *See also* International Olympic Committee
*On Germany* (de Staël), 288
Oosterwyck, Maria van, 241
Oppenheim, Meret, 480
Order of St. Ursula, 228, 229, 244, 250
orgasm, 552-553
*The Origin of the Species* (Darwin), 314
*The Origins of the Family, Private Property, and the State* (Engels), 359
*Orlando* (Woolf), 456
Ospedale della Pietà, 273
*Ostéologie* (d'Arconville), 262
Ottawa Treaty, 589
Otto, Louise, 320, 341, 347, 348
*Our Fate (Nasha dolia)* (Kobryns'ka), 367
*Our Freedom and Its Results* (Strachey), 464
*Out of Africa* (Dinesen), 392
Owens, Robert, 339

Pacifists and pacifism. *See* Activists and activism; Peace organizations
Paintings. *See* Artists and art
"Pale Horse, Pale Rider" (Porter), 441
Palestine: displaced Jews and, 518; gendered division of labor in, 405, 406; Jewish immigration and, 405
Palmer, A. Mitchell, 442
Pankhurst, Christabel, 421, 425
Pankhurst, Emmeline, 421, 422, 425
Pankhurst, Sylvia, 421, 425
Papandreou, Margaret, 573
Pappenheim, Bertha, 406
Paradis, Maria Theresia von, 273
Parent-Duchâtelet, Alexandre-Jean-Baptist, 310
*Parenthood and Race Culture* (Saleeby), 315
Parisian Royal Academy of Science, 261
Parisian Society for the Emancipation of Women, 341
Parks, Rosa, 554
Parr, Catherine, 224
Partido Socialista Obrero Español (PSOE), 573
*The Passion of the Soul* (Descartes), 245
Pasteur, Louis, 327
Patmore, Coventry, 312–313

Patriotic Women's Societies, 363
Patriotism: food rationing programs and, 433; military women and, 429; volunteerism and, 432; women's short hair and, 439
Patronato Español, 405
*Patterns of Culture* (Benedict), 456
Paul, Alice, 423, 444, 464, 465
Paulía y Aguirre, María, 278, 279
Paul III, Pope, 225
Paul I (Russian ruler), 271
Paulson, Charlotte, 322
Payen, Alix Milliet, 357
Peace of Westphalia, 237
Peace organizations, 354, 550. *See also* Activists and activism; Women's movements
Peasants: Aragón Muslims as, 234; conscripted Prussian, 268; French Revolution and, 280, 281; production of wealth and, 258; profits of the landowner and, 258; revolutionary solutions of, 345; rural life and, 258, 259; Russia and revolution of, 475; Russian rebellion of, 271
Pechey, Edith, 389
Pedro III, Dom (Portugal king consort), 257
Peeters, Clara, 241
Peisley, Mary, 276
Pelletier, Madeleine, 318, 419
Penis envy, 317
People's Will, 369
*Peregrinations of a Pariah* (Tristan), 339
Perestroika, 575
Pérez, de Cuéllar, Javier, 584
*Perfect Health for Women and Children* (Sloan-Chesser), 424
Perkins, Frances, 466
Perovskaia, Sofia, 368–369
Perre, Madame van den, 389
*The Persian Letters* (Secondat), 274
Pétain, Marshall Philippe, 508
Peter I (Peter the Great) (tsar of Russia), 270
Peter II (tsar of Russia), 271
Peters, Carl, 381
Petit, Gabrielle, 428
Petitt, Ann, 588
Pétroleuses, 357
Pfeiffer, Ida, 400, 401
Philadelphia Anti-Slavery Society, 335
Philip II (king of Spain), 227, 241
Philip III (king of Spain), 234, 237

Philip IV (king of Spain), 248

Philippines: nurses as prisoners of war in, 501; prostitutes and prostitution in, 379; United States and the, 374

Phillips, Catherine, 276

Philosophers and philosophy: Guillaume Thomas François Raynal, 276; Jean-Paul Sartre, 546; "mind has no sex" as, 262; philosophes as, 263, 264; René Descartes, 245, 262; Simone de Beauvoir, 500, 546, 556; Simone Weil, 472

Philosophes, 263, 264

Photographers and photography: Dada artists and, 479; Dorothea Lange, 461; Margaret Bourke White, 461; military ban and, 509; Therese Bonney, 506; women travelers and, 402

Physicians: abortions and Russian, 477; Aletta Jacobs, 435; Josef Mengele, 514; Marie Stopes, 454; Russia and, 444; Russian women, 326–327; shell shock and, 439; sterilization and Germany's, 489; World War I and women, 428

Pickford, Mary, 414

Pietà, Anna Maria della, 273

Pimentel, Eleanor, 274

Pinckney, Eliza Lucas, 275

Pincus, Gregory Goodwin, 551, 553

Pirckheimer, Caritas, 221

Pius IX, Pope, 365

Pizzey, Erin, 571

Plat, Sylvia, 599

Playwrights and plays: Aphra Behn, 244; Caryl Churchill, 596; *Clitnotes,* 596; *The Doll's House,* 317; Eve Ensler, 597; *Fires in the Mirror,* 596, 597; Holly Hughes, 596; *Owners,* 596; *Top Girls,* 596; *Vagina Monologues,* 597. *See also* Theaters

Pocahontas, 252

"Poems on Several Occasions" (Egerton), 242

Poets and poetry: Anna Akhmatova, 542; Ann Yearsley, 276; Coventry Patmore, 312–313; D. H. Lawrence, 439; Gisèle Prassinos, 480; Joseph Brodsky, 542; Osip Mandelstam, 542; Sarah Fryge Egerton, 248; Sarojini Naidu, 543

Poisson, Jeanne, 258

Poland: abolition of serfs and, 299; abortion laws and, 576, 577; abortions and, 539; Calvinism and the, 223; Chelmno, 512; de-Stalinization and, 541, 542; divorce and, 539; extermination camps in, 514; ghettos in, 511, 512; Hasidism and, 321; Hitler's invasion of, 493; labor camps in, 512; the Resistance in, 512; Solidarity and, 576; witch-hunting in, 231; world's largest Jewish community in, 234

Polygyny, 223

Pompadour, Madame de, 264

Pompadour, Marquise de, 258

Ponsonby, Sarah, 317

Ponte, Carla del, 586

Pope, Alexander, 266

Popes: Clement VII, 224; Leo XIII, 365; medical missionaries and the, 384; Papal States and the, 363; Paul III, 225; Paul VI, 554; Pius IX, 365; Urban VIII, 229; women's rights and the, 365

Porter, Katherine Anne, 441

Portugal: authoriarianism in, 473; colonization by, 246; egalitarian wage structure and, 594; Estado Novo (New State) of, 473; Inquisition and, 227; Judaism and, 232, 233; Napoleon and, 286; Napoleonic Code and, 286; orphans and, 246; Salazar and women in, 473

Pottery, 416

Poullain de la Barre, Francois, 262

Poverty: aging women and, 592, 593; mixed-race children and, 380; reforming urban, 310, 311; widows and, 260

Prague Spring, 555

Prassinos, Gisèle, 480

Praunheim, Rosa von, 572

Presley, Elvis, 560

*Pride and Prejudice* (Austen), 274

Primo de Rivera, Miguel, 470

Primo de Rivera, Pilar, 472, 473

Prince, Mary, 336

*Principia mathematica* (Newton), 261

Prisoners of war: communication methods of, 503; communications and, 509; conditions of, 503; Germans and, 509; Philippines and nurses as, 501; World War II nurses as, 499

Prohibition. *See* Temperance organizations

Propaganda: Nazi sex ideology as, 492; posters and, 437, 438; Russian women and, 445; Soviet political, 478–479; wartime work and, 505; women and Nazi, 492

Prophets and prophecy: Anabaptists as, 223; new congregations and, 238; political, 239; Quaker visionaries as, 238

Prostitutes and prostitution: attitude toward, 307, 308; colonial officials and, 379; in concentration camps, 513; Crispi regulations and, 353; diseases of, 311–312; female behavior and, 311–312; Jack the Ripper and, 308; Josephine Butler and, 352, 353; lifestyle of, 307, 308; Magdalene houses and, 227; Mexican Revolution and, 379; Nicotera Laws and, 353; in Palestine, 406; political activism and, 352; Portugal incentives for, 246; POW's wives as, 508; reasons for, 307, 308; Soviet women and, 520; sterilization of, 489; suffragists and, 422; Ursulines and, 229; Veronica Franco and, 244; view of working women as, 297; women activists and, 353

Protestant missionaries, 381, 382, 385, 386

Protestant reformation: Anabaptism, 223, 224; Calvinism 221, 222; English reformation, 225; Lutheran reformation, 218–221; Puritans, 225

Protestants and Protestantism: Anglican Church and, 224; Calvinism and, 223; Catholic doctrine challenged by, 219; city government and, 221; impact on merchants, 221; Mary and, 224, 225; predestination and, 222; witches and witchcraft and, 231; women and, 221

Protoindustrialization, 258

Proudhon, Pierre Joseph, 347

Prussia: abolition of serfs and, 299; and coalition against Maria Theresa, 267; Franco-Prussian War, 356; German Confederation and, 342; law code and, 270; masculine, military society of, 268; Napoleon and, 286, 289; Pragmatic Sanction and,

267; Silesia and, 267; women and politics of, 348
Psarouda-Benaki, Anna, 581
Psych et Po (Psychanalyse et Politics), 595
Public health, 436, 584
Pugwash Movement, 550
Puerto Rico, 374
Pugachev, Emilian, 271
Puritans: Anne Hutchinson and, 250; Charles I and persecution of, 238

Quakers: abolitionist and, 276; as activists, 335; female preachers and, 238; Grimké sisters as, 335
Querelle des femmes, 239, 241, 246

Radical Hungarian Women, 348
Radio, 481, 507
Rankin, Jeannette, 462
Raskova, Marina, 498
Rathbone, Eleanor, 467
Raynal, Guillaume Thomas François, 276
Read, Catherine, 272
Reagan, Ronald, 575, 588
Recolhimentos, 246
Recusants, 225
Red Cross: *See* International Red Cross
Red Stockings, 571
Reform Dress Movement, 416
Reitsch, Hannah, 499
Relationships: cohabitation and, 591; end of war and, 519; equal partners in sexual, 474; European same-sex laws and, 572; importance of sex in, 456; nonmarital or domestic partnership, 591, 592; of servicemen and European women, 519; single women and, 591, 592
Religions: fulfillment in non-Christian, 393; Khrushchev and, 538; missionaries and native, 382; Owenites and, 339; Peace of Augsburg and, 221; Sunday school movement and, 273. *See also* Christianity, Islam, Judaism
*Remonstrance*, 423
Rémy, Carolyn, 354
Rent Restriction Act, 437
Representation of the People Bill, 442, 443
Republican motherhood, 278
*Requiem* (Akhmamtova), 542
La Revue Negre, 481
Rice, Harriet, 323

Richards, Amy, 569
Richer, León, 354, 355
Richthofen, Frieda von, 434
Riess-Passer, Susanne, 583
Riley, Bridget, 599
Riot Grrrls, 597
Riots: racial tensions and, 505; Stonewall, 572; Zoot Suit, 510
Rist, Pipolotti, 596
Robespierre, Maximilien, 285
Robinson, Mary, 582, 586
Robinson, Vera, 497
Rogers, Edith Nourse, 498
Rogers, Mary Josephine, 383
Roland, Pauline, 338, 340, 346
Rolfe, John, 252
Rolfe, Rebecca, 252
Roma. *See* Gypsies
Roman Academy, 272
Romania: abortions and, 539; collectivization and, 541; denial of rights in, 444; divorce and, 539; labor shortages and, 434, 435; nurses and, 428
Romero Masegosa y Cancelada, María, 274
Rookwood Pottery, 416
Roosevelt, Eleanor, 459, 466, 498, 528, 556
Roosevelt, Franklin Delano, 459, 466, 495, 510
Rousseau, Jean-Jacques, 258, 263, 265
Rouzade, Léonie, 310
*The Rover, or the Banished Cavaliers:* (Behn), 244
Royal Academy of Arts, 272
Royal Aragonese Economic Society, 265
*The Royal Dildo*, 284
Royal Society of London, 261
Royal Society of Sciences, 261
Royer, Clémence, 354, 415
Rubenstein, Helena, 453
Rumiantseva, Nadezhda P., 417
Russia: abandoned children and crimes in, 433; abolition of serfs and, 299; abortion and, 477; Academy of Sciences, 271; Academy of the Study of the Russian: Language, 271; Assembly of Russian Factory Workers, 419, 420; authoritarianism and, 445; Bering Strait, 270; "Bloody Sunday" in, 420; China and, 373; civil war in, 445; class ten-

sions in, 271; collapse of, 444; collectivization and, 475; Communist Party in, 475; Crimean War and, 299; division of socialist movements and, 444–445; divorce in, 474, 476; economic revolutions of, 475, 476; Enlightenment, 271; European culture and, 270; expeditions and, 270; Family Code of 1926 and, 476, 477; female honor and, 240; Finland and tsar of, 365; gender equality and, 477; gender tensions and, 474; Great Reforms of, 299; independence and, 365; Industrial Home in, 310; industrialization of, 475, 476; inequities and class division in, 433, 434; International Woman's Day and, 444; Jewish pogroms and immigrants from, 403; Jews and immigration from, 405; Komsomol (Young Communist League), 474, 475; Lenin's social policy in, 474; lifestyle of Soviet hierarchy in, 475; Marriage, Family, and Guardianship law, 474; marriages in, 474; mixing of sexes in public, 270; Muslims and the Zhenotdel of, 474; Napoleon and, 286, 289; nationalism and, 365–369; New Economic Plan (NEP) and, 475; peasant rebellion in, 259, 271; persecution of women in, 369; political modernization and, 369; Red Army and, 445; reformers in, 310; Revolution and, 420, 421; Soviet economy and, 475; strikes in, 444; terrorism and assassinations in, 367, 369; Terrorist Brigade and, 420; tsarist government and, 365; Union of Russian Workers, 442; uxoricide and, 240; "White" forces and, 445; "white marriages" and, 367; witchcraft and, 231; women physicians and, 326–327; women rulers of, 270, 271; women's issues in, 476; women's labor in, 476; World War I and women from, 429; Zhenotdel and, 474. *See also* Soviet Union; USSR
Russian Academy of Science, 270
Ruysch, Rachel, 241

Saint Bartholomew's Day Massacre, 222, 236
Saint Petersburg Soviet of Worker's Deputies, 420
Saint-Simon, Henri de, 338

Saint-Simonians, 338
Salazar, Antonio de Oliveira, 473
Saleeby, Caleb, 315
Salieri, Antonio, 273
Salonières, 263
Salons, 263, 264–266, 267, 279, 284, 480
Saltykova, Praskovia, 270
Salvation Army, 323
Samizdat, 542
Samoa: fa'a Samoa (marriages), 379; mixed marriages and, 380
Samson, Deborah, 278
Sand, George, 341, 599
Sandwich Islands' Maternal Association, 385
Sanger, Margaret, 454, 455, 551
Sanz de Santamaría, Manuela, 279
Sappho, 599
Sardinia, 363
Sartre, Jean-Paul, 500, 546
Sati, 382
Satyagraha, 543
Savage, Augusta, 480
Saxony, 267
Schafly, Phyllis, 569
Scharlieb, Mary, 389
Schepeler-Lette, Anna, 355
Schlegel, Dorothea von, 265
Schlegel, Friedrich, 317
Schneeman, Mariechen, 513
Scholtz-Klink, Gertrud, 493
Schreiner, Olive, 396
Schroeder, Patricia, 582
Schröter, Corona, 273
*Science and Health with Key to Scriptures* (Eddy), 320
Scientific revolution: mathematics and astronomy, 261. *See also* Enlightenment
Science: Darwin's theories and, 314; early modern 245, 246; graduate education and, 326–328; psychology as, 316; sexology as, 315, 316; women in the, 326–328
Scotland: Elsie Inglis and, 428; John Knox and, 222, 235; Mary Stuart, 235, 236; rent strikes in, 437; Scottish Enlightenment, 265
Scottish Women's Hospitals (SWH), 428
Sculptors: Augusta Savage, 480
Seacole, Mary, 322
Sección Feminina (Women's Section), 472

Secondat, Charles-Louis de, 274
*The Second Sex* (Beauvoir), 556
Second Wave Feminism. *See* Feminists and feminism
Sedition Act, 434
Selbert, Elizabeth, 532
Selective Service Act, 437
Separate spheres, 312, 313, 383
Sephardim, 233
Serbia, 426; Kingdom of the Serbs and, 442; rape of Muslim women in, 577; United Nations and, 577, 578
Serfs: abolition of, 324, 325; Europe and abolition of, 299; Joseph II abolishes role of, 268; as landowners and the Habsburg monarchy, 237; reduced to slave status, 271; work decrease of, 268
*Service Social* (of *Combat*), 500
Seven Years' War, 275
Séverine, 354
Sewell, Wright, 354
Sex and sexuality: artistic rivalry and, 272; attitude towards, 318; bicycles and clothing, 304; bisexual experimentation of, 456; Catholic Church and, 226; cold war norms of, 551; Geneva, 222; consumerism advertisements and, 306; Council decrees on, 226, 227; cultural construction of, 456; differences of men and women, 262; domination through, 278; double standard of, 337; equal partners in relationships of, 474; European same-sex relationship laws and, 572; French revolutionaries use of, 284; gender debate and, 249, 250; gender expectations of queens and, 236; German soldiers and Mädelgruppe, 501; harassment and factory workers, 297; Inquisition and, 227, 228; Italian fieldworkers and, 299; "Jewish cosmopolitanism" as, 492; Kinsey Report and, 551–553; Marie Antoinette and, 284; masculinity ideas and, 376; missionaries and, 382, 385; native men and, 381; Nazi regime and, 492; 1960s music and, 560, 561; 1960s sexual revolution, 551, 554; non-European women and, 376; nurses and reputation of promiscuity, 389; orgasm, 552–553; parallels of slavery and, 398; personal and political goals with, 258; priests and concubinage,

226; psychology and, 315–317; radicalism and deviant, 437; scientists and female, 456; servicewomen and, 497, 498; sexual identity with, 315–318, 319; sexual revolution and, 559, 560; single women and, 260; slaves and, 249; Social Darwinism and, 314, 315; Soviet military service and, 498; student and free love, 556; value of reproductive abilities, 249; war effort and affects on women's, 438, 439; Western philosophical traditions and, 595, 596; wives of POWS and, 509; women and witchcraft with, 230; women musicians and, 273; women's relationships and, 317, 318; of working women, 297; World War I posters and, 438. *See also* Sciences
*Sex and the Single Girl* (Brown), 554
*Sex in Education* (Clark), 325
*The Sex That Is Not One* (Irigaray), 595
*Sexual Behavior in the Human Female* (Kinsey), 551
Sexual inversion, 316
*Sexual Politics* (Millet), 595
Seymour, Jane, 224
Shakhovskaia, Eugenie, 429
Sharaawi, Huda, 398
Shaw, Flora, 394
Shearer, Norma, 452
Sheppard-Towner Maternity and Infancy Act, 466
Shirelles, 560
Siberia, 270
Sidgwick, Henry, 325
Sieveking, Amalie, 321
*Silent Spring* (Carson), 549
Silesia, 268
Singapore: Changi Prison in, 503
Singers: Billie Holliday, 481; Faustina Bordoni, 273; school for male and female, 273. *See also* Musicians and music
Sinn Fein, 397
Sipilä, Helvi, 585
Sirmen, Maddalena (Lombardini), 273
Sisters of Mercy, 320
Sisters of Saint Joseph de Cluny, 383, 384
Six Point Group, 465
Slaves and slavery: abolitionist movements and, 276, 277; abolition of, 334–335, 336; antislavery groups

and, 276; France and abolishment of, 346; French National Assembly and, 281; Great Britain and, 333; impact of mercantilism on, 275; Inquisition and, 228; married women and, 360; Morisca resistance and, 234; native women as, 252; parallels of sexism and, 398; sexual relations with, 249; United States and, 276, 333; white slave trade as, 406

Sloan-Chesser, Elizabeth, 424

Slovenia, 577

Smith, John, 252

Smith, Margaret Chase, 582

Smith, Mary, 337

*The Social Basis of the Woman Question* (Kollontai), 474

Social Darwinism, 314, 315, 376

Social Democratic Party, 532

Socialism: feminism and integration of, 418, 419; Finland and, 365; revolution and, 418

Socialist Democratic Party (SPD), 359, 362, 418, 442

Social protest movements, 555, 556

Social Revolutionary Party (PSR), 420

Society for Social and Political Interests of the Jews, 322

Society for the Emancipation of Women, 346

Society for the Mutual Aid to Working Women, 421

Society for the Protection of Women, 406

*Society in America* (Martineau), 340

Society of Decorative Arts of New York City, 416

Society of Friends. *See* Quakers

Society of Jesus. *See* Jesuits

Society of Maternal Breastfeeding, 322

Society of Revolutionary Republican Women, 281, 284, 285

Society of the Friends of Blacks, 276

Somerset, Isabel, 398

Sontag, Susan, 599

Southeast Asia: Portugal and colonies in, 246

Soviet Union: Allied forces and the, 493; atomic testing and the, 549; Berlin blockade and, 531, 532; détente and U.S., 575; Duma and, 580; economic policies and the, 576; end of, 580, 581; end of the war and

women of, 520; female pilots in, 461; feminist movement in, 575, 576; feminists in, 576; Germany and pact with, 493; glasnost and, 575, 576; Great Terror of 1936–1939, 478; Jewish partisans and partisans of, 501; KGB and, 575; Korea and the, 530; New Family Code of 1944, 519; 1936 law and women of, 477; perestroika and, 575; Petersburg Centre for Gender Issues and, 576; postwar, 519; POWs in Nazi Party camps, 514; refugees, 518; Russian women and the, 478–479; Soviet Women's Committee (SWC) in, 575, 580; "The Special Camps for Wives of Traitors to the Motherland," 478; Union of Women of Russia in, 580; Warsaw Pact and the, 528; women and politics of the, 477, 478; women and the, 580, 581; women as industrial workers in, 506; women's military service and, 498; women's organizations in, 580, 581. *See also* Russia

Spain: anarchists and anti-fascism in, 472; Basque Homeland and Freedom, 583; beneficent societies and, 405; birth control and, 454; charitable organizations and, 322; civil war in, 470, 471; and coalition against Maria Theresa, 267; colonization and, 249; Economic Society of Madrid, 265; expulsion of Jews from, 232; Falange Party and Sección Feminina, 472; fascism in, 470–472, 473; female mystical activity in, 228; feminist movement in, 573; Franco and Catholic ideals for, 472; French expansion and, 285; gender norms and, 244; gender roles and, 470; Habsburg monarchy and, 267; independence and colonies of, 373; Inquisition and, 227; Institute for Women in, 573; Joseph Bonaparte and, 288; "La Pasionaria" and, 471, 472; lesbian subcultures and, 317; military suppression in, 348; Mussolini and, 468–469, 470; Mussolini and modernization of, 469, 470; Napoleon and, 286; Napoleonic Code and, 286; nationalization of women in, 468–469, 470; "New State" and, 472, 473; opposition to Napoleon

and, 288; reforms and, 353; revolutions and, 347; Roman Academy, 272; Royal Pragmatic decree and, 279; Second Republic of, 470; social reforms and salons in, 265; strikes in, 297; suffrage and, 470; UCD (Union of the Democratic Center), 573; unification of, 363–364, 365; uxoricide and, 240; witches and, 231, 232; witch-hunting in, 231; women and socialism in, 419; women in the military and, 470, 471; women's labor militancy in, 459, 460; women's status and rights in, 363–365; women's status in, 355; women's unions in, 459

Spanish America, 278, 279

Spartacus League, 441, 442

Speght, Rachel, 240

Spencer, Anne, 482

Spencer, Herbert, 314

Spies and spying: Mata Hari, 439; for the Red Army, 445; surveillance and, 434, 437

Spock, Benjamin, 534

Sprenger, Jacob, 230

Sri Lanka, 246, 249

Stagg, Ann, 238

Stalin, Josef, 475, 493, 519, 528, 541

Stanton, Elizabeth Cady, 336, 340, 355

Stanton, Theodore, 355

Steel, Flora Annie, 388

Stein, Gertrude, 480, 599

Steinem, Gloria, 568

Stephens, Uriah, 297

Stewart, Maria W., 335

Stöltz, Gunta, 479

Stone, Lucy, 360

Stone, Mary (Shi Meiyu), 392

*The Stoning of St. Stephen Martyr:* (Fontana), 241

Stopes, Marie, 454, 456

*Story of an African Farm* (Schreiner), 396

*The Story of Miss Von Sternheim:* (von La Roche), 274

Strachey, Ray, 464

Strickland, Susannah, 336

Strikes: boycott of sugar and, 335; female glassworkers and, 337; Finland and national, 366; in France, 297; Jewish boycott of meat prices and, 404; in Madrid, 297; Poland's Solidarity and, 576; reasons for, 459;

Strikes (cont.)
Russian Revolution and, 420; suffragists and, 422; textile workers and, 404; women employees and, 296; women's unions and, 459. *See also* Labor union(s)
Stuart, Mary, 235
Student Nonviolent Coordinating Committee (SNCC), 556
Students for a Democratic Society (SDS), 556
Student social movements, 555, 556
*Studies in General Science* (Blackwell), 314
*The Subjection of Women* (Mill), 360, 361, 363, 366
Suchocka, Hanna, 576, 577
Suffrage: debates of, 394; Euro-American women and, 399; in Europe after World War I, 442; Finland and universal, 366; Great Britain and, 421, 422; Hawaiian Islands and, 399; hierarchical and imperialist efforts of, 398; men and, 346; "motherhood franchise" and, 444; Mozzoni and, 365; Native Americans and, 444; "Night of Terror" and, 423; opposition to, 394, 423; Russian women and, 421; Spain and, 470; United States and, 423; women's movement and, 355; "women's year of service" and, 432. *See also* Voters and voting
Suslova, Nadeshda, 324, 326–327
Suttner, Bertha von, 354
Swanwick, Helena, 397
Sweden: laws and women's status in, 360, 361; pacifist groups in, 354; Peace of Westphalia and, 237; Thirty Years' War and, 237
Swetnam, Joseph, 240
Switzerland: Anabaptists and, 223; Calvinism and, 222; female workers limited in, 310; French expansion and, 285; John Calvin and, 222; Napoleonic Code and, 286; witchcraft in, 231; women and universities in, 324–325; women's issues and, 354

Taeuber-Arp, Sophie, 599
Taft, Helen Herron, 423
Tallit, 321
Tandel, Laure, 428
Tanganyika, 544
Tanner, Sarah, 308
TANU (Tanganyika African National Union), 544, 545, 547, 548

Tanzania, 545, 547, 548. *See also* Tanganyika
Tassi, Agostino, 241
Taylor, Harriet, 359, 360
Teachers: communism and, 531; interwar years and, 461; as missionaries, 385; pay equal to men's, 414; virginity and Russian, 417. *See also* Education
Teahouses, 260
Technological innovations: aviation as, 461; for birth control, 454; birth control methods, 318; electrical appliances as, 453; electric lighting, 305; medical treatments, 312; narrative film, 481; new appliances and postwar, 558; photography, 313; rayon, 451; sewing machines, 305; tractors, 536, 537; Tupperware, 559; typewriters as, 414; weapons, 353
Teleki, Blanka, 348
Television and television industry: *The Adventures of Ozzie and Harriet,* 560; *Coronation Street,* 560; *The Donna Reed Show,* 560; *Father Knows Best,* 560; gender norms and, 600; *Leave It to Beaver,* 560; *What Do You Think About It? The Grain of Sand,* 560; women in, 559, 560
Temperance organizations: American Temperance Society, 322; American Temperance Union, 322; British Women's Temperance Association, 398; prohibition and, 464; Women's Christian Temperance Union (WCTU), 323; World's Women's Christian Temperance Union (WWCTU), 398
*The Tenant of Wildfell Hall* (Brontë), 349
Teodoroiu, Ecaterina, 429
Terem, 240, 270
Teresa of Avila, 228
Tereshkova, Valentina Vladimirovna, 531
Terrorism: ETA and, 583; radical women and, 574, 575; Social Revolutionary Party and, 420; Terrorist Brigade and, 420
*Testament of Youth* (Britain), 428
Thatcher, Margaret, 550, 582
Theaters: film industry and, 414; At the Foot of the Mountain, 596; The Other Place, 596; plays and, 417; Spiderwoman, 596; Split Britches and, 597; women and, 304

Thiers, Adolphe, 356, 357
*Thinking About Women* (Ellman), 598
Third Order Regular of Mary, 384
Third Wave Feminism. *See* Feminists and feminism
Thirty Years' War, 237
Thomas, Martha Carey, 317, 318, 324, 325
Thompson, Dorothy, 506
Thornton, Willie Mae "Big Mama," 560
Tiffany, Lewis Comfort, 416
Titi, Bibi. *See* Mohamed, Bibi Titi
Tito, Josef, 577
Toklas, Alice B., 480
Toomer, Jean, 482
Trade and trading: colonial, 276; mercantilist policies and, 275; state-sponsored companies of, 275
Transportation: aviation and, 461; bus lines as, 305; modern women and, 452; during the 19th century, 302; theater and, 304; women's travel and, 400
Transvestism: Spanish America, 248; in British America, 249–250
Trapnel, Anna, 239
*Travels in West Africa* (Kingsley), 401
Treitschke, Heinrich von, 425
Triangle Shirtwaist Fire, 404
*The Tribune of the People* (Bazán), 352
Trimmer, Sarah, 273
Trinity Sisters, 384
Tristan, Flora, 339
*Trooper Halkett of Mashonaland* (Schreiner), 396
Troy Seminary, 324
Truffaut, Francois, 560
Truman, Harry S., 515, 528
Tucker, Helen, 549
Tupper, Earl, 559
Tupperware, 559
Turati, Filippo, 419
Tverdost, 445
Twinings Company, 260
*Two in the Far North* (Murie), 549
*Two Treatises on Government* (Locke), 262

Ukraine: gulag rebellion and women of, 541; massacre of Jews, 514; nationalism and women's movement in, 367
Undset, Sigird, 416
*Undine* (Schreiner), 396

UNESCO, 558, 559
Union des Femmes (Union of Women), 357
Union of Kahlmar, 235
Union of Unskilled Women Workers, 459
Unions. *See* Labor union(s)
United Artist Studio, 414
United Auto Workers (UAW), 505, 506
United Electrical (UE), 505, 506
United Kingdom. *See* Great Britain
United Nations: creation of the, 528–529; equal rights and, 528; International Year of the Woman and, 585; resolution 1325 and, 590; Serbia and, 577; Tanganyika and the, 544; women and the, 585, 586; women's voting rights and the, 529; Yugoslavia war crimes and, 577, 578
United Service Organizations for National Defense (USO), 509
United States: antiwar protest movements and the, 555, 556; atomic testing and the, 549; citizenship qualifications, 278; cold war arms race and USSR, 530; Cuba and, 374; détente and Soviet Union, 575; displaced Jews and the, 518; effeminacy and the men of the, 378; first federal welfare law in the, 466; first women's antislavery society and, 335; flappers in the, 450; Great Society and, 535; Greek Communist Party and the, 530; Hawaii and, 373; intelligence service and, 499; internment in the, 510; kitchen debate, 559; "the Kitchen Front" in, 507, 508; Korean War and the, 530; legal sterilization and, 489; Lend-Lease Act and the, 495; limitation of "rights" during World War I, 434; Marshall Plan and the, 528; McCarthyism and the, 531; military and women from the, 429; military auxiliaries and the, 498; military service and women of the, 498; pacifist organizations in, 354; Pearl Harbor and the, 495; Philippines and the, 374; Puerto Rico and, 374; racial discrimination in the, 424; reasons for suffrage in, 423; "Red Scare" in the, 442; slave trade and, 333; student social movements in the, 555; Truman Doctrine and the,

530; U.N. Convention on Eliminating Discrimination Against Women and the, 585; Vietnam War and the, 545; volunteer services and World War II, 499; war brides and, 519; war's effects on wives in the, 509; women activists undermining the, 378; women and military, 520; women and political candidates in the, 582; women's reaction to Pearl Harbor, 497; women and workforce during World War I, 434; World War I and women from, 428
Universal Declaration of Human Rights, 528, 529
Universal Peace Union, 354
Universities and colleges: student protests and, 555; women and, 245, 320, 325, 326–328, 482, 550, 555, 584, 598; women's studies at, 595; women students at, 460
*Urania propitia* (Cunitz), 245
Urban life: activities of, 304–305; consumer-oriented society and, 259, 260; domestic work and, 298; illegitimacy and, 310; life choices in, 260; married women and work, 260; mobility and, 302–305; new woman and, 412, 414; occupations of women in, 260, 414; problems of, 306–308; rural life replaced by, 536, 537; talents of middle class women and, 272; teahouses and coffeehouses of, 260; widows and, 248, 260
Urban VIII, Pope, 229
U.S. National Committee for a Sane Nuclear Policy (SANE), 548
USSR: abortion laws and, 538, 539; agricultural reforms and, 540, 541; Brezhnev and, 542; cold war arms race and U.S., 530; communal living and, 539; de-Stalinization and, 537; divorce and, 539; era of dissidents, 542; family housing and, 539; gulags and, 541; KGB and the, 555; Khrushchev and the, 537; persecution in, 542; secret police and, 538; space travel and the, 530, 531; Virgin Lands program and, 538; women and economy of, 539, 540; women and politics in, 537, 538. *See also* Russia; Soviet Union
Utopian socialism, 338–339
UWT (Umoja wa Wanawake wa Tanganyika), 548

Valadon, Suzanne, 599
Van Hyning, Lyrl Clark, 495
Varda, Agnés, 560, 597
Vasari, Giorgio, 241
Verbermacher, Hannah Rochel, 321
Verein Frauenwohl (Women's Welfare Association), 353
Verona Fathers, 386
Vérone, Maria, 463
Vickery, Alice, 318
Victor Emmanuel II (king of Italy), 363
Victor Emmanuel III, (king of Italy), 468
Victoria League, 394
Victoria (queen of England), 313, 398
Viet Minh, 544
Vietnam: description of men from, 376; French colonies and, 544; Ho Chi Minh Trail, 545; "New Life Movement," 544; Viet Minh, 544; women and, 544; women and the Communists of, 545
Vietnam War, 545, 555
Vigée-Lebrun, Elisabeth-Louise, 262, 599
*Vindication of the Rights of: Woman* (Wollstonecraft), 284, 285
Virginity: male writers and, 240; Mexican convents and, 250; Old Christian women and, 227; Russian teachers and, 417; Russian women's quarters and, 240; sexual revolution and, 559; women's honor and, 240
Visiting Nurses Association, 440, 441
Vivaldi, Antonio, 273
Vives, Juan Luis, 240
Vlachou, Eleni, 530
VOC. *See* Dutch East Indies Company (VOC)
*The Voice of Industry,* 297
Voltaire, 261, 271
Voluntary Aid Detachments (VADs), 428
von La Roche, Sophie, 274
Von Trotta, Margerethe, 597
Vorontsova-Dashkova, Ekaterina: (Russian princess), 271
Voters and voting: attempts at, 346; Equal Franchise Act and, 462; fundamental right and, 355; gender gap and, 581, 582; Great Britain and rights of women, 360; individual states and women, 278; Martineau and right to vote, 340; Reform Bill and right to vote, 337; reform in Great Britain after World War I, 442,

Voters and voting (cont.)
444; Republican motherhood and, 278; Twenty-first and Nineteenth amendments, 444. *See also* Suffrage

Wages: cheap workforce and, 310; collective bargaining and, 459; discrimination of women's, 594; Enlightenment women and, 259; Great Britain and military, 429; immigrant women and, 296–297; male counterparts and, 460; Mussolini and lowering of, 469; USSR women and, 539, 540; women and decline in, 297, 298; women's vs men's, 505
Wald, Lillian, 404
Walesa, Lech, 576
Walker, Rebecca, 569
Ward, Mary, 229
Warfare: Boer War, 396, 401; camp followers and, 288, 289; Crimean War and, 299; France and Austria, 285; Franco-Prussian War, 356; Korean War, 530; Napoleon and European, 288; nurses and fundraisers during, 363; pacifist organizations and, 354; Seven Years' War, 275; War of the Austrian Succession and, 267; women divided and, 425; women's organizations and, 495; World War I, 425–442; World War II, 493–521
Warren, Mercy Otis, 277
Warsaw ghetto, 511, 512. *See also* Ghettos; Nazi Party
Wars of Religion, 237
Warville, Jacques-Pierre Brissot de, 276
Washington, George, 277
WAVES (Women Accepted for Volunteer Emergency Service), 530
Weber, Lois, 481
Wedgwood, Josiah, 259, 260
Weil, Simone, 472
Welch, Joseph, 531
Welfare: maternity allowances and British, 467; New Deal reforms and, 466; United States first federal law, 466
*The Well of Loneliness* (Hall), 456, 457
Wells-Barnett, Ida B., 424
Wesley, John, 313
*West African Studies* (Kingsley), 401
West Germany. *See* Germany, West
We the Mothers Mobilize for America, 495

We Women Demand, 570
Whately, Mary Louisa, 382
Wheeler, Anna, 337
Wheeler, Candace, 416
White, Margaret Bourke, 461
Whiteley, William, 306
White Sisters, 383
Whitney, Gertrude Vanderbilt, 481
"Why Have There Been No Great Women Artists?" (Nochlin), 598–599
Wicksell, Anna Bugge, 465
Widow(s): Catherine de Médicis' power as a, 236; French conscription and, 288; Iberia and, 246; Maria Theresa as empress-widow, 268; self-supporting, 260
Willard, Emma, 324
Willard, Frances, 323, 398
William of Orange, 239
Williams, Jodi, 588
Williams, Mary Lou, 481
Wilson, Helen C., 397
Wilson, Woodrow, 435, 437, 441
Winfrey, Oprah, 600
Wise, Brownie, 559
Witches and witchcraft: demonic possession cases and, 232; disappearance of trials and, 232; Inquisition and, 227; interrogation and torture as, 230, 231; profile of typical, 231, 232; role of sex in trials of, 232; sex of accused, 231; sexual relations as, 230; *The Witches Hammer* and, 230
*Within the Whirlwind* (Ginzburg), 542
Wobblies. *See* International Workers of the World
Woker, Gertrud, 465
Wollstonecraft, Mary, 284, 285
Women Airforce Service Pilots (WASPs), 499
*Women and Economics* (Gilman), 314
*Women and Labour* (Schreiner), 396
*Women and Socialism* (Bebel), 359
*Women in the Past, Present, and Future* (Bebel), 359
Women's Aid Centre, 571
Women's Alliance of America, 405
Women's Armed Services Integration Act, 530
Women's Army Auxiliary Corps (WAACs), 429, 498

Women's Army Corps (WAC), 499
Women's Association for the Support of Poor Relief, 321
Women's Auxiliary Air Force (WAAF), 497
Women's Auxiliary of the Anti-Imperialist League, 397
Women's Caucus for Gender Justice, 586
Women's Christian Temperance Union (WCTU), 323
Women's Crusade, 323
Women's Enfranchisement League, 396
Women's International League for Peace and Freedom (WILPF), 435, 465, 466–467, 528
Women's Land Army, 497
Women's Liberation Front, 573
Women's movements, 556–557, 558; Anti-League and, 425; division within, 356; egalitarian communes and, 338; European reforms and, 355; goals of, 341; lesbian rights as, 571, 572; Marxism and, 359; middle class and founding of, 340–341; similarities of African Americans and women, 336; in Ukraine, 367; utopian socialism and, 338–339
Women's rights: to abortion, 569, 570; activists and, 355; British politics and, 337; campaigns for, 352, 353; Chartists and, 337, 338; conventions for, 340; economic independence as, 359; in Egypt, 398; end to sexism as, 568, 569; end to violence against women as, 570, 571; Enlightenment's influence on, 284, 285; equality feminists and, 596; Frederick Douglass and, 340; Germany and, 347; human rights and, 528; International Exposition and, 355; in Italy, 363–365; organizations and welfare states, 594; Pope and, 365; in Russia, 474; social and economic transformation as, 339; work at home, 346; World War II and, 498. *See also* Equal rights
Women's Royal Air Force Service, 429
Women's Royal Naval Service, 429
Women's Social and Political Union (WSPU), 421
Women's Strike for Peace (WSP), 555
Women's Suffrage League, 435
Women's Suffrage Union, 424

Women's Trade Union League, 404
Women's Voluntary Services (WVS), 497
Woolf, Virginia, 456, 463, 599
Worcester Foundation for Experimental Biology, 554
Workers and work: apprenticeships and, 264; characteristics of female, 593, 594; childcare and, 535; clerical, 414, 460, 461; conditions of, 308–310, 311; discrimination of women and, 297; dramatists in 17th century and, 244; Europe and revolutions by, 347; gender equity and, 593–594, 595; gender norms at, 594, 595; immigrants as, 404; independence and women at, 296–297; leisure time and, 417; married women and, 457, 458; Mussolini and gender norms for, 469; nationality dominance and gendered, 404; oppressed mothers as, 337; pacifist organizations and, 354; reasons for reforms of, 347, 348; regulating women's, 308–309, 310; the salon as, 264; science as men's, 261; sex segregated, 457; single women and, 414; type of woman as, 505; women during World War I as, 434; working-class wives and, 313–314; working conditions and, 345, 404, 505; during

World War II, 504–505, 506. *See also* Employers and employment
Workers of Northern France, 297
*The Workers Union* (Tristan), 339
Working Women's Association, 459
Works Progress Administration (WPA), 459
World Anti-Slavery Convention, 336, 340
World Commission on Environment and Development: *See* Brundtland Commission
World Health Organization (WHO), 584
World's Women's Christian Temperance Union (WWCTU), 398
World War I: emasculation of men and, 439; end of, 441, 442; home front and, 432–434; preservation of life style and, 438; reversal of gender roles and, 439; women and, 425–439, 440
World War II: economic and human cost of, 515; effects on Germans, 510; effects on U.S. wives, 509; end and results of, 514–520; food rationing during, 507, 508; Germany's expansion of Aryan nation and, 493–494, 495; the Resistance during, 500, 501, 502; science, 550; U.S. volunteer services and, 499; USO

and service women in, 509; women in military service and, 497–499; workforce of women during, 504–505, 506
*The Worth of Women* (Fonte), 240
Wright, Fanny, 339
Wu Yi-Tang, 529

Yearsley, Ann, 276
Yeltsin, Boris, 580
Yugoslavia: authoritarianism and, 473; Germany's attack on, 493; women Resistance fighters in, 500. *See also* Serbia

Zaharias, Babe Didrikson, 453
Zander, Elsbeth, 493
Zappi, Gian Paolo, 241
Zasulich, Vera, 369
Zayas y Sotomayor, Maria de, 244
Zell, Katherine, 244
Zelle, Margaretha Geertruida, 439
Zemliachka, Rozaliia, 445
Zenana, 382
Zetkin, Clara, 318, 359, 418, 419, 435
Zetkin, Ossip, 359
Zheliabou, Andrei, 368
Zhenodtel, 474, 477
Zhhensovety, 537, 538
Zietz, Luise, 318
Zionism, 405